Hitler's Airwaves

Hitler's Airwaves

The Inside Story of

Nazi Radio Broadcasting

and Propaganda Swing

Horst J.P. Bergmeier & Rainer E. Lotz

Yale University Press New Haven & London

Set in Walbaum
Printed in Great Britain by Biddles Ltd, Guildford and Kings Lynn

Library of Congress Cataloging-in-Publication Data

Bergmeier, H.J.P.
  Hitler's airwaves: the inside story of Nazi radio broadcasting and propaganda swing/Horst J.P. Bergmeier, Rainer E. Lotz.
  Includes bibliographical references and index.
  ISBN 0–300–06709–7 (cloth: alk. paper)
  1. World War, 1939–1945—Propaganda. 2. Radio in propaganda—Germany. 3. Propaganda, German. I. Lotz, Rainer E. II. Title.
  D810.P7G318 1997
  940.54'88743—dc20   96–36617
                                                                            CIP

A catalogue record for this book is available from the British Library.

10 9 8 7 6 5 4 3 2 1

Contents

Preface and Acknowledgements

The authors of this book were at primary school during the Second World War. We had no direct experience of the operation of Nazi propaganda, nor of Germany's English-language radio propaganda more specifically. It was much later that we came upon the subject, circuitously and almost by chance.

During the 1950s, when jazz clubs mushroomed in Germany in the wake of the Dixieland Revival, we encountered Anglo-American jazz music for the first time, and were hooked. Even before each knew the other, we had this interest in common. And in addition to enjoying the music, we wanted to know everything about it. We wanted to know about its roots and the ways in which it had developed, particularly in our own country. We wanted to know about the performers and their professional backgrounds, and about the detailed circumstances of the recordings. This inquisitiveness led to the collecting of records and the tracking down of musicians and band-leaders. Nothing was too much trouble. We set about the task of interviewing them meticulously, the Germans as well as the 'visiting firemen' from abroad, and indeed anyone who had shaped and influenced the development of German jazz.

Our enthusiasm for jazz and its history had, however, to take second place as we pursued our separate careers in commerce and banking in many parts of the world. Perhaps it was inevitable, given the specialist nature of our hobby, that our paths would again cross, sooner or later. So when we both found ourselves back in Europe, we decided that we should pool our knowledge and publish the research we had amassed over the years. We had, after all, already published a substantial amount in the form of monographs, bio-discographies and articles on German jazz history in Germany, Great Britain, The Netherlands and the United States. There must, we imagined, be other jazz enthusiasts with whom to share the results of our work, and we could combine what each knew best. One of us, Horst Bergmeier, could specialise in the biographical material, and the other, Rainer Lotz, could concentrate on the discographies.

Early in our quest we had encountered rumours of alleged 'jazz' recordings, made in Berlin by a group called 'Charlie and his Orchestra' during the Second World War, a time when the performance of jazz was strictly prohibited by the Reich. We had consulted Joachim Ernst Berendt's *Das Jazzbuch* (first edition 1953) and *Die deutsche Jazz-Discographie* by Horst H. Lange (first edition 1955), which were in their time the leading sources on German jazz history. Berendt's book left us none the wiser: it

viii | **Preface and Acknowledgements**

contained no reference to this orchestra. Lange's work did at least confirm its existence. He listed forty-five 'Charlie' titles, and noted that 'The unidentified personnel consists of the best German and Italian musicians as well as musicians from occupied countries (Netherlands and Belgium)'. Once Lange's book appeared, reports of additional 'Charlie' numbers flooded in from collectors all over Europe.

Berendt's *Jazzbuch* has been revised and re-issued several times over the years, yet 'Charlie and his Orchestra' is still not mentioned. The 1992 edition of the Lange discography, on the other hand, lists a greater range of 'Charlie' titles than its predecessors. But the names and dates which give it a sense of authenticity are not always supported by documentary references.

Some twenty years after hearing the rumours about 'Charlie', and when Horst Bergmeier was living in The Netherlands, he made contact with Dutch and Belgian musicians whom we believed might have been active in Berlin during the war. But the meetings led nowhere. It clearly remained a very sensitive subject: the musicians still feared the stigma of collaboration with the German occupation. Similarly, Rainer Lotz's interviews with German musicians proved unproductive. The musicians we contacted frequently claimed they had been unaware of the purpose of the recordings with which they had been involved. Their accounts were like brief snapshots within a musical career, and yielded little about the circumstances in which the recordings had occurred, or why they had occurred.

Apart from what we could glean from the musicians themselves, the one certainty was that the recordings made by 'Charlie and his Orchestra' were political parodies of well-known and mainly American hit-songs. It became clear that they represented an official enterprise of wartime propaganda, authorized and financed at the highest levels of Nazi hierarchy.

By the mid 1970s, Rainer Lotz had accumulated what was probably the largest collection of 'Charlie' records in the world. In 1975 he compiled a selection for re-issue on the German Discophilia label, accompanied by a text which set down everything then known about this mysterious orchestra . But it was too soon for a straightforward and impartial discussion of the subject: an American music publisher threatened legal action over 'unauthorised bowdlerisation of original material' and the anti-Semitic tone of some of the parodied texts. The LPs had to be withdrawn and are consequently as scarce today as the original 78 rpm shellacs.

Ten years on, Rainer Lotz tried again. This time the 'Charlie' anthology was very successfully re-issued in collaboration with the British Harlequin label. Reviews from around the world acknowledged the selection as a scoop of historic importance. The journalists Florian Steinbiss and David Eisermann collaborated with Lotz on a feature for the German magazine *Der Spiegel* which was syndicated internationally and led subsequently to the making of a television documentary.

At last a few 'Charlie' veterans felt prepared to speak about their wartime experiences on the fringes of the Nazi propaganda machine. By now most were well into retirement, and sadly their recollections were often vague and incomplete. Since many were already dead, it seemed that the opportunity to piece together a reliable account of 'Hitler's band', as the orchestra was sometimes mistakenly called, was over.

But then we had an unexpected stroke of luck. Early in the 1990s, parts of the recording ledgers of Deutsche Grammophon, the company that had processed the original records, surfaced, and Rainer Lotz was able to obtain copies. The company's management had assumed that the ledgers had been lost when the factory was bombed or in the turmoil that followed the war. But they had survived in other hands, and Lotz could now reconstruct the recorded output of 'Charlie and his Orchestra', complete with recording dates, alternate takes and unissued material. The discovery coincided with the ending of the Cold War and the opening of the archives in the former East Berlin and in Czechoslovakia, providing further sources on German Radio recording activities during the war.

These events encouraged us to think that it was now possible to make available the ultimate 'Charlie' discography, presented within the overall context of Germany's English-language radio propaganda, the only way in which the story can be properly understood. Rainer Lotz's discography and transcription of the lyrics are fundamental to the book, and to this Horst Bergmeier has added detailed notes on history, personnel and instrumentation, together with biographical sketches of the musicians, the chapters on jazz and Nazi ideology, and on the development of the various radio orchestras.

What we had begun by imagining as a 'hipster history' of Nazi Germany's radio propaganda, by way of an introduction to the 'Charlie' discography, turned into an arduous task of basic research which overran our original conceptions of subject, time and place. Most existing studies seemed to focus on propaganda directed *at the German home front* through press and cinema. Considering that the war was fought to a background of radio noise, they were surprisingly unhelpful in relation to radio propaganda generally, and to Germany's foreign propaganda effort in particular.

One reason is obvious: compared to print and film, recorded sound has survived relatively rarely. Only very special radio programmes were thought to merit the costs of recording on disc. The clandestine nature of much of Germany's foreign propaganda, and the fact that few people, apart from supervisors and others directly involved, knew anything about the operations, helped to keep them shrouded in mystery. With the propaganda operation run on a need-to-know principle, many participants have been genuinely surprised to learn the degree to which foreigners were involved. Furthermore it is painfully true that historians do not pay sufficient attention to light entertainment – the best bait for all radio propaganda.

The organization and intentions of the book require explanation. The principle subject is the growth of the 'Reich Ministry for Public Enlightenment and Propaganda' (the 'Ministry for Propaganda', or simply 'ProMi' in abbreviated form) and the subordinate and satellite units active in Germany's foreign-language radio propaganda after 1933. Since the propaganda machine comprised several quite different but overlapping elements, the material does not lend itself to a single continuous narrative. Instead we have found it best to provide, chapter by chapter, a series of parallel histories, cumulatively making a total account. The first two chapters explore the establishment of the German Ministry for Propaganda and the workings of the Nazi broadcasting apparatus. Chapter 3 looks at overseas propaganda broadcasts on short-wave, and at the individuals – including a number of Americans – involved in its dissemination. Chapter 4 focuses on medium-wave propaganda, principally targeted at Britain, and involving William Joyce and other expatriate broadcasters. The fifth chapter presents the story of propaganda jazz, and of the orchestra fronted by Charlie Schwedler. Chapter 6 documents the struggle for control of the German broadcasting system within the Nazi party itself, while Chapter 7 considers the so-called 'secret' radio stations which operated covertly throughout the war. The final chapter gives an account of Radio Arnhem and of the 'clandestine' stations across Europe. Appendices provide a complete discography of the recordings, issued and unissued, of 'Charlie's Orchestra', and the full texts of the propaganda lyrics.

Fundamental to Goebbel's ministry – surely the most powerful PR and promotion machine of the twentieth century – were the individuals involved in it. We have therefore included organisational details and personal backgrounds which may appear, at first sight, to have little to do with the main theme of broadcasting and politics. The careers of the Germans at the helm of the system were perhaps predictable, but what of the many foreigners who joined German radio during the war? We have sought to place both broadcasting and broadcasters in the broadest possible context. And, since the bulk of the biographical material presented in the book is wholly unknown or unobtainable elsewhere, we offer it as a source of reference for future work.

This study would have been impossible without the unselfish assistance of a great number of people. Our work received a timely fillip when we made the acquaintance of Michael and Doreen Forman. Michael Forman – a collector whose remarkable archives intersect with a large area of our interests – had asked the recording engineer John R.T. Davies for advice on restoring some old gramophone records of historical interest. Davies mentioned similar work he had done in preparing masters for the Harlequin release of Rainer Lotz's 'Charlie' material. A few weeks later we met the Formans, and the vast amount of unpublished material they hold has proved to be of the highest importance for the research towards this book.

Over many years, Michael and Doreen Forman have sought to acquire anything connected with the broadcaster William Joyce ('Lord Haw-Haw'), including letters written to his wife Margaret during his trial and while awaiting execution in Wandsworth prison, and indeed Margaret Joyce's own estate. Of even greater importance has been the Eduard Roderich Dietze archive. The late Dr. Edith Dietze-ter Meer, Eduard's widow, had entrusted the Formans with the preservation of their vast collection of private papers. As we show in this book, the bilingual Dietze was a relatively inconspicuous 'cog' in the English-language broadcasting operation, but such was the range of his responsibilities and contacts that his papers facilitate an intimate understanding of the workings of the *Reichsrundfunk* from the outbreak of war until the last transmissions in May 1945.

Much valuable original information was made available to us by the various branches of the *Bundesarchiv*, whose technical facilities undoubtedly set the standard for other research institutions around the world. The same must be said about the superior competence of its staff – in their various fields of specialisation – who proved ceaselessly co-operative: Dr. Ritter, Dr. Hoffmann, Mr. Scharmann and their staff at the *Bundesarchiv*, Koblenz; Dr. Oldenhage, Mrs. Gronau and Mrs. Roeske at the *Bundesarchiv – Abteilung Potsdam*, the former Central Library of the German Democratic Republic; David G. Marwell and the staff at the Berlin Document Centre; Mr. Dillgard at the *Bundesarchiv-Zentralnachweisstelle*, Aachen; Major Diefenbach at the *Bundesarchiv-Militärgeschichtliches Forschungsamt*, Freiburg.

The kindness of Dr. Freifrau von Boeselager at the *Politisches Archiv* of the *Auswärtiges Am*t, Bonn, proved limitless when it came to providing us with information on the organisation of Kultur-R and other broadcasting activities of the Berlin Foreign Ministry. By examining the wartime budgets of Kultur-R, the Foreign Ministry's broadcasting activity, we obtained the first biographical information on 'Charlie' himself. Armed with this information we initiated a search for the musician. Beginning at his home town, we were passed from one registration office to the next. Mrs. Wessollek at the *Ordnungsamt*, Duisburg, and Mrs. Thol at the *Amt für Einwohnerwesen*, Düsseldorf, showed tremendous patience in answering what must have seemed to them the most trivial of questions. At the end of this journey we even enlisted the services of the Genealogical Society of Utah, which claims to have data on half of mankind on its computerised archive. Stephen S. Barthel was kind enough to screen his files – only to admit defeat.

Without the generous assistance of Ansgar Diller and Klaus Stoessel, Walter Roller and Mrs. Kerbel at the *Deutsches Rundfunkarchiv*, Frankfurt, we would not have been able to obtain access to several specialised publications – books, periodicals and dissertations together with photographic material and background information on some musical items.

The understanding and support of Mrs. Rosenberger of the *Gesellschaft für musikalische Aufführungs- und mechanische Vervielfältigungsrechte* (GEMA), Berlin, Mrs. Fried of the American Society of Composers, Authors and Publishers (ASCAP), New York, and Mrs. Mitchell and Peter L.T. Stroud of the Performing Rights Society (PRS), London, proved invaluable in identifying composers and lyricists.

Among the many people who deserve our primary gratitude we would like to mention Kenneth D. Schlesinger and Jo Ann Williamson for their patience in guiding us through the technicalities of US legislation and the maze of the National Archives in Washington, as well as Mr. C. de Roo of the *Ministrië van Justitie*, The Hague, and Mrs. van Bockxmeer and Mr. E. Somers of the *Rijksinstituut voor Oorlogsdocumentatie*, Amsterdam, for providing us with information relating to Dutch radio during the German occupation.

Early in our research, Horst Bergmeier 'discovered' the late Dr. Erich Hetzler, the wartime head of Germany's secret stations. By all accounts Hetzler was already an almost mythical figure during his time in office. At the end of the war he appeared to have vanished from the surface of the earth. Reading a local paper while waiting for his lunch, Bergmeier spotted the name 'Hetzler' among a list of the bereaved in an obituary announcement. Some weeks later he contacted Hetzler, and the former chief of the secret stations and his charming wife, Erika, were kind enough to receive him for a valuable discussion on a number of contentious issues, and agreed to examine parts of the manuscript.

The flawless memory of alto-saxophonist Franz 'Teddy' Kleindin, and *via* him of pianist Primo Angeli, has proved invaluable in preparing the sections on the various radio orchestras studied, their personnel and instrumentation. His forbearance in the face of repeated nagging queries over an extended period is greatly appreciated.

Among those who deserve our very special gratitude is James Clark. We sought initially to trace him, as a former Nazi broadcaster, for advice and information. At that time James was working on a memoir of his life in Berlin, and had made contact independently with Michael Forman on an issue relating to William Joyce. Michael introduced us and suggested that James might be able to assist in the editing of our work for publication. James Clark's contribution to this study cannot be overemphasised, as he has worked as a professional editor since the war and is fluent in several languages. Most of the translations we quote from original German documentation are by him. His intimate knowledge and personal experience inside the German propaganda apparatus, combined with his careful eye and meticulous attention to linguistic detail, saved us from certain embarrassment at a number of points.

There were many others whose generosity and assistance in a variety of contexts were invaluable to us. For advice of various kinds we are deeply indebted to Bruce Bastin, Freddy Brocksieper (†), Gerhard Conrad, Martin Doherty, Dr. Hans-Heinrich Düsel, Dr. David Eisermann, Tony Fletcher, Clive Garner, Jan Grundmann, Harold S. Kaye (†), Peter Köhler (†), Dr. Klaus Krüger, Dr. Richard Kupsch, Carmen Litta-Magnus, Gunther Lust, Friedrich Meyer-Gergs, Wolf Mittler, Herman Openneer, Werner Ripske, Günther Schifter, Joachim Schütte, Klaus Schulz, 'Marquis de Slade', Gert Spahn, Florian Steinbiss, Wolfgang Stenke, Stefan Streif, Mrs. Wagenführ and Karlheinz Wendtland.

Finally, we record our gratitude to our wives, Petra Bergmeier and Birgit Lotz, for their understanding and patience when at times the clattering of the printer tended to shake the house for hours on end.

Despite the tremendous amount of support we have received and the care we have taken in the evaluation of the information, some oversights or errors of interpretation may remain. We alone bear responsibility for them.

Horst J.P. Bergmeier   Rainer E. Lotz
Apeldoorn, The Netherlands   *Bad Godesberg, Germany*

Illustrations and Charts

Illustrations

Charts

Abbreviations

Abbreviations have been used sparingly but could not be wholly avoided. German terms and titles have generally been rendered in the most appropriate English form, but the original has been given in parenthesis where a translation does not convey the full original meaning or intention. The authors have followed the Civil Affairs Guide – German-English Dictionary of Administrative Terms prepared by the Library of Congress for the War Department in Washington, DC, and published in a restricted edition in July 1944. After the war, this dictionary was adopted for use by the International Military Tribunal, Nuremberg.

AA	*Auswärtige Amt* – Foreign Ministry
AA-PA	*AA – Politisches Archiv*, political archive of the Foreign Ministry
BA	*Bundesarchiv* – Federal Archive, mainly in Koblenz, otherwise branches as indicated
BDC	Berlin Document Centre
DRA	*Deutsche Rundfunkarchiv* – German Broadcasting Archive, Frankfurt/Main
DTU	*Deutsches Tanz- und Unterhaltungsorchester* – German Dance and Entertainment Orchestra
FA	Forman Archive
Gestapo	*Geheime Staatspolizei* – secret state police
HJ	*Hitlerjugend* – Hitler Youth (founded in 1926 as the youth organization of the NSDAP, legally extended on 1 December 1936 to embrace the training of the entire youth of Germany)
KPD	*Kommunistische Partei Deutschlands* – German Communist Party
KWS	*Deutsche Kurzwellensender* – German Short-Wave Station (*Die Deutschen Überseesender* – German Overseas Stations from 30 January 1943)
NA	National Archives, Washington, DC
NSDAP	*Nationalsozialistische Deutsche Arbeiterpartei* – National Socialist German Workers' Party (the only political party permitted by law in Germany after 14 July 1933; founded in 1919 as *Deutsche Arbeiterpartei*; renamed NSDAP on 24 February 1920)
OKW	*Oberkommando der Wehrmacht* – High Command of the Armed Forces (the head of the OKW was subject directly to Hitler, who became *Oberster Befehlshaber der Wehrmacht* – Supreme Commander – by decree on 6 March 1935)
Party	NSDAP
PK	*Propagandakompanie* – war correspondents' unit attached to the armed forces
PRO	Public Record Office, London
ProMi	a term generally applied to the RMVP (*q.v.*)
RBT	*Radio Berlin Tanzorchester* – Radio Berlin Dance Orchestra
RIOD	Rijksinstituut voor Oorlogsdocumentatie – State Institute for War Documentation, Amsterdam
RKK	*Reichskulturkammer* – Reich Chamber of Culture (the official body established to administer the full range of cultural activities of the German nation, and to represent the various 'chambers' under which professionals were grouped)
RMK	*Reichsmusikkammer* - Reich Chamber of Music (established as part of the RKK)
RMVP	*Reichsministerium für Volksaufklärung und Propaganda* – Reich Ministry for Public Enlightenment and Propaganda, generally referred to as the Propaganda Ministry or simply as the ProMi
RRG	*Reichs Rundfunk GmbH* – German Broadcasting Company Ltd. (founded as a public company on 15 May 1925, and from 1933 supervised by the ProMi)
SA	*Sturmabteilungen der NSDAP* – Storm Troops (the 'brown-shirts', established 11 November 1921 as the organised stewards at NSDAP meetings; reorganised 1925)
SD	*Sicherheitsdienst* – Security Service (part of the SS)
SS	*Schutzstaffel der NSDAP* – Security Squad (annexed from the SA in the spring of 1925 as the Führer's personal bodyguard; became a para-military political group in wartime, with a death's head cap badge)

CD Contents

The contents of the accompanying CD are given below. Where applicable a page reference indicates where to find the full lyrics in Appendix II.

Further videos, CDs and audio cassettes of German propaganda broadcasts in English are available from Historia Publishing, P.O. Box 5276, Bromsgrove, Worcestershire, United Kingdom B61 0HZ.

1   The Making of the German Ministry of Propaganda

German Paranoia over the Allied Psywar, 1914–1918

Field Marshal von Hindenburg, chief of staff of the Imperial German Armed Forces, was disgusted by the idea. He was reading a letter dated 4 July 1917 – the third year of the First World War, with America already three months into the conflict on the Allied side – from General Erich Ludendorff, the military brain behind the German war effort, to the War Ministry in Berlin. The letter urged the German film industry to counter the Americans' world-wide anti-German campaign. An unsoldierly proposal! The revered field marshal would have nothing to do with 'poisoning enemy minds', as he put it. A decent soldier, he believed, should fight with only a weapon in his hands. So it was not until August 1918, two months before the end of the war, that Germany first used written propaganda as a deliberate policy action, and a German aircraft first dropped propaganda leaflets over Allied lines. By October, while German troops on the western front were experiencing the full force of the American army, German aircraft had delivered 876,169 leaflets. Set against that were the 65,595 *million* leaflets the Allies had dispersed throughout the war.[1]

The Allies did not make the similar mistake of underestimating the value of war propaganda. The French government had established the Maison de la Presse as a central propaganda agency in October 1915 and, given official status by Clemenceau, it later expanded. By June 1917 the British government had sent the press magnate, Lord Northcliffe, to New York where, as chairman of the British War Mission, he orchestrated the anti-German campaign.[2] The following February, Lloyd George appointed him Director of Propaganda in Enemy Countries, with headquarters in Crewe House, London.

When the United States entered the war in April 1917, President Woodrow Wilson established a Committee on Public Information, selecting the journalist George Creel as chairman. It was Creel who became famous for marshalling America's film industry in support of the war. As Ludendorff realised, by ensuring that American movies and newsreels where shown in the cinemas of the neutral countries of Europe and around the world, Creel could influence people in a way that the Imperial German Army could not. Chaplin's *Shoulder Arms*, in which Charlie dreams of kidnapping the German emperor, and *The Kaiser – The Beast of Berlin*, the most venomous of the US-sponsored anti-German movies, were products of this period, as were such musical numbers as

'We'll knock the Heligo out of Heligoland' (Theodore Morse/John O'Brien, 1917), 'We're going to take the Germ out of Germany' (Frederick V. Bowers/Arthur J. Lamb, 1917), 'Just like Washington crossed the Delaware (General Pershing will cross the Rhine)' (Howard E. Johnson/George W. Meyer, 1918) and 'If he can fight like he can love (Good Night Germany!)' (Grant Clarke/George W. Meyer, 1918).

Many ordinary Germans were in a real sense surprised in November 1918 when the imperial régime collapsed and the army sued for an armistice. There was no German agency that could have prepared the home front for the rapid surrender. As late as October that year, Germany's future prospects seemed reasonable, even after four years of war. Stunned by the unexpected destruction of their country, people wanted to know how it could have happened. Whose fault was it?

The legend of the 'stab in the back' was to provide a consoling answer: it was not the enemy forces, but the 'enemies within' that had brought the country to this eventuality. During the preliminaries to the armistice negotiations, the head of the British delegation, General Sir Neill Malcolm, overheard Ludendorff berating German politicians and civilians, and remarked to him: 'You mean that you were stabbed in the back?' German military circles adopted this as their slogan, and when, in November 1919, a German parliamentary committee investigated the causes of the collapse, Hindenburg and Ludendorff – in a stroke of propaganda that was to haunt German politics for the next thirty years – testified that '*as a British general has said, the German army was stabbed in the back.*'

As this myth was created and nurtured, so was the somewhat exaggerated idea of the power of insidious and unscrupulous enemy propaganda to sap a nation's strength. Basil Liddell Hart has referred to the 'unwilling tribute paid by the Germans to the effectiveness of Allied, and especially British, propaganda. In the later stages of the war it was skilfully directed and intensively developed.' But he added that, 'though we should recognise the value of the more discriminating propaganda [...] it was the kernel of essential truth upon the bigger issues which was digested by the German people and [...] weakened the will to continued sacrifice.'[3]

Ludendorff, not surprisingly, was a leading political proponent of the paranoid theory of propaganda, but even writers at the bourgeois centre of the political spectrum, like Edgar Stern-Rubarth, (until 1933 chief editor of *Wolffs Telegraphisches Bureau*, a German news agency) took it on board:

> Here we can see the explanation of the propaganda success of the British and other Allies, in that they clearly recognized the potential that this weapon had, and that in a sense, they were prepared to put more energy into developing it to the highest degree than they did into the struggle of arms, the quarrel of the guns.[4]

The Reich Ministry for Propaganda ('ProMi')

The theory that the failure of Germany's political and military leadership was explicable in terms of the 'decisive role' of hostile propaganda was strongly endorsed by the

National Socialists; after their electoral victory in 1933, it became an axiom of their policies. Propaganda was seen as a self-fulfilling activity, as Willi Münzenberg, a perceptive but ambiguous German Communist exile, described it in 1937:

> Where propaganda was formerly a function of policy, it is now policy which has become a function of propaganda, that is to say, measuring how far, at a given moment, a particular political action should go, has instead been subordinated to the measure of its propagandistic impact. [...] Indeed, this makes propaganda – particularly in international affairs – itself into a form of policy in action.[5]

Once the National Socialists, obsessed with the importance of propaganda as an active political force, had gained power, they could implement the theory on both the national and international stage. In this they were immeasurably helped by recent advances in radio technology. On 29 October 1923 the '*Sendestelle Berlin*' had been launched with a regular service for its first 461 headphoned listeners . By 1933, the wireless set was becoming an increasingly common household item in Germany, and radio communication had already become the most powerful instrument of political influence. The Nazi leaders were able to manipulate their broadcasting system in a way not previously imagined in a democratic state.

For Joseph Goebbels, the Reich's future propaganda minister, radio was central to the concept of an all-embracing propaganda operation at home and abroad. In an emerging strategy of total warfare, he saw the combination of air strikes and 'mind-bombing' as an irresistible strategy. On 22 January 1932 – almost exactly a year before Adolf Hitler became chancellor – Goebbels noted in his diary that he had discussed his own future role with him. In *Mein Kampf*, Hitler had made only general observations about the uses of propaganda, on the lines of 'the bigger the lie, the more easily it will be believed, provided it is repeated vigorously and often enough'. Not long after this meeting, Hitler is recorded as having commented:

> Artillery preparation before an attack, as during the World War, will be replaced in a future war by the psychological dislocation of the enemy through revolutionary propaganda. The enemy must be demoralized and driven to passivity. [...] Our strategy is to destroy the enemy from within, to conquer him through himself. Mental confusion, contradictory feelings, indecision, panic – these are our weapons.[6]

Devoted follower and amplifier of Hitler's vision that he was, Goebbels frequently found that the Führer presented other's ideas as his own.

On 5 February 1933, six days after Hitler assumed power, Goebbels spoke for the first time in concrete terms about the envisaged new Ministry for Public Enlightenment and Propaganda (*Reichsministerium für Volksaufklärung und Propaganda*), generally known as the Ministry for Propaganda, or in German simply as the 'ProMi'. On 8 March he confided to his diary that the outlines of the ministry were now clear, so by the time he was appointed minister on 13 March, Goebbels was prepared for the immediate implementation of his plans and the realisation of his dreams.[7]

Of the leading Nazi Party figures close to Hitler in 1933, Paul Joseph Goebbels was one of the best educated. He had been born on 29 October 1897, in Rheydt, Rhineland, into a devout Catholic family; his father was a bookkeeper. With financial assistance from the Catholic 'Albertus Magnus Society', Goebbels was able to study philosophy, and German language and literature (*Germanistik*). He was rejected for military service in the First World War on medical grounds. In 1921 he completed his studies with a doctorate in literature at Heidelberg university, and to earn a living became a trainee in the Cologne branch of the Dresdner Bank. It was during this period, after he had rejected Catholicism, that he wrote a novel entitled *Michael – Ein Deutsches Schicksal in Tagebuchblättern* (Michael – A German Destiny in Diary Form), published only in 1929, and then by the Nazis' own Eher Verlag. The novel is a heroic fantasy in which a Communist party member becomes a National Socialist and dies a hero's death resisting the French army of occupation in the Ruhr. The language of the novel is permeated with the nationalist cult of exemplary heroism, sacrifice and death.

During 1921–24, Goebbels made the transition from literary romantic to man of politics – as much out of frustration and distaste for the life of the bourgeois intellectual as a response to the political situation in Germany – and began to apply his sharp mind and rhetorical skills to political demagoguery. In 1924, he joined the NSDAP. Here, 'the little Doctor with the club-foot' excelled in Party doctrine and ideology, perhaps in compensation for his physical disability.[8] In 1925 he became the Party's executive manager (*Geschäftsführer*) in the region of Rhineland-North, and the following year enthusiastically supported Adolf Hitler against his rivals within the Party, earning him the position of regional Party leader (*Gauleiter*) for Berlin-Brandenburg. By 1927 Goebbels was the unchallenged head of the NSDAP in the German capital. In 1929 Hitler appointed him his *Reichspropagandaleiter*, the Party's national director of propaganda. Goebbels' brilliant, if cynical, manipulation of the electorate was a decisive factor in Hitler's triumph in 1932–33.

On 17 March, only four days after his appointment, Goebbels confided in his diary that 'Broadcasting is now totally in the hands of the state. We have put a stop to endlessly swinging this way and that; we have thus ensured that there will be uniform control.'[9] The way was now clear for him to transform German radio into the most powerful instrument of political warfare the world had seen.

The German Broadcasting Apparatus

Until 1933 the German broadcasting system had been a loosely knit network of financially independent regional companies. In the technical, financial and administrative spheres the German Broadcasting Company (*Reichs-Rundfunk Gesellschaft mbH*), or RRG, exercised a limited control over the regional stations. Fifty-one per cent of RRG shares were held by the Reichspost which owned the fixed assets and provided certain types of transmission. These included the Wireless News Service (*Drahtloser Dienst*), which, on behalf of the government, selected and distributed news features for the regional broadcasting companies to use as they thought fit, and for the marine radio service to transmit to ships at sea. The Reichspost also collected licence fees from the public.

Berlin had only marginal political influence on the local broadcasting stations. Regional committees, which included a representative of the Berlin Ministry of the Interior, controlled the political programmes, while a local committee called the *Kulturbeirat* advised the regional stations with regard to cultural and scientific programmes.

Hindenburg's appointment, on 1 June 1932, of Franz von Papen as chancellor triggered the nationalization of the German broadcasting system. Papen belonged to the right-wing of the Catholic Centre Party. Since his government had only limited support, principally from business and the military, Papen had to provide substantial assurances, including the promise of new elections if he could win a majority in a general election to the *Reichstag*, to Hitler, who had mass support among the unemployed. In June, Papen ordered that each regional station should allocate an hour a day to a Berlin programme called '*Die Stunde der Reichsregierung*', or 'The Voice of the Reich Government'. But even this did not bring the necessary majority in the elections of 6 November 1932, and Papen resigned.

After three months of hectic negotiation, on 30 January 1933, Papen succeeded in persuading the 86-year-old Hindenburg to appoint Adolf Hitler his successor as chancellor and leader of a right-wing coalition government. By means of the deal with Hitler, Papen hoped to return to power, and was rewarded with the post of vice-chancellor in Hitler's first cabinet, providing the NSDAP with a façade of respectability behind which the Nazis could consolidate their power. Although compromises were necessary, Hitler ensured that all cabinet posts vital to his political survival were entrusted to solid party members. Wilhelm Frick, one of the new chancellor's closest advisors, became minister for the interior and hence responsible for the German broadcasting system. Goebbels' high-flown radio commentary on the torch-light procession organized for the Führer in Berlin on the evening of 30 January provided a foretaste of the new character of German radio.

The new parliamentary elections, to which Hindenburg assented on the appointment of Hitler, were set for 5 March. The competing parties were banned from the radio by cabinet decree, but in practice only the leftist parties were excluded. In spite of all the propaganda, including nearly fifty radio broadcasts, and heavy-handed partiality on the part of the police, the NSDAP gained only 43.9 per cent of the poll, and in order to secure a parliamentary majority of 51.8 per cent had to continue to govern as part of a coalition.[10] A few days later, during a cabinet meeting on 11 March, Hitler introduced the concept of a propaganda ministry, specifically mentioning the importance of radio access to the population 'in the event of war measures'.[11] On 13 March Hindenburg signed the draft of the relevant bill, and Joseph Goebbels was appointed head of the new ministry.

A decree on 30 June made the propaganda ministry responsible for 'all means whereby influence on the mind of the nation, the promotion of national, cultural and economic issues, and the information of the public at home and abroad concerning these, can be effected, and for the administration of all establishments serving these purposes'.[12] Thus the ProMi became solely and exclusively responsible for German radio, and other institutions – including the Reichspost, the Ministry of the Interior and the regional governments – were required to transfer most of their rights to the new Goebbels ministry. On 8 July, a new charter was imposed on the RRG, making it responsible for the 'political, cultural, administrative and technical management of the German broadcasting system'.[13] Its personnel was altered and its structure reorganized accordingly. At the same time, Goebbels established a Broadcasting Division within his ministry that would exercise control over every aspect of radio.

'The most direct instrument'

'What the press was to the nineteenth century, radio will be to the twentieth', Goebbels declared as he opened the tenth *Deutsche Funkausstellung* (German radio show) in Berlin on 18 August 1933. Radio was the 'chief and major mediator between the Movement and the Nation, between Idea and Man [...] We need broadcasting that is in step with the nation, radio that works for the people'. Two men played a key part in this riveting of Nazi ideology upon the German people through broadcasting: Wulf Bley and Eugen Hadamovsky. Wulf Bley (1890–1961) was chief radio commentator for the Storm Troopers of the Party. In 1933 he wrote a pamphlet, *Deutsche Nationalerziehung und Rundfunkneubau* (Nationalist Education and Radio Reform in Germany), in which he demanded that 'The German radio under National Socialist auspices must become the clearest and most direct instrument for educating and restructuring the German nation'. Reich Programme Director Hadamovsky (1904–1944) put it more forcefully: 'Radio programmes must mould the character and will of the German nation and train a new political type'. On another occasion he declared that 'the National Socialist movement alone gave radio its proper function'. Radio was to be the 'characteristic means of political expression of the National Socialist', possessing 'all the inner and outward elements from which he will construct the image of his new values.' National Socialism had identified 'the positive laws' of broadcasting, among which was the 'leadership-principle': 'Propaganda, in short, is pure mental creativity emanating from a central will. Broadcasting is propaganda's perfect instrument.' The radio, in Hadamovsky's view, was 'the strongest weapon ever given to the mind – opening hearts and neither halting at city gates nor turning away from closed doors, leaping rivers, mountains and seas, and swaying the people under the spell of a single powerful idea.'

Later Dr. Adolf Raskin (1900–1940), one of Goebbels' most capable broadcasting specialists, endorsed Hadamovsky's view in an article headed *'Dramaturgie der Propaganda'* (The Dramaturgy of Propaganda) in the *Handbuch des Deutschen Rundfunks 1939–40*:

Broadcasting in the full and true sense is propaganda, it is what 'propaganda' means, if one examines the content of the word properly: 'propaganda' means

1. Aerial view of the Berlin Funkhaus, 1932.

reaching out, making known, pressing forward, spreading new ideas and insights, taking arms on every battlefield of the mind, fertilizing and doing away with, clearing and extirpating, building and tearing down. Both the means and the objective are implicit in the term 'propaganda'. [...] The parameters of propaganda are set exclusively by what we mean by 'German', 'race', 'blood' and 'nation [Volk]'.[14]

The editor of the annual *Handbuch*, Hans-Joachim Weinbrenner, who was responsible within the Party structure for 'cultural-political' broadcasts, reinforced the line in the same edition under the heading '*Die Grundelemente des Rundfunks*' (Fundamentals of Broadcasting):

It must be made emphatically clear that broadcasting consists of two elements. Propaganda is a civilizing influence and at the same time an instrument of persuasion. These two aspects must not be confused. [...] Propaganda is like a bombardment softening up the five senses. The more basic the propaganda message is, the stronger will be the impression it makes on the masses, whose feelings and attitudes are of a similarly basic kind. You will not rouse the enthusiasm of the masses with scholarly talks, but by presenting them with simple, everyday illustrations that correspond with their own experiences.

By the time of the Berlin Olympics of 1936, the German foreign-language broadcasting system was significantly ahead of that of all other countries in terms of technology and equipment, staff numbers, and expertise in the manipulation of listeners. In a 1936 ProMi circular, Goebbels noted with satisfaction: 'We National Socialist propagandists have transformed the radio into the sharpest of propaganda weapons. Before we took power, the German radio was run by amateurs. What we have now made of it is a tool for ideological education and a top-class political force.'

The 'People's Set'

Having defined the political nature of German radio, Goebbels' next task was to ensure that every German household could receive its programmes. He might well have preferred a broadcasting system such as that of the Soviet Union, where uniform programmes were distributed by wire throughout the country. But the Russian system was an innovation of the very beginning of radio technology, whereas the Nazis had inherited an already sophisticated, working system. Goebbels' solution was to launch an inexpensive, mass-market radio set, the 'People's set' (the *Volksempfänger*). On 25 May 1933 production began on the first 100,000 sets, aiming to have them on the market in time for the first radio show in August. The prototype model was the VE 301, or '*Volksempfänger 30. Januar*', commemorating the date Hitler came to power in 1933. The set was launched at a retail price of 76 marks, which compared well with the existing average market price of 150 marks for a simple set and up to twice as much for a more powerful, quality model. Using the 'People's set' the nearest *Reichssender* (regional station) could be received on medium wave and the *Deutschlandsender* (national station) on long wave. For obvious reasons, short-wave reception was not provided. In 1936 an improved version was introduced at the price of 65 marks, and in 1938 a compact and even cheaper model, the DKE 38, or German Mini Receiver (*Deutscher Kleinempfänger*), was launched at the aggressive price of 35 marks.

2 **German working-class family listening to the 'People's Set', or Volksempfänger.**

The 'People's sets' were a tremendous success: propaganda objectives apart, the Nazi government now had direct access to the entire population at any given moment. A total of 4.3 million receivers had been registered by 1 January 1933. By the following year the figure had climbed to 8.2 million, and on 1 January 1938 there were 9.1 million sets in the country – one for every second household – and the number was climbing steadily. This ratio of 121.5 sets per thousand inhabitants put Germany in fifth place in Europe, after Denmark (187), the UK (176), Sweden (171) and Holland (124). On 1 January 1939, 'Greater' Germany (including annexed territories) had 10.8 million receivers, and by 1 January 1941, just under 15 million, reaching a total of about fifty million listeners.

The policy of maintaining a deliberately low retail price for radio receivers clearly worked: of all sets sold between August 1933 and July 1934, 37 per cent were People's sets, climbing to 44 per cent in the following twelve months. Eventually the percentage declined to 24 per cent during 1936–37, when sales of higher-priced sets began to climb.[15] Paradoxically, by that point Goebbels' political objective may have been exceeded: those who could afford it were selecting more expensive sets through which, by short wave, they could receive foreign stations.

The 'Broadcasting Division' in the ProMi

From modest beginnings the Broadcasting Division grew steadily. In 1933 it consisted of just three departments: Broadcasting Affairs (*Rundfunkwesen*), dealing generally with technical matters, Political and Cultural Aspects (*Politische und kulturelle Angelegenheiten des Rundfunks*), and Organization and Administration (*Organisations- und Verwaltungsfragen*). By 1945, however, there were twenty-one departments and a staff of about two thousand. During the ProMi's twelve-year existence, broadcasting evolved into the ministry's largest and, after propaganda, second most important division. As the representative of the interests of the sole shareholder it controlled everything from planning through to the last detail of presentation, to political commentaries, entertainment programmes, and financial and technical operations. And as if it were not already clear, Goebbels emphasized at the beginning of the war that the political direction of the German radio operation was the exclusive responsibility of his ministry's Broadcasting Division, and that all ideas and suggestions were to be brought to its attention. The ruling applied also to all RRG employees: the ProMi alone would decide what was to be broadcast, not the regional directors nor programme supervisors, let alone the editors.[16]

The first head of the ProMi's Broadcasting Division was Horst Dressler-Andress, appointed in July 1933. He succeeded Gustav Krukenberg (*b.* 1888), who had been the Reich Broadcasting Commissioner since February 1933. Dressler-Andress, born in Zeitz in 1899, was an actor trained in the famous Reinhardt school at the Deutsches Theater, Berlin. A volunteer in the First World War, he returned to the theatre in 1919. From about 1927 he began to develop ideas on the impact of radio broadcasting on the theatre. Goebbels noticed his pamphlet on 'Radio as a Propaganda Instrument

3 Horst Dressler-Andress, first head of the ProMi's Broadcasting Division.

for the Arts' (*Rundfunk als Propaganda-Instrument für die Kunst*) and as a result Dressler-Andress became involved in the formulation of Nazi broadcasting policy. Party members regarded him as a left-winger, a National Socialist with the emphasis on the term 'socialist'.

By February 1936, the Broadcasting Division consisted of four departments and one 'Special Tasks' (*Sonderreferat*):[17]

- Political and Organizational Matters (*Politische und Organisatorische Angelegenheiten*);
- Cultural Matters (*Kulturelle Angelegenheiten*);
- Legal and Administrative Matters (*Rechts- und Verwaltungsangelegenheiten*);
- Technical Matters (*Technische Angelegenheiten*);

The *Sonderreferat* was responsible for liaising with the Party's leisure organization *Kraft durch Freude* (Strength through Joy), which had been founded in October 1933 under the German Labour Front to develop a programme of recreational activities for the workers.

In the spring of 1937 the broadcasting system began a second phase of administrative centralization. On 19 March Dressler-Andress, whose belief in broadcasting as a means of bringing culture to the masses and not simply as a propaganda vehicle for the state and ruling party led to his political demotion, was replaced by Hans Kriegler.[18] Hans Gottfried Kriegler, born in Breslau in 1905, had left school in 1921 to begin an apprenticeship in the building industry. After three years as a journeyman carpenter and further training in a technical college, Kriegler described himself as an architect. More important in the light of his future career was his early involvement – at eighteen – with several right-wing groups. In December 1926 he joined the NSDAP, and in 1929 became a member of Alfred Rosenberg's Campaign for German Culture (*Kampfbund für deutsche Kultur*). A year later, he became a Storm Troop leader. Kriegler's political connections then secured him a full-time party career and, after Hitler came to power, he emerged as the director of the regional station at Breslau. Kriegler was a loyal follower but no leader, and Goebbels' motive for calling this technician to Berlin may have been an acknowledgment of his serf-like diligence.

Early in 1937 the top echelons of the RRG management were reorganized, with regional vacancies arising from internal promotion to several key positions. In a circular dated 15 August 1937, these measures were explained as 'consistently implementing the authoritarian principle in practice', and at the same time achieving a 'substantial administrative decentralization and consequently an increase in independence for the individual *Reichssender* with enhanced responsibility for the *Intendanten*'.[19]

From then until the beginning of the war there were only minor changes: Kriegler moved to Political and Organizational Matters; the department of Cultural Matters was enlarged to include Foreign Broadcasts under Hans-Joachim Weinbrenner, who was also deputy head of the division; Legal and Technical Affairs were combined under Herbert Dominik (*b.* 1902); Hans Schaudinn (1901–1945?), a personal friend of Hadamovsky, headed Special Tasks. Originally a stage actor, he had become a Storm Trooper in 1930, rising to the rank of brigade commander in January 1941. He had joined the Party in 1931. Finally, a new section, Radio Industry (*Rundfunkwirtschaft*) under Dr. Horst Schaefer, was created to oversee the restructuring of the German radio industry along ProMi guidelines. Schaudinn, a personal friend of Eugen Hadamovsky, was deputy head of the division, which he had joined in 1938.

On 29 August 1939, just before the German attack on Poland, Goebbels gave Kriegler's job to Alfred-Ingemar Berndt. Kriegler had made little impact on German broadcasting history, and his term of office is notable only for the substantial increase in the number of listeners.[20] Berndt, however, became one of Goebbels' closest colleagues.

Berndt was born, in 1905, into a peasant family living in Bromberg/Bydgoszcz, near what was then the German-Polish border. Leaving Berlin University before his studies were complete, he joined the *Deutsches Tageblatt* as an editor in 1924, later working as a freelance journalist. In 1923 he joined the NSDAP, leaving it the following year but rejoining in May 1932, when he was sent to the Party's regional press office in Berlin. Here Berndt soon became a confidant of *Reichspressechef* Dietrich, in whose name – and wearing Storm Trooper uniform – he was responsible for the reorganization of the German news agencies along Party lines and the centralization of all news services in the German News Bureau (*Deutsches Nachrichtenbüro*) – with himself at the helm. Between 1936 and 1938 Berndt was head of the ProMi's Press Division. When this was divided into two separate divisions,

Inland Press – later renamed German Press – and Foreign Press, he briefly lead the *Schrifttumabteilung* (the ProMi's division for literature) before becoming head of the Broadcasting Division.

Berndt was a notably unsavoury character: Goebbels and his senior officials were frequently astounded by his slyness and cunning, fabrications and lies. At the Nuremburg tribunal, Moritz Augustus von Schirmeister, Goebbels' personal press secretary, described Berndt as a 'typical sledgehammer politician (*Holzhammerpolitiker*)'. Wilfried von Oven, Schirmeister's successor, called him 'an unscrupulous and ambitious, but not untalented young man. In February 1940, after only a few months in office, Berndt surprised the regional directors with the news that he had completed his assignment and successfully placed the German broadcasting system on a wartime footing. He announced that he had decided to join the forces, since 'no-one who had not served at the front had the right to be called a propagandist.'

With Berndt temporarily absent in the army, the Broadcasting Division was run by Hadamovsky, the RRG's Programme Director, showing how close was the integration of ProMi and RRG at the highest level. In August 1940 Berndt returned to the ministry as director of broadcasting but left much of the daily work to his deputy, Wolfgang Diewerge. Berndt occupied himself by trying to persuade the Party's governor of the Warthegau region, annexed from Poland, to provide him with a country

4 Goebbels at the microphone, with Hadamovsky (*left*), Diewerge and Berndt looking on.

retreat, 'in recognition of his war service'. Goebbels continued to shield Berndt and in September 1941 appointed him head of the ministry's all-important Propaganda Division, in place of Ernst Braeckow, while Diewerge took full control over Broadcasting. Finally, after Berndt was caught shooting at crashed Allied pilots on the open roads, Goebbels was forced to act, dismissing him, but with an honourable discharge, in December 1944.[21] A few weeks later Berndt was killed in action as a member of an SS-unit.

Wolfgang Diewerge, born in Stettin in 1906, turned to politics after completing a law degree, and in 1930 joined the Party — and enlisted in the SS — under the name of 'Diege'.[22] Three years later he joined the newly established ProMi and turned into a fanatical Nazi and anti-Semitic 'expert'. In the autumn of 1933, Goebbels sent Diewerge to Cairo to report on a trial of Jewish underground fighters. After April 1934 he was the ProMi's advisor on France, North Africa and Switzerland and, in this capacity, reported on the assassination of Wilhelm Gustloff, head of the Nazi movement in Switzerland, by a Talmudic student, David Frankfurter, in Davos in 1935.[23] Diewerge was also responsible for the ProMi's investigation of the killing of Ernst vom Rath, an attaché at the German embassy in Paris, by the seventeen-year-old Polish-German, Herschel Grynszpan, on 7 November 1938, the murder which provided the Nazis with the pretext for the *Kristallnacht*, the pogrom of the night of 9–10 November 1938. With customary diligence Diewerge set about assembling in an official Yellow Book (*Gelbbuch*) records of all acts of violence involving Jews.[24] In 1939 Goebbels posted him to the new regional propaganda office in Danzig from where he promoted racial humiliation and extermination in annexed western Poland until recalled to Berlin to deputize for Berndt.

In October 1941, during Diewerge's tenure as head of Broadcasting, another of Goebbels' confidants, Hans Hinkel, was commissioned to produce a plan for a major reorganization of the RRG's musical and entertainment programmes. Goebbels accepted Hinkel's proposals in February 1942 and put him in charge of all radio entertainment, thus further centralizing power in the ministry.[25] And since Hinkel reported directly to Goebbels, Diewerge's responsibilities in the Broadcasting Division were curtailed accordingly.

Hans Hinkel, born in Worms in 1901, was the son of a wealthy industrialist. He dropped out of university in 1923 and began working as a journalist, initially for various Bavarian daily newspapers. He had joined the National Socialist Party as early as 1921 and by 1928 was on the editorial board of two Nazi newspapers, the *Völkischer Beobachter* and *Der Angriff*, and serving as the Party's regional press watchdog (*Gaupresseleiter*) in Berlin. Skilfully reading the political signals, Hinkel had surrendered his membership of the SA in 1928 and transferred to the SS in March 1931. His career leapt ahead in January 1933 when he was appointed state commissioner at the Ministry of Sciences, Arts and Education. Three years later Goebbels appointed him head of the index of cultural personalities (*Kulturpersonalien*), later the division for special tasks: cultural life (*Besondere Kulturaufgaben*). In this guise Hinkel assumed responsibility for the purging of Jews from German cultural life, and became one of the ProMi's most feared operators and its highest ranking SS-officer.[26] In November

1940 he was promoted *SS-Brigadeführer*, the equivalent of major-general, and in 1943 to *SS-Gruppenführer* (lieutenant-general).

Even though Goebbels, in his 1938 diary, termed Hinkel a 'loathsome intriguer' and 'bug', he seems to have valued his henchman's abilities. In 1940 Hinkel was appointed chief executive of the Reich Chamber of Culture and head of the ProMi's special department (*Sonderreferat*) for forces entertainment. A year later he was given the newly-created title of secretary general of the Reich Chamber of Culture and, from February 1942, was effectively responsible for all radio entertainment.

1942: Reorganization of 'Broadcasting' in the ProMi

Two weeks after endorsing the Hinkel plan for the entertainment sector, Goebbels turned his attention to the 'political-propaganda' agenda of his Broadcasting division. On 26 February 1942 he announced that Diewerge would work on the reorganization of all spoken-word schedules other than entertainment, a shake-up which left the Broadcasting division in seven departments:[27]

- The Control Section (*Kontrollreferat*) which, under Seitz, checked the content of the RRG's foreign-language broadcasts. This function was later transferred to Foreign Broadcasts (*Auslandsrundfunk*).[28]
- The Broadcasting Command Post (*Rundfunkkommandostelle*) which, together with the Mobilization Centre (*Mobilmachungs-Referat*), was responsible for all security matters and for liaison with the military. It was headed by Ernst Apitzsch.[29] The Command Post had been established by Berndt in August 1939 to tighten control over German radio. It was the ministry's official channel of communication with the RRG – except when Goebbels by-passed it and gave instructions direct to RRG officials, as was often the case. The Command Post relayed Broadcasting's daily instructions to the RRG, emphasizing political items to be highlighted, and directing the use of broadcasting time, and the selection of quoted material from foreign stations and the Wireless News Service (which had been transferred back to the RRG from Broadcasting at the beginning of the war.)
- Foreign Broadcasts (*Auslandsrundfunk*) which, under Werner Knochenhauser until November 1942 and Fritz Noack thereafter, was the division's means of communication both laterally with the ProMi's own Foreign Policy Division and externally with the Foreign Ministry. It also had the authority to grant individual permits to listen to foreign radio stations.
- Programme Control (*Rundfunkprogrammbetreuung*) which, headed by Wilhelm Bartholdy,[30] maintained contact with the Party's various propaganda offices and with Himmler's dreaded Security Service, the Sicherheitsdienst . At the same time, it served as an internal audit, ensuring that the minister's instructions were promptly and effectively executed.
- the *Rundfunk-Organisation*, which was led by Arthur Freudenberg, the

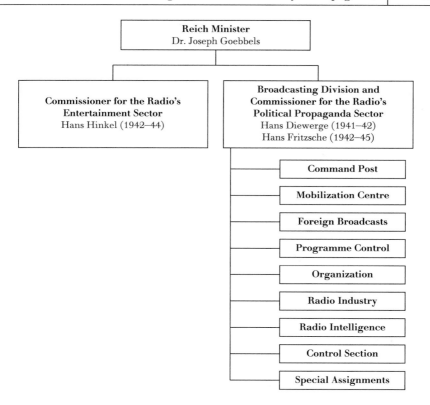

Chart 1: Organization of the ProMi's Broadcasting Division (1942–45)

ProMi's first broadcasting delegate in the occupied Netherlands, until he was recalled to Berlin in March 1941.[31]

- the Radio Industry (*Rundfunkwirtschaft*), which under Heinrich Müller (and Hellmuth Bruchmann after November 1942) was responsible for radio set production and production control.
- Radio Intelligence (*Rundfunkerkundung*) which, under Rudolf Stache, was one of the many competing agencies monitoring and evaluating foreign broadcasts, as well as Germany's own foreign-language programmes. It was established by Goebbels to avoid overdependence on the Foreign Ministry's facilities and favours.

By the autumn of 1942 the war against Russia was approaching its second winter and, despite early successes, the devastating self-inflicted disaster of Stalingrad. Public morale was at an all-time low and the performance of the reorganized Broadcasting division fell short of Goebbel's expectations. On 27 September1942, during his daily ministerial conference, he spoke of the 'inadequacies of German propaganda methods' which, with their 'stale and cheap' (*'abgegriffen und schäbbig'*) language and content, left the public cold both within Germany and abroad. Someone had to pay, and

Diewerge's was the head to roll. Early in November he was demoted to his previous job in Danzig – ostensibly transferred for 'special assignments' by the minister's office.

Wolfgang Diewerge settled in Opladen after the war, working as an advertising manager in Essen. He joined the Free Democrats, at that time a kind of catchment party for former Nazi officials, rising to the position of personal secretary and adviser to the party's chairman in North-Rhine Westphalia. By 1966 Diewerge was managing director of a business in Wiesbaden. His name was frequently in the headlines: when expelled from the Free Democratic Party in 1953, when imprisoned in 1966 for perjury before an inquiry into the Herschel Grynszpan case, and when revealed to be involved in a bribery case.[32]

Hans Fritzsche

The fifth and final head of Goebbel's Broadcasting Division was Hans Fritzsche, an experienced journalist and chief of the ministry's German Press Division. Here at last was an able administrator, though by no means a political fanaticist to the degree of his predecessors.

Like many of his colleagues, Fritzsche, born in Bochum in 1900, had dropped out of university to become a full-time journalist. After a period as editor of the *Preussische Jahrbücher* (Prussian Annuals) he joined the *Telegraphen-Union*, the country's next most important news agency after *Wolffs Telegraphisches Bureau*. Here he became editor of the foreign correspondents' column, the so-called *Auslandsbriefe*. In 1932 Fritzsche joined the RRG as head of the Wireless News Service, moving to become head of the Press Division's news section when it was absorbed into the ProMi's Press Division the following March. At the same time he belatedly joined the NSDAP, one of several prominent Nazis ridiculed as the March Victims ('*März-Gefallene*').[33] In December 1938, after splitting the former Press Division into its two new divisions, Goebbels appointed Fritzsche as director of Inland Press, later called the German Press Division. If his career until then could be described as that of a very capable journalist, passively entangled in politics because it went with the job, Fritzsche now became a willing tool for Goebbels, earning the nickname 'His Master's Voice'.

Prior to and early in the war Fritzsche was an almost daily presence on German radio. His commentaries were marked by an absence of the crude lies and polemic so common to most of his colleagues. Instead he 'analysed' the political situation with an irony and intelligence that appealed to many listeners, and delivered his broadcasts with rare skill and urbanity. Fritzsche's tone was reassuring rather than provocative: following the pogrom of 9–10 November 1938, for example, he reported in characteristic style:

> Over there, they cling to their 'one salvation' – Judaeo-democracy, under which, like mediaeval bigots, they would like to see anyone they regard as politically heterodox dragged to the stake – while here, we have a nation that wants nothing more than to be allowed to get on with our work and put our house in order the way we like it!

5 Goebbels broadcasting to England, with Berndt (*left*) and Hans Fritzsche observing, October 1939.

In April 1942, however, Fritzsche resigned from his post, apparently over differences with 'Reich Press Chief' Dietrich. He delivered his final broadcast from Berlin on 14 April.[34] For a while thereafter he served with the propaganda unit of the Sixth Army, storming towards Stalingrad, until Goebbels recalled him to the ProMi in October 1942. He returned then as head of the Broadcasting division as well as *Beauftragter für die politische Gestaltung des Grossdeutschen Rundfunks*, the official directly responsible to the minister for all political spoken-word programmes. His counterpart as *Beauftragter für den unterhaltenden und künstlerischen Programmbereich*, responsible for all entertainment and musical programmes, was Hinkel. The only other departmental change, apart from the departure of Diewerge, was the appointment of Karl Scharping (*b*. 1908), a Party member since March 1940, whom Fritzsche knew from the German Press division, as his deputy in place of Schaudinn.[35]

All radio propaganda now emanated from Fritzsche: the Foreign Broadcasts section declined in importance since he dealt directly with the RRG and the Foreign Ministry. Eventually, at the end of May 1944, Fritzsche became head of an undivided Broadcasting division, following the removal of Hinkel to the Film Division.[36] In addition, in a defining move, Goebbels – now empowered as the 'Reich Commissioner for the Total War Effort' – informed Fritzsche that he wished to be involved only in key issues of broadcasting policy. Now, and effectively until the end of the war, Fritzsche was in sole charge of all German broadcasting. Paradoxically, however, by the time his career reached its zenith, the war was already lost.

Fritzsche remained in Berlin until the very end. On 21 April 1945 he spoke for the last time on the radio. On the evening of 1 May, after the *Reichssender* Hamburg had announced Hitler's death, Fritzsche ended all transmissions from the capital. The following day he was taken prisoner by the Russians. With Goebbels having committed suicide, and the other senior ProMi officials, such as Otto Dietrich and secretary of state Dr. Werner Naumann, having vanished,[37] it was Hans Fritzsche who came before the Nuremberg Tribunal as the most prominent surviving representative of the Nazi propaganda operation. While in Moscow's Lubianka prison awaiting trial, Fritzsche planned his defence carefully and rehearsed the role of one 'misled about the aims of German policy' and 'exploited' by both Hitler and Goebbels. The Soviet judges, who wished to prosecute, were out-voted and Fritzsche, though unquestionably one of the Third Reich's more significant officials, was acquitted of war crimes on 1 October 1946. Following his release from Allied custody, however, proceedings against him were begun by a German de-nazification court. This time the judges were not seduced by his rhetoric or his claims to innocence, and Fritzsche was sentenced to ten years hard labour and the loss of pension rights. During this period he wrote his memoirs, entitled *Es sprach Hans Fritzsche*,[38] and in September 1950 was released from custody and settled in Cologne. He died there in September 1953, following a cancer operation.

The Penetration and Alignment of the RRG

When the ProMi 'took charge' of the RRG in 1933, Goebbels had ensured it would not be able to act independently. The RRG's supervisory board was to consist of five members – three appointed by the ProMi, and one each by the Reichspost and the Ministry of Finance. The ProMi's secretary of state assumed the position of overall chairman and the political alignment of the RRG was guaranteed.

Under the existing structure of the broadcasting company, senior operational responsibility was vested in the technical director, the director of administration and the programme director. In 1933, the then technical director, Walter Schäfer, committed suicide and his two colleagues resigned 'voluntarily'. Their replacements were Dr. Claus Hubmann, engineering, Hermann Voss, administration, and Eugen Hadamovsky as Reich Programme Director. Hubmann (*b.* 1898), was a member of both the NSDAP and the SS, and decorated with the death's head ring (*Totenkopfring*) and the blood order (*Blutorden*). Voss too (*b.* 1880) was a trusted Party member, previously responsible for the Party's 'economic-political affairs' in Greater Berlin. Hadamovsky however was undoubtedly the most influential official in the shaping of the National Socialist broadcasting system, though this did not prevent ProMi staff members from despising him as heartily as they did Berndt.

Hadamovsky was born in Berlin in 1904 and attended the local technical high-school. As a young man he was a member of the underground paramilitary organization *Schwarze Reichswehr*, and after this had been dissolved, he worked as a mechanic in Austria, Italy and North Africa. Back in Berlin and unemployed, he joined the NSDAP in December 1930, and became the Party's regional broadcasting watchdog (*Gaufunkwart*). From 1932, Hadamovsky worked for the Party's central propaganda office (*Reichspropagandaleitung*) and in this capacity organized many of Hitler's rallies and broadcasts. In recognition of his services, Hitler appointed him programme manager of the *Deutschlandsender* in March 1933, and promoted him to Reich Programme Director of all stations in July.

The RRG's Programme division was charged with ensuring the ideological balance of both national and regional broadcasting, and the output of topical comments on the daily news. 'The one thing that matters in broadcasting', Hadamovsky observed, 'is the Führer's voice', and indeed the home service was henceforth dominated by Party rallies, military parades, triumphal celebrations and, above all, by news of Hitler's speeches and appearances. The engineering and administration departments oversaw the studios, equipment and recording machinery, though the Reichspost retained responsibility for the channels on which programmes were transmitted: the RRG outlined its requirements and the Post Office carried them out.

It was not only at the senior level that RRG personnel was sifted. A task force from the ProMi assessed the political trustworthiness and Aryan credentials of the entire work force. By June 1933 a total of 136 employees had been dismissed or taken into 'protective custody', 98 of them senior officials accused of corruption. On 5 December 1934, criminal charges were levelled against eight former RRG executives, though proceedings were abandoned six months later for want of hard evidence. But formal charges were never withdrawn. With or without conclusive verdicts, the accused were jailed or vanished into concentration camps as inconvenient opponents of the new régime: the goals of the new rulers were achieved through intimidation. The German broadcasting system was now fully centralized and the regional directors reduced to ProMi puppets. On 1 April 1934, all regional stations were uniformly titled *Reichssender*, proclaiming, as Hadamovsky put it, that the German radio was at one with the people and the state, *Volk und Reich*.

In March 1937, this concentration was intensified by creating the positions of a *Reichsintendant* and a director general of the RRG. Goebbels selected Dr. Heinrich Glasmeier, the former director of the Cologne station, for both tasks – as *Reichsintendant* to keep the regional directors under control, and as director-general to oversee the three RRG directors, and Hadamovsky in particular, whose Nazi fanaticism failed to compensate for his managerial incompetence.

Glasmeier was born in Dorsten, Westphalia, in 1892. An archivist by profession he had served as an officer in the First World War and subsequently joined a free corps in the Ruhr to fight the Communists. In 1923 he was appointed director of the Westphalian Archives of Nobility, and became an expert on Westphalian genealogy and heraldry. In February 1932 he joined the NSDAP and became a regional cultural supervisor (*Gaukulturwart*), soon afterwards being promoted to captain (*SS-Hauptsturmführer*). From this base, Glasmeier was appointed director of the Cologne radio station in April 1933, replacing Ernst Hardt, an actor. In practice, however, the placid and genial Glasmeier was no match for the unscrupulous Hadamovsky. Although Glasmeier held the senior post and was responsible for carrying out the ProMi's directives in relation to organization and personnel, Hadamovsky was still Reich Programme Director and the number two in the system.

Early in 1940 Goebbels further tightened his grip by dissolving the supervisory board, thereby excluding the representatives of the Ministry of Finance and the Post Office.[39]

6 Heinrich Glasmeier (*right*), in uniform, greeting Queipo de Llano, the Spanish nationalist general and radio propagandist, June 1939.

Next, on the pretext of saving manpower – broadcasting staff were not exempt from military service – but essentially to clip the wings of the regional stations and, at the same time, to clear the way for expansion of foreign broadcasts, the RRG introduced the centralized national programme (*Reichsprogramm*) of the *Deutschlandsender* in May 1940. By December that year a quarter of all male employees of the German broadcasting system had been called up.

Hadamovsky and Glasmeier in decline

By mid-1941 Glasmeier had been eased out of Goebbels' daily ministerial conference and in a letter to the minister in June, Diewerge signalled Glasmeier's acceptance in principle of the ProMi Broadcasting division's 'commanding role'. It seems that Glasmeier was not even consulted when in October 1941 Goebbels charged Hinkel with reorganizing the radio's entertainment sector. As a result of Hinkel's proposals, submitted on 15 February 1942, the ten broadcasting sections (*Sendegruppen*) set up for various types of entertainment music were to report directly to him.[40] At that point the integration of the broadcasting system within the ProMi was complete, and there remained no place for either Glasmeier or Hadamovsky. According to the minutes of the broadcasting planning meeting of 22 April 1942, Goebbels relinquished his former Reich Programme Director on 11 or 12 May. Hadamovsky was assigned as an aide to the rising Dr. Werner Naumann, soon to become secretary of state at the ministry. This too did not last, and within weeks Hadamovsky was transferred to the the Party's national propaganda centre (*Reichspropagandaleitung*) in Munich, where he had begun his political career in 1932, and 'where he could do no more damage'. Towards the end of 1943, Hadamovsky volunteered for active service and was killed in action on the eastern front in 1944.

Although Glasmeier's sphere of influence had been substantially curtailed, leaving him with only managerial and technical responsibilities, and then only through his colleagues on the board (Voss, Hubmann or, from July 1942, Herbert Dominik), he retained his posts as *Reichsintendant* and director general of the RRG until October 1944. After 1942 however he was employed mainly on special missions, and hardly ever in Berlin. At a broadcasting planning meeting on 15 May 1942, Hinkel reported that the minister had asked Glasmeier 'to look after certain matters relating to the broadcasting stations in the east', and in the autumn of 1943, Glasmeier was dispatched on a delicate mission to Paris to persuade the military High Command against transferring local propaganda activities to Ribbentrop's Foreign Ministry.[41] Finally, on 3 October 1944, Goebbels released Glasmeier from his post at the summit of the RRG, 'in view of his imminent call to the colours'.[42]

In fact however, deprived of most functions and all power, the *Reichsintendant* had been spending much of his time in Austria. When the former monastery of St. Florian, near Linz, was requisitioned by the local Party branch, Glasmeier (who in 1938 had been awarded the International Bruckner Society's certificate of honour) became obsessed with the idea of creating within its precinct a '*Kulturstätte von Weltgeltung*' – a shrine to German culture of world-wide standing.[43] Since one of Hitler's dreams was to transform Linz into 'a German city on the Danube, that must outshine the beauty of Budapest, and demonstrate the supremacy of German intellect and creativity in the arts and crafts',[44] he was fascinated by Glasmeier's proposal and appointed him 'special commissioner' to oversee the scheme.

In September 1942, the RRG took over St. Florian, and from that point Glasmeier was principally occupied with matters related to the development of the Bruckner Foundation at Linz. With the blessing of both Hitler and Goebbels, Glasmeier picked the best available musicians from the already depleted radio orchestras in Berlin, Hamburg, Leipzig, Munich and Stuttgart and established an eighty-member symphony orchestra, a chamber music society and a choir of about forty voices. Besides giving public concerts, the Reich Bruckner Orchestra recorded for broadcasting until the final days of the Third Reich.

Heinrich Glasmeier remained at St. Florian until the end of the war. He was last seen on 5 May 1945, when he left the complex by car, and is presumed to have been killed.

2   Foreign Policy by Radio

The RRG's Foreign Broadcasts Division

Before 1938 the only foreign-language programmes regularly presented on German medium-wave broadcasting were the so-called 'midnight concerts' of the *Reichssender* Frankfurt and Stuttgart. These were announced in five languages, and cut in with foreign-language texts promoting Nazi cultural achievements or 'lessons' on the elements of National Socialism. From May that year the ProMi began to focus on the expansion of foreign-language broadcasts. Thereafter the medium-wave transmitters of these and other regional *Reichssender* began to be regularly used to target specific foreign audiences, over and above the programmes already being broadcast by the German short-wave station (KWS). Programmes in Czech were transmitted from Vienna; in French from Stuttgart, Frankfurt and Saarbrücken; in English from Hamburg and Cologne and, starting in the spring of 1939, in Polish from Breslau. Only the national *Deutschlandsender* and regional *Reichssender* Berlin were reserved for German broadcasts, at least for the time being.

By the beginning of the war, twelve *Reichssender* and twenty-seven secondary stations were involved, and a ProMi circular of 23 October 1939 put the RRG's foreign-language output at 113 hours each day, in fourteen languages. By January 1940 the number of languages had risen to twenty-two, and by the summer of that year to thirty-one, including Gaelic and some dialects. By then fourteen *Reichssender* and twenty-one secondary stations, including the new *Reichssender* in Prague and Danzig, with their sub-stations, were involved. By the end of 1940 the RRG employed about five hundred people in its foreign-language service. From a base of two hours of foreign broadcasts a day in 1933, in just two languages, the service had grown, after a decade of Nazi rule, to 147 hours of foreign broadcasts in fifty-three different languages.

The *Auslandsdirektion* of the RRG

The task of overseeing foreign-language broadcasts was originally a subsidiary function of the *Intendant* of the German Short-Wave Station, Dr. Kurt von Boeckmann, appointed in April 1933. Von Boeckmann, born of German parents in Italy in July 1885, studied law in Bonn, Heidelberg and Freiburg. After taking his degree in 1911 he became a lawyer, later served as an army officer in the First World War. After the war von Boekmann immersed himself in the study of the history of culture and, in 1920, was appointed a director of the Research Institute for Cultural Morphology in Munich. In 1925 he joined the Bavarian radio as an adviser, becoming its *Intendant* and sole director later that year.

Kurt von Boeckmann was one of the few radio executives to survive the Nazi purge and continue in his post after 1933: at the time of his appointment as head of Short-Wave broadcasting, the *Bayerische Rundfunk-Zeitung* observed that his diplomatic skills appeared to have saved him from the fate of most of his colleagues. At the beginning of the Second World War, von Boeckmann (who seems to have been connected with the German resistance) requested early retirement. It was denied and he sought escape on medical grounds, having suffered for many years from malaria. Although he was replaced *de facto*, von Boeckmann remained the titular *Intendant* of the German Short-Wave Station until the end of the war.

In March 1940 Dr. Adolf Heinrich Raskin was appointed acting head of the German Short-Wave Station, and given the additional brief to reorganize the foreign-language operation. Highly intelligent, dynamic and full of ideas, Raskin was a close confidant of Goebbels, and a fellow Rhinelander. Born in Cologne in November 1900, he graduated in 1923 with a study of Johann Joachim Quantz, flautist and composer to Frederick the Great. After a period as a bank clerk in Saarbrücken, he became a journalist with the *Saarbrücker Zeitung* and, in 1928, joined the *Rheinisch Westfälische Zeitung* in Essen as arts editor. In May 1933, Glasmeier, then director of the Cologne station, selected Raskin to head the station's music department. About this time Raskin became a Party member, like Fritzsche, as a so-called 'March Victim', and later the same year Goebbels picked him to direct the *Westdeutscher Gemeinschaftsdienst*, the radio propaganda campaign which was to schedule fifty Reich broadcasts and more than a thousand individual programmes ahead of the Saarland referendum due in January 1935.

Since the Treaty of Versailles, the Saar region had been under the jurisdiction of the League of Nations. The point of the 1935 referendum was to decide whether the population wished to remain under the existing administration, join France, or be reunited with Germany. The Saarland referendum was the first international political event in which radio broadcasting played a significant, and possibly decisive, role. It marked Hitler's first international triumph and was a considerable personal success for Raskin: 91 per cent of the Saar population voted in favour of integration into the Reich. The same year Raskin became the first National Socialist director of Saarbrücken radio.

In March 1938, Goebbels again called on Raskin's organizational skills to mastermind the absorption of the Austrian broadcasting company, RAVAG, into the German system. (Broadcasts from Munich had already provoked the abortive 1934 *coup d'état* in Vienna, when the Austrian chancellor, Dr. Engelbert Dollfuss, was assassinated, and in 1938 radio played an even greater part in preparing for the bloodless take-over of the country.) The next year, Goebbels brought Raskin to Berlin to head the RRG's Current Affairs (*Zeitgeschehen*) division, and in March 1940 he was put in charge of

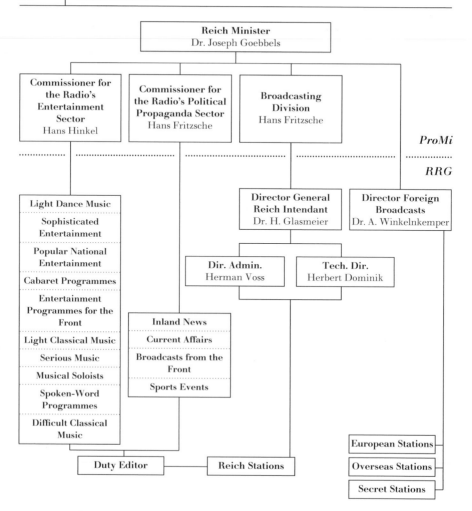

Chart 2: Organization of the German Broadcasting System (1942–45)

Foreign Broadcasts. But in November 1940 he was killed in a plane crash near Dresden, travelling to Sofia to establish a secret station targeting Greece, known later as the 'Patris' station.

Raskin's death was a serious blow to Goebbels, and in January 1941 he appointed Dr. Anton 'Toni' Winkelnkemper, a bull-necked Westphalian and loyal Party member, to replace him. Winkelnkemper had been born in Wiedenbrück in October 1905.[1] After school and an apprenticeship he lived for a time in France and Italy, sojourns described as 'study visits' in later biographies. He joined the Nazi Party – and later the SS – in 1930, soon afterwards becoming *Gaupropagandaleiter* in the Rhineland. Expelled from Cologne University for his political activities, he was elected a member of the provincial parliament in March 1933 and a member of the *Reichstag* later the same year.

7 Anton Winkelnkemper, in uniform, 1941.

Winkelnkemper then returned to university, at Bonn, completing his law studies with a thesis on *Der strafrechtliche Schutz der NSDAP* (The Rights of the NSDAP under Criminal Law). In 1937 he succeeded Glasmeier as director of the regional station at Cologne, before being summoned to Berlin on the death of Raskin, to become one of Goebbels' closest collaborators.

On 21 April 1941 the Foreign Broadcasts department was re-shuffled and renamed the *Auslandsdirektion*, with Winkelnkemper as director. According to a ProMi circular of 26 February 1942, directives came straight from Goebbels, and Winkelnkemper was a regular member of the daily ministerial briefing. With the formation of the *Auslandsdirektion*, Foreign Broadcasts fell into three main activities:

- the European Foreign-Language Services (*Die Europäischen Fremdsprachendienste*), renamed the German European Stations (*Die Deutschen Europasender* – DES), to which Walter Wilhelm Dittmar (1898–1945) was appointed as *Intendant*. Dittmar was a professional journalist who had been chief editor of the *Nationalzeitung* in Essen when he succeeded Fritzsche as head of the Wireless News Service (*Drahtlose Dienst*). But he was prevented from taking up the DES post on account of receiving his call-up papers the same month.[2] The previous head of the RRG's European foreign-language services, Walter Kamm (*b.* 1906), who had been designated programme controller (*Sendeleiter*) of the DES under Dittmar, remained in

---

Foreign Broadcasts
Director of Foreign Broadcasts (from early 1943)
(September 1933 – March 1940: Dr. Kurt von Boeckmann)
March 1940 – November 1940: Dr. Adolf Raskin
April 1941 – May 1945: Dr. Anton Winkelnkemper

The German Short-Wave Station (KWS)
The German Overseas Stations (DÜS) (from early 1943)

European Foreign-Language Services
The German European Stations (DES) (from April 1941)

The Secret Stations/Bureau Concordia (from November 1939)

International Programme Exchange (IPA)
Office for International Broadcasting Services (from April 1941)

Chart 3: Organization of the RRG's Foreign-Language Broadcasting Activities

charge, while Johannes Schmidt-Hansen – until then head of the English service – replaced Kamm as programme controller.

- the German Short-Wave Station (*Der Deutsche Kurzwellensender* – KWS), in 1943 renamed the German Overseas Stations (*Die Deutschen Ueberseesender* – DÜS). Horst M. Cleinow (*b.* St. Petersburg, 1907), who had succeeded Raskin as head of Current Affairs, became its acting head when Winkelnkemper moved to his new post, with Adalbert Houben as programme controller.
- the Secret Stations (*Die Geheimsender*), which was run by Dr. Erich Hetzler under the bland title of 'programme controller for special assignments'.

In August 1944, after D-Day, the department acquired a fourth section, for Battle Stations (die *Kampfsender*).

From 1942 until the end of the war the 'permanent deputy of the director of Foreign Broadcasts' was Hans Häuschen (*b.* 1910), whom Winkelnkemper had brought from Cologne to head the International Programme Exchange (*Internationale Programm-Austausch*-IPA). Häuschen became acting head of the DES on 21 September 1943 and was confirmed as Intendant on 10 May 1944. Other staff changes in the 1943 shuffle involved Dr. Kurt Rathke as head of IPA, and Dr. Harald Diettrich, who had worked for the RRG since 1931, as controller of the foreign stations.

Winkelnkemper remained in charge of Foreign Broadcasts until the end of the war, when he was held in Dachau by the Americans until taken to the United States, along with other former officials of the German radio, to serve as a witness in the federal court cases against American pro-Nazi propagandists. Winkelnkemper appears to have settled in the US thereafter.

News Services

Early in 1940 Goebbels reorganized the RRG's 'political propaganda' section into five departments headed by individuals selected for their political reliability:[3]

- the Inland News Services (*Nachrichtendienste für das Inland* – NI) was led by the Austrian Franz Wildoner (*b.* 1883), who had joined the ProMi's Press Division in 1937 and later headed the RRG's Information Department;
- Foreign Broadcasts (*Nachrichtendienste für das Ausland* – NA), under Winkelnkemper;
- Current Affairs (*Zeitgeschehen* – NZ), the political division, which was headed by Paul Müller-Franken;
- Broadcasts from the Front (*Frontberichte* – PK *Propagandakompanie*), under Karl-Heinz Richter (*b.* 1910), an early member of the Hitler Youth and a Storm Trooper, and
- Sports Events (*Sportberichterstattung* – SP), which was headed by Rolf Wernicke (*b.* 1903).

Current Affairs, Broadcasts from the Front and Sports Events reported directly to Ernst Apitzsch, head of the Broadcasting Command Post in the ministry. Inland News Services included the Wireless News Service, which in March 1933 had been transferred from the RRG to the ProMi and integrated in the Press Division with Hans Fritzsche at the helm. In December 1938, when the Press Division was split and Fritzsche appointed as director of the new Inland Press Division, Dittmar succeeded Fritzsche as head of the Wireless News Service. Then, in September 1939, the Wireless News Service was transferred from the ProMi back to the RRG and combined with the Foreign Language Service (*Fremdsprachendienst*) in Inland News Services.

Inland News compiled, wrote and translated all news for foreign-language broadcasts until April 1941, when Winkelnkemper established his own News and Information Department, (*Nachrichten- und Informationszentrale*) generally referred to as NIZ. All foreign-language staff were transferred to NIZ. The Wireless News Service was reduced to its original role of handling inland news, and its head, Dittmar, was promoted to *Intendant* of the European Stations, with Wildoner taking over from him.

Inside the RRG's Foreign Broadcasts Division

Two extensive statements, written in English in April 1946 by Eduard Roderich Dietze, wartime head of all broadcasts to the British Isles, provide a revealing insider's view of the workings of the *Auslandsdirektion*. The following account relies substantially on Dietze's statements.

The apex of all propaganda operations was Goebbels, who delivered his instructions during his daily ministerial briefing (the awesome *Ministerkonferenz*), which normally began at eleven in the morning. In the early months of the war about twenty people attended. Later as many as fifty or sixty were present, including heads of departments and their deputies, radio officials, representatives of news agencies, and noted individual commentators. As issues involving Britain grew in importance, Winkelnkemper took Dietze along to assist him at these briefings.

> For Goebbels, the *Konferenz* was his way of personally 'selling' policy from the top and committing his senior staff to the Party line. It consisted of a monologue of varying length, with very few and invariably short exchanges, mostly following questions from Goebbels. Suggestions from the conference members were not impossible, but invariably risky, and often led to the reverse of the speaker's intentions. It was this fact, more than fear of consequences, which resulted in the monologue habit. Even at this level [...] many outspoken words of criticism were heard, before and after Goebbels was there. Many were so genuinely in despair – even *Reichstag* members and bearers of the golden Party badge – that I could not help wondering at the rigid Party discipline which forbade even them from voicing their views in the proper quarters.[4]

Following the briefing, departmental heads, together with other high-ranking specialists, would remain to draw up a *précis* of Goebbels' instructions. This customarily involved Fritzsche with his deputy, Karl Scharping (ProMi – Broadcasting Division), Heinrich Hunke or his deputy (ProMi – Foreign Division), Winkelnkemper and his deputy, Häuschen (RRG – Foreign Broadcasts), and Rühle or his deputy (Foreign Ministry – Broadcasting Division). The resulting summary was returned to the minister for approval and then read out by Fritzsche at a more general meeting, and enlarged upon by Scharping. Occasionally this was followed by a talk by a guest speaker, or a 'confidential' report on the military situation.

Fritzsche's briefing was carried by land lines to the RRG and Königs Wusterhausen, where members of NIZ listened and took down the *précis* verbatim, while a summary report of the rest of the conference was prepared – apart from the 'confidential' military report, during which the microphone was switched off. Thus NIZ in Berlin and the news centre at Königs Wusterhausen were able to issue copies of the *précis*, called the *Tagesparole* (daily 'watchword' or slant), and a report of the Fritzsche briefing, complete with advice from the Foreign Ministry.

At this stage the personal rivalry between Winkelnkemper and Fritzsche was plainly evident. Once Goebbels had approved the *précis*, Winkelnkemper would slip away with Häuschen and Dietze and immediately head back to the *Rundfunkhaus* in Charlottenburg, to deliver his own briefing to staff. The head of NIZ, however, and – so long as they were still operating out of Berlin – the heads of the DES and the DÜS, or their deputies, would normally remain to represent the *Auslandsdirektion*.

The Winkelnkemper meeting was attended by all section leaders, and most editors and chief commentators; 'only [William] Joyce was always exempted'. In Winkelnkemper's absence Cleinow, Houben or Kamm chaired his meetings, until evacuation to Königs Wusterhausen in August 1943. The officer representing the high command (OKW) would make a short statement and Dietze would then be called upon to provide an account of Goebbels' instructions. The presentations were frequently followed by 'lively and outspoken discussion' which was minuted for Winkelnkemper's files. 'They often used to need a good deal of editing in view of the frankness with which certain views were sometimes expressed.'

There were, additionally, weekly liaison meetings between the ProMi and the Foreign Ministry at which representatives regularly exchanged views on propaganda abroad. The Foreign Ministry had established specialized committees for the major target countries, with chairmen directly responsible to Ribbentrop. It was a full-time job for each of them. Dr. Fritz Hesse (1898–1980), who chaired the 'England committee' was born in Baghdad and had fought in the First World War. He was a representative of the German News Agency (*Deutsche Nachrichtenbüro*) at the German embassy in London from 1934 until the beginning of the war. Dr. Colin Ross (1885–1945), chairman of the 'America committee', was born in Vienna and became known as a travel writer and novelist. He was to commit suicide at the end of the war.

The country committees were purely advisory. They met once a week at the Foreign Ministry and were attended by the desk chiefs (*Länderreferenten*) of the Foreign Ministry's Broadcasting Department and of the ProMi's Foreign Department, the heads of the RRG's broadcasting zones, often some editors and senior commentators and, at the invitation of the chairman, occasional experts on specific agenda points or journalists with specific knowledge of the country in question.

About once a week the RRG's *Auslandsdirektion* called a meeting of the heads of the broadcasting zones, with a similar gathering of participants, which was chaired by either Winkelnkemper or Häuschen. While during liaison meetings at the Foreign Ministry the emphasis was on practical problems and suggestions for broadcasts, the RRG's *Zonenkonferenzen* were primarily a forum for high-level discussion of ProMi/RRG – Foreign Ministry disagreements when lower levels had been unable to reach a working compromise.

As part of the spring 1941 reshuffle, Dr. Herbert Schröder became head of NIZ, with Erwin Barth von Wehrenalp (*b.* 1911), as his deputy. Schröder had joined the German Short-Wave Station in 1933. Not a Party member himself, he managed over the years to keep the departments he was responsible for relatively 'Nazi-free'. Indeed Günther Weisenborn, a prominent member of the German resistance movement, was a member of Schröder's staff at NIZ.[5]

The function of NIZ was to gather news from the military High Command, the Foreign Ministry and the various news agencies, to sift, correlate, subedit and issue it. 'The material produced by NIZ and issued by the *Nachrichtenstelle* was practically the only source of news. Material obtained from other sources was considered as uncensored. In cases of doubt even an item published in a German newspaper was not 'free' and gave no alibi to the chief editor responsible.'

8 Winkelnkemper (in SS uniform) chairing a weekly *Auslandsdirektion* meeting of heads of the RRG's broadcasting zones, 1942. On Winkelnkemper's right is his deputy Hauschen, KWS-Intendant Cleinow and KWS-Sendeleiter Houben.

In the course of an average day, NIZ would receive new or additional telephone instructions from Fritzsche's office, or from Goebbels' personal press officer, often acting on direct orders from the minister. If these instructions were relevant to more than one broadcasting section, they were copied and issued under the heading 'On higher instructions'. On some occasions, orders would come through to cancel an item which had already been released.

> Stopping such items on one authority after they had been released on another, and *vice versa*, was a great game and played a large part in the general activities. Sometimes flat contradictions were demanded – for ProMi and AA [*Auswärtiges Amt* – Foreign Ministry] rarely were in full agreement, practically only on the handling of the Jewish problem, and even then there were occasional differences – and we had our work cut out to save what face we had left.[6]

Most talks and features were written by commentators on the staff of, or freelancing for, the various broadcasting zones, but suggestions came also from the Foreign Ministry, NIZ and from *Dramaturgie*, a special production unit for radio plays. Generally the commentators did not write strictly to order, but worked out their own ideas. They then submitted the script to the chief editor for clearance. If he could not agree to a certain sentence or line of argument, there would be a discussion which generally ended in a compromise acceptable to both. 'In extreme cases – it happened more often with Kaltenbach [the American Nazi propagandist] then with anybody else – we just had to agree to differ and the talk was withdrawn by the commentator, or it was handed back as quite unsuitable, which was rare.'

Editors were frequently issued with propaganda points or positions (*Thesen*) which they were responsible for working into their scripts. An example from fairly late in the war (5 January 1944) was the Foreign Ministry directive, headed 'New Themes for Propaganda to England':

1 Britain cannot win this war.

2 Any action Britain undertakes against Germany in this war benefits Bolshevism and compromises the British Empire.

3 Britain openly supports Bolshevism since by tying down German forces in Italy, France and the Balkans with her own and America's armies she tries to weaken the German front in the east.

4 The British government openly states that the bombing offensive against German industry and homes is the best help it can give the Bolsheviks.

5 Even if it actually proved possible to overpower Germany, it would require a military campaign lasting many years that would destroy every part of Europe.

6 Britain hopes that both Germany and Russia are being so weakened by this war that they will remain weak for a long time to come and that neither will be able to wage war against Britain in the future.

7 Germany has the best soldiers in the world.

8 The British assertion that Bolshevism would withdraw to its pre-war territories after the war and that it would not entertain any expansionist aims is a delusion, which can be put down to astute Soviet propaganda.

9 The peace which Britain wants to impose on Germany would lead to the Bolshevization of Germany.

10 The dismemberment and disarmament of Germany demanded by Britain would only be detrimental to her own interests, but would benefit the Soviets.

11 It is idle for Britain to hope she can revive her old 'Balance of Power' policy, using France as her continental cat's paw (*Festlanddegen*).

12 Similarly, Britain's Balkan policy only serves Bolshevik interests, not her own.

13 Britain's abdication in the face of Bolshevism is just one aspect of Churchill's catastrophic policy.

14 This catastrophic policy can be explained by the fact that the government of Britain is not motivated by her own true interests but by the hatred, vengefulness and lust for power of Jewry.

15 Churchill is blind to all this.[7]

Each point was followed by a degree of exposition, usually in the form of press quotes. Testifying after the war, Winkelnkemper set out five central themes upon which the Nazi propagandists were required to develop an infinite number of variations:

- *anti-Communism*: Bolshevism anti-Christian and a world menace; Germany the only dependable stronghold against it.
- *anti-Semitism*: Jews the instigators of Bolshevism and destroyers of Christian economic systems.

- *social policy*: Germany's superior progress in comparison with that of other countries.
- *military power*: Prohibitive cost in bloodshed to defeat Germany; the Wehrmacht the only strong defence against Bolshevism.
- *Britain's economic doom*: Britain to lose her empire and fall as a world power if she continued the war.

Material from NIZ or *Dramaturgie* first had to be translated, and was frequently drastically edited in the process. Material from the Foreign Ministry came as finished scripts. If RRG officials could not agree with a proposal or with parts of it, a compromise was negotiated. Sometimes the Foreign Ministry suggested a broadcaster, but normally professional radio speakers would read out the Foreign Ministry material.

There was not much exchange of programmes between the various English-language zones and the *Ländergruppe Nordwest* [broadcasting zone north-west, i.e. Britain] as might have been expected. Personal ambitions and jealousies were one reason, the lack of land lines between Königs Wusterhausen [location of the short-wave transmitters outside Berlin] and the Funkhaus the other, and more important one.[8]

The *Auslandsdirektion* maintained its own music department, which produced light and dance music of a type considered likely to attract foreign listeners, but which was not allowed to be played on the home service. 'There were constant difficulties to maintain this production, since Schönicke was constantly opposing it on 'Nat. Soc. principles' and could not be persuaded to take a more broadminded view.'[9]

All material had to be submitted to military censors for clearance. Military clearance was generally sought at the source of an item of information or of a report. All news items and scripts emanating from the Foreign Ministry were deemed to have already been passed by the military censors. At any given time several censorship officers, among whom were *Kapitänleutnant* Ernst von Kunsti, an Austrian, *Korvetten-kapitän* Paetzold and Dr. Wünsche, an army officer, as well as Major Doye, Captain von Matsch, Captain Berghaus, Lieutenant Kurs and Second Lieutenant Obermeier, were in attendance at the *Funkhaus*, and scripts could be submitted at short notice. 'However, not infrequently this military censorship was by-passed, mostly because people were in a hurry.' In the case of material written by staff members, 'we often did not trouble to submit them to the censor, but regarded them as censored news'.

Political censorship was even less uniformly strict. Some section leaders submitted their scripts for clearance to their counterpart in the ProMi's Foreign Division. 'But Winkelnkemper encouraged his staff to take the responsibility themselves, and by 1943 this had become the general practice.' After the shock of the 'Schotte Incident' in June 1943, when the head of the North America zone was fired for alleged 'sloppy censorship control', Winkelnkemper directed that every item to be broadcast should be heard by an independent officer, who would read a copy script whilst it was being read, in order to guard against all possible leakages or *ad lib* alterations. Within the narrow limits of their instructions, the chief editors of the various broadcasting sections were able to select news items at their discretion, edit them if necessary, and have them translated. The translation was vetted again, and the service completed by the duty editor. The text was then passed to the speaker, who often doubled as translator between broadcasts, and read in direct transmission. Only in isolated cases involving rare languages and specialized foreign announcers was the news broadcast recorded in the presence of an editor. 'Although the order to follow the reading of a news service by a copy, to check the announcer, stood, it was rarely observed in the English section.'

Each day the heads of the broadcasting zones were required to scrutinize their broadcasts under specific categories, anti-Soviet arguments or sociological critique, for example, and submit a response to the *Auslandsdirektion*. The procedure was to ensure that all types of propaganda were adequately presented in the course of a day's programme, and if not, why not. The *Auslandsdirektion* had its own monitoring service, headed by Walter Ziebarth, which, among other duties, regularly prepared the so-called *Kategorienberichte*, or reports grouped by category of information, to enable the *Auslandsdirektion* to check that the broadcasting sections had complied with official directives and rulings. In order to simplify the work of the broadcasting zones, NIZ issued a daily index of headings (*Kategorienspiegel*) which enabled editors and commentators to respond quickly with arguments in a particular category, if no other lead had been given.

There were also about half-a-dozen a day special *Hauptsprachleitungsmeldungen* which was a more impressive way of telling editors that these items had to be featured verbatim and without fail, and if possible repeated at least twice.[10]

Once each month section leaders were required to compile for the *Auslandsdirektion* a report detailing evidence of the impact or effectiveness of his output. The primary source used to prove that broadcasts were being heard was the daily 'bible' from the Foreign Ministry's monitoring service. Foreign newspapers should have been another appropriate source, but the RRG seems only to have received the occasional spare copies. Personal statements by prisoners-of-war in German hands passed on by the military High Command, or reports by war correspondents, neutral observers and repatriates passed on by the Foreign Ministry, were too infrequent to be significant. There may in addition have been reports from Intelligence agents, but if there were, 'they were not disclosed as such'. Finally, the Foreign Ministry carefully scrutinized all foreign broadcasts put out by its arch-rival, the Propaganda Ministry, and was quick to report any deviation from official guide-lines. These 'fraternal' reports were referred to as *Thesis 17b*.

In spite of these elaborate routines it remained difficult to enforce compliance with the rules, or indeed check the quality of the propaganda output. Hans König, a journalist and former member of Foreign Broadcasts, explained in an affidavit after the war:

It was often impossible to rely on broadcasts being properly checked, since there were not enough people available who knew foreign languages sufficiently well to do so. I know of several cases where one got away with broadcasts that deviated completely from the line laid down, and had been the subject of official complaints, by using the 'foreign mentality' argument or by playing on linguistic nuances. Not infrequently, advantage was taken of such gaps in people's knowledge or experience, despite the network of tale-tellers that naturally flourished in this sector. I have reason to believe that there was a relatively high rate of convictions for political offences with concentration camp sentences, as well as of membership of resistance groups, among the foreign broadcasting staff. The wider horizons of the mainly non-Party staff members, subjected as they were to draconian thought-control and eavesdropping, bred a spirit of opposition among people of their intellectual training, especially when their professions and their life abroad had largely inclined them to liberal attitudes.[11]

Talks and features were pre-recorded as a matter of routine. The American broadcaster Mildred Gillars used to *ad lib* a good deal, and as a result her programmes in particular were played back before transmission, with at least one other section member listening in to offer a second opinion. Dietze was the only person in the English-language broadcasting zone to give extempore comments live, 'but only in emergencies'. Normally, he did an *ad lib* recording and played it back to a staff member. 'I often decided to repeat the recording and have a second shot. It was then copied out from the recording for the files.'

3   Short-Wave Propaganda to North America

Genesis, 1926–1939

Goebbels and his team wasted no time in pushing forward with the development of the still embryonic German short-wave system. The World Broadcasting Station (*Weltrundfunksender*) was to become their 'long-range propaganda artillery'. Its name was changed to the German Short-Wave Station (*Der Deutsche Kurzwellensender*) on 1 April 1933, with the shorter form, *Kurzwellensender*, abbreviated to KWS, widely used, even on official stationery. The KWS comprised a cluster of transmitters situated between Zeesen and Königs Wusterhausen, some thirty kilometres south of central Berlin. Test transmissions had begun in August 1926, and three years later, on 15 August 1929, the RRG signed a contract with the National Broadcasting Corporation (NBC) for the exchange of programmes. The first of these, between Zeesen and Schenectady, New York, took place on Christmas Day 1929, with Zeesen using a new 8 kW transmitter provided by the Telefunken company. By early 1933, the KWS had two short-wave transmitters available – the Lorenz company having installed an additional 5 kW transmitter the previous year – as well as a directional beam antenna serving North America.

Since the autumn of 1932, Dr. Kurt Rathke, deputy head of the programme committee of the RRG, had been pressing for a regular service to North America. Rathke was one of the pioneers of short-wave journalism, and on 12 January 1933, shortly before Hitler came to power, he put his proposals to the then RRG director, Dr. Kurt Magnus. On 16 March, a few days before his dismissal by the new administration, Magnus authorized a regular two-hourly short-wave service to the USA, beginning on 1 April. The National Socialists were therefore able to claim credit for having begun regular broadcasts to America. The first programme was transmitted on 2 April, between 01:00 and 03:00 Central European Time. It featured a brass band performing martial music, followed by a news bulletin in German and English, incorporating a recording of a speech by Hitler, and an interview by Rathke with the aviator Wolfgang von Gronau. The programme ended with a medley of students' songs sung by Franz Baumann, with Erich Ernst Buder at the piano.

On April 15 Dr. Kurt von Boeckmann was appointed *Intendant* of the KWS, a post he was to hold, at least nominally, until 1945. It was von Boeckmann who was responsible for appointing some of those who became the bedrock of Germany's foreign-language

9 **Kurt von Boeckmann,** *Intendant* (1933–39) of the KWS, the short-wave station broadcasting propaganda to North America.

broadcasting system. These included the producer and occasional vocalist Ernst Wilhelmy as speaker, Karl Schotte as English-language announcer, Horst M. Cleinow[1] as translator and announcer, and Dr. Herbert Schröder to handle public relations and advertising.

A second English-language service was introduced in June and when, at Christmas 1933, Hitler's deputy, Rudolf Hess, made a broadcast to the nation, three new short-wave transmitters began testing. Regular broadcasts to Africa, Latin-America and the Far East were added to the North America service on 1–2 February 1934, and on 1 January the following year, a regular service to South-East Asia was launched, targeting the Dutch colonies (now Indonesia) and Australia.

The staff and equipment of KWS quickly outgrew the facilities of the new Rundfunk building on Masurenallee, and the team moved into Soorstrasse 33, the nearby villa of the former technical director of the RRG. These premises were soon outgrown, and the expanding KWS studios were relocated to the *Deutschlandhaus*, a modern building on the Reichskanzlerplatz (later Adolf-Hitler-Platz, and today Theodor-Heuss-Platz) in Berlin-Charlottenburg, where a television team was also testing. The technical staff moved into prefabricated huts in Bredtschneiderstrasse, between the Rundfunk building and Kaiserdamm, in 1936.

In 1935, Rathke took the decision to concentrate on the expansion of the international programme exchange business, now being run as a department called *Internationaler Programmaustausch* or IPA. *Intendant* von Boeckmann selected Dr. Gerhart von Westermann *(b.* Riga, 1904), until then responsible for music programmes at the Munich station, to succeed Rathke as programme director, and as his own deputy. By the time of the Berlin Olympics in 1936, eight new 50 kW short-wave transmitters had been installed at Zeesen. Eight radio announcers were reading news bulletins in German, English, Spanish, Portuguese and Dutch, a total of twenty-two times each day.

In 1937, Schröder, the PR and advertising manager, was placed in charge of all KWS broadcasting zones. He himself was directly responsible for North America, with Gerhard Pyper responsible for Spanish-speaking Latin-America, Heinrich Harm for Portuguese-language broadcasts, Alfred Merklein for the Far East and Australia, and Walter Grohé for Africa. The KWS now offered free re-transmission rights in its programmes to overseas stations. By 1937, for every British transmission, two hundred German programmes were being re-broadcast in South America, according to a survey quoted by Charles Rolo.[2]

By 1938, the KWS employed over a hundred people. Its headquarters were now in an old building at Kaiserdamm 77, while its studios remained in the *Deutschlandhaus* with technical staff accommodated in the Bredtschneiderstrasse prefabs. Early in 1939, four 'primary' German-language programmes were broadcast regularly, along with versions in English, Spanish and Dutch. Arabic and Afrikaans were added in April, and in May the Portuguese service was expanded to cover Brazil.

10 **Villa Concordia, Berlin, the first headquarters of the short-wave service and, subsequently, of the Secret Stations.**

Mobilization, 1939 – 1941

At the outbreak of war in September 1939, the KWS staff numbered 150 people, including freelance contributors. Ten transmitters served its six overseas zones, introducing 69 programme hours each day in six languages: English for North America, Asia, Australia, and parts of Africa; Spanish for Central and South America; Portuguese for Brazil and parts of Africa; Dutch for the East Indies; Arabic for the Middle East; and Afrikaans for South Africa.[3] Three departments covered the main activities of the KWS: programme control (*Sendeleitung*), current affairs (*Zeitgeschehen*), and special foreign-language cultural broadcasts (*Fremdsprachige kulturelle Sondersendungen*).

The last of these departments – which was soon to grow into a vehicle for the whole of Germany's overseas short-wave propaganda – was made up of the six broadcasting zones. Its head at the time was Dr. Karl Andreas Wirz, who had joined the KWS from the *Deutschlandsender* in April 1939, replacing Dr. Eugen Kurt Fischer. Wirz also doubled as the KWS programme controller, with Cleinow – now head of current affairs – as his deputy. Schröder, who had led the North America zone since 1937, was moved to East Asia, while continuing to oversee the work of the other five zones

Wirz returned to the *Deutschlandsender* in 1940 and the appointment of Winkelnkemper as director of foreign broadcasts in April 1941 was accompanied by other changes. Cleinow became acting head of the KWS, with von Boeckmann still *Intendant* in name. The East Asia zone was eliminated in the April 1941 reshuffle and parts were transferred to one or other of two new zones, Orient and Empire. Schröder was placed in charge of Foreign Broadcasts' newly created news and information centre (NIZ).

The Broadcasting Zones at War

The zonal teams were made up of editors, commentators, presenters and a large number of freelance translators and contributors. The staff members were chosen for their familiarity with the political, economic and cultural aspects of their target region and their fluency in its language. Most in fact were either foreign nationals who had elected to work for the German propaganda machine or German repatriates.

Each zone was normally headed by a dependable German official and, in the interest of effective propaganda, section leaders were permitted a relatively broad latitude of expression – within the constraints of ProMi guidelines. Eduard Dietze, later the head of the English section, commented:

> Few of the commentators were ardent Nazis, comparatively few were Party members, and even most *Zonen-* and *Ländergruppenleiter* were very critical of the Party line. They had been chosen for their job by virtue of their knowledge of foreign affairs and languages, and that practically excluded all Nazis from the very first. Winkelnkemper, Häuschen, and Kamm were notable exceptions, to a great extent

also Houben, but even they were far more liberal-minded than the Party would have wished them to be. Quite a number were potential oppositionists, and one or two may have been active members of the underground. Most men, I think, were loyal because they could not see themselves acting against their Government in wartime, but all had misgivings and more, in varying degrees. Nearly all strove, according to their ability and courage, if not for reform, at least for a certain moderation. I make that assertion fully conscious that it may appear absurd to people who listened to the German broadcasts, but I maintain that they are not in a position to judge what these broadcasts would have been like *without* these modest efforts. We were.[4]

As the war escalated, the technical facilities of the KWS were continuously enhanced to cope with the requirement for the Nazi message to be heard on every continent. By 1941 eleven transmitters, with a combined power of 467 kW, were operational at the Zeesen complex. Four additional transmitters later became available at Munich-Ismaning, two with a combined power of 150 kW in 1941, and a further two of 100 kW in 1942. In January 1942, the short-wave transmitter at ...Öbisfelde on the Aller, north-east of Brunswick, came on line, providing an additional 300 kW *via* its three transmitters; by 1944 the complex was expanded to include eleven transmitters with a combined power of 825 kW. Then, in June and November 1943, two transmitters of 50 kW each became operational at Elmshorn, north-west of Hamburg. These were backed by short-wave transmitters throughout the occupied territories, including the powerful stations at Podiebrad in Bohemia-Moravia, Huizen-Kootwijk in the Netherlands, and the French short-wave centre at Allouis-Issoudon-Pontoise, as well as weaker transmitters in Belgium, Norway, Greece and the Ukraine.

By 1943 the KWS was using twenty-three transmitters – and, if minor stations are included, close to thirty – with a combined total power of 1500 kW. They were coded DXO, DXM, DJL, DJX, DZD etc. ('D' was the international designation for Germany; the second character indicated the type of service, e.g. 'J' for broadcasting; and the last character signalled the frequency used.) On 30 January 1943 the KWS was renamed the German Overseas Stations (*Die Deutschen Überseesender*), to match its medium-

11 Transmission centre of the German short-wave station, 1941.

The German Short-Wave Station
The German Overseas Stations (from early 1943)
(September 1933 – March 1940: Dr. Kurt von Boeckmann)
March 1940 – November 1940: Dr. Adolf Raskin
January 1941 – April 1941: Dr. Anton Winkelnkemper
April 1941 – May 1945: Horst M. Cleinow

Programme Controller:
April 1939 – 1940: Dr. Karl Andreas Wirz
1940 – April 1941: Dr. Gerhart von Westermann
April 1941 – May 1945: Adalbert Houben

Duty Editor/Zone Heads/all Broadcasters/Production Office/Gramophone Records:
Königs Wusterhausen

> **Broadcasting Zones**
>
> > **North America:**
> > – 1938: Dr. Herbert Schröder
> > 1938 – September 1939: Dr. Harry Eisenbrown
> > September 1939 – August 1943: Karl Schotte
> > September 1943 – November 1944: Hans von Richter
> > November 1944 – May 1945: Heinrich 'Henry' Maurice Schafhausen
> >
> > Commentators: Jane Anderson, Robert Best, Douglas Chandler, Constance Drexel, Gertrud 'Gertie' Hahn, Fred Kaltenbach, James Monti, etc. and Donald Day, Edward Delaney, Prof. Otto Koischwitz *from AA*/Broadcasters/Translators/Clerical Staff
>
> > **Ibero-America:** Spanish-language countries
>
> > **Brazil:** Portuguese
>
> > **Empire Zone:** Far East/Australia
>
> > **Orient Zone:** Middle East
>
> > **Africa Zone:** English/Afrikaans/Portuguese
>
> > **German Zone**

Chart 4: Organization of the RRG's German Overseas Stations

wave counterpart, the German European Stations (*Die Deutschen Europasender*). The daily output now amounted to two hundred and twenty-eight broadcasting hours in thirty-one languages. The staff totalled about six hundred people, of whom between 175 and 200 were on the direct payroll.

The North America zone of the KWS, which was of such major political and strategic importance as to over-shadow the output of all the other zones put together, is described below.[5] Here, first, is an account of the work done by the other five zones with their very differing audiences.

From its launch in February 1934, the RRG's Latin America service was highly successful in propaganda terms, thanks to the poor quality of local programmes and the absence of serious competition from any of the other major powers. The section had been headed by Gerhard Pyper since 1937, and Juan Iwersen (*b.* Mexico City, 1901), broadcasting as 'Don Juan', was the zone's chief commentator. Until 1934 Iwerson had

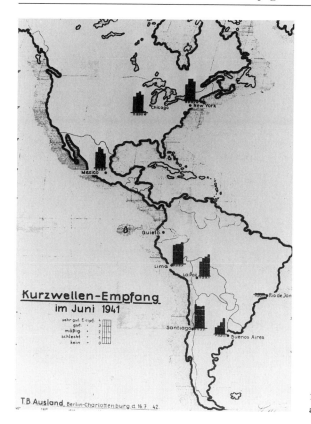

Kurzwellen-Empfang
im Juni 1941

12 Short-wave map of North
and South America.

worked as an export manager in the USA. He came to Berlin in 1938, joining the RRG in January 1939, where he proved an accomplished journalist and broadcaster. To listeners in Latin America, he projected Germany as an enlightened and progressive country ruled by orderly and civilized leaders. Since the propaganda objective was to alienate Latin Americans from Washington, 'Don Juan' would ridicule the Pan-American ideal as an 'instrument of US expansionist policy' and warn his listeners to beware of 'dollar diplomacy'.

Early in the war, Iwersen was appointed head of his zone, remaining so until the end of 1942 when he asked to be relieved to concentrate on his work as a commentator. He was replaced by Leo Anton Ribitzki, a German (*b*. Luenten, Westphalia, 1904), who had lived in Chile between 1927 and 1931 before returning to Germany. He joined the RRG in December 1935 as an announcer for Spanish and English-language broadcasts, along-side presenters such as Ludwig Maurer and Maximo Pavese, *alias* 'Don Maximo'. During the war, this team was expanded to include nationals from Chile, Ecuador, Honduras and Peru.

Broadcasting in Portuguese to Brazil began in May 1939. Initially headed by Heinrich Harm, with Gerhard Dohms (who called himself 'Enrique Micus') as chief commentator, this section soon included Otto E. Schinke, Dr. José Fernandez and Dr.

Karl-Heinz Hunsche, *alias* 'Sebastiano Sampaio da Silva'. In September 1941, Dohms succeeded Harm as head of the section, and Hunsche and Maximilian Stahlschmid, *alias* 'Mario de Andrade', became commentators. During the second half of the war, the section's staff numbered about twenty, including clerical staff and freelance contributors.

South Africa was seen as a promising target for Nazi propaganda, playing on the anti-British sentiments of many Afrikaners. Walter Grohé headed the section throughout the war, with Dr. Sidney-Erich Holm, *alias* 'Neef Holm', as his chief commentator and deputy. Holm originated from the former German South-West Africa (now Namibia) and had studied in Germany. Eckhart W. Becker (*b.* 1912), a German who had studied in the Cape, and two South African students who were in Germany when war broke out, Dr. Jan Adriaan Strauss, *alias* 'Neef Burman' (*b.* 1916) and Michael Johannes Pienaar, completed the team.

Strauss joined the Africa section in September 1939 and eventually became editor. Another South African, Johannes Jacobus Snoek, who had earlier been employed in Leipzig, joined the KWS in 1941. There were also several freelance contributors, including Dr. Edith Dietze-ter Meer (1904–1993), the daughter of the Dutch taxidermist and animal sculptor, Herman ter Meer, and married to Eduard Dietze, the head of all broadcasts to the British Isles. After the war, in autumn 1946, the three South African propagandists were tried for treason in Pretoria. Holm was sentenced to ten years imprisonment, Strauss to three years, and Snoek was fined, though on appeal all three were acquitted.

In April 1941, the original Middle East section was extended to include India, and renamed the Orient zone. Both the Foreign Ministry and Goebbels' propagandists regarded this region as of equivalent strategic importance to South Africa, especially after Rommel's Africa Corps had introduced a German military presence to Egypt. Winning Arab sympathy for Germany and supporting the call for the 'liberation of the Arab lands from Zionism and British imperialism' were key propaganda themes. The enlarged zone was headed by Dr. Gustav Bofinger, with Christian Kölbach as his deputy. It consisted of some eighty full- and part-time contributors. Several prominent exiles enjoying the protection of the Reich were encouraged to broadcast home through RRG facilities. These included the spiritual leader of the Palestine Arabs, the Grand Mufti of Jerusalem, Hajji Amin al-Husayni (1897–1974), as well as an ex-prime minister of Iraq, Rashid Ali el-Ghailani (c.1892–1965).

The Grand Mufti had helped engineer the Axis-backed Iraqi coup of April 1941, but when the insurrection collapsed in May, al-Husayni fled to Rome and thence to Berlin in October 1941. Rashid Ali had led the revolt, but the Iraqi army capitulated by the end of May and Rashid Ali fled *via* Iran to Germany.

Another member of the Orient section was Elsa Gertrude Brietzmann. Born in Brighton to a German father in 1910, she had been living in Germany from the age of twelve and, at the beginning of the war, joined the KWS as a typist. Given the shortage of qualified foreign-language broadcasters, Brietzmann was soon put on the air to urge Indian listeners – in English – to take part in the 'great Indian revolution' and 'unite to deliver a crushing blow to British imperialism'.[6]

The Orient zone was hampered by a shortage of specialists capable of handling the many cultures and languages of this vast region. About two dozen translators and presenters were recruited through advertisements in the Berlin press, and a number of German journalists were simply pressed into service (*dienstverpflichtet*). Many of the contributors had never visited their target country, but drew their 'expertise' from newspaper reports and relied on specialized input from the Foreign Ministry.

At the beginning of the war, Christian Kölbach was in charge of the Arabic team, succeeded in 1942 by Rudolf Nowasad. Egon Grossmann headed the Indian and Heinz Lubbers the Turkish teams. Alin Idris — born to Turkish parents in Kizlyar, north Caucasus, in 1887 and a professor of Islamic theology living in Berlin since 1915 — was the expert on first Balkan and then Turkish affairs. For almost two years the Persian team had no German editor and Nezzameddin Akhavi was its acting head. For the whole of the war the Indian team managed without a German specialist, the commentator, Dr. Raoul Abdul Malik, doubling as its acting head, assisted from March 1943 by Abdul Rashid Malak (*b*. Lahore, India, 1899).

Alfred Merklein led the South-East Asia zone in 1939, but in the 1941 reshuffle it was absorbed in a new Empire zone embracing the entire English-speaking world outside Great Britain and North America. Its programmes were broadcast in English and Dutch. Towards the end of 1943, broadcasts in Japanese and Manchurian were added. The new section head was Dr. Egon Strohm (*b*. Trossingen, 1904), the son of a wealthy brewery owner, who had joined the RRG in August 1938. Strohm had a team of about twenty full-time and ten freelance contributors, his key man being Dr. Rudolf Böhringer, head of the region's news service. Strohm, however, was dismissed in September 1942, following an irregularity involving a trip accompanying his English-born wife, the opera singer Margery Booth, to an engagement in Budapest. Böhringer now took over, but Strohm was allowed to continue working for the zone as chief commentator.

Emil Beckmann (*b*. Gevelsberg, Westphalia, 1909), a former graphic artist and cartographer, was one of the editors of the Empire section after October 1942. Beckmann had been living in Washington, DC, since 1929, but in June 1941 was repatriated under an exchange programme. Erwin Günther Hansen, born in England of a German father and an English mother in 1913, worked for the Empire zone on a freelance basis throughout the war. Having left England after the First World War, he returned there in 1933. In September 1939 he was back in Germany, ostensibly on holiday, although a MI5 report suggested that he went there deliberately in anticipation of the war.[7]

The North America Zone

The central feature of the broadcasts to North America was of course the news service. By 1943, up to nine prime-time news schedules were being transmitted each day, at hourly intervals. There were in addition up to five 'talks' a day, usually political commentaries on topical themes: after June 1941 the most frequent topic was the

'Communist-Jewish conspiracy'. In addition to the broadcasts in 'American English', there were also broadcasts in French for francophone listeners in Canada.

The service that was to become the North America zone had originally been coordinated by Dr. Herbert Schröder and, briefly in early 1939, by Dr. Harry Eisenbrown, a former Princeton professor who had studied at Heidelberg, where he met his German-born wife. After living in the United States between 1931 and 1938, the couple returned to Germany where Eisenbrown joined the staff of Berlin University. Until 1943 the region was headed by Karl Schotte. A German repatriate with a US passport, Schotte had joined the KWS as a news reader as early as 1933. Ten years later he was made to take the blame for some 'off-limits' remarks by one of his contributors. Eduard Dietze is the source of the following account of the 'Schotte incident'.

Just before the Roosevelt-Churchill summit at Quebec on 20 August 1943, Schotte approved a script by a certain Harl, in which it was suggested that in the event of a mutually acceptable conclusion to the war, the German people would be prepared to make considerable adjustments to the present National Socialist policy. Associated Press interpreted the broadcast as a 'semi-official peace feeler', and Ribbentrop immediately complained to Goebbels that it could be seen as a sign of German weakness, and encourage the Allies rather than push them in the direction of compromise. Goebbels, clearly wrong-footed, demanded the immediate arrest of the responsible section leader. Dietze reveals that Schotte admitted to having approved, consciously if not deliberately, of the passage in question, and remained of the opinion that Harl's remark was good policy from the German point of view – an admission which would almost certainly have meant Schotte's execution if brought to the attention of Goebbels or Ribbentrop. Winkelnkemper however presented the incident as a blunder and suggested that Schotte had been under strain from overwork and had *not* read the script. Schotte was nevertheless arrested and taken to a concentration camp, but released just before Christmas 1943 and returned to the *Auslandsdirektion* as producer – together with Dietze – of a new daily feature directed at the invasion forces gathering in England. This programme, initially called 'D-Day Calling', later became 'Invasion Calling' and 'Jerry Calling'. Schotte was responsible for the entertainment side – on Goebbels' instructions, he was to have no further political responsibility – while Dietze was placed in charge of the political content.

Schotte's deputy had, initially, been Gerdt A. Wagner, who joined the zone in May 1941. Wagner was born in Berlin on 27 July 1902, and had emigrated to the United States in 1924, settling in New York where he ran a company specializing in mosaic work. In 1936 he became an American citizen. His business took him abroad, and he frequently visited Europe, including Germany. In America Wagner was loosely associated with anti-Nazi circles, and when in Berlin at the beginning of the war, he offered his services to the Wehrmacht, which sent him back to New York on a special mission.[8] US officials learned of the mission, however, and on his return to America Wagner's passport was confiscated. Eventually, in July 1940, after several appeals, Wagner was permitted to leave the US, without his wife and son, on condition that he repatriated himself as a German citizen. On arrival in Berlin in August 1940, he joined the RRG's Wireless News Agency, from which he was transferred to the KWS.

But Wagner's appointment was not an unmitigated success, since he appears to have antagonized the American broadcasters working under him. In January 1943 Burgman complained to Schotte about Wagner's alleged continued sabotage of his work as a Nazi propagandist. A few weeks later, Douglas Chandler, the American Nazi propagandist, denounced Wagner to the Gestapo in respect of his 'outspoken viewpoint of antagonism to the German government which he is serving and an outspoken partiality for the Jews,' claiming that Wagner had been a member of the Communist Party while he lived in the United States.[9] Wagner was replaced as Schotte's deputy in the spring of 1943 by Hans von Richter (*b.* 1910), formerly on the staff of the German consulate in Cleveland, Ohio, who, after Schotte's removal from office, became the acting head of the North America zone. The final head, before the team dispersed in April 1945, was Heinrich 'Henry' Maurice Schafhausen.

'Semi-detached patriots': The American Propagandists

On 26 July 1943 — nearly eighteen months after Hitler's declaration of war on the United States — six US citizens were indicted *in absentia* by a federal grand jury in Washington, DC, on charges of wartime treason. These, all members of the RRG's North America service, were Fred Kaltenbach, Edward Delaney, Constance Drexel, Douglas Chandler, Jane Anderson and Robert Best. Although there had been short-wave broadcasts to North America since 1933, it was not until the eve of the Second World War that Goebbels agreed to staff it with authentic American propagandists. On the air, these expatriates from the still neutral United States assumed the role of semi-detached patriots motivated by their country's best interests. ProMi officials tolerated their often absurd exaggerations and fantastic assertions, so long as they meshed sufficiently with the overall propaganda strategy. Nor did the position alter significantly after Pearl Harbor.[10]

The circumstances of the individual expatriate broadcasters were obviously diverse.[11] But most were part of the American emigration to Europe following the first world war. There were times in the late 1920s and early 1930s when Paris, Berlin and Florence were crowded with American writers and artists — not to mention the rich. In 1933 the National Socialist regime inherited a fair number of them.

As in any totalitarian state, the new rulers of Germany ensured that their socio-economic and political goals and achievements were proudly projected on every conceivable occasion — at the opening by local officials of a neighbourhood kindergarten as much as at spectacularly choreographed party rallies. At a time when American liberals were wrestling with the problem of the integration of ethnic communities within their own country, and progressive voices in Britain articulated Socialist ideals, the Nazi message was loud and relentless in print, on the radio, in documentaries and in feature films. It may be that under such bombardment, expatriates and drifters, their own allegiances diluted by prolonged residence abroad and bewildering changes at home, were attracted to the growing fascist trend in Europe.

At the time of the German census in May 1939, there were 6,177 United States citizens living in the Reich.[12] Of these, seventy per cent had German ancestry. Others had dual citizenship, since American law recognised the children of first-generation immigrants as Americans, whereas under German law these were Germans. Technical citizenship is not however a sure guide as to whether loyalty remains with the country of ancestry or of residence. Indeed, two of the accused at the Nuremberg Tribunal may technically have been US citizens. The parents of former *Reichsbank* president Hjalmar Horace Greeley Schacht (named for the American liberal journalist and politician) had returned to Germany for his birth, the father being very probably a US citizen. Both parents of Reich Youth Leader Baldur von Schirach were US citizens by birth.

As the war escalated and the German propaganda machine moved into top gear, Berlin radio needed an increasing number of foreign-language broadcasters to add variety to its programmes, as well as translators to handle the mass of scripts. Many civilian internees and POWs succumbed to the recruitment drive of the German authorities, and were glad to exchange the tedium and shortages of camp life for a comparatively easy time in Berlin. Very few American and British nationals joined primarily out of political motivation, and even fewer were dedicated Nazis. Most turncoats joined the propaganda apparatus out of convenience and seem to have been little more than hucksters in search of an easy life and a ready pay-packet.

One of the first Americans to join was Fred Kaltenbach. William L. Shirer, CBS's celebrated Berlin correspondent, noted in his *Berlin Diary*, that:

> Fred Kaltenbach [...] is probably the best of the lot, actually believing in National Socialism with a sincere fanaticism and continually fighting the Nazi Party hacks when they don't agree with him. He is not a bad radio speaker. I [...] have seen Kaltenbach only once. That was at Compiègne when he was having one of his periodic feuds with the Nazi radio authorities. They gave orders that he was not to be taken from Paris to Compiègne, but he stole a ride with some army officers and 'gate-crashed' the ceremony. He was continually being arrested by the military and ejected from the grounds, but he came back each time. Most Nazis find him a bit 'too American' for their taste, but Kaltenbach would die for Nazism.[13]

Frederick Wilhelm Kaltenbach, the son of an immigrant German butcher, was born in Dubuque, Iowa, on 29 March 1895. On graduating from high school in 1914, he and one of his brothers were sent – with remarkably unfortunate timing – on holiday to Germany, where both were interned at the outbreak of the First World War. After his release and return home in December 1914, Kaltenbach entered Grinnell College in Ames, Iowa. In the summer of 1918, he enlisted with the coastal artillery, but never saw active service. At the end of the war, he entered Iowa State Teacher's College and received a BA in 1920, and subsequently an MA at Chicago University before settling as a schoolmaster in his home town. In 1932, Kaltenbach revisited Germany and was impressed by the National Socialists' economic programme. Shortly afterwards his tenure at Dubuque High came to a sudden end as he was dismissed for organizing a

Hitler Youth-style 'club'. In June 1933, Kaltenbach returned to Berlin, ostensibly to study for a doctorate, and later married a German secretary. Eventually, probably some time after he had obtained his Ph.D in 1936, he joined the RRG and, in 1939, began his regular broadcasts to the USA. Later, he would also regularly provide material for broadcasts to Britain, initially up to six talks per week. Throughout his career Kaltenbach claimed dual patriotism: proud of his German ancestry, he somehow simultaneously described the United States as his 'sweetheart'.

Kaltenbach was utilized by German radio propaganda in several ways. From October 1939, 'Fred W. Kauffenbach' broadcast a 'Weekly Letter' to his friends in Iowa. Accounts of the letters survive through the records of the BBC monitoring service. This is a summary of the second 'Letter to Iowa':

All well in Berlin, American films showing, plenty of food, foreign culture appreciated (e.g. presentation of play by Hungarian); no enmity to French, present conflict senseless, Germany no aggressive design in West, only looks East, Germany broken ring round her and retains only peaceful reconstruction to do. Why does England want to continue war? She can't beat Germany by blockade. On the contrary Germany will increase use of submarine aginst English shipping.[14]

Soon Kaltenbach gave his 'Letter' a personal touch:

Dear Harry, don't forget to send your next letter the way I instructed you – if you do, I'm hoping to put one over on the English letter openers. A while ago I got the following telegram addressed: 'Iowa, c/o German Short-Wave Station, attention: British censor'.

'Harry' was in fact an old schoolmate called Harry Hagemann, by that time a practicing lawyer, no doubt made increasingly uncomfortable by this embarrassing and one-sided relationship. From February 1940, Kaltenbach added curious 'News Flashes' to his 'Weekly Letter':

News Flash: The Mongrovian Government sends a cruiser to protect Mongrovian mail for Europe. Bravo, good people of Mongrovia, that is the only kind of protest the English Government will listen to.

News Flash: The Indian Branch of the British Lion Tamers' Club has increased its membership since Zetland's statements; and the Irish branch has been further augmented since the hanging of the Irish patriots and martyrs, Barnes and Richards. [15]

At an even less sophisticated level, Kaltenbach had his 'Friendly Quarrel between Fritz and Fred'. As honest American, Kaltenbach ('Fred') would support British policies until 'Fritz', a smart German of course, played by the former assistant professor at

Hunter College, Otto Koischwitz, demolished Fred's views with compelling arguments spiced with heavy-handed wisecracks. As the monitors heard it in January 1940:

This is a talk between two men who discuss the introduction of rationing in England and its effects. Fritz, for example, contends that the rationing will do the English people good as it will teach them to be moderate and not to eat so heartily. He says: 'There are plenty of fat people walking around the streets of London who will grow fitter than fatter if they eat less bacon'. Fred agrees that Churchill could certainly afford to lose a few pounds, and will benefit by the rationing system. But Chamberlain, on the other hand, hasn't much to lose. Fred asks whether rationing will affect unemployment, and Fritz answers that they will not notice the difference, being already used to minimum rations. Fred is puzzled. The Ministry of Food said that British sailors should not be asked to risk their lives bringing food cargoes. He asks his friend why, if Britain dominates the seas, can she not protect her ships. Fritz says that the submarine is the reason. Churchill had said many weeks ago that the British Admiralty had succeeded in eliminating this danger. But he can't have been well informed etc.[16]

A week later the Friendly Quarrellers were on the air again:

'What news, Fred?'
'Nothing, I've stopped reading the papers. I'm not interested any more.'
'But I have news for you. Interesting and rather embarrassing, Fred. It is from America this time. University Professors are going to investigate propaganda methods, particularly on the radio. So watch out, Fred, they are going to listen to you today. Their investigation will reveal all the tricks of propaganda.'

After some derogatory remarks by Fred on professors in general, and the teaching profession of which he was once a member, Fritz continues: 'The American professors are listening carefully and if you say something unpleasant they will publish it all.' Asked by Fred what he knows about propaganda, Fritz replies: 'First of all, you must take a fact. A fact you find in books; e.g. suppose we were English and had to do propaganda for the British. We would take a sentence out of some book. There is in front of me Duff Cooper's book, *The Second World War*, and on page 86, I find: "England's policy was, and always will be, to fight domination of Europe by any Power. For this reason, the English fought Philip II, Louis XIV, and Kaiser Wilhelm" ' (here Fred interposed: 'And against Hitler'.) 'Yes', replied Fritz, 'and here is a passage about the technique of starting a war. It says on p. 215, "We guarantee the frontiers of a State, not for love of that particular country, but for our own security" '.

Fred: 'That is a fact? And what do you do with a fact?'
Fritz: 'You create the impression that you know something, but you ignore the fact. The next item in propaganda is flattery. For instance, the

	British say: "American national heroes are always made of ... stuff. Men who will never rise above the common rut."
Fred:	'That is not much flattery.'
Fritz:	'Maybe not, but it must be so because otherwise the British would not say so.'
Fred:	'You have done all this. What next?'
Fritz:	'You misquote the enemy. You say, for instance, that the Germans want to dominate the world.'
Fred:	'But the English always have, and always will, dominate the world.'
Fritz:	'But don't you see you must never let anyone see that that is what you are driving at?'
Fred:	'Ah, that's what they call subtle propaganda.'
Fritz:	'Finally, you frighten your audience. With a ghost story something like this: "You, my dear American listeners, must not think you are safe in your homes... is after your fortune, your freedom, etc."'

Fred, however, is not impressed by such stories so Fritz promises him some entertainment next week.[17]

Later, as Jim, the smart milkman, Kaltenbach lectured a naive colleague, Johnny, on world affairs. At the end of the programme, Johnny usually dashed home to tell it all to his wife, who was amazed at her husband's understanding of world politics.

In addition to his propaganda broadcasts, Kaltenbach kept himself busy advancing the Nazi cause in other ways. He translated a radio play by Erwin Barth von Wehrenalp, deputy head of the KWS' own news bureau (NIZ). Called 'Lightning Action', it concerned the 1940 campaign in Norway. The twelve scenes were recorded on 5 April 1941, the speaking parts being taken by Georg H. Schnell, Henry Stuart (possibly the Irish broadcaster Francis Stuart), Dr. Philipp Manning, the British film actor Jack Trevor, Richard Ludwig, Gösta Richter, Gretl Hartmann, London-born Erwin Hansen and Elisabeth Stein.[18] Kaltenbach also wrote a series entitled 'British Disregard for American Rights'. On the passing of the Lease-Lend Act on 11 February 1941, Kaltenbach began the programme with the words 'Lend or lease me your ears!', and continued: 'Now that Roosevelt has signed the Lease-Lend Bill, I suppose the Germans should be bowing before the new Lords of the universe, George VI and Emperor Roosevelt I. The Germans have been too busy dropping their iron pellets on Englishmen to worry about the Union-Now boys in Washington [...] Compared with the patriots of 1941, Benedict Arnold was a mere piker. All he did was to betray a fort to the Red Coats. The Union-Now boys have betrayed the whole country.'

Kaltenbach's style was loaded with puns and jingles. On a speech by 'Roly-Poly Windsy' Churchill dealing with British losses at sea, Kaltenbach commented: 'Figures don't lie but liars figure.' He called Chamberlain the 'Umbrella Man' and Eden the 'Nincompoop – famous for his good suits and bad speeches'. The BBC became the 'Bullitt-Biddle Corporation – Atrocity Manufacturers Unlimited'. In spite of Kaltenbach's laboured jocularity which, branded as typically Teutonic by American listeners, often defeated his own purpose, he was able to introduce some astutely provocative opinions:

- He urged the Canadians to secede from the Commonwealth and tried to incite the Americans to appropriate all British property in the United States.
- He charged the 'Roosevelt Column' with stirring up a civil war in Central America so that the United States 'could take over' — a theme also plugged by Juan Iwersen on Berlin's Spanish-language service.
- He called for the abolition of money and thus of the class system in the United States.
- He called for anti-Semitic pogroms, strikes against the US adminstration and similar revolutionary action.

Fred Kaltenbach's wartime role was amply documented, but he never faced trial. On 14 July 1945 he was captured by the Russians and interned in a camp near Frankfurt-on-the-Oder, where he died in October 1945, reputedly of natural causes.

Another early American Nazi propagandist was Leo Delaney, whom William Shirer described as having 'a diseased hatred for Jews, but otherwise is a mild fellow and broadcasts the cruder type of Nazi propaganda without questioning'.

Edward Leopold Delaney, the son of Irish immigrants, was born in Olney, Illinois, on 12 December 1885, and raised in Glenview, a suburb of Chicago. Around 1910, he embarked on a career as a stage actor, initially in San Francisco, and later in New York, before eventually signing on with a road company. For several years Delaney toured North America until noticed by an Australian film producer and offered work in the movies. He was cast by Cecil B. de Mille opposite the silent movie star Blanche Sweet in *The Thousand Dollar Husband*. But in an argument over pay, he threatened to walk out before the end of the shooting. The studio relented, but Delaney was blacklisted. With no chance of further films, he toured South America, showing American silent films with Spanish subtitles.

About the time of America's entry into the First World War, Delaney left for the Far East as a representative of an Australian company. Then, in 1920, he moved to South Africa to join the staff of fellow-American Isidore William Schlesinger's theatre chain. The following year he was in Paris and London, involved in several unsuccessful road company productions and, from 1924, worked as marketing manager for MGM. After the stock market crash of 1929 Delaney was made redundant, spending the following years in and out of the United States. Little is known of his activities, except that his apparent open criticism of President Roosevelt was noted by the German embassy in Washington and resulted in an invitation to Berlin in July 1939. He was received by Dr. Hans Schirmer, and offered a position countering anti-German propaganda abroad. Delaney was promised editorial freedom and unrestricted travel, and in September 1939 returned first to the United States and then to Britain 'to study wartime conditions'. His conclusion, predictably, was that the British were willing to accept Poland's absorption by Germany in order to 'get on with their lives'.

13 The American Nazi propagandist, Leo Delaney, 1943.

Towards the end of 1939 Delaney began working for the Berlin radio, using the name 'E.D. Ward' and describing himself as an 'American correspondent and observer'. He followed hard on the heels of the advancing German armies, reporting their entry into various European capitals, reiterating throughout his independence as a news commentator and distance from National Socialist doctrine. In fact, however, Delaney's scripts needed no censoring, for by this time his reasoning was fully Nazified.

When some American correspondents painted a depressing picture of wartime Berlin, Delaney took it upon himself to counteract the impression of gloom: 'Naturally things are not the same as in peacetime, but the surprising thing is that they are not worse. That they are not is due to the amazing organization of economic genius.'[19] He warned his listeners that an over-zealous U-boat commander might fall into Roosevelt's trap and attack an US naval convoy. At the time of the 1940 Republican convention, Delaney applauded ex-President Hoover for backing US neutrality. After Henry Ford's refusal to manufacture airplane engines, Ward-Delaney exclaimed: 'Would that there were more Fords in America!'[20] He frequently interviewed Europeans who had just returned from a visit to the United States, confirming his view of war hysteria there. After Germany's invasion of Yugoslavia in 1941, Delaney visited Belgrade, where he convinced himself that the vast majority of the Yugoslavian population supported the ousted pro-Axis government.

Not long before Pearl Harbor, Delaney accused Roosevelt of endangering America with his aggressive policies:

The declaration of war will be catastrophic for the United States. Not only in men and materials, in blood and tears, but in the loss of our priceless heritage of independence and principles. The meaningless and deceptive slogans about salvaging democracy and upholding the principles of Christian civilization will prove to be but shibboleths that lead to the shambles. This war is for control of European politics and the economic life of Europe's many nations, regardless of the phrases used to camouflage it.'

As the war progressed Delaney became increasingly bitter and his broadcasts vitriolic: 'The real enemies of the United States', he claimed in one programme, 'are in the service of the government. Care for American interests went out with the Model-T Ford.' In another he referred to reports the Duke of Windsor was going to be First Viceroy in Washington. Would he be 'a sort of assistant to the president. Or would the president be subordinated to him? Who knows? Not the people of America. They'll be told when the details are all worked out – only then. Just now you're informed in advance by E.D. Ward in Berlin.'

Within Berlin, however, Delaney was becoming increasingly isolated. Edwin Hartrich, CBS's Berlin correspondent, reported that 'after a while he became rather a tragic figure. He couldn't find an audience to listen to his line of preaching. Even the Nazis avoided him.' William Shirer described him, in his latter days, as simply 'bored and boring'.

Eventually, in April 1943, Delaney ended his tenuous releationship with the Foreign Ministry and left Berlin for Slovakia. By the time of the Red Army's occupation, he was living in Prague, and when two *Stars & Stripes* correspondents, Klaus Mann, son of Thomas Mann, and Howard Byrne, visited the city in May 1945, Delaney could not resist being in contact. He boasted about his Berlin broadcasts, and the journalists reported him to the Czechoslovakian authorities. He was first detained, then arrested, and in June 1945 handed over to the US Army Counter-Intelligence Corps, before being released. In March 1946 he was again taken into custody and interned in the US Army detention centre at Oberursel, near Frankfurt-on-Main. In August he was released a second time, though, without a passport, could not leave Germany. Eventually, in July 1947, Delaney's repatriation was arranged but he was re-arrested upon arriving in New York City. In detention he told the press that he was being prosecuted for writing anti-Soviet literature. The jury seems to have agreed, since the indictment was dismissed. In subsequent years Delaney toured the lecture circuit as an ardent anti-Communist campaigner, maintaining links with other anti-Bolshevik activists and organizations around the world. On 1 July 1972, by then 86-years-old, he was hit and killed by a motor car at his home in Glendale, California.

Nobody in Berlin took Constance Drexel seriously. On 26 September 1940, William Shirer noted in his *Berlin Diary*: 'The Nazis hired her, so far as I can find out, principally because she's the only woman in town who will sell her American accent to them. Bizarre: She constantly pesters me for a job. One American network hired her at the beginning of the war, but dropped her almost at once.'[21]

Constance Drexel was born in Darmstadt, Germany, on 28 November 1894. Her father was a businessman and her mother the daughter of a Swiss watchmaker. In

1895 her father brought his baby daughter to Roslindale, Massachusetts, where Constance attended school. Later she went to school in several European countries and eventually completed her education at the Sorbonne in Paris. In 1914 Drexel was living in France with her mother and, at the outbreak of war, volunteered as a nurse at a French hospital. In April 1915 she attended the International Women's Congress in The Hague and reported on it for the *New York Times* (it marked her début both as a journalist and a campaigner for women rights) and she later covered the Paris peace conference for several other American papers. After the peace, the Polish and Czechoslovakian governments invited her to tour their countries and study the role of women. In 1920 she returned to the USA and, over the next twenty years, worked for several papers, dividing her time between Europe and the US. In the mid-1930s in particular she visited Germany frequently, was received by Party officials and given writing assignments. Colleagues began to notice an increasing bias in her journalism toward the social reform programme of the National Socialists, their health cult, and in particular the enhanced role that they claimed to give to women: by 1937, Drexel's pro-Nazi stance was undeniable. Early in 1939 she joined the staff of publisher Richard H. Waldo but soon, in May, left her job, and the United States, for Germany, ostensibly to visit her ailing mother. Dietze mentions Miss Drexel in his 'agendas' on 3 September 1939. Shortly afterwards, on 11 September, she was introduced to the Berlin press corps. The following year she began broadcasting for the German radio,

14 Constance Drexel, cleared of Nazi charges, is released from Ellis Island, October 1946.

which grandly introduced her as a 'famous American journalist' and as a 'Philadelphia socialite and heiress'. At first she covered the social activities of Berlin's American colony, but the longer she remained the more she enthused over Nazi cultural life — based, she claimed, on 'aesthetic principles handed down from Ancient Greece, that is, truth and beauty'. Drexel was reputed to have exclaimed, on catching sight of Winifred Wagner at a reception in Bayreuth, 'Oh, you are the girlfriend of Adolf Hitler...!'

The further Drexel moved from her original role as saleswoman for 'Nazi culture', the more embarrassing her programmes became for German officials. When Washington sent the liner *American Legion* to repatriate US citizens stranded in Europe, for example, she suggested: 'It is possible the government deliberately sent the ship through the war zone in the hope that it might create an international incident which would arouse American public opinion to the point of entering the war.'

The triviality of Drexel's propaganda role was matched by the bathos of her decline. On 16 August 1945, she was arrested by American GIs in Austria. She had naively contacted a *Stars & Stripes* journalist and divulged her wartime broadcasting activity. She spent the next twelve months in American internment camps and prisons. Eventually released, she arrived back in the USA in October 1946. In April 1948, a federal judge dismissed the treason indictment on the ground that her programmes were 'purely cultural'. Drexel died at the home of a cousin in Waterbury, Connecticut, on 28 August 1956.

Another flapper on Berlin's North America service was a squeaky-voiced young woman who called herself 'Gertie'. This was the German actress Gertrud Hahn, better known by her maiden name Seitz, who was born in Stuttgart in September 1905, and lived in the USA between 1923 and 1925, when she returned to Germany. There she took drama lessons from Emil Hess in Stuttgart, followed by engagements in Stuttgart and Ingolstadt.

Early in March 1940, BBC monitors recorded the broadcast dialogue between two American girls, Gertie and Nancy, about the Nazi leisure and welfare organization, 'Strength through Joy', and summarized its contents:

> The girls discuss the results of the 1914–18 war and agree that America is gaining nothing; England's war debts were still not paid. America's entry into this war would be 'terribly-plumb crazy'. Jewish newspaper owners in America twisted the news against Germany, says one of the girls, quoting from a boy-friend's letter. She describes visits to theatres, cafés and holiday resorts — all at low prices in National Socialist Germany. 'What I like about Germany', she says, 'is that even in wartime there is no profiteering — not like the last war ...'.[22]

In her series 'Hot Off the Wire' Gertie is a switchboard operator at the *Pittsburgh Tribune* reading letters from her friend 'Joe', its Berlin correspondent. In his letters Joe praises Nazi achievements and complains bitterly about the editors of his paper, 'Rosenbloom and Finkelstein', 'because they change his wires 'round and won't tell the truth about Germany'.

Gertie's monologues were interrupted by 'phone calls from readers' asking her to interpret certain information for them: 'Hello. Yes, I read this rumour about the tunnel from France to England. It just shows the nervous conditions of the English. Impossible for the Germans? Oh, I wouldn't say that. However, I personally think they would not need it.' For one inquiring caller she explained the intricacies of the Stuka dive bomber; for another she explained the concept of the German counter-blockade; for yet another caller she would describe in glowing terms the treatment of prisoners-of-war in Nazi camps.

One of Gertie's assignments was to encourage her listeners to buy short-wave radios:

I still don't know why you don't have a short-wave radio. Oh, I see, you went to your grandmother last night and tuned in to Berlin. Didn't I tell you it came in crisp like a local station? You've missed a lot already. Never mind – there will be plenty more interesting news from Germany in the future.

Otto Koischwitz

Late in 1939, a more substantial figure, Otto Koischwitz, a German repatriate and assistant professor at Hunter College, joined the North America section of the KWS. Like Drexel, Koischwitz sought to sell the virtues of German culture to his American audience. Max Otto Koischwitz was born on 19 February 1902, in Jauer, Silesia, the son of a physician. Having completed his studies at Berlin University, and unable to find employment, he emigrated to the United States, finding temporary posts at Columbia and New York universities, and at Hunter College and, in 1926, a more permanent position in the German department of Columbia's Lincoln School. In his first major American publication, *Our Textbooks and Kulturkunde* (1928), Koischwitz insisted that a pupil must comprehend both the language and literature of a nation, as well as the temper of its people. Louis J. Halle, a former pupil, recalled to John Carver Edwards: 'He was a man whose mind dwelt always in the empyrean, in a world of epic visions from which the petty practical affairs of our day-to-day world were excluded.'[23] His lectures frequently digressed into musings on German mythology, Oswald Spengler's vision of human history, Einstein's theory of relativity and the universe, and other themes far beyond the subject at hand.

In 1928, Koischwitz was appointed assistant professor in the German faculty at Hunter College, and by 1934 had won something of an international reputation. He failed however to achieve promotion and, increasingly embittered, seemed to focus in his lectures on the contrast between western decadence and corruption and the glories of Teutonic civilization – the heroism of Siegfried and genius of Richard Wagner in particular. He openly attacked 'the frauds committed by Jewish writers', asserting that people 'think with their blood, not with their intellect' and sneering at 'degenerate western literature'. Yet his classes were popular, baited perhaps by his reported leniency over grades.

In August 1939, New York's anti-Nazi League notified the department of education of Koischwitz's political ramblings, concluding: 'Whether under the circumstances[...] he is a fit person to remain a teacher of youth in the city of New York is, we believe, of major importance, particularly at this time when Nazi-inspired incitements to racial hatred and fratricidal strife are so much to the fore'. The board of higher education granted Koischwitz a leave of absence, without pay and, in September, shortly after the outbreak of war, he and his family returned to Europe, settling first in Denmark, before answering 'the call of the blood' and moving to Berlin. There he joined the USA zone of the Foreign Ministry's newly created broadcasting depart- ment,[24] and was soon on the air with Fred Kaltenbach as 'Fritz and Fred, the friendly quarrellers.[25]

On 19 January 1940, Koischwitz introduced his own series on the North America service, 'Dr. Anders and Little Margaret'. 'Little Margaret, an American girl who had come to Germany to see her grand-mother', described to her friends at home her daily routines, sumptuous meals, plays, songs and bedtime ritual.[26] By the early spring of 1940, 'Dr. Anders' was broadcasting his observations on American life and society. Early in May, Koischwitz proposed a new radio series, a 'special college hour', for transmission during the American universities' summer vacation and on 27 June he, as 'Dr. Anders', presented the first programme, 'The Law of Historical Evolution – Part I'.[27] To promote his programme, Koischwitz dispatched dozens of letters to for- mer colleagues and academic contacts in the United States, detailing the frequency, time and themes of his forthcoming broadcasts. For the remainder of 1940 and well into 1941 he was on the air for a quarter of an hour every Thursday evening, dealing with such subjects as 'Typology' (11 July), 'Surrealism' (29 August), 'The Problem of Freedom' (7 November) and 'Physical Deficiencies of 50% of all Genii [sic]' (5 December). *The New York Post* of 24 September 1940, observed that his programme was 'cultured, gentle, intelligent and charming'.

By early 1941, however, Koischwitz's lectures had declined into raw Nazi polemic. After 'Numerology' (9 January 1941) and 'James Joyce' (16 January), 'Dr. Anders' spoke about 'The Name of Germany' (23 January), followed by talks on 'A Thousand Years of German History' and 'Mirror of German Progress' later in the year. In these, he described the war as the product of 'inscrutable' historical forces, with the 'predes- tined evolution' of which the United States should not interfere. Germany's ultimate victory, he asserted, would be the inevitable triumph of youth and vigour over age and decay.

In his 'O.K. Speaking' broadcasts, he posed as 'The Man Who Knows' and claimed an arcane insight into 'alien elements that are administering American policy and diplomacy'. After the US government had announced its intention to give aid to the Soviet Union, 'O.K.' had 'confidentially' heard of Roosevelt's interest in equipping the Russian army with boots because he has shares in the shoe industry.

Throughout, Koischwitz hammered away at the theme of Anglo-American friction in history, that by becoming a wartime partner of 'the forces of yesterday', the US had consigned itself to national degeneration. On 4 June 1941, 'O.K.' concluded that the United States was no longer a democracy, as Roosevelt had extended the defence of

15 Otto Koischwitz

America 'to the Maginot Line, the Danube and Dakar' without public sanction. 'It is surely a calamity that in one of the gravest hours in the history of mankind, one of the greatest nations of the earth is ruled by a man with a fevered mind.'[28] On 17 October, in one of his 'College Hours', Koischwitz concluded that this 'abnormal' alliance had taken its toll on the life of the American people:

> Life in the USA becomes more and more abnormal. The standard of living is going down; the cost of living is going up; the 'land of the free' has become a one-man dictatorship. In time these conditions may appear so usual that they will be regarded as normal. It is doubtful whether a 'return to normal' is desirable, for every 'normal' period in history has been marred by a succession of wars. Since life is growing steadily more abnormal, we may be progressing to a period of 'abnormal' peace.

During the Stalingrad winter of 1942–43, 'O.K.' argued that the German withdrawal from southern Russia was planned before the Soviet offensive began, and that 'the Russians could have occupied the area without firing a shot.' On the Allied counter-offensive in North Africa, he commented: 'Was this worth the loss of the *Prince of Wales* and *Repulse*, of Hong Kong, Malaya, Luzon, Guam, Wake, etc.?' After the first appearance of US planes with American crews over the European continent, Koischwitz commented:

> The other day I saw a letter which was found in the pocket of an American pilot who met his death on the way to the Rhineland. In that letter an American mother writes to her son. It's one of those tender, motherly letters which to read publicly over the radio would be out of place. But there is one short passage I'd like to quote: 'While I'm writing you this letter, Roosevelt is speaking over the radio and I can't

help thinking of all his pledges.' Many American mothers will feel the same this Christmas season.[29]

Listeners in Germany could hear Koischwitz in their own language on the home service. On 16 June 1942, he spoke on the subject of '*Hier irrt Onkel Sam*' ('Where Uncle Sam gets it wrong'). According to Gestapo reports, German listeners regarded the talk as 'impartial', 'enlightening in the best sense of the word' and 'informative'. [30]

Between 1942 and 1944, Koischwitz partnered Mildred Gillars, a prominent American Nazi propagandist in her own right,[31] visiting PoW camps, telling listeners of their 'amazement' at the friendly treatment afforded to American prisoners, interviewing internees for broadcast messages home – or describing the funeral of two Americans who had died of their wounds.[32] A close bond grew between the two broadcasters.

Koischwitz had been acting head of the Foreign Ministry's USA broadcasting zone since 1941 and, some time after July 1942, was confirmed as its head. But, after the Schotte incident in July 1943, Goebbels confronted him with the alternative of either 'becoming a full member of the RRG staff and severing his Foreign Ministry ties, or resigning as head of the zone'. He chose to resign, and was succeeded by Dr. Dietrich Ahrens (*b.* 1916).[33] Shortly after this, on 24 August, Koischwitz's wife, Erna Keller-Koischwitz, died within a few days of giving birth to their son, Otto, who survived only a few hours.[34]

On 11 May 1944 a doomsday drama written by Koischwitz and entitled 'Vision of Invasion' was beamed to Americans at home and to US troops mustering for the Normandy landing. Mildred Gillars played the part of the mother of a GI (with Ulrich Haupt as her son),[35] lamenting:

Everybody says the invasion is suicide. The simplest person knows that. Between seventy and ninety per cent of the boys will be killed, or crippled for the rest of their lives!

After the Normandy landing, Koischwitz was despatched to the front to explain away the unfolding military crisis. On 15 June 1944, he reported from Hilversum in Holland: 'War profiteers on the London and New York exchanges go wild with joy, whilst tens of thousands of bodies litter the beaches of north-western France, waiting in vain for a decent grave'. From New York, William Shirer mocked:

Otto Koischwitz [...] long ago discontinued his breezy broadcasts under the name of 'O.K.'. Goebbels, for some reason, sent the professor to the firing line as a 'front-line reporter'. His speciality was broadcasting eye-witness accounts from the various battle fronts on which the Americans were facing Germans. Since General Bradley's Americans began their race through France, I have not been able to catch any more broadcasts by him. Presumably he began moving too fast to allow for a pause at the microphone.'

Koischwitz concluded his tour with a broadcast from Paris on 26 July. A little more than a month later he was dead, of tuberculosis of the lungs and heart failure, in a Berlin hospital on 31 August 1944.

Douglas Chandler

On 13 April 1941, the North America service announced:

> Stop – look – listen! Paul Revere is going to ride again! Stand by on next Friday the 18th of April at 11:30 p.m. Eastern Standard Time, to hear a message brought to you by the hero of that daring ride immortalized in Longfellow's poem. From that date, Paul Revere, the new American commentator, will speak to you every night over the German shortwave.[36]

Revolutionary hero Paul Revere rode from Charleston to Lexington in 1775, but on 18 April 1941 nothing happened, and the announcer asked listeners to contain their excitement until the following week. This time, introduced by piccolos playing 'Yankee Doodle' over a clatter of coconut husks, 'Paul Revere' attained the microphone. 'Your messenger, Paul Revere, greets you, friends and compatriots.' A few weeks later he revealed his true identity: Douglas Chandler.

Douglas Arnold Chandler was born in Chicago on 26 May 1889, and raised in Boston and Baltimore. During the First World War, he served briefly in the US Navy, and after it became a freelance columnist. In August 1924, he married the Pittsburgh heiress Laura Jay Wurtz, great-grand-daughter of John Jay, the first chief justice of the United States, and daughter of the Carnegie professor and wealthy Westinghouse inventor, Alexander Jay Wurtz. Until the 1929 Wall Street crash, Chandler cast himself as a financial expert. Subsequently, he worked as assistant editor on the Baltimore *Sunday American* while brooding over the 'deeper causes' of his misfortune, somehow concluding that it was a Jewish conspiracy. Appalled to think this could happen in America, the Chandlers departed for Europe in September 1931, settling on the French Riviera. In March 1933 they rented a villa on the Starnberger See, near Munich. Here Chandler became acquainted with two officials of the NSDAP's foreign press department, Ernst 'Putzi' Hanfstaengl and Rolf Hoffmann. Hanfstaengl was the son of a fine-arts publisher and a mother of old American lineage. He was educated in the USA and, on his return to Munich, became a personal friend of Adolf Hitler. Hoffmann had studied at Glasgow University and had lived much of his life in Britain.

During the winter of 1933–34, the Chandlers lived in Austria, and went on an extensive tour of the Balkans during the spring of 1934. In June the family moved to northern Yugoslavia, close to the Austrian border, but was still not settled, making several visits to Greece and Corfu, followed by several months in Innsbruck, and ending up at Freudenstadt in the Black Forest, where the Chandler children were dispatched to boarding school. Here Hoffmann was again in touch, showing Chandler around factories, schools, youth camps and hospitals, and flattering him with an invitation to a Party rally at Nuremberg, and to an anti-Comintern congress.

After touring North Africa in 1936 with a new German camera, Chandler sent samples of his work to the *National Geographic Magazine*, and several were accepted. It established his association with the magazine as a contributing correspondent. Beginning with a substantial illustrated article on Berlin in February 1937, he accepted various assignments, travelling extensively during the next three years.

In November 1936 the Chandlers moved to Göttingen. They were frequently in Berlin and there became acquainted with Dr. Ernst Ulrich von Bülow (1891–1945), the son of a wealthy Mecklenburg landowner and his wife, Ida Thomas, an American heiress from Michigan. Von Bülow was on the editorial board of the Nazi propaganda periodical *News from Germany*, and in May 1941 was to become chairman of the Foreign Ministry's expert committee on propaganda for America.

In the autumn of 1937, Chandler accepted another Hoffmann invitation to a Party rally in Nuremberg. Here he met the Belgian linguist Charles Sarolea, a retired professor of French literature at Edinburgh University, who invited him to lecture on Anglo-German relations and on the Führer's constructive vision of a 'new order'. In January 1938, after a fortnight in Edinburgh, the Chandlers proceeded to London as guests of Admiral Sir Barry Domvile and his German-born wife, Alexandrina von der Heydt, and other British Nazi sympathizers. Domvile had established an Anglo-German exchange organization, *The Link*, and founded a periodical of the same name to which most of the proponents of appeasement contributed. (Domvile himself was detained in Brixton prison in 1940 for his pro-Nazi sympathies.)

In February 1938 the Chandlers moved to Potsdam. Later that year, on a *National Geographic* assignment in Yugoslavia, Chandler 'discovered' the Dalmatian coast and settled on the island of Korcula. Early in August 1940, however, their residence permit was withdrawn: according to Chandler, the island's Jewish community regarded him as a Nazi and engineered his expulsion. The couple then moved to Florence, where Chandler perceived that the local American colony was greatly disturbed by Roosevelt's growing involvement in European affairs. He later claimed he was 'urged from all sides to employ his talents and his name' to try and stop any attempt at intervention by the US government.

Chandler offered his services to officials of the Italian radio, but was rebuffed. He then contacted von Bülow, and a meeting with Dr. Hans Schirmer, son of a German general and an American mother, and deputy head of the German Foreign Ministry's broadcasting organization, was organized. Chandler offered to act as a 'freelance radio commentator without compensation'. Schirmer however dismissed this as unworkable: Chandler's services, he declared, could not be accepted without payment. Somewhat flabbergasted, Chandler again contacted von Bülow and was introduced to Dr. Hans Theodor Froelich of the ProMi's Press Division and, through him, to the ministry and the RRG. A salary was fixed at 1,800 marks, and an initial six months' contract signed. 'I was overjoyed', Chandler explained, 'because America is my home, and I love it'.

In March 1941 Chandler and his family returned to Berlin, where he began to develop ideas for his broadcasts. The idea of a pseudonym was mooted, but Chandler insisted on using his real name, as listeners could then associate him with his writings.

With the anniversary of Paul Revere's ride only a few days away it was suggested that Chandler be launched to the sound of galloping hooves and the strains of 'Yankee Doodle'. The anniversary was missed, however, and the *bravura* arrival of 'Paul Revere' on German radio occurred a week late, on 25 April. Over the next six months, Chandler delivered his fifteen-minute broadcasts six times a week, battering away at America's pro-British stance: 'With bloodshed and agony we freed ourselves from England. Are we going to enslave ourselves today?'[37] 'Can you not grasp the reason for Europe's determination to hack off Britain's shackles? It was America who first set the fashion.'[38]

But Chandler was irritated by the working conditions at the KWS. He had been promised an office and a secretary, but found himself sharing with 'chattering colleagues and clattering typewriters'. He later recalled 'an atmosphere which was strangely unfriendly and disappointing [...] throughout my entire activities in the Berlin station, I encountered increasingly this attitude of unwilling cooperation'. Nor was Chandler assisted in finding accommodation for his family, and often his salary was paid months in arrears. Even worse, he found himself required to read news bulletins as a preface to his own programmes, and to weave ProMi-supplied material into his commentaries. 'I would be seized by a violent paroxysm which centered in my solar plexus and caused me during the time of writing a violent diarrhoea each day. I was suffering from acute headaches and experienced great difficulty with my eyes.'

In September 1941, at the end of his first term of employment, Chandler took leave of absence and indicated that he might not return unless conditions improved. At the time of Pearl Harbor, however, he was back in Berlin and negotiating a new contract. This time he was promised 'full official support in matters of daily existence', a reduction of broadcasts by half, and regular meetings with Karl Schotte, head of the North America zone, to resolve possible problems. Three separate contracts were signed, giving Chandler a monthly salary of 2,500 marks, making him one of the highest paid members of the KWS staff.[39]

In January 1942 Chandler was back on the air. But he was not easy to satisfy – nor, for that matter, to supervise. His behaviour was erratic and increasingly eccentric. He drove a maroon Mercedes with a US flag painted on its doors. In the studio he wore a lapel emblem of a swastika set against a background of crossed Axis flags. Laura Chandler died in July 1942, after which he fell into a depression, drinking heavily and needing sedatives to sleep.

Chandler's broadcasts essentially followed the standard Nazi clichés, seeking to exploit any domestic opposition to the Roosevelt administration. His prime target was the government in Washington which, in his view, was manipulated by Jewish advisers: 'Roosevelt, himself an off-spring of Spanish Jews, is a mere tool of the Jewish conspiracy against all Nordic Aryans.'[40] In one of his broadcasts he nominated the president for the 'Meddle Medal', for carrying out 'Jewish plans for world domination': 'Yes, by all means let Pearl Harbor be avenged, but not upon the Japanese, who have been forced into a struggle – no, not upon the Japs, but upon the real authors of this war, the Jews.'[41] Chandler reiterated his claim that 'international Jewry' had driven him from Korcula – the Dalmatian island where he had been living since 1939 – and wrecked his career as a writer.

Chandler was equally quick to denounce the many flaws, organizational and technical, in the German broadcasting system. He frequently criticized the output of other broadcasters, notably those of Leo Delaney, and abused the reputation of his German superiors. In February 1943 he went so far as to denounce a colleague to the Gestapo:

I therefore feel it my imperative duty to submit certain facts relating to the political viewpoint (an outspoken viewpoint of antagonism to the German government which he is serving and an outspoken partiality for the Jews) of the chief of the American *Redaktion* in the Rundfunk, with whom I have been associated in my work as commentator for nearly two years. The person in question is Gerdt Wagner, now *pro-tem* in Rome.[42]

Chandler sought 'to remain anonymous in this matter,' and indeed when interviewed at the Gestapo headquarters was ordered not to speak about it to anyone.[43] But his denunciation was leaked to the RRG and he was dismissed. Having taken legal advice he was reinstated, only to be immediately suspended as a security risk and well-known troublemaker.

Later that year Chandler's relations with his superiors eased when, with his second wife, Maria 'Mia' Moorgat, from Kleve in the Lower Rhineland, he was transferred to Vienna and settled in Schloss Seuftenegg. Chandler continued to record programmes, in the RRG's Vienna studios, for onward dispatch to Berlin. In February 1944 he launched a series on American poetry that continued for the remainder of the war. That spring nervous exhaustion forced him to take time off from his schedule, but he was back by the end of June. Faced with the Allied landing in Europe, Chandler moderated his tone, as he later admitted at his trial: 'I realized that perhaps my continued adherence to my course of action had been the result of colored thinking'. In October the Chandlers moved to Durach, near Kempten, in Bavaria, and it was there that he was apprehended in May 1945. He was released after an initial interrogation, but re-arrested in February 1946 and held in the US Army detention centre at Oberursel. There he was joined by Robert Best, a fellow American Nazi propagandist, and the two were flown to the USA in December 1946.

When their joint trial opened in Boston on 12 February 1947, the defence filed for a court inquiry into Chandler's mental condition. Two experts concluded that he was mentally equipped to stand, while a third claimed he was suffering from paranoia and 'not responsible for his actions from the time he left Italy to go to Germany in 1941'. The judge ruled that Chandler was sane and the trial began on 6 June. The prosecution exposed the direct chain of command from Goebbels, Fritzsche and Winkelnkemper to Chandler, tabled documents and scripts, and presented monitorings of his broadcasts. Several of his former Nazi colleagues, including Winkelnkemper, Wagner, von Lilienfeld and Ahrens, appeared as witnesses. After proceedings lasting three weeks, Chandler was found guilty and, on 30 July, sentenced to a fine of $10,000 and life imprisonment.

Sixteen years later, in January 1962, the office of the US Attorney-General announced its intention to release the seventy-four-year-old Chandler from

16 Robert Best (*second from left*) and Douglas Chandler (*third from left*), escorted by US Marshals when charged as Nazi propaganda agents, Washington D.C., December 1946.

Lewisburg penitentiary, on condition that he returned to Germany in the care of the daughter of his first marriage. The release was hampered by the fact that the fine remained unpaid, and in any case the Bonn Foreign Ministry barred Chandler's re-entry into Germany. In July 1963 his daughter Sylvia appealed to John Kennedy and, on 5 August, the president commuted the remainder of Chandler's sentence. He left the United States to settle finally on the island of Tenerife.

Jane Anderson

About the time that Douglas Chandler arrived in Berlin – March 1941 – Jane Anderson, a renowned journalist, also joined the KWS. Anderson was probably the most dedicated foreign propagandist on the German radio. She had been born in Atlanta, Georgia, on 6 January 1893; orphaned by the age of ten, she was raised by her grandparents. Entering journalism she moved first to New York and then, in 1915, joined the staff of the London *Daily Mail*, soon proving herself a daring reporter in dispatches from the Western Front. The owner of the *Daily Mail*, Lord Northcliffe, introduced her to such figures as H.G.Wells and Joseph Conrad, and in 1917 she was living flamboyantly in Paris, moving in political and diplomatic circles. (A 1942 FBI study reported that: 'In Paris, Jane Anderson had no reputation of promiscuity, but was not a woman of entirely rigid virtue.') Back in New York after 1918, she revisited Paris in the early 1930s and in Spain married a wealthy aristocrat, the Marquis Alvarez de Cienfuegos.

Upon the outbreak, in July 1936, of a civil war on her doorstep, the new Marquesa Jane Anderson could not resist the urge to return to journalism. A cable to London was enough to secure the position of the *Daily Mail's* war correspondent, reporting from the front with Franco's forces. Late in September she was captured by government forces and charged with spying for the Nationalists. Held in appalling conditions in several Madrid prisons for six weeks, she contrived to get a message to the US embassy and, on 10 October, was released on condition that she immediately left the country.

Anderson went to Paris to be reunited with her husband. Burning for vengeance, she launched a propaganda campaign against her former jailers, which soon grew into a major crusade against Communism. On the American lecture circuit, she vividly described the trauma of her imprisonment. The *Catholic Digest* proclaimed her 'the world's greatest woman orator in the fight against Communism', *Time* magazine quoted Monsignor Fulton Sheen – a lecturer at the Catholic University of America in Washington, and regular presenter of the 'Catholic Hour' on NBC – who annointed her a 'living martyr', and she was taken up by the ultra-conservative Merwin Hart. In November 1938 the Cienfuegos were able to return to Spain.

Anderson appears to have been noticed by Goebbels, who noted in his diary that her campaign in New York was 'the big sensation'. After her return to Europe in November 1938 she found herself in Berlin at the time of the German invasion of Poland. A year later she joined the broadcasting staff of the North America zone, but did not go on air until 14 April 1941, when she was introduced as 'the world-famous Catholic, twice condemned to death by the firing squad in Spain, whose lectures in the United States were endorsed by the Archbishop of Washington'. In her first broadcast she proclaimed that: 'Germany gives the Church the strength of her sword, the weight of her wealth, and the protection of her law'. A week later she described to her listeners the 'dynamic life of the Reich' and compared Hitler to Moses: 'He had reached to the stars, and the Lord's will would prevail.'[44]

Towards the end of May, Anderson joined the Foreign Ministry's newly founded 'expert committee' on propaganda to the USA, chaired by von Bülow. Opinions of her usefulness were mixed; in the opinion of Gerhard Rühle, head of the Foreign Ministry's Broadcasting Division, she proved herself particularly suited for Catholic propaganda. 'Apart from that she has little use. For example, we received a cable from the Washington embassy, telling us we must tone down her style at all costs, since her bombastic and histrionic expression was having a negative effect on American listeners.'[45] On 14 June, however, Diewerge, head of the ProMi's Broadcasting Division, reported to Goebbels that they were giving Jane Anderson her own slot, entitled 'Voice of Europe'. Anderson's broadcasts usually began and ended with the slogan, 'Always remember, progressive Americans eat Kellogg's Corn Flakes and listen to both sides of the story', delivered to the sounds of the nonsensical 1939 hit *Scatterbrain*, popularized by the Benny Goodman orchestra. It was on 'Voice of Europe', on 21 November, that Anderson and William Joyce exchanged reminiscences of their respective adventures in the cause of National Socialism.

During her earliest broadcasts, the non-aggression pact with Moscow restricted outright anti-communist propaganda on the German radio. With the June 1941 attack on the Soviet Union however, that changed. In their wartime study *The Goebbels Experiment*, Derrick Sington and A.G. (later Lord) Weidenfeld observed:

17 Jane Anderson, US journalist and Nazi propagandist, 1937.

Since the invasion of Russia an Englishwoman [*sic*] named Jane Anderson has moved into the foreground of German broadcast propaganda to North America. This somewhat hysterical woman, who claims to be an ardent Roman Catholic, used to broadcast accounts of the 'toleration' shown in the Third Reich for the Roman Church. She reverts continually to the subject of the 'maltreatment' by the Republicans during the Spanish Civil War [...] Her talks, which nearly always contain highly coloured accounts of atrocities committed by the 'Reds' during the Spanish war, occasionally border on the pornographic.[46]

At the same time an American monitor noted: 'If her microphone hysteria is any clue to her personality, she is probably mentally unhinged'.

After Pearl Harbor, Anderson's efforts became even shriller. British monitors noted that her broadcasts had become wildly denunciatory in tone, less structured, and often incoherent:

So the American people have gone to war to save Stalin and the international bankers. The American brains trust, alien to and superimposed upon the land of Old Glory, is nothing but a branch of the Communist international secret super-state – and this superstate holds Soviet Russia, plutocratic England and Roosevelt's America in the hollow of its filthy, hybrid hand [...] Roosevelt and Churchill secretly arranged to declare war upon Japan just to help the Communist leaders who are now fleeing for their lives before the advancing power of the

German armies [...] Remember, when Roosevelt offered the wealth of the American nation to the support of Communism, he offered it as a footstool to Stalin, the mightiest murderer of modern history!

Anderson charged Roosevelt with having communication with the 'Red Antichrist' who is beating children 'black and blue for their religion', proclaimed that the Roosevelt administration was guilty of 'diabolical, infernal sabotage against the Catholic faith', and denounced Churchill for allying himself with the devil residing in the Kremlin.

On 9 February 1942 she alleged that US troops had been stationed in Northern Ireland at Stalin's direction to crush the Catholic faith: 'Though it was the smallest of the Catholic citadels, Eire was called upon to withstand the might of the united Anglo-Saxon world, which would never break its spirit.' The thought that her personal war against Soviet Russia put her in conflict with the official policy of the US government, never seems to have entered her mind.

A few months later, Anderson's career as a Nazi propagandist came to a premature end, when, provoked by Anglo-American 'lies' about food shortages in Germany, she unwisely decided to describe a visit to a Berlin cocktail bar in her broadcast on March 6:

Last night my gentleman friend and I went to the bar at the Hotel Adlon. There, on silver platters, were sweets and cookies galore. I ate Turkish cookies, a delicacy I happen to be very fond of. My friend ordered great goblets of champagne for the two of us, and into the champagne he put liberal shots of cognac to make it more lively. Sweets and cookies and champagne, not bad!

Not good, either! US radio monitors recorded the broadcast and the following night a translation of the programme was beamed back to German listeners who were by then having to exist on *Ersatz* coffee and other concoctions. Anderson was promptly taken off the air. Although in the US it was generally assumed that she had met a violent death in a concentration camp, she in fact returned to the airwaves on 12 June 1944 with a talk on 'America in the hands of the Jews and Bolshevism'. A week later, she announced that she had come to Germany 'to add the weight of her valor and her international prestige to the world conflict'.

At the end of the war, the Cienfuegos were living in Austria. Eventually Anderson was arrested in Innsbruck in April 1947, and placed under restriction until the Franco government engineered her release. In view of her acquired Spanish nationality, the US Department of Justice publicly declined to prosecute.

After Pearl Harbor, Helen Davis was on the air every Sunday as 'your American correspondent', broadcasting her impressions of Germany. One of her series of features, entitled 'An American Girl sees Wartime Germany', included an interview with Margaret, the wife of William Joyce.

Helen Davis was formerly Martha Helene Freifrau von Bothmer. Born in Bolivar, Missouri, on 8 December 1908 into a pioneer family who numbered Jefferson Davis among its forbears, she studied fashion design in Chicago before joining a New York fashion house in 1930. Here she met, and in 1936 married, Heinrich Freiherr von Bothmer (*b.* 1897), apparently a German consular official and SS member, and a relative of Ulrich von Bothmer, the NSDAP's labour leader (*Arbeiterführer*). Late in 1941, upon Germany's declaration of war on the United States, the Bothmers left New York for Berlin, where Mrs. von Bothmer joined the KWS, broadcasting to the United States, Britain, Australia and the Far East.

Robert Best

A late recruit to the Berlin corps of American Nazi propagandists was Robert Best. He, like Jane Anderson, was a professional journalist. Born in Sumter, South Carolina, on 16 April 1896, the son of a Methodist preacher, Best taught at a school in Spartanburg, South Carolina and, upon America's entry into the First World War, served as a non-combatant officer in the US Army. He resigned his commission in 1920, and enrolled at the Pulitzer School of Journalism at Columbia University. Taking his degree he won a travelling scholarship to Europe, where he settled in Geneva, covering the League of Nations for the *Independent* magazine. On the expiry of his scholarship, Best secured a post with the Berlin Bureau of United Press as stringer for south-eastern Europe. Based in Vienna, where he spent the next eighteen years, he continued to write for a large number of US and British publications.

The favourite journalists' hang-out in Vienna was the Café Louvre on the Ring-Strasse. Here Best's huge frame was a familiar sight. According to William Shirer, he spent most of his waking hours glued to his table, haranguing anyone who would listen to him about the petty politics of Vienna.[47] Gradually, however, Best's professional enthusiasm evaporated: while colleagues were promoted, he remained a stringer, later portraying himself as the victim of Jewish interests:

> Over the past years there has been an increase in the number of non-Jewish correspondents who [...] chose to covet favour of the Jews as a certain road towards notoriety and, therefore, towards a small fortune. They chose to do this instead of telling the truth. In my own nineteen years as a journalist in Europe [...] I chose, I am proud to say, an uncompromising stand, and I remained, in consequence, comparatively unknown to the wider public in America and Britain.[48]

Best monitored the poser struggles of the Dollfuss and Schuschnigg era 'with only occasional lapses into wondering whether there wasn't something in the Nazi business', as William Shirer put it. The president of United Press, Hugh Baillie, later recalled: 'Of course we watched his copy for any signs that he was slanting it pro-Nazi, but he never did. He was far too foxy for that' .[49] 'At that time', Shirer noted, 'he was not a Nazi'. Indeed at this time Best appeared to be genuinely concerned for the safety of his Jewish colleagues. On one occasion he designed an elaborate plan to smuggle into Hungary a Jewish UP staffer sought by the SS, and on another campaigned for the release of an employee arrested for illegal political activity.

A few weeks after the German annexation of Austria in March 1938, however, Best exhibited a wholly pro-Nazi attitude. As recalled by Baillie: 'One night at dinner he gave us the full treatment, enthusiastically explaining the Nazi idea of brotherhood. From others we heard about his liaison with [...] the most extreme local Nazis.' While most of his colleagues returned home, Best remained in Vienna and, following Pearl Harbor, was arrested as an enemy alien and sent to an internment camp at Bad Nauheim, near Frankfurt-on-Main, for repatriation with other American newsmen and diplomats. Instead of accompanying them, however, he wrote to the Gestapo asking for permission to stay, on the grounds that he wanted 'to work towards the construction of a new European federation built upon a new order of social and economic justice' – and also because he wanted to marry Erna Maurer, an Associated Press writer from Carinthia.

In March 1942, Best was invited to Berlin and asked to contact the Foreign Ministry. He was asked if he was interested in working for the German radio, whereupon he was promised that he would be able to broadcast to the United States as a staff member of the Ministry, with a salary of 1,500 marks a month.

But there may have been a further pretext for Best's remaining in Germany. According to Shirer, dubious deals with the Vienna-based Credit Anstalt bank were an open secret. Later Louis Lochner, the former Associated Press bureau chief in Berlin, was to suggest that the Nazis may have coaxed Best into treason with the promise of quick riches in Germany's lucrative black market. Indeed, shortly after his arrival in Berlin, Best wrote to former colleagues interned at Bad Nauheim and offered to provide foodstuffs and other necessities to their relatives inside the Reich, for a price.

On 10 April 1942, Best went on the air as 'Mr. Guess Who, your self-appointed correspondent for the new world order'. On 21 May, 'Mr. Guess Who' revealed his identity to his listeners. In programmes styled 'BBB – Best's Berlin Broadcast' – or, as he preferred to call them, 'Berlin's Best' and 'Best's Little Life-Savers' – this new voice blasted 'the Jews and Jewed-up gentiles', who were, he alleged, the enemies of Germany in America, with a vehemence that had not been heard before over the Berlin airwaves. With such an 'important' message to impart, Best banned any form of music or light relief.

Best was often at loggerheads with German officials over his coarse microphone style and unpredictable stunts. The censors deleted some of his favourite lines and scrapped whole passages of his scripts. When they insisted on a disclaimer preceding a piece by him on the Archbishop of Canterbury ('Although he [Best] enjoys the privilege of this station, his views are not necessarily identical with our own'), he hit back, staging a sit-down strike in his office.[50]

Early in July, Best took two months leave for a honeymoon. Once back on the air, his broadcasts became even more extreme. A stunt in October had him running for Congress: 'Elect me to Congress as your protest candidate and I shall do my best to bring about peace before America has fallen into a state of complete chaos and Jewish slavery'. Then he announced he was going to run for President, greeting his indictment for treason in July 1943 as a Rooseveltian smear tactic to compromise his presidential candidacy. In January 1943 he warned listeners: 'US newspaper and radio editors have been trying to deceive you with announcements concerning the alleged plan of Churchill and Roosevelt to open a second front in the near future. Any time you hear it spouted out you should shout "The Judocrats should first take Tunis", and then talk.' On 13 May, Tunis – Hitler's last bastion in North Africa – fell to the Allies. On the defeat of the Sixth Army at Stalingrad, Best commented:

> The disengagement of the Caucasus divisions and their withdrawal to positions suitable for an offensive later in the year [...] is a feat which ranks with Xenophon's. Similarly, the German troops sacrificing their lives in a defense of civilization are making Stalingrad a new Thermopylae. They recently became hopelessly trapped but they never considered retreat. They died to save the world from the Jewish evils of Communism and Plutocracy. My mission is to rouse you to action to end this holocaust of the international Jew.[51]

Later in 1943, after a strained eighteen months', the RRG transferred Best – and Chandler – to Vienna. Here his programmes would be recorded and sent to Berlin for transmission. It was from Vienna that Best commented on the Normandy landing:

> D-Day will begin a flow of death from Europe to Britain and the USA. [...] The new flying projectiles which are being launched against England are stacked not in mere hundred of thousands, but in tens of hundreds of thousands. [...] So far the V1 has been doing more practice shooting than otherwise but by the time it reaches its climax, V2, V3, V4 etc. will be ready to step into the ring with deadlier punches.[52]

After Arnhem, however, Best began to moderate his message and urge the United States to allow 'Europe to pursue its own destiny', while suggesting that only Hitler was able to 'settle the hash of the Bolshevik beast' and generally be 'a valuable partner to the USA in the fruitful exchange of cultural and material values.'[53]

When the Russians occupied Vienna in April 1945, Best fled to his wife's home-town of Villach, in what was soon to become the British-occupied zone of Austria. Here he remained until February 1946, when British security police apprehended and passed him to the American authorities. After ten months in an internment camp near Salzburg, he was transferred to the US Army detention centre at Oberursel for the flight back to the States with Douglas Chandler.

At their successive trials in Boston in 1947, Chandler appeared upright, well-dressed and spruce – in the judge's words, 'a snob who did what he did in order to get attention, especially of persons in high places'. Best, in contrast, was thick-set, balding and dressed in crumpled clothes. If Chandler remained arrogant and tight-lipped throughout the proceedings, Best conspicuously lobbied for approval. He showered the court with arguments and objections which exasperated officials and delighted the spectators. On the opening day of his trial, Best informed the bench that he would 'rely for his defence upon the Holy Trinity of God – the Father, the Son and the Holy Ghost'. Like Chandler before him, Best was examined by court-appointed psychiatrists who, when hearings began on 24 September, agreed that he was aware of his situation, sane and competent to stand trial. Best retorted: 'Is the prosecution convinced that each of the psychiatrists is sane and normal?', arguing that if the prosecution were entitled to ask the doctors any questions that might reflect against him, he in turn was also entitled to examine the experts. After a couple of hours the judge stopped the exchanges and a week later ruled that Best was fit to stand.

Apart from Best's outbursts, the proceedings essentially followed those of the Chandler trial. Several former Nazi officials who had worked with Best in Berlin were called to the witness box. Best responded that he did what he did because the Germans were 'the one and only people who could be considered a bulwark strong enough to withstand the Bolshevist threat'. He closed his statement by saying:

> The fact that my activities might be viewed by some persons as treason was never absent from my mind. I fully realized what I was doing, and did what I did because of the fact that to have done otherwise would have caused me to consider myself a real traitor. [...] In other words, I place loyalty to my country far above what some people construe as a technical loyalty. [...] I should not hesitate for one moment to repeat my actions.

Asked about his reaction when he heard of the treason indictment against him in 1943, Best declared, 'I said I would prefer to be denounced as a traitor by people who were traitors themselves than actually to be a traitor'. The conclusion of the prosecution case was that: '[Best] sold out his native country. This was cold, unadulterated treason.' He was found guilty on 16 April 1948, his fifty-second birthday, and given life imprisonment and a fine of $10,000. After two years of appeal proceedings, the conviction was upheld. In August 1951, after suffering a cerebral haemorrhage, Best was transferred to the medical centre for federal prisoners in Springfield, Missouri, where he died on 16 December 1952.

Donald Day

One of the last American Nazi propagandists to join forces with Radio Berlin was Donald Day, for many years the controversial Baltic correspondent for the *Chicago Tribune*. Like Best, Day had lived in Europe since the early 1920s.

Donald Day, born on 15 May 1985 in Brooklyn, NY, was the child of a newspaper-owning family. When he was eight his parents settled in Oakland, California, and then, after the 1906 earthquake, in Chicago. On leaving school Day joined the local *City News* bureau and, by the age of twenty-three, was sports editor on the *New York Morning Telegraph*. After serving in the navy, he returned to New York, writing on labour affairs for the *World*, which led to a contract with publisher William Randolph Hearst. Both Day and Hearst followed developments in Russia after the October Revolution with great interest. Since western journalists were barred, Hearst signed

Day to mole his way into Russia and feed Hearst's papers with first-hand news from within. As a first step, Day married a staff member of the then controversial Ludwig Martens agency in New York. Ludwig Karlovich Martens had been a professor at St. Petersburg University until arrested for Marxist revolutionary activities in 1896. After three years in prison, he was expelled from Russia, moving to London in 1906 and later to New York. After October 1917 Martens was named the first Soviet 'ambassador of the new Russia', but was not recognized by the US government. When anti-Soviet hysteria swept America, Martens was investigated and expelled from the USA. He, his family, and forty-six members of his agency — including Day and his wife — left for Russia in January 1921. At the border, however, Day was singled out as an agent of the capitalist press and sent back to Riga. Hearst's response was to fire his stranded journalist. After working for a time as the *Daily Mail's* stringer in Riga, he was taken on by Robert McCormick's *Chicago Tribune* as a regular correspondent, covering the Soviet Union from the Baltic.

At the beginning of the Second World War, Day's view was that Britain should appreciate the 'terrific vitality' of Hitler's 'new order', and he attributed Germany's bad press to 'international Jewry'. He was still in Latvia when the Soviet army occupied Riga in June 1940. Four weeks later he was expelled and went to Helsinki. From there, he reported deteriorating German-Russian relations and Moscow's internal political tensions. After the German invasion of the Soviet Union, he predicted a quick German victory, a generous armistice with Britain, and an Anglo-German campaign against Bolshevism. The German army showed the American journalist round the smouldering ruins of liberated Tallinn, and took him to the front at Leningrad: 'The Soviet "diggers"', he wrote, 'are preparing mass graves instead of trenches in the suburbs of Leningrad.'[54] Perplexed by stiffened Soviet resistance and Germany's sputtering winter campaign, Day warned that Roosevelt's allies were plotting a course that would not be in the best interest of the United States and that the appointment of Sir Stafford Cripps to the British cabinet would drag the United States into a Scandinavian theatre of war.[55] A few weeks later he wrote:

> There were persistent rumours in Stockholm about negotiations between the Soviet and German governments which may lead to a truce on the eastern front. [...] There is a mutual respect developed by eight months of ferocious fighting. The Soviet government was the first to make the advances now said to be under discussion. The chief reason for Moscow's proposals was to pressure the Allies into opening up a second front on the continent of Europe.[56]

A week later, a New York daily singled out Day and his publisher:

> What is the purpose of *Tribune* publisher Robert McCormick and his associates in printing such stuff as that dispatch from Stockholm? [...] If he doesn't know that the above story is a message which Berlin-Tokyo-Rome is trying to dump on us; if he doesn't yet know that the Axis' divide and conquer strategy is designed to split England, Russia and the United States [...] his paper should be suppressed for the

duration. [...] Neither freedom of speech nor freedom of press permits McCormick or any political Quislingist to drive a wedge between the United States and its Allies. He, and his *Tribune*, and 'his allies' have gone too far this time.[57]

The State Department seems to have shared *P.M.'s* views and instructed its Stockholm embassy to impound Day's passport. He then advised his editor that he was returning to Helsinki to enlist in the Finnish army, a step the US ambassador in Finland declared would be interpreted as 'an unfriendly act'.[58] Day then settled in Helsinki and worked on his memoirs, *Onward Christian Soldiers*, earning a living translating for the Finnish government. When in the summer of 1944 the advancing Soviet army began to penetrate the Finnish defences, he left Helsinki for Berlin.

The German Foreign Ministry welcomed Day as a committed American anti-Communist journalist, whose support was offered even when the German armies were retreating on all fronts and Berlin was being reduced to rubble. He was offered a salary of 1,500 marks a month, together with a monthly bonus of 6,000 marks. (Berlin's star foreign Nazi propagandist, William Joyce, was at that time earning the same amount, with a smaller, 5,000 marks bonus.) By the end of the year, Day's name headed the Allied list of almost one hundred suspected American and British rene-gades.[59]

On 21 August, Berlin radio introduced its new recruit as a '20-year-veteran corre-spondent for the *Chicago Herald Tribune* [sic]'. Three weeks later, Day announced himself as a US newspaper correspondent whom 'Mr. Roosevelt and his friends have placed, through their intrigues, on the other side of the fence.'[60] On 7 October, he praised life in Berlin, which, in his words, was far from bleak, and flatly denied the existence of a black market 'because money could not corrupt justice in Germany as it did in the democracies'. However, as conditions worsened so Day's spirit grew more sombre. On 17 February 1945, after the Allied bombardment of Dresden, he conferred the nominal 'Order of the White Feather' upon US Air Force General Spaatz, 'for acts of exceptional cowardice in bombing German cities filled with pitiful refugees'. A week later, on 24 February, he told listeners:

Berlin hotels and private homes are without heat and hot water. Eight weeks' food coupons must last for nine weeks, and we must make up with uncouponed vegeta-bles. The horrors of life are enhanced by the air raids, and the need to dress in a cold room at every alert. [...] I thought so little of Berlin had been left to bomb that these large-scale raids would cease; but I was mistaken. [...] Sleeping in a room with no windows in freezing weather is not pleasant. Life would be unendurable, but for the unostentatious heroism of everyone.

At a reception early in 1945, the German foreign minister had received a taste of Day's vehement opinion. Dietze recalled an observation by Ribbentrop to the effect that Jews had no particular power or influence in the Soviet Union. 'Here Day firmly contra-dicted and in the ensuing discussion with him, Ribbentrop considerably modified his assertion.'[61] In mid-April, Day and his wife left Berlin for Bavaria. Here he contacted

US Army officials, but was allowed to leave after an interrogation. In March 1946 he was arrested and interned at the US Army detention centre at Oberursel. By December, however, army officials informed him of his pending release: the Department of Justice was 'no longer interested in his case' in view of the shortness of his involvement in Nazi propaganda and the nature of his broadcasts.

Prohibited from returning to the United States, Day and his wife settled in Bad Tölz, in Bavaria, writing for the *Daily Press* in Ashland, Wisconsin, and for Stockholm's *Fria Ord*. Late in 1953, the couple obtained permission to return to Finland. In 1962, Day underwent surgery for cancer, and by the time he had recuperated, he had been granted a new US passport, thanks to the efforts of colleagues and of he US ambassador to Finland. He was also reinstated by the *Chicago Tribune* as a stringer in Helsinki. Donald Day died of a heart attack on 30 September 1966.

Ezra Pound

One of the most celebrated American propagandists in Europe before and during the war was the poet Ezra Pound. And one of the most improbable, and indeed ultimately fruitless, associations, was that between Pound and the most infamous British propagandist, William Joyce, 'Lord Haw Haw'.[62] A resident of Rapallo, Italy, since 1908, Pound was one of the only Americans to play a part in the foreign-language broadcasting propaganda of Germany's Axis partner, Italy.

Technically, the Italian radio was a very competent partner for Berlin, the *Ente Italiano per le Audizione Radiofoniche* (EIAR) having been, in the service of the Fascist régime, one of the pioneers of international radio propaganda. Right up until the Italian armistice on 9 September 1943, the propaganda division of Italy's *Commando Supremo* still insisted on clearing all German broadcasts prior to transmission on EIAR. Berlin's propaganda partnership with Tokyo, in contrast, did not go beyond the ProMi's extensive and grateful coverage of Japan's early military successes in the Pacific and south-east Asia, at a time when blows were showering on German morale in Russia and the Mediterranean, and the tide began to turn against the Wehrmacht.

The voice of the irascible and controversial Ezra Pound was first heard by American listeners on Rome radio in January 1941, ripping into the policies of Roosevelt and 'his gun-making pals'. Ezra Loomis Pound was born in Hailey, Idaho, on 30 October 1885, and raised at Wyncote, near Philadelphia. In the autumn of 1902 he enrolled at the University of Pennsylvania, followed by two years at Hamilton College in Clinton, New York. In 1906, he was awarded a Harrison fellowship and departed for Europe to study for a thesis on the Romance languages. But after seven months abroad, the university scratched his travelling scholarship and Pound was forced to return to the United States. He settled briefly as a teacher of languages at Wabash College in Crawfordsville, Indiana, but after only a few months decided to leave the Mid-West and the United States to live as a poet in Europe. Early in 1908, Pound arrived aboard a freighter at Gibraltar and traversed Europe, walking long distances, before settling in Venice. Here he lived with a pianist fifteen years his senior, acting as her impresario. During this period Pound published at his own expense his first collection, *By a Dark Lantern (A Lume Spento)*. But soon Venice seemed too restricted for his energies and in August 1908 he arrived in London, then still the centre of a world empire.

Pound swiftly gained entry to literary circles in London and, through his many contacts, became a promoter of and agent for the literary *avant-garde*. In 1914 he married Dorothy Shakespear, a talented painter whose mother ran a literary salon. The same year he met T.S. Eliot and began promoting other young writers. His most important contribution was probably his fostering the early works of James Joyce, whom he also supported financially. After a tour of continental Europe in 1920, the Pounds settled in Paris early in 1921, where the literary dynamo continued promoting rising authors, in competition with Gertrude Stein. In Paris, Pound met the American violinist Olga Rudge, the daughter of a wealthy real estate broker from Ohio, who had been raised in England and Italy, and who was to become Pound's life-long partner.

By 1924 the restless poet probably felt that his own literary work was suffering. In the 1925 spring edition of *This Quarter*, Hemingway remarked that Pound spent about one-fifth of his time working on his own poetry and the remainder trying to secure the literary and financial future of his friends. After an extensive tour of Italy during the autumn of 1924, Ezra and Dorothy Pound settled in Rapallo on the Riviera di Levante. In July 1925 Pound's daughter Maria (Mary) was born to Olga Rudge in Brixen (Bressanone), north of Bozen (Bolzano), in the South Tyrol. Mary was raised by step-parents in Gais, South Tyrol. Just over a year later, in September 1926, Dorothy Pound gave birth to a son, Omar, in the American Hospital at Neuilly, near Paris. Omar was raised by his grandmother, Olivia Shakespear.

During his years in Rapallo, Ezra Pound withdrew from the hectic life of a promoter of *avant-garde* literature and concentrated on his labyrinthine life-work, the *Cantos*, a kind of a journey through the story of mankind. One of the central themes of the *Cantos* is USURA, Latin for profiteering from usury and extortionate interest. For Ezra Pound, USURA became the embodiment of evil and the destroyer of all beauty and values. In *Cantos XIV–XV* Pound directly attacked war profiteers, high finance, politicians and imperialists alike, as well as all liars, orators and preachers. Because many banks were owned and managed by Jews, Pound developed a blind hatred of them. When literary friends accused Pound of ideological confusion, he retorted that he was crying out for humanity in a world cauterized by usury.

On 30 January 1933 – a date that was perhaps some kind of omen – Mussolini received the American poet. Beside a special edition of his *Cantos XVI*, Pound presented the Duce with an eighteen-point programme summarizing his economic and political ideas. The dictator described his visitor's writings as 'entertaining', but paid no attention to his opinions.

After 1933 Pound spent more and more time on his theories of world economy and finance. Between 1933 and 1939 several German writers, including Gerhart Hauptmann, made a pilgrimage to Rapallo, while most of his former Anglo-American literary friends turned away from him. Pound's crude conclusion that all European politicians other than Mussolini were rogues was more than they could bear. Pound was probably beginning to feel his growing isolation, and sense that he was losing ground, when he began to immerse himself in the study of Confucius.

In April 1939 Pound visited the USA, hoping to meet the president and persuade him to keep out of a possible Second World War. But Roosevelt had no intention of meeting the expatriate. Instead Pound was received by the agriculture secretary, Henry A. Wallace, and by some senators. The trip was not a success, and Pound's experiences in Washington only intensified his burning hatred of the Roosevelt administration. Wallace later recalled that Pound appeared perfectly normal, but gave the impression that he inhabited a different world. Early in the war, Pound is recorded as having proposed that the US government should present the Japanese government with Wake Island in exchange for a complete set of *Noh*-plays, and thereby avoid an armed conflict with the Japanese.[63]

From the start of the war, when Italy still held 'non-belligerent' status, Pound canvassed Italian radio officials to let him go on the air to address the American people. Eventually, beginning on 23 January 1941, he was given a ten-minute slot every three days in the 'American Hour'. This marked the beginning of an unprecedented one-man peace movement. To record his talks, Pound had to travel from Rapallo to the Italian capital. For each broadcast he was paid the equivalent of fifteen dollars. In his broadcasts, Pound blasted the 'money-hungry' Americans for sending aid to Britain, warned against the cost of intervention in terms of lives and blood: 'For God's sake, don't send your boys over here to die for the Shell oil company and the Jewish war profiteers'. He blamed the Jews for most of the wars in history, and held forth on just about anything that popped into his mind – venereal disease, carving in wood, the price of potatoes, health diets – laced with homely American slang and quotations from ancient Greek, Chinese and Japanese poetry.

'Ezrapunto' Corresponds with 'Lord Haw-Haw'

On 5 May 1941, Pound wrote a letter to a Miss Beveridge in Berlin, apparently enquiring about times when he could listen in to William Joyce's talks. This letter was passed on to Joyce who replied on 3 June, giving the schedule and promising: 'In the very near future I propose to inflict a real letter on you. Meanwhile all the best. Heil Hitler.'

Pound's response was a three-page barrage of suggestions covering a wide variety of subjects, commencing with: 'I don't suppose you have time to listen, but shd/ be glad to profit by experienced criticism. God knows HOW one gets an idea into a lunatic asylum. And the idea that Brits/ are subject to REASON is probably an error if not downright lunacy. Can't remember when I first heard of yr/ transmissions, but have been hearing 'em daily ever since.' Pound complained that he was suffering from the lack of new information; recommended that Berlin translate 'an excellent book in japanese/ title meaning British Empire and Brit. people/ dope on the Sassoons in Shanghai etc/' by a 'bloke named Itoh'; continuing: 'Weltdienst is good/ Germany and You is no longer sent me/ I dont know why. mebbe they dont like my front name.

I am not going to change it/ believe the yidds swiped it from the Egyptians/ but at any rate the bloody pilgrim farvers took over and it is rural and Bauernfahig in up state N.York as is Jack in Deutschland.' Ezra Pound signed off with "HEUL [*sic*] HITLER and nach Vladivostock.'

On 30 June 1941, William Joyce thanked him somewhat formally 'for the valuable hints which you gave me', continuing: 'Unfortunately, I cannot write a real letter as yet because, as you can imagine, my work is heavier than ever just at present. [...] I agree with you that it is not easy to make an impression of an obvious nature on the thing called the British public, but I nevertheless think that we are succeeding and that the results will be cummulative [*sic*] when they emerge.'

Ezra Pound responded with another three-page letter: 'I think I was right to transmit from Rome/ I know this country and do not know Germany and can not speak German well enough to make my ideas clear/ Also I cd/ never stand a winter in Berlin.' Later Pound hinted that he would like to visit Berlin: 'Money tied up/ I couldn't get to Berlin except by official invite with paid expenses.' Then, turning to his favourite subject, "Can't you put a proper Berlin psycopath [*sic*] onto the FILES of the newspapers, to see, if Roosevelt gets worse at full moon? A good [...] thorough Grundlichkeit study of the kikeology of the president ... I haven't the files or material here.'

The poet followed this letter with a note dated 29 July, drawing Joyce's attention to a radio talk from Rome by Princess Troubetzkoi on 'Russian bolchevik Dumoing', ending with 'ever, Heil Hitler'. William Joyce acknowledged the tip with a brief note, dated 19 August, and promised: 'I shall try to procure a copy of Princess Troubetzkoi's talk. With kindest regards and Heil Hitler!'

Pound's next letter to Joyce, dated 16 September 1941, opened with a blast against Roosevelt: 'Dear Joyce – Am still feeling lack of coordination. Faint down of hope, or fat faith in the American people, I mean IF we can hold out a few months longer, the American electorate will I think squash that unspeakable louse, that cunt of all infamy Roosevelt at the autum[n] elections next year. I dont want to mention this; and dont want it mentioned it wd/ only accelerate his devilments: (if it isn't al[r]eady doing so anyhow.) [. . .] I am not convinced the kikes meant England to WIN/ or that the drive to war is the same as a drive to WIN a war/ . the buggars [*sic*] want DEBT/ vide Herzl ten or was it 20 years ago, or the Hazard circular of 1861 (or thereabouts) too late this evening to look up the detail. [...] Comment, preceding yr/ last this evening/ at 11.30, was very good, 4 days guns etc/ for Eng/ in 6 months/ GOD damn Roosevelt, and the brit. gang. ANYhow/ what shit/ what [. . .] muckers !!' The letter ended with another plea for new information: 'BUT I want more printed matter from Germany/ Weltdienst O.K. but I want MORE. I cant keep up my particular kind of barrage without nutriment/ facts and more facts/ Fuller reports from the public I am supposed to be shootin AT. Is there anybody in the Rundfunk that can send 'em to me/ stuff ABOUT the U.S. that I would be able to interpret, even if it means nothing to Europeans/ personal news/ even the NEW directory of congress/ for Krizake realize that I am not even SURE which congressmen have been reelected last autumn, Jo Martin is gunnin for Ikes/ GOOD but what doesit mean in Bucarest ??'[64]

It is not known whether Joyce replied, or whether Pound continued his largely one-way correspondence in the three months that remained before Pearl Harbor. By this time, Pound was classified as a Fascist, and the US embassy in Rome extended his US passport by only six months. After America entered the war, the Italian government arranged for the evacuation of war-trapped Americans from Italy to Portugal for onward transport to the United States. Pound wanted to leave Italy with them, but embassy and consular staff refused to allow him to board the diplomatic train.

By the end of January 1942 Pound was back at the Rome microphone and resumed his pounding more intensively than before. From then on his radio talks concentrated on the danger of the Communist menace, now that Washington and Moscow had become wartime allies. Sometime during this period, possibly in April 1942, he may have visited Berlin and spoken on the radio to the United States, as recalled by Dr. Richard Kupsch, who believed that Pound also met William Joyce, though the two did not, apparently, mesh well.[65] The German Foreign Ministry in Bonn has not been able to confirm this visit, and pointed out that if the American was a guest of the Reich he would not have required a visa.

On 26 July 1943 a federal grand jury in Washington indicted Ezra Pound, along with the Berlin Americans, on charges of wartime treason. Pound received the news with disbelief, and sent a letter to Washington arguing that the simple fact that someone expresses his personal views could not possibly be taken as evidence of treason. The dismissal and arrest of Mussolini on 25 July 1943 had in any case put an end to Pound's career as a pro-Axis radio propagandist. On 10 September Pound left Rome and headed north towards Gais, where his daughter was still living with her step-parents and working at a German military hospital in Cortina d'Ampezzo.

Back in Rapallo, Pound plunged into the translation into English of a voluminous novel by Enrico Pea, and the translation of the work by the economist J.P. Arnold into Italian. In addition, he provided the Fascist government at Salò, set up after Mussolini's rescue by a German glider commando, with a continuous stream of propaganda material, and continued his studies of Confucius.

When the German army evacuated the population of the region around Rapallo in anticipation of a possible Allied landing, the Pounds withdrew to an apartment which Olga Rudge had bought in the hills above Rapallo. On 2 May 1945, the German army in Italy surrendered, and the following day partisans forced their way into Pound's retreat and took the writer to their camp at Zoagli. On 5 May, Pound was handed over to US Counter-Intelligence in Genoa.[66]

On 22 May 1945 the US military received orders from Washington to transfer Pound to a camp for defectors and criminals in Pisa, demanding top security precautions. Here the poet was detained in a specially constructed cage in the open. Because of Washington's instructions, Pound was kept under guard twenty-four hours a day, with searchlights at night. His belt and laces were taken away from him and nobody was allowed to speak to him. After three weeks, Pound complained about hallucinations and nightmares. He ate little and was rapidly losing weight. An army psychiatrist found that he Pound was suffering neither from psychosis nor neurosis, but recommended that he be transferred to the camp's sick-bay. Here, Ezra

18 Ezra Pound, charged with treason, in Washington D.C., November 1945. On the right is Chief Deputy Marshal Kearney.

Pound began working on his *Cantos LXXIV–LXXXIV*, later published as *The Pisan Cantos*.

In November 1945 Pound was flown to Washington to stand trial. The judge ordered his mental examination by court-appointed specialists. In January 1946 these submitted their reports. Although differing as to the category of mental disorder into which to fit him, they agreed in their verdict: 'Insane and mentally unfit for trial'. The judge ordered Pound to be detained in a mental institution. For the next twelve years the Chestnut Ward of the St. Elizabeth Hospital for the criminally insane, on the outskirts of Washington, was Ezra Pound's home.

Dorothy Pound visited her husband daily, and many literary friends also visited him at the institution. Pound wrote many letters, received even more mail, and continued working on the *Pisan Cantos*. They were published in July 1948 and won him the Bollingen Award. The jury's decision caused a public uproar between pro- and anti-Pound forces, involving poets, literary critics, politicians, psychiatrists and just about everybody who had ever heard the name of Ezra Pound. But the poet remained locked away, ignoring his surroundings and working painstakingly on his *Cantos*. To an enquiring journalist Ezra Pound once remarked sarcastically: 'An insane asylum is the only place I could bear to live in, in this country!' Meanwhile circles in the United States began lobbying for Pound's release. These were strengthened when Ernest Hemingway, after receiving the 1954 Nobel Prize for literature, commented that Ezra Pound ought rightfully to have been the recipient.

Eventually the US attorney general accepted a petition by a committee of prominent literary and public figures, and the presiding judge ruled that Ezra Pound was 'not too dangerous to go free in his wife's care, but too insane ever to be tried'.

In April 1958 the poet was released from hospital. On 30 June, Pound left the USA for Italy, where he and his wife Dorothy settled with his daughter's family at the Brunnenburg, near Meran (Merano), in South Tyrol. Towards the end of 1961, Pound ceased writing. His health was beginning to decline and, between travels, he frequently had to be admitted to hospital. On 1 November 1972, two days after his eighty-seventh birthday, Ezra Pound died in Venice. He was buried on the island of San Michele, not far from the tombs of Diaghilev and Stravinsky.

The last volunteer

Almost certainly the last American to join the German propaganda apparatus was Martin Monti, a young second lieutenant of the US Army Air Force who presented himself unexpectedly to the Nazi propagandists in a P-38 fighter aircraft. Martin James Monti was born on 24 October 1921 in St. Louis, Missouri. His father, a respectable stock-broker, was the child of an Italian mother and Swiss father, while his mother was a first-generation American born of German parents. The Monti family were staunch Catholics, and the father a fervent isolationist, strongly opposed to the United States taking any part in the war, though without expressing any pro-Axis or un-American sentiments. Monti left school prior to graduation in August 1938, and with his older brother was dispatched to relatives in Switzerland and Italy. On his return to St. Louis, Monti got a job in a warehouse but, alienated by rules and discipline, left in March 1940 to work in an Oregon lumber camp. In the summer of 1941 he returned to Missouri and went to work as a rivetter in the Curtiss Wright aircraft company. When he realized that he was going to be drafted, he enlisted as an air force cadet, though, after a disagreement with officials, not in fact joining until January 1943. After pre-flight training at Santa Ana, California, Monti was posted to Hamilton Field, San Francisco. In August 1944 he was posted as a P-38 replacement pilot to an air-strip near Karachi, India, while most of his contemporaries were sent to Italy.

As a result of his views on America's participation in the war in Europe, Monti was not popular with his fellow-pilots. Increasingly wild and disaffected, he declared he wished to be assigned to a squadron in Italy so he could take off, bail out with a distress signal over Switzerland and be reported missing in action. On 2 October he did in fact go AWOL, hitching a ride from Karachi to Cairo on a military aircraft. After a couple of days he continued to Tripoli and thence to Naples by sea. He tracked down his comrades in the Foggia area, and applied unsuccessfully to be transferred there. On 10 October a fellow pilot flew him to Pomigliano air base, near Naples. There Monti managed to persuade mechanics working on a P-38 fighter that the plane needed 'test hopping'. Referred to the engineering officer, Monti instead boarded the aircraft and took off without permission. He reached German-controlled air-space unmolested and landed the aircraft behind German lines, near Milan, and was taken prisoner.

Monti was held first at a PoW camp in Verona, and later transferred to the Luftwaffe's interrogation and transit camp at Oberursel, where he informed German officials that he had deliberately landed behind German lines. The claim led to interrogation by members of the military assessment centre – west (*Auswertungsstelle West*) who discovered that the American PoW was strongly anti-Communist and wanted to help the Nazi cause. Monti was then turned over to Luftwaffe Lieutenant Bönninghaus, a former war correspondent attached to the propaganda section of the High Command. Bönninghaus signalled to radio officials that the American airman might be useful as a broadcaster.

By the end of November, Monti was in a PoW camp in Berlin, where Heinrich Schafhausen, the current head of the RRG's North America zone, and the commentator Edward Vieth Sittler, from Ohio but by then a German citizen, appraised Monti's usefulness. Although Schafhausen found him 'on the whole immature and lacking in general education', he recommended that Monti be employed to relieve pressure on the other announcers. For a week or two Monti was kept under observation by the military, before being released and transferred to Königs Wusterhausen. After a microphone test, he was asked to deliver his impressions of the food situation, the effects of the bombing, the morale of the German people and similar general topics. With Sittler's help, Monti (as Martin 'Wiethaupt', his mother's maiden name) wrote and presented several talks on the North America service. But his youth, inexperience and fundamental lack of talent ensured he did not become a regular broadcaster. After the war Sittler recalled that: 'He labored for some weeks with monumental minuteness on several small talks, but he was too engrossed in vague and vast feelings and too little used to formulating ideas and impressions to be very adept at the task'.

Meanwhile, Monti-Wiethaupt had made the acquaintance of Pierre de la Ney du Vair (*d.* 1945), an American from Louisiana who had been a member of the French volunteer anti-Bolshevist Legion fighting alongside the Wehrmacht on the eastern front. At the time Monti encountered him, du Vair was a captain (*Hauptsturmführer*) with the *Standarte Kurt Eggers*, the SS propaganda unit.[67] Du Vair arranged for Monti to visit Hungary early in 1945, accompanied by Railton Freeman – the RAF officer who had been writing scripts for the Foreign Ministry, and had enlisted in the Waffen-SS in August 1944 – to see evidence of atrocities committed by Soviet troops in a city which had been retaken by the Wehrmacht. Monti's reports on this expedition formed the basis for his regular participation as 'an American captain' in du Vair's weekly 'Round Table Conferences'. Other participants in the programme were Schafhausen, Sittler, Dr. Curt Eduard Friese of the Foreign Ministry, Leon Ribitzki, as well as Margaret Hermann, a radio announcer, and Mrs. Katherine Bussman-du Vair.

Monti-Wiethaupt's friendship with du Vair frequently took him to the *SS-Standarte Kurt Eggers* quarters in Berlin-Zehlendorf, and he was eventually absorbed by the unit 'as he believed he would be treated in a less step-motherly way by them than by the RRG'. He made several recordings for use by the *Standarte*, '[...] at least one of which, possibly two, were also run over the short-wave transmitters in our programme', according to Schafhausen. Early in April 1945, with the Soviet Army

19 US pilot, Martin J. Monti, arraigned on charges of treason by US Commissioner Fay, Brooklyn, 1945.

closing in on Berlin, Monti-Wiethaupt was formally admitted to the SS and ordered to report to a propaganda unit stationed on the shores of Lake Como in northern Italy, near the Swiss border. When he had crossed the Brenner Pass he encountered, probably to his amazement, a situation far from that he had been led to expect. The chaos he found prompted him to desert once again and await the arrival of the US Fifth Army. At the end of the month he reported to the American authorities in Milan, omitting of course to mention that he was AWOL, let alone a deserter. He manufactured an account that he had been shot down by German flak over Milan on 13 October 1944, taken prisoner and shifted to PoW camps in Verona, Frankfurt and Wetzlar. He also claimed to have escaped from a train between camps and to have roamed the countryside for two months with the help of German, Austrian and Italian farmers; he had eventually reached Milan by cart, explaining that the SS uniform he was wearing had been given him by members of the Italian underground.

The story stuck and Monti was left free to go. But the Counter-Intelligence Corps then began its own checks, since he had made no attempt to conceal his identity, and on 14 May the 'escaped Allied PoW' was apprehended at the American Red Cross Club in Bari and put on trial by general court-martial. He admitted going AWOL from Karachi and taking the P-38 from Pomigliano , claiming that he simply wanted 'to get into the fight' and that 'it was his intention to see action'. For the rest, he repeated his earlier story. On 18 September Monti was found guilty of 'desertion and misappropriation of government property', dismissed and sentenced to fifteen years hard labour. No treason charge was brought against him: the military authorities did not have the evidence, and Monti had no intention of incriminating himself. He was returned to the US and confined in the disciplinary barracks at Green Haven, NY. Protests by Monti's family to their congressman and to the under-secretary of war led to press interest and a review of the case by the classification board. The result was a 'no clemency' recommendation, but assignment to a disciplinary company with a view to eventual restoration to duty. On 4 February, however, the under-secretary of war remitted the rest of Monti's sentence upon his re-enlistment in the army as a private.

It was some time before the truth about Monti emerged. When the Justice Department began probing other treason cases, traces of his adventures came to light. On 24 January 1948 FBI agents arrested him and two days later he was discharged from the army. At his trial at the Brooklyn federal court a year later, Monti pleaded guilty to all charges and was sentenced to twenty-five years imprisonment and fined $10,000. He was paroled in 1960.

Final Broadcasts

In August 1943, the German Overseas Stations (formerly the KWS) were evacuated from Berlin to Königs Wusterhausen, a few miles miles from the transmitter complex at Zeesen. Winkelnkemper and his staff transferred to the Schenkendorf Palace, while the programme directors and producers, and some broadcasting sections, moved into the Station Hotel. Roughly eighty members of the Orient zone moved into a home for the blind – the former occupants being hurriedly removed to an asylum in Teupitz. The North America zone and some parts of the German zone now operated from a rustic inn in nearby Gussow. The studios were crammed into the basement of the local post office in Königs Wusterhausen, which, conveniently, had already been handling all broadcasting traffic between Berlin and Zeesen. But primitive working

20 The German Overseas Station studios at Königs Wusterhausen.

21 Maintenance of broadcasting installations at Königs Wusterhausen.

conditions, frequent interruptions by Allied bombing, and concern for families remaining in Berlin, depressed morale and undermined vigour.

Nine of Zeesen's twelve short-wave transmitters were put out of action when Allied bombing destroyed the power station at Finkenheerd on the river Oder, and services to the USA, Africa, the Far East and some European regions temporarily ceased. When the amplifier-modulator at Magdeburg was hit, the landlines to the short-wave stations in north-west Germany were cut, and on another occasion the landlines to the transmitter complex at Munich were interrupted at Weimar.

A series of five large-scale RAF attacks on Berlin began on 18 November 1943. By 3 December, 8,600 tons of bombs had been dropped on the capital and 2,700 people killed. A quarter of a million were made homeless. One of these raids demolished what was left of the Overseas Stations' facilities in Berlin. Steps were then taken to replace the makeshift arrangements in the Station Hotel and the post office, and proper broadcasting facilities were installed in the former home for the blind. Further facilities were provided in Helmstedt, Lower Saxony, and in Landshut, Lower Bavaria. After 1944, broadcasts to India were engineered from the basement of the Hotel Pätzold in Helmstedt, where the German Secret Stations were later to take refuge. At the same time, new facilities became operational in Königs Wusterhausen, but, with the advance of the Soviet Army, had to be evacuated, and most broadcasting teams moved to Landshut. Here the remnants of the former German Overseas Stations moved into a country inn, the *Goldene Sonne*, and from its dance hall the last programmes – directed at Asia – continued to be broadcast until the US Army overran the town at the end of April 1945.

4   Fighting Great Britain on Medium-Wave

Harnessing the Medium-Wave System for Foreign-Language Propaganda

Europe was a fundamental target of Nazi Germany's propaganda operation. In 1938, when the European Foreign-Language Services (*Europäische Fremdsprachendienste*) first harnessed the short-wave transmitter DJA at the Zeesen complex for its early broadcasts, the objective was defined as 'to promote a new European order, and combat the inflammatory lies of her enemies and seek recognition and support for Germany's political, military, economic and cultural goals and achievements'. As the war progressed the goal became more focussed: 'To be a weapon against England, and interpreter for allied [i.e., Axis] and neutral nations'.[1] Medium-wave transmission, which became possible when a new 100 kW transmitter (Bremen I at Osterloog, near Norddeich on the North Sea coast)[2] began broadcasting on 24 November 1939, was the means through which it would be attempted.

By the time the Foreign-Language Services were renamed the German European Stations (*Die Deutschen Europasender*) on 21 April 1941, the systematic construction of a homogeneous European broadcasting network was almost complete. The DES were then regularly broadcasting programmes in twenty-seven languages – twenty-nine by 1944 – to six broadcasting regions:

- *Bremen I* effectively covered north-west Europe and the British Isles;
- the new 100 kW medium-wave transmitter *Donau* at Dobrochow u Litomysle, in former Czechoslovakia, covered south and south-east Europe and North Africa;
- the 100 kW medium-wave transmitter *Alpen* at Graz-Doble in Austria, was directed at south-west Europe, including Vichy France, Spain and parts of North Africa;
- the long-wave transmitter *Weichsel* (also referred to as *Bremen II*), at Warsaw-Raszyn in Poland, was primarily directed at eastern Europe, but transmitted programmes in eight different languages, including clandestine programmes in French;
- a 120 kW long-wave transmitter, *Friesland*, at Kootwijk in Holland, covered northern Europe;

- the French 100 kW medium-wave transmitter *Calais* – which was actually located about 120 km north-east of Paris – now served the DES, covering the western region and the British Isles;[3]
- and, in adddition, the 40 kW short-wave transmitters DXX and DXM at Zeesen were received reasonably well in even the remotest corners of Europe.

This basic grid was boosted by up to eighty long, medium and short-wave stations. The powerful 165 kW Luxembourg transmitter at Junglinster was the most important in terms of boosting English-language broadcasts. First used by the Wehrmacht as a 'black' station against France, it was taken over by the RRG in November 1940 and integrated into its European network. The Dutch transmitter complex at Lopik was also effective for coverage of the west.

Mobile stations were added to the transmitter grid as and when needed. These emergency back-up stations had been made available to the RRG since 1934, and the propagandists soon perceived how useful they could be as secret stations. In November 1937, Goebbels' ministry had provided Franco with a mobile 20 kW medium-wave transmitter. Stationed on a football pitch in Salamanca, it enabled *Radio Nacional de Salamanca* to support the Nationalist side while suggesting it was operated by the Republicans, hence creating confusion behind Republican lines.

By 1939 five mobile transmitters were available to the ProMi – four medium-wave and one long-wave. Each unit consisted of a convoy of twenty or more trailers of up to 20 metres long, 2.5 metres wide and 3.5 metres high, and weighing up to 20 tonnes – too wide for most roads and bridges, too high for underpasses. During the war these were used mainly by the military, while the ProMi relied on its network of stationary transmitters across Europe and the short-wave stations at Zeesen.

Apart from the regional *Reichssender* Berlin and the national *Deutschlandsender*, regional stations in Germany and all stations in occupied territories were compelled to give priority to DES material fed into the network by landline from Berlin. The English-language news, for example, went out over Calais, Breslau, Cologne, Luxembourg and the short-wave station DXX (8 April 1943), and later over Calais, Cologne, Luxembourg, Friesland and the short-wave station DXQ (30 August 1944).

In May 1939 a new triple-power 165 kW long-wave *Deutschlandsender* transmitter at Herzberg, on the river Schwarze Elster, came on air, replacing the old 60 kW *Deutschlandsender* at Zeesen, thereafter used almost exclusively for clandestine broadcasts.

Production teams comprising editors, commentators, translators, presenters and clerical staff, generally under the direction of a German zone chief, and largely self-sufficient, ran the regional programmes. Compared to their colleagues at the Short-Wave Station, the European teams had an easier task, thanks to their broadly shared cultures, their closeness to events and the live interviewing of local and foreign personalities that was feasible for them.

European Foreign-Language Services
The German European Stations (from April 1941)
1938 – April 1941: Walter Kamm
April 1941 – 1941: Walter Wilhelm Dittmar
1941 – September 1943: Walter Kamm
September 1943 – May 1944: Hans Häuschen *acting* head
May 1944 – May 1945: Hans Häuschen

Programme Controller:
April 1941 – 1941: Walter Kamm
1941 – May 1945: Johannes Schmidt-Hansen

Duty Editor/Zone Heads/all Broadcasters/Production Office/Gramophone Records

Broadcasting Zones

North: Scandanavia

North-West: Britain
     – 1941: Johannes Schmidt-Hansen
1941 – May 1945: Eduard Roderich Dietze

Chief Commentator: William Joyce ('Lord Haw-Haw') from June 1942
Commentators/Broadcasters: Norman Baillie-Stewart, Frances Bothamley,
Edward Bowlby, James Clark, Frances Eckersley, Jack Trevor, etc. and John Amery,
Ralph Baden Powell *from AA*

North-West: Ireland
1942: Prof. Ludwig Mühlhausen
1942 – May 1945: Dr. Hans Hartmann

Commentators/Broadcasters: Susan Hilton, Gertrud 'Madeleine' Meissner,
Ella Neher, John O'Reilly, Francis Stewart etc.

West: Benelux/France

South: Italy/North Africa
1941 – March 1943: Wolf Mittler

Commentators/Broadcasters: Mildred Gillars ('Axis Sally') etc.

South-East: The Balkans

East: Poland/Soviet Union

Chart 5: Organization of the RRG's German European Stations

Mental Missiles on the Airwaves

Given Britain's failure to fill its designated role in Hitler's foreign policy scenario – as a natural ally in Germany's struggle against the Soviet Union – it became, not surprisingly, the most important European broadcasting target. Hitler's vision of a universal empire, based on perceived racial superiority and a deep-rooted belief in an Anglo-German alliance, did not seem as odd at the time as it may today. Similar ideas had been expressed in Britain itself during its imperialist heyday at the turn of the century. In 1896, for example, an anonymous scientist published an article in which he detected in the racial closeness of the two peoples the threat that Germany would become Britain's natural rival in world affairs, and advocated a four-step 'biological' approach for British foreign policy:

> First, federate our colonies and prevent geographical isolation turning the Anglo-Saxon race against itself. Second, be ready to fight Germany, as *Germania est delenda*; third, be ready to fight America when the time comes. Lastly, engage in no wasting wars against peoples from whom we have nothing to fear.[4]

But Hitler had completely misjudged Britain's strategic and political priorities during the 1930s, and Britain declined the alliance. Without it the German attack on the Soviet Union in 1941 was Hitler's last gamble to realize his global ambition.

The prospect of a radio war between Britain and Germany was anticipated in January 1939, three months before the annexation of Prague, when the Berlin Foreign Ministry floated the idea of an Anglo-German cultural agreement involving, amongst other areas, broadcasting. The proposal was summarily vetoed by Sir Reginald (Rex) Leeper, the fiercely anti-German head of propaganda at Woburn Abbey, without even consulting his superior, the permanent under-secretary at the Foreign Office, Sir Alexander Cadogan, or the foreign secretary, Lord Halifax. The German Foreign Ministry then made a second approach, this time through the BBC, suggesting that each leader should address the other country, Hitler speaking to Britain over the radio. In April 1939, soon after the British government had rebuffed the proposal, the English-language programmes of the medium-wave regional stations at Hamburg and Cologne, which had been broadcasting occasional items across the North Sea since the previous year, began to assume the form of a focussed propaganda campaign. In a minute to Cadogan Leeper observed: 'I don't think it matters in the least if they repay the compliment of broadcasting in English. Their propaganda here will have little effect.' Cadogan agreed: 'I should not be afraid of German broadcast propaganda in this country'.[5] The accuracy of the judgement remained to be seen.

Eduard Dietze, a bilingual freelance reporter at the RRG, was one of the early pre-war contributors to the European Stations' English service, as was Rolf Hoffmann, of the Party's foreign press office. (The operation seems to have been directed by Johannes Schmidt-Hansen.) Until the outbreak of war the programmes comprised a varied repertoire of news and commentaries, together with fairly pounderous comedy sketches. Among the characters presented were 'good old Bumbleby Mannering', a hypocritical cleric with a flair for timely investment in armaments; the Foreign Office's 'Sir Jasper Murgatroyd', with his insight into the government's acts of aggression; and 'Mr. Smith', a 'typical' upper-class Englishman who, from his Swiss retreat, poured scorn on his country's rotten workers and socialists. This embryonic and largely amateur propaganda apparatus survived until early September 1939, when a specialized English section was established within the European foreign-language services.

In September 1938, when it seemed probable that the Munich crisis would precipitate a war, Dietze had been asked by Rathke, head of the IPA, to edit the news in English. The offer was repeated several weeks later by Dr. Adolf Raskin, head of foreign broadcasts. Although Dietze accepted, he did not get the appointment, apparently because he was not a Party member and, as an Anglophile, regarded as not politically reliable. Nevertheless a year later, soon after the beginning of the war, and following complaints about the quality and professionalism of the news service in English, Dietze was again approached. On 20 October he was invited to submit 'proposals for appropriate foreign-language propaganda in support of the war effort, taking foreign mentality into account'.[6] Several days later he was called to discussions at the Foreign Ministry with Dr. Wanninger and Dr. Schulte-Strathaus, followed by a meeting with Gerhard Rühle, head of the Ministry's broadcasting department, and Professor Reinhard Haferkorn, head of its English-language section.

In short Dietze, on pain of being drafted into the forces, was prevailed upon to join the English section of the Wireless News Agency (*Drahtloser Dienst*) as a language corrector, with a view to becoming joint editor. He succeeded in making it a condition of the appointment that he should not be required to join the RRG's permanent staff. But from that moment Dietze's career would be inextricably bound to the history of the RRG's English-language broadcasting operation.

Eduard Dietze

Eduard Roderich Dietze was born on 1 March 1909, in Glasgow, to a half-German, half-Hungarian father and a Scottish mother, and raised in Erith, near London. In August 1914 Dietze senior returned to Germany to join the army, and in 1916, after he had been wounded, his wife and son followed him, eventually settling in Hamburg. As a boy Eduard was obsessed with radio technology and, while still at school, constructed his own well-equipped electro-physical laboratory. At Hamburg University Dietze read natural sciences, mathematics and later philosophy, and in the summer of 1928 was chosen by the young physicist and inventor, Manfred von Ardenne (*b.* Hamburg, 1907), to accompany him as interpreter on a study trip to the United States. By 1929 Dietze had founded his own company, specializing in radio amplifiers and loud-speakers, and in April 1930 joined Siemens & Halske in Berlin as an electrical engineer. Two years later, in April 1932, he left what appeared a promising career in technology to join German radio as a freelance reporter, and within a few

22 Eduard Dietze, lecturing
Rundfunk students, 1940.

years had become one of the country's leading radio journalists. He launched a crisp daily news summary (*Echo des Tages*) which went on air on 5 March 1934, and produced the short-wave programme *Deutschland-Echo*. In 1933 Dietze became the BBC's Berlin commentator, and from 1936 that of the NBC, specializing in covering key events in the German capital with simultaneous translations or instant summaries in faultless English.

When Dietze joined the Wireless News Agency in October 1939, among its senior English section staff were Margarete 'Maja' Guth (*b*. Lübbenau, Brandenburg, 1893), who had joined the RRG as secretary in June 1932, and Peter Adami. Both took shifts with Dietze as duty editors. Another early member of the emerging team was Helen Sensburg, who had been born in Britain in 1913 and come to Berlin with her German husband at the beginning of the war.[7]

In May 1940 Dietze was appointed acting head of the English section. At that point his political views were comparatively moderate, and his commentaries appeared reasonable to British ears. During this phase of German propaganda in English, from the 'phoney war'[8] to the fall of France, amiable buffoonery gave way to political commentary intended to engender despondency and defeatism among British listeners rather than, as yet, a full collapse of confidence. And here lay the origins of the mutual dislike between the infamous and best-known English-language broadcaster, William Joyce, and his direct superior. Between Dietze the moderate and Joyce the political agitator there was a substantial intellectual divide. After the war Joyce's widow,

Margaret, recalled that 'D. [Dietze] thought W. [William Joyce] a Nazi and W. thought D. anti-Nazi and a careerist. Later they got on better, although never close friends. [...] D. did have the grace to laugh when W. wrote in D's. copy of *Twilight Over England*: With the best respects of Faust to Mephistopheles!'

Goebbels swiftly ordered a change of attitude when, in spite of Dunkirk and the fall of France, Britain continued to reject a settlement. In July 1940 German psychological warfare entered its third phase, that of a full-scale propaganda offensive.

In April 1941 the Wireless News Agency was transferred to the RRG's newly created *Auslandsdirektion*.[9] Although not a Party member, Dietze now became editor-in-chief, responsible for all spoken broadcasts, including the news, which had so far been the responsibility of Schmidt-Hansen. His position was now comparable to that of Karl Schotte, the head of the Short-Wave Station's North America zone, the difference being that Dietze was an independent freelancer while Schotte was a permanent RRG staff member.

In October 1943 a ProMi survey claimed that of the 204 hours of programming produced by the European Stations each day, fifteen hours were directed at Britain. Unlike the German home service, which mainly featured music, about seventy per cent of the European Stations' air time was devoted to information and news. A surviving programme schedule from 1944 gives an idea of a typical day's programme schedule:

1   Views on the News (daily commentaries by either William Joyce or Eduard Dietze)
2   Matters of the Moment (news from the front; news letter; special commentaries)
3   Forces' Hour (PoW greetings & the reading of names of PoWs, casualties and those killed in action)
4   On the Spot (news from the military 'propaganda companies')
5   Have-it-out Club (dialogue about the general & political situation)
6   Progress Parade (information from all over the world; progress of science; economic report)
7   Jazz Cracks (satirical comments served with jazz music)
8   Calais Magazine (news summary; commentary; announcement of the names of PoWs)
9   The End of the Welkin (hits and popular melodies)

Early Voices

Wolf Mittler, the bilingual KWS announcer and reporter, was one of the early RRG voices available for reading the news and for commentaries in English. When the programmes acquired a more overtly political slant in 1939, Mittler found himself reluctantly acting as an English-language propagandist for Nazi achievements and goals. 'It can't have been more than five or six times', he told Denys Blakeway, when interviewed for BBC-Radio 4 in 1991. In his autobiography Mittler recalled:

Soon after the outbreak of war, the Propaganda Ministry decided to beam anti-British propaganda to Britain on medium wave. I was supposed to take part as one of the speakers, and was told it would be starting very soon. Luckily for me, it did not come to that, as two Britons turned up in the nick of time (others came later) who were prepared to go on the air in this unpleasant business. They were Norman Baillie-Stewart and William Joyce.

Wolf Müller-Mittler was born in Munich on 1 January 1914. His maternal grand-father had been born in Königsberg but for much of his life had lived in Ireland, where Mittler's mother was born. His father was a legal expert who, after the First World War, had represented the Bavarian government in the Geneva Red Cross negotiations on the release and eschange of prisoners-of-war. Mittler was bilingual, but had never been to school in England. When his parents separated, the boy fol-lowed his mother to Berlin and, on her remarriage, began work in his stepfather's insurance company. During the summer of 1935, however, Mittler resigned and, with a friend, was hired as cabin boys by a Hamburg shipping company. Mittler later wrote a travel piece which he placed with the *Berliner Tageblatt*. The item was noticed by the chief of the local United Press office, and he was invited to join the operation, collating reports from all over the world for distribution in Germany and neighbour-ing countries. It was late in 1937 that Mittler joined the RRG as reporter for English-language broadcasts.

Norman Baillie-Stewart

One of the first British-born speakers to join the English-language service was Norman Baillie-Stewart. Born Norman Baillie Stewart Wright in London on 15 January 1909, he later acquired the name Baillie-Stewart by deed poll. At eighteen he left the Royal Military College, Sandhurst, and joined the Seaforth Highlanders, where his compe-tence and a marked mechanical gift attracted the attention of his superiors. Having been promoted to captain, however, Baillie-Stewart's army career came to an abrupt end when, during a holiday in Berlin in August 1932, he contacted the *Reichswehr* head-quarters in Berlin, offering to sell classified technical information. Baillie-Stewart's motivation has never been satisfactorily explained: the material offered was little more than could have been gathered from a study of British military journals, and the approach merely aroused the suspicions of his German contacts, who tipped off the British authorities. After some further contacts with representatives of the German army in Holland, all of them monitored by the British War Office, Baillie-Stewart was arrested in January 1933, held in the Tower of London and, in March, court-martialled under the Official Secrets Act. The case, the first of its kind in living memory, inevitably caused a press sensation. Baillie-Stewart's action was seen as naïve and ludicrous, and he was sentenced to five years' penal servitude.

On his release in 1937 Baillie-Stewart settled in Vienna, where he came under the wing of a Nazi agent, an English or English-speaking woman who used the name

'Edith Shackleton' and claimed to be a sister of the explorer. But in February 1938 he was declared an 'undesirable' by the Austrian police and ordered out of the country. He returned in March 1938, immediately after the Nazi annexation of Austria, and in September applied for German citizenship, gaining it in July 1940. Six months later Baillie-Stewart contacted the Vienna branch of the ProMi, criticizing the poor quality of Berlin's English-language broadcasts. He was invitated for a voice test and, in August 1939, asked to Berlin for a three-week trial as an announcer.

In Berlin he was received with suspicion, the German propagandists believing him a British agent — or at least a Foreign Ministry 'plant'. Like many other foreign employees of Nazi institutions, Baillie-Stewart was required to conceal his identity and adopted the name 'Manfred von Krause', apparently that of a German forbear. But his relationship with the RRG did not last: during September William Joyce — whom Baillie-Stewart vehemently detested — gradually usurped the position of Germany's Number One English-language mouthpiece.

In December 1939, after some incautious remarks about the scuttling of the German pocket battleship *Graf Spee* off Montevideo, Baillie-Stewart was temporarily replaced as news reader by the sixteen-year old Jim Clark. A few months later, on 26 September 1940, William Shirer noted in his *Berlin Diary* that 'He [Baillie-Stewart] is now off the air and working as a translator in the Foreign Office.' After the war Margaret Joyce recalled that: "He [Baillie-Stewart] was getting more and more drawn to the Foreign Office, where, if you were a good boy, there was more money to be earned.'

At that point Baillie-Stewart indicated he wished to return to Vienna, but the Foreign Ministry offered him a place in its own English-language broadcasting team.[10] He now produced and presented radio programmes (under the name 'Lancer') as well as giving lectures at Berlin University and writing for *The Camp*, a German-sponsored four-page illustrated weekly tabloid distributed to British PoWs.[11] In 1943 he also tried his hand as a librettist, adapting current German hits for the singer Lale Andersen to record in English for the RRG. In May or June 1944, the Foreign Ministry transferred Baillie-Stewart to Vienna, where he was to produce propaganda programmes for the local *Reichssender*.[12]

After the war Baillie-Stewart was arrested in the Austrian lake-side village of Altaussee and put on trial in the Central Criminal Court at the Old Bailey in London. The capital charge of treason was dropped on condition that he pleaded guilty to having 'aided the enemy' under the Emergency Defence Regulations of 1939. In comparison with William Joyce and John Amery, Baillie-Stewart was politically harmless and had done little real damage: in his defence, he gave his affection for a German woman as the deeper cause for his actions. Since he had abjured his British nationality long before the war, and had technically been a German citizen after 9 July 1940, the idea was mooted that Baillie-Stewart might be released to Germany, on condition that he undertook never to return to Britain. The judge declared that 'the sooner this man is got away from this country the better'. But when the attorney-general pointed out that the Allied Control Commission was bound to penalize Nazi collaborators, Baillie-Stewart was

23 Norman
Baillie-Stewart,
at the time of his
court-martial,
March 1933.

sentenced, on 10 January 1946, to five years' imprisonment on charges of aiding the enemy. The judge recorded that he was 'one of the worst citizens that any country has ever produced'.[13] After a short time in Brixton prison, Baillie-Stewart was transferred to Wakefield prison in Yorkshire and, after an escape bid, removed to the high security centre at Parkhurst, on the Isle of Wight. At the time of his release, in May 1949, he remained barred from Germany. At first he lived in Quaker guest houses, under the name 'James Scott', and in October 1949 entered Ireland, on false papers provided by the Quakers, and settled in Dublin. Here, in November 1950, and aged forty-one,   he married a Dublin shop assistant. Norman Baillie-Stewart died on 7 June 1966.

Jack Trevor

After the quarrel between Baillie-Stewart and William Joyce late in 1939, the British actor Jack Trevor became the RRG's number two speaker in the English service. Trevor was born Anthony Cedric Sebastian Steane in London on 14 December 1893. After Westminster School and New College, Oxford, Steane served as captain with the Manchester Regiment until invalided out of the War in 1916. At the end of the war Steane married an Austrian, reputedly the illegitimate daughter of the fatal liaison between the heir to the Austrian throne, Rudolf von Habsburg, and Baroness Mary Vetsera, but after a year his new wife mysteriously committed suicide. He then met and married the divorced wife of Harry Penton, a rich land owner. After 1922 Steane, as 'Jack Trevor', had acted in several silent movies, and in 1925 was brought into the German film industry by the director, Friedrich Zelnik, who cast him in *Die Venus vom Montmartre*. That year the Trevors moved to Berlin and settled in some style at

24 Jack Trevor
with guitar and
typewriter.

Bendlerstrasse 8, later the headquarters of the military high command. From then, Trevor featured as the 'typical English' gentleman, officer, ambassador or adventurer in many silent movies, including Georg Wilhelm Pabst's *Geheimnisse einer Seele* (1926) and Gerhard Lamprecht's *Der Katzensteg* (1927). In 1928 he took a part in Hitchcock's *Champagne*, of which a parallel German version was produced, directed by Geza von Bolvary. The same year he featured in Martin Berger's production of *Rasputin's Liebesabenteuer*.

The advent of the talkies did not hinder Trevor's career: indeed, his halting German accent probably added to his appeal. His first speaking part was in the successful movie *Die grosse Sehnsucht* (1930), starring Camilla Horn and Theodor Loos, followed by *Das Lied der Nationen* (1931), a Franco-German co-production, and *Die fünf verfluchten Gentlemen* (1932), starring Adolf Wohlbrück (later Anton Walbrook) and Camilla Horn. After interludes in London and Hollywood, Trevor returned to Berlin for the filming of *Henker, Frauen und Soldaten* (1935), starring Hans Albers. The family now settled in Oberammergau, spending the summers at their villa near Villefranche-sur-Mer. Bit parts followed in musical comedies such as *Engel mit kleinen Fehlern* (1936) and *Napoleon ist an allem schuld* (1938), and in adventure films like *Unter heissem Himmel* (1936), starring Hans Albers.

When war broke out, Trevor was filming aboard a cruiser in the Baltic Sea, his family at home in Oberammergau. On 11 September 1939, returning to harbour, he was arrested by the Gestapo, losing several teeth in subsequent 'interrogations' during which he refused to give the Hitler salute. Shortly before Christmas Goebbels sent for the actor and requisitioned his services as a news reader in English-language broadcasts. In view of his own and his family's precarious situation, Trevor accepted. But when he declined to continue in May 1940, Gestapo agents again visited him and forcibly compelled a change of mind. Trevor was required to appear in three anti-British propaganda movies, *Mein Leben für Irland* (1941), *Carl Peters* (1941) and

Ohm Krüger (1941), and he also featured in the wartime productions of *Geheimakte WB.1* (1942), *Rembrandt* (1942) and Veit Harlan's treatment of *Immensee* (1943), the novella by Theodor Storm.

In July 1945 Trevor was arrested and interned by the American military authorities, and a year later handed over to the British. He stood trial at the Old Bailey, was found guilty of aiding the enemy and, on 15 January 1947, sentenced to three years' imprisonment. After serving only three months, however, he was paroled, probably on the grounds that he had been forced to collaborate with the Germans. Thereafter Jack Trevor lived with his family in France, and occasionally returned to Oberammergau, though he never again entered a film studio. The family eventually settled in Deal, on the Kentish coast, where Trevor died on 19 December 1976.

Frances Eckersley and James Clark

Among the other early broadcasters on behalf of Nazi Germany were Frances Dorothy Eckersley (1893–1971), a member of the literary Stephen family, and James 'Jim' Royston Clark (*b.* 1923), her son by her first marriage to Edward Clark, an employee in the BBC's music department who had studied composition with Schönberg and Busoni in Berlin. Eckersley was the second wife of Peter Pendleton Eckersley, the well-known former chief engineer of the BBC.

Dorothy Eckersley had once been a member of the Independent Labour Party. In 1935 she and her husband visited Germany and admired the country's progress, still desperately lacking in Britain, in relation to unemployment and other social problems. From that point the Eckersleys were frequent visitors to Germany, and Dorothy joined the Anglo-German Fellowship. P.P.Eckersley, after a period of private ventures in broadcasting technology between 1930 and 1937, became consulting engineer on a secret project, conceived by Sir Oswald Mosley, for the development of a commercial radio station. The station, privately owned and outside British jurisdiction, reflected Mosley's ambition, having been banned by the BBC in 1936, for political extremism, to win a British audience. Mosley, having founded a company called Air Time Ltd., was seeking a site for a station on the lines of Radio Luxembourg or Radio Normandie. After plans had fallen through for a transmitter on Sark, in the Channel Islands, Eckersley helped identify a potential location on the Frisian coast of Germany, from where good reception across the North Sea could be assured. Through his second wife, Diana, and her sister Unity, daughters of Lord Redesdale and both ardent followers of Hitler, Mosley had already established close links with the Nazi hierarchy. In mid-1938 the British syndicate, headed by the bill-board mogul W.E.D. ('Bill') Allen, reached agreement with the Reich Minister of Posts, Dr. Wilhelm Ohnesorge, and a joint company, Gemona AG, was registered in Germany. Fifty-five per cent of the equity was owned by the *Reichspost*, and the remaining forty-five per cent by Air Time Ltd. By the time the agreement was signed – after the *Anschluss* in March – Germany was able to allocate a previously Austrian medium wave band (the former Polish Kattowitz frequency) to the transmitter, then under construction at Osterloog near Norddeich.

On completion in November 1939 the station went on the air as Bremen I, beaming propaganda to the British Isles.[14]

By 1938 Frances Eckersley had moved well to the right of Oswald Mosley, as well as of her husband: eventually she and her teenage son joined the Imperial Fascist League of Arnold Leese, a former veterinary surgeon of the British Army. The password of the League was 'P.J.!', for 'Perish Judah!'. They also began attending meetings of the National Socialist League and the Carlyle Club, founded by William Joyce. On one or possibly two occasions Mrs. Eckersley bailed Joyce from police custody, and it was probably her advice that led the Joyces to turn to Berlin in August 1939.[15]

In August 1939 Mrs. Eckersley enrolled her son at the Humboldt School in Berlin-Tegel. Later, on her return from a visit to Budapest, she stopped in Berlin to see James, and when the war broke out they both remained in Germany. Initially Mrs. Eckersley was convinced that 'the Polish business', as she called it, would soon be over. Her primary German contact in Berlin, whom she had met at one of the Nuremberg Party rallies in 1937 or 1938, was Dr. Erika Schirmer, a lecturer at the *Hochschule für Politik* and protagonist of Anglo-German understanding. In December 1939 Mrs. Eckersley was contacted by Schmidt-Hansen of the RRG, invited to a microphone test, and appointed to the English section of the German European Stations as an announcer. She was however taken off the air in October 1941, following complaints about her 'plaintive' voice, and in February the following year was shunted to a lesser job in the archive, trawling the English-language press for information that could be used in anti-British broadcasts. Eventually, from late 1942, she worked for the German Short-Wave Station.

Sometime during the second half of December 1939, and a few days after his mother had been contacted by Schmidt-Hansen, Jim Clark was called for an interview at the *Funkhaus*. Following a brief meeting, he received a letter from the RRG, instructing him to report to Dr. Hetzler at Kaiserdamm 77, home of the German Short-Wave Station, just before Christmas. Clark was immediately put on the air as a news-reader, replacing Baillie-Stewart. At just sixteen, however, his voice must have come across as obviously underaged, and on New Year's Eve Jack Trevor was brought in to replace him. But early in 1940 Clark was again summoned by the RRG and, after a thorough voice test in the presence of Kamm and Dr. Hetzler, was re-appointed. He became, after William Joyce, the English section's number two speaker, earning an average of 400 marks a month.

Late in 1942, according to RRG reports, Jim Clark was compelled to give up broadcasting because of severe malnutrition, tuberculosis, and scarlet fever which had brought on temporary blindness.[16] According to Clark himself, however, this was a pretext worked out by his mother to release him from the German propaganda apparatus: 'There's no getting out for us in our silent disaffection. We can only shrink down as far out of sight as possible where we are. Survival through invisibility. The doctors have been understanding.' According to his statement to MI5 on 18 June 1945, Clark made his last broadcast on 19 July 1942. Since Dr. Richard Kupsch, repatriated from Manila, had been brought in to join the English team as third news-reader early in 1941, it was relatively simple for Clark to slip away. Shortly afterwards, in January 1943, his mother tripped and fell in the archive office, suffering concussion. On 8 April the personnel department informed the various RRG departments that Mrs. Eckersley was too ill to work, even in the archive. Cleinow, head of the European Stations, and Winkelnkemper, director of foreign broadcasts, both agreed to give financial support to the Eckersleys, referring to the 'political importance of the work of Mrs. Eckersley and her son, and the political consequences which a passive attitude of the RRG would engender. Considering the political and military situation it is almost essential to support Mrs. Eckersley with a one-off payment of 1,000 marks.'[17] Soon afterwards, in September 1943, the ProMi began paying her 500 marks a month. Mother and son augmented their income by selling their cigarette ration on the black market, with Jim Clark also giving English lessons and dubbing German films at the UFA studios.

In November 1944 Mrs. Eckersley received a visit from a ProMi official. After an introductory chat, he came to the point, reminding her that Goebbels had authorized the payment of a subsidy without requesting anything specific in return, and enquiring what she and her son proposed to do now that the war had entered a critical phase. According to Clark, his mother thanked the ProMi representative for the minister's kind help: she informed him they had managed to survive without touching the money and that she was pleased to return the whole sum.

On Christmas Eve 1944 Eckersley and Clark were finally arrested by the Gestapo. After some weeks in Berlin's Alexanderplatz prison, they were transferred to internment camps, she at Libenau on Lake Constance, he at Spittal, Carinthia. After the war, they were held in Germany and Italy respectively, until simultaneously repatriated on 29 October 1945 to face charges, under the Defence Regulations, of aiding the enemy. At an MI5 interrogation at Recklinghausen camp, in the Ruhr district, prior to her repatriation, Mrs. Eckersley claimed:

The reason I worked for the Germans was for money. When I began I had no more thought I was working for the Germans than anything. I was only doing it to get

25 James Clark with his parents, Frances Eckersley (*left*) and Edward Clark (*centre*), at Bow Street Police Court, November 1945.

the money to support myself. The only work that I could have done which could have been of assistance to the enemy was in the archives section, but as my work was never used it was of no assistance to them.[18]

When, on her arrival at Croydon airport on 1 November 1945, a warrant of arrest was read to her, Frances Eckersley said: 'It seems comic that anything I have done should be so tremendous'. And when formally charged at Bow Street police station, her reply was: 'I am bowled over by the wording. I never did anything with intent to help the enemy. I only did it to get our bread and butter. What I did did not help the enemy one ha'p'orth.'[19] Eckersley's MI5 statement, given as evidence at her trial, stated:

> My trouble was how was I to live. I had my son dependent upon me, and had managed to keep him from broadcasting since July 1942. I resorted to selling articles of personal property, sufficient to bring us in 500 marks a month. The Rundfunk sent me 1.000 marks on July 9, 1943, a gratuitous payment. I suppose so that they could have a hold over me. [20]

In Jim Clark's statement, given at Terni Internee Camp in Italy, he argued that:

> I merely read the scripts handed to me. I appreciated that my broadcasts were entirely anti-British, but I had at that time no objection to this, as I was still in a hysterical state of mind which had been fostered by the Nazis. I remained in this state of mind until approximately August 1940, when I was somewhat shocked by the air raids on London and other towns in England. It was this news that brought me to my senses, and I began to feel that I had a certain pride in being an Englishman with a correponding hate of the Germans, although in my circumstances I was unable to say so.[21]

Both defendants pleaded guilty to the charges at the Old Bailey. The judge was however not convinced by Mrs. Eckerley's explanation: 'you gave yourself wholeheartedly to the Germans. You were perfectly willing to, and did, assist in the propaganda which you yourself describe as propaganda against England', and sentenced her to twelve months' imprisonment. To her son, whom he bound over for two years, he said: 'I do not believe that you are or ever have been a traitor. I think you caught up with many others in that abominable, and most insidious propaganda which was imbued with the so-called tenets of the Nazi youth organization.'[22]

During the early years of the war P.P. Eckersley had continued as a government servant until his absent wife was identified as a speaker on the German radio by a feature article in the *Daily Mail* on 12 May 1940. Interviewed by the Special Branch. Eckersley convinced the authorities of his loyalty and remained at liberty, but was removed from official work. In a semi-autobiographical book written at this time, *The Power Behind The Microphone* (1941), he set out the case for unrestricted access to independent radio stations.

William Joyce

Probably the only truly professional foreign political agitator working on the Berlin radio was William Joyce, the first radio propagandist to become an international celebrity. Joyce was the most successful, but also the most resented, of all English-language Nazi propagandists.

Joyce was born on 24 April 1906, in Brooklyn, New York, to British-born parents. His father, Michael Joyce, came from County Galway in Ireland, but had become an American citizen in 1894. In 1909 the family returned to Galway, where William received a traditional Catholic education. Loyalists during the struggle for Irish independence, the Joyces left Ireland after July 1921, and settled in England. Later that year William enlisted in the British army, giving Galway as his birthplace and his age as eighteen. When asked to produce his birth certificate, he claimed never to have posessed one. But his military career came to a precipitate end when, four months later and in hospital with rheumatic fever, his true age was discovered. Joyce returned to school and, after matriculation, enrolled first at Battersea Polytechnic and then, in September 1923, at Birkbeck College. He became president of the student Conservative Society and joined the British Fascist Party, an early grouping inspired by the example of Mussolini. In June 1927 he took a first-class degree in English literature and embarked on a Ph.D. course at King's College, London, doing research in English phonetics.

For a time thereafter Joyce lost interest in politics. Observing that the Conservative Party was unprepared to respond to the bidding of a 22-year old, he left it. And with no revolution at hand nor any 'Bolsheviks' in sight – not even during the 1926 general strike – the first British Fascist movement petered out. Joyce did some tutoring and considered returning to university to study for a doctorate in educational philosophy. But in 1933 he returned to politics, joining Oswald Mosley's British Union of Fascists. He became an energetic party speaker and street fighter: indeed it was in a 'political' brawl that he received the razor cut that left him permanently scarred from the corner of his mouth to the lobe of his right ear. Joyce soon graduated from the street corner soap box to deputizing for the leader, and was appointed the party's propaganda director. But in March 1937, along with four-fifths of the BUF's inflated payroll, he was fired.

Unperturbed, Joyce now founded his own party, the National Socialist League. The principal message was clear: 'Britain and Germany, particularly with the assistance of Italy, can form a bulwark much too strong to invite attack from Bolshevism and international finance, twin Jewish manifestations'. As a committed Fascist, Joyce became increasingly aware that, in the event of a war with Germany, he risked being interned or deported: indeed his name was on the original 18b list for immediate detention.[23] In August 1939, alerted that he was about to be detained under the Emergency Powers Act, Joyce and his second wife, the Manchester-born Margaret Cairns Joyce (1911–1972), left London for what seemed their only logical destination – Berlin.

On Sunday 27 August the Joyces arrived in the German capital, with little money and no useful contacts. They sought out Frances Eckersley who suggested they accompany her to the home of Dr. Erika Schirmer. There Joyce met Schirmer's brother, Dr. Hans Schirmer, a high-ranking official at the Foreign Ministry, who undertook to investigate the possibility for work for the Englishman. The following day, Monday 28 August, the British ambassador in Berlin handed a note to the Führer, demanding that the German and Polish governments return to the negotiating table and expressing the British government's determination to fulfill its obligations towards Poland. War now seemed inevitable and the Joyces decided to return to London rather than await certain internment in Germany. But, shunted from travel agency to the British Embassy, and thence to the British consulate in Cologne, they abandoned their plan and remained in Berlin.

On 31 August Dr. Schirmer arranged an interview for Joyce with Foreign Ministry officials. The meeting yielded only a part-time translation assignment, and over the following few days it became plain that little more could be found. Eventually Dr. Hetzler, formerly a member of Ribbentrop's private office and now on the staff of the RRG's English-language section, introduced Joyce to Walter Kamm, head of the European Stations, who agreed to test him as a news reader. On 6 September, Joyce read his first bulletin on German radio, and on 18 September received his contract. To conceal his identity he adopted the name 'Wilhelm Fröhlich' – *fröhlich* being a German equivalent of 'joyous', from which 'Joyce' may have been derived.

Almost at once Joyce began to criticize the quality of the material he was expected to present. He was convinced that he alone could make an effective impression on the British public, and argued that he should be allowed to write and present his own commentaries. 'He had battles almost all the time about the muck the Propaganda Ministry kept turning out as suitable for the talks in English and the badly formulated and inaccurate news. A great deal of material which would have been useful was not allowed, a lot that was bad, had to be used at all costs.'[24]

Joyce's wife Margaret was also given an opportunity to broadcast. Contemporaries described her as a 'compulsive babbler', without a 'microphone voice'. On 2 April 1940, for example, she opened a 'Talk Frau Fröhlich' with the words:

> The other day a friend, who takes an interest in these things, said to me: 'Look here, the BBC and the press have been saying recently that women are unable to buy any clothes in Berlin, and that although the windows are full of nice things, if you go into the shops one can't buy anything. You ought to write a talk about that.' I said: 'Thanks for the tip'.[25]

She proceeded to marvel at the pretty objects she has seen, and might have bought, in Berlin shop windows, ending her talk predictably with the observation: 'There is certainly no need for the BBC to sympathize with the Berlin woman because she can't get clothes – the great trouble is not to want to acquire too many – and too many bills'.

During the first few months of the 'phoney war', tuning in to the voice on German radio universally dubbed 'Lord Haw-Haw' (Joyce himself had still not been publicly identified) seemed to British listeners harmless and amusing, whomever they imagined him to be. The ProMi's English-language broadcasts still

26 William Joyce
(Lord Haw-Haw)
behind the micro-
phone.

reflected an element of restraint. So long as there was – at least until the occupation of Denmark and Norway in April 1940 – the possibility of an accommodation with Britain, Joyce, no man for diplomatic overtures, was kept somewhat in the background. But his opportunity soon came. In January 1940, Hetzler, one of Joyce's early Berlin contacts, was assigned to coordinate and develop the RRG's 'secret stations', and Joyce was invited to join the project. Since the covert stations were free of some of the restrictions applied to the established programmes, they offered Joyce a conspicuous platform to demonstrate his skills. In addition to his work for 'Germany Calling', he now produced, almost single-handed, the bulk of the material used in Germany's secret radio war against Britain.

In Goebbels' diary, Joyce makes the first of many appearances on 5 January 1940:

Our English-language broadcasts are stirring things up in London. Our speaker has the nickname Lord Haw-haw [*sic*] over there. Everyone is talking about him, and that is important for us. In London they are planning to put up a counter-speaker. We could not ask for anything better. Then we'll be in the driving seat.

Here and in all subsequent references, Goebbels designates Joyce as 'Lord Haw-Haw' (or 'Haw-haw'). Joyce himself only began to trade on the notoriety of the nickname more than a year later, on 3 April 1941, when he announced himself as 'William Joyce, otherwise known as Lord Haw-Haw', despite the fact that in Britain 'Lord Haw-Haw' was associated with the voice of someone quite different.

A few days after the first mention, on 9 January 1940, Goebbels refers to Joyce again: 'The Führer heaped praise on our radio propaganda. He is particularly interested in our Lord Haw-Haw. He is a Mosleyite.' (This is a significant misunderstanding: either

Goebbels was unaware of Joyce's breach with Mosley, or had reasons for concealing the information from Hitler.)

But the popularity of 'Germany Calling' soon declined, and by the summer of 1940 'Coopers' Snoopers', of the Ministry of Information, reported that 'his Lordship's audience has shrunk to a fraction of its former size'.[26] As William Shirer observed, 'like a drug too often given, it is losing out what little force it had'.

Goebbels, however, found his British protégé's work greatly to his liking: 'Lord Haw-Haw's voice is now reaching America, and causing a sensation there. The man is a pearl!' (14 March 1940). The following day: 'I told the Führer about Lord Haw-haw's successes, which are positively staggering. He complimented our broadcast propaganda abroad.' (15 March 1940). And again, under the same date: 'Lord Haw-Haw is the great mouthpiece of [Britain's] profound dismay.' Joyce's talks were indeed now being picked up on short wave in the United States. Soon he was giving three talks a week for American listeners, and the press could not ignore him. Goebbels noted that 'He has really become a sort of world-wide celebrity. And does us incalculable service.' (26 April 1940).

On 19 July 1940 Hitler, in a speech to the *Reichstag*, offered a settlement, but Halifax rejected it. The British, said the Foreign Secretary, would go on fighting no matter what the odds. Three days later Goebbels ordered a full propaganda blast, to spread 'alarm and fear among the British people', demonstrating that they had provoked the Führer to the point where he had to mete out the punishment they deserved.[27]

Joyce's aggressive style was a good fit with the new mood. The *BBC Daily Digest of Foreign Broadcasts* of 4 June 1940 noted that: 'Hate along the whole line is the outstanding new feature of this week's broadcasts from *Deutschlandsender*'.[28] The second phase of propaganda attack began with the promise that the end of Britain would come, 'not within a few years but within a few days. Any day now, any moment indeed, the invasion of this country may begin with all its horror, bloodshed and destruction.'[29] Radio Stuttgart claimed confidently on 29 July 1940: 'The way the situation in England is going is very much like that of France before she collapsed'. And in July and August other supposedly 'clandestine' stations were added in support of Operation Sea Lion (*Unternehmen Seelöwe*), the projected German landing in Britain and Hitler's triumphal entry into London.[30]

Joyce now saw himself as the effective, though invisible, leader of a 'Fifth Column' in Britain, urging his listeners to take action against the government.[31] 'The government is faced with an organization which cannot be stamped out. I know that any instruction I give will be carried out in every city, town and village in the United Kingdom.'[32] The style of his scripts grew daily harsher, and by late summer 1940 the little-known Fascist agitator had become Britain's leading figure of hate. Hitler, Göring and Goebbels were remote cartoon figures, but on the 'wireless' Lord Haw-Haw was very much in their midst.[33] He seemed to know every detail of their lives, spoke their own language, and insulted them with bitter cynicism in their homes. It was as if, like some supernatural being, Joyce was running the war on the German side.

On 26 September 1940 the Joyces became naturalized German citizens. It made William liable for military service, and on 12 February 1941 he was issued with a German *Wehrpass* (serviceman's papers) in his own name, and classified a *Reservist*. He was now eligible for more strenuous effort on behalf of the Reich: on 29 March Goebbels noted in his diary that '[Göring] thinks highly of the job Lord Haw-Haw is doing. The best runner I've got in my stable.' The Foreign Ministry, which had not been willing to employ Joyce in the summer of 1939, now commissioned him, for an outright fee of 10,000 marks, to write a full-length work of propaganda for distribution in neutral countries and in the United States. The script was required to be cleared by the Foreign Ministry prior to publication and, in view of the German-Soviet non-aggression pact of August 1939, neither Communism nor the Soviet Union could be ridiculed. *Dämmerung über England* was published by the Internationaler Verlag, Berlin, in September 1940. The book was a personal statement by William Joyce, speaking almost exclusively to a British readership, and hitting out randomly at whatever came into his mind. In 1942 an English edition, *Twilight over England*, was published in The Hague. Of the 100,000 copies printed, none, so far as is known, reached the British Isles until the war was over.

With Joyce involved in intensive broadcasting and writing, his wife Margaret took a lover, Nicky von Besack, a Wehrmacht Intelligence officer. In August 1941 William Joyce sued for divorce on grounds of his wife's infidelity, while Margaret cross-petitioned, alleging cruelty. The court accepted that the marriage had broken down

27 Margaret Joyce, at the Olympic Stadium, Berlin, then home to the Secret Stations, 1942.

and a divorce was granted. But when von Besack was posted to the Baltic, Joyce made a determined effort to win Margaret back, and in February 1942 they remarried in Berlin in a ceremony as discreet as their divorce had been. Shortly afterwards, that June, Joyce achieved his personal ambition when he was appointed chief commentator on the European Stations's English-language service, at a salary of 1,200 marks a month. Later that same year Margaret Joyce joined the English section: 'Dietze had, for some time, been wanting to get me away from Hetzler, (we had moved from the Villa to *Reichssportfeld*) and in October he made a definite move to get me transferred and I started translating at Masurenallee'.[34]

In March 1945, towards the end of the war, the entire English section was transferred from Berlin to rural Apen, near Oldenburg. There, on 7 April, an instruction arrived from the ProMi that the Joyces were, 'at all cost', to be kept out of Allied hands. As a first step they were taken to Hamburg, where William Joyce resumed his 'Germany Calling' broadcasts from the Hotel Vier Jahreszeiten. At the same time he was issued with a new German passport, in the name of Wilhelm Hansen, a teacher born in Galway but later resident in Hamburg.

Joyce made his final broadcast on 30 April. After it, the Joyces were driven to German-occupied Denmark from where they were to travel to neutral Sweden. But British forces had landed in Denmark and the route to Sweden was closed. They returned to Flensburg, in Germany, where they remained until 4 or 5 May, slipping discreetly away when the British army requisitioned the hotel in which they were staying. They moved in with another refugee and ex-Nazi propagandist,

28 **William Joyce, captured, May 1945.**

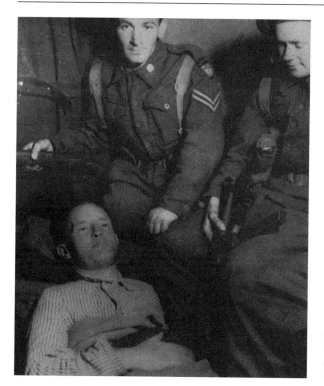

29 William Joyce,
wounded and on a
stretcher, with British
captors, May 1945.

Edward Bowlby and his German fiancée, at nearby Wassersleben, until they found
accommodation at a private lodging in Kupfermühle. Here, on 28 May, while on a
stroll, William encountered two British officers. He might have avoided them, but
could not resist the temptation to chat. The officers appeared to recognize his voice
and asked to see his papers. Thinking that he was reaching for a weapon, one of
them fired a revolver, and Joyce was wounded, and arrested. Detained first in a
military hospital at Lüneburg, he was then transferred to Brussels. On 16 June he
was flown to England and held in Brixton prison, later being moved to Wormwood
Scrubs.

On 17 September 1945 Joyce was charged with treason in No. 1 Court at the Old
Bailey. For the most part the proceedings which followed concerned technicalities,
and in particular the issue of whether an American citizen who had acquired his
British passport under false pretences, and was now a naturalized German subject,
could in fact commit treachery against the British Crown. The judge eventually ruled
that, by obtaining a British passport, Joyce had placed himself under the protection of
the Crown and was 'clothed with the status of a British subject'. In return this required
from him the 'duty of faithfulness and allegiance to the British Crown, between
September 18, 1939, and July 2, 1940 [the expiry date of his British passport]'. On 20
September 1945, William Joyce was found guilty of high treason and sentenced 'to be
hanged by the neck until you be dead'.[35]

Appeals to the Court of Criminal Appeal and the House of Lords both failed. After the House of Lords rejection, 'letters poured into Buckingham Palace and Whitehall pleading for his life', according to David Millward, reporting on the release of government files in 1995.[36] 'Several hundred people signed a petition claiming the execution would be merely vindictive and serve no useful Christian purpose'. And the Duke of Bedford wrote to the Prime Minister, Clement Attlee: 'I gather he has never been charged with betraying military secrets. I must say that I feel his execution would be an act of quite unjustifiable vindictive severity involving a not inconsiderable degree of hypocrisy as well. [...] Joyce, when telling the British people in his broadcasts that their real enemy were the international financiers, spoke no more than the truth.'[37]

On 17 November 1945 Margaret Joyce was transferred from custody in Brussels to Holloway prison in London so that she might visit her husband regularly at Wandsworth prison. Just over six years later, on 19 December 1951, she sent a letter to Dr. Hetzler, passing on her husband's farewell note to his former boss:

> My dear Erich,
> Damn it – and I had such a good conscience – I was sure I'd answered your last letter! [...] When I was over in England, Quentin[38] gave me a book in which he had made notes of Will's last messages to his friends over here. Quentin had never dared to send it but had waited till he could give it to me.
> 'For Dr. Hetzler.
> I regret never having said good-bye to him in Berlin, but my failure to do so was deliberate because I could see the tragedy coming and I had no wish to take a final leave of him after such a happy association and deep friendship. Tell him I was true to the Hakenkreuz till the end and I salute him with the *Deutsche Grüss* [*sic*] – *Heil Hitler.*'
> I thought you would like to have his message at last, although it is just about six years since it was given. He began probably the day – the 19th. December, to put his affairs in order, for it was on the afternoon of the 18th. that we heard, he in Wandsworth and I in Holloway, that the appeal had been dismissed and he was to die. [...]
> Ever yours Margaret.[39]

On the afternoon of 2 January 1946, the day before he was to be executed, Joyce handed a statement to Quentin:

> In death, as in life, I defy the Jews who caused this last war: and I defy the power of darkness which they represent. I warn the British people against the aggressive Imperialism of the Soviet Union. May Britain be great once again; and, in the hour of the greatest danger of the West, may the standard of the Hakenkreuz be raised from the dust, crowned with the historic words '*Ihr habt doch gesiegt!*'. I am proud to die for my ideals; and I am sorry for the sons of Britain who have died without knowing why.

On the morning of 3 January 1946, half-an-hour before his execution at 09:00 hours, William Joyce wrote his last letter to his wife. In it he repeated the message he had given to his brother for publication. The letter concluded with the words: 'I salute you, Freja, as your lover for ever. *Sieg Heil! Sieg Heil! Sieg Heil!* – Your Will.' He added a footnote in German: '*Beim letzten Appell, Volkssturmmann des Bataillons Wilhelm-platz.* [At the last roll-call, *Volkssturm* soldier of the Wilhelmplatz battalion].'[40]

In August 1976, thirty years after Joyce's execution, the then Home Secretary, Roy Jenkins, acceded to the wish of Joyce's family for his remains to be exhumed from the prison grounds and reinterred, in a Catholic ceremony, at Boher More Cemetery, in Galway.

After Joyce's execution, Margaret Joyce was returned to Germany and interned at Sennelager while her case was considered. She was never charged and eventually released on 1 January 1948. Later, under the name of Margaret Brooke-Joyce, she settled in Hamburg, finding work as a translator and supervisor at the Deutsche Maizena Werke, an international foodstuffs company. She and von Besack, her wartime friend, encountered each other again and, according to Hetzler, resumed their affair and planned to marry. But, as Margaret later wrote, in her curious admixture of languages:

> Besack left me flat for good and all – his wife had a baby mitten in den Vorbereitungen zur Scheidung (my German is as bad as ever)! That was too much for me and I at last believed all the people who told me he was rotten – it left rather a hole in my Seele![41]

At Christmas 1962 she was married again, to Donald John Alban May, an accountant more than ten years her junior. May was employed by a company in Casablanca, and they married in Gibraltar. Margaret Joyce later returned to England and settled in Hammersmith, London, where she died of cirrhosis of the liver on 19 February 1972.

The 'Lord Haw-Haw' Myth

On 14 September 1939 Jonah Barrington, radio critic of the *Daily Express*, remarked that 'A gent I'd like to meet is moaning periodically from Zeesen. He speaks English of the haw-haw, damn-it-get-out-of-my-way variety and his strong suit is gentlemanly indignation'.[42] On 18 September – the day William Joyce received his contract from the RRG – 'Lord Haw-Haw' was born. The headline in that day's *Express* ran: 'Warsaw Winnie finds a Friend: Jonah Barrington, listening at the *Daily Express* short-wave station in Surrey[43] to the war on the radio, introduced "Lord Haw-Haw" '.[44] The name was not, in fact, entirely original: William Thackeray had already used something like it in *Vanity Fair*. Barrington was later to lament that 'Haw-Haw hangs round my neck like the "buried-alive" Prelude hangs round Rachmaninov's: it is an achievement I would sooner forget'.[45] But in the last months of 1939 he was able to profit from his 'invention' by means of a hilarious 128-page collection of spoof programmes, illustrated by the cartoonist 'Fenwick'.[46] This spoof collection was inspired by programmes monitored by Beaverbrook's staff between 14 September and 1 November, with one earlier programme around 10 September. Under careful scrutiny, Barrington's little book offers clues as to the identity of the cast of 'Germany Calling' at the outbreak of the war.

Aside from Barrington's comic interventions, the actual texts can be seen to follow the general pattern of the peacetime German programmes, incorporating little skits, commentaries and news bulletins, except that the tone is now more sarcastic and the emphasis is on making the point that the war is barely impacting on daily life in the Reich. Barrington had already assigned humorous names to other English-language Nazi propagandists, such as 'Winnie the Whopper' (or 'Winnie of Warsaw', since her broadcasts were received on the wave length of Radio Warsaw's transmitter), 'Ursula the Pooh', 'Auntie Gush' (because she spoke so much and so fast), 'Uncle Smarmy' *alias* 'Uncle Boo-hoo', and 'Weepy', with the plaintive microphone manner. In all probability, 'Auntie Gush' and 'Uncle Smarmy' were Edith and Eduard Dietze who, as a duo, broadcast a long-running German language programme for British listeners. Edith Dietze has herself identified 'Winnie' as Gerda Nebbe. Author Charles Rolo described 'Weepy' as a former English actor who sold his voice to the Nazis for the sake of a steady job: Jack Trevor. 'Lady Haw-Haw', announced as 'an Englishwoman living in Berlin', may well have been Mrs. Margaret Bothamley.

The monitors at the BBC listening post also did their best to allocate descriptive names to the voices on Germany's English-language service. On 5 January 1940, one described a voice as 'Sinister Sam'; on 9 January, another voice was identified as 'Surbiton Syd', and on 13 January a BBC monitor designated one as 'Racing Reg'.

The link between Jonah Barrington's discovery and Joyce's advent on the German propaganda scene was coincidental. Barrington's description of a speaker with an exaggeratedly upper-class accent provoked immediate public debate, with correspondents arguing the unlikely view that the style and accent of the speaker were 'conditioned by residence oversea' (Rose Macaulay), or that 'I am never quite sure what an Oxford accent is like, but I am sure that this is not his' (Lady Cynthia Colville). The real William Joyce spoke with a sarcastic, emphatic and occasionally drawling monotone.

The stages by which the lordly designation passed from the original voice – whomsoever it may have been – to William Joyce, as his contribution both in style and content grew, can be traced in the weekly magazine *News Review*. In response to a reader's enquiry, it 'disclosed' in its issue of 19 October 1939:

No Englishman is [station] DJA's 'Lord Ha Ha' [*sic*], but a propagandist named Hoffmann, who three years ago married a Manchester girl. Son of a wealthy tea importer, he worked for some years in the USA, and now lives in Munich.

The *News Review* even published a photograph of Rolf Hoffmann in its 11 January 1940 issue. Eventually, on 7 March 1940, the paper made a connection with William Joyce, noting that he had fled to Germany, 'where he was said to have become one of the English-speaking radio announcers'. This article prompted a letter from an observant Mrs. M. Kelly of Galway:

As one who knew Willie Joyce from the time he arrived in Galway (an infant) until he left rather hurriedly in 1922, I am quite certain that he is the 9.15 pm and 11.15 pm English announcer from Hamburg, Bremen etc. Ever since those broadcasts started I was struck by the familiarity of that voice. I often mentioned that I heard that voice before but could not place it, but the minute I saw your photograph and read the paragraph, I knew at once it was Willie.

The struggle to identify the protean broadcaster continued. For some, it had to be Eduard Dietze. For Basil Nicolls, Controller (Programmes) at the BBC, it was 'quite clear' that Haw-Haw was neither Dietze, Baillie-Stewart nor William Joyce. He wrote to J.C.S. Macgregor, Empire Service Director at the BBC before the war and now seconded to the Ministry of Information, at the end of February 1940: 'I am personally quite certain he is a German and that we cannot say much about him being a traitor'.[47] Others suggested that 'Lord Haw-Haw' might be Eric Dorn, the son of a South African rabbi. It is Norman Baillie-Stewart who, in his post-war autobiography, identified the original 'Lord Haw-Haw': The first 'Lord Haw-Haw' of the Berlin Rundfunk was not William Joyce or myself, but handsome, six feet two inches tall, Wolff [sic] Mittler, a man with both snobbish manners and an aristocratic voice. Mittler was a PolishGerman with curly blond hair, who had received his secondary education in Britain. He was a playboy of the first order. He drove big high-powered sports cars and he was a great attraction for women.'

James Clark recalled Wolf Mittler as having 'been doing English programmes since well before the war in his Woosterish voice [...] his must be the voice that Jonah Barrington of the *Daily Express* listened to when he coined the nickname "Lord Haw-Haw". Nobody else's fits so well.' German jazz guitarist Coco Schumann remembered Mittler as 'a weird guy – always wore English gear and drove an MG'.[48] When interviewed by Denys Blakeway for a BBC Radio 4 programme in 1991, Mittler himself laughed off the honour of the title, admitting to only five or six broadcasts to Britain.

The 'Lord Haw-Haw' character, simultaneously lampooning an effete British class stereotype and the Nazi leadership in Germany, was an immediate hit with the British public in the early months of the 'Phoney War'. 'His listening figures crept up – 40, 50, 60, 70 per cent of all listeners in Britain nightly' claimed Barrington. Smith's Clocks issued an advertisement, depicting a monocled donkey at a microphone, with the caption: 'Don't risk missing Haw-Haw – Get a clock that shows the right time always, unquestionably'. In December 1939, Philips ran a series of advertisements for radios in the British press, featuring the schedule of the broadcasts from Hamburg and Zeesen. And comics picked up the theme. A musical revue entitled *Haw-Haw* played to packed houses at the Holborn Empire, Arthur Askey presented 'Baron Hee-Haw' in the BBC's *Band Waggon* programme on 18 November 1939, Michael Moore and Paddy Browne toured the music halls in a double act as 'Lord Haw-Haw and Winnie the Whopper', and in October 1939 the then famous Western Brothers, sporting monocles and tails, recorded 'Lord Haw-Haw Of Zeesen'.[49]

But the laughter gradually faded. From early 1940, talks broadcast by the real William Joyce – still concealed by the 'Lord Haw-Haw' cover – gave the 'Germany Calling' propaganda a sharp edge of a taunting contempt that was politically motivated and a long way from the complacent and good-natured mockery of P.G. Wodehouse or Jonah Barrington. F. Tennyson Jesse wrote to friends in America:

> By about May 1940 I found I could no longer listen to Haw-Haw. Nor could any- one else. He was no longer amusing when his boasts had changed to a recital of facts, although these were cleverly interspersed with lies.[50]

Later Voices

The turnover of staff and collaborators within the English section was rapid, and it is almost impossible to track its members accurately. A memo dated 10 June 1942 listed the following German commentators as members of the English service: Johannes Schmidt-Hansen, Eduard Dietze, Dr. Egon Strohm, *alias* 'Scrutator' (from the Empire zone), Dr. Fritz Peter Krüger, *alias* 'Peter', Professor Reinhard Haferkorn (head of the Foreign Ministry's English broadcasting section), Dr. von Losch, *alias* 'Range Finder', and Dr. von Kries.[51] It also identifies the foreign English-language broadcasters work- ing for the European Stations: William Joyce and his wife, the American Fred Kaltenbach, Mrs. Margaret Bothamley, Mrs. Jeanne Lange, *alias* 'Anne Thomas' (a former British actress, married to an Austrian), and Norman Baillie-Stewart. The same memo lists the Short-Wave Station's English-language commentators as Dr. Egon Strohm, *alias* 'Scrutator', Wolf Müller-Mittler, *alias* 'Wolf Mittler', Baron von Andrep, *alias* 'Swedish Observer', Helen Freifrau von Bothmer, *alias* 'Helen Davis', Dr. Erika Schirmer, Constance Drexel, and Dr. Vivian Stranders, *alias* 'Mediator'.[52]

From May 1940 the American actress Mildred Gillars worked as a duty announcer for the English zone, until she established herself as the producer of her own programmes and joined the Short-Wave Station. At various times, Martin Erle, a naturalized German, Dr. Joachim Schaede (*b*. 1910) and Dr. Edwin Schneider (real name Edwin Herman Frederick Lynn) belonged to the core of the European Stations' English section. Others, on the German side, were Benecke, Gerhard Heydebreck, Hans Hupfeld, a nat- uralized German who had served in the 30th Middlesex Regiment during the First World War, Alain de Kergoër from Brittany, Lenzner, Heinz Mitschke, Miss Gerda Nebbe and Dr. Kurt Vaessen (1909–1987). Despite its fullness, this list is probably incomplete.

From June 1942 until November 1943, Norman Baillie-Stewart shared his office at the Berlin Foreign Ministry with another renegade British officer. Pilot Officer Benson Railton Metcalf Freeman, of the RAF, was born at Newbury, Berkshire, on 6 October 1903, the son of a commander in the Royal Navy. Freeman, like Baillie- Stewart, was a graduate of Sandhurst. He embarked on what appeared a promising career with the King's Own Royal Regiment, and also developed an interest in flying. In 1926 he was posted to an RAF flying school and, on completion of his training, transferred to the RAF as a flying officer and instructor. But in 1931, Freeman chose to retire, and settled as a farmer in Gloucestershire. During this period he studied Communism, and was later to explain:

> I have been bitterly opposed to the appalling menace of Soviet Communism for a long time. I have studied Moscow propaganda for about 15 years and its hideous exploitation by world Jewry and I am more than dismayed at the fearful fate that awaits this country and western Europe and eventually the world when this menace overpowers them.[53]

Freeman rejoined the RAF on the outbreak of war and was captured by the Germans during a combat mission in France in May 1940. During interrogation at the *Luftwaffe* transit centre at Oberursel, it quickly became apparent that Freeman was a Nazi sympathizer and he was appointed to positions within the camp administration which might draw him towards German Intelligence, which was running the camp. At one stage, the camp commandant engaged Freeman in a discussion on the effect of William Joyce's broadcasts on British listeners. Freeman exploded, saying that he 'considered this man a howling disaster and a hate-maker of the worst possible type', whereupon the German officer suggested that 'if Joyce could come down one night Freeman could enlighten him as tactfully as he could as to the breach he was making'.[54] Soon after, Freeman was called to a meeting with the head of the Foreign Ministry's English-language broadcasting section, and the chairman of the Foreign Ministry's committee for British PoWs. He was invited to broadcast, or write for *The Camp*, the Foreign Ministry's tabloid for British PoWs, but declined.

In the spring of 1942 Freeman was transferred to a farm near Berlin, ostensibly owned by a *Luftwaffe* intelligence officer, and, in June, taken to a meeting with Dr. Hesse of the Foreign Ministry's England committee. Giving a detailed exposition of his views on the 'Communist menace', Freeman forecast that German's summer offensive in Russia was doomed, and that the country would be the first to succumb to the Soviets. Despite his directness and candour, he was invited to undertake some broadcasts for the 'promotion of peace and the frustration of Bolshevist plans'.

Under the name 'Royston', Freeman began writing scripts for 'Germany Calling'. But he refused to broadcast: indeed he was constantly at loggerheads with German officials until November 1943, when he simply resigned after a fierce row with Hesse and 'retired' to a farm owned by some Foreign Ministry official.

Sometime in 1944, however, Freeman was introduced to Gunter d'Alquen, the commanding officer of the *SS-Standarte Kurt Eggers*, who offered to let him join the propaganda unit and vet propaganda material. Later, at his court-martial in Uxbridge, Freeman was to claim that 'he signed a letter that he would join the Waffen-SS, the agreement being that he could go with them, and that if there was anything he could do to help handing them over to the British and Americans instead of the Russians he would do it.'[55] But he maintained that he was, throughout, 'untouchable'.[56] And a German officer confirmed to the court that 'Freeman refused to broadcast. No information of the slightest use to the Germans was obtained from him.'[57] Nevertheless he was found guilty of 'aiding the enemy while a PoW by having joined the Waffen-SS in August 1944, written scripts for German propaganda broadcasts, accepting a salary of 200 marks a week', and sentenced to ten years' imprisonment.

Lewis Barrington ('Barry') Payne Jones was born in Birmingham on 20 May 1914. Number thirty-three on the British Renegades Warning List, his short-hand entry there described him as a 'pro-Nazi sympathiser who went to Germany in May 1939, as English teacher at Berlitz school, Cologne. Not interned. Broadcaster on German radio since 1940. Married German girl, Gretel Becker, 1944.' At some time during this period Jones became a naturalized German, and was classified as indispensable '(*unabkömmlich*)' for his work as a commentator and broadcaster for the European Stations' English service.[58] In May 1945 he was arrested in Apen and, after initial interrogation, transferred to a military prison in Brussels.

Ralph Baden Davenport Powell (*b*. 1910), who claimed to be a nephew of the founder of the Boy Scout movement, had married a German in 1938 and settled as a teacher at the Berlitz school in Haarlem, Holland. Interned at Ilag VIII, a camp for civilian internees, after May 1940, he was later attached to the Foreign Ministry's language service as a translator. In the summer of 1942 he was recruited by the RRG as a reader of straight news material, to relieve pressure on William Joyce. After August 1943 he broadcast from Luxembourg, and later from Apen, rotating with Barry Jones, but wrote no propaganda material.

Dr. Richard Kupsch, who joined the English section early in 1941, was the child of a German father and a Franco-Irish mother. Born near Hamburg in December 1910, he was brought up by his maternal grandparents and educated in England. Having studied linguistics at the Sorbonne, he took a first degree at Budapest University, returning to Paris for his master's degree. After a period teaching at the University of the Philippines at Manila, Kupsch was repatriated to Germany in 1941 as part of an exchange programme organized by the International Red Cross.

Shortly after his arrival in Berlin, Kupsch was visited and auditioned by William Joyce, and joined the English zone as a translator and third news reader after Joyce and James Clark.

'Plum' in Nazi-Wonderland

During the summer of 1941 British listeners were surprised to hear Eduard Dietze introduce a series of five broadcasts by the celebrated humorist P.G. Wodehouse. Pelham Grenville Wodehouse (1881–1975) had lived abroad since 1902, dividing his time mainly between the United States and France. 'Plum', as he was affectionally known, was living in Le Touquet when German troops overran France in May 1940. He was there, as he later observed in one of his Berlin broadcasts, because the BBC had led him to believe that the Germans would be driven out of France. Unlike Knut

Hamsun and Ezra Pound, who were keen to mount a platform on behalf of Nazi policies, Wodehouse had no political message to peddle.

Under German occupation, life in the holiday resort of Le Touquet continued without incident until July 1940, when all British subjects were arrested and interned at Loos, a suburb of Lille. Wodehouse himself was eventually transferred to an internment camp at Tost, near Gleiwitz, in Upper-Silesia. On 21 June 1941 he was unexpectedly released and taken to Berlin, probably as a result of representations by American friends to the German embassy in Washington.

Wodehouse was put up at the top-ranking Hotel Adlon, where he was welcomed by a former Hollywood friend, Baron Eric von Barnekow, an officer in von Richthofen's squadron during the First World War.[59] The same afternoon, Wodehouse and Barnekow were joined by Werner Plack, a Foreign Ministry official responsible for liaison with foreign collaborators. Plack too had spent some years in Hollywood, initially as an actor though later as a wine merchant. When war appeared inevitable, he gave up his business and joined the staff of the German consulate in Los Angeles, from where he was posted back to Germany. Plack apparently offered Wodehouse an opportunity to speak to his friends in America over the radio. It was a skilful and organized deception: Plack had been alerted to Wodehouse's release from Tost and was able to stage-manage his reception. In 1945, Wodehouse told British Intelligence: 'I think I can say what chiefly led me to make the talks was gratitude.'

The day after his arrival in Berlin Wodehouse was taken to meet Paul Schmidt, the Foreign Ministry's chief interpreter. He and Plack explained the broadcasting process, emphasizing that broadcasts were not transmitted live, but recorded, and Wodehouse agreed to write and deliver five programmes. The following day his passport was returned and, within certain obvious limits, he was once again a free man. The first programme, an interview with a CBS correspondent, Harry Flannery, was recorded on 25 June and broadcast to America on short wave on the evening of 27 June. In it Wodehouse described his experiences in Le Touquet from the German occupation up to his internment:

> Young men starting out in life have often asked me how can I become an internee? Well, there are several methods. My own was to buy a villa in Le Touquet on the coast of France and stay there till the Germans came along. This is probably the best and simplest method. You buy the villa and the Germans do the rest.

Flannery was strongly anti-Nazi and the interview ended with his speaking candidly about conditions in German internment camps and about Wodehouse's release. It led to the banning of Flannery from the RRG studios and the cancellation of the CBS's Berlin broadcasts, an action by Glasmeier which resulted in a forceful protest by the Foreign Ministry, stressing the importance 'in foreign policy terms' of the CBS broadcasts from Berlin, and the Wodehouse interview.[60]

In the remainder of his five broadcasts, Wodehouse's accounts were straightforwardly factual and uncontroversial. Following the broadcasts he was taken to the country estate of Barnekow's fiancée in the Harz mountains, returning to Berlin on two occasions to record further talks. In August 1941 the broadcasts were repeated, this time by the ProMi side of the German propaganda apparatus, to British listeners, on long wave. On 2 August Wodehouse's name appears for the first time in Dietze's agenda, according to which the Wodehouse talks were re-broadcast on the English service, introduced by Dietze, between 8 and 15 August.

In Britain and the United States Wodehouse's Berlin broadcasts were interpreted as pro-Nazi propaganda, and provoked a storm of protest. On 15 July – responding, presumably, to the first short-wave transmissions – William N. Connor, author of the 'Cassandra' column in the *Daily Mirror*, launched a vitriolic attack on Wodehouse on the BBC:

> I have come to tell you tonight of the story of a rich man trying to make his last and greatest sale – that of his own country. It is a sombre story of self-respect, of honour and of decency being pawned to the Nazis for the price of a soft bed in a luxury hotel. It is a tale of laughter growing old and of the Judas whine of treachery taking its place. It is the record of P.G. Wodehouse ending forty years of money-making fun with the worst joke he ever made in his life. The only wisecrack he ever pulled that the world received in silence. The last laugh bought from him by that prince of inno-cent glee – Dr. Paul Joseph Goebbels.[61]

Given the option of moving to a neutral country or remaining in Germany, Wodehouse chose to stay. After a further visit to Berlin, and the recording of his fifth talk, he was reunited with his wife who had arrived from France. But in September 1943, during the heavy bombing of Berlin, the Wodehouses were moved to Paris. Immediately after the Liberation, Wodehouse reported to the British authorities, and was extensively interrogated. He eventually settled on Long Island, New York, where he died on 14 February 1975, at the age of 93. A few weeks earlier he had been knighted for services to literature, the honour having been denied him for many years.[62]

Accompanying Wodehouse out of the intern camp at Tost had been the Yorkshire-born Noel Barnard Teesdale Mackintosh (*b*. 1885), a schoolmaster who had left England to live in France in August 1939 'to avoid arrest on homosexual charges'.[63] Between 1919 and 1924 Mackintosh had been registrar of Hong Kong University, but was never a professor.

The circumstantial manner by which some Britons found themselves in wartime Germany is exemplified by Mackintosh's history. Upon his arrival in Berlin it was discovered that he had in fact been mistaken for a 'McKenzie', also interned at Tost. He nevertheless remained in Berlin, employed as a translator for the International Social Economic Institute and later for the Foreign Ministry's Language Service, and supplementing his income by giving bridge lessons and by betting on the horses. Here Mackintosh was in the company of other British renegades, including Edward Bowlby, William Henry Howard, Gordon Perry, Ralph Baden Powell, Harold Rasmussen, Reginald Walford and his wife Edith, as well as several British women married to Germans.

After the war Mackintosh explained, in a statement to MI5, that he had worked for the Germans for a living, and that he had conscientiously refused to be involved in any way in anti-British propaganda.[64]

John Amery and the Legion of St. George

In October 1942, John Amery arrived in Berlin. The former playboy turned political visionary (1912–1945) persuaded Foreign Ministry officials to allow him to make radio broadcasts, arguing that both Baillie-Stewart and Joyce had failed because their message was hostile when they should have been trying to win over the British public. Amery's activities in Berlin were a particular embarrassment to Whitehall: he was after all the elder son of the distinguished statesman, Leopold Stennett Amery, former First Lord of the Admiralty and Colonial Secretary, and now Secretary of State for India and Burma in Churchill's war cabinet.

From boyhood John Amery revealed himself to be profligate, obsessive and reckless. As a schoolboy of fifteen, he launched a film company and collected money from possible investors. He later developed a passion for fast cars, and in due course alienated his family by marrying a woman much older than himself, the actress Una Wing. By the autumn of 1936, aged only twenty-four, Amery was bankrupt; the following year, granted an allowance by his family, he left England for the continent. More out of love of adventure than political conviction, he enlisted with Franco's forces in the Spanish Civil War. After some time as a gun-runner, Amery became a liaison officer with the French Royalist *cagoulards*, where he encountered the leaders of the French fascist movements: Jacques Doriot (1898–1945) – the proletarian dare-devil and hero – and Marcel Déat (1894–1955) – the intellectual. It was they who provided the susceptible Amery with a political education, persuading him of the virtues of fascism and the dangers of communism.

Jacques Doriot was a passionate public speaker and ruthless tactician, and for many years the glamour figure of the French Communist Party, even to the extent of becoming an executive committee member of the Comintern. But when, after resisting Moscow directives in 1934, he was expelled from the Communist Party, Doriot transformed himself into a vehement opponent of Communism. His colleague Marcel Déat was a member of France's Socialist Party at the age of twenty, and at twenty-six a professor of philosophy at the Ecole Normale Supérieure in Paris. For years, Déat had brooded over a concept of socialism which in due course led him towards extreme fascist views.

At the outbreak of the Second World War, Amery was living in San Sebastian, Spain. Travelling to the south of France in April 1940 he found himself, upon the French collapse, trapped in the unoccupied zone. Since visas were not granted to British nationals of military age, he remained for the next twelve months in a Savoy village.

The German invasion of the Soviet Union in June 1941 was a turning point in Amery's political consciousness, though he remained inactive until the tide clearly

30 John Amery as a young man.

turned against Germany. In a statement prepared after his arrest in 1945, Amery recalled that:

It was my considered opinion that Europe was in the greatest peril of a Communist invasion; that this invasion would sweep the whole of Europe; and that nothing could stop it unless the different countries of Europe pushed through a social revolution which would spike the guns of the Communists in their world-wide revolutionary activities.

In February 1941, Déat and Doriot had combined to found the *Rassemblement National Populaire* (National People's Grouping), a French version of the Nazi party. The group's aims included 'cooperation with Germany' and 'defence of the race', and it raised an 'Anti-Bolshevik Legion' to fight alongside the Wehrmacht on the eastern front. Even with 13,400 volunteers, the radical collaboration did not impress Hitler, and by May 1943, only about 6,400 French volunteers still served in the *Légion Tricolore*.

The notion, instilled by his French and Spanish collaborators, of a united front of European nations to combat Communism, became a fixation with Amery. He attempted to present his ideas to Vichy officials, but was rebuffed, and indeed imprisoned. 'Vichy was an ultra-reactionary government of priests, the worst type (in my opinion) of French industrialists and militarists'. Released after three weeks, Amery next sought to contact Count Dino Grandi, the former Italian ambassador in

London, through the Italian consul in Grenoble. Nor did the Finnish authorities show any interest. It was only when he approached a German liaison officer that his luck changed: Berlin was of course interested to meet the son of a British cabinet minister who expressed a desire to address his fellow countrymen on German radio.

Soon after his arrival in October 1942, Amery outlined his ideas to two senior officials of the Foreign Ministry, Dr. Friedrich Hansen and Werner Hallmann. According to his subsequent confession, Amery informed them that he was not interested in a German victory as such: 'What interested me was a just peace where we could all get together against the real enemies of civilisation, and that the British Empire must be part of this'. After some persuasion, Hansen agreed to forward a favourable proposal to the Propaganda Ministry, and a fortnight later Amery received a positive response. He was invited to stay at the Hotel Kaiserhof as a guest of the Reich and to broadcast a series of seven talks, transmitted live each week until New Year's Eve, with repeat broadcasts of each recording. Amery's first talk was broadcast on 19 November 1942. It opened with the words:

Listeners will wonder what an Englishman is doing on the German radio tonight. You can imagine that before taking this step I hoped that someone better qualified than me would come forward. I dared to believe that some ray of common sense, some appreciation of our priceless civilization, would guide the counsels of Mr. Churchill's government. Unfortunately this has not been the case! For two years living in a neutral country I have been able to see through the haze of propaganda to reach something which my conscience tells me is the truth. That is why I come forward tonight without any political label, without any bias, but just simply as an Englishman to say to you: A crime is being committed against civilization. Not only the priceless heritage of our fathers, of our seamen, of our Empire builders is being thrown away in a war that serves no British interests but our alliance with the Soviets!

For seven weeks Amery lashed out at Churchill and Roosevelt, Whitehall and Washington, advocating an anti-Bolshevik Nordic bloc under Anglo-German leadership. In his final address he argued that: 'It can never be treason, in wartime or any other time, to love ardently one's country and to take up arms because all things that are sacred to us are being systematically violated'.

While John Amery broadcast from Berlin his father, Leo, was active as a regular German-language commentator for the BBC, regularly addressing the German people from London in its 'German Workers' programme.

In January 1943, at the end of his series of broadcasts, Amery travelled to Paris with Walter Plauen, a Foreign Ministry official and effectively his 'minder' and guide through the intricacies of German military bureaucracy. There, in discussions with Doriot and Déat, he developed the idea of an anti-Bolshevik legion, recruited from Britons held in German PoW and intern camps. Returning to Berlin with plans for such a force, and the draft of a book entitled *England faces Europe*, Amery impressed Hansen with the concept of a 'Quisling' army and obtained support for an initial recruiting drive at the civilian internment camp at St. Denis, near Paris.

On 21 April 1943, accompanied by Walter Plauen and several other German military and diplomatic aides, Amery arrived at St. Denis to raise his volunteer army, the British Legion of St. George. Assuring the British captives that they would be fighting against the Red Army and would never be called upon to attack their own country, Amery's first address – to a hand-selected group – was a flop. Faced with hecklers raising such issues as the status of Legion members if taken prisoner, or their fate after the war, and reminding Amery of the treasonable nature of their acts, the visiting party was booed away by a hostile crowd. Several days later, having returned to the camp and conducted a number of personal interviews, Amery had mustered precisely three volunteers: a professor who wanted to study Plato in Greece under German auspices (whom Amery's minders gladly left in the custody of the German embassy in Paris), a naturalized British internee of French birth, who soon vanished once released from internment, and Edward Berry, a seventeen-year-old deck-hand, captured in September 1940 when the ammunition ship on which he was serving was sunk by a German raider.

The St. Denis fiasco confirmed the scepticism of many in Berlin. If the playboy-politician had been perhaps a few degrees more eccentric, he might have been sent home into obscurity. But the German Foreign Ministry continued to rate the project as a means of achieving a propaganda coup. Himmler also perceived an opportunity to extend his power and seconded an English volunteer in the Waffen-SS, Thomas Cooper, to the Foreign Ministry.

Tom Cooper, Vivian Stranders and the British Free Corps

Thomas ('Tom') Haller Cooper was born in London in 1919 to a British father and a German mother. At school he proved gifted at languages, and studied Chinese and Japanese in his spare time. After matriculation in December 1936, he endeavoured to join the Metropolitian Police, the Royal Air Force and the Royal Navy. But because his mother had never taken British nationality, Cooper was rejected and had to settle for a job as a clerk in east London. Probably largely out of frustration, he joined the British Union of Fascists and sought official recognition from the Reich as an ethnic German (*Volksdeutscher*). At the same time he applied for a job in Germany through the German Academic Exchange Organization. In July 1939 he travelled to Germany to join a summer camp organized by the National Labour Service (RAD – *Reichsarbeitsdienst*), only to learn that the requisite paperwork had not arrived from London. Eventually he secured a position as a language teacher at a school near Frankfurt-am-Main, only to be dismissed as an enemy alien at the beginning of the war. Cooper was arrested and risked being interned until documents arrived from his mother certifying him as a *Volksdeutscher*.

Rejected by the Wehrmacht on the grounds of his British nationality, Cooper joined the Waffen-SS in February 1940 and, using the name 'Peter Böttcher', saw action in Poland and Russia, where he was wounded in February 1943. Leaving hospital in June, he was contacted by the Foreign Ministry and invited to prepare two pamphlets on National Socialism for distribution among British PoWs, later visiting a prisoner-of-war camp apparently used as a indoctrination centre. Soon afterwards, in August 1943, Cooper became a naturalized German.

At about the same time Dr. Vivian Stranders (1881–1959), an *SS-Sturmbannführer* (major), set about supplanting John Amery as the imaginary leader of a secessionist force. Amery's elderly rival was an Englishman by birth and habits, but a German by inclination and naturalization.

A graduate and a linguist, Stranders was a captain in the Royal Flying Corps during the First World War, and a member of the Inter-Allied Control Commission after it. When demobbed in 1921, he established an import company in Düsseldorf, later transferring to Cologne and Berlin where his post-war duties had brought him into contact with leaders of the hobbled German aircraft industry. Stranders' business venture collapsed when the French secret police discovered a security leak and began a large-scale investigation, culminating in his arrest in Paris in December 1926. The following March he was found guilty of industrial espionage, imprisoned for two years, and fined.

Released after eighteen months, Stranders returned to Berlin where he concentrated on journalism. In 1931 he settled in the Thuringian town of Weimar, where local National Socialist Party leaders welcomed him as a sympathetic Englishman. Stranders was soon speaking at political rallies, and sporting the Party badge and SS insignia. In April 1933 he became a naturalized German citizen. He registered as a student of philosophy at Bonn University, where he also gave English lectures, and in March 1936 was awarded a doctorate.

At the beginning of the war, Stranders sought a position in the inner sanctum of one of the many Berlin-based Nazi organizations, but without success. However he made himself useful to the propaganda authorities, as a commentator under the name 'Mediator', and eventually, during the summer of 1943, obtained a position at SS headquarters.[65] Here, handling routine matters marginally connected with British PoWs, Stranders developed a scheme for absorbing John Amery's Legion of St. George, soon to be renamed the British Free Corps, into the Waffen-SS – perhaps even seeing himself leading it into battle in the 'defence of Europe'. The senior officer of the BFC until November 1944 was Thomas Cooper.

But Stranders' army of renegades never really established itself. In March 1945, the full strength of the BFC – a grand total of ten – clad in regular SS outfit adorned with a Union Jack flash, were merged with an SS unit that was being held in reserve at Stettin on the Baltic coast. Soon the remnants of the Corps, now reduced to five, straggled south-westwards until they encountered the advancing American troops on the middle Elbe, and were arrested.

By February 1945, Stranders was busy outlining a new propaganda offensive codenamed 'Operation Königgrätz', which involved setting up a 'European-British Peace League' among British PoWs, at that time being herded westward into the Reich to avoid the rapidly advancing Soviet army. With the Russians threatening the capital, Stranders sought sanctuary near Bremen before fleeing, in April 1945, to Tyrol where he joined the provisional SS at St. Johann.

At the end of the war Stranders disappeared without trace. But, using documents captured in Berlin and elsewhere, British Intelligence gradually established a picture of his wartime role and instigated a manhunt. In November 1945 he was detained in Garmisch-Partenkirchen by the US military. But in interviews MI5 officials confirmed that, as a naturalized German, Stranders could not be charged with treason. After his release, he settled in North-Rhine Westphalia, where he died after a long illness in 1959, at the age of 78.

It is not easy to establish the extent of membership of the Legion of St. George, or the BFC, but it probably numbered about sixty men in all, including those coerced into joining but permitted to leave after the first few weeks of indoctrination. The highest number at any one roll call was twenty-seven, at Christmas 1944. Compared with its prototype, the French *Légion Tricolore*, the British Free Corps seems never to have been anything more than an incarnation of British music hall's 'Fred Karno's Army'.

A number of the renegades faced trial by courts-martial or in criminal courts. In January 1946 Thomas Cooper was charged with treason at the Old Bailey, found guilty and condemned to death. On appeal the sentence was commuted to life imprisonment on the grounds that Cooper had been a follower rather than a leader. Released in January 1953 Cooper left Britain for Japan, where he is believed to have lived as a Buddhist monk before marrying and returning to England in 1975. He died in south London, in 1987, aged 67.[66]

Though without his Legion, John Amery was still usefully employed by the Propaganda Ministry which, early in 1944, invited him to tour France, Czechoslovakia, Norway and Belgium to speak with local journalists. Back in Berlin in August 1944, Amery broadcast once more on the radio, because 'it was being thought I was a prisoner of the Gestapo'. According to the Dietze agendas, his talk was recorded on August 2 and broadcast on August 17. In September the Italian government invited Amery to a meeting with Mussolini on the shores of Lake Garda, and the impressionable Englishman found a new cause. The Duce outlined his scenario of a 'social republic' in northern Italy and promised to throw 'his whole person into the balance in obtaining the peace we had for years been seeking. In this line he asked me to assist him. I consented readily [...].' Amery set to work by broadcasting, in Italian, on the radio and delivering speeches in Italian towns. On 25 April 1945, while driving between Milan and Como, he was arrested by Italian partisans and later handed to the British military authorities in the person of Captain Alan Whicker of the Intelligence Corps – later famous as a British television personality. On 30 July Amery was charged with treason. The case was delayed on the defence grounds that he had become a naturalized Spanish citizen during the Spanish Civil War, but no conclusive evidence could be produced. Eventually, on 28 November, Amery stood trial in No.1 Court at the Old Bailey. Appearing frail and unhealthy, he pleaded guilty to all charges and the trial lasted only eight minutes. The judge sought confirmation from the defence counsel that Amery comprehended the inevitable result: the death penalty. Conviction for treason carried no alternative sentence, and as Amery had pleaded guilty, he had no right of appeal. If it gave him the moral satisfaction of dying as a martyr for fascism, it certainly had the effect of sparing Amery and his family the agony of a trial. On 19 December he was hanged, Albert Pierrepoint, the Home Office's official executioner until 1956, later claiming in his autobiography that Amery was the bravest man he executed.[67]

31 John Amery and
his French wife in
Antwerp, April 1944.

According to David Millward, Amery was executed 'against advice' and 'despite evidence from Government psychiatrists that he was "abnormally defective" '.[68] Amery was 'a sexual deviant with a pathological inability to distinguish right from wrong', declared Alan Hamilton.[69] 'A psychiatrist who examined him in his prison cell reported Amery to be 'a severe and long-standing case of psychopathic disorder of the type at one time called "moral insanity" or "moral imbecility". His conduct of life is determined by diseased mental processes.'[70]

The Irish Zone

The German European Station's Irish broadcasting zone team was small and, in effect, little more than an annexe to the English zone. Indeed although the RRG's 1942 internal directory gives a Flemish, Finnish and an Iranian zone, it does not mention the Irish section, listing its staff in a supplement under the heading '*DES Ländergruppe West*'. The nominal head of the Irish zone in June 1942 was Professor Ludwig Mühlhausen (*b.* Kassel, 1888), an academic at Hamburg University since 1922. He was succeeded later that year by Dr. Hans Hartmann, a lecturer in Celtic studies, who, according to a post-war affidavit by Eduard Dietze, was 'one of the very few Germans who had a perfect command of spoken and written Irish'. Dietze described Hartmann as a 'true scholar, whose judgement was never clouded by Nazi propaganda,' and mentioned how surprised he had been when Hartmann told him, towards the end of the war, that he had been a Party member since 1933:

Considering what one could call the virtually opposite attitude he displayed, which had struck me from the first time I met him, Dr. Hartmann's membership of the NSDAP only seems explicable on the grounds that otherwise he would have been unable to obtain official support for his academic plans, in particular for his studies in Ireland.[71]

The subordinate staff of the zone, however, included some native Irish speakers.[72] Its most prominent broadcaster was the Irish poet and novelist Francis Stuart. A colourful and somewhat complex character, Stuart was the child of Protestant Irish parents, though born in Townsville, in Queensland, Australia, on 29 April 1902. He was brought up in Ireland, where the family had returned after his father's death, and became involved in the 1922–23 uprisings as a young IRA volunteer. He carried out an arms-purchasing mission to Belgium before being arrested and interned by the Irish (Free State) government. 'Neither a liberal nor a Socialist, and not impressed by democracy', Stuart, as his biographer, Geoffrey Elborn remarks, remained sympathetic to the Republican cause, although 'naive and vague about the political arguments of both sides'.[73]

In April 1939 Stuart undertook a lecture tour of Germany under the auspices of the German Academic Exchange Service in Ireland, an organization sponsored by the Berlin Foreign Ministry. During the visit he was offered the post of lecturer in English and Irish literature at Berlin University and, needing an income, accepted. He declared himself impressed by Hitler and, after attending a military parade during the visit, was convinced, Elborn observed, 'that this was preparation for some revolution which he had longed for all his life'.

The Berlin appointment was delayed, however, and in July 1939 Stuart returned to Ireland. By the time the contract was confirmed, in December 1939, Europe was at war, and Stuart travelled to Germany via Switzerland, to mislead British Intelligence. In Berlin he called on the Foreign Ministry and was received by Ernst von Weizsäcker, the secretary of state, and was soon offered work by the English-language broadcasting section, writing talks for William Joyce. Stuart agreed on condition he would not be required to supply anti-Semitic material. 'I agreed and wrote three, the first of which Joyce will broadcast tonight [February 18, 1940]. The theme of my contributions, which I know is not exactly what either the Germans nor Joyce want, is a recollection of some historic acts of aggression on part of the United Kingdom, similar to those which British propaganda is denouncing the Nazis for.'[74]

Stuart's overall contribution to Germany's propaganda effort was slight, in part because he and Joyce did not mesh. Stuart despised Joyce's heavy drinking, and Joyce, who mistrusted Irishmen with anti-British sentiments but without National Socialist convictions, insisted on writing his own scripts. Stuart was soon little more than a translator and editor of news items, and in autumn 1941 moved to join the Irish section as a broadcaster. He gave his first radio talk on St. Patrick's Day, 1942, the theme being Ireland's place in Europe, independent of Britain, and from the summer of 1942 was broadcasting regularly to Ireland.

Stuart's motivation is not clear. Elborn suggests that he 'deliberately wanted to expose himself to humiliation'. Stuart himself admitted: 'I somehow felt the necessity to broadcast. I could never be a writer in the "bosom of society". Being in Germany was one thing, lecturing at Berlin University was bad enough – but going over to the other side of the street, slinking down a street, was something a writer could not do in peacetime.' 'Having finally given up betting, drink and the rest, I came here [in Berlin] and was plunged into a kind of whirlpool.'

Personally Stuart was also in turmoil. Though already married, he formed a relationship with Gertrud 'Madeleine' Meissner, a former student now working for the Irish zone. And his attitude towards Germany was changing. In 1942 the ProMi forbade him to publish a novel, and the Irish Chargé d'Affaires in Berlin refused to renew his passport. In subsequent broadcasts, Stuart now swung between a growing distaste for the Nazis and glowing praise for Hitler's own achievements. He did not however confront the issue of Ireland's status following a German victory, on which he, designated 'Ireland's Haw-Haw, Frances [*sic*] Stuart', was challenged by the British weekly *Picture Post*.[75]

Along with most of the DES staff, Stuart was transferred to Luxembourg in August 1943, though he refused to commit himself to further broadcasts. In February 1944 he was released from his assignment in Luxembourg and sent back to Berlin on condition that he reported back to the RRG, which he did not. Within days he was visited by the police who confiscated his passport and identity papers. Since Berlin university had been bombed into rubble, there was little for him to do. He and Meissner left for Munich, joining the crowd of miscellaneous refugees criss-crossing southern Germany in an attempt to find an escape route to Switzerland.

The end of the war found the couple in Dornbirn, on the Austro-German border. When French troops occupied the town in May 1945, Stuart was interned in a repatriation camp at Bregenz. In August, leaving Meissner in Dornbirn, he was able to travel to Paris and visit the Irish Legation, only to be told that his presence was an 'embarrassment' and that there was 'not the foggiest chance' of Meissner being permitted to accompany him to Ireland. Stuart's return to Dornbirn was now blocked. Early in September he managed to leave Paris on a train crowded with Yugoslav ex-partisans, bluffing his way through the French border controls and jumping out near Dornbirn. But the reunion with Meissner lasted only a couple of weeks. On 21 November, they were arrested by French security forces and the following year transferred to Freiburg-im-Breisgau on the German-Swiss-French border, where they were released on condition they remained in the French occupation zone.

In October 1948 Stuart was informed that he was free to leave Freiburg, but warned by a friend, Basil Liddell-Hart, the British military historian, that the British government would not welcome him in the UK. From the summer of 1949, the couple were in Paris, and two years later succeeded in returning to London, where they scraped a living. After the death of his first wife in March 1954, Stuart married Meissner, and the couple moved to County Meath, and then to suburban Drumdun, in Dublin, in August 1970.

Defending the 'Soft Underbelly'

The Italian invasion of British Somaliland on 6 August 1940 marked the beginning of the African theatre of war. On 11 November three Italian battleships were sunk at

Taranto by the Fleet Air Arm, and on 7 December British forces in Egypt opened an offensive against the Italians in Libya. Hitler reacted on 11 January 1941 by ordering an armoured force into North Africa, and on 4 April the counter-offensive, under Rommel, began to roll. Propaganda broadcasts to the region immediately became critical, and Wolf Mittler was appointed head of the Short-Wave Station team charged with directing programmes at enemy forces in the Mediterranean and North Africa.

Mittler himself was principal announcer and presenter of the lead radio programme:

> We called the feature 'Anzac Tattoo', which was the abbreviation for the troops of the Australian-New Zealand Army Corps in North Africa. We consciously choose the subtitle 'From the Enemy to the Enemy!' The opening melody was 'We'll Meet Again', which was then very popular with the troops on the other side. [...] I was responsible for the programmes, contributors from the Foreign Office were Werner Plack and Charlie Schwedler, who took care of the music part of the programmes.[76]

'Anzac Tattoo' went out on Saturdays at 11.00 hours; it was a programme of about thirty minutes, and was repeated at 16:30 hours. It was a rapid success with the Eighth Army, partly because it was short on propaganda and long on light entertainment, but also because Mittler used regularly to interview two or three prisoners-of-war whose names and addresses he announced well in advance. German guitarist Heinz 'Coco' Schumann recalled that the radio team were given considerable freedom:

> [Mittler] was at the Propaganda Ministry, doing propaganda broadcasts for abroad, though he wasn't even a Nazi. He was into music and his job was getting it across to the other side. And Middler [sic] knew the form down in the Groschenkeller. One time Middler came round with the recording van, and came in with a Telefunken mike and said: 'Boys, swing it, give it everything!' So our pianist, we called him Cab Calloway, sang 'Hi de hi de ho', and Ilja Glusgal sang 'Alexander's Rag Time'. [...] And it all went on the air over to England.[77]

But Mittler overestimated the Gestapo's patience. About 20 April 1943, at the conclusion of a performance by the Fud Candrix band at Berlin's Delphi-Palast, Mittler talked the Belgian band leader into staying on for a live broadcast of a jam session, pointing convincingly to his microphone and saying something about authorization 'from above'. On this particular evening, the Candrix band played the kind of music which had long been banned on German radio, including 'In the Mood', 'Sugar Foot Stomp' and similar numbers. The authorities would probably not have noticed had they not been tipped off, but Mittler was promptly suspended, pending an investigation.

By this time some of Mittler's friends, including Paul Schmidt, the Foreign Ministry's influential interpreter, had become concerned about his safety and had contacted General Oster, a key figure in the German military resistance, who apparently arranged for Mittler's transfer to an army unit in North Africa.[78] But Mittler's 'fall from grace' had been expected for some time. While he himself proudly recounts in his autobiography a successful interview with PoWs after the British débâcle at

Dieppe (19–20 August 1942), Edith Dietze noted in her diary that 'Mittler interview with PoWs at Dieppe misfired …Trouble over Mittler's fiasco at Dieppe'.[79] Mittler, however, made his way from Berlin to Italy, and was apprehended by the Gestapo in Naples. During an RAF raid he managed to evade the restrictions and link up with the Italian resistance movement until, with their help, he succeeded in escaping to Switzerland during the autumn of 1943.

After the war Mittler returned to Italy where, for five years, he worked for the British Forces Network, *The Rome Daily American*, the International Refugee Organisation and the French radio in Rome. During the early 1950s he was an editor with the radio branch of the Marshall Plan Information Division in Paris, eventually returning to Munich in 1953, where he joined the Bayrischer Rundfunk as aviation and space editor.

But the unquestioned star of 'Anzac Tattoo', before and after Mittler's defection, and the most glamorous figure at the RRG's *Auslandsdirektion*, was the American 'actress' Mildred Gillars. Dark-haired, sly-eyed, coquettish, and stage-struck, Gillars earned herself the nickname 'Axis Sally', particularly after the Allied landings of 8 November 1942 brought tens of thousands of American servicemen into the Mediterranean theatre of war. It is often alleged that the Americans landing in Sicily in July 1943 were met with leaflets, enticing them to desert, which read: 'With love from Axis Sally!' and 'A date with Mildred keeps you fit for your return home after the war!'.[80] The leaflets were said to show the photograph of a young girl with blonde hair – an image the 43-year-old Mildred Gillars sought to create in her listeners' minds. But the story is aprocryphal: there is no evidence that such a leaflet existed, and indeed the first propaganda leaflet issued in Italy by the Wehrmacht dates from January 1944.[81]

Mildred Elizabeth Gillars was born in Portland, Maine, on Thanksgiving Day, 29 November 1900. Her natal name was Sisk, but she adopted that of her step-father, Dr. Robert Bruce Gillars, a dentist. The family moved frequently and Mildred attended schools in several towns before earning her high school diploma in 1917, after which she studied English and drama at Ohio Wesleyan University. When forced to chose between marriage and the stage, she opted for the latter and moved to Cleveland where she worked by day and studied at night. The early 1920s saw Gillars in New York, unsuccessfully canvassing the theatre agents. The nearest she came to the lime-light was in 1928, by means of a dubious deal with the promoters of a third-rate movie, *Unwanted Children*.

In 1929 Gillars went to Paris where she worked as an artist's model. The following year she was back in New York and in 1933 went to Algiers to meet a gentleman at the British consulate whom she knew 'rather fleetingly'. Whatever she had anticipated did not, apparently, succeed, and Gillars found herself working as a shop assistant with a dressmaker in Algiers until able to depart for Naples. From there she moved to Budapest, arriving eventually in Berlin in September 1934, where she found a job at the Berlitz language school. In her free time she took classes in expressive dance (*Ausdruckstanz*), dubbed German films and wrote film reviews. Later she became private secretary to the German film star, Brigitte Horney.

But at the outbreak of war, Mildred Gillars had no regular employment. On 6 May 1940 she was engaged as a duty announcer for broadcasts to Britain *via* Bremen I, at forty marks a week. American embassy officials urged her to return home, but she replied: 'Go home to what? To poverty again?' At her post-war trial she claimed that the Gestapo had also tried to entice her to return to the United States to work for them as an undercover agent at the Wright aircraft factory in Dayton, Ohio.

While employed on Bremen, Gillars read some of the messages from British PoWs to their families, which Dietze used to record in the *Dulag Nord* transit camp at Westertimke/Farmstedt, near Bremen. She would add her own impromptu comments, and the readings would be set against music provided by 'Charlie and his Orchestra'. In the spring of 1941, Gillars sought an extension to her passport from the US embassy in Berlin, but her papers were confiscated by the vice-consul.

At about this time Gillars fell in love with Otto Koischwitz, the former American professor and by then influential broadcaster on the North America service. Koischwitz, two years her junior, was already married and the father of three daughters, but may have been attracted by Gillars' flair for the dramatic or sympathetic with her difficult personal situation. During her post-war trial Gillars said: 'I feel if Professor Koischwitz had not been in my life, I would not be fighting for my life today. [...] I consider him to have been my man of destiny'. Indeed, from the start of the relationship, Koischwitz had sought to persuade her to feature in his propaganda broadcasts. Later, she was to claim that she was adamant about not working on the North America service and that she did not read German newspapers so as not to be subjected to or influenced by Nazi propaganda. Instead Gillars wanted her own programme slot in order to interview PoWs as Dietze had been doing since 1940, and Koischwitz since 1941. During her trial she claimed, somewhat disingenuously: 'I told him [Koischwitz] I felt my only reason for being was to go to prisoner-of-war camps. I told him the only thing that would give me some happiness in the chaos of war was to feel I'd be of some service to the people of the United States.' Eventually, by the summer of 1943, Koischwitz succeeded in having Gillasrs transferred to the German Short-Wave Station, and obtained authorization for her to visit PoW camps, record interviews with prisoners and internees and broadcast them under the title 'Medical Reports' to North America. But in Washington, DC, on 26 July 1943, a federal grand jury indicted Gillars, along with other American propagandists, *in absentia*, on charges of wartime treason.

From mid-1943, Mildred Gillars, accompanied by Koischwitz and a technical crew, motored from camp to camp interviewing Allied prisoners-of-war. By Nazi standards she was a success. She produced and presented 'Home Sweet Home' and 'Medical Reports', and became the highest paid broadcaster on German foreign-language radio, at her peak earning 3,000 marks a month, on a par with Winkelnkemper's own salary.

Her then still raven-black head of hair, black silk pants, three-quarters length sealskin cape and ever-increasing pay demands combined to make her one of the most striking personalities in the *Funkhaus*. Should her pay fail to arrive on time, she would steam in to the station management and make her indignation known.[82]

But not everything went smoothly. In March 1944, Gillars and Koischwitz visited a camp for American PoWs near Hammerstein. Introduced as Red Cross representatives by the camp commandant, they offered internees an opportunity to broadcast a message to their families and friends in the US. The interviews came to an abrupt end, however, when one of the PoWs offered Gillars a thank-you present – a cigarette carton which turned out to be filled with horse manure. Following the Allied landings in Normandy, she travelled to interview Allied prisoners-of-war in France: 'Hello, boys. I'm here to make recordings so your folks will know you're still alive.' She continued to suggest she was working for the International Red Cross, but her interviews were edited and broadcast from Paris and Chartres, interpersed with a sprinkling of Nazi propaganda, though Gillars later claimed she always resisted pressure for the broadcasts to be used as propaganda.

Gillars left Paris on 15 August to record some broadcasts at the Hilversum studios in Holland. The Dutch crooner Jan de Vries later testified that one night, during an edition of 'Home, Sweet Home', she asked him to speak some propaganda material into the microphone. Gillars became 'very furious' when he refused, and it may not entirely be a coincidence that Jan de Vries was arrested shortly afterwards and dispatched to a concentration camp.

According to an agreement between the military, who were responsible for all active propaganda into enemy lines, and the ProMi, the RRG had been supporting military operations in Italy with English propaganda on short wave from late in 1943. Gillars, as 'Axis Sally', played her part: her programme, 'Midge at the Mike' (dubbed 'Bitch at the Mike' by her audience), made her notorious among GIs. She was the girl next door who sympathized with 'the boys in their odious task of having to carry out the orders of Roosevelt, Churchill and the Jewish gangsters'. Her voice brought an illusion of warmth and intimacy, and many appreciated the music she played – familiar, pleasant and soothing. But at the same time it was plain that many resented 'Axis Sally's' often sarcastic delivery. Between sentimental ballads and swing music, she would taunt the 'boys' about wives and girl-friends at home:

And what are your girls doing tonight, fellows? – You really can't blame them for going out to have some fun, could you? It is all so empty back there now – better to got out for some drinks with that 4-F boy friend than to sit and wait forever, doing nothing. [...] You may dislike my repeating this to you, but it's the truth, especially if you boys get all mutilated and do not return in one piece. I think then you'll have a pretty tough time with your girl. Any girl likes to have a man in one piece, so I think in any case, you've got a pretty hard future ahead of you.[83]In February 1944 German troops on the Italian front bombarded advancing American units with a leaflet depicting 'Sally's Complimentary Return Ticket' on its front, with the following printed on the back:

SALLY, the RADIO-GIRL from station 'JERRY'S FRONT' invites you to a FREE RETURN TRIP TO AMERICA via Germany. Sally says YOU CAN LIVE IN

PEACE and COMFORT at one of the camps operated under the auspices of the International Red Cross. She thinks you ought to take a long woolen blanket, some underwear and an extra pair of pants. DON'T HESITATE to make good use of this offer while there is a chance. 'SUMMER IN GERMANY IS THE PERFECTION OF THE BEAUTIFUL.' (Mark Twain)[84]

The following month, leaflets plugged 'Jerry's Front Radio':

What about Sally? — GI's Radio Dial: You won't see her but every evening you can hear her most fascinating voice. If you like to get a sweet kiss from Sally — tune in to Jerry's Front.

Leaflets gave the programme schedule and wave lengths of programmes directed at the Allied forces in Italy, and invited GIs to give their names and write a message they would like to have broadcast to 'their folks back home' if they were taken prisoner.

By the autumn of 1944, with the Allies were closing in on Germany from all sides, Dietze, in his capacity as Winkelnkemper's adviser on English-language broadcasts, wanted to give the Reich the fullest benefit of Mildred Gillars' celebrity status and recommended transferring her to one of the Battle Stations (*Kampfsender*) operated by the military. But Gillars objected violently and, in the end, remained in Berlin with the KWS.

Accounts of Gillars' role have suggested that she was solely responsible for radio propaganda directed at the Allies. The tone and character of her programmes reflected her talents, of course. But in terms of their content and objectives, she was but a part of a much larger scenario. In the 'Guidelines for Propagandists at the Front' ('*Richtlinien für Kampfpropagandisten Nr. 3*') the target audience is described as follows:

The average American GI is decidedly basic in his attitudes. Generally un-political and apathetic. Most of the officers have little interest in politics, and compare poorly with British officers in bearing and turn-out. It follows that propaganda directed at American forces needs to stick to clear-cut issues and must not rely on above-average educational responses. What most American soldiers care about chiefly is their own well-being. If they have been in action for any length of time, they want to know how soon they can go home. [...] If PoWs are asked what the United States are fighting for in Europe, hardly any know what to say. [...] Most American soldiers have a strongly developed family feeling and if taken prisoner are grateful for any opportunity to tell their people back home what has happened to them. As home leave is only granted at long intervals in the American forces, concerns about how true the sweetheart or wife is being loom very large.[85]

In accordance with this perception, the primary themes of German propaganda were laid down as follows:

1 Fear of being killed:

e.g. 'Stop, watch your step, it's five minutes to twelve!

Five minutes to twelve:

Luftwaffe down and out.

German war industry smashed.

Russians threatening Berlin.

The end in sight.

Five minutes to twelve:

And so nobody wants to be killed in these last five minutes.

That's common sense.

Watch your step!'[86]

2 Sexual anxieties:

e.g. 'Gentlemen prefer blondes – but blondes don't like cripples.'[87]

3 Personal resentment, whether against higher ranks at the front, or jealousy of suspected rivals back home: e.g. 'For men only – for officers only.'[88]

4 Home-sickness and nostalgia, particularly in a family context:

e.g. 'Come back home alive, Daddy'

'Where might Daddy be on this Holy Night [*Heiligabend*, i.e. Christmas Eve]?'[89]

By the end of 1944, 'Axis Sally' was past her heyday, as was the Reich itself, but she was clearly still worth discrediting. Dietze reported to Winkelnkemper that an Italian on the Allied controlled Rome station EIAR had slandered 'Sally, the famed broadcaster', by informing listeners that 'she was ugly and cross-eyed, had bandy legs and, to top it all, that she was pregnant. This tit-bit quickly made its round among the [enemy] troops.'[90]

During the early months of 1945, the German consul-general in Mussolini's 'Social Republic', Dr. Hans-Otto Meissner, threw several parties in the castle in Fino, one of which Gillars attended as a guest of honour. The remnants of the military propaganda unit 'Southern Star' (*Südstern*), was also there. It included the 'Radio Liberty' outfit and the mobile medium-wave transmitter 'Fritz', so was able to beam these *danses macabres* live to the advancing Allies in the south:

Enemy personnel tuning in to the 'Liberty-Station' got an earful of laughter and the sounds of clinking glasses. Yanks in their tanks, curious to catch what the Krauts had to say for themselves on 9011, picked up dance tunes and popular songs, wisecracks and girls' voices through their head-phones. That's what the party here was all about, a hell of a party. [...] The music cuts out. A middle-aged lady, tall, lean, with loose hair, picks up the mike. Her eyes shine with excitement, she gives a big smile: 'Hello, boys ... How are you tonight ...? A lousy night it sure is ... Axis Sally is talking to you ... you poor silly dumb lambs, well on your way to be slaughtered!'[91]

Even John Amery turned up at one of these parties, shouting into the microphone: 'This is Germany calling ... Germany calling! Listen, boys, what a happy time we're having!'

At the end of the war Mildred Gillars went into hiding in Berlin, until apprehended

32 Mildred Gillars ('Axis Sally'), arriving back in the US to face charges of treason, January 1949.

by US Counter-Intelligence in March 1946. She spent the next six months in the US Army detention centre at Oberursel, together with Chandler, Best, Burgman and Day. While Chandler and Best were flown back to the US in December 1946, the others were set free, on condition that they reported every two weeks to the military authorities in Frankfurt.

Without identity papers, ration cards, money or helpful friends, Gillars took a desperate gamble. She called a press conference and informed the stunned audience of her background and her intention to return to her 'rightful home in the United States. I always considered myself an American. [...] I only joined the German radio because it gave me the outlet for dramatic expression that I have always sought. [...] I only tried to warn America against Communism and Judaism. All the things I warned against have since become actualities. Oh, if only those poor GIs who sacrificed their lives and futures had realized what was going on!' The US authorities were forced to react. On 21 January 1947 the Army received orders from Washington to re-arrest Gillars, pending further investigation into her role in Nazi Germany. After nineteen months in a US Army prison in Germany, 'Axis Sally' was flown to Washington, and her trial began on 24 January 1949.

After all the bad luck in her life, she now has her great opportunity – though it would also be her last. Mildred Gillars is to appear before the federal court in Washington, DC, to face the charge of high treason. [...] Mildred E. Gillars makes the most of her final but starring role. She tosses a silvery shoulder-length mane seductively round her neck. With a figure, at 48, still worth looking at, she eloquently swings a hip before her judges and her public. Varying expressions as the occasion demands, she gives a glamorous smile, or displays the tears of injured innocence. With virtuoso skill she plays upon the scales of American PR to the full. But the court declines to be taken in.[92]

On 25 March 1949 Gillars was found guilty of treason and sentenced to between ten and thirty years imprisonment and a fine of $10,000. Her sentence was stated to be lighter than that imposed on others because there was no evidence that she had helped formulate broadcasting policy. Gillars spent the following twelve years in a federal women's reformatory at Alderson, West Virginia. On 10 July 1961, she was paroled and began a fresh career, teaching German, French and music at a Catholic convent in Columbus, Ohio. On retirement she returned to Ohio Wesleyan University and completed her bachelor's degree in speech, at the age of seventy-two. On 25 June 1988, Mildred Gillars died in Columbus, Ohio.

Last Words from 'Germany Calling'

When the Allied round-the-clock 'combined bomber offensive' against Germany began in June 1943, landlines linking the studios in Berlin with Königs Wusterhausen and the transmitters in the west were frequently cut, and normal schedules became unreliable. In August 1943, sections of the editorial staff were moved to Luxembourg.

The English team in Luxembourg was headed by Dr. Joachim Schaede (*b.* 1910) and included Dr. Edmund Dondelinger (*b.* 1913), Martin Erle (a naturalized German), Dr. Hans Hartmann (responsible for broadcasts to Ireland), Hesse, Heydebreck, Knipping, and Helen Sensburg as commentators and readers. The Luxembourg contingent's political briefing was the responsibility of Dr. Friedrich Wilhelm Schoberth (*b.* 1905) of the Foreign Ministry's broadcasting activity. The first locally produced programme was broadcast on 12 August 1943. A year later, in September 1944, the station was evacuated again, before Luxembourg could be over-run by the Allies.

At this time Dietze had a further crisis on his hands. The head of the Party's regional office decided to suspend the 'indispensable' status of six members of Dietze's section and ordered them to be handed over to the military authorities 'with immediate effect'.[93] Dietze appears to have won and some of the English section were transferred to Hilversum in the Netherlands, while other members of the former Luxembourg team were transferred to Apen, near Oldenburg, in the north-western corner of the country, where emergency studio facilities were established in Bremers Hotel, a country inn. K.O. Koch, who had previously worked for the RRG in the Netherlands, was the station head (*Sendestellenleiter*) and Willi Günther (*b.* 1900) was responsible for engineering. On 24 August 1944, the English section of the German European Stations began broadcasting from Hilversum. Apen became operative on 25 October.

Dietze himself remained in Berlin. In summer 1944 he was appointed advisor and inspector of all broadcasts in English, including those of the USA section and the newly created Battle Stations (*Kampfsender*). In March 1945, when it became impossible to maintain even a skeleton programme with any regularity, the last of the English section in Berlin were transferred to Apen and to an intermediate base at Hamburg.

It was from Hamburg that William Joyce made his valedictory broadcast, the BBC recording of which has become well-known. On 30 April 1945, the station staff was summoned to a meeting and informed that both their minister and the Führer were dead, and that Admiral Dönitz was taking over as Hitler's successor. At the conclusion of the meeting the staff was invited to a buffet meal: they ate and drank, laughed and shouted as if celebrating a victory. From the party Joyce went directly to the studio to record his last broadcast. The text of his commentary had been cleared by Gustav Grupe, director of the Hamburg station, before the party began. Joyce spoke slowly, with long pauses, sometimes slurring his words, sometimes raising his voice to a shout, then dropping it until he was almost inaudible. The recording engineers seem to have been as drunk as he was, or they might have cut him off. 'Lord Haw-Haw' opened his final performance with the words: 'I'm speaking now personally. I want to talk to you about what I know and what I feel. Germany – if you will – is not anymore the chief factor in Europe. Germany may be – I may be wrong – I will only say – the German arms have been defeated in many battlefields. I've always hoped that in the end there would be an alliance of combat and understanding between England, America and Germany. Well, at this moment, that seems impossible.' He concluded with the words: 'You may not hear from me again for a few months – I say: *Es lebe Deutschland! Heil Hitler!* – And farewell!'

Dietze had left Berlin for Apen on 13 April, after the last landline to Hamburg had broken down. The remnants of the former *Auslandsdirektion* in Berlin were now completely cut off from their editorial offices and transmitters. A few days later, on 30 April and 1 May 1945, Dietze and sixteen volunteers moved to an old fortification, Fort Altona, at Fedderwardergroden, a suburb of Wilhelmshaven. From there, on 2 May, they began to provide the rudiments of a German home service over a local 1.5 kW station which until then had only been used for air-raid warnings. They also maintained the 'Germany Calling' programme on the former Stuttgart wave-length, *via* Bremen I. Apen was occupied by the British on 3 May. Later that day, the regional substation at Flensburg, near the Danish border, announced it had become a *Reichssender* and the mouth-piece of the last Nazi government under Grand Admiral Dönitz.

Wilhemshaven continued its English-language programme and home service until 5 May 1945. In the end, Dietze reported:

I had to handle the entire programme alone – and struggle with the local *Kreisleiter* [Horsmann, the regional Party leader] and Seiffe [the Party's regional propaganda head at Oldenburg] who wanted to take the air on Bremen with a most harmful last speech, which I managed to divert to the small low-power station only – while I received no guidance whatever from Flensburg, although there was a line available.[94]

The Dönitz administration was seeking to correct as far as possible the impression created by its predecessors, particularly in the final phase of the war, that Germany would be 'fighting to the last man and the last bullet'. The new propaganda themes were 'a sense of responsibility towards the welfare of the people' and 'consideration for the people'. On 1 May 1945, at 22:26 hours, in his first broadcast to the German people, Dönitz declared: 'It is my first task to save German people from destruction by the advancing Bolshevik enemy. For this aim alone the military struggle continues.'

A day later, on 2 May at 21:00 hours, the acting head of the new Reich government and foreign minister, Graf Schwerin von Krosigk, spoke to the German population via Radio Flensburg:

A great flood of desperate and starving people is pouring westward along the roads of the still unoccupied parts of Germany. [...] An iron curtain[95] is sweeping relentlessly forward from the east. [...] The German nation, its suffering women and mothers, pray God to spare the world yet another war with all its horrors. In company with us, all the nations of Europe, threatened with famine and Bolshevik terror, are looking to a new order that will assure us of a true and lasting peace, and the opportunity for a free and secure life.

Later in his radio address, Schwerin von Krosigk was clearly appealing to the Allies rather than to the German people when he referred to the San Francisco conference (from 25 April 1945), at which the United Nations charter was drafted. He argued that the German people were now cured of any warlike inclinations and were therefore the best security for world peace, and played on what he supposed were western fears of famine and Communism in Europe. He was succeeded by Albert Speer on 3 May at 19:45 hours, on Kalundborg and Copenhagen, as well as the former wave-length of the *Deutschlandsender*. Speer was almost entirely concerned with the immediate restoration of supply lines, and the revival of food production and the railway system. He urged the German people to overcome their natural dejection: 'We must not mourn and weep over the past at this moment. Only dogged work will make it possible for us to continue to bear our lot.'

Though these messages from Flensburg were favourably received in London, the effect was somewhat spoiled by a broadcast in English to the United Kingdom on the same day.[96] The perpetrator was Dietze, and the programme, 'Views on the News', was broadcast from Wilhelmshaven. Considering the circumstances of this broadcast, from a makeshift studio with the world around it sinking into chaos, Dietze's material displayed a remarkable lack of reality. He began with his views on the 'final stages of the great struggle':

So, there would have been no point, from the German military angle, in ceasing fire in Holland ['fortress Holland'] at so early a date. But consideration for the civilian population, which should not be subjected to further suffering senselessly, was, I think, the main operating thought which actuated the German command in the area in agreeing to cease hostilities. There we have another instance of that great sense of responsibility towards the welfare not only of the German population but of all European peoples. This sense of responsibility goes so far as to maintain the most stubborn resistance in the European interest on the eastern front whenever possible against the Soviets. For the German soldiers fighting there know that they defend not only their homeland, the fatherland, but also all European civilization and culture. So, I believe, I am quite justified in saying that Germany today is fighting a pioneer's battle against forces of destruction that evidently have not yet been fully realized by the western powers. Forces of destruction which threaten Great Britain and, in the long run, the United States, just as much as they at present do the German people.[97]

Further into the broadcast, Dietze mentioned some strikes in London, conceding that they were small scale, but citing them as remarkable evidence of 'burning social problems calling for a solution of labour unrest' and warning that 'the straws which show which way the wind is blowing may soon blow to the tune of a regular hurricane'. Dietze ended what he termed 'this extempore marshalling of thoughts and facts' with a personal tribute 'to the great leader of the German people, Adolf Hitler, whose memory, I believe, will be immortal in the minds of every German':

I was a loyal supporter of this great figure in world history, because he had achieved what I had believed for many years to be impossible, the unity of the German people. [...] That to me is the reason why I firmly believe that his name will always be a name connected with Germany's future. The name of Adolf Hitler will be eternal, it will never be eradicated from the hearts and the minds of Germany's youth. And whatever we think of Germany's greatness, of Germany's unity, of the nation of all Germans, of the Reich which is eternal, we will think of Adolf Hitler, the man who united the Germans for the first time in history as they had never been before, Adolf Hitler, the author and creator of the greater German Reich.[98]

Hearing the recording some fifty years later, former members of the RRG's English section reacted with disbelief. Mrs. Luzie Henze, a member of the Dietze team from late in 1941 exclaimed: 'This can't be him!'. James Clark shook his head saying: 'He must have lost his sense of proportion!' Although comparatively young, Dietze was generally called 'Papa' in the section because of his caring attitude. His former colleagues remembered him as a professional radioman and efficient administrator, obviously working under enormous pressures and never showing the feelings to which his intelligence and divided loyalty condemned him.

On 5 May 1945 Dietze addressed his fellow-countrymen for the last time in a broadcast on the home service:

So I decided to wind up with a German comment in which I called upon the German people to cease destroying means of traffic, to maintain and repair communications as far as possible, give precedence in all workshops to such repair work, and to continue to produce as much food as possible and maintain the rationing system in working order. To give it added weight with the more ardent Nazis, I quoted a last speech of Speer's on a low-power German station on similar lines. I concluded with an appeal to maintain a certain dignity towards the Allies, and not to lose all honour into the bargain.[99]

On 12 May, Allied military authorities arrested Dietze for having, as a British subject by birth, assisted the enemy. Dietze spent the next six months at a British internment camp at Esterwegen. On 12 November he was released and informed that he should expect proceedings against him should he ever return to Britain. For a time, Dietze earned a living as a translator and freelance journalist in Apen, while working on several inventions in his laboratory. In 1950 he returned to the air with a live broadcast from the Hamburg Derby for the Norddeutscher Rundfunk (NDR), Hamburg. Around this time, he became involved with the Südwestfunk (SWF), Baden-Baden, and frequently lectured at the institute for journalism of Münster University. In July 1953, as the SWF's television delegate, he was the station's driving force in developing a local TV capability. Subsequently, Dietze continued as a freelance radio and television journalist for the SWF and other stations. On 25 May 1960, at the age of 51, Eduard Dietze died of a heart condition, at Bühlertal, near Baden-Baden.

5   Propaganda Swing

Nazi Ideology and Jazz

From the earliest years of the Second World War the RRG, the German Broadcasting Company, used popular music, swing and jazz as calculated bait to attract listeners to its foreign-language propaganda broadcasts. While Goebbels was at loggerheads with hard-line Party officials over the type of music to be played on the German home service, there was from the start no argument about the type of music to accompany propaganda broadcasts targeted abroad. Even Hitler was in agreement: on 10 April 1942 he held forth over lunch on aspects of propaganda for foreign listeners:

> Broadcasts aimed at England need to include a lot of musical material of a kind that appeals to the British, so as to get them more and more accustomed to tuning in to our stations if they cannot get what they want on their own stations.[1]

But it was only a few days later, on 22 April, that Goebbels' right-hand man and recently appointed overlord of entertainment, Hans Hinkel, was minuted as saying at the broadcasting planning meeting:

> On no account should the stations in question be allowed to frame any political news bulletins targeting a particular country with music that is representative of that country. For example, imitating distinctively English and American music is in his [Hinkel's] opinion undesirable, and on the contrary, he is firmly of the view that this kind of broadcast must be framed with really good German music.[2]

Hitler may have shared – or been influenced by – Goebbels' empirical outlook, but the fact that the principal policy-makers, Hinkel and Goebbels, were so completely at odds over a key point of Nazi ideology illustrates the difficulty of interpreting the true nature of German light entertainment, and in particular of popular jazz music, an issue still unresolved at the end of the Nazi period. The explanation lies in the course of Germany history after 1918. The first world war had swept away the monarchy and much else, and a whole society of petty-bourgeois 'rabbit breeders and allotment holders' felt it had been left abruptly shelterless, as if a storm had blown the roof off.

With the decentralization of state power, few Germans could do much with their newly-gained political freedom. They were not accustomed to democracy, and did not feel comfortable with the new republic. If the new Germany did not see revolution, it did indeed see social and cultural ferment: forces unleashed in the post-war social upheaval had a dramatic effect on art and music, and for a brief period between the end of inflation in 1924 and the beginning of the world economic crisis of 1929 – or even up to Hitler's seizure of power (*'Machtergreifung'*)[3] in 1933 – Berlin could claim to be the creative metropolis of Europe. These forces of change and dislocation were incomprehensible to a narrow-minded bourgeoisie, and were bitterly rejected by the political right – traditionalists and opportunists alike – who sensed their days might be numbered.

When Adolf Hitler was appointed chancellor on 30 January 1933 the nation acquired, in its new leader (*'Führer'*), a dictator with an ideology. Party doctrine would now be enshrined in German law. Expressionism, Suprematism, Constructivism and Dadaism, as well as 'Nigger' music and modernist atonal composition, in short 'the refuse of a rotting society', were banned, and the perceived source of it all, the Jews, could begin to be barred from the life of the Reich.[4]

Bolstered by pseudo-scientific theories, the right-wing parties worked hard after 1918 to assuage the nation's damaged pride and restore a sense of collective self-respect. They argued that despite the defeat, the Versailles treaty and national disgrace, 'Aryan' Germans remained at the apex of humanity's ethnic pyramid, with blacks at its base, barely superior to primates. Before 1914 the average German was unlikely to have encountered black people, except as 'exotic' attractions in the secure environment of theatres, night-clubs or circuses. So the presence of a contingent of coloured troops from France's colonies during the French occupation of the Rhineland between 1919 and 1925 became a symbol of the 'Shame of Versailles'. It was exemplified by the central character of the popular 1927 jazz opera, *'Jonny spielt auf'* ('Johnny Strikes Up'), by Vienna-born Ernst Krenek, in which white girls succumbed to the magic of an Afro-American's jazz fiddle.[5]

Because of its black origins, and its 'pulsating, sensual' rhythm, jazz was considered to be below German moral standards and aesthetically inferior to German culture. When Dr. Bernhard Sekles instituted a jazz class at Frankfurt's prestigious Hoch'sche Konservatorium in January 1928, it provoked an outcry from traditionalists, including respected members of the musical establishment, who denounced jazz as the 'rhythm of belly-dancing Negroes'.[6]

A pervasive anti-Semitism was intrinsic to such attitudes. Although even anti-Semites acknowledged that the demonstrable intellectual powers of Jews placed them 'higher' than blacks in the racial scale, they had as much trouble with the sound of modernist compositions as with 'Nigger' music. While black people were supposed to revel naively in the perceived erotic ingredient of jazz, Jews were alleged to exploit it as part of a systematic conspiracy to corrupt the 'Aryan' German culture through acts of 'musical race defilement'.[7]

Even before Hitler came to power, jazz had already been banned by some provincial guardians of German culture. In September 1930 Thuringia's newly-appointed

Minister of the Interior, Wilhelm Frick – the former head of the political police in Munich and an early supporter of Hitler and the political Right – prohibited the playing of jazz in *his* province. Frick's decree was entitled 'Against Negro Culture – For German Nationhood' and opened with the words:

> For years now, alien influences have been gaining ground in all fields of cultural life with effects which tend to undermine the moral strength of the German nation. To a very large extent, they are products which glorify the Negro – such as jazz and percussion music, Negro dancing, singing and drama – and are an affront to German cultural sensibilities. For the sake of conserving and strengthening German nationhood, a halt needs to be called to corrupting influences like these.

Frick's dominion in Thuringia provided a first taste of what to expect were the NSDAP to win an election: licensing rules for theatres, restaurants, clubs and bars were tightened to enforce the ban on 'Negro dancing, singing and drama';[8] the showing of the anti-war movie 'All Quiet on the Western Front' (*'Im Westen nichts Neues'*) was prohibited; ministerial staff, including the police, were purged of all elements considered disloyal to the Nazi cause, and on Frick's instruction the schoolday was expected to begin with a prayer for Germany's honour and military strength.

With Hitler's accession to power in 1933, all types of conservative authorities – local politicians, university professors and schoolmasters, provincial police chiefs and Storm Troopers as well as leaders of all variety of racially-inspired movements on the margins of the Party – were able, by the banning of jazz, to define themselves as executors of Reich policy. And they were correct.

The Third Reich at War with Jazz

In March 1933 Germany's new rulers banished jazz from all radio programmes on the grounds that it was a form of 'musical decadence'.[9] Earlier that month the RRG had informed the press that:

> The Berlin programme is banning all the dubious dance styles that healthy public opinion calls 'Nigger music', in which provocative rhythms predominate and melody is violently abused.[10]

However it took more than a further two years for the ban to be effective. On 12 October 1935, Eugen Hadamovsky, the RRG's programme director, outlined the 1935–36 winter programme to an assembly of regional directors and leading composers. He expatiated on the 'disintegrating effects of cultural Bolshevist-Jewry', concluding, 'We also mean to eradicate every trace of putrefying elements that remain in our light entertainment and dance music', and proclaimed, 'As of today, Nigger jazz is finally switched off on the German radio.'[11]

But what jazz was, exactly, was nowhere clearly defined. Hans Otto Fricke, director of the regional radio station in Frankfurt, jointly with the Reich Chamber of Music, put together 'From Cake-Walk to Hot', a programme intended to provide listeners with criteria for identifying jazz and to demonstrate its questionable history. The programme, first broadcast by Radio Frankfurt on 9 December 1935 and later networked by other stations, included several numbers, performed by American bands, that were intended to ridicule hot music. In doing so it unwittingly won new friends for jazz.

At the same time German composers were called upon to develop a contemporary national music style, and dance band competitions were organized to introduce the public to the 'new' music. But the very composition of the assessment committees and competition juries ensured that the selected 'model' orchestras were mediocre at best and the winning tunes decidedly old-fashioned. The chairman of the jury was none other than Hadamovsky himself, and other members included Paul Graener, vice-president of the RMK and a classical composer, Dr. Fritz Stege, chief critic of the prestigious journal *Zeitschrift für Musik*, and Dr.Willy Richartz, a composer and RRG administrator who had been instrumental in removing the very popular, Berlin-based, *Goldene Sieben* jazz band from German radio the previous summer. All were known jazz-haters.

A contrary argument, though cautiously expressed, was made by Richard Litterscheid who, in 'An Obituary on Jazz', gave a new slant to the ban: 'All the same, we must not over-react against jazz, and allow ourselves to slide back into the cosy, superficial and sentimental palm-court music ['*Salonmusik*'] of pre-war days.[12] Two years later, on 17 December 1937, Goebbels decreed that 'The recording of music by Jewish composers and of works presented and performed by Jews is forbidden'. The following day, Dr. Peter Raabe, former music director of the Aachen Opera and a fervent Nazi who had replaced Richard Strauss as president of the Reich Chamber of Music in October 1935, expanded on his minister's decree and declared that all foreign music published or distributed in the country had first to be vetted by an agency of the Chamber.

At the same time, Dr. Hans Severus Ziegler, director-general of the German National Theatre in Weimar, Thuringia, and the Party's provincial 'culture watch-dog', organized an exhibition of 'Degenerate Music' patterned on the notorious 1937 Munich exhibition of 'Degenerate Art'. Ziegler was a pioneering National Socialist, his Party membership number being 1317, and having been charged in January 1935 with homosexual offences, was now engaged on a conscientious demonstration to re-emphasize his political reliability and loyalty. 'Degenerate Music' was to be presented as a special feature within the Reich Music Conference (*Deutsche Reichsmusiktage*) in Düsseldorf, opening on 24 May 1938.

The 1937 Munich exhibition had been personally authorized by Hitler, confident of his own knowledge of art and intending to pillory artists whom he saw as enemies of the state. 'Degenerate Music', on the other hand, was a semi-official affair for which the Führer saw little or no need, as all the performing music media – radio, theatres and orchestras – were already tightly controlled by loyal Party members. But both Goebbels and Dr. Heinz Drewes, head of the ProMi's Music Division, favoured

Ziegler's initiative as an opportunity for the publicizing of official policy on German music. The press obediently heralded the event as a 'Panorama of German Musical Art', a 'Festival of a truly Musical Nation' and the 'German Music Olympics'. If the objective was the wholesale denunciation of modern music, the show was not a success. The visuals presented were familiar caricatures of a very primitive nature, and the audio material consisted of examples taken overtly out of context. Early visitors to the exhibition displayed incredulity and irritation and a subsequent national tour was cut short when it was noticed that among the musicians pilloried by Ziegler were some, like Igor Stravinsky, who were officially tolerated in some areas, and others who were Party members, such as Hermann Reutter, director of the Hoch'sche Konservatorium in Frankfurt, whose politically-approved musical paean, 'Gesang des Deutschen', was dedicated to Dr. Fritz Krebs, an influential NSDAP member and lord mayor of Frankfurt.

Undeterred by this embarrassment, the campaign against jazz persevered as a fundamental feature of musical life throughout the Nazi period. In 1941, Max Merz, a folksong researcher and dance instructor, declared to members of the Vienna branch of the Reich Chamber of Music that:

> Jazz is the product of a featureless existence deprived of any striving towards a higher vision, of any sense of uplift. We need to protect ourselves as a nation against mental infections of alien origin lest we lose the inward sense of our own proper identity and choke the wellsprings of what we are ... The perpetual pounding, this whole jerking rhythm, comes across like something machine-made, fragmented images in sound, like some kind of mechanical formula, deviating from all that is human.[13]

The nearest to an authoritative definition of the abhorred features of jazz came from Goebbels himself. The minutes of his daily ministerial briefing on 1 February 1941 indicate that:

> With regard to the question of playing jazz music on the German radio, the minister laid it down that the following are banned on principle:
> 1 music with distorted rhythms,
> 2 music with atonal melody line,
> 3 the use of so-called 'stopped' horns.[14]

'The Most Effective Weapon'

Hitler – the vegetarian and bachelor, who neither smoked nor drank – resented modernism in whatever field or form, and favoured a generalized kind of neo-classical monumentalism. He admired Richard Wagner's music-dramas and Anton Bruckner's symphonies, but apart from his table-talk opinion for listeners to the German radio's English-language programmes, there is little evidence of theoretical pronouncements by him on music. So far as jazz was concerned Hitler, like any other right-wing politician, regularly played the 'black shame' card in his early Rhineland speeches as a small-town agitator. His opinion of jazz was doubtless implicit in his belief in the creative superiority of the 'Aryan' race.

For his part Goebbels, with a degree in German literature and a moderate talent as a pianist, had a penchant for light classical music and operettas, and occasionally attended one of the big Berlin revues, despite his declared disgust of Berlin's night life during the Weimar years (a 'Babylon of sin', as he described it in his diary). Goebbels had nothing but scorn for the Nazi ideologist Alfred Rosenberg's Campaigners for German Culture (*Kampfbund für deutsche Kultur*) with its naive offerings of folk-singers and dancers. 'So this, then, is "German culture"!', he exclaimed after attending one of the *Kampfbund's* events.[15] Goebbels was aware that 'National Socialism set to music' was not what most listeners wanted when switching on their radio sets, and throughout his twelve years in office sought to provide quality light entertainment, sandwiched between the martial music of Party ideologists and the unrelieved classical diet of the musical traditionalists.

At the opening of the 1936 Berlin Radio Show (*Funkausstellung*), he outlined his programme philosophy:

> The broadcasting programmes need to be put together in such a way that while they still cater for sophisticated tastes, they are also pleasing and accessible to less demanding listeners […] They should offer an intelligent and psychologically skilful blend of what is informative, stimulating, relaxing and entertaining. Of these, relaxation in particular deserves special care, for the life of by far the greater number of all radio listeners engages them in a tough and merciless everyday struggle that wears at their nerves and their strength, giving them a right to recuperate and refresh themselves during the few hours when they are off work.[16]

This directive had the result of increasing the proportion of musical programmes to nearly seventy per cent in 1937, compared with sixty per cent in 1934. At the opening of the 1939 *Funkausstellung*, Goebbels again emphasized the importance of relaxation and entertainment on the radio, in addition to spiritual uplift and political dedication, pointing out that this made it, 'next to the press, the most effective weapon in our struggle for national existence.'[17]

Music and Morale on the Home-Front

After the lightning victories in Poland and the West, expectations of an early final victory were high. But public morale soon faded when it became clear that the Battle of Britain had not in fact pushed Britain out of the war. The military successes in the Balkans and North Africa during 1941, however, as well as the sweep towards Moscow, temporarily restored public confidence before the shock of 'General Winter's' 1941–42 counter-offensive made it clear that the campaign in Russia would not be a quick one.

During the third year of the war, words such as *Belastungen* (burdens), *Einschränkungen* (restrictions) and *Opfer* (sacrifices) dominated German propaganda on the home service, and listener reactions were marked by deep anxiety.[18]

As the war continued and public gloom deepened, Goebbels became increasingly emphatic about the importance of programmes which offered light relief to the nation – entertainment on the level of the enormously popular radio feature, the '*Wunschkonzert für die Wehrmacht*' ('Forces' Choice') with its mixture of sentimentality, old favourites and current hits – martial music such as '*Es ist so schön Soldat zu sein*', '*Siegreich woll'n wir Frankreich schlagen*', or '*Bomben auf En-ge-land*', with cheerful greetings from the front and for the family. Even before the invasion of the Soviet Union, Goebbels had announced, in June 1941, that he was putting more light entertainment on the radio. The people, and in particular the soldiers at the front, required some distraction from the hardships and exertions of daily life.[19] 'Monotonous and boring' programmes were to be deliberately enlivened.[20] In order for this to be achieved prohibitions needed to be relaxed and concessions made.[21] During the annual RRG staff assembly in October 1941, the head of the RRG sound archive, Dr. Fritz Pauli, gave a talk on 'Dance Music on the Radio' in which he spoke about a 'German dance music that doesn't get all its ideas from abroad', even while conceding that there was 'a shortage of good German dance bands'. Pauli established two criteria for 'German dance music': 'Melody over rhythm' and 'step up the emphasis on the melody: the violin carries the melody'. He described the orchestra at the *Deutschlandsender*, directed by Willi Stech, as an 'ideal formation', and went on to propose a 'German model dance band' consisting of twelve violins, four violas, four saxophones, three trombones, three trumpets, piano, zither, percussion, bass, as well as two bassoons and two bass-clarinets.[22]

Goebbels' confidant Hans Hinkel at once set to work to reform radio entertainment. At meetings on 14 and 15 October he discussed objectives with Winkelnkemper and Dr. Schönicke of the RRG, the composers Norbert Schultze and Dr. Willy Richartz, the musicians and orchestra leaders Franz Grothe, Georg Haentzschel and Theo Mackeben, and the cabaret artists Willi Schaeffers and Ludwig Manfred Lommel. It was agreed that programmes be interspersed with orchestral music, the tone varied by means of contrasts between 'lyrical' and 'strongly rhythmic' pieces, and that breaks by announcers in mid-music be scrapped.[23] Above all Hinkel ensured that not the slightest hint of jazz was to be heard in the home services; the minutes of programme planning meetings reveal that: '[Singer] Rosita Serrano and the Hohenberger band are to be off-air until further notice'.[24] Dr. Richartz suggested that the word 'Jazz-music' be generally replaced by the term 'dance music', and Hinkel specified that after the news and before any subsequent light entertainment programme, 'a neutral march or overture or something of the sort should be played'.[25] Diewerge informed a meeting on 7 January 1942 that 'in future up-beat hits are to be played individually and no longer coupled', and that 'rhythmic music is not to be ignored, but without overdoing it'. Prompted by a letter from the Reich Chamber of Music complaining that on 8 March 1942 a band directed by Adalbert Lutter had, contrary to the ProMi's instructions, played the Harold M. Kirchstein number '*Du bist meine grosse*

Leidenschaft', Hinkel confirmed that compositions by the German-American guitarist were banned.[26] (The Chamber of Music pointed out that Kirchstein had returned to the United States in 1938 and was to be regarded as an American, and that his music should not be played on the German radio 'particularly because of his suspected non-Aryan ancestry'.) On 29 April, Hinkel reiterated that 'in future the term "Jazz" was to be avoided'.[27]

Lightening the tone of German radio programming was not a straightforward matter. Goebbels encountered resistance from Party fanatics, but remained adamant: 'We must provide opportunities for relaxation through lighter reading matter, lighter music on the radio and so forth...When the war is over we can get back to discussing the ideological aspect.[28] A few days earlier, he had railed at 'ignorant music experts, who have no idea what ordinary people feel they want most.'

Hinkel's proposals for the reformation of German radio broadcasting were delivered on 12 February 1942 and immediately accepted by Goebbels. On 15 February, the RRG was divided into ten separate broadcasting groups, each one responsible for a particular sector of radio entertainment, and headed by an expert in its field.[29] The group heads constituted a 'Programming Board for the Music and Entertainment Sector' and were to report directly to Hinkel at the ministry, completely bypassing existing RRG structures. The two groups which principally concern us here are Group A, 'Light Dance and Entertainment Music', headed by Georg Haentzschel, and Group B, 'Sophisticated Entertainment Music', which included film music and contemporary operettas, headed by Franz Grothe.[30] Haentzschel and Grothe now both became employees of the RRG, on a salary of 2,000 marks a month.

The Berlin-born pianist Georg Haentzschel (1907–1992) had worked for Berlin radio since 1926, freelancing with other bands in his spare time. In 1928 he joined the orchestra of violinist Marek Weber, which included several Americans. Later that year Lud Gluskin, leader of an American society orchestra, selected Haentzschel to replace his regular pianist. During the early 1930s Haentzschel played and recorded with a good many jazz groups including The Virginians, directed by the Americans Teddy Kline and Mike Danzi, and with symphonic jazz orchestras such as the one directed by the conductor Mitja Nikisch. In 1935, he was one of the founder members of The Golden Seven (*Die Goldene Sieben*), which included some of the finest jazz musicians in Germany, among them the American guitarist Harold M. Kirchstein. When The Golden Seven disbanded at the beginning of the Second World War, Haentzschel worked mainly for the German film industry.

The pianist Franz Grothe (1908–1982) also hailed from Berlin, and was Haentzschel's life-long friend. As an eighteen-year-old he had joined an orchestra directed by violinist Dajos Béla, but was soon to concentrate on writing operettas and musical scores for the nascent German film industry. By the time of his death, Grothe had provided the music for more than two hundred movies.

With the confirmation of Hans Hinkel as head of all radio entertainment at the beginning of March 1942, the reconfiguration of the service was complete. And it appeared to be successful. Two months later the *Sicherheitsdienst*, the security service which monitored all aspects of German civilian life in regular secret bulletins to the

SS, assessed the reaction of the listening public: 'Reports say that the musical content of programmes is felt generally satisfactory, so long as there was no slipping back into "jazz", and not too much "serious" [classical] music'.[31]

Light entertainment was acceptable, but jazz remained the antithesis of the Reich. In an article on 'Jazz on the Radio' in the weekly, *Das Reich*, Goebbels addressed the issue of whether the medium and the music were complementary:

> The answer to this question has to be negative if by jazz we mean a form of music that totally ignores melody, indeed even makes fun of it, and is based on rhythm alone, rhythm which manifests itself principally in a cacophonous instrumental squawk that offends the ear. This alleged music is revolting, being in reality not music at all, but talentless and unimaginative juggling with notes. On the other hand, it must not be suggested that our grandparents' waltzes were the apex of musical development, and that nothing since then has been any good. Rhythm is fundamental to music. We are not living in the Victorian age [*'in der Biedermeierzeit'*], but in a century that takes its tune from the thousandfold humming of machines and roar of motors. Our war songs today are set to a different tempo from those of even the First World War. The radio people need to pay due attention to this, if they do not want to get left behind in the era of stiff-collars and frock-coats [*'beim Bratenrock stehenzubleiben'*]. This is not intended as a personal criticism of anyone in particular, yet we feel we have, all the same, a duty to respond to the justifiable demands of our fighting and toiling people in this respect.[32]

But try though Hinkel might to keep jazz off the German airwaves, hard-boiled Nazi fanatics were never satisfied. Norbert Salb, a retired Vienna publisher, put the standard argument to Hinkel on 18 July 1943:

> Jazz music is a Jewish-American invention, which one could call musical Bolshevism. We have to defend ourselves against Bolshevism in all its forms. Yet there is so much jazz on the radio that for years now the programmes have been grating on the ears of truly musical, German-feeling listeners. [...] But our protests have been fruitless! It seems, on the contrary, as though these Jewish cacophonies enjoy special promotion. [...] Considering the abundance of beautiful melodies by German composers there is really no need to borrow from Judaeo-Americans and from our misguided composers. Are we, the world's leading musical nation, to let ourselves be put to shame by the Japanese, who are by no means on a level with us musically, when, some six weeks ago, they quite simply banned the whole jazz spook from their East Asian hemisphere? [...] in the hope that you [Hinkel] will be able to cut off the head of this music hydra. You will be assured of the thanks of many millions of musical Germans.[33]

The Reich Dance and Entertainment Orchestra

As early as September 1941 Goebbels had taken the decision to establish a German

Dance and Entertainment Orchestra (*Reichsorchester für Unterhaltungsmusik*', the later *Deutsches Tanz- und Unterhaltungsorchester*, or DTU) to implement his ideas on musical quality and variety. On 29 September that year Leopold Gutterer, Goebbels' secretary of state, had informed Hinkel that this new orchestra was to have a status in popular music equivalent to that of the Berlin Philharmonic in the classical sector, and that Franz Grothe should be its Furtwängler. The orchestra's début concert was set for 29 October, though in the event rehearsals, at the Delphi Palast in Berlin, did not begin until 1 April 1942.[34]

A meeting in October 1941 to discuss the formation and funding of a 'forty-strong' state orchestra was chaired by Dr. Lucerna of the ProMi's finance department and attended by Franz Grothe, Georg Haentzschel, (the 'conductor designate'), and other musicians. Having agreed a budget allocation of 130,000 marks to fund the orchestra's first six months, the musicians went on to discuss questions of repertoire, instrumentation and personnel.[35] It was to be run as a commercial business, a limited company (*GmbH*) with a managing director, bookkeeper and requisite clerical staff. Dr. Hans Kunitz (1907–1969) was appointed the orchestra's first managing director, replaced in April 1942 by Sergius G. Safranow (*b.* 1898). Though Safranow's own father had been a conductor and composer, the boy, having lost his parents at an early age, was brought up by step-parents who decided he should train for a commercial career. As a side-line the enterprising young Safranow became consultant and promoter to several music publishers. He was appointed the German representative of Bosworth & Co., of London, and of other foreign publishers, as well as business manager of several German dance band leaders including Oscar Joost and Gerhard Hoffmann. In 1936 he joined the music publishers Meisel & Co. Two years later he was recruited by the CrescendoTheaterverlag to develop its dance and entertainment repertoire and, in 1939, put in charge of the Tauentzien publishing firm.

In October 1941 Grothe and Haentzschel were engaged by the *Deutsches Tanz- und Unterhaltungsorchester* at monthly salaries of 2,000 and 1,700 marks respectively, plus a bonus of 200 marks for each public or radio performance.[36] The two musicians had already drawn up a provisional list of candidates for the new orchestra, which, in full, gave forty-eight names:[37] Franz Grothe (*musical director*); Georg Haentzschel (*conductor*); Fritz Petz, Erich Puchert, Karl Kutzer (*trumpets*); Erhard Krause, Willy Berking, Walter Dobrzynski, Walter Krug (*trombones*); Franz Thon, Kurt Wege, Franz Kleindin, Helmut Friedrich (*saxophones*); Kurt Henneberg, Adalbert Luczkowski, Walter Leschetitzky, Helmut Zacharias, Gustav Klein, Kurt Senz, Adolf Linnartz, Friedrich Friebe, Alfons Hartmann, Ludwig Hörmann, Horst Rosewscy (*violins*); Hermann Hirschfelder, Willi Hanuschke, Karl Urahne, Hermann Däubner (*violas*); Helmut Steinmann, Fritz Buchwitz (*cellos*); Albert Vossen (*accordion*); Fritz Stamer, Franz Mück (*pianos*); Hans Korseck (*guitar*); Rudolf Wegener, Max Schönrade (*string-basses*); Waldemar Luczkowski, Hans Klagemann (*drums*); Friedrich Schröder, Ernst Fischer, Adolf Steimel, Friedrich Meyer, Horst Kudritzki, Werner Eisbrenner (*arrangers*); an addendum mentions Fritz Müller, Werner Ahlers, Detlev Lais and Horst R[amthor] as substitutes.

By the standards of the time this was an ambitious and comprehensive array of musical talent, and the selection a kind of 'wish list' addressed to Hans Hinkel. Many names on the surviving document appear to have been annotated by hand, presumably by Hinkel or a member of his staff: '*Soldat*' (soldier), '*Ostfront*' (Eastern Front), or, as in the cases of Erich Puchert and Erhard Krause, '*abgelehnt*' (rejected). The latter was probably excluded because he was married to an American.

Based on this list, with fresh names added for those that had fallen out after a first screening, letters were dispatched on 10 March 1942 to the UFA film company and to Berlin theatres and variety houses requisitioning the immediate release of the named musicians, or alternatives, under contract to them. Four days later the situation was assessed and minuted: 'Metropol theatre: Director Haenschke [*sic*] would also have been willing to release Hartmann if the ministry (probably section RV) had not already required the release of a number of other musicians'. Nollendorf theatre, on releasing trombonist Willy Berking from his contract: 'I again pointed out that it was totally pointless to resist, since the minister himself would intervene if required'. 'Scala: Herr von Garczynski tells us that he is prepared to let Herr Krause and also Herr Krug go, but that he must at all cost be permitted to keep Herr Hohenberger. He had already let the Berliner Künstlerfahrt. (front-tour by Berlin artistes) take Herr Stamer. Removing Herr Hohenberger would very seriously undermine the orchestra's performance. It should be noted in this connection that Hohenberger was only added to the DTU list in replacement for a musician who had been called up and whom we are at present unable to recall.'[38]

After long wrangles over the exclusivity clause, both Grothe and Haentzschel eventually signed their contracts on 27 March. By the first rehearsal, on 1 April, the DTU in fact consisted of Franz Grothe (*musical director*); Georg Haentzschel (*conductor*); Hendrik Bruyns, Karl Hohenberger (*trumpets*), Erich Puchert (*trumpet/violin*); Erhard Krause (*trombone*), Willy Berking (*trombone/saxophone*), Walter Dobrzynski (*trombone/string-bass*), Walter Krug (*trombone/guitar*); Herbert Müller, Helmut Friedrich, Detlev Lais, Hans Meyer (*saxophones/clarinets*); Kurt Henneberg (*concert master*); Adalbert Luczkowski, Gustav Klein, Kurt Senz, Friedrich Friebe, Alfons Hartmann, Fritz Müller, Gustav-Adolf Linnartz, and, from 23 May, Paul Richter (*violins*); Willi Hanuschke (*viola/violin*); Karl Urahne, Hermann Däubner (violas); Helmut Steinmann, Fritz Buchwitz (*cellos*); Albert Vossen (*accordion*); Franz Mück (*piano*); Erwin Gotschalk until 1 August 1942 and then Serge Matul for Gotschalk (*guitar*); Rudolf Wegener, Max Schönrade (*string-basses*); Hans Klagemann (*drums*), Waldemar Luczkowski (*percussion*); Horst Kudritzki, Adolf Steimel, Walter Leschetizky, Ernst Fischer (*arrangements*).[39]

Bruyns, Berking, Krause, Müller, Henneberg, Mück, Vossen and Matul were graded as 'top soloists' and employed at a salary of 1,500 marks per month; Puchert received 1,450 marks and Hohenberger, Dobrzynski, Krug, Friedrich, Lais, Luczkowski and Klagemann 1,400 marks each.[40] All became full-time employees of the *Deutsche Tanz- und Unterhaltungsorchester GmbH* 'on exclusive contracts which stipulate that they may only perform with this orchestra', and were classified as being '*unabkömmlich*' (indispensable) and thus exempt from military service.[41] Alto-saxophonist/clarinetist Teddy Kleindin testified that 'Because of their contracts with the RRG the DTU-musicians were not allowed to do any other work; though, with the daily rehearsals they just would not have had the time anyway'.

When the original target for the orchestra to begin broadcasting on 29 October 1941 proved unfeasible, the debut was changed to 1 June 1942, though the DTU was in fact christened with the performance of three pieces on 19 April as part of a radio series called '*Fortsetzung folgt*' ('To be continued'). Hinkel himself introduced the orchestra as a surprise for listeners on the eve of Hitler's birthday celebration.[42]

Regular broadcasts began on Saturday 1 August, at 22:30 hours, in the series 'Melody and Rhythm'. 'On the home service [*Reichsprogramm*] the German Dance and Entertainment Orchestra directed by Franz Grothe and Georg Haentzschel introduced itself to listeners for the first time with its own programme.'[43] Dr. Fritz Stege reviewed the performance in the following issue of *Das Podium*: 'The orchestra plays exclusively their own arrangements. Some of the best composers are writing technically challenging movements for them, with harmonic embellishments which approach the borders of modern art-music.'[44] Henceforth the DTU could be heard every fourth Saturday evening, and from 10 October the programme was repeated on Wednesday afternoons so that 'café musicians could have a chance to check the quality of the orchestra's performance. [...] No musician who wants to keep abreast of contemporary style can afford to miss the Wednesday programme.'[45]

The DTU performed in public for the first time in March 1943, at the Philharmonie in Berlin, with a concert in aid of the Winter Relief Work (*Winter-hilfswerk*), and gave its last public concert of the season on 24 April. Already however there were difficulties. Safranow complained about the indiscipline of the orchestra's two musical directors, while conceding that some of the musicians had objected to his own rigid management style. On 16 September the orchestra's second trumpeter, Karl 'Säckel' Hohenberger, was involved in an incident in Berlin. In a drunken state Hohenberger had attempted to persuade the pianist of the *Cantina Romana* restaurant to perform the Yiddish songs appreciated by German officers on the eastern front. When the owner intervened, Hohenberger pointed at the man's Party badge and shouted 'You can't be proud of that thing! Adolf Hitler is finished anyway!'[46] Hohenberger was arrested by the Gestapo and, in December, sent to Sachsenhausen concentration camp, pending trial for defeatism. (In June 1944, he was sentenced to two years penal servitude. In the general confusion at the end of the war he escaped from the camp, only to be shot dead by Soviet soldiers during a routine check.)

An internal report of a meeting with Safranow included the comment:

[...] a right dressing down would do the gentlemen of the orchestra a world of good. It's no news to me that musicians generally behave badly. However, I stand by my assertion that thirty musicians together in one place constitute a political danger spot. Nowhere do you find as much gossiping and grumbling as among musicians, especially when since 1939 – due to their regular evening duties – they have never been trained to understand (if they ever even knew) what it means, for example, to serve in the SA [Brownshirts]. So it is hardly to be wondered at if, in the whole orchestra, there is literally only a single Party member.

After the rehearsal hall in the building of the Reich Chamber of Theatre in Berlin was bombed, the DTU was transferred in November 1943 to Prague. There matters soon came to a head. Hinkel and other ProMi officials had complained that Grothe's and Haentzschel's individual preferences were predominating in the broadcast repertoire and both were dismissed, by letter, on 24 January 1944.[47] Late the following February they were replaced by the Budapest-born violinist Barnabás von Géczy (1897–1971) and the pianist Willi Stech (1905–1979) who, though a founder member of the *Goldene Sieben*, had acceptable Party credentials. Under von Géczy's direction, as might be expected, the violins were soon carrying the melody again in accordance with the ProMi's guideline, and discipline had been restored. A listing dated 14 September 1944 gives the following DTU personnel and instrumentation:

Barnabás von Géczy (*musical director*); Willi Stech (*1st conductor*); Franz Stolzenwald (*2nd conductor*); Hendrik Bruyns (*trumpet*), Curt Dillenberg (*trumpet/ violin/accordion*), Erich Puchert (*trumpet/violin*); Erhard Krause (*trombone*), Willy Berking (*trombone/saxophone*), Walter Dobrzynski (*trombone/string-bass*), Walter Krug (*trombone/guitar*); Herbert Müller, Helmut Friedrich, Detlev Lais, Hans Meyer (saxophones/clarinets), Hans Friedl (*saxophone/bass/accordion/guitar*); Kurt Henneberg (*concert master*); Adalbert Luczkowski, Gustav Klein, Friedrich Friebe, Alfons Hartmann, Fritz Müller, Gustav-Adolf Linnartz, Paul Richter, Erich Heinecke (*violins*); Rudolf Schanz (*violin/saxophone*); Willi Hanuschke (*viola/ violin*), Karl Urahne, Hermann Däubner (*violas*); Helmut Steinmann, Fritz Buchwitz (*cellos*), August Gerhardt (*cello/guitar*); Albert Vossen (*accordion*); Franz Mück (*piano*), Erich Kaschubec (*piano/accordion*); Serge Matul (*guitar*); Rudolf Wegener, Max Schönrade (*string-basses*); Hans Klagemann (*drums*); Waldemar Luczkowski (*percussion*); Georg Braun (*drums/violin*); Horst Kudritzki, Adolf Steimel, Ernst Fischer (*arrangements*).[48]

The imprisoned Hohenberger had been replaced by Curt Dillenberger, drafted in from a band directed by Rudi Rischbeck. Friedl, Heinecke, Schanz, Gerhardt, Kaschubec and Braun all joined in Prague. But even this line-up soon altered: five of the musicians (including the Russian-born guitarist, Matul) were called up for military service towards in end of the year and, in January 1945, Linnartz and Urahne were both hospitalized.[49] When the war ended and the Czechs regained control of their capital, the German musicians hid in their hotels until they found an opportunity to leave, in small groups, for an uncertain future in their occupied homeland.

Singin' to the Foe

The first recording known to have been made by the RRG for the specific purpose of introducing or leavening propaganda broadcasts beamed at enemy or neutral countries was a coarsely satirical and viciously anti-semitic rendering of the martial hymn 'Onward Christian Soldiers'.[50] This version of the Salvation Army favourite went by the title 'British Soldier's Song'. Though there is no entry for it in the surviving recording ledgers, we know from the diary of one of the musicians, guitarist Fred Dömpke, that the swing orchestra of Erhard Bauschke recorded it for Deutsche Grammophon on 11 October 1939. Unless it was included in a separate and as yet unidentified block of matrices, this may point to the unusual and secret nature of this session. The performance sounds stale, certainly not swinging. The record was released as record Number I in the RRG's Lyra label series. Whether it was actually broadcast, let alone monitored in Britain, is unknown.

The reverse side of 'British Soldier's Song' carries, for no very clear reason, a reissue of the title 'Could Be' (Lyra II), which was recorded by the Bauschke orchestra in May 1939 and released commercially on the Deutsche Grammophon and Polydor labels.

The title of the third record in the series is not known. Record Numbers IV to VII are sung in French to piano accompaniment. The label credits Pierre Lapaix with the music and lyrics, but does not mention the performers. From recordings of the same titles cut about the same time, and which survived for the best part of fifty years in Czech archives (*Archiv Českého Rozhhlasu*), it can be deduced that the German operatic baritone Karl Schmitt-Walter (*b.* 1900) was the vocalist, accompanied by Dr. Rosen at the piano.

Record Number XVII is the only side in the series known to have been sung in German. While Number XVII remains anonymous, Number XXVI is credited to 'Charlie and his Orchestra', a name that appears here for the first time and was to appear on almost every subsequent recording in the series. The name is a camouflage for the Lutz Templin orchestra, fronted by the crooner Karl 'Charlie' Schwedler, of whom we shall learn more later.

Birth of a Band

The nucleus of the Lutz Templin orchestra came into being in May 1935, when reed player Erhard 'Funny' Bauschke (1912–1945) took over (probably with the consent of the new régime) the leadership of James Kok's swing band. Rumanian-born Arthur 'James' Kok (1902–1976) was partly Jewish. It was he who, during a pre-war engagement of the British Jack Hylton dance orchestra at the Berlin Scala in May 1939, had presented the band leader with a wreath inscribed '*In defiance of all moustachioed critics – come back Maestro Hylton*', commemorating the death of German jazz – an action which earned him an immediate performing ban (*Spielverbot*). Deprived of his income, Kok was forced to emigrate.

From the spring of 1936 Bauschke and his orchestra recorded many sides for Deutsche Grammophon, though few of those were in any sense 'hot'. But when war broke out in 1939, ProMi officials invited him to provide the backing for 'British Soldier's Song'. A brief excerpt from one of the Bauschke band's pre-war commercial releases, '*Nachtexpress nach Warschau*' ('Overnight Express to Warsaw', 1937), was used in the ProMi's 1940 film-short, '*Tran und Helle hören fremd*' ('Tran and Helle listen to foreign broadcasts').[51] This was one of sixty-three sketches which, between

September 1939 and the autumn of 1940, German cinemas were required to show before the main feature. Directed by Johannes Guter, the sketch depicts two nice German kids, Tran (meaning 'dull, slow-witted'), played by Ludwig Schmitz, and Helle ('bright, smart'), played by Jupp Hussels, set out to enlighten the audience about Party doctrine and warn it of the dangers of enemy espionage, alcohol abuse, black-market dealings, the occult and similar offenses. They remind the public of the prohibition on listening to foreign broadcasts, and of the death penalty for the dissemination of information obtained in this way. Tran seeks to tune in to a foreign station while Helle advises against it on the grounds that (a) it is forbidden, (b) no 'good German' would do anything like that, (c) foreign stations only tell lies anyway, and (d) there is already plenty of good dance music to be heard on German radio. To emphasize the last point, a short excerpt of hot music is performed by an unnamed band: Erhard Bauschke's version of '*Nachtexpress nach Warschau*'.

Because the Bauschke band was frequently on tour and unavailable at short notice, the broadcasting authorities engaged the pianist Willi Stech to recruit an in-house dance and entertainment orchestra for use by the *Deutschlandsender* in its home service. About the same time the RRG invited Edmund Kötscher (1909–1990) to organize and direct an orchestra for use specifically with foreign-language broadcasts.[52]

Edmund Kötscher had been born in Berlin in April 1909. After a classical education, he moved into light entertainment, accompanying silent movies and writing musical scores for the burgeoning German film industry. In 1933–34 he was first violin and concert master of the orchestra at Berlin's Admirals-Palast, recording separately with a studio formation. When an engagement at the Hotel Excelsior, Berlin, fell through at the beginning of the war, Kötscher returned to the Admirals-Palast until approached by the RRG late in 1939.[53]

At the same time Ernst Wilhelmy, head of foreign-language productions in the KWS's foreign-language cultural broadcasts department, and one of the pioneers of the German short-wave system, had hired his nephew, the trumpeter Arnd Robert, to organize an occasional formation for radio work.[54] Arnd Robert came from a prosperous Berlin family and performed on the trumpet through inclination rather than necessity. Before the war he played with a group called 'The White Ravens' (*Die Weissen Raben*), performing in cafés and clubs, at cabaret evenings and benefit concerts in and around Berlin.[55] Robert may also have been the owner or manager of Arnds Bier-Bar, a popular watering-hole on Pariser Strasse at Olivaer Platz, Berlin-Wilmersdorf, where during the early years of the war, pianist-vocalist Bully Buhlan, drummers Ilja Glusgal (or Bobby Schmidt) and jazz-violinist Helmut Zacharias used to meet after closing time for a jam-session.

These radio bands were not fixed ensembles: the musicians, usually members of the Admirals-Palast orchestra known to Kötscher from his previous engagement, were hired only when needed. According to Teddy Kleindin, 'various musicians played with Kötscher; Heinz Munsonius was always there.' Tenor-saxophonist Lutz Templin was a regular member of these formations, and alto-player Teddy Kleindin used to sit in occasionally until he was called up in December 1939. Karl Kutzer and Otto Türksch (*trumpets*), Helmut Wernicke (*piano*), Paul Henkel (*bass*) and Meg Tevelian (*guitar*) were probably all regular members of these ensembles.

When Kötscher was himself called up in April 1940, Wilhelmy nominated Arnd Robert as his successor. Werner Bergold, the KWS production manager (*Oberspielleiter*), agreed, provided the decision was endorsed by the musicians themselves. But it was not: they did not think highly of Robert's ability as an orchestra leader, and preferred Lutz Templin. Robert received his call-up papers shortly afterwards, and Templin was duly entrusted with the leadership of the combination.

Lutz Templin and the Propaganda Cabaret

Thus the thirty-nine-year-old Templin, himself not even a Party member, became the unchallenged leader of the RRG's propaganda orchestra, an ensemble made up of the personnel of both the former Kötscher and Robert formations.[56] Lutz, known to his friends as 'Stumpie', was born Ludwig Templin in Düsseldorf on 18 June 1901. After apprenticeship to a goldsmith, he studied violin and composition. During the late 1920s and early 1930s Templin worked as violinist, tenor-sax and arranger for various dance-band leaders, including an engagement at St. Moritz-Bad around January 1932. On 12 April 1934, he applied for membership of the Reich Chamber of Music, giving the following details:[57]

Name: Templin, Ludwig
Professional Name: (Lutz)
Questionaire No.: 0185
License No.: 105.832   *Category*: II, Iᵃ
Address: ~~Berlin, Eislebenstra_e 16, W.50~~
            ~~W.15, Lietzenburgerstr. 7a~~, Augsburgerstr. 23
            ~~Wilmersdorf, ?Kärtnerstr 29~~
Date of Birth: 18/6/1901   *Place of Birth*: Düsseldorf   *Nationality*: Pr[ussian]
Religion: Catholic   *Aryan*: Yes   *Membership No. of the NSDAP*: –
Main Instrument: violin, composer
Other instruments: tenor sax, clarinet
Potential Employment: as above, dance
Married – Single – Divorced
Date of Membership Application: 12/4/34
Previous Engagements/Months: Radio, gramophone records, abroad, Kristall;
Palast 6; Carlton Bar 24; Cascade 5; Delphi Palast 4; Charlott Bar, Cologne 6.

During the summer of 1934, Templin played tenor-sax with Georg Nettelmann's Kristall recording orchestra.[58] In 1935, at the recommendation of Teddy Kleindin, he joined the orchestra led by violinist Ilja Livschakoff, replacing Otto Henkis, whose style was felt to be too old-fashioned. During the summer of 1936, when Livschakoff left for a long residency in Karlsbad, Czechoslovakia, most of the others, including Templin and Kleindin, remained in Berlin to enjoy the opportunities offered by the 1936 Olympics and the crowds it drew. Kleindin joined the pit orchestra at the Charlottenburg opera, before assembling a band for an engagement at the Atlantic-Bar, Berlin, and recalls that:

AUFNAHME

LUTZ TEMPLIN

33 Lutz Templin, a postwar advertising postcard from Polydor, 1949.

spielt auf Polydor Schallplatten

'Templin formed a small bar combination after I. Liv. had disbanded. He [Templin] replaced me at the Insel-Bar [*should be* Atlantic-Bar], because I had joined Emil Roosz for 2 months in Breslau followed by 2 months at the Westerland Trocadero.'[59] From about April until October 1937, the 'Ludwig Templin Quartett' and the 'Barkapelle Ludwig Templin' (of four Musicians) worked at the Atlantic-Bar.[60] At this time the Templin band probably included violinist and reed player Rudi Rischbeck and pianist Franz 'Baby' Neukum. After the war Templin recalled that for seven winter seasons he led his own formation at the Palast-Hotel in St. Moritz, Switzerland, during which time he and his wife Anni encountered many notable personalities, including Charlie Chaplin and the Prince of Prussia.[61]

By 1939, Templin was freelancing with several studio groups in Berlin, including the foreign-language service radio orchestra he was soon to lead. The arranger Friedrich Meyer, who worked with him from about March 1939, recalled of that period:

Then there was the war, and in the very early days a Herr Martin from the ProMi came along to the *Pension* where I was staying and asked: 'Would you like to record a title for us – the 'Siegfried Line' with the famous Lord Haw-Haw?'. And then along came Templin and said: 'Do the arrangement for me'. After that I was doing records with Franz Mück for a long time. [...] They let me pick what I liked. Schwedler took care of the lyrics [...] and got laughed at for it. He was just happy to get exemption and not to have to go and play soldiers. Charly Tabor gave him hell over his idiotic texts. [...] But the lyrics were quite good and we had a good laugh at the time.[62]

I wrote arrangements for Erhard Bauschke and his orchestra. Deutsche Grammophon had signed me. I was to arrange accompaniments and direct them. My stars were Mimi Thoma, Maria von Schmedes, Iska Geri, Joan Even [sic], Rudi Godden and Carmen Lahrmann, who used to do the [German] synch for Shirley Temple's voice. I did a series of recordings with the Danish singer Fine Ohlsen [sic]. Nothing but the latest American tunes. The Nazis would sell their Aryan souls when it came to exports. I even went on television with Fine Ohlsen [sic] at the Adolf-Hitler-Platz studios.

'Total' war began for me on September 1, 1939. I was tickling the ivories in theatres, accompanying Johannes Heesters and Lil Dagover. In February, 1940, Polydor renewed my contract. Under the name Friedrich Meyer-Gergs I made some swing-type recordings and wrote a lot of compositions for Hans Rehmstedt. The ProMi objected to a piano piece called '*Teufelchen*' ('Little Devil') that had a shot of Dixie sound, and Franz Lehèr had my treatment of '*Komm in den kleinen Pavillon*' banned on account of my taking liberties with it.

In 1941 Willy Berking introduced me to the pianist Willy Stech, who was departmental head at the RRG. He had got together a band of freelance musicians, and all composers who were anybody in the light muse's service took part. I was also allowed to put on some light-classical pieces. The Willy Stech orchestra's first programme was to go on the air during the winter of 1941–42.

About Lutz Templin: he blew a good tenor-sax on a number of recordings with Rehmstedt and Meyer-Gergs. And when he teamed up with Charly [sic] he got Franz Mück and me to work out the arrangements. I can't recall individual titles any more. I was allowed to choose what I liked, whether by Jews or not didn't matter, as long as the lyricists could do something with the material. I must have been doing arrangements for Templin right up to the time I got my Death-on-the-Field-of-Honour summons (22 June 1941).[63]

The Christening of 'Charlie'

On 4 January 1940, and every successive second Thursday at 02:30 GMT, the RRG broadcast on short wave for North America a series entitled 'Political Cabaret'. A memo from Dr.Timmler, the Foreign Ministry's liaison officer at the RRG, to Gerhard Rühle, head of Kultur-R, on 18 March, reveals that one Karl 'Charlie' Schwedler, had featured on the programme as a vocalist on several occasions. Schwedler and Templin must therefore have worked together on the cabaret programmes, known either as 'Charlie And His Gang' or 'Charlie's Political Cabaret', long before the earliest recordings of 'Charlie and his Orchestra', which themselves date from the autumn of that year. Their signature tune was Walter Kollo's '*Unter'n Linden*'.

Karl Emil Heinrich Schwedler, to give him his full name, was born in Duisburg on 13 August 1902. His father, Wilhelm August Emil Schwedler, was a plumber. Little is known of Schwedler's early life other than that he lived in Cologne until the end of the 1920s and moved to Düsseldorf in 1930. By November 1939, he was employed by the USA section of the Foreign Ministry's broadcasting department (Kultur-R), sharing an office with Georg von Lilienfeld, the first section head.[64] The Kultur-R budget for 1943 defined the scope of the section as: 'Coordination of broadcasts to the USA/cabaret broadcasts.'[65] In January 1940 it consisted of von Lilienfeld, Dr. Rieder, Dr. Anders (the German cover name of Professor Otto Koischwitz, the German-American Nazi propagandist) and Schwedler.[66]

Within the broadcasting department, Schwedler was termed a foreign-language employee (*Fremdsprachiger Mitarbeiter*), and by July 1942 was receiving a monthly salary of 489.80 marks.[67] His status brought him other privileges and indulgences. Norman Baillie-Stewart, in his autobiography, described Schwedler as a 'playboy':

One of my 'protectors' in the Foreign Office was Dr. Schernier, whose weakness was snobbery. Two of his playboys were Werner Plack [68] and Kalk [*sic*] Schwedler who were permitted to do almost anything they liked in the name of Germany and the Nazis throughout the war. They were given every facility to travel to neutral countries. There they stocked up with every conceivable commodity that was scarce or rationed in Germany – silk stockings, liquor, soap, chocolates, cigarettes, and so on.

Schwedler was perhaps the more colourful character of the two. He was, amongst other things, a crooner and his voice was often heard on musical broadcasts to England. His trips to neutral countries and to countries that had been recently occupied were for the alleged purpose of collecting the latest English dance music for his broadcasts [...] In fact he had received unprecedented benefits from the Nazis and both he and Werner Plack were permanently exempt from military service.

On the left breast of Schwedler's superlative silk shirts was a finely stitched coronet with the initials 'SS' [*sic*] underneath. On a finger of his left hand was a massive signet ring engraved with a bogus coat-of-arms. At times he even sported the Old Etonian tie until I mentioned the fact. Schwedler and Plack possessed charm and cheek that prevented anyone disliking them despite their scandalous behaviour. Both spoke excellent English.[69]

Top officials at the Foreign Ministry evidently held Schwedler in high esteem, and in September 1940 he was appointed to the so-called '*Einsatzgruppe* (task force) England', chaired by Rühle's deputy, Dr. Hans Schirmer. Even Ribbentrop was aware of Schwedler's propaganda work and seems to have appreciated his recordings, as reported by Dr. Timmler in a memo of 10 March 1941, detailing a meeting with the Foreign Minister:

34 Charly Tabor (*with trumpet*), Charlie Schwedler (*right*) and an unidentified female singer, at the microphone.

Further, I was able to bring to the Minister's notice the work which Kultur-R has been doing. He was particularly interested in what was being directed to North America and was clearly aware of the cabaret of which Herr Schwedler is the author, having listened to some of the records. In this connection, the Minister expressed a wish to have a record of the English song 'We Are Hanging Our Washings On The Siegfried-Line' [*sic*]. I believe that Lord Haw-Haw once glossed this song. It would be desirable if the recording could be obtained as quickly as possible.[70]

The general character of the cabaret broadcasts, and Schwedler's impact on them, may be judged from the reports of the BBC radio monitors. On 25 October 1939, the reports summarized an item on short-wave for North America as follows: [71]

WE ARE HANGING OUT OUR WASHING ON THE SIEGFRIED LINE: Sir Kingsley Wood went to Paris and there, between one good dinner and another, he allowed himself to be photographed on an old bus on which was an inscription: 'Evening Tours to Siegfried Line and beyond'. He listened in vain for patriotric cries of 'À Berlin! À Berlin!'. Maybe that dance tune as well as the charabanc [*sic*] in which Sir Kingsley Wood allowed himself to be photographed meant to be taken figuratively. If so we enjoy the talk without reserve.

The 11 January programme included a version of 'The Lambeth Walk', the hit from the popular 1938 musical, 'Me And My Girl': [72]

LAMBETH WALK – NEW VERSION:

At the great Maginot Line,
right opposite the Siegfried Line,
don't think it's talk,
they're doing the Lambeth Walk.
They dance together just like pals,
they're only dancing, they have no gals,
don't be surprised New York,
they're doing the Lambeth Walk.
Everything's free and easy,
clapping their hands and swing it,
Germans also sing it
Now lest you fight by any chance,
we thank you for the lovely dance.
Let the British shout and talk,
we're all doing the Lambeth Walk.

On 8 February, BBC monitors took down *verbatim* an entire 'Political Cabaret' broadcast:[73]

Song: 'Skits at Britain'.
The band played six dance tunes, some vocal, with straight announcements.
   At 02:55 the cabaret was announced. It began with [the] song 'Goody Goody', then 'Little Ditty' was announced, being verse to the same tune to the effect that when Winston Churchill spoke to the House of Commons last week, he was greeted with catcalls and booing. The Government now realise that the Empire is breaking to pieces in spite of their efforts and that they are sitting on a keg of dynamite.
   This was followed by two straight songs, then apparently, a skit of some sort, but interferences rendered it almost unintelligible. One of the 'wisecracks' related to the opening of US mail.
   Further musical items followed and finally there was another song, 'Jeepers Creepers', in which was introduced a verse to the effect that the British Minister of Air does not like Messerschmitts.

Two weeks later, on 22 February 1940, the monitors summarized another 'Political Cabaret':

Parodies on the 'Lambeth Walk' and 'Three Little Fishes' and a dialogue the tone of which may be gathered from the following extract:
Woman: I want to see the film 'The Lion has Claws'.
Man: I don't like animal films.
Woman: It's wonderful. All about England's struggle for world domination. England is fighting for you and me. We owe her a lot.

Man:	And she owes us three billion dollars –
Woman:	our law – our liberty –
Man:	and our declaration of independence.
Woman:	... My father came over in the 'Mayflower' –
Man:	mine came over in the steerage.
Woman:	... except for England. We are so lucky in many things. England and America have so much between them.
Man:	They have the Atlantic Ocean between them![74]

Their Kind of Music

It was long assumed that the 'Charlie' recordings featured hot jazz because the Templin orchestra included some of Europe's best jazz musicians. This is one of the myths surrounding these recordings. The music in this series was cleverly selected and arranged with a particular target audience in mind: the general public which regarded Paul Whiteman as the 'King of Jazz'. Hot jazz, even in the United States, was appreciated by a small minority only. The Nazi propagandists accordingly choose popular titles which were sufficiently Anglo-American to be mistaken for the real thing but not too advanced to cause listeners to switch off the radio.

About sixty per cent of all 'Charlie' titles were standards first published during the 1930s, with about fifteen per cent from the 1920s and another fifteen per cent more recently in the early 1940s. Nearly ninety per cent of all 'Charlie' recordings are American, usually songs from Broadway musicals and Hollywood movies. Only fifteen per cent may be termed jazz standards, and none of these thanks to German arrangers. In fact all 'Charlie' titles are heavily scored and leave little opportunity for improvisation. Only here and there is room left for an occasional solo. The result is pleasant swing music in the Dorsey Brothers, Harry James, Glenn Miller or Benny Goodman mould.

A lengthy memorandum heavily criticizing the Reich's propaganda efforts to the United States was written by the American-born broadcaster Edward Vieth Sittler, an ardent Nazi, in December 1942. In respect of the jazz content of German propaganda Sittler had this to say, using the series 'Dance Tunes and Cabaret' as a example:

> The 'Dance Tunes and Cabaret' programme is trying to build a bridge of jazz between Germany and America. The broadcast assumes that thousands of friendly disposed Americans have gathered round their loudspeakers to hear how in poor old Hunland they treasure the cultural legacy of Jewish-American jazz. 'Listen! We Germans can do it too!' is what the announcer seems to be saying. The choice of material would make you think you were in the heart of New York's black ghetto – well, a few years back, actually, as the latest hits have not yet filtered through to us barbarians.[75]

In January 1943 Sittler addressed an addendum to his superiors. The last part, headed 'Concerning Music Programmes' (*Etwas über Musiksendungen*), read as follows:

Music is a major ingredient of our broadcasts, not merely in terms of airtime, but also as propaganda. Music is more of a German thing than English or American. But this is no longer so the moment jazz turns up. Jazz is an expression of the American and British way of life, and has little in common with the German mentality. It is therefore wrong to cram German overseas broadcasts with transplanted jazz music. We cannot possibly perform this decadent 'hot' jazz as 'well' as Negroes and Jews, and this is a question of more than just a lack of technical virtuosity. Imitating, or wanting to imitate, this kind of music and the life-style that goes with it is an unconscious form of sabotage of the German propaganda effort. Anyway, Americans actually want to hear 'German' music. [...] Broadcasts of light entertainment and dance music should consequently consist of purely German pieces, without endeavouring to sound 'New-Yorky'.[76]

But, according to a report in the *Daily Express* of 11 September 1944, quoted in a so-called impact report by Eduard Dietze, the British audience seems to have liked the music:

The musical part of his [William Joyce's] programmes was excellent, but his sour insertions of mockery and threats [...], and other attempts at intimidation merely proved irritating interruptions.[77]

The Charlie Orchestra: Personnel and Instrumentation

The membership of the Templin orchestra fluctuated considerably, and cannot be precisely known. As the war progressed the pool of Berlin-based musicians from which both Lutz Templin, for foreign-language broadcasts on short wave, and Willi Stech, for broadcasts on the *Deutschlandsender*, could draw dwindled. According to Teddy Kleindin, who worked frequently for both leaders, the pool included Templin's stalwarts, the pianist Primo Angeli and the drummer Fritz Brocksieper.

Several of the German musicians were exempt from military service: the bass player, Otto Tittmann, for example, was a diabetic. Others were called up but stationed locally and thus able to come into the city to join friends for musical evenings at a night club, at the *Funkhaus*, or in a recording studio. Kleindin, for example, was stationed at Döberitz, on the outskirts of Berlin, for most of the war, and able to slip away and join Templin and Stech for broadcasting or recording dates, including several sessions with a studio formation under his own name. When on leave from the front musicians were also happy to augment the Templin orchestra in order, as Kleindin recalled, 'to forget it all'. In terms of personnel the Templin and the Stech formations came to be almost identical, the main difference between them being the kind of music they played. The Templin band played jazz-inclined music and swing arrangements in the mornings. During the afternoons most of the players regrouped with string musicians in another studio to play, under Stech, the standard repertoire of German dance and entertainment music for home consumption. The duplication even went as far as Templin's directing the Stech orchestra at the *Deutschlandsender*, when it was due to perform one of his own compositions.[78]

As more and more German musicians went into the forces or were requisitioned by other state organizations, notably the *Deutsche Tanz- und Unterhaltungsorchester* (DTU), the few remaining band leaders in Berlin, including Templin and Stech, began to hire foreign musicians to fill the vacancies. By the autumn of 1943, the Templin orchestra numbered only four Germans, other than its leader. First-class Italian jazz formations had played in Berlin before the war, and later other Italian bands, such as that of tenor-saxophonist Tullio Mobiglia, visited Berlin. After the German occupation of the Netherlands and Belgium in May 1940, entire orchestras were compulsorily contracted ('*dienstverpflichtet*') to provide the quality light entertainment that was then officially approved. These foreign orchestras provided Germany's state-established band leaders with a much needed source of musical talent. And some Italian, Dutch and Belgian musicians found it impossible to resist the good salaries and relatively privileged life on offer to jazz musicians in Berlin, and joined the German propaganda apparatus by way of its radio orchestras. The Italian trumpeter, Nino Impallomeni, later recalled that Templin paid him sixty marks for a broadcast or recording session – considerably more than the going rate with one of the bar ensembles.[79]

Hans Hinkel, however, the self-appointed warden of Aryan culture, was not comfortable with the RRG's policy on the employment of foreign musicians and orchestras. In April 1942, when the Belgian tenor-saxophonist Fud Candrix's hot combo was performing at Berlin's Delphi-Palast, the KWS broadcast sections of its programme on 'Germany Calling', complete with political commentary by William Joyce and the customary greetings of British PoWs to families and friends at home.[80] At the broadcasting planning meeting on 13 May 1942 Hinkel raised the matter with his colleagues:

> Means should be agreed with the Short-Wave Station for finding and engaging German musicians for unavoidable music programmes, instead of employing foreign bands like the one directed by Fud Candrix, which openly play hot music of a kind that we would never tolerate in the air.[81]

Lutz Templin, however, remained secure of support at the highest level. When the *Reichsintendant* and director-general of the RRG, Heinrich Glasmeier, raided the already depleted symphony orchestras of the regional broadcasting stations to furnish musicians for his Reich Bruckner Orchestra, the question of disbanding the regional radio orchestras altogether was raised. But Goebbels ruled in their favour, and indicated that the requisitioned players should instead be replaced by 'new musicians from Flanders, Holland, France, Norway and the *Generalgouvernement* [i.e. German-occupied Poland outside the Reich]'.[82]

The basic formation of Templin's orchestra – thirteen or fourteen players – was occasionally augmented by a soloist or string set, taken from the musicians whom Willi Stech regularly employed at the *Deutschlandsender*. 'The violinists suitable for this type of work were, besides Helmut Zacharias, Bruno Sänger as concert-master, [Ernst] Zeebe, [Karl 'Carlo'] Hönsch among others, at that time from the orchestra at the Scala or the opera.'[83] Helmut Zacharias had been called up in 1941 but was stationed near Berlin and able to travel to town for broadcasts and recordings until 1942, when he was transferred to Hilversum in the Netherlands.

The surviving recording ledgers contain little information on personnel. And the musicians themselves, in particular the foreigners, being seen as Nazi collaborators, were understandably reticent about this phase of their careers. But there are several pointers which help to establish the personnel of the Templin orchestra with reasonable certainty. The German singer and dancer Evelyn Künneke (b. 1921) recalled that: 'All the musicians in the Charly-gang [sic] − I'm thinking specially of for instance the Czech trombonist Ferri Juza, of Meg Tevelian, the Armenian guitarist, and also Detlev Lais und Kurt Abraham − they were all masters of their craft, real "hot" specialists.' Künneke toured the battle fronts with an entertainment unit until arrested by the Gestapo over casual remarks she was reported to have made. In January 1945 a summary court found her guilty of 'defeatism and denigrating of the fighting troops'. Her release was engineered by an SS-officer admirer who claimed she was urgently required for a propaganda recording of Ella Fitzgerald's 'My Guy's Come Back'.[84] But the recording never took place and instead Evelyn Künneke was attached to the SS-*Standarte Kurt Eggers*, the propaganda unit of the SS.

Künneke herself never recorded with the 'Charlie' orchestra, which she described as consisting 'mainly of Italian, Belgian and Czech musicians; there were even half-Jews and Gypsies there, Freemasons, Jehovah's Witnesses, homosexuals and Communists − not exactly the type of people the Nazis normally wanted to play cards with. But because their work was classified as being important for the war effort, they sat at music-stands in Berlin, and not behind barbed wire, and made swing.'

Like Templin and Stech, Deutsche Grammophon drew on this same small reservoir of 'hot' musicians in Berlin. In December 1940 and January 1941, Templin's arranger, Friedrich Meyer, recorded several sides for Deutsche Grammophon with a studio formation. Meyer reported the orchestra's personnel as follows: Alfredo Marzaroli (*trumpet*), unidentified (*trombone*); Benny de Weille (*clarinet/alto-sax*), Eugen Henkel (*tenor-sax*), Mario Balbo (*alto-sax*); Willy Berking (*accordion*); Primo Angeli (*piano/celesta*); Meg Tevelian (*guitar*), Cesare Cavaion (*string-bass*), Fritz Brocksieper (drums).[85] These were all musicians working also for Lutz Templin at the time. When Deutsche Grammophon reinstated its Brunswick label and invited Templin's favourite drummer to do a series of recording sessions, Brocksieper organized his studio combinations as a band-within-the-Templin-orchestra. He also insisted on his session musicians being individually credited on record labels, a convenience in terms of identifying members of the Templin orchestra.

The DTU had requisitioned three musicians from the Short-Wave Station: the trumpeter Karl Hohenberger, as well as the reed players Helmuth Friedrich and Detlev Lais. Other musicians were contracted from other organizations, trombonist Willy Berking from the Theater am Nollendorfplatz, trombonist Erhard Krause from the Scala, violinists Kurt Henneberg, Willi Hanuschke, Waldemar Luczkowski and

35 The Ernst van 't Hoff orchestra on stage in Dresden.

Hermann Steinmann from the UFA film company, and violinist Gustav Klein from the Volksoper; other members of the DTU were pianist Franz Mück and bass-player Rudi Wegener.[86] So after 1 April 1942, when the newly formed DTU commenced rehearsals, none of these musicians was available to play with Templin – or any other formation for that matter, and replacements had to be found.

In some cases musicians were acquired from the ranks of other formations which failed or were deliberately disbanded. One such was the band founded in autumn 1940 by the Dutch pianist Ernst van 't Hoff.[87] This group, which opened with engagements at the Eden Hotel, Dresden, and the Delphi-Palast in Berlin, was widely seen as one of the most superior swing orchestras of its time: 'The Band played with a dragging rhythm and cracking 'Tuttis' of the kind which was then favoured by the most advanced American swing orchestras, especially the generally highly esteemed Artie Shaw'.[88]

In April 1942 the security branch of the Gestapo accused Ernst van 't Hoff of 'having played "wild", that is to say Jewish hot music to the displeasure of the audience' during an engagement at the Hindenburgbau in Stuttgart, and demanded that his orchestra be banned by the Reich Chamber of Music. Van 't Hoff may have come to the notice of the Gestapo a few weeks earlier when some members of his orchestra, at the invitation of the (illegal) Berlin Melody Club, participated in a jam session at the Delphi-Palast.[89] The Chamber of Music did not accept the Gestapo's interpretation, however, pointing out that 'the location was always packed'.[90] But van 't Hoff was arrested in Stuttgart and his orchestra folded.[91] Several former members of his 1942 orchestra then joined Templin in Berlin – either voluntarily or under some persuasion. Trumpeter Rimis van den Broek apparently went back to the orchestra he had already

36 The Lutz Templin orchestra, 1942.

worked and recorded with in the autumn of 1940, bringing with him trumpeter Herman 'Herre' Jager, trombonist Folke Johnson, reed-player Tinus Bruijn and pianist Joop 'Tip' Tichelaar. Bass-player Otto 'Titte' Tittmann had joined the Templin orchestra in April, replacing Rudi Wegener who had left for the DTU. He recalled that:

When the *Deutsche Tanz- und Unterhaltungsorchester* was going to be set up in Prague[92], many good musicians left Berlin. Two bass players were in line for it: Rudi Wegener, my predecessor with Templin, and myself. As I wanted to stay in Berlin, I teamed up with Templin's band at the Short-Wave Station on April 1, 1942. We were on duty five days per week, from nine in the morning till noon. We did broadcasts for the Anglo-American area, plus South America and South Africa. We came under the Propaganda Ministry.[93]

A rare photograph of the orchestra provided an opportunity to identify its members. Teddy Kleindin and trombonist Jos Breyre examined the image at different times, and a collation of their evidence suggests the following as the orchestra's leading players in 1942: Alfredo Marzaroli, Rimis van den Broek, Tip Tichelaar, possibly Herre Jager (though not in the photograph) (*trumpets*); Jos Breyre, Henk Bosch, Folke Johnson, Josse Beeckmans (*trombones*); Erich Kludas, Kurt Wege, Teddy Kleindin, Bob van Venetië, possibly Tinus Bruijn (*reeds*); Primo Angeli (*piano*, not in photograph); Meg Tevelian (*guitar*); Frando Chrpa (*string-bass*); Fritz Brocksieper (*drums*).

Jos Breyre could not recall the name of Folke Johnson, whom he identified as 'Swiss or Swedish', while Kleindin could not remember the name of Josse Beeckmans. Breyre mistakenly identified Teddy Kleindin as Detlev Lais, and gave the name of the fourth reed-player as Cor Koblens, but Kleindin was adamant that the person on the photograph was Bob van Venetië. Breyre named the bass-player 'Frand, a Czech'.

With the exception of Erich Kludas and Kurt Wege – who according to Kleindin were under contract to Otto Stenzel at the Scala and had little time for outside engagements – this line-up of musicians is identical with that of the Lutz Templin orchestra at the same time. Jos Breyre dated the photograph 'about 1941', but it was probably taken after that. The inclusion of Rimis van den Broek and Tip Tichelaar, who are known to have joined Templin in May 1942, and the absence of any DTU members, suggest a date after May 1942. According to Kleindin, the photograph was taken during a recording session in a nearby warehouse, used as a store for mattresses:

> When the DTU was set up, it claimed all studios for rehearsals, and Stech was made to move out of the *Rundfunkhaus*. So, we ended up in this store for mattresses next to the *Funkhaus*.[94]

The next date at which the personnel can be positively identified is in November 1943, when Templin photographed them at Jos Breyre's wedding. Both Jos Breyre and Teddy Kleindin independently identified the following:

Alfredo Marzaroli, Nino Impallomeni (*trumpets*); Henk Bosch, Jos Breyre, Robby Zillner (*trombones*); Jean Robert, Francesco Paolo Ricci, Bob van Venetië, Mario Balbo, Renato Carneval (*reeds*); Primo Angeli (*piano*); Max Gursch (*guitar*); Otto Tittmann (*string-bass*); Fritz Brocksieper (*drums*).

In addition Teddy Kleindin recalled other excellent players who passed through the ranks of the Templin orchestra:

37 Members of the Lutz Templin band attending the wedding of Jos Breyre, November 1943.

Cuban trumpeter Fernando Diaz and Czech trombonist Ferri Juza; tenor-saxophonist Eugen Henkel; "[...] not forgetting 'Wernimäuschen' Neumann. [...] Initially Paul or Kurt Henkel was the bass-player. He was killed in the first air-raid on Berlin.[95]

The likely make-up of the Templin orchestra can be refined by eliminating musicians who are known not to have played in any of its formations. Kleindin comments:

> [Trumpeter] Karl 'Säckel' Hohenberger *never* played in the Templin orchestra. They may have played together earlier, somewhere. – But I say 'no': K. Hohenberger did not belong to this gang. [Trombonist] R. Zillner was not a member of the orchestra as long as I played with L. Templin at the European Station, Berlin. I suppose he was with the L.T. orchestra when it was transferred to Stuttgart – see the photograph. Tenor-saxophonist Detlev Lais only guested in the Templin orchestra at a few recording sessions but never participated in any broadcasting work. [Alto player and clarinetist] Kurt Wege never blew in the Templin orchestra. Baldo Maestri – never – as long as Benny de Weille was a member of the Templin orchestra or I led the sax-set. Never.[96]

The tenor-saxophonist and clarinetist Kurt Abraham is sometimes mentioned as a member of the Templin orchestra; but in an autobiographical sketch compiled for the Frankfurt jazz fan and promoter Alexander Loulakis, Abraham listed the many formations he had played with, including those where he substituted. None of them was directed by Lutz Templin.[97]

According to some sources, accordionist Albert Vossen occasionally augmented the Templin orchestra before 1 April 1942, when he joined the DTU. Teddy Kleindin, who took the trouble to listen to representative samples of most recording sessions, and comment on the instrumentation and soloists, was adamant: 'Albert Vossen was *never* a member of the L. Templin orchestra, not even as a soloist'.

Putting together the information from each source – photographic and documentary evidence, interviews and audio checks – the following picture of the membership of the Lutz Templin orchestra seems as definitive as possible (*see* Chart 6 opposite).

'Charlie's' Musicians

The basic instrumentation of the Templin orchestra included three trumpets:
Marinus 'Rinus', called 'Rimis', van den Broek came from the province of Friesland in northern Holland. In 1938 he travelled with a friend, the clarinetist and alto-saxophonist Kees Verschoor, to Amsterdam where both joined the *Rhythm Sheiks* of American pianist Eddie Oliver at the Carlton Hotel. Van den Broek remained with this formation when it was taken over by violinist Jascha Trabsky, after Oliver's return to the United States, and then joined Jack de Vries' *Internationals*. During the summer of 1940, van den Broek featured in the band of German refugee 'Secco' Selichson – a violinist from Berlin whose real name was Hans Michael Seligsohn. Following this engagement, van den Broek joined the Lutz Templin orchestra in

	Autumn 1940	1941	Mid-1942	1943
1rst trumpet	Rimis van den Broek	Nino Impallomeni *or* Rimis van den Broeck	Rimis van den Broek *or* Nino Impallomeni	Nino Impallomeni
2nd and 3rd trumpets	Charly Tabor *and/or* Fernando Diaz *and/or* Helmuth Friedrich *and/or* Fritz Petz	Charly Tabor *and/or* Alfredo Marzaroli *and/or* Fernando Diaz *and/or* Helmuth Friedrich *and/or* Fritz Pietz	Alfredo Marzaroli *and/or* Herre Jager *and/or* Tip Tichelaar	Alfredo Marzaroli E. Schmidt-Schulz
trombone	Willy Berking *and/or* Henk Bosch *and/or* Ferri Juza	Willy Berking *and/or* Jos Breyre *and/or* Henk Bosch *and/or* Ferri Juza	Jos Breyre *and/or* Henk Bosch *and/or* Josse Beeckmans *and/or* Folke Johnso	Jos Breyre *and/or* Robby Zillner
tenor-sax/clarinet	Mario Balbo	Mario Balbo *and/or* Francesco Paolo Ricci	Mario Balbo *and/or* Francesco Paolo Ricci *and/or* Jean Robert	Mario Balbo
tenor-sax	*and/or* Bob van Venetië *and/or* Eugen Henkel	*and/or* Bob van Venetië *and/or* Eugen Henkel *and/or* Detlev Lais	*and/or* Bob van Venetië	Bob van Venetië
clarinet/alto-sax alto-sax/clarinet	Benny de Weille *and/or* Teddy Kleindin	Benny de Weille *and/or* Teddy Kleindin *and/or* Cor Koblens *and/or* Tinus Bruijn	Benny de Weille *and/or* Cor Koblens *and/or* Teddy Kleindin	Renato Carneval
piano	Franz Mück	Franz Mück *or* Primo Angeli *or* Werner Neumann	Primo Angeli *or* Tip Tichelaar	Primo Angeli
guitar	Meg Tevelian Cesare Cavaion *or* Paul Henkel	Meg Tevelian Rudi Wegener	Meg Tevelian Otto Tittmann *or* Frando Chrap	Max Gursch Otto Tittmann
string-bass				
drums	Fritz Brocksieper	Fritz Brocksieper	Fritz Brocksieper	Fritz Brocksieper
plus as required strings accordion				Walter „Jacky" Leschetizky / Bruno Sänger / Ernst Zeebe / Karl „Carlo" Hönsch Walter Munsonius

Chart 6: Charlie Orchestra Personnel

Berlin until transferring, late in December 1940, to the newly formed Ernst van 't Hoff orchestra, continuing to augment the Templin formation for recording work whenever possible. He rejoined the Templin orchestra on a more permanent basis around May 1942.

Milan-born Giuseppe 'Nino' Impallomeni (1917–1994) replaced Rimis van den Broek as Lutz Templin's regular first trumpeter in 1941, alternating with the Dutchman whenever the latter was in town. During the 1930s, Impallomeni had been a member of the *Nuovo Ritmo* band under the direction of bass-player Michele d'Elia, after which he had joined the hot combination of Italian accordionist Kramer Gorni. According to Italian discographies, Impallomeni recorded in Italy until mid-1941.[98]

Karl 'Charly' Tabor (*b*. Vienna, 1920) was Templin's regular second trumpeter until mid-1942. In 1940 Tabor had been a member of the Berlin Carlton Club band which included trombonist Willy Berking, pianist Franz Mück and drummer Fritz Brocksieper: Templin hired all three. Tabor frequently played and recorded with the Templin orchestra until he was called up on 21 May 1942. Later he occasionally sat in when on home leave.

In April 1941, Alfredo Marzaroli came to Berlin with the combo of Italian tenor-saxophonist Tullio Mobiglia for residencies at the Patria and Rosita Bars. He worked additionally for Lutz Templin, in whose radio orchestra he shared the position of second trumpeter with Charly Tabor from mid-1941. (Marzaroli had earlier visited Berlin, with the band of violinist Nanni dal Della, in 1938.)

Helmuth Friedrich, Fritz Petz and Fernando Diaz probably alternated on second and third trumpet, when one of the key players was unavailable, from about 1940 until 1941–42.

Enrique Rivero was the original trumpeter with the *Lecuona Cuban Boys* until 1934. 'In his place we got a Cuban whom we met in Spain, Fernando Diaz – an excellent musician, and very useful for us, as he could not only play the trumpet, but also the saxophone, the guitar and the violin.' During a booking in Berlin, Diaz fell in love with a German girl and stayed on to live with her. 'Later on we heard that Hitler put him in the military band of Berlin, as first trumpeter. It is true that he lost his life in San Pablo [São Paulo], Brazil, through jealousy.'[99]

In May 1942 several Dutchmen from the van 't Hoff orchestra, including Herre Jager and Tip Tichelaar, augmented the depleted roster of Templin musicians. Trumpeter and accordionist Hermanus 'Herre' Jager (1912–1973) had begun his career as a professional musician in January 1935 when he joined the band aboard the liner *Costa Rica* which operated on a regular shuttle between the Netherlands and South America. By April 1938 he was playing second trumpet under the direction of Pi Scheffer in the *Blue Ramblers*, which then included tenor-saxophonist Bob van Venetië. Tichelaar joined the orchestra as alternate pianist but stepped in as third trumpeter whenever his services were required.

The orchestra included two trombonists to whom a third was occasionally added when called for by the arrangement:

Initially Willy Berking (1910–1979) was Lutz Templin's favourite trombonist. He was born, like Templin, in Düsseldorf, and besides being one of Germany's best swing musicans, was also a competent arranger and composer. Berking had been selling musical arrangements and instruments in Düsseldorf until 1930, when a regular customer, bandleader Eddie Dittke, invited him to join his *Royal Syncopators*. Berking initially joined as a pianist in the Dittke band but as Dittke himself was a pianist he soon took up the trombone, which was to become his standard instrument. Berking left the *Royal Syncopators* in the summer of 1932 to join the José Wolff orchestra. Two years later he joined Heinz Wehner who was then augmenting his swing orchestra for a first Berlin engagement, at the Europa-Pavilion. In addition Berking recorded with the enlarged formation of the *Goldene Sieben* whenever his services where required. During the early 1940s he was a member of the orchestra directed by Erhard Bauschke, and from there linked up with Lutz Templin. Berking worked regularly for Templin until March 1942, when he joined the *Deutsches Tanz- und Unterhaltungsorchester*.

Hendrik 'Henk' Bosch (*b*. Amsterdam, 1903), a former member of Melle Weersma's *Red, White and Blue Aces*, was second trombonist. Bosch had an active performing career in Germany before the war, including an engagement with Oskar Joost.

Templin's alternate trombonist during the early months was the Czech Ferri Juza, a regular member of the Willi Stech orchestra at the *Deutschlandsender*. Before the war, Juza had toured with the Italian band of John Abriani until the latter returned to his native Italy.

In the autumn of 1941, Joseph 'Jos' Breyre (1902–1995) – born in Malmedy, then part of Germany – joined the Templin orchestra from a return engagement with the van 't Hoff orchestra at the Delphi, sharing first trombone with Willy Berking. Breyre had already subbed in the Templin orchestra during the first Berlin engagement of the van 't Hoff orchestra, in the spring of that year. Breyre was one of the Templin orchestra's most accomplished musicians. After seven years in the Belgian army, he embarked on a jazz career, eventually playing in the orchestra directed by Gus Deloof. In 1932 he joined the *Internationals* of Dutch trombonist Jack de Vries and, three years later, returned to Belgium and joined the Fud Candrix orchestra, followed by an engagement with Stan Brenders. From 1937 until the summer of 1939, Breyre was a member of the French Ray Ventura orchestra, then one of Europe's leading dance orchestras.

In September 1939, Breyre replaced Billy Burns in the orchestra led by alto-saxist/clarinetist Willie Lewis at the Tabaris in The Hague. At that time he was the only white musician in this all-American formation. In January 1940, the Dutch authorities informed the Tabaris management that it should employ at least eight Dutch nationals. Since the Willie Lewis band included only one Dutchman, the pianist Joop Tichelaar, he, together with the Tabaris' second band, a local tango formation of six, made a combined total of seven nationals. As a result Breyre was let go: he joined the Joe Andy orchestra, followed by a stint with drummer Nico de Vries' *Rascals*, from where he linked up with the van 't Hoff orchestra at the end of 1940.

When Jos Breyre succeeded Berking as the band's regular first trombonist, two new trombonists joined the roster of Templin musicians: the Swede Folke Johnson from the van 't Hoff orchestra, and Josse Beeckmans, a Belgian, who joined from a tour with the Jean Omer orchestra. By 1943, Alois Robert 'Robby' Zillner (*b*. Starnberg, 1900) was the regular trombonist. Before the war Zillner had been sideman in several name bands, including those led by Eric Borchard, Ben Berlin, René Dumont, Joe Bund, Hans Busch and Peppi Schuber.

Templin included four players on reed instruments, occasionally augmented by a guest soloist:

Clarinettist/alto-saxophonist Bernhard 'Benny' de Weille (1915–1977) was a regular member of the orchestra from its beginnings until some time in 1942 or 1943. De Weille was born to a Dutch father and a German mother in Lübeck, Germany, and attended school in Hanover. Beginning as a piano student he continued his musical education at a conservatory where he discovered his love for 'hot' music, and the saxophone became his favourite instrument. Around 1931 the family settled in Amsterdam: de Weille took clarinet lessons with Hans Helmke and was, for some time, a member of the famous *Concertgebouw Orchestra*. De Weille seems to have given up classical music altogether in 1935 when he joined the *Adventurer*s, a small formation directed by Dutch trumpeter Louis Bannet. In the autumn of 1937, he came to Berlin, where he replaced Eugen Henkel in the Teddy Stauffer orchestra towards the end of its engagement at the Femina. At the end of the 1937–8 winter season in St. Moritz, de Weille briefly returned to the Netherlands and augmented a hot combination at the Tabaris, which included Eddy Meenk on trumpet and tenor-saxophonist/violinist Jascha Trabsky, before returning to Berlin. After engagements in Belgium, the Netherlands and London, the Stauffer orchestra returned to Berlin where de Weille, in November 1938, finally resigned. He remained in Berlin and became one of the capital's most sought-after studio musicians. As a foreigner he intially had difficulty being recognized by the Reich Chamber of Music, appealing to its president on 3 March 1939: 'You will understand that I am severely handicapped in my work, because I have to apply for your permission for every little extra job.'[100] As late as September 1939, de Weille was still listed, by the Kristall-Schallplatten company, among the foreign musicians who had participated in session work during August and September 1939.[101]

Another important member of the Templin orchestra was alto-saxophonist/clarinetist Franz 'Teddy' Kleindin (*b*. Berlin, 1914). He and Templin had first met as members of the Ilja Livschakoff orchestra during 1935–36. Kleindin had been a member of the Teddy Stauffer orchestra from March 1937 – which accounts for his nickname – and from December 1938 was a member of the orchestra directed by Heinz Wehner. He was called up for military service at the beginning of 1939, but when his medical examination revealed a perforated ear-drum he was sent home. Between April and December 1939, when he was drafted into the army and stationed at Guben for basic training, Kleindin was a member of the 'hot' combo directed by Kurt Hohenberger. Because of his ear condition, however, he was soon transferred to a training unit (*Lehrregiment*) at Döberitz, on the outskirts of Berlin, from where he was able to slip away and cycle into the city to join friends for a jam session or a recording date. Until June 1941, when his unit was transferred to the eastern front,

Kleindin frequently augmented the Templin orchestra for broadcasts, usually as leader of the sax-set when Benny de Weille was not available, but rarely played on recording dates.

When Kleindin ceased to be regularly available, the Dutch members of the orchestra contacted their fellow-countryman Cornelis 'Cor' Bernadus Koblens – *not* Koblenz – (1911–1942), an experienced radio musician, and persuaded him to come to Berlin. Koblens had been a member of the *AVRO-Dansorkest*, the dance orchestra of the Dutch AVRO broadcasting station, from its foundation in the spring of 1936 until it was disbanded in December 1939. Koblens fell to his death from a balcony during a drinking bout late in 1942.[102]

By this time another Dutchman, alto-saxophonist/clarinetist Tinus Bruijn (*b.* Wormerveen, 1914), had joined the Templin orchestra after an engagement with the van 't Hoff orchestra. He had previously been a member of Jack de Vries' *Internationals.* During the summer of 1939, Bruijn linked up with John Fresco for an engagement at the Kurhaus-Foyer, Scheveningen, from where he rejoined the *Internationals* until 1941, when it disbanded.

Ultimately, Renato Carneval became the orchestra's regular alto-saxophonist during its final phase.

Mario Balbo, the band's first tenor-saxophonist, had toured with John Abriani. He remained in Germany, joining Templin in the autumn of 1940, and staying until its final days in 1945. The second tenor-saxophonist/clarinetist was a Dutchman, Barend Johan 'Bob' van Venetië (1916–1966). During the spring of 1938 van Venetië had been a member of Pi Scheffer's *Blue Ramblers*, which then included Herre Jager on trumpet. Later that year, he joined the *Golden Stars* of Dutch bass-player, Will Hildering, at La Gaité, the dance-restaurant at the Tuschinski Theatre in Amsterdam. During the spring of 1939, van Venetië was with Eddy Meenk's *Sweet Music* at the House of Lords in The Hague. At the time he joined the Templin orchestra, in April 1941, he was living in Berlin and studying to become a singer. In the Templin orchestra van Venetië alternated with the Italian Francesco Paolo Ricci of the Mobiglia band. Eugen Henkel (1909–1978), who, in spite of having only one Jewish grandparent, was classified by the Nazis as a 'half-Jew', also occasionally subbed during the orchestra's early years.[103]

Around July 1942, Templin was joined by the Belgian multi-instrumentalist, Jean Mathieu Joseph Robert (1908–1981). After Jos Breyre, Robert had the most international experience of all Templin's players. His favourite instrument was the tenor-sax, but he was equally at home on bass-saxophone, piano, clarinet, trombone and trumpet.

As a student Robert was inspired by the Belgian jazz pioneer, Peter Packay. He began in 1927 as a jazz pianist, but soon switched to trombone. Subsequently he played and recorded with many Belgian jazz bands, including those of Gus Deloof, Charles Remue and Robert de Kers. In Amsterdam after February 1938, Robert played first with the band of Jascha Trabsky, which then included Rimis van den Broek on trumpet, and then with the hot trio directed by Afro-American pianist Freddy Johnson at the Negro Palace. Back in Brussels, he joined the band of American trumpeter Joe Smith and, from May 1941, the Jean Omer orchestra. After the band's visit to Berlin in July 1942, Robert stayed behind and joined Lutz Templin.

The tenor-saxophonist Detlev Lais (*b.* Frankfurt, 1911) joined the standard formation as guest soloist for occasional recording dates, but never took part in broadcasts with the Templin orchestra. Lais was a member of the Kurt Hohenberger orchestra until March 1942, when he joined the DTU. And, last but not least, Lutz Templin himself occasionally played tenor-solo on a few recording dates.

Lutz Templin's rhythm section:

Templin's original pianist was Vienna-born Franz Mück (1898–1957). Second pianist from early 1941 was the Italian Primo Angeli (*b.* Bologna, 1908). Mück joined the DTU in March 1942, and Angeli emerged as Templin's regular pianist up until the orchestra finally collapsed in 1945.

Angeli first came to Germany in September 1937, a member of the Italian band of violinist Nanni dal Della (which then included Alfredo Marzaroli on trumpet), for engagements at the Hotel Esplanade, Hamburg, and the Frasquita Bar in Berlin. He married Henriette Schäffler, Kleindin's cousin and a singer, and settled in the German capital.

According to Kleindin, Werner Neumann (1913–1992) occasionally played and recorded with the Templin orchestra during 1941–42. Neumann was the regular pianist of the band which, throughout the war, trombonist-vocalist Kurt 'Kutte' Widmann led at the Café Imperator.

In May 1942, Joop 'Tip' Tichelaar briefly joined the roster of Templin musicians from the van 't Hoff orchestra as alternate pianist and third trumpet player. In 1933 he had been a member of the short-lived *Swantockers*, directed by clarinetist/violinist Antoon Swaan and drummer-entertainer Eliazer 'Eli' Tokkie, which included the famous Dutch trumpeter Louis de Vries and German star-saxophonist Ernst Höllerhagen. In January 1940, Tichelaar joined the Willie Lewis band, replacing Freddy Johnson, who had left in October 1939 to form a trio for an engagement at Amsterdam's Negro Palace. From the summer of 1940, Tichelaar was a member of a band directed by guitarist/violinist Lex van Spall until joining the newly formed Ernst van 't Hoff orchestra at the end of the year. By early 1943 he was back in the Netherlands as a member of Borge 'Börke' Boyd Bachman's show-band.

Armenian-born guitarist Meguerditsch 'Meg' Tevelian (1902–1976) played and recorded with the Templin orchestra from the autumn of 1940 until 1943. He came to Berlin in 1921, where he worked as a bank clerk until, encouraged by the pianist Hans Bund, he decided to become a professional musician. Around 1928–29, Tevelian joined the band directed by fellow-Armenian Grégoire Nakchounian at the Café am Zoo, Berlin, followed by a European tour with the band of Belgian drummer-vocalist Eugène 'Bobby' 't Sas, playing alongside pianist Franz Mück. By 1932 he was with René Dumont in Vienna, alongside Lutz Templin at the piano, and in the following years played and recorded with a variety of dance bands, including those directed by Oskar Joost and Heinz Wehner. With the return to the United States of the guitarists Harold M. Kirchstein (1938) and Mike Danzi (1939), and the death of Hans Korseck

(1942), Tevelian was very much in demand as a session musician. When he was transferred to the *Reichssender* Vienna in 1943, he was replaced in the Templin orchestra by Max Gursch.

Italian bass-player Cesare Cavaion alternated with Paul Henkel until 1941, when Rudi Wegener (*b.* 1907) became Templin's favourite bass-player. Wegener had belonged to the roster of *Goldene Sieben* musicians and was added to the basic formation whenever the arrangement called for a string-bass. At the beginning of the 1940s he was probably a member of the Bauschke orchestra. After Wegener left the Templin orchestra for the DTU in March 1942, Otto Tittmann, who had been with the Wehner orchestra since March 1939, replaced him. Cavaion too withdrew around this time and the Czech Frando Chrpa took his place as alternate bass-player. Up until September 1941, Chrpa had been a member of the Karel Vlach orchestra.

Fritz Brocksieper (1912–1990) was Lutz Templin's drummer throughout the existence of his orchestra and participated in all recordings and broadcasts. Largely due to his work with Templin – and because of his talent as a Gene Krupa-type artist – Brocksieper became Germany's most popular drummer of the 1940s and 1950s. He was born Bruno Hans Friedrich Brocksieper, in Constantinople, to a German father – an engineer on assignment in Turkey – and a Greek mother. The family settled in Munich in 1918 where Fritz too trained as an engineer, taking drum lessons on the side and playing with dance bands in and around Munich. In the summer of 1938 he moved to Berlin and was soon at home as a drummer in the bars and recording

38 Fritz ['Freddie'] Brocksieper, the drummer, Munich, 1931.

studios, playing with many of Germany's top jazz musicians. When ordered to report at a garrison at the beginning of the war, Brocksieper avoided the draft by swallowing a medication that induced vomiting. Dispatched to hospital for treatment of a suspected ulcer, he was later discharged from both the hospital and the army.[104]

Since most able-bodied German males had been called up for military service, the remaining Berlin-based musicians were under pressure to play – and in the case of official engagements were compelled to play – in various and different formations almost day and night. The musicians who worked for Templin were no exception. The recordings of Fritz Brocksieper, made with a combo formation from the 'Charlie' orchestra, are listed in the discography. But there were other combinations of 'Charlie' musicians: the Cuban trumpeter Fernando Diaz and Italian bass-player Cesare Cavaion, for example, recorded a large number of sides with the Cuarteto Argentino and the Quinteto Tipico for the German Overseas Station in 1943. These were sessions of mainly Latin-American music, but the recordings also produced jazz standards such as 'Saint Luis [*sic*] Blues' – with Duke Ellington wrongly credited as composer – and 'I Can Nobody" [*recte* 'I Ain't Got Nobody'], as well as popular German tunes of the time, like Theo Mackeben's *'Bei dir war es immer so schön'* and Michael Jary's *'Ich liebe die Sonne, den Mond und die Sterne'*.[105]

Lutz Templin's arrangers:
Templin's arrangements were orchestrated by himself, together with several members of the orchestra, including Franz Mück and Willy Berking (until they joined the DTU in March 1942), and with Friedrich Meyer-Gergs until he was called up in June 1941. Templin had a permit that allowed him to listen to foreign stations and hear the latest tunes and arrangements. As the bass-player Otto Tittmann recalled: 'Templin had a listening-in permit. He was allowed to tape American numbers straight off the air. These would be taken down by the various arrangers in the band. We were the only band in the whole of the [German] radio doing this. Because our recordings were so important, the few Germans in the orchestra were exempted from military service.'[106]

In May 1943, the ProMi summoned Czechoslovakian accordionist Kamil Behounek (1916–1983) to Berlin and contracted him as Templin's arranger. Behounek later recalled his introductory visit to Berlin:

In his office Herr Bauer said to me: I've got you an assignment in Berlin as arrranger at the Short-Wave Station on Masurenallee. Here's the train ticket. You're leaving on May 17. I wondered what sort of village band I was going to be working for. But orders is orders. I got to Berlin in the evening. In the darkness I could make out the ruined buildings which bore witness to the devastating air raids. Next morning I went to the huge broadcasting centre on Masurenallee. The producer welcomed me and took me straight away to a studio where the orchestra I was going to work for was playing. I felt like Alice in Wonderland. Here was this big dance orchestra with three trumpets, three trombones, four saxes, a full rhythm group. And were they swinging it! And how! They were playing up-to-date hits from America! Lutz Templin had got together the best musicians from all over

Europe for his band. There was the Belgian [*sic*] clarinetist Benny de Weille, the two Balbos from Italy, Willy Berking on trombone, and the well-known, technically brilliant Freddy Brocksieper. They played absolutely spot on. Our Vlach orchestra would have had to hide their heads in the ground.

During the lunch break, the leader, Lutz Templin, invited me to his flat. And he already had my first job waiting for me. It was a slow waltz that needed arranging for a small group. Back at the studio he fixed me up in an empty room at a piano. I got down to work. I really prefer doing arrangements with an accordion on my lap. All the same, I finished it in two hours, to Lutz's satisfaction.

Next day my boss showed me what my job involved. The Berlin Short-Wave Station was broadcasting propaganda programmes to America and England. For that, only the latest swing music was suitable. They were recording American programmes on flexible acetate discs [Decelith], which I was to listen to and do fresh arrangements for the Templin orchestra. And what great stuff there was among the recordings! Glenn Miller, Harry James ... the cream of American swing.

I picked out ten of these discs [and] proposed taking them home to Prague where I would work on them and post the completed arrangements back to Berlin. The producer, thank goodness, agreed. He wrote me a warrant that I was under compulsory contract [*dienstverpflichtet*] to the Berlin Short-Wave Station, on 'essential war work'. The words 'Reich Ministry of Propaganda' graced the top of the letter. It covered me against the labour office right up till the end of the war. I don't have that on my conscience. My mates were filling shells – I was making music. I don't see that that is any worse.

Listening to these discs was not as easy as it looked. They had been picked up on short or medium wave. A lot of passages were almost impossible to hear due to

39 Fritz Brocksieper and his wife, Charlie Schwedler (*centre*), with the pianist Werner Scharfenberger and his wife, *c.* 1949.

atmospherics or fading. So you had to help out with a bit of imagination. Smart as I then was, I used to keep a second copy of each arrangement. So by the end of the war a stash of about sixty manuscript arrangements had built up in my desk drawer. Finding material for six saxophones in Prague was as good as impossible. Nobody had anything like that. That was the foundation for my post-war big bands.

Soon after I got back from Berlin I went on an extended tour with the Vlach orchestra in Moravia. Then back in Prague I put together the first combo of my own: the Kamil Behounek Septet. They were dedicated jazzmen, one and all.[107]

Occupation Epilogue

On 16 April 1945, the Soviet army launched its final offensive against Berlin. On 25 April the German capital was cut off from all land communications, and house-to-house fighting had reached the Hohenzollerndamm, close to the radio tower (*Funkturm*) and the radio building (*Funkhaus*) itself. On 26 April, Werner Naumann, Goebbels' secretary of state, made a radio appeal to the population to fight to their last drop of blood. It was probably the last radio broadcast from a Berlin station in the Second World War. On 30 April 1945, hard on the heels of the Soviet forces, Walter Ulbricht (the future prime minister of the German Democratic Republic, 1955–60) and his group were flown from Moscow to Berlin to begin preparations for the implementation of the new, Communist order in Germany.

The *Funkhaus* on Masurenalle in Berlin-Charlottenburg had survived the war with little actual damage, the Soviets having apparently spared the building during the battle of Berlin. The transmitter of the former *Reichssender* Berlin in Berlin-Tegel had also survived in working order. Early on 2 May a Soviet unit under Major Popov entered the

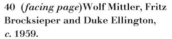

40 (*facing page*)Wolf Mittler, Fritz
Brocksieper and Duke Ellington,
c. 1959.

41 Lale Andersen (who launched the
song 'Lili Marleen') with the Lutz
Templin orchestra, after the war.

Funkhaus to inspect the building, remove all Nazi insignia and repair what needed to be repaired. Alexander Stepanovich Popov was no stranger to the building. From 1931 until early 1933 he had worked there as a trainee engineer, and in May 1941 had again inspected the installations as a member of a Soviet delegation.

On 10 May, only one day after the signing of the German capitulation at Karlshorst – and while the Dönitz government was still transmitting *via* the station at Flensburg, albeit with the consent of the British military authorities – the first Russian commander of Berlin, Colonel-General Nikolai Erastovich Berzarin, ordered Hans Mahle (*b.* 1911), the former deputy chief editor of the Soviet 'Free Germany' station, to restore regular programmes from Berlin as soon as possible. On 13 May, at 20:00 hours – the British forces having closed Radio Flensburg down, after strong Soviet protest – Radio Berlin was back on the air, broadcasting from a hastily repaired studio in Berlin-Tegel. In May 1945 Theodor Mühlen, Radio Berlin's first head of light entertainment, selected Michael Jary as leader of the envisaged *Radio Berlin Tanzorchester*. Having tracked Jary down in Berlin, the two began searching for suitable musicians, eventually selecting forty-eight instrumentalists for their orchestra-to-be: six trumpets, four trombones, six reed instruments, two pianos, two basses, two guitars, drums and percussion, together with a string section of twelve violins, four violas and four cellos, as well as three woodwind instruments and a harp. Mühlen and Jary contracted Horst Kudritzki, Werner Eisbrenner, Georg Haentzschel and Walter Leschetitzky to act as arrangers. Rehearsals began immediately and on 27 May the *Radio Berlin Tanzorchester* (RBT) was on the air, broadcasting American hits and swing music from the auditorium of the Berlin *Funkhaus*, at a time when all other stations in Germany remained off air.

Kudritzki, Haentzschel and Leschetitzky had been working for the *Deutsches Tanz- und Unterhaltungsorchester* (DTU), which is why the two formations sounded alike and why the RBT is sometimes referred to as the successor of the DTU. Michael Jary left Berlin at the end of 1945 and Horst Kudritzki took over as leader of the RBT. If Jary had founded the orchestra, Kudritzki was the one who polished it.

In June 1952 British military police cordoned off the *Funkhaus* as their contribution to the cold war. In July Soviet military police occupied the enclave, while the British guarded the building from the outside. Four years later, on 5 July 1956, the Soviet commander in Berlin handed over the *Funkhaus* – intact but gutted – to the Berlin city administration, 'free of charge' ('*unentgeldlich*') as the Soviet statement put it.

Fade-out

In 1943, when Berlin was reeling under the Allies' saturation bombing and normal work became impossible, the broadcasting authorities had evacuated their foreign-language activities to locations outside Berlin. First each member of the Lutz Templin orchestra received a personal letter instructing him to prepare for a transfer to Breslau, but this plan was abandoned when it became apparent that working conditions were no better there. Most members of the Templin orchestra were instead evacuated to Stuttgart after the summer holidays, early in September 1943. (Charlie Schwedler was among the few who stayed on in Berlin).

At the new location, Stuttgart's '*Haus des Deutschtums*' (House of the German Nation) on Neckarstrasse, near Charlottenplatz, home of the local *Reichssender*, there was no access to Deutsche Grammophon's professional recording equipment. As a consequence, no further shellac pressings of recordings by Charlie and his Orchestra were made. However, when the Templin orchestra was playing in Stuttgart on propaganda broadcasts, the ProMi in Berlin continued making records for the clarinet & mandoline label until the series was finally closed in November 1943.

Lutz Templin and the remnants of 'Charlie and his Orchestra' were in Stuttgart when the war ended. On 5 April 1945 the *Reichssender* Stuttgart transmitted its last broadcast. The following day an SS unit blew up the facilities. On 22 April French troops occupied Stuttgart and eventually the region was handed over to the American occupation forces.

Germany's leading wartime swing orchestra finally collapsed when most of its members dispersed in all directions. The stalwart pianist, Primo Angeli, had already left the orchestra. He and his wife had departed for her birthplace, Karlsbad, Czechoslovakia, and during the orchestra's final weeks an unidentified Dutch pianist, possibly Tip Tichelaar, had taken Angeli's place. By then the Templin orchestra consisted almost entirely of foreign musicians, and most of those were to return to an uncertain fate in their own countries, while the few remaining German players left for their own home towns.

Lutz Templin himself stayed on in Stuttgart, and, towards the end of 1945, organized a new formation from the musicians at hand. But his new orchestra played no role in the post-war history of German jazz. Between broadcasting assignments for the local station, he mainly toured holiday resorts in southern Germany, in autumn 1947 accompanying singer Lale Andersen at engagements in Lindau, Konstanz and other vacation resorts in the area. For a brief period in the 1950s Templin was music director of the dance orchestra of the *Süddeutscher Rundfunk* in Stuttgart until, on the recommendation of orchestra leader, Bert Kaempfert, he was appointed A & R manager of the Polydor record company in Hamburg. During this period, Templin developed his own music publishing business in Hamburg.

During the 1960s Templin and his wife Anni retired to Warder, a small village in Schleswig-Holstein, where he had been building a home since 1958. He died there on 7 March 1973, Anni dying in 1981.[108]

The drummer Fritz Brocksieper, star soloist of Templin's wartime orchestra, survived the last weeks of the war on a farm in the Tübingen area, near Stuttgart, after which he returned to Munich where he directed a band at American clubs in and around the Bavarian capital. Initially this included the trumpeter Charly Tabor and tenor-saxist Eugen Henkel, both former wartime colleagues. Brocksieper remained musically active and continued to record, on both coarse-groove shellac and microgroove EP's and LP's, until his sudden death in Munich on 16 January 1990.

Karl 'Charlie' Schwedler, who had remained in Berlin in September 1943, may still have been there at the end of the war. Teddy Kleindin recalled Schwedler working as a croupier at the Europa Pavillon, Berlin, after 1945. Later, Schwedler settled in Schwanenkirchen, Bavaria, until 1951, when he moved to Düsseldorf. Eventually, in August 1960, at the age of 58, Karl Schwedler, his wife and two children, Bernd and Scarlet, emigrated to the United States, where the former Nazi crooner slipped into obscurity.

6 Farcical Feuding: the Nazi Propaganda Battle

The Goebbels-Ribbentrop Rivalry

Goebbels' twelve years in office saw a relentless battle between German ministries, beginning with the creation of the Propaganda Ministry out of departments removed from the Foreign Ministry, the Ministry of Economic Affairs and of the Interior, and from the Post Office. Relations between the departments were not helped by the fact that the lean and mean organization Goebbels had sought ('a tool unfettered by red tape, flexible and with quick reflexes'), and the propaganda coordination office ('*Propagandaleitstelle*') his cabinet colleagues had envisaged, turned out to be an administrative leviathan. In 1933 it had five divisions (propaganda, broadcasting, press, film and theatre) with about 350 employees. By 1941, three secretaries of state managed an organization of nearly two thousand employees across seventeen divisions, each of them made up of different jurisdictions (*Ressorts*) and desks (*Referate*). By the end of 1942 it comprised as many as twenty-one major divisions.

Obsessed as he was with the spoken word, it was natural for Goebbels to attach enormous importance to radio. But achieving control over broadcasting went beyond personal preference: radio was vital to Goebbels' personal standing in the Party, since he could use it far more directly than he could the other mass media – press, books, periodicals and posters. In determining Nazi press policy, Goebbels had to contend with Max Amann, the president of the Reich Press Chamber, and with Otto Dietrich, the Party's press chief. To complicate matters further, Hitler had installed Dietrich as secretary of state to the ProMi in 1937, replacing Walther Funk, in spite of Goebbels' protests. Within the ministry Dietrich of course reported to Goebbels; but in the Party, he, as a member of the Party directorate (*Reichsleiter*) and Goebbels were of equal rank. Furthermore there was the dreaded Martin Borman, Hitler's influential secretary and head of the Party chancellery, to contend with. Goebbels was cowed by Borman's ideological interventions, as Hans Fritzsche testified to the Nuremberg Tribunal: 'A telex from Bormann to Dr. Goebbels was quite enough for Dr. Goebbels to put the entire apparatus into top gear'.[1]

Early in 1938 Hitler strengthened his hold on the government machine. The faithful Joachim von Ribbentrop was appointed foreign minister, replacing Konstantin von Neurath, whom Hitler distrusted. At the same time Hitler's military critics, war minister Werner von Blomberg and commander-in-chief of the army Werner

Freiherr von Fritsch, resigned 'for health reasons'.[2] The ministry of war was dismantled and converted into a new Supreme Command of the Armed Forces (*Oberkommando der Wehrmacht*, OKW) under General Keitel, with Hitler himself as supreme commander. Sixteen generals were compulsorily retired, with another forty-four re-posted. Goering, whom, it was believed, coveted the title of war minister, had to be content with promotion to field marshal.

In Ribbentrop Goebbels was to find a serious contender for control of foreign-language broadcasts. In 1933, when the newly-appointed propaganda minister laid claim to two of the Foreign Ministry's responsibilities, Press Relations (*Nachrichtenwesen*) and Foreign Intelligence (*Auslandsinformation*), Neurath had protested. Hitler compromised by ruling that the Foreign Ministry should continue in its 'traditional' tasks of disseminating the government's official view, while the new Propaganda Ministry should 'actively' support and advance the government's foreign policy, whatever that might mean. And there the matter rested until Ribbentrop's appointment as Foreign Minister on 4 February 1938.

Joachim von Ribbentrop was born the son of a Prussian officer – and without the 'von' – in Wesel, in the Lower Rhine region, on 30 April 1893. Educated in Metz – then part of the Reich – and in Grenoble, France, he subsequently worked as a bank trainee, labourer and journalist, before spending some time in Canada. Ribbentrop fought as a volunteer in the First World War (including a period as a military adviser in Istanbul), ending as a lieutenant. The war over he settled in Berlin, taking a job in the cotton industry. His marriage in 1920 to Anneliese Henkell, daughter of the head of Germany's largest champagne makers, gave Ribbentrop an entry into Berlin's high society. In 1925 he gratified his vanity by adopting the 'noble particle' *von*, and officially joined the ranks of the nobility.

In May 1932 – comparatively late – Ribbentrop joined the Nazi Party, and met Hitler for the first time in August of that year. The Ribbentrop villa in exclusive Berlin-Dahlem became Hitler's preferred refuge, and there the future chancellor developed and discussed his strategy for the January 1933 elections with his closest advisors. A year later Ribbentrop was an NSDAP member of the *Reichstag* and an SS-colonel, as well as Hitler's foreign affairs adviser, a rôle he shared with Foreign Minister Freiherr von Neurath and Alfred Rosenberg, the Party's ideologist and head of its foreign-policy office.

Ribbentrop first came to international prominence when he negotiated the Anglo-German naval treaty of 1935. Between August 1936 and February 1938 he served, without great success, as ambassador in London, returning to Berlin as Minister for Foreign Affairs. Before long, particularly after the *Anschluss* with Austria in March 1938, and during the international crisis leading to the annexation of the Sudetenland in September 1938, Ribbentrop decided he was not being kept properly informed about opinion in the foreign press. He also absorbed the value of propaganda in preparing the ground for international negotiations and diplomatic manoeuvres. In the autumn of 1938 he instructed the head of his Press Division to establish a news gathering apparatus, or '*Nachrichtenbeschaffungsapparat*'. Ribbentrop seems also to have lobbied Hitler for the transfer of the crucial Foreign Intelligence function back from the ProMi, a move which would have involved reversing the ruling of June 1933. Ribbentrop must have convinced himself that he had the Führer's approval, for directly after signing a German-Danish non-aggression pact on 31 May, he informed key members of his Cultural Policy Division (*Kulturpolitische Abteilung*) that the Foreign Ministry was to be in charge of all propaganda abroad. The duties of the ProMi were to be restricted to the provision of the technical facilities for carrying out Foreign Ministry policy.

Ribbentrop gave orders for a foreign-language broadcasting capability to be created immediately:

> The requisite staff are to be engaged forthwith and the necessary [financial] resources must be made available. [...] This is to be accomplished without entering into any disputes with the Reich Ministry for Public Enlightenment and Propaganda over issues of demarcation.

The Foreign Ministry's new broadcasting activity gave rise to a new department within the Cultural Policy Division, headed at that time by a conservative career diplomat, Dr. Fritz von Twardowski (1890–1970), a former ambassador to Moscow. Until July 1941 the department was officially known as the *Kulturpolitische Abteilung – Rundfunkreferat*, or simply Kultur-R, and provided with an office in the Moltkehaus at number sixty Saarlandstrasse (now Stresemannstrasse).

Since 1933, as policy gave way to propaganda, the Cultural Policy Division had been increasingly sidelined. Its main activity was not unlike the administration of today's Goethe Institutes abroad, an operation which was increasingly hampered by the elimination of Jews from German cultural life. But the creation of a broadcasting outfit within its framework gave it a new lease of life. The man chosen by Ribbentrop to run it was Gerhard Rühle, a loyal Party man who had no foreign or broadcasting experience, but was a versatile manager.

Rühle was born at Winnenden, near Stuttgart, in March 1905. An early member of the Nazi Party, he wore the gold-wreathed Party badge, an honour accorded to those who were considered to have suffered from political discrimination during the Party's 'years of struggle'. Rühle was a Reichstag member, an SS-colonel, and had held some twenty-six different Party posts since 1925. In 1933 he was made personal adviser to the regional Party leader (*Gauleiter*) of the Kurmark region, and in 1935 appointed a councillor for Calau district in the Prussian province of Niederlausitz. He joined the Foreign Ministry in February 1939, at the rank of *Vortragender Legationsrat*.

The structure of Kultur-R was quickly established, but without the cooperation of the ProMi, which stubbornly resisted the Foreign Ministry's abrogation of its business. After some of Rühle's officers had 'raided' the *Funkhaus* and occupied its offices, they found their furniture piled up in the corridor. Another such foray led to the cutting off of power and telephone connections, after which Rühle's men threatened to wreck the switchboard. This petty warfare was halted when ProMi officials telephoned Ernst von Weizsäcker, the Foreign Ministry's secretary of state, on 17 June 1939 and informed him the Führer had ruled that nothing was to be changed and that the Foreign Ministry was to cease all broadcasting activity.

Early the following month the German ambassador in Washington, Dr. Hans Heinrich Dieckhoff, complained to Ribbentrop that 'particularly at the present time no adequate foreign-language news service is at the service of Germany's foreign policy'. He deplored the fact that the Foreign Ministry had the appropriate 'machinery', which it was not allowed to use, while the ProMi itself had none. 'It is all the more deplorable that, when in spite of all efforts our public relations work abroad is coming up against very considerable difficulties, the most effective weapon – radio – is not being exploited as it should be.' Goebbels did not compromise, but the triumph over his arch-rival lasted only a few weeks.

The Hitler Ruling of 8 September 1939

A week after the outbreak of war, in September 1939, Ribbentrop obtained a ruling from the Führer which reversed that of 30 June 1933. At that point Ribbentrop was at the peak of his political career, having just concluded the German-Soviet non-aggression pact of August 1939, which effectively indemnified the German invasion of Poland, clearing the way for the offensive in the west without risking a second in the east. The new ruling established that 'as regards propaganda relative to foreign policy [...] general guidelines and directives will be issued by the Reich Foreign Minister. [...] The whole of the propaganda facilities of the Reich Propaganda Ministry may be called upon in putting this directive into effect.' Weary of the squabbles between the two ministers, and angry at the resulting demands on his own time, Hitler further stipulated that the ministers should agree an operational solution, in future only approaching him jointly, and after consultation with the head of the Reich chancellery, Hans Heinrich Lammers.

Goebbels, however, was not about to accept the implied demotion of his ministry into a tool for Foreign Ministry policy, but at Hitler's insistence agreed to the stationing of Foreign Ministry personnel within his department to support the ProMi and safeguard the interests of the Foreign Ministry. But in practice Goebbels never permitted Foreign Ministry representatives into his inner sanctum, and the broadcasting liaison office of Kultur-R (*Funkverbindungsstelle*) remained the Foreign Ministry's only foothold. So far as Goebbels was concerned nothing had altered, and the acrimonious struggle between two of Hitler's most senior ministers continued, each invoking Hitler's views and directives, without their being able to be verified or confirmed.

The conflict was rooted in personal resentment: Goebbels wholeheartedly despised Ribbentrop. Throughout his diaries are references to Ribbentrop as a sleazy opportunist and belated Nazi: 'I regard Ribbentrop as a dud card *(Niete)*' (1 February 1938), 'a megalomaniac (*Grössenwahnsinnigen*)' (6 February 1940), 'a creep (*üble Type*)' (12 July 1940), 'a typical political parvenu (*Emporkömmling*)' (1 April 1941), and more. The view of the Foreign Ministry was that the loudmouth ProMi, staffed by Nazi fanatics, lacked experience in dealing with foreign powers, and was wholly deficient in tact. As Wolf Mittler described it:

The Foreign Ministry and the ProMi were poles apart regarding the broadcasts in English. While Goebbels and his stooges – Fritzsche and the fanatical *Reichssendeleiter* Eugen Hadamovsky at their helm – stuck to the hard line [...] the Foreign Ministry pursued a 'velvet glove' approach.

Ribbentrop made maximum capital out of Hitler's September ruling, even though the Foreign Ministry had not budgeted for the additional expenditure: the entire expansion was met by the special war resources fund, the *Kriegskostensonderfond*. At this point – the beginning of the war – the Foreign Ministry's propaganda personnel consisted of between ninety and a hundred people. In November Ribbentrop appointed Theodor 'Theo' Habicht (1898–1944), under-secretary of state and deputy head of the Political Division, as his special delegate for propaganda, answerable directly to him for the coordination of both the Information Division and the Broadcasting Department. In January 1940 Ribbentrop gave Dr. Markus Timmler (formerly on the RRG staff) responsibility for liaison between the ministry and the RRG's Foreign Broadcasts Division.

Timmler, born in Königsberg in August 1906, had joined the KWS in 1935. At first he coordinated programme take-over from regional stations, but in 1936 was placed in charge of radio drama in the KWS' entertainment section. Dr. Georg Heinevetter was Timmler's deputy, and Kurt Georg Kiesinger (1904–1988), later West German chancellor, was, from April 1940, adviser on broadcasts to the former German colonies. Timmler and his team attempted to influence the RRG's foreign-language services, but it was wishful thinking. Irked by the Foreign Ministry's efforts, Goebbels sought to streamline his own ministry's communications with the Foreign Ministry, and appointed Dr. Ernst Brauweiler head of the ProMi's Foreign Division.

Like Goebbels himself, Brauweiler (1889–1945) came from the Catholic Rhineland. After graduating, he became chief editor of the national-liberal *Hannoverscher Kurier* in 1926. In 1932 he joined the NSDAP's press office, which was amalgamated with the new ProMi in 1933. When the Press Division of the ProMi was divided in April 1938, he became deputy head of the Foreign Press division under Professor Karl Bömer, whose dramatic disgrace in the summer of 1941 opened the way for Brauweiler to succeed him.

Throughout the winter of 1939–40 and the period of the 'Phoney War', Goebbels worked hard to win back the ground he had lost to Ribbentrop. On 10 January 1940 he sent Hitler an extensive report on the successes of his foreign-language broadcasting, which – he was informed – the Führer studied 'with interest'. Two days later he noted in his diary: 'Coordination with the Foreign Ministry has become a dead end. For the time being I am letting the matter ride.' On 6 February he observed: 'Ribbentrop sends me another offensive ten-page letter. How does he find the time? I'm not answering. He'll have a long wait before I run to his whistle.' Soon afterwards, Hitler rewarded Goebbels' patience and trust by ordering the ProMi, rather than the Foreign Minstry, to prepare the propaganda campaign in support of the planned military offensive in the west. Early on 10 May, as the Foreign Minister was polishing the communiqué he planned to deliver later the same day, Goebbels delivered the radio announcement signalling the beginning of military operations. Ribbentrop was furious: 'My entire Broadcasting Department, including its head, is dismissed instantly for incompetence!'

As the urgencies of war took over, the feuding between Hitler's two ministers began to wane; and at an operational level close contact between the two departments led to a reasonable degree of cooperation and mutual respect. By then Kultur-R had established regional broadcasting teams (Länder-Referate) which interfaced with the RRG's broadcasting zones. Reports from German embassies abroad on reception quality and propaganda effectiveness, via Foreign Ministry representatives, were of particular value to the RRG.

The Organization of the Foreign Ministry's Broadcasting Zones:

Interestingly, a number of the principal section heads had British or United States connections. Professor Hermann Reinhard Haferkorn was head of the English-language broadcasting section throughout the war. Born at Waldheim in December 1899, he became, before the war, a lecturer at the technical high school in Danzig, from where he joined the Foreign Ministry on 1 September 1939. In March 1941 he was appointed professor at Greifswald University. In 1945 he was interned and brought to Britain as a witness for the prosecution in the trials of several British Nazi propagandists. He eventually settled in Speyer, and in 1961 was made an honorary professor of Heidelberg University. He died on 24 May 1983.

Haferkorn's deputy was Dr. Friedrich Wilhelm Schoberth. Born at Nuremberg in June 1905, he was lecturer in German and French at Newcastle-upon-Tyne, Liverpool and Cardiff universities between 1928 and the beginning of the war, when he returned to Germany as a lecturer at Berlin University. Schoberth retained his university position on joining the English section of Kultur-R on 25 October 1939. In November 1940 he was sent to The Hague to run the Foreign Ministry's broadcasting activity there, and about that time became a Party member. On returning to Berlin in December 1942, he became the Ministry's liaison officer for broadcasting to Britain. From September 1943 he was responsible for 'political guidance' (Gruppe Politik) at the Luxembourg station. Eventually, in June 1944, Schoberth was made deputy head of the European Station's English-language zone.

After Schoberth moved to The Hague, Dr. Edgar Mertner became second in command of Kultur-R's English-language broadcasting section. Mertner was born in Gurten, West Posen, in December 1907, and had studied at Marburg, Breslau, Berlin and Halle, before obtaining his M.A. at Cardiff. He taught at a high school in Saxony from April 1931, and from August 1938 was a lecturer at Halle University, and later at Greifswald and from 1944 at Rostock.

Professor Adolf Mahr, born in Trieste in May 1887, was a prehistorian and archaeologist, and keeper of Irish antiquities at Dublin's National Museum. Returning to Germany at the beginning of the war he became the Foreign Ministry's liaison officer with 'Concordia' – Dr. Hetzler's 'clandestine' radio stations for British listeners (see Ch. 7). Mahr shared responsibility for the Irish section with Haferkorn from 1942.

	REGION	5 January 1940	14 October 1940	7 June 1941	1 July 1941	5 March 1943	
I	WEST	H. Schlottmann	Dr. Fritz Bran	Dr. Fritz Bran	Dr. E. Weinhold	Dr. R. Lappla	(I)
II	GREAT BRITAIN IRELAND	Prof. H. Haferkorn Dr. Schoberth —	Prof. H. Haferkorn Dr. Schoberth —	Prof. H. Haferkorn Dr. E. Mertner	Prof. H. Haferkorn Dr. E. Mertner Prof. A. Mahr	Prof. H. Haferkorn Dr. E. Mertner Prof. A. Mahr	(II) –
III	SOUTH-EAST	Kurt Alex. Mair	Kurt Alex. Mair	Franz Schaub	Franz Schaub	Franz Schaub	(IVb)
IV	NORDIC AND HOLLAND	Dr. L. Lienhardt	(Erwin Gross)	Dr. L. Lienhardt	Dr. Zimmermann	Dr. Zimmermann	(VI)
V	ITALY	Prof. Werner	Martin von Bruch	Klaus Rühle-Fecht	Klaus Rühle-Fecht	(Wendenburg†)	(IVa)
–	EASTERN EUROPE	—	—	—	Dr. Josef Luckau	Dr. Josef Luckau	(V)
VI	SPAIN/PORTUGAL/ LATIN AMERICA	Josef Schoof	Gustav Bannach	Gustav Reder	Dr. W. Haverbeck	Dr. G. Reichel††	(III)
VII	USA	G. von Lilienfeld	G. von Lilienfeld	(Prof. O. Koischwitz)	(Prof. O. Koischwitz)	Prof. O. Koischwitz Dr. H.D. Ahrens†††	(IX)
VIII	ORIENT	—	Dr. Georg Kaspar	Dr. Georg Kaspar	Kurt Munzel	Kurt Munzel	(VII)
–	FAR EAST	—	—	Erwin Gross	Franz Ferring	Dr. E. Poensgen	(VIII)
IX	SOUTH AFRICA	Dr. W. Oetting	Dr. W. Oetting	Dr. W. Oetting	Dr. W. Oetting	Dr. W. Oetting	(Xa)

Dates are of announcement; the second name is the deputy, bracketed names refer to acting heads of broadcasting zones.
Numerals in margins indicate divisions, those in brackets reflect final zonal regrouping.

† Dr. Dietrich Suenkel succeeded Wendenburg as head of section IVa (Italy).
†† Adolf Lichtenberger succeeded Reichel as head of section III (Spain/Portugal/Latin America).
††† Ahrens succeeded Koischwitz as head of section IX (USA).

Chart 7: Organization of the Foreign Ministry's Broadcasting Zones

The first head of the American broadcasting section, Georg von Lilienfeld, was born in Riga, Latvia, in December 1912 and brought up in Düsseldorf and Munich. Von Lilienfield studied law, journalism and geography at various universities, including the Fletcher School of Law and Diplomacy at Tufts University, Massachusetts, and Columbia University, New York. He remained in the United States until 1938, when he returned to Germany, joining the Foreign Ministry in January 1939 and being attached to the Press Department later that year. During this period he met Douglas Chandler and introduced him to the Berlin propaganda system. In the summer of 1941, von Lilienfeld became the Foreign Ministry's liaison officer with the Army Command North. He left Kultur-R in September 1943 and was appointed radio attaché at the German embassy in Rome, staying in Italy until the end of the war.

Von Lilienfeld appeared as a prosecution witness at the trials of Douglas Chandler, Robert Best, Mildred Gillars and other American Nazi propagandists, after which he remained in the United States, as a riding and ski coach, until May 1951 when he took over the USA and South America section of the West German government's press office in Bonn. He returned to the Foreign Ministry in April 1954, serving at Geneva, Ankara and Washington, before going to Teheran as West German ambassador in August 1968. He died in Munich in December1989.

Dr. Hans Dietrich Wolfgang Ahrens, who succeeded von Lilienfeld as head of the North America broadcasting section in 1943, was born in Wiesbaden in July 1916. He studied philosophy – for a time as an exchange student at Haverford College, USA – and on graduating was one of the first to join Kultur-R.

Flawed Champions of their Masters, 1940-41

In the autumn of 1940, after only a short period as head of the Foreign Division, Ernst Brauweiler reported to Goebbels that he had restored order where there had been 'anarchy' at the beginning of his appointment. In reality, however, little had changed. Brauweiler's directives were often vague, making it easy for the ministry's core activity, the Propaganda Division, to carry on as before. In November 1940 Kiesinger, from Kultur-R, described the atmosphere at the RRG building as 'unendurable'. Within a short time tension had reached crisis point: Goebbels' officers once again ejected the staff of the *Funkverbindungsstelle* – Timmler, Kiesinger and others – from their offices in the *Funkhaus* in retaliation for the Foreign Ministry's latest ploy of not issuing visas for ProMi employees and affiliates visiting other countries. Brauweiler seems to have been conscientious but lacking in flexibility and diplomatic flair, and while he maintained his position, relations with the Foreign Ministry deteriorated to their worst point. Goebbels decided to look for a more effective administrator, and in December 1940 appointed Professor Heinrich Hunke to Brauweiler's position.[3]

In Hunke (*b.* 1902) Goebbels had finally found an experienced official with diplomatic skills. Hunke had been a Party member since 1923 and, from 1924, regional Party leader (*Kreisleiter*) for the Lippe-Westphalia district, the region in which he was born. In 1927–1933 Hunke had served as an adviser to the *Reichswehr* Ministry, and from 1929 was the Party's top organizer for Greater Berlin. In 1932, Hunke became a member of the Reichstag. In 1935 he became professor of political economy at the technical high-school in Berlin, from where he moved to the ProMi.

Meanwhile Ribbentrop was rapidly constructing his own information and broadcasting network. As an early military victory became less and less likely, Germany's relations with allied and neutral countries became correspondingly less close. In the face of dwindling political opportunities abroad, Ribbentrop adopted propaganda as a *de facto* substitute for foreign policy. The Foreign Ministry turned itself into a kind of 'mini-ProMi' of the Wilhelmstrasse, with propaganda serving to justify a huge ministerial staff and compensate Ribbentrop for his loss of political power and Party standing. The driving force behind this development were the unscrupulous and power-hungry Nazi fanatic, Martin Luther, and his accomplice, Ewald Krümmer.

Luther proved to be the ideal champion of Ribbentrop's ambitions. Committed to the extermination of the Jews as the supreme agenda of foreign policy, Luther had powerful allies in Himmler and Heydrich, and was thus able to create a personal power base with which Ribbentrop himself, as much as Goebbels, needed to reckon with

Martin Luther (1895–1945), a former furniture remover who spoke with a broad Berlin accent, had joined the Party on 1 March 1933. From 1936 he worked in Ribbentrop's personal office (*Dienststelle*) and, when transferred to the London embassy, Ribbentrop left him in charge of the sensitive issue of Party liaison back in Berlin. When Ribbentrop became a minister, Luther moved with him, and the former Party Advisory Office, *Büro Luther* for short, acquired semi-official standing when re-named Sonderreferat Partei (party special relations) and, in May 1940, made responsible for the production and distribution of propaganda material. In September 1940, Luther replaced Habicht as the Foreign Ministry's chief propaganda coordinator.

Luther's close collaborator, Dr. Ewald Ludwig Krümmer (1896–1968) had joined the Foreign Ministry in 1920, immediately after leaving university. By 1940 he was head of Organization, a task force primarily concerned with personnel. But because the ministry's Information Division freely interfered with the propaganda domain of the Cultural Policy Division, and Organization was either unable (or, more likely, unwilling) to rationalize the overlap, Krümmer seized the opportunity to assume personal responsibility for the propaganda activities of both divisions, reporting to Luther. As a result the stage was now set, by spring 1941, for the Foreign Ministry's boldest move in the competition with Goebbels.

Ribbentrop's *Coup*

On 21 February 1941 the Foreign Ministry registered the *Deutsche Auslands-Rundfunk-Gesellschaft 'Interradio' GmbH* (German Foreign Broadcasting Company 'Interradio') in Zürich. The operation was masterminded by the versatile Kurt Alex. Mair, already running the South-East section as well as the Seehaus monitoring post. Five weeks later, on 1 April, the ProMi, together with the National Advertising Council of German Industry, of which Hunke was president, retaliated by founding the

Radio-Union, a supposedly independent radio advertising agency sponsored by German industry, including Siemens, AEG and Telefunken, for the purpose of promoting its products and services abroad. Goebbels' real objective was obviously to influence opinion in neutral and occupied territories by insinuating 'covert' propaganda into advertising material supplied to foreign broadcasting stations. Horst Schaefer and Horst Cleinow were appointed general managers of Radio-Union.[4]

In a crowning manoeuvre on 24 May, Ribbentrop disclosed that the Foreign Ministry, in cooperation with the High Command, had purchased Radio Belgrade, in newly-occupied Serbia, together with its medium-wave transmitter at Makis, in suburban Belgrade, and the short-wave transmitter at Zemun, across the river Sava on the other side of the city. On 29 May Mair signed a contract with the Serbian post office by which it sold fifty-one per cent of the medium-wave station, and the entirety of the short-wave station, including broadcasting rights, to Teleradio AG Belgrad, itself registered on 10 June. The Foreign Ministry's legal expert, Dr. Kurt Böhlhoff, became chairman of the supervisory board, while Mair himself became president of the management committee. A German radio pioneer, Robert Weege, was appointed Teleradio's local managing director. The operational management of both Radio Belgrade and Radio Zemun were hence largely the same.

This surprise acquisition of Radio Belgrade by the Foreign Ministry outraged Goebbels. His arch-rival would now be able to place on air his own radio propaganda, unhindered by the ProMi's Nazi fanatics, and indeed proceeded to do precisely that with considerable success. Goebbels' response was an angry note to Secretary of State Lammers on 16 June 1941, headed 'Compliance with the Führer ruling of 8 September 1939', in which he complained that the Foreign Ministry had acquired broadcasting stations in occupied territories completely by-passing the ProMi, even when some of the stations were maintained and operated by ProMi staff. Lammers, the head of the Reich chancellery, did not even answer, and on 10 July Goebbels complained again. This time he received a predictable reminder from the chancellery: differences of opinion were to be settled by Goebbels and Ribbentrop themselves, before *jointly* approaching the Führer.

Radio Belgrade

The medium-wave Radio Belgrade was managed by the broadcasting unit of the forces' propaganda region south-east (*Rundfunk-Kompanie der Wehrmachts-Propagandaabteilung Südost*) under Dr. Julius Lippert (1895–1956), a Party member since 1923 and lord mayor of Berlin since 1937. Its day-to-day operation was in the hands of two radio professionals, Karl-Heinz Reintgen and Hans-Jürgen Nierentz.

Reintgen, born in Wilhelmshaven in November 1915, had joined the *Deutschlandsender* in 1935 as a trainee. After 1937 he had served with an armoured reconnaissance unit until transferred at the rank of lieutenant to the army's propaganda corps in 1940. After launching Radio Belgrade, Reintgen succeeded Franz Huber as head of the *Reichssender* Vienna in 1944. Following the war he joined Baden-Baden station, operating from Kaiserslautern, and in 1961 transferred to Radio Saarbrücken, becoming the station's editor-in-chief in 1968, and deputy *Intendant* in 1974.

Nierentz was born in Posen in September 1909 and raised in Berlin. He began writing for local papers in 1927, and for radio in 1932. In 1934 he was editor for arts and ideology at the local *Reichssender* Berlin. Appointed deputy to the *Reichs-filmdramaturg* (national film '*dramaturg*') in 1935, he assumed the post himself a year later, in April 1936. Nierentz was appointed the first *Intendant* of Germany's experimental television station (named *Paul Nipkow* after the German TV pioneer) in April 1937. He was drafted into the army at the outbreak of war and transferred to the army's propaganda corps in 1941. After the war he settled as an advertising consultant in Düsseldorf.

The early days of Radio Belgrade were humble, but promising. A daily newspaper served as the basis of its news script, and it possessed a library of only about sixty gramophone records. Reintgen sought to borrow additional items from the local Viennese *Reichssender*, but found the people un-cooperative and obtained only records which were either out of date or had been banned by Goebbels. Among these was one that would make itself – and the station – world-famous virtually overnight: 'Lili Marleen', sung by Lale Andersen.[5]

Lale Andersen (1908–1972) had originally sung the song, but it was not a commercial success and Anderson remained largely unknown until the summer of 1941. When, for want anything else, Radio Belgrade repeatedly aired 'Lili Marleen', German and Allied troops alike responded to its melancholic melody of love and loss. When Reintgen, seeking variety, sought to drop the song from the station's programmes, letters of protest came in from listeners all over Europe. He ruled that 'Lili Marleen' was to be played only once daily, as the station signed off at 22:00 hours.

Goebbels himself disapproved of the song, saying it had a 'cadaverous smell', and Hinkel once described it as 'defeatist chirping which tends to undermine the fighting spirit of German soldiers'. In the summer of 1942, after the Gestapo had intercepted a letter from Andersen to a friend in Switzerland, the composer Rolf Liebermann, asking for help in arranging her escape from Germany, Goebbels banned the song and prohibited Andersen from performing in public. But owing to the song's immense popularity, the ban was largely ignored: Radio Belgrade still ran it when going off the air, and Anderson recorded it, with Charlie Schwedler, for none other than the ProMi's own clarinet & mandoline label. Parodies of the song, with seditious lyrics, circulated in Germany, and after Stalingrad the BBC broadcast the emigrée cabaret artist Lucie Mannheim singing her version in German.

Reintgen, Nierentz and a handful of other uniformed professionals pulled Radio Belgrade together. These included Johannes Ferger as the technical manager; Richard Kistenmacher (later with the station *Freies Berlin*) for light entertainment; Willi Opitz (from the *Deutschlandsender*) for current affairs; Heinz-Rudolf Fritsche (after the war with the *Süddeutscher Rundfunk* in Ulm), Walter Jensen, Hermann Kaufmann and Hans Werner Krüger (later a theatrical director in Oldenburg). About three hundred locally recruited staff, operating from offices in the former Serbian Ministry of Agriculture, produced a varied and entertaining schedule. Although the medium-wave transmitter at Makis was not particularly strong, it was received by listeners across Europe and North Africa, thanks to favourable ground conditions in the marshes between the Danube and Sava. Radio Belgrade (including, from April 1942, the military stations Athens and Salonika) rapidly acquired the flavour of a 'European' station.

Friedrich Meyer (1915–1993) became one of the station's musical directors in June 1942. In Berlin Meyer had provided arrangements for Hans Rehmstedt, Erhard Bauschke, Oscar Joost and Lutz Templin. At Radio Belgrade he assembled a jazz orchestra with Serb and Gypsy players – his Berlin connections enabling him to get the latest sheet arrangements. He was also able to persuade such top artists as the vocalists Evelyn Künneke and Kary Barnet, and the clarinetist and vocalist Horst Winter, to appear on his programmes. Evelyn Künneke (*b.* 1921), daughter of the operettist Eduard Künneke, having been 'called up' for forces entertainment in September 1943, was posted to Radio Belgrade in mid-1944. At the time Lale Andersen remained out of favour and 'Lili Marleen' was proscribed for German home consumption:

> 'We're just getting together an English version of this song', they told me at the station. 'It's only the German version that is banned. But our battle stations have got Allied listeners too. We are doing it for them.' [...] So, together with the Vienna cabaret artiste Peter Wehle and composer Friedrich Meyer who were both working in Belgrade, I reconstructed from memory the English lyric for 'Lady Of The Lamplight'. And then I sang it accompanied by the Belgrade Forces Orchestra. 'We can at least let the Tommies have their Lili Marlen back', I kidded. Our recording brought the international forces sweetheart back to life; we'd given her the kiss of life – in English.[6]

As Tito's partisans and the Soviet army closed on the Serbian capital late in 1944, Radio Belgrade shed all its foreigners and most of its German staff. A few days prior to the occupation of the city, on 14 October, the last Germans fled the broadcasting building. Since July the military had been operating a mobile station on the Belgrade wave-length from Hungary. At first using the name 'Q', for '*Quelle*' (source), it now titled itself 'Battle Station *Prinz Eugen*'[7] and used the identification 'Studio Belgrade *Lili Marleen*'. As the Soviets advanced from the east and the German army withdrew westward, their transmitter went with them. During the final weeks of the war, 'Prinz Eugen' criss-crossed the Alps until it finally came to rest at Maria Pfarr at the foot of the Hohen-Tauern-Pass. From there it continued broadcasting until 8 May 1945, when its staff learned that Germany had capitulated. Because no Allied soldiers were in evidence in the vicinity, the broadcasters put together a farewell programme, signing off appropriately with a final rendition of 'Lili Marleen'. Soon afterwards a British officer arrived and ushered the survivors of Radio Belgrade to a PoW camp.

The 1941 Truce and Interradio

Having acquired Radio Belgrade in May 1941, Ribbentrop looked further afield. On

14 July the Foreign Ministry created an agency called Radio Mundial, aiming to win access to and influence over foreign stations through a nominally 'neutral' international radio news agency. For this reason Radio Mundial SA was registered in Lisbon. Next, on 22 July, Ribbentrop removed Kultur-R from the Cultural Policy Division and made it a division on its own, called the *Rundfunkabteilung* (and, from 13 February 1942, *Rundfunkpolitische Abteilung*), with Rühle at its helm and Dr. Hans Heinrich Schirmer (*b*. 1911 – the post-war West German ambassador to Canberra and Vienna) as his deputy. The new division had two functions, Ru-A, which under Kurt Alex Mair supervised technical and legal matters, and Ru-B, which under Kurt Georg Kiesinger looked after propaganda content, ProMi relations and the coordination of the new division's regional teams. After Schirmer was called up for military service early in 1943, Kiesinger became deputy head of the Foreign Broadcasting Division.

By mid-1941 the Foreign Ministry had two hundred and sixty staff, spread over twenty departments, working on broadcasting activities. So, to match his arch-rival's appetite for new propaganda initiatives, Goebbels doubled his Foreign Division staff to ninety-three. Both the ProMi and the Foreign Ministry were now apparently so engrossed in encroaching upon the other's territories that neither paid much attention to the provision of propaganda back-up for the German attack on the Soviet Union. Hitler therefore placed responsibility for all propaganda in the area with Alfred Rosenberg, recently created minister for the occupied territories in the east.

Goebbels and Ribbentrop were both losers as a result, which may account for the fact that each ministry soon redefined its propaganda activities and agreed to adhere to Hitler's September 1939 ruling. Hunke led the consultations for the ProMi and Krümmer for the Foreign Ministry. On 22 October 1941 the ministers signed a fourteen-page working agreement which seemed more a truce than an end to feuding. According to the document:

- Foreign broadcasting stations in occupied territories should be consolidated in a jointly controlled holding company, Interradio AG;
- the Foreign Ministry should transfer its Seehaus monitoring activity to Interradio;
- the Foreign Ministry would refrain from active propaganda and restrict itself to providing guidelines to the ProMi;
- the importance of liaison officers was reconfirmed and their functions re-defined.

Krümmer was now the Foreign Ministry's chief liaison officer with the ProMi and the RRG and as such attended Goebbels' daily ministerial conference and conferred with Goebbels' secretaries of state each afternoon. Under the new agreement the ProMi recognized and approved a further three top Foreign Ministry representatives, including Mair on broadcasting matters and Kiesinger on cultural and propaganda matters. Kiesinger thus became the Foreign Ministry's official link with Winkelnkemper. Further Foreign Ministry representatives were installed in the RRG at an operational level.

On 26 January 1942 Interradio A.G. was restructured, and four weeks later registered, with four board members from each ministry, including Mair (Foreign Ministry) as chairman, Diewerge (ProMi) as his deputy, Diettrich (RRG) and Kiesinger (Foreign Ministry). The company was based in offices in the Lessinghaus at Schiffbauerdamm until September 1943, when it was bombed out and transferred to the Seehaus complex at Wannsee. On 1 February the Seehaus monitoring post became part of the new Interradio AG, and in May Radio Mundial SA was shut down, after eleven months of existence.

Radio Metropol

In March 1942, soon after the restructuring, Interradio launched Radio Metropol, which was to become one of the most popular stations of the Second World War. Although the Foreign Ministry originally planned to use the Zemun short-wave transmitter for general overseas broadcasts, it first went on the air as the 'covert' station Radio Metropol, with programmes in Russian, Ukrainian, Georgian and Tatar directed at the eastern front, in addition to English and Persian broadcasts. Soon afterwards French broadcasts were added and, in the summer of 1942, programmes in Uzbek introduced in support of the thrust towards Stalingrad. After the German defeat, Radio Metropol's schedule to the Soviet Union was substantially curtailed and, in the summer of 1943, dropped altogether.

At the beginning of 1943 the focus of Radio Metropol's broadcasts had begun to shift towards North Africa. In May its schedules were extended to include the Middle East, with programmes in English, French, Polish, Arabic and Persian. There were three transmissions in English and French, each lasting a full hour, every day. The programmes were carried by cable link to Zemun for transmission, initially from Berlin and later from Graz, in Austria, where the RRG's current affairs section had been evacuated. The station's news bulletins were drawn largely from information provided by German sources to which items of Allied origin were added in order to give an appearance of balance. Current affairs commentaries were included, with the usual helping of familiar official interpretations. The Interradio studios in Berlin provided Radio Metropol with light-hearted sketches and relaxing entertainment music.

Dr. Harald Diettrich, controller of the RRG's foreign stations after April 1941, was Interradio's head of musical programming and largely responsible for Radio Metropol's success. A note on Metropol drawn up by the BBC monitors in February 1944, and cited in a 1945 MI5 report, observed that: 'The speakers are well trained and have an excellent command of their respective languages'.[8] Among its staff were several British-born broadcasters, of the now familiar polyglot backgrounds, chiefly Birmingham-born John Ward and the journalist Baer Kospoth; others were Henry William Wicks, before the war a right-wing activist in Britain, and James Blair.

John Alexander Ward was born at Birmingham in November 1885. Between 1908 and 1911 he was in Frankfurt-on-Main, learning German. During the First World

War he served briefly with the 3rd Battalion of the Gloucestershire Regiment, and in December 1921 returned to Germany to settle near Frankfurt as an interpreter-translator. At the beginning of the Second World War he was interned, initially at Würzburg and later at Tost, Upper Silesia. Having spent nearly three years in German internment, he offered his services to the German authorities, which brought his release in May 1943 and transfer to a so-called 'holiday camp' at Genshagen, a Berlin suburb, for observation and political indoctrination. This was one of two 'holiday camps' – the other, for officers, being in a villa at Berlin-Zehlendorf. These camps came under the Army High Command and were supervised by the counter-intelligence (*Abwehr*), but effectively run by Arnold Hillen-Ziegfeld, the Foreign Ministry's special representative for British PoWs.

Six weeks later, on 19 June 1943, Ward was required to report to Dr. Harald Diettrich, who later recalled the circumstances in a statement to MI5:

> I first heard of Alexander Ward through Wicks who had been with him in an internment camp. Wicks knew we were short of British announcers and he suggested we should get Ward out of the camp. We did manage to do this, although it took some time, and we were very glad to have him. He was made an announcer in the English Section. [...] His wife came to see me once or twice, seeking my assistance in getting her husband out of internment.[9]

Ward himself later described his duties for Radio Metropol:

> For the first two months, my work consisted of reading news and announcing musical programmes. Later on I drew up programmes of music, took part in sketches and wrote a few sketches myself. The idea was to entertain the troops and by that means to induce them to listen to the news. This was full time work, for which I was paid a salary of 600 marks and extras for any manuscripts or any taking part in sketches that I did. The gross salary averaged from 800 to 900 marks a month.[10]

After Radio Metropol closed in August 1944, Ward briefly worked as a speaker of commentaries in the programme 'Jerry Calling' of the German European Stations. In November 1944 he joined the Empire zone of the German Overseas Station at Königs Wusterhausen, working mainly as a news translator. From January 1945 he wrote and read a regular Monday evening talk, under the name 'Donald Hodgson'.

Baer Joseph Kospoth, the illegitimate son of an American lawyer and Countess Margaret Kospoth, of Briese, Silesia, was born in October 1881 at Weymouth, in Dorset. To avoid a scandal the Countess had travelled to England for the birth, and registered the child under the name of Russell. At the age of four Baer Russell was taken to New York, where he attended Berkeley School until the age of twelve, when he and his mother settled at Vevey, in Switzerland. Around the turn of the century Russell entered Berlin University as a student of philology, registering under his mother's name. Upon completion of his studies, Kospoth became a freelance journalist. In 1904 he married a Dutch woman in Berlin, being issued with a British passport to do so. In 1906 Kospoth joined the staff of the *Kleines Journal*, a left-wing Berlin paper. Upon the outbreak of war in 1914 he was arrested and released only on condition he reported to the police daily. To avoid internment, he now claimed German nationality on the grounds that his mother was German, and was eventually issued with German papers. When Kospoth was suspected of having leaked classified military information to American contacts, the publisher of the *Kleines Journal* sent him as correspondent to Geneva, where, chameleon-like, he claimed British nationality, was issued with a British passport, and worked for the local British Intelligence station until its closure in 1918.

Between the wars Baer Kospoth worked as a correspondent for American papers in Paris until, in 1940, he was arrested and interned as a British subject. Once again he claimed German nationality on the strength of the papers issued to him in 1914, and was released to work as a clerk at a military hospital and later as an interpreter and translator for the German administration in Paris.

In the spring of 1943 the local branch of the Nazi Party's foreign organization sent Kospoth to Germany for indoctrination. There he was made clearly to understand that he was expected to support the German war effort. Through James Blair, an Irishman and fellow-internee in France, Kospoth was introduced to Dr. Diettrich, who recruited him for Radio Metropol. From August 1943 Kospoth played in French radio sketches, of which he wrote three himself, read the news in English about six times a week – alternating with Blair – and worked in the editorial offices.

Radio Monitoring by the Foreign Ministry

The Foreign Ministry began monitoring and evaluating foreign broadcasts only in July 1940, during the battle of France. The operation, under Kurt Alex Mair, was based at a villa in Berlin-Wannsee, generally therefore referred to as the special agency Lakeside-House (*Sonderdienst Seehaus*). The Seehaus service concentrated initially on foreign stations not already monitored by agencies such as the RRG, the High Command, the Counter-Espionage or Göring's so-called research office (*Forschungsamt*) of the Luftwaffe. In December 1940 Göring, in his capacity as chairman of the Ministerial Council for the Defence of the Reich (*Ministerrat für die Reichsverteidigung*), was apparently receptive to the idea of integrating all monitoring activities in the Seehaus operation – but this never materialized.[11]

At its peak the Seehaus staff of 580 evaluated some 360 foreign stations across thirty-one languages, with monitoring facilities all over Germany, in Bucharest, Paris, Marseilles and Shanghai. Further listening posts in Casablanca and in the Crimea were to follow. The Seehaus daily analysis of foreign broadcasts, commonly referred to as 'the bible', was circulated to a very restricted and highly-supervised top-level readership.

Double Nemesis – Ribbentrop and Luther

After the October 1941 agreement between the two ministries, Krümmer organized the 'Propaganda Control Apparatus' as an annex to his *Sonderreferat Organisation* in order to streamline communication over propaganda within the Foreign Ministry. In addition, in December, Ribbentrop appointed Dr. Karl Megerle (*b.* 1894), a freelance journalist working on several assignments for the Foreign Ministry, as his special delegate for propaganda. Megerle was also an NSDAP member in the *Reichstag*. His task was to interpret developments to the minister and pass on ministerial views and directives. Habicht and Luther had also been appointed special delegates for propaganda, but within the Foreign Ministry structure, whereas Megerle was attached to the minister's personal office. Megerle's deputy was Werner von Schmieden of the Foreign Ministry's Political Division.

In October 1942, a year after the 'truce', Luther finally consolidated his position when Ribbentrop appointed him as under-secretary of state. Luther was now head of the Foreign Ministry's German Division; *via* Krümmer's *Sonderreferat Organisation* he was involved in all organizational and personnel matters; and as head of a new division, *Auslandspropagandaleitstelle* (the former *Propagandakontrollapparat*), he was now directly responsible for all propaganda within the Foreign Ministry. Six months later, however, this elaborate structure collapsed when Luther's conspiracy to topple his minister was exposed and he was dispatched to Sachsenhausen concentration camp. It is generally accepted that Luther was plotting to replace Ribbentrop with an SS-man, probably Werner Best. The plot came to light when Himmler's adjutant, SS-General Karl Wolff, sent Ribbentrop a copy of Luther's plan. Hitler wanted to hang Luther, but Ribbentrop persuaded him to sentence the culprit to detention. With his superior's ignominious departure, Krümmer too was finished, and posted to a consulate in Turkey.[12]

By this time military solutions had replaced foreign policy and Goebbels had emerged the victor in the battle for control of propaganda abroad. In April 1943 he instructed Hunke to amend the October 1941 agreement with the Foreign Ministry. Later that year Hunke retired from the ProMi to take up a directorship of the Deutsche Bank.[13]

Martin Luther died of a heart condition in a Berlin hospital in May 1945, having just been released from Sachsenhausen by the Soviets.

Ribbentrop's foreign-policy base and Party standing evaporated as the war reached its climax. By 1945 he had no influence over Hitler. At the end of the war Allied Intelligence, which sought quickly to track down 'war criminals', had little initial success in finding the former Reich foreign minister. Ribbentrop had registered in a hotel in Hamburg under the name 'Reiser'. By day he strolled the streets in double-breasted suit and bowler hat, concealing his face behind sunglasses. Eventually, on 13 June 1945, he contacted a local wine merchant, an acquaintance from the past, saying 'You've got to hide me [...] it is important for Germany's future'. But the police were informed and, the following day, Ribbentrop was arrested. The Nuremberg Tribunal found him guilty, on 1 October 1946, and two weeks later he was the first to be hanged, at 01:14 hours, on 16 October.

7   Voices from Nowhere – the 'Concordia' Story

'Black' and 'White' Propaganda

In addition to its overseas and European services, German broadcasting also operated a third foreign-language outlet.[1] This was the Secret Stations, the so-called *Geheimsender*, also known – for reasons that will be explained – as the 'Büro Concordia'. These 'covert' or 'clandestine' stations, run by the Germans – and equally by the Allies – during the Second World War, were secret only in the sense that they did not in fact transmit from the location they claimed. They existed to deceive foreign listeners as to where the signal came from, what their real agenda was, and who was behind it. The art of creating successful 'covert' stations lay in appearing to be unofficial – or even illegal – organizations, operating in the listeners' own country as the voice of dissidents seeking to undermine the government or of patriots resisting foreign occupation.

Sefton Delmer coined the term 'black' propaganda for covert activities where the source is disguised. 'Black' propaganda mixes verifiable information with falsifications and fabrications aimed at undermining the morale of the target population. Overt, or legitimate, stations do of course occur, such as when a front organization, with government funds, obtains control of a foreign station – usually one with a well-known advertizing schedule. Nor is war the only pretext for 'black' propaganda, which can also be harnessed to aggravate a political crisis, or exploit conflicts as a means to destroy national cohesion.

Before the Second World War Germany's broadcasting policy concentrated on 'white' propaganda. This involved leading foreign opinion, through the selection and presentation of news and background material, towards a favourable view of political developments in the Reich, and of its economic achievements, without a sense that either could be a threat to peace. But 'black' propaganda came of age during the War, and it too fell under the central control of Joseph Goebbels. In Britain, by contrast, the BBC remained 'white', while 'black' stations came under the Political Warfare Executive, itself answerable to the Foreign Office and the Ministries of Economic Warfare and Information. Although the BBC was not mobilized as a 'weapon of war' on the lines of its German counterpart, its role in the war effort, for all its prized independence, is revealed by the growth of its personnel. According to the broadcasting historian Asa Briggs, the BBC and the RRG each employed a staff of about 4,800 at the beginning of the War. From 1943 the BBC increasingly took the initiative, and by March 1944 its staff had risen to 11,600, while that of the RRG had begun to decline from a peak of about 10,000.

The Beginnings: Radio Stuttgart

The Nazi experience of 'black' propaganda began in July 1934, when Berlin remote-controlled an unsuccessful armed uprising on the part of the Austrian SS in Vienna. In November 1937, during the Spanish Civil War, Goebbels' ministry provided the Nationalists with a mobile medium-wave transmitter which was stationed first on a football field in Salamanca, and later in Burgos and at La Coruña. Radio Nacional de Salamanca professed to be operated by the Republicans and created confusion within the Republican camp, to Franco's military advantage. And 'black' propaganda played its part, of course, in disabling resistance to the annexation of Austria in March 1938, and of the Sudetenland, the German-populated part of Czechoslovakia, in September.

In 1937, Nazi-sponsored programmes in French were introduced onto the Stuttgart wave-length. 'Radio Stuttgart' purveyed an intermediate kind of 'black' propaganda: it did not conceal from its French listeners that its programmes emanated from Germany, but offered an alternative, pro-Nazi viewpoint. Its programmes were presented by two French speakers, Paul Ferdonnet, who adopted the *nom-de-guerre* 'Stoessel', and André Obrecht. Beginning with two programmes a day, it rose to nine by 1939, broadcast from the 100 kW transmitter at Mühlacker-Dürrmenz, backed by local stations in Frankfurt, Cologne and Saarbrücken.

Ferdonnet and Obrecht were sensitive communicators: they identified whole-heartedly with their audience, dwelt sentimentally on the charms and beauty of France, and knew when logic should give way to emotion. As the political crisis in Europe escalated in 1938 and 1939, they took a more divisive tack, beginning to attack the French bourgeoisie, inciting workers against bosses, and citizens against the 'war-mongering' government. They appealed to lingering Anglophobia among the older generation and reiterated the theme that the conflict with Germany was the consequence of the French government's alliance with the 'British imperialists', out to plunder both France and Germany. Ferdonnet hammered away at the slogan: 'England means to fight this war to the last Frenchman'.

So long as the 'Phoney War' lasted, Radio Stuttgart's programmes were never dull. Ferdonnet and Obrecht made it appear that their source was well-connected sympathizers within France who fed them privileged information. When King George VI's driver lost his way en route to an inspection of the British Expeditionary Force, Radio Stuttgart sneered: 'The king should have asked us!', and went on to identify the unit's exact location. It 'reported' the daily catch at Boulogne, as well as the crash of a French fighter plane at Orleans, proffering the pilot's name, rank, age and even the number of his children. On 3 March 1940 Radio Stuttgart correctly informed the French *'Division des Bidons'* (roughly, the 'Flask Force') that they were to break camp at Mourmelon ten days later than planned. Most perplexing to the hard-drinking forces

Secret Stations (from November 1939)
November 1939 – November 1940: Dr. Adolf Raskin
April 1941 – May 1945: Dr. Erich Hetzler

Stations targetting France

Radio Humanité	December 1939 – June 1940
Poste de Réveil	December 1939 – June 1940
La Voix de la Paix	February 1940 – June 1940
Camarade du Nord	June 1940
Voix de la Bretagne	June 1940

Stations targetting Britain

New British Broadcasting Station	February 1940 – April 1945
Radio Caledonia	June 1940 – July 1942
Workers' Challenge	July 1940 – End 1944
Christian Peace Movement	July 1940 – February 1942
Welsh National Radio	July 1940 – August 1940
Radio National	July 1943 – April 1945

Stations targetting the British Sphere of Influence

The Voice of the Free Arabs	May 1941 –
The Voice of Free India	January 1941 –

Stations targetting the Balkans

Radio Velebit (targetting Croatia)	April 1941 –
Patris (targetting Greece)	April 1941 –

Stations targetting the Soviet Union

Lenin's Old Guard	June 1941 – February 1943
For Russia	June 1941 – February 1943

Stations targetting the USA

Debunk – Station of all Free Americans	March 1942 – 1943
Katos	May 1942 – July 1942

Stations targetting the Netherlands

De Notekraker	March 1942 – July 1942

Chart 8: Organization of the RRG's Secret Stations

was that their division's nickname was known in Stuttgart. In April 1940 a Czech army unit in France was ordered to march from Agde on the Mediterranean coast to Pézenas. The same night the 'Traitors of Stuttgart' (as the press now dubbed them) provided a detailed account of the excercise. When four British officers had a row with a waiter in a Dieppe café, Radio Stuttgart described the incident nine hours later, with precise details of the menu and of the drinks served. Members of a French air force unit first learned from Stuttgart that they were about to be moved to another base. The legend of the omniscience of the 'Stuttgart Traitors' became such that – as with 'Lord Haw-Haw' – they were often credited with wholly mythical scoops.

Ferdonnet, born at Niort in June 1901, was a right-wing journalist with a strong professional reputation. He went to Berlin in 1927 as correspondent for Jacques Doriot's paper, *La Liberté*.[2] In 1934 he founded a press agency in Paris, called *Prisma*, and wrote and published several pro-Nazi brochures, including *Face à Hitler* and *Le troisième Reich*, paid for by the Press Department of the Berlin Foreign Ministry.[3] In March 1940, his participation in Radio Stuttgart having been identified, Ferdonnet was sentenced to death *in absentia* by a Paris court. By this time he had moved from Stuttgart to Berlin to work for the RRG's Foreign Languages Service. But at the end of September 1941 he was declared redundant, on the grounds of being 'impossible for his colleagues to work with'.[4] Eventually, early in 1942, he was transferred to the European Stations' French editorial staff where he operated under the cover name of 'Peter Hörbiger'.

By this time, however, Ferdonnet had become very much a problem. In December 1940 his seventeen-year-old daughter had suddenly arrived in Berlin from France. After her father's sentence earlier in the year she had been expelled from the convent at which she was studying and been living on the streets of Paris. In Berlin, Ferdonnet refused to look after his daughter, who had to be put up in an institution. From early in 1942, the broadcaster was too ill to work, suffering from heart disease and, according to a contemporary medical report, 'Thyreotoxicosis with a considerable psychological element'. But, despite criticism from the foreign language service and the European Stations, the RRG's personnel department recommended that Ferdonnet receive a pension of 500 marks a month: 'in recognition of his undoubted successes and merits in Germany's French propaganda during the years 1937 to 1941, it appears to be desirable that the Reich should magnanimously support him now'.[5] At the end of the war Ferdonnet was living in Schwenningen, where a French army commando arrested him in April 1945. He was immediately tried for high treason, found guilty, and executed by firing squad on 4 August 1945.[6]

'Concordia' is Born

After the signing of the German-Soviet non-aggression pact of 23 August 1939, the French Communist Party switched its target from the Nazi party to the government of France. This in turn gave the French authorities the pretext for treating the Communists like a German fifth column: the party was outlawed on 26 September and its leadership rounded up. At the same time the opportunity for a radical shift to a more subversive propaganda line presented itself to Goebbels. On 30 October, in expectation of a (soon countermanded) German offensive in the west, Goebbels instructed the head of his ministry's Broadcasting Division, Alfred-Ingemar Berndt, to develop, in coordination with the Foreign Ministry and the military High Command, propaganda stations targeting French and Irish listeners.[7] Britain was excluded since, at that time, Nazi leaders still considered the possibility of a peaceful settlement with Her Majesty's Government.

Berndt charged the energetic and experienced Dr. Adolf Raskin, head of the RRG's Current Affairs Division and future head of all foreign broadcasts, with overall

42 Adolf Raskin, head of the RRG's
foreign broadcasts, 1940.

responsibility for a new secret special agency (*geheime Sonderdienststelle*) called
Bureau (*Büro*) Concordia, and Walter Kamm was appointed its deputy head and pro-
gramme controller. Initially Concordia consisted of two broadcasting sections,
'*Redaktion I für Ost und West*' and '*Redaktion II für Königs Wusterhausen*'. '*Redaktion I*'
covered French-language broadcasts on medium wave and was headed by Raskin.
French Communists were recruited to write the scripts, read at first by Theodor
Thony, a German-born actor who had been brought up in France. Other members of
Concordia's French section were Friedrich Dambmann, Josef Haafs and Anna
Jankowski, with Dr. Karl Bartz and Otto Mohri as freelances. The Foreign Ministry's
liaison officer was Otto Abetz, later the German ambassador to Vichy France, with a
Mr. Diehl as his deputy.[8]

Dr. Erich Hetzler headed '*Redaktion II*' for English-language broadcasts on short
wave. The Foreign Ministry's liaison officer with Concordia's English section was
initially, and for a brief period only, Dr. Rösel, a journalist who had been before the
war with a trade magazine in London. After a clash with Hetzler, the Foreign
Ministry withdrew Rösel and replaced him with Professor Adolf Mahr. In 1942 Mahr
also became head of the Foreign Ministry's Irish broadcasting section.

The *Büro's* tendentious claim to the patronage of the Classical goddess of harmony
stemmed from the address of its original headquarters in the basement of the 'Villa
Concordia' at Soorstrasse 33 in Berlin. The house had belonged to the RRG's pre-war
technical director, and lay conveniently close to the *Funkhaus* in Berlin-
Charlottenburg. From 1942 Concordia operated from the press boxes of the Olympic
stadium. Most of its foreign broadcasters were also accommodated in the stadium's
spacious facilities, where they turned the Olympic turf into a vegetable garden. The
RRG's 1942 internal telephone directory gives the new location as '*Lager Osterhof*'

(roughly, eastern camp), although in fact it lay two and a half kilometres north-west of the *Funkhaus*.

After the beginning of the Allied saturation bombing of German cities in June 1943, Hetzler, by then head of the Secret Stations, was instructed to investigate emergency quarters in Dresden and ready Concordia for evacuation. But he rejected the premises as unsuitable, and Concordia remained in the Olympic stadium. In September 1944, for protection from the bombing, the full staff moved into the cavernous corridors beneath the spectators' terraces. Finally, at the end of March 1945, Concordia was evacuated to Helmstedt, until all clandestine radio activities ceased on 10 April 1945.

The Battle of France

Concordia commenced operations on 12 December 1939. From the outset the RRG paid for everything – management, staff, accommodation, technical facilities – on top of which an additional sum of 22,000 marks per month, earmarked for extra foreign-language staff, was promised by the Propaganda Ministry from its war funds. The initial target was France, and on 16 December the first French-language station – on long wave – went into action from Saarbrücken.[9] In internal correspondence Raskin and Berndt had been referring to the station as either Concordia East or The Free Word (*La Franche Parole*), but it went on the air as *Radio Humanité*, making for French listeners an obvious connection with the Communist Party newspaper, *l'Humanité*. Of the stations he was about to launch, Raskin saw this as 'the more objective, harder hitting, more serious and higher standard operation'.[10] *Radio Humanité* claimed to be the underground voice of the French Communist Party and made the most of the Party's hostility to the French government. The Concordia editors had indeed no need to fabricate Communist defeatism: the French Party's official line at this time often sounded as if it had been written by Nazi propagandists. *Radio Humanité* presented itself as pacifist and called for peace demonstrations. It opposed overtime at arms factories and called on men to refuse conscription. But apart from the music it played – principally records of *chansons* performed by Lucienne Boyer and Tino Rossi – *Radio Humanité* programmes were dull and lacked general appeal.

Two more 'clandestine' stations began broadcasting against France on short-wave during the 'Phoney War': *Poste du Réveil de la France*, meaning France's Watch Station, and *La Voix de la Paix*, or The Voice of Peace. It has been suggested that *Poste du Réveil* and *La Voix* were one and the same station, called *Le Réveil de la Paix*, but this is not borne out by BBC monitoring service transcripts and other sources.[11] *Poste du Réveil*, or *Radio Révolution* as its was also called, began broadcasting from Stuttgart on the 41 metre band on 27 December 1939. Originally referred to in the files as Concordia West, it was named (perhaps by mistake) *La Réveille de la France*, meaning France's Alarm Clock. Its signal was weak and the presentation of material deliberately amateurish, doubtless to convey the impression of a station operated by well-meaning but non-professional Frenchmen. In his strategy paper, Raskin described its approach as 'the more popular, more down-to-earth and more reckless operation' in comparison with Concordia East. Like Radio Stuttgart before it, *Poste du Réveil* asked its listeners why the French were at war with the Germans, and all through the early months of 1940 the station repeated the message: France was weak, Germany was strong, and Britain was using France for its own imperialist purposes.

In February 1940 a third station – *La Voix de la Paix* – was launched, with a more bourgeois approach and delivery, and transmitted on the Warsaw wave-band. One of its slogans was: 'We have lost – stop the war!' In addition to the Saarbrücken, Stuttgart and Warsaw wave-lengths, Concordia's French-language programmes also had the use of a mobile long-wave transmitter at Schopfheim, near Lörrach, Baden, in the German-Swiss-French triangle.

To coincide with the beginning of the German *Blitzkrieg* of May 1940, the ProMi stepped up its psychwar. *Poste du Réveil* now went out on long wave in addition to its short-wave transmissions, and *La Voix* also appeared on medium wave. The regional stations at Cologne and Leipzig, the *Deutschlandsender* and the station in newly-occupied Luxembourg, were linked in a concerted propaganda barrage on the French population.

The ProMi now solicited the services of several prominent German Communists, including Ernst Torgler (1893–1963) and his partner, Maria Reese, to write scripts for *Radio Humanité*. Torgler and another German Communist, Karl Albrecht, an ex-commissar from the Soviet Union, later worked for a clandestine German station broadcasting to the Soviet Union.[12] After the war, Torgler denied that Maria Reese had written any texts for *Radio Humanité* and stated that, apart from himself, only Wilhelm Kasper, a Communist friend and pre-1933 member of the Prussian diet who had also been released from concentration camp, and Karl Albrecht, were forced to write appeals to French workers not to resist the German army and to 'avoid unnecessary bloodshed'.

Torgler had joined the German Communist Party in 1920 and later became the party's spokesman in the *Reichstag*. During the 1920s he, with Ernst Thälmann, was one of Germany's most prominent Communists. '*Zum Schutz von Volk und Staat*' (for the protection of the nation and the state), the decree-law hurriedly enacted by Hitler on 28 February 1933, was the instrument used for the arrest of Torgler and many other critics of the Nazi régime. As the last to leave the burning *Reichstag* building on 27 February, Torgler was charged with arson, but acquitted by the jury. Goebbels raged over this 'misverdict' and Torgler was promptly re-arrested and dispatched to a concentration camp. On several occasions over the next two years the foreign press reported his death, but the Nazis repeatedly produced him alive. Torgler presented his mutilated fingers to the journalists, praised his treatment, and declared all he wanted was to return to a normal family life outside politics. He was released in 1935, and almost simultaneously expelled from the Communist Party. Torgler's son, who had fled to the USSR in 1933, was sentenced in Moscow to ten years' hard labour. After the war the West German Communist Party rejected Torgler's application for membership, and he joined the Social Democrats.

During the campaigns of May-June 1940, the German secret stations worked assiduously to foster a mood of panic in France. Access to familiar wave-lengths such as Radio

Brussels and Radio Paris added force and plausibility to their propaganda. *Poste du Réveil* gave the impression it was calling up a Fifth Column ready to direct a national revolution. It directed passionate appeals to the French army to capitulate or face a bloodbath, and routinely exaggerated the ferocity of the German *Blitzkrieg*. *La Voix* 'revealed' deficiencies in the French armament industry and expressed concern for the country's future following its army's loss of tactical cohesion and fighting spirit. It demanded Paris be declared an open city and delivered alarmist news flashes such as the one on 12 June: 'All Paris is at risk [...] since Fifth Columnists succeeded in poisoning several reservoirs of drinking water. [...] Will Paris be another Warsaw [with] our women and children's blood running in the gutters?' The stations 'reported' that the French government had fled the country, leaving the people to fend for themselves, 'knew' of cases of cholera in Paris, and 'advised' listeners to withdraw their savings from bank accounts and stock-pile food. Smears against political and military leaders were daily events.

Early in June two further German-sponsored 'clandestine' stations began broadcasting to France, *Camarade du Nord* (Northern Comrade) and *Voix de la Bretagne* (Voice of Brittany). Both declared they spoke for local opponents of government policy who sought peace, but significantly they addressed the sensitive zone within which the German offensive of 5 June needed to make its first decisive gains. *La Voix de la Bretagne's* regional appeal was based on its claim to be run by Breton separatists seeking German support. On 1 June an Italian-sponsored station, *Radio Corse Libre* (Radio Free Corsica), which had been broadcasting intermittently throughout 1939, returned to the air. On 10 June, four days before the German army entered Paris, Italy declared war on France.

On 12 June, Goebbels confided to his diary that he had justified hopes that the population of Paris would start a revolution against their government. At his 18 June ministerial briefing he is minuted as follows: 'The minister reported that an analysis made by our diplomatic services confirms the effectiveness of our broadcasts, that their success is one hundred per cent, and that the collapse in the enemy camp can be attributed to a major degree to these broadcasts'.[13]

On 24 June, a couple of days after the surrender of France, the German secret stations closed down. They had achieved what they had been created to do. Later, analysts such as Charles Rolo and Edmond Taylor (a psychological warfare specialist with the US Office of Strategic Services) indeed attributed France's sudden collapse in large part to the effects of German propaganda. But another American analyst, Dr. Muehlen, observed in 1941 that extreme right-wing political trends *within* France were more relevant than the influence of Nazi propaganda. Since the political and social crisis of the early 1930s, France had exhibited many signs of 'defeatism, incompetence and divided counsels at the head of an undermined morale among the rank-and-file', and German propaganda found in the French body politic a highly receptive mentality.[14]

Build-up to 'Operation Sea Lion'

In a report on Concordia's activities, dated 25 June 1940, Raskin reaffirmed his overall managerial and political responsibility, with Walter Kamm as his deputy and programme controller and Erich Hetzler as head of the English section. 'Lord How How' [*sic*] was described as a '*beratender Mitarbeiter*', that is to say, a consultant and contributor to the programmes.

Norman Baillie-Stewart described Hetzler as a 'fanatical Nazi [who] always wore his black SS uniform in the broadcasting station. He was never known not to have worn his uniform, even when he was doing occasional broadcasts to Britain. He strutted around the station not merely in his impressive uniform but wearing his sword as well.' In a ProMi document of 26 June 1942, Winkelnkemper reported that Hetzler had 'first-hand knowledge of England from a 13-year stay in that country, including four years as English affairs specialist on the staff of Reich Foreign Minister von Ribbentrop. [...] Clever, flexible propagandist, with proven success. Adheres consistently to our political propaganda line.' But Winkelnkemper's account was not quite accurate: Hetzler had in fact spent precisely thirteen *months* in England, and it was as a Party activist and highly decorated SS-officer that he rose to his position in Ribbentrop's circle.

Kurt Erich Werner Hetzler, to give him his full name, was born in Mannheim on 15 January 1910. In 1919 he followed his divorced mother to Munich, attending schools in Munich and Aschaffenburg, and finishing his secondary education in Darmstadt in 1929. Subsequently he joined the Britannia Batteries company in London as an apprentice, and in October 1929 enrolled at the London School of Economics and Political Science. In May 1930 Hetzler returned to Germany to become assistant operations manager with a wholesale paper business in Salach, Württemberg. A year later, in the summer of 1931, he enrolled at Berlin University, and in February 1932 joined the NSDAP, the National Socialist German Students Organization and became a Storm Trooper. At about the same time he enrolled at Munich University to study under Otto von Zwiedineck-Südenhorst, an authority on national economics, 'to whom I felt ideologically closer than to the mainly Jewish lecturers at the Berlin High School', as Hetzler stated in his 1937 curriculum vitae.[15]

43 Erich Hetzler, photograph from his internment camp pass, July 1948.

In April 1935 Hetzler gained his master's degree with a thesis on 'Reichsbank and Business in the aftermath of Economic Stabilization' (*Reichsbank und Wirtschaft in den ersten Jahren nach der Stabilisierung*).

Hetzler sought to join the staff of the Reichsbank, but his chances were diminished in the light of some critical opinions aired in his thesis. Instead, von Zwiedineck-Südenhorst introduced him to one of his private pupils, Rudolf Hess, Hitler's deputy, who recommended Hetzler to Ribbentrop. On 1 July 1935, Hetzler joined the '*Dienststelle des Beauftragten für aussenpolitische Fragen der NSDAP im Stab des Stellvertreters des Führers*', in other words he became a member of Ribbentrop's foreign policy office 'on the staff of the Führer's deputy', as the official designation went. Initially he reported to Otto Abetz, but after a few weeks was transferred to the newly created England section (*Hauptreferat X*) headed by Professor Graf von Dürckheim, while Abetz concentrated on France. At the point Hetzler joined Ribbentrop, Walter Kamm was responsible for the Netherlands section, but left in 1938 to join the RRG's European Stations.[16]

Shortly afterwards, in September 1935, Hetzler was 'transferred' from the SA to the SS, in which Ribbentrop himself had the rank of colonel. He rose to SS-captain and by 1941 had accumulated several esteemed awards: the death's head ring (*Totenkopfring*), the sword of honour (*Ehrendegen*) and the pseudo-Germanic yuletide lantern (*Julleuchter*). Ribbentrop sent Hetzler to London for the funeral of King George V, early in 1936, partly to sound out Labour leaders and others with whom German diplomats had no official contact on the likely British reaction to a German re-occupation of the Rhineland. Hetzler subsequently returned to London on several occasions as a special emissary of Ribbentrop. Once he was tempted to accept an offer to join the *Frankfurter Zeitung's* economics desk, but was not let go. When Ribbentrop was appointed German ambassador to London in August 1936, he sought to transfer Hetzler to the Foreign Ministry. But Hetzler declined, seeing himself neither a civil servant nor a diplomat.

During a reception for the Italian foreign minister, Count Ciano, in the spring of 1939, Hetzler met Walter Kamm, his former colleague from the Ribbentrop office but now head of the RRG's European foreign-language service, who introduced him to Heinrich Glasmeier. He was offered a position at the RRG, but Ribbentrop once again refused to release him. Nevertheless, Glasmeier invited Hetzler to visit the *Funkhaus*, where he was shown round by Kamm. When war seemed inevitable, Hetzler volunteered for service in an anti-aircraft unit with which he had earlier trained, but the RRG now laid claim to his services, and on the very day the Second World War began, Hetzler joined the RRG as senior specialist (*Hauptsachbearbeiter*), on a salary of 680 marks a month. Propaganda was now more important to the war effort than foreign affairs.

When German clandestine operations against France ceased with the armistice of June 1940, and Britain became the primary target of German propaganda, Erich Hetzler emerged as effective head of all the German secret stations. After the death of Adolf Raskin in November 1940 and the reorganization of the German broadcasting system in April 1941, Hetzler's position was reconfirmed and he was appointed a 'programme controller with special responsibilities' (*Sendeleiter mit besonderen Aufgaben*). His salary was raised to 800 marks per month, with 150 marks performance bonus and 150 marks for expenses.[17]

William Joyce, king-pin of the RRG's English-language service, was Hetzler's most valued British Nazi propagandist. While continuing his 'overt' broadcasts on the Hamburg and Bremen medium wave-lengths, Joyce prepared much of the output of what eventually became a cluster of specialized clandestine stations, each designed to appeal to a different segment of the British target audience. But because his voice was so well known in Britain, Joyce never featured as a speaker on these stations.

The 'New British Broadcasting Station'

Between 25 February 1940 and 9 April 1945, for about half an hour every evening, British listeners could tune in to the so-called 'New British Broadcasting Station' – NBBS, on short wave.[18] The station's German code was 'N' (for 'New'). The original wave-length was 41.07 metres, to which 25.08 and 30.77 metres were added in July 1940. Later the 25.08 metre channel was switched to 47.83 metres.[19]

The NBBS broadcasts invariably opened with 'Loch Lomond', followed by a medley of traditional melodies designed to disarm the listener, such as 'Comin' through the Rye' and 'When Irish Eyes are Smiling'. The programmes closed to the strains of 'God Save the King', as of course did the BBC. The early programmes seemed quite balanced and the speakers well chosen. The fact that the NBBS programmes were 'uncensored' and appeared to deliver accurate news bulletins drew frequently comment. The programmes were listed alongside those of the BBC in British newspapers, and in May 1940 small posters and announcement stickers even appeared in London and the home counties. They were monitored and analysed by the BBC, parodied by comedians and – at least in the early days – discussed in parliament.

Soon however William Joyce, the station's brain and driving force in all but name, began to introduce attacks on the British government. Far less restrained in his NBBS scripts than over Hamburg and Bremen, Joyce termed the British government Jewish-controlled and imperialist. It was they, he said, not Germany, that had started the war and that it was the 'patriotic duty' of British subjects to oppose their government's war policy. Joyce hated the Soviet Union and Communism as intensely as he hated Jews, but during 1939 and 1940 the existence of the German-Soviet pact prevented him from articulating what he profoundly believed, that Britain was fighting the wrong enemy and should side with Germany in a war against Russia. Later the NBBS's line was that it was neither pro-American nor anti-Russian, but purely pro-British. It professed to be 'entirely run by British people who put their country above their own interest and are resolved to speak the truth for their country's sake'.[20]

That the NBBS broadcasters were largely British can hardly be denied. Kenneth Vincent Lander was born in London in May 1904 and educated at Ampleforth College, Yorkshire, and Pembroke College, Oxford. From 1926 Lander regularly vacationed in France and Germany, and in 1930 studied for some time at Munich

University. He became a language teacher but was made redundant in 1932 and, after a period of private tutoring, secured a job in May 1933 at the exclusive Hermann Lietz Schule, at Schloss Bieberstein, near Fulda. During his years at the school, Lander regularly returned to England and travelled widely throughout Europe. Schloss Bieberstein was converted into a military hospital at the beginning of the war, and the school moved to nearby Buchenau. Late in 1939 Lander applied for German naturalization, but was turned down. But in mid-February 1940 he was called to Berlin for a meeting at the RRG:

> I at once said that if they expected that I should give anti-English talks I should like to decline forthwith. They said they did not expect me to do this but I should speak English to English people and give even an English point of view. It seemed to me to be their wish to prevent the actual clash of arms between Germany and Britain, although a state of war existed. They said they were planning a secret radio transmitter in Berlin, the idea of which was that it should appear to the listeners that it was coming from England. They wanted to change the attitude of the English people and thus avoid the clash of arms. It occurred to me then that I in a small way could contribute to this end particularly as I, somewhat influenced by German propaganda admittedly, feared that as a result of this clash of arms Britain might well be the loser.[21]

Lander accepted the offer and joined Concordia's English section in March 1940. At first he read notes supplied by the German news service and scripts written by William Joyce. But from about the end of May 1940, he broadcast his own material, and used his own name.

By this time, Leonard Banning had joined the NBBS, and he and Lander broadcast alternately, regardless of where the material came from. 'After the fall of Norway, Belgium, Holland and France, I [Lander] began to wonder if I was serving the cause for which I enlisted my services, namely the avoidance of this very clash of arms. [...] About the second week of June 1940, Brown [?] broadcast a new service, which seemed to have as its object the creation of chaos among the people and the traffic system in England, and threatening an invasion, but of course pretending to prepare Britain against German attack, but as he admitted to me with the idea of creating panic. I broadcast some of this material but by now I was in a bit of a panic myself and didn't think I could continue much longer'.[22] On 15 July 1940 Lander was released from his contract, only to be rearrested on 30 July 1940 as a security risk, and interned at Würzburg. The camp was closed on 1 October 1941 and he was moved to Tost with the rest of its inmates. He remained an internee until March 1943 when his application to resume work as a teacher at the schools in Bieberstein and Buchenau was approved. In November 1945 Lander was arrested by British troops. After a first interrogation at Lüneburg, he was taken to Brussels *en route* to Britain.

Leonard Banning (*b.* 1910) was the NBBS's principal announcer. During the early 1930s he had been an active member of the Conservative Party, but later joined the British Union of Fascists. After he had left Britain and settled as a language teacher and journalist in Cologne, Banning continued writing contributions to various Mosley papers. After a brief period of internment in Germany at the beginning of the war, he came to Berlin in March 1940 and worked for Concordia from 10 April 1940.

Banning appears to have been a valuable asset to the English-language service. Early in 1944 Arnold Hillen-Ziegfeld, the Foreign Ministry's special representative for British PoW camps, tried to entice him away from Concordia in order to campaign for the British Free Corps. But Hetzler refused to accept Banning's letter of resignation, and complained to the ProMi that Banning's release from internment stipulated his sole employment at Concordia. Eventually, on 7 March, a compromise was reached and Banning allowed to write texts for the recruitment of Free Corps volunteers in his spare time.

At Bow Street in November 1945, Leonard Banning was charged with 'having between March 1, 1940, and March 1, 1945, committed acts likely to assist the enemy and to prejudice the efficient prosecution of the war by broadcasting propaganda from Germany, contrary to Regulation 2A of the Defence (General) Regulations 1939'.[23] On 22 January 1946 he was found guilty on five out of seven counts and sentenced to ten years penal servitude.

Lander's replacement at the NBBS, Charles Patrick Kenneth James Gilbert, used to broadcast under the names of 'Kenneth James' and 'Chris Artus'. (The latter was the maiden name of his German wife, a former typist at Concordia, also variously spelt Althus and Artios.)

Gilbert was born at Poona, India, in March 1917. In 1939 he was living at Sandhurst, Kent, where he was known to the police as a Fascist sympathizer and 'heavy drinker of violent disposition'.[24] In December 1939 he registered as a conscientious objector and was sent to Jersey to work as a farmhand. Following the German occupation of the Channel Islands in July 1940, Gilbert contacted the new rulers and offered 'to do anything he could to help bring about peace'. Shortly afterwards, in December 1940, he accepted an offer to go to Berlin, where, after interviews at the ProMi and at the RRG, including meetings with Dr. Hetzler and William Joyce, he began work as a broadcaster and script-writer for NBBS.[25]

After about a year Gilbert was invited to provide scripts for another secret station, Workers' Challenge, in addition to his work for the NBBS. In October 1942, however, he was involved in a brawl with an SS-guard when, unable to produce his pass, he was refused entrance to Concordia. A fistfight ensued and, despite representations from Hetzler, Gilbert was investigated and in January 1943 sent to a forced labour camp. He claimed, during MI5 interrogation after the war, that Hetzler had instigated his imprisonment as a kind of warning when he tried to resign from Concordia in order to work for the Foreign Ministry's Interradio.

I was kept there (two camps) for nearly five months and kept under appalling conditions. I was constantly beaten by privileged prisoners, but not so much by the German guards. This had a bad effect on my health, so much so that I had no alternative but to go back to Hetzler, or otherwise die.[26]

After his release, Gilbert returned to Concordia and to the NBBS, where he stayed until April 1945, when the whole operation was evacuated to Helmstedt and quickly petered out. After the German surrender, Gilbert remained in Germany, successfully posing as a Dutchman who worked for a United Nations agency, until British Intelligence caught up with him in the spring of 1946.

Other British subjects working for the NBBS were Ronald Spillman, a lance-corporal from London, Peter Kosaka, one of whose parents was Japanese and, for a time, Douglas George Skene Johnston. Johnston, like Gilbert, had registered as a conscientious objector and been sent to work in Jersey. After the German occupation he was interned. When a camp official asked for candidates to work in Berlin, Johnston volunteered and was taken to the capital in August 1943, together with two other civilian internees, a certain Thomas and John Lingshaw.

Johnston joined the NBBS as a speaker, calling himself 'Barrington'. He was later transferred to one of the Foreign Ministry's listening posts, until he disappeared with a German girl who was working with him. When recaptured, Johnston was sent to a concentration camp.

Some speakers on other Concordia stations which came into existence after 1940 – for example William Colledge, *alias* 'Winter', previously with Workers' Challenge – also worked for the NBBS. The Irish writer Francis Stuart occasionally contributed until about 1942, but because Joyce had reservations about his motives, Stuart's contribution was small. Edda Fromeyer, according to Hetzler a widow from South Africa whose husband's ship had been torpedoed, worked on the NBBS programme 'Between Ourselves'. Later she re-married and settled in Germany.

The NBBS – or any of the other German clandestine stations, for that matter – aroused far less public attention in Britain than the RRG's overt broadcasts, if only for the fact that only thirty-eight per cent of British listeners could pick them up, provided they had suitable receivers. A survey by the British Institute of Public Opinion in November 1939 indicated that fifty per cent of those who listened to foreign stations listened to German medium-wave broadcasts in English from Hamburg and Bremen, compared with seven per cent before the war, and with two per cent who listened to New York and ten per cent who listened to Paris. According to Silvey of the Institute of Public Opinion, in a letter to Sir Stephen Tallents, the BBC's Controller of Public Relations, on 17 November 1939, twenty-seven per cent of the British audience were listening regularly to 'Lord Haw-Haw' on Hamburg and Bremen.

Silvey's final report on *Hamburg Broadcast Propaganda: An Enquiry into the Extent and Effect of its Impact on the British Public during the mid-Winter 1939–40* was published in March 1940. It was based on 34,000 interviews and 750 questionaires. The report concluded that one person in six was a regular listener to 'Lord Haw-Haw' and that three were occasional listeners, while two never listened. Some sixteen million listeners heard the BBC nine o'clock news every night, and about six million of them would switch straight over to Hamburg afterwards. The Silvey report also showed that the habit of listening to German broadcasts was on the decline: the novelty was wearing off. On 10 May, the day Germany invaded Holland, Belgium and Luxembourg, only 13.3 per cent of the British population was listening to Hamburg.

Switching Masks – 'Workers' Challenge', 'Radio Caledonia', 'Christian Peace Movement'

After the collapse of France, Britain became Germany's major target. Hitler had hoped for a second 'Munich' which would at last allow him a free hand on the Continent, but Britain proved unreceptive to the plan. Above all Germany remained unprepared to carry out an invasion across the Channel. Such was the situation when, on 16 July, in his directive No. 16, the Führer ordered preparations for Operation Sea Lion (*Unternehmen Seelöwe*), the landing in the British Isles:

> Since England, despite its hopeless military situation, still continues to give no sign of a willingness to reach an understanding, I have made the decision to commence preparations for, and if necessary carry out, an invasion of England.

In parallel with these preparations, 'clandestine' broadcasts in English were stepped up. In a letter dated 5 July, Rudolf Stache, head of Radio Intelligence, presented Goebbels with a survey of all existing and projected secret stations against Britain:

> With the aim of disrupting the British home front on a scale comparable with what was achieved in France, we are currently extending the operations of Concordia with more powerful transmissions and new programmes.
>
> The programme that causes the English authorities the greatest anxiety, the New British Broadcasting Station, previously carried by one transmitter, will with immediate effect be heard on three short-wave stations on a variety of frequencies. This programme is hostile to the government, and agitates for an England of peace and prosperity.
>
> Concordia North-West is now operating as Caledonia, which is ostensibly an amateur station dedicated to the ideal of Scottish independence.
>
> A third secret station has just been launched. It is called Concordia Plan S, a medium-wave programme based on a mobile transmitter hitherto used for Brussels II. Plan S targets the working masses, inciting them to prepare for, and initiate, direct action. This station has a revolutionary socialist tone.
>
> Two further secret stations, both on short wave, are being readied to go on the air in the immediate future. One of these will be a secret station, Plan W, which will support the efforts of the Welsh separatists in reaction to the prevailing social conditions in Wales. The fifth Concordia transmission to England, Plan P, which will represent a purely pacifist standpoint of Christian inspiration, goes on the air in three or four days.
>
> All programmes are transmitted between 20:30 and 23:30 hours. The New British Broadcasting Company and Plan S programmes are broadcast three times daily, while at present the rest of the stations are giving only one transmission a day.[27]

On 27 June 'Radio Caledonia – The Voice of Scotland' went on the air for about half-an-hour daily on the 42.86 metre band. Its programmes were aimed at the dockyards on Clydeside, appealing largely to Scottish nationalist sentiment. Although Foreign Ministry officials were dubious about the likely receptivity of the Scots, they approved the ProMi plan.

In a letter of 25 June, Dr. Raskin had described 'Mr. Palmer' and 'Mr. MacDonald' as the main speakers of Radio Caledonia.[28] 'Donald Palmer' (real name Donald Alexander Fraser Grant) was a journalist and one-time BUF member. Until July 1942, when the station was taken off the air, he wrote and presented most of the broadcast material. Grant was assisted by a Sergeant MacDonald between June and November 1940, and, for a few weeks during the winter of 1941–42, by Susan Hilton, *alias* 'Ann Tower', who also worked briefly for the DES's Irish zone in 1942, as 'Susan Sweeney'.[29]

Each station's propaganda was carefully targetted to exploit perceived social differences and class distinctions. 'Plan S' – Workers' Challenge – began broadcasting for about fifteen minutes a day on 7 July on the former Brussels wave-length of 212.4 metres. The transmitter was the mobile medium-wave station 'Anton' at a location near Ghent on the estuary of the Scheldt in Belgium, and, after D-Day in 1944, at Wipperfürth, near Cologne. Workers' Challenge kept up its broadcasts until 26 January 1945, aiming at disgruntled workers and taking a straightforward Marxist line, with attacks on capitalists in general and on 'Churchill, Bevin, Attlee and the whole filthy, lousy gang who have betrayed you and exploited you' in particular.[30] It called on the British working class to stop the war by organizing strikes at arms factories. A typical programme opened with: 'Here is Workers' Challenge calling, the movement for revolutionary action against the bosses and war-mongers', and included passages such as: 'Organize a real working-class meeting, a march, a demonstration; get the banners out. Churchill means hunger and war. Down with Churchill. Up with the workers' Britain. No bloodshed for capitalism. Let the bosses fight for their profit. Kick 'em out of Westminster into the Thames.'[31] 'If we had it our way we would dislocate the capitalists' necks', was the blunt message on 21 July 1940. Ernest Bevin, the powerful trade unionist, then Minister of Labour and National Service in the coalition cabinet, was a favourite target: 'Sir Ernie Bevin [...] just think of the bloody rat sitting in his office, drawing his dough and telling us that we ought to work eighty-four blinking hours a week!'.[32]

The novelty of the Workers' Challenge broadcasts was that they were copiously larded with what was – by contemporary standards – relatively bad language. Leonard Ingrams of British Intelligence said that 'old ladies in Eastbourne and Torquay are listening to it avidly because it is using the foulest language ever'.[33] The jazz musician Spike Hughes recalled these broadcasts:

Dr. Goebbels' Workers' Challenge Station had quite a vogue at one time but tended to bore the English listener once the novelty had worn off. This programme was another first-hand example of German bungling. Somebody had obviously told the *Reichspropagandaminister* that the British working classes swore a lot; so with great industry all news items and talks were translated into what the Germans thought was the British working class idiom. After the German attack on the Soviet Union in June

1941, Workers' Challenge, in order to maintain its camouflage and credibility, also urged workers to demonstrate in favour of a second front in support of Russia.

Raskin's letter of 25 June says that 'Mr. Beasley', a former sergeant, was the chief speaker of Workers' Challenge. Most of the talks were written by Gilbert of the NBBS, who described them after the war as 'revolutionary'. He excused himself with the observation that he 'could not imagine that anyone in England would take any notice of the broadcasts'.[34] Another member of the Workers' Challenge team in 1942 and 1943 was William Colledge (cover-name 'Winter'). Colledge had been with the North Somerset Yeomanry in North Africa, where he was captured. After interrogation, German Intelligence passed him on as cooperative. After working for Workers' Challenge he was transferred to the NBBS and then to one of Concordia's listening posts. Grant *alias* Palmer joined Workers' Challenge from Radio Caledonia in 1942.

In Stache's report of 5 July, 'Plan P' (for peace) and 'Plan W' (for Wales) were to be implemented around 10 July. But the plan had to be delayed until 24 July, when the Christian Peace Movement station opened, on 31.75 metres, for some ten to fifteen minutes a day between 20:45 and 21:45 hours.[35] The broadcasts were first monitored in Britain on 15 August 1940.

In sharp contrast to the others, this fourth secret station purported to be the voice of pacifists of the Christian Peace Movement, urging 'every good Christian to join in an effort to make the government stop the war while there is something worth living for. Women are the greatest sufferers. You have most to lose. It is possible for you to bring the war to an end.'[36] On 21 August, BBC monitors recorded the following homily:

'Judge not that ye be not judged, and with what judgement ye judge ye shall be judged, and with what measure ye mete, it shall be measured to you again.' From this warning it is clear that Christ does not expect us to judge others. Judge not, that ye be not judged. Beware of judging, and of judging too hardly. The severity with which you deal with others will recoil upon your own head. For when it is time for you to be judged, you shall be judged. For with what judgement ye judge, and with what measure ye mete, it shall be measured to you again.

This command we should bear in mind when we blame Germany for causing the war. Are we not as much to blame as she is? [...] Why did we refuse Germany's peace offer last October [1939]? Why did we again ignore her peace proposal last month?

Once again the Government has misled us into a dreadful war, the result of which many of you have yet to see. How can we pretend to achieve anything good by committing fearful slaughter? Before another million of our men are sacrificed, let us ask ourselves: 'What does this war mean to me? What am I asked to fight for? And what will the result be? Can I, as a Christian, support the war?' The answer is simple: You cannot.

The sermon ended with the words:

War is not Christianity. God's will is peace. Remember Christ's words: 'Blessed are the peacemakers, for they shall be called Children of God'. Pray for peace. Work for peace. Demand peace.[37]

The Christian Peace Movement station's theme music was the hymn 'O God, Our Help In Ages Past', which was particularly likely to affect listeners who had lost relatives at Dunkirk. The station was probably the most insidious of all, not only because of the large number of genuine pacifists in Britain who believed that the war was wrong, but also because it linked pacifism with the German-Russian pact – a central theme for many Labour Party speakers since the beginning of the war.

The speakers were Corporal Jones, a Welshman, and Dublin-born Reginald Arthur Humphries[38] (b. 1916), a former seaman in the Royal Navy, who was announced as 'Father Donovan'. Most of the material was supplied by Rifleman Cyril Charles Hoskins (b. London, 30 November 1918). After the war Hetzler described Hoskins in an affidavit for the MI5:

Hoskins was one of eight prisoners-of-war whom William Joyce selected at a POW Camp near Thorn after the battle of Dunkirk for work at the Rundfunk. At first H. wrote manuscripts for the 'Christian Peace Movement', a phoney wireless station with a pacifist tendency set up according to Joyce's ideas. As far a I can remember H. also spoke a few times in these broadcasts. [...]

Hoskins was an educated, unassuming, quiet character who gave me the impression of trying to escape the dull camp life. He certainly did not act from a profit motive and has to my knowledge never asked for a rise in salary – his salary having been about 350 to 500 marks a months. He appeared to have spent most of his money on literature and was very happy when he had succeeded in getting a copy of Shakespeare's works.[39]

The Christian Peace Movement station remained in operation for nearly two years until February 1942, at which time Jones was returned to a PoW camp, while Hoskins was transferred to one of Concordia's listening posts.

At about the same time the fifth secret station, Welsh National Radio, was launched. Its programmes were designed to appeal to separatist tendencies in the principality and within the armed forces. Reports as to the effectiveness of its propaganda were poor and it was soon taken off the air. The chief speaker, according to Raskin's letter of 25 June, was William Humphrey Griffiths (b. 1911), a former Welsh Guardsman with a rough voice who spoke perfect German. Margaret Joyce said Griffiths was 'one of the original army men who worked for Hetzler on the *Geheimsender*' – 'one of the first picked by W[ill]'. In October 1945 a Chelsea court-martial sentenced Griffiths to seven years' penal servitude 'for voluntarily aiding the enemy while a prisoner-of-war by broadcasting'. In his defence Griffiths claimed:

[...] that after he had been taken to a prison camp in Poland he was 'lured' to Berlin. He volunteered to do work, but he did not know the nature of the work he would be called upon to do. In October 1942 he told Dr. Hetzler, who was in charge of the men, 'I am finished, I will do no more work'. The next day Joyce threatened his life if he did not carry on, and he was subsequently told that if he did not carry on he would be sent to a concentration camp. [...] Macdonald [Radio Caledonia] and Beasley [Workers' Challenge] subsequently refused to do the work and were taken away by the SS. The scripts were written by a mystery man named Brown, who was said to be in Germany before the war. [...] It meant five years in a concentration camp or the bullet, and when I escaped I preferred the bullet. I had a wonderful welcome when I returned home, and I was hurt because I knew I was not worth it.[40]

While Hitler clung to the vague hope that Britain would succumb, and the world waited for the launch of a German invasion in the summer of 1940, the German clandestine stations did their best to alarm listeners by exploiting the fear of a Fifth Column. In scripts written for the NBBS, William Joyce claimed: 'Among the 64,000 persons of German and Austrian nationality on our soil there is a powerful nucleus for the kind of work undertaken by the Fifth Column'. Without much distinction in listeners' minds between 'white' or 'black' stations, German broadcasts were generally believed to have described specific targets for attack in the British Isles, in a manner suggesting intimate knowledge of Britain's cities and factories, aided by a flow of information from Fifth Columnists. The imagined 'predictions' were often such that a nervous public might apply them to almost any Luftwaffe attack – after the event. In this way, the 'Lord Haw-Haw' myth added a bonus to the efforts of the Concordia stations.

The escalation of the war on the air waves, as perceived by Goebbels, is reflected in various observations within his diaries:

Deepening depression grips London and, even more, Paris. The devastating effect of our secret stations. [...] Hard Times for Albion! Have set down what the secret station have got to do: calls to prayer, panic-mongering, sensational news flashes and British press quotes [...], encouragement to desertion etc. We are seeing the results clearer day by day. Raskin is doing a tremendous job. (23 May 1940)

We are stoking up panic. [...] Have pushed secret stations into top gear. [...] Churchill keeps up the bluster, but fear sweats from every pore of his body. [...] We haven't yet turned up full blast in our broadcasts. Waiting for that until just before the catastrophe. (29 May 1940)

British press is keeping desperately stiff upper lip. But it's all put on. [...] For our part, the German media are back on the offensive. Keynote: Attack! (4 June 1940)

Shattering descriptions from London. An inferno on an appalling scale. [...] Slight signs of failing morale can be detected. [...] We are retuning our radio message. Straight and secret broadcasts both to focus on creating alarm and panic. We are putting on the big squeeze. Lord Haw-Haw is at the top of his form. (11 September 1940)

Initially the British government tried to suppress all references to the German clandestine stations. In July 1940 it became an offence to spread rumours and the Ministry of Information asked the public to join the 'silent column' and report defeatist talk. When the whispering continued and rumours gained a spurious authenticity by attribution to 'Lord Haw-Haw', the British government established the Anti-Lie Bureau as a department of the Central Office of Information.

The bureau's job was to counteract alleged German propaganda lies with the truth, but did themselves little good by giving the lie to rumours which were in fact true. For example, 'Lord Haw-Haw' reported that a woman had closed her nursing home in Beaumont Street, London, and moved to Blackwell because air-raids on London had made her work there impossible. This was publicly denied by the Anti-Lie Bureau, but a subsequent internal investigation revealed that the item had been broadcast, and had been based on an advertisement in 'The Times.'

On 14 August 1940 the NBBS 'reported' that German spies in British uniform and civilian clothes had dropped by parachute into the country, and that the parachutists had not been located because Fifth Columnists were giving them shelter. This story gave rise to further rumours. On 26 September, the CoI's Beckenham representative wrote to the Anti-Lie Bureau about persistent rumours that a parachutist had landed and been captured at Denton, Northampton. The Anti-Lie Bureau duly stated there was no substance to these rumours. However, on 11 October, the bureau had to admit that the story was apparently true, as a Swedish citizen, Gösta Caroli, had indeed landed in the area. Caroli was a British-controlled double-agent who fed information to the Germans.

Concordia's source for most of the genuine 'scare' items that went into the NBBS and other scripts were reports extracted from British newspapers by Donald Grant *alias* 'Donald Palmer', of Radio Caledonia, and later by Dorothy Eckersley and others, in the RRG's *Information-Archiv* headed by Dr. Hans Heuermann. The Nazi propagandists had access to the full range of the British press within twenty-four hours of publication. The newspapers were delivered by plane to neutral airports, usually in Spain and Sweden, from where they were flown to Berlin. Occasionally the propagandists were fed highly sensitive information. On 4 September 1940, for example, the NBBS mentioned negotiations for the acquisition by Britain of fifty destroyers from the United States, which seems to point to a security leak on the British side.

Topical material was also gathered *via* radio monitoring. Several services were competing with each other, but none was of much use to Concordia: the RRG's central monitoring service seemed to be mainly interested in gathering news favourable to Germany, while the RRG's Foreign Broadcasts' service primarily checked on the compliance of its programmes with official directives; the so-called 'research office' (*Forschungsamt*) was primarily interested in military matters; the ProMi's service tended to duplicate the work of the RRG, while the Foreign Ministry's service was rather standoffish towards the others. None dealt with internal conditions in the target countries. So Concordia launched its own monitoring service, headed by Walter Ziebarth. Mrs. von Petersdorf, an American skater who had remained in Germany at the beginning of the war, was responsible for monitoring American broadcasts. But Concordia had to surrender its independence and, in the spring of 1943, its monitoring service was combined with that of the Foreign Ministry's Seehaus operation.

All outgoing Concordia broadcasts were first recorded on Magnetophon tape and then, usually an hour or two later, played over a cable link to a transmitter, as the electrical engineer, Herbert Krumbiegel (*b.* 1911), recalled in an MI5 statement:

> I recorded in this way talks in English, Polish, French, Belgian, Persian and Indian dialects (Hindustani, Bengali, Tamil, etc.) [...] I recorded a few speeches by Subhas Chandra Bose. Nearly 50 per cent of the recordings I made were English talks.[41]

Krumbiegel had been doing this job since June 1940. A Party member since 1933, he had been in the employment of the RRG since 1935, first in Berlin, then in Saarbrücken, and then again in Berlin.

In time, fresh voices and a wider range of them were needed to maintain the deception. To this end William Joyce made a second visit to a German camp for British PoWs, in search of volunteers.

> It must have been January 1941 when Will did his big trip for Hetzler and the 'Villa'. [...] I am fairly sure it was January 1941 when Will suddenly announced that H. was sending him on a trip. It had been decided, after studying Wehrmacht interrogation reports, that there were quite a number of ex-Mosley men in camps now and that they might be prepared to help National Socialism. William was to make a two-day trip, incognito, to Thorn, to a big camp and interview likely candidates. What he really thought of the whole thing, I never knew, but he was dying to do the trip just to see more of the things going on around us. Thorn, now again with an unpronounceable Polish name, was built by the Teutonic Knights when they were bashing Christianity and 'civilization' into Eastern Europe and doing rather well for themselves. Will said it was 'rather nice' and the pictures of it were rather romantic. However, as I know camps, the PoW camp wasn't particularly romantic, but the interviews seem to have been interesting. Will was treated very VIP and very top secret. Even he was somewhat disconcerted, according to him, when an interviewee left the hut or whatever it was at a gallop calling to the whole camp 'I've just been talking to Lord Haw-Haw'. Within 24 hours he was back, 24 hours before schedule and vanished to the villa. He had got a few men together, one a convinced Mosleyite, the others of whom he said he thought it was more the cakes and ale than anything else but they'd got the voices they wanted. Some civilians had also been found, in and out of camps and work started. [...] The military prisoners were kept out of the way of the ordinary *Rundfunk*, next door, for the time being. The whole scene changed later.[42]

Other radio officials also passed on potential foreign speakers to the secret stations. Eduard Dietze, head of the English section, frequently visited *Dulag Nord*, the naval transit camp at Westertimke/Farmstedt, near Bremen, to interview PoWs and solicit broadcast messages for families back home. During a visit in February 1943, Dietze noted in his agenda: 'Hetzler could use people. They will later be interned in the High Command's special camp for security risks.'

At the beginning of 1941, Germany had four English-language 'clandestine' stations, all allegedly operating from inside the United Kingdom. But Berndt, the head of the ProMi's Broadcasting Division, was not satisfied, which probably meant that Goebbels himself had voiced doubts about the effectiveness of these broadcasts. In a secret report dated 16 January 1941, Berndt informed the minister that he had taken over direct control of the Secret Stations, the broadcasts being currently rather weak and in need of improvement. 'Since the death of Dr. Raskin the day-to-day initiative and psychological flair have been lacking.'[43]

Berndt's criticism was that the Secret Stations were merely reacting to British propaganda, thereby turning them into no more than a 'refutation and debating machine'. By relying on news material as the basis of their programmes, rather than defining their own propaganda agenda, and using the material to fit it, they were losing the game. British telephone directories, newspapers and periodicals should be scoured for businesses and individuals who should be addressed directly. In this way *they* would be forced to respond, provoking public discussion of the broadcasts in Britain. 'No Plutocrat should feel safe from our spotlight!'

> Suppose a businessman advertises in an English newspaper. That gives us the chance to target him at an appropriate moment. One can hint at fraud in big companies and accuse the owners of sending their capital abroad. One can blame them for shortages among the working class caused by their hoarding of goods and foodstuffs. One can weaken share prices by planting rumours – in short, one can create confusion in every conceivable area of life by increasing the personal element in our broadcasts.

During the summer of 1943, by which time Radio Caledonia (in July 1942) and The Christian Peace Movement (in February 1942) had been taken off the air, a new German secret station commenced operations against Britain. This was called Radio National, code named 'F' (for Fascist), operating on 208.6 metres, and the German propagandists rated it almost as highly as the NBBS. Hetzler had nothing directly to do with this station, since Radio National was the brain-child of and managed by the Foreign Ministry, and thus its programming can be assumed to have been, at least to some extent, influenced by the people behind the British Free Corps, with Concordia providing simply the technical facilities. Radio National was run as a frankly Fascist political station and, not surprisingly, its programmes therefore included a great deal of anti-Jewish propaganda.

Peter Adami, a former senior staff member and colleague of Eduard Dietze in the Wireless News Agency, was put in charge of Radio National. While the other secret stations were closely supervised by Hetzler and his staff, Adami appears to have been given considerable administrative independence. His personnel consisted largely of British PoWs, the chief contributors and broadcasters being Roy Purdy, Frank Maton and Roy Courlander.

Roy Walter Purdy (*b.* Barking, Essex, 1918) had been a member of the BUF. He had served as engineering officer aboard an armed merchant ship which was sunk by a German raider off the Norwegian coast in June 1940. Rescued and captured by the Germans, he spent time at several PoW camps before ending up at *Dulag Nord* until about June 1943, when he was taken to Berlin to meet William Joyce.

Joyce may have remembered Purdy and heard about his imprisonment, though it is more likely to have been because Purdy had been boasting about his past and his friendship with 'Lord Haw-Haw'. Purdy indicated willingness to co-operate, but failed a first voice test. The Foreign Ministry's broadcasting section seems to have been less fussy, hired Purdy, and attached him to Radio National as – according to his own story – script writer and broadcaster of ten programmes, in exchange for which he believed he was to have an opportunity to escape to a neutral country. From about 24 August 1943 Purdy was on the air, calling himself 'Pointer' and 'Ronald Wallace', on programmes such as 'The Air Racket – Jewish ICI Profiteering in War' (2 August 1943), and 'The Tilbury Dockyard Racket' (10 August 1943).

Six months later, towards the middle of February 1944, Purdy decided it was time to leave and escape to Sweden, but a German sentry picked him up and sent him back to Berlin. He now feigned illness, bribed a doctor to provide a certificate, and tried to persuade Adami to send him for special treatment to Vienna. But instead of travel documents, two Gestapo agents arrived at his flat and arrested Purdy, in March 1944, and sent him to *Oflag* (*Offizierslager*, officers' camp) IVC, better known as Colditz Castle, where he was questioned by British camp officials. The renegade spoke about his deal with the Berlin Foreign Ministry and waxed eloquent on the favourite subject of all turncoats: sabotage. Purdy claimed he had prowled the deserted streets of the German capital during air-raid alarms and had, on several occasions, thrown Molotov cocktails into official buildings and stolen top secret technical drawings from the German admiralty when the building burned after a direct hit. Short of claiming that he had joined the Berlin propaganda apparatus for the sole purpose of carrying out sabotage, Purdy 'disclosed' during this interrogation that he had made two attempts to kill William Joyce. The British camp officials were not impressed, and placed Purdy in solitary confinement.

The Colditz proceedings were apparently brought to the attention of the German authorities, and Purdy was then accused of sabotage and espionage during a preliminary investigation by the German camp authorities. Rejected by his fellow-prisoners, and threatened with a death sentence by his captors, he sought to escape by applying for acceptance in the British Free Corps. During his MI5 interrogation, Purdy admitted to this application, only to claim a few sentences later: 'It was never my intention – even if offered a commission – to join the Free Corps.'[44]

At the end of November 1944, according to his MI5 statement, two SS officers informed Purdy that he could choose between working for the SS propaganda unit *Standarte Kurt Eggers* or the death sentence. Purdy accepted the first, and was attached as an interpreter to the operation *Skorpion West*. According to his subsequent self-justifying testimony, he now resumed his acts of sabotage by 'allowing many mistakes to pass in the English texts he was to correct and edit so as to reduce the propaganda effect', and by dropping sugar into a petrol tank used to refuel German military vehicles.[45] In April 1945 Purdy tried to escape through Italy, but was stopped by partisans and handed over to the advancing Americans.

On 29 May, Purdy arrived in Glasgow, where he gave himself up to Naval Intelligence. During his four-day trial in December 1945, he repeated his earlier claims to anti-German sabotage. But the judge concluded that there was no reason to suppose that there was a single grain of truth in this defence, and he was sentenced to death. However, a few days before the date fixed for his execution, Purdy was reprieved on the grounds that he had been a follower in treason rather than a leader and the sentence was commuted to life imprisonment. Following his release from prison in December 1954, Purdy left Britain to settle in Germany.

Francis 'Frank' Paul Maton is described in a MI5 report of 27 March 1945 as a man 'whose make-up is fertile ground for Nazi ideas with which, on his own admission, he is impressed'. When captured on Crete in 1941, he was a corporal in a Commando unit. His pro-Fascist outlook was quickly noted by the PoW camp authorities and earned him a transfer to the indoctrination centre at Genshagen, a Berlin suburb, in June 1943. Genshagen was one of two 'holiday camps' administered and staffed by the Army High Command and supervised by the counter-intelligence (*Abwehr*), but effectively run by Arnold Hillen-Ziegfeld, the Foreign Ministry's special representative for British PoWs. Here Maton found himself in the company of Roy Purdy and Arthur Chapple, a sergeant in the Royal Army Service Corps. Maton and Chapple both declined, for the time being, to join the Legion of St. George, the later British Free Corps, but agreed to join the staff of Radio National where they broadcast as 'Maxman' (Maton) and 'Lang' (Chapple). Early in June 1944 Maton decided to join the Free Corps after all, assuming the name of 'Frank MacCarthy', only to realize within a couple of days, after the successful D-Day landings, that he had been a 'bloody fool'. He and Roy Courlander – another Free Corps member and one-time broadcaster – saw a way of improving their records in the event of being captured: in August they volunteered for the SS propaganda unit, *Standarte Kurt Eggers*, with a view to defecting at the earliest opportunity. In September both were posted to Brussels where they handed themselves over to a British officer.

Roy Nicholas Courlander, soon to become a leading member of the British Free Corps, was another of the original Radio National team. Courlander was born in London in the early 1920s, the illegitimate son of a businessman from Lithuania who owned a copra plantation on a remote South Sea island in the New Hebrides, where the boy went after leaving school in 1933. At the beginning of the war, Courlander enlisted in the New Zealand Expeditionary Force, serving in North Africa and Greece, where he was taken prisoner in April 1941. He was transferred to the Genshagen 'holiday camp' at the beginning of June 1943.

In Berlin Courlander was taken to the Foreign Ministry to meet John Amery, who outlined his vision of the 'Legion of St. George', and Dr. Fritz Hesse, who suggested he should make some broadcasts on Radio National. Courlander accepted and was given civilian clothes and a pass which allowed him to travel regularly between Genshagen and the *Funkhaus*.

In November 1943 the Foreign Ministry and the SS renewed their drive for volunteers among the thousands of British PoWs in their hands with a view to forming a unit that would fight alongside the Wehrmacht on the eastern front. Courlander joined the British Free Corps under the cover-name of 'Roy Regan' and was put in charge of recruitment. In this way he became one of the 'Big Six' in the hierarchy of the Free Corps.[46] In August 1944 he left the BFC to join the *Standarte Kurt Eggers*, was posted to Brussels, where, with Maton, he surrendered on 4 September 1944.

After the war Maton was sentenced by court-martial to ten years' penal servitude. Courlander was court-martialled at Westgate in October 1945 on a charge of voluntarily aiding the enemy by broadcasting and joining the BFC and the SS, and sentenced to fifteen years' penal servitude, of which he served seven. After his release Courlander settled in New Zealand, where he died in 1970.

Reginald Arthur Humphries, who had been the 'Father Donovan' of The Christian Peace Movement station, joined Purdy, Maton and Courlander at Radio National. In December 1945 Humphries was found guilty at the Central Criminal Court of 'assisting the enemy and doing acts likely to assist the enemy and to prejudice the efficient prosecution of the war – to wit, broadcast propaganda from Germany, contrary to Regulation 2A of the Defence (General) Regulations, 1939', and sentenced to five years' penal servitude.[47]

At the end of October 1943, a further PoW joined Radio National. Raymond Davies Hughes (*b*. Mold, Flintshire, 1913) was an RAF air gunner who had been shot down over Peenemünde, the German experimental rocket station on the Baltic coast, in August that year. After interrogation at the Luftwaffe transit camp at Oberursel, he agreed to cooperate and broadcast on Radio National. In April 1944 he was switched to Radio Metropol to make broadcasts in Welsh. In September 1945 Hughes was dishonourably discharged and sentenced to five years' penal servitude by an Uxbridge court-martial for 'aiding the enemy by asking prisoners of war to give information regarding RAF formations; making German propaganda records at the Rundfunkhaus; lending money to persons engaged in the formation of the British Free Corps; accepting employment from the German Foreign Office at 350 marks; and from Radio Metropol at 600 marks a month'.[48] In his defence he claimed that he had been forcibly taken by the Germans to Amery and Baillie-Stewart and intimidated by them into serving the enemy. 'I was under under mental strain at the time. I was constantly reminded of people who had been shot and how uncomfortable the prisons were in Germany.'

William Joseph Murphy (*b*. Bessbrook, County Armagh, 1898) had been teaching at various Berlitz schools on the Continent since 1926. At the outbreak of the war he was arrested but as an Irish national soon released and required only to report regularly to the police. In August 1943 he moved to Berlin where, two days after his arrival, the local Berlitz school was destroyed in an air raid, leaving him with no job or regular income. By this time he was toying with the idea of returning to Ireland, and was in contact with people connected with German Intelligence. They promised to take care of all arrangements, in exchange for information on the effects of German blitzes on Britain. The intended mission had to wait while Murphy sought to make up his mind, during which time he was introduced to William Joyce, who agreed to take him on as a translator at Luxembourg. But Murphy's work was unsatisfactory, his voice unsuitable and, after four weeks – at the end of January 1944 – he was discharged and returned to Berlin. He then renewed his contacts with German Intelligence, and plans were resumed for the intended mission. While waiting for his travel documents, Murphy encountered Francis Stuart who recommended he contact Peter Adami with a view to joining the German secret stations. But though offered broadcasting training by Radio National, Murphy changed his mind once again, returned to Luxembourg and awaited its liberation by American troops on 10 September 1944.

'Black' Stations for the USA

Dr. Herbert John Burgman was employed at the US embassy in Berlin at the time the United States entered the war, and when American diplomats and journalists were assembled at Bad Nauheim for repatriation, he elected to remain and join the Foreign Ministry branch of the German propaganda system. In 1942 he began broadcasting to the US on 'Station Debunk', trying to foment disquiet and suspicion over President Roosevelt's 'catastrophic' policies. As 'Helmuth Brückmann', the German name he assumed, he was attached to the North America zone of the RRG's Foreign Broadcasts division, at a salary of 1,500 marks a month.

Burgman was born at Hokah, Minnesota, in April 1896, his parents originating from Pomerania in Germany. He worked first as a newspaper compositor and printer, then in 1914 for a railway company and subsequently for a grain wholesaler in Minnesota. After another spell with a railway company he joined a government department in Washington DC as a junior clerk. In 1920 he travelled to Germany, married a music teacher in Koblenz, and entered Berlin University to study political economy. With a doctorate of political science, Burgman became an administrative staff member of the US embassy in Berlin. By December 1941 he was the embassy's economic affairs specialist.

From 12 March 1942 Burgman broadcast regularly to North America, under the name 'Joe Scanlon' – a fictitious figure associated with the isolationist, anti-communist Christian Front movement – *via* the 'clandestine' station 'Debunk – The Station of all Free Americans'. On the day of its first broadcast, Diewerge briefed Goebbels:

> The station is using the call-sign D-E-B-U-N-K, i.e. the station that 'debunks' the war, 'debunks' war propaganda, and so on. 'To debunk' is a typically American expression meaning more or less the same as 'to strip off the nonsense'.[49]

Under his contract dated 19 June 1942, Burgman was not to receive any instructions as to the direction and contents of his programmes, but from the end of October that year, and much to his fury, his direct superiors, Karl Schotte and Gerdt Wagner, insisted on censoring his scripts.

Initially Debunk claimed to be broadcasting in Iowa, a rural area of the Mid-West with a strong evangelical tradition, using false Federal Communication Commission registration numbers. On 12 November 1942 the *Saturday Evening Post* reported that the Foreign Broadcast Intelligence Service had identified Debunk as the former DJH short-wave station in Germany. Subsequently the programmes were transmitted *via* the French short-wave station at Allouis, in order to create at least the impression that the station was operated by Americans in the non-occupied zone of France.

Burgman's collaborators as announcers were Edward Vieth Sittler and his elder brother, Charles Sittler, as well as Julius Kraus. In his programmes, Burgman regularly played a worn copy of 'Carry Me Back To Old Virginny', and always concluded his programmes with the American national anthem.

Debunk's programmes were a strange mix of appeals to pacifism, to group prejudices, to defeatism and to personal selfishness rolled into one. 'Joe Scanlon' excelled in the wildest fantasies. One programme began: 'Who killed the Duke of Kent? This is the question of the day throughout England!', continuing the view that the duke's death was 'an act of sabotage by Welsh miners whom the duke had visited – an act approved by Churchill and Eden, stock-holders in the coal mines who wanted to eliminate the next successor to the throne.' 'Joe Scanlon' accused '99 per cent' of the officers in the US Army of embezzling government funds, naming several generals. In another broadcast, 'Joe Scanlon' carefully spelled out the names of the wives of several US Army officers who were reputed to be prostitutes. A Debunk speciality was its 'news flashes', a propaganda technique introduced by fellow-American broadcaster Fred Kaltenbach in 1940:

> *Flash from Australia*: General MacArthur driving an open car has run over several American soldiers and killed them!
> *Flash from Stockholm*: Molotov, the Soviet Foreign Commissar, has arrived in Berlin for a negotiated peace!
> *Flash from Denver*: The citizens of Denver suggest that this war should be called 'Franklin's Last Experiment'!

Another peculiarity of Debunk was its preacher-man style, primed with Scriptural phrases. 'Scanlon' referred to New York and Washington DC as 'Sodom and Gomorrah'. Farm boys were being sacrificed on the 'Altar of Mammon'. 'The New Order cometh' and 'the Old Order passeth away'.

After the war, Herbert Burgman was found guilty of treason and sentenced to between six and twenty years imprisonment. He died in prison.

Propaganda with an astrological and occult slant, to which the Anglo-Americans were supposed to be particularly receptive, was the subject of a study presented to the ProMi by Berndt in May 1942. As a result a secret station was proposed which was to beam predictions of an alarmist nature to the United States. The name suggested for the station was 'Katos', from κατ, the word for *downward* in classical Greek, implying all sorts of dire eventualities. But soon, early in July 1942, all parties concerned at the ProMi and the Foreign Ministry agreed to drop the idea. It was partly due to the difficulty of providing material for this kind of psychological sabotage – presumably because Himmler had rounded up the majority of occultists in the aftermath of Rudolf Hess's traumatic flight to Scotland in 1941. Instead, Debunk was to cast Roosevelt's horoscope from time to time.

The Voices of Subject Peoples

To help undermine Britain's position as a world power, two secret stations were directed at subject peoples in British-occupied areas of the Middle East and India:

- From 9 May 1941, Concordia A, 'The Voice of the Free Arabs' (*Saut al-Urubah al-hurrah*) broadcast daily for about half-an-hour on the 30 metre short-wave band to Egypt. The Austrian Dr. Gerhard Rott, the ProMi's expert on the Middle-East press, was responsible for this secret station, and contributors included the journalist Dr. Kama-Eldin Galal, as well as Nashed, Safty and Achmed, according to Hetzler. Hajji Amin al-Husayni, the Grand Mufti of Jerusalem, and leader of the Palestinian Arabs, was the station's adviser.[50]
- From 7 January 1942, Concordia H, 'Free India Radio' (*Azad Hind Radio*) bombarded India for about four hours a day on 20.34 and 26.16 metres. The Foreign Ministry's secretary of state, Wilhelm Keppler, was responsible for this station. He was assisted by Ernst Meissner from Concordia, and the militant Indian exile, Subhas Chandra Bose, was its most prominent contributor and speaker.[51] Bose (1897–1945) came to Berlin in October 1941 *via* Afghanistan, but failed to find the political support he had anticipated. The Nazi leaders were doubtful about his plans for an Indian uprising, they rejected his idea of an Indian government-in-exile and were not prepared to make any statement with regard to India's sovereignty after the war. Instead, Bose was kept in Berlin like a rare bird in a golden cage. He was given an Italian passport in the name of Orlando Mazzotta and lived with his entourage in the former residence of the US ambassador in Sophienstrasse, while the world speculated about his whereabouts.

After Pearl Harbor and the Japanese advance through Burma, the Foreign Ministry decided to take an active interest in the Indian nationalist's plans, and provided his Free India organization with air-time. Bose's refuge was still kept secret, even after he had read his 'freedom manifesto' on *Azad Hind Radio* on 27 February 1942. Eventually, at the end of May, Hitler was prepared to receive Bose in a meeting that officially disclosed he was in Berlin, but did not bring him nearer to his political goal – an Axis guarantee for India's sovereignty after the war.

Disillusioned, and feeling he had been misled and misused by the Nazi leadership, Bose now prepared for his return to Asia – in fact to Japanese-occupied territory. After delays he was taken aboard a U-boat at Kiel on 8 February 1943 and brought to Penang Island off the Malayan coast, from where he flew to Tokyo to seek Japanese support for the struggle for Indian independence.

What was probably the last – and without doubt the strangest – secret station to be planned was one targeting Jews in the United States. The minutes of a meeting with the head of the ProMi's Broadcasting Division on 21 December 1943 record that Rühle of the Foreign Ministry confirmed that the editorial team (*Redaktion*) for the '*Jüdischer G-Sender*' would be in place by early January. The programme was intended to be on the air for thirty minutes between 1 and 3 a.m. on short wave. We do not know, however, whether this station ever went beyond the planning stage. The mind boggles at the intentions that may have lain behind this Nazi scheme for a 'Jewish secret station'. In the absence of any documentary evidence, we can only leave this to the reader's imagination.

1945: The End of all Clandestine Broadcasts

On Good Friday, 30 March 1945, the Concordia staff, with the exception of William Joyce, was evacuated to Helmstedt where the clandestine operations were resumed from the basement of the Hotel Pätzold, using the Oebisfelde transmitter. From Helmstedt the German secret stations – or what was left of them – continued operation until American forces arrived in nearby Brunswick on 10 April, whereupon the staff scattered in all directions. A Luftwaffe officer of Polish stock, Kowalski, was the last to broadcast for Concordia. At the end Hetzler instructed the staff at the local county council (*Landratsamt*) to issue all foreign broadcasters with passports in the names and other details of their choice. Shortly afterwards military sappers arrived from Berlin and destroyed the Oebisfelde transmitter.

At that point Hetzler made a bonfire in the hotel yard of all scripts, papers, tapes and discs. He then set out, by bicycle, for Wernigerode in the Harz mountains to join his family, who had fled there from Berlin. On 13 May 1945 the US Military Police found him, in bed in a mountain hut, suffering from fever generated by an abscess in the ear. Hetzler was interned at the Sennelager camp where he was soon joined by other members of the former Büro Concordia. Margaret Joyce too was interned at Sennelager after her husband William's execution. Later the Americans handed the camp to the British authorities; John Alfred Cole, a future biographer of William Joyce, was the camp's chief interrogator. Eventually Hetzler was held at the nearby No. 5 Civilian Internment Camp at Staumühle until his release on 3 April 1947. Subsequently he worked for the British camp authorities as a civilian employee until August 1948, when he returned to civilian life. Initially he found employment with relatives at his home town of Mannheim. Later he worked as an import/export manager for various commercial businesses in Stuttgart and Frankfurt, until he retired to the province of Baden in 1972, where he died on 27 August 1994.

8   The 'Battle Stations' and Radio Arnhem

Front-line Propaganda

On 6 June 1944, Operation Overlord was launched across the English Channel, and Total War reached its turning point. From that day until the end of July, the Allies pumped fresh troops ashore day after day, until they had massed on their beachhead more than one and a half million men and huge quantities of armour and supplies. For the depleted German forces facing them, there were no reserves to summons. On the last day of July, the Anglo-Americans began their offensive in the west. On 17 August Dietze – whom, the month before, Winkelnkemper had appointed *Inspektor* of all English-language broadcasts, including the USA zone and the newly-formed Battle Stations, but excluding Concordia's secret stations – noted in his agenda: 'Mobile station! Siegfried Line'.

> Soon after the invasion orders were received from Goebbels to intensify the broadcasts to the Allied forces on lines that were thought to have had a certain measure of success in the Mediterranean area, thanks in part to the peculiar gifts of Miss Gillars and certain Italian announcers in 'American-English'. Special mobile transmitters were established in the west in co-operation with units of the Wehrmacht Propaganda Department (OKW/WPr) and the 'SS-Standarte Kurt Eggers', which had a broadcasting section of its own under *SS-Obersturmführer* [Konrad] Buchholz. A special department – called '*Kampfsender*' – of the *Auslandsdirektion* was formed, parallel to DÜS [*Deutsche Überseesender*, German Overseas Stations] and DES [*Deutsche Europasender*, German European Stations] and placed under Buchholz, who retained his other capacities as well.[1]

Here we see the new concept of *Kampfsender* or Battle Stations coming into full play. These were front-line 'sneak' stations equipped, manned and operated by the military for their own largely autonomous purpose of supporting the fighting front. Their function was to carry propaganda actively into the advancing enemy lines, stirring up confusion and undermining morale. Since the military leadership conceded that the SS 'war correspondent' units had done a good job with this technique on the eastern front – all through the defensive battles since the retreat from Russia began in mid-1943 – these were permitted free rein to organize the Battle Stations on the invasion front. Dietze's statement shows how *Wehrmacht* personnel commingled with Waffen-SS in the Battle Stations. At the operational level rank mattered less than language skills and propaganda flair.

Landlines carrying conventional news and propaganda broadcasts in English from the studios in Berlin to transmitters in the west were now constantly interrupted, and as the delivery of recordings by courier was almost as hazardous, Dietze contemplated switching some of his editorial staff directly to the Battle Stations. On 21 August 1944, he noted: 'Mrs. Joyce? Gillars!' Four weeks later, on 20 September, he noted: 'Battle propaganda group: Schaede, Mitschke, Erle, Klöden, Gerz; Frau Klöden, Frau Bierbrauer, Frau Klokow'. A further four weeks later, on 20 November: 'Schaede begins assignment near the Rhine, in November 1944. Battle Station with Gernet', and 'Gillars? Ward? Donald Day?'. Under 25 November, Dietze jotted down: 'Kaltenbach for Ida and Gustav, Donald Day dto.' ('Ida' and 'Gustav' were the code-names of two mobile stations.)

Dietze had at first considered Margaret Joyce for transfer to one of the Battle Stations in the west, but then favoured Mildred Gillars, so as to 'exploit her great appeal to the full'.[2] However 'Mitch' flatly refused and enlisted the support of Horst Cleinow, who in turn procured the backing of the Foreign Ministry, and in the end she remained where she was, based at the Short-Wave Station in Berlin.

Meanwhile another new approach was brewing among members of the English section of the editorial staff who had been evacuated from Berlin to German-occupied Luxembourg in August 1943. It was an approach pivoted on the general longing for an end to the fighting in 1944–45, and which proposed a message in tune with that mood, very different from the ProMi's official 'life-and-death-struggle' line. Commentator Helen Sensburg and translator/typist Gerda Eschenberg were part of the team, headed by Dr. Schaede, that had been sent to Luxembourg to carry on broadcasting with locally-produced programmes whenever the lines from Berlin failed. An opportunity for them and for some of their colleagues to put their ideas into practice presented itself just as the German position in the west began to crumble.

The Hilversum Option

With the Allied advance, the RRG lost one station after the other – first Rennes, then Calais, and on 22 August 1944 Luxembourg itself had to be evacuated. The team was transferred either to Hilversum, the Dutch broadcasting centre near Amsterdam, or to Apen, near Oldenburg, in north-west Germany. Helen Sensburg and Gerda Eschenberg were both in the Hilversum group, and after the botched Allied air drop behind the German lines at Arnhem on 17 September, they and most of their colleagues were ordered back to Berlin. Around this time Helen Sensburg learned about plans being laid by the ProMi's broadcasting delegate in the Netherlands, the energetic Eberhard Taubert.

Helen Sensburg was born Helen Margaret Edwards in Britain in 1913. At the beginning of the war she returned to Germany with her German husband,

Maximilian Andreas Sensburg. She joined the RRG's English-language section in 1939 and became a practised broadcaster. Gerda Eschenberg (*b.* 1921), who was raised in the United States and spoke better English than German when she returned to Germany at the beginning of the war, joined the RRG's English zone on 1 September 1940 as a typist. She became a broadcaster one afternoon when the duty announcer failed to show.

Propaganda policy in the still-occupied Netherlands was in disarray. Dr. Halm, a member of the ProMi's Propaganda Division, observed: 'Seeing that Reich Commissioner [for The Netherlands] Dr. Seyss-Inquart has packed the entire staff of his propaganda division off to Berlin, apart from Messrs. Dittmar to supervise the press and Taubert for broadcasting, seems to indicate that the Reich Commissioner no longer believes in the possibility of undertaking any official propaganda in The Netherlands. Thus our work has to be restricted to spasmodic clandestine activities.'[3] But Berlin would have none of this, and insisted that there must be no 'pussy-footing' with propaganda in the Netherlands. 'There is still plenty of scope for positive, insidious and − above all camouflaged − subversive propaganda'.[4]

This was an ideal platform for Taubert who, in the spring of 1942, had master-minded the ill-fated *Notekraker* station. Eberhard Karl Theodor Ferdinand Taubert, by profession an electrical engineer, was born in Oberhausen, North Rhine-Westphalia, in December 1904.[5] From 1928 to 1932 he had been working at a radio factory in Amsterdam, and was probably living in the Netherlands at the time of the German occupation in 1940, as may be deduced from one of his post-war statements: 'Being a Reich German I was drafted and thus became a member of the German occupation forces in the Netherlands'. On 18 May he was attached as technical expert with the special rank of a *Sonderführer Z* to the military propaganda unit that had occupied the Hilversum broadcasting complex on 15 May 1940. In March 1941 Taubert became the ProMi's broadcasting delegate in the Netherlands, in succession to Arthur Freudenberg who had been recalled to Berlin to head the department *Rundfunk-Organisation* of the ProMi's Broadcasting Division.

'De Notekraker'

The 'clandestine' Dutch station called The Nutcracker (*De Notekraker*), supposedly operating from inside the German-occupied Dutch capital, The Hague, was set up by Concordia early in 1942. Its purpose was to try to influence uncommitted sectors of Dutch public opinion by ostensibly undermining both the pro-German Dutch National Socialist movement and pro-British sentiment among the population. The station was probably operated from the private villa occupied by Taubert as the ProMi's broadcasting delegate in the Netherlands, at Utrechtseweg 30, Hilversum. On 1 January 1942 Winkelnkemper telexed Taubert to come to Berlin to discuss the proposal, a discussion which appears to have been successful since from mid-January parts of the villa were rebuilt, and technical equipment and office furniture installed on the premises.[6] Taubert later charged part of his rent to a special account designated 'PR'. When the RRG's accounts department queried this detail, Taubert explained that it was in connection with a 'secret project' cleared by the ProMi. He also set the cost of two Dutchmen against the same account. These were Gerrit van Duyl (*b.* 1888), until January 1942 pastor of the Dutch Reformed Church at Blokker and a dedicated activist of the Dutch National Socialist movement (NSB), and possibly Johan Hendrik Lodewijk de Bruin (*b.* 1896), another NSB activist. But by 15 February the underground paper *Zij van den Omroep* had already warned: 'The Dutch freedom station "De Notekraker" is another Fascist attempt to create dissension among the Dutch people'. The Dutch government-in-exile's station, Radio Oranje in London, soon afterwards exposed the identity of this station. 'De Notekraker' was eventually taken off the air on ProMi orders. On 14 July 1942 a cable was sent to The Hague in Goebbels' name, '[...] since it would be scarcely plausible for a secret station in The Hague to remain undetected by the occupying power, on account of the severe security restrictions, its [political] objective is consequently unattainable'.

A New Start

With ProMi backing Taubert now started several other secret stations, two or three of them broadcasting in Dutch, including *De Polder* and the Station of the Free South (*De Zender van het vrije Zuiden*). One was an English-language station intended to promote 'the reconciliation of the people of all nations'.

Full of enthusiasm to produce English 'reconciliation' programmes for Taubert's 'independent' station, Helen Sensburg decided to return to Hilversum as soon as she could. After a few days in the German capital, according to the Dietze agenda of 3 October, she returned to Holland to rejoin her colleagues and implement a plan which, Gerda Eschenberg later claimed, Helen had confided to her:

We have got to do something about reconciling the Germans and the British, ordinary Tommy and German *Landser*, before the shooting stops. Can you bear to hear the way they talk over there, calling all Germans fanatical Nazis and saying the only good German is a dead German?[7]

Helen Sensburg's plan was:

[...] to do pacifist programmes, counteract all the hatred, dwell on what we have in common, the shared humanity that links soldiers on every front with each other, both them and us! [...] We're setting up [...] a totally new station, on a new wave length, with a new name and programme, the like of which has never been known, half BBC, half our own stuff, and as little *Reichs-Rundfunk* as possible. A radio station in between the front-lines, speaking for both sides, and with its own anti-war views. We've got to stick together, we mustn't let anyone fire out of line. The

Redaktion in Berlin will cover us and here in Holland Gerhard [Eberhard Taubert] will make sure of that.

Taubert's proposed 'peace' programme was classified as a Battle Station within the propaganda operation '*Skorpion-West*' headed by *SS-Sturmbannführer* (Major) Dr. Hans Damrau. Dietze managed the operation for the first ten days before putting Taubert in control. Apart from the two enthusiastic female pacifists from the English *Redaktion*, the German members of the team were Heinz Mitschke, Martin Erle, Miss Gerda Nebbe, Mrs. Till Klokow and a '*Skorpion-West*' detachment named *Kampfsenderstaffel* 'Arnhem' under Lieutenant Hajo Hübener.[8] Jan Moene, a Dutch radio engineer, recalled to author Dick Verkijk in 1972 that the technical brains behind the new station was called 'Peacock'. W.A.Boelcke, in his book '*Die Macht des Radios*', states (without giving his source) that 'Peacock' was Moene's nickname, but this could be a misinterpretation of the Moene/Verkijk interview. Boelcke might be on the right track, however, for in 1933 Moene had masterminded a secret station (call-sign PA.AR – 'AR' for *Arbeiter-Radio*, Workers' Radio) in order to keep Dutch Socialists in touch with their comrades underground in Germany. During the German occupation Moene, a former member of the League against War and Fascism, was behind numerous incidents against Dutch Nazi supporters at Radio Hilversum, though generally they seem to have been more practical jokes than actual sabotage.

Radio Arnhem at Work

Taubert's private villa in Hilversum served as the station's headquarters. The programmes were broadcast from studio A in Hilversum. When Helen Sensburg arrived on 5 October, preparations for the launch of the new station were in their final stages: BBC programmes were monitored, details of their schedule were noted, the pattern of BBC presenters and their idiosyncracies analysed, and own programmes developed that would dove-tail with the BBC output. Taubert testified to the State investigation (*Rijksrecherche*) before the Special Court (*Bijzondere Gerechtshof*) in Amsterdam on 29 October 1947, in the course of an inquiry into the Dutch radio during the German occupation:

As distinct from the Propaganda Ministry's 'hate propaganda', I started 'Radio Arnhem' on 10 October 1944, with the objective of promoting the reconciliation of the people of all nations. We transmitted on 375 metres *via* the Dutch station Lopik I and broadcast every day in the week, including Sundays, commencing seven o'clock in the morning until eleven o'clock at night.[9]

On 1 December, Dietze reported to Winkelnkemper:

Of course the station is not actually at Arnhem, but at Lopik, south-west of Utrecht, and currently a mere 30 km behind the lines. This is the big Lopik I transmitter, not a mobile unit.[10]

The station was named 'Arnhem' to rub salt in the wounds left by the Allies' costly setback there just three weeks earlier. Radio Arnhem was without doubt the only truly innovative and effective operation the Nazi propagandists ever created during the Second World War – and ironically it was in part thanks to plugging an anti-war message.

The 120 kW transmitter at Lopik ensured that listeners on the Allied front in Belgium and the Netherlands would receive the Arnhem signal louder and clearer than the original BBC broadcasts. 'Peacock' flawlessly mixed BBC transmissions with programmes taken from Berlin and local productions. He would deftly splice into the relay of a BBC transmission at the announcement of the news, with Gerda Eschenberg or Helen Sensburg reading their news bulletin, continuing afterwards with the BBC's original music programme. Occasionally, a Radio Arnhem relay of the BBC news would have an impromptu commentary by Helen Sensburg tacked on to the end.

The BBC commentator 'Brent Wood' (actually Edgar Lustgarten) described these methods on the Overseas Service on 12 January 1945, concluding:

> The listener doesn't know there's been a switch unless, of course, he guesses it from the curious nature of the news, and the curious slanting of the comment. Apart from that it sounds exactly like a continuous uninterrupted programme, put out from London and filled with London's information and opinions. [...] It all serves to show that enemy propaganda is still intensely active, and that those who carry it out have lost neither their malice nor their courage.

In his evidence, Taubert described the programming of Radio Arnhem:

> Basically, we re-broadcast one of three BBC programmes, either the 'Home Service' or the 'Light Programme' or the 'Allied Expeditionary Forces Programme'. We stayed tuned in to each of these programmes on three radio receivers, and used to switch over from one programme to another and do the announcements while the previous programme was still on. We always introduced a programme along the following lines: 'This is Arnhem calling, we now bring you (for example) the Light Programme'. We did not have a fixed schedule and were very flexible as far as programming was concerned. If none of the three English programmes carried anything interesting for the Allied soldiers we would broadcast our own musical programme from gramophone records.
>
> One part of our programme consisted of music and cabaret transmissions which we took over from the English stations – but well adapted for our puposes – while the other part mainly consisted of news and talks.

A typical day's programme on 'Radio Arnhem' ran like this:

> *07:00 – 08:00*: Music taken over from the BBC and own gramophone records;
> *08:00 – 08:02*: News summary from Reuter, DNB and other agencies;
> *08:03 – 09:00*: Music and/or cabaret, maybe some own chats;
> *09:00 – 09:02*: News summary from Reuter, DNB and other agencies;

09:03 – 12:00: Music and/or cabaret, maybe some own chats, and so on until 12:00.
12:00: Re-broadcast of English 'slogans' such as: 'Don't take a drink with a
German'. We used to fade-in to these BBC programmes our answer immediately
following this slogan: 'For he stands it better than you' or something like this. We
were able to do this because the British radio always repeated the same five
slogans which generally aimed at non-fraternization with the Germans.
12:15 – 14:00: Music as before.
14:00 – 14:10: Own news service based on reports from Reuter, DNB and other
agencies; military reports from the British and German front lines.
14:10 – 17:00: Music and cabaret.
17:00 – 18:15: Own music programme from gramophone records interleaved with
greetings from Allied PoWs to their families at home as well as information
gathered during PoW interrogations.
18:15 – 19:00: Music.
19:00 – 20:00: Transmission of the Berlin programme 'Jerry Calling'. This was a
kind of cabaret programme with clumsy German propaganda.
20:00 – 21:00: Own music and cabaret programme, alternating with 'Hans
Speaking', 'Her Point of View' aiming at reconciliation, and a military
commentary by 'Captain Borrel'.[11]
21:00 – 21:20: Re-broadcast of the BBC news.
21:20 – 21:30: Music from gramophone records.
21:30 – 21:40: English-language reports taken over from Berlin.
21:40 – 21:55: Broadcast of the William Joyce talk from Berlin. We used to
announce this talk by saying that one should listen to both sides to be able to
form an objective opinion.
22:00 – 23:00: Re-broadcast of a BBC music programme or own music from
gramophone records.
23:00: Close down.

According to Taubert, 'This is Arnhem calling' was followed by 'It's A Long Way To
Tipperary', and the PoW greetings section was introduced by 'Home Sweet Home'.

Helen Sensburg, the commentator and 'brain' behind the programmes, was introduced on air as 'Molly', and Gerda Eschenberg, the 'voice', as 'Ann'. Gerda Nebbe was
the other female speaker. All three merged into 'Mary of Arnhem' for the station's
Allied audience, and were known to them collectively by this name.

The BBC mentioned Radio Arnhem for the first time on 21 October 1944, quoting
war correspondent Frank Gillard at Eisenhower's headquarters. On 10 November, the
Daily Express carried a story about the new station. By early January 1945 the Allies
were seriously concerned about the effects of Radio Arnhem's message. On 6 January
the BBC reported:

Mr. Roosevelt gave what he called a 'very serious warning against the poisonous
effect of enemy propaganda'. The wedge which the Germans tried to drive in western Europe was less dangerous in actual terms of winning the war, than the wedges

they are continually trying to drive between the United States and her Allies. There were evil and baseless rumours against the Russians, against the British and against the Americans. Every one of the rumours bore the same trade mark: made in Germany.

A day later, the Allies installed three mobile stations on the western front to relay the BBC's 'Allied Expeditionary Forces' programme and out-blast Radio Arnhem. Winkelnkemper now recommended his minister 'to extend Radio Arnhem's schedule – even beyond 23:00 hours – and also to carry the programme over Holland II on 301 metres.' In the same letter, Winkelnkemper proposed Taubert should be nominated for the war merit cross and Helen Sensburg for the war merit medal.[12] About the same time Radio Arnhem pulled off one of its best coups, to which the BBC gave prominence on 10 January 1945:

> German propaganda methods aimed at causing dissention between the Allies were strikingly illustrated by a recent incident. Yesterday, some New York papers commented in very unfavourable terms on an alleged BBC broadcast which gave all the credit for stopping Rundstedt's push to Field Marshal Montgomery. [...] Not unnaturally the American newspapers resented this so-called BBC broadcast and one carried the headline: 'Monty gets glory – Yanks get brush-off'."

The BBC commentator then went on to insist that the broadcast did not come from London:

> This is part of the Germans' ingenious technique for spreading doubt and confusion. [...] The most significant feature of this fake broadcast is the subtle form of the propaganda which is clearly designed to embitter relations between American and British troops fighting side by side on the western front.

Next day the *Daily Telegraph* quoted an official of the Department of Counter Propaganda at the Ministry of Information as saying: 'Subtle distortion of the truth such as this case causes indignation in America and is typical of the line they [the Germans] have recently adopted.' Later the same day, the BBC reported that the Minister of Information, Brendan Bracken, had sent a message to General Eisenhower about the recent broadcast in which a German radio station, 'masquerading' as the BBC, denigrated Eisenhower and exaggerated British military performance. Bracken was anxious to emphasize that the BBC had nothing to do with this broadcast:

> I need hardly tell you that the BBC would never broadcast anything which would be offensive to American troops, or to you, the C-in-C. On the contrary, the BBC has always done everything in its power to do justice to the great achievements of America's gallant armies. Like the rest of the British people, the governors of the BBC have the greatest admiration for General Eisenhower. They are grateful to

him for his shining leadership and for the truly marvellous job he has done in creating unity among the Allies.

What had happened was that German Intelligence had intercepted a report by Chester Wilmot, the British journalist, on a press conference by Montgomery on January 7, and had passed it on to Radio Arnhem for appropriate action. A few hours later, a willing prisoner-of-war, calling himself Chester Wilmot, read a doctored version of the British journalist's script on Radio Arnhem. This now claimed:

Field Marshal Montgomery came into the fight at a strategic moment. He scored a major success across the La Roche road, which American tanks cut on Saturday. [...] In the three weeks since Montgomery tackled the German Ardennes offensive he has transformed it into a headache for Rundstedt. It is the most brilliant and difficult task he has yet managed. He found no defence lines, the Americans somewhat bewildered, few reserves on hand and supply lines cut. The American First Army had been completely out of contact with General Bradley. He [Montgomery] quickly studied maps and started to tidy up the front. He took over scattered American forces, planned his action and stopped the German drive. His staff, which has been with him since Alamein, deserves high praise and credit. The battle of the Ardennes can now be written off, thanks to Field Marshal Montgomery.

A few days later the BBC had to disclaim yet another broadcast attributed to the BBC:

Mary of Arnhem [...] is at it again. This time she said that the wife of the Portuguese ambassador to London, the Duchess of Palmella, had stated in Lisbon that V-bombs were doing untold damage to London, particularly to military installations, and she would not return until after the war. There is no truth in the statement. It was stated at the Portuguese embassy in London last night that the duchess went to Lisbon fairly often to see her eleven children, who are at boarding schools. She is expected back in London with the ambassador in the first week of February.

American swing in the Glenn Miller vein dominated the music programmes of Radio Arnhem. In the proven manner, already skilfully exploited by 'Axis Sally' (Mildred Gillars), the Radio Arnhem staff gave Allied PoWs captured in the northern sector the opportunity to record messages to their families back home.

Allied PoWs were roped in for an American-style radio music programme, 'Golden Pirate Club', scripted by Willem W. Waterman (*alias* Willy van der Heyden, *alias* Victor Valstar, *alias* Sylvia Sillevis *et al*).

His proper name was Wilhelmus Henricus Maria van den Hout (1915–1985), one of the most non-conformist of Dutch Nazi supporters. Waterman began as a journalist with the Catholic newspaper *Het Huisgezin*, and was corporate director of the Philips press office, Eindhoven, 1936-38. After briefly serving in the Dutch army, he became a member of the *Nationaal Front* in December 1940. This was a right-wing organization in which he soon became responsible for propaganda, and in 1944, when the head of the Reichskommissar's press office invited him to contribute to the German propaganda effort in 1944, he accepted. Waterman launched the German-sponsored satirical weekly *De Gil* and a radio programme called 'De Radio Gilclub'. After Hilversum had been transformed into a 'battle station', he wrote the scripts for the English-language series, the 'Golden Pirate Club', presented on Radio Arnhem by Ferdinanda 'Nan' Weckerlin de Marez Oyens (*b.* 1918) as 'Leonie Miller'. This was an all-music programme with plenty of American jazz and current hits. Waterman's collaboration during the German occupation earned him three years in prison after the war.[13]

Some PoWs were so delighted by the atmosphere at the station that they volunteered to stay on. Gerda Eschenberg fondly recalled a Canadian who, after some weeks' work at the station, parted with the words: 'It was a tremendous experience working with you folks. This was the best time of my life.' But Radio Arnhem programmes also had their downside:

I have in front of me the pocketbook of a British lance-corporal. His Christian name was Thomas. His surname has been obliterated by his blood. From letters and photographs he carried with him it is clear, however, that he was the dearly beloved husband of Hilda and the daddy of Geoffrey, aged one. [...] Hilda's husband Thomas was a religious man – a good Roman Catholic. He carried with him a little medal with the image of the Saviour, a little embroidered cross and, encased in red velvet, consecrated wax blessed by his holiness the Pope in Rome. Both are inscribed Agnus Dei. Perhaps [he was] persuaded to carry them with him, in the hope that they might give him protection, but Providence decided otherwise, and Thomas has been gathered to the fold of the Almighty. May his soul rest in peace and may life be merciful to his young wife and son.[14]

Private Robert Raymond Dorion died on the 23th of November 1944, where three roads meet at Horst in Holland. We know a little more about Robert Raymond Dorion. He was wounded in the chest by shell splinters – his pocket-book and the letters he carried with him show us that. When he was found he was already beyond human aid – and died soon afterwards – 19-year-old Robert. [...] When he died, he had nearest to his heart a birthday rosary from '*ta mère, Maman*'.[15]

In the *Daily Mail* of 20 February 1945, Noel Monks sensed that 'Mary has gone soft':

During the past two weeks there has been a noticeable change. A tender, wheedling note has crept into Mary's vapourings. Says she: 'The British and Americans are both good fellows – as are their opponents, the Germans. Why go on killing each other?' [...] This is in striking contrast to broadcasts of two weeks ago when British and Americans were urged by sweet little Mary to slit each other's throats.

'Mary of Arnhem' Signs Off

On 3 March 1945 Helen Sensburg presented 'Her Point of View' in the Radio Arnhem 'Forces Hour':

> I don't know how you feel about it, Forces, but I think the men have been having it all their [own] way lately. That's why it's high time for the woman's point of view to be heard for a change.
>
> You've been hearing Captain Borrel every evening with his military commentary, carefully weighing the possibilities of every situation. Peter Collins on politics, the three Musketeers with all problems, big and small, that worry a soldier, Eddy Foster with his human touch, the voice of William Payne speaking to you through his diary, and then, of course, Hans, our philosopher and bitter opponent of all who sow hatred and discord in the world. But they are all men. – Just like most of us here, I get a lot of letters and talk to many people, men and women – chiefly women – of all types, rich and poor, happy and unhappy, educated and uneducated, hopeful and pessimistic, but on one point they all agree – that this war must come to an end and that there must not be another one.
>
> I'd like to tell you a bit about some of the girls and women who speak and write to me – that will show you how war is affecting them.

Helen Sensburg then went on to speak about Margaret, who 'decided to wait until it [the war] was over before thinking of additions to the family. Margaret is nearly thirty now and a very unhappy woman'; about Susan who has 'three children now, but no husband. He has been killed in action'; and about Ann, who 'is bombed out and living under very primitive conditions with her two children while her husband 'was always being seen with different girls'; ending her talk with a kind of outburst:

> Women don't want honour and glory and heroes – they want a home, the companionship of a husband, and children. Can you wonder that women hate war?![16]

Soon afterwards, on 23 March 1945, Radio Arnhem ceased to exist.[17] On 17 April Hilversum had to be evacuated and the German broadcasting staff was transferred to The Hague, where the local transmitter proved to be too weak to be of any effective use.

Eventually, on 9 May, Canadian soldiers arrested Eberhard Taubert and the remnants of his staff. All were placed under house arrest in The Hague, until transferred, on 6 June, to the Oranje Hotel at nearby Scheveningen, the former Gestapo internment camp for prominent prisoners. Later Taubert was interned in Belgium, and later still in Herford and Minden, Germany, until he was handed over to the Dutch authorities in November 1946 as a prosecution witness in proceedings against the former AVRO director, Willem Vogt, and Johan(nes) Paardekooper, the former Radio Arnhem broadcaster. Taubert was eventually released and returned to Germany. He died in Hamburg on 13 February 1965.

Helen Sensburg and Gerda Eschenberg were transferred from Scheveningen to an internment camp at Delft. Eschenberg managed to escape in February 1946 and returned to Germany, where she eventually married and settled in Bremen. After Helen Sensburg's release from internment, and her divorce, she remarried and settled in Hamburg as Taubert's wife.

Postscript

Accounts of the cessation of the Nazi radio propaganda campaign in April-May 1945 have been provided in the closing pages of each of the chronologically parallel Chapters 3, 4, 7 and 8. On a different level, the ludicrous media rivalry between the ministries headed by Ribbentrop and Goebbels, traced in Chapter 6, impinged on all the other narratives.

As indicated in the Introduction, the information presented in this book has been accumulated, piece by piece, and the story that emerged from the archives and from the testimony of survivors led in many different directions.

What we have described is very far from the 'monolithic' propaganda machine that Dr. Goebbels had sought to create, and it has defined the structure of this book. When the end came, and the system disintegrated, the individuals involved in putting 'Germany Calling' on the air disappeared, sporadically, into history.

Notes

Chapter 1: The Making of the German Ministry of Propaganda

1. Thimme (1932).
2. Alfred Harmsworth (1865–1922), owner of the *Daily Mail*, was created Viscount Northcliffe on his return from the USA in November 1917.
3. Liddell Hart (1970).
4. Stern-Rubarth (1921).
5. Münzenberg (1937).
6. Rauschning (1939).
7. Goebbels, *Vom Kaiserhof zur Reichskanzlei* (1934).
8. At the age of seven, Goebbels had to undergo surgery on his left thigh because of osteomyelitis, in consequence of which his left leg remained thin and weak, and about eight centimetres shorter, and he needed to wear an orthopaedic shoe. Goebbels never spoke about his childhood disease and crippled leg, so that even close Party friends believed him to have a club-foot.
9. Joseph Goebbels, *Vom Kaiserhof zur Reichskanzlei.*
10. Erdmann (1980); Diller (1980).
11. BA: R43II/1149.
12. Rühle (1934).
13. Diller (1980).
14. Weinbrenner (1939).
15. Weinbrenner (1938 & 1939).
16. BA: R55/436.
17. BA: R55/1317.
18. In 1939 Dressler-Andress was made the Party's propaganda chief in occupied Poland. After the war he was given a post by the East German Foreign Minister, Lothar Bolz, until, in 1954, he went back to his first love as director of the 'Agit-Prop' theatre. He died in Berlin-Karlshorst on 19 December 1979.
19. Pohle (1955); in German the term *Intendant* is applied to the artistic and administrative head of a theatre, opera house or radio station.
20. After his removal from office, Kriegler joined a propaganda unit and covered the Battle of Britain, before running the stations at Lodz, Warsaw and Cracow in occupied Poland. From August 1941 until 1944 he headed the Baltic broadcasting group 'Ostland', with stations in Riga, Vilnius/Vilna and Kaunas/Kowno. After the war, Kriegler worked as a building contractor in Duisburg and Dortmund, and died on 30 December 1978 while on a visit to Neumünster in Holstein.
21. Keitel, IMT, Vol. V.
22. BDC.
23. Diewerge, *Der Fall Gustloff – Vorgeschichte und Hintergründe der Bluttat von Davos,* (Munich: Eher, 1936); ditto: *Ein Jude hat geschossen – Augenzeugenbericht vom Mordprozess David Frankfurter,* (Munich: Eher, 1937).
24. Diewerge, *Anschlag gegen den Frieden,* Munich: Eher, 1939.
25. BA: R55/439. For details of the Hinkel plan, *see* pp. 142–8..
26. It is probably a coincidence that Charlie Chaplin gave the 'Great Dictator' the name Adenoid Hynkel.
27. BA: R55/430.
28. BA: R55/13.
29. Born in 1900, Apitzsch had been a salesman, coal dealer, peddler, theatre actor and journalist prior to joining the RRG. He was a Party member and Storm Trooper from 1931.

30. Born in 1907, Bartholdy was a university drop-out. A Party member from 1930, he was a lecturer at a Party-sponsored school after 1934.

31. Born in 1903, Freudenberg had worked in broadcasting since 1933. After an enforced break due to 'political unrelia-bilty' in 1934–36, he served with the two Berlin stations, the *Reichssender* and the *Deutschlandsender*, as well as with the KWS.

32. Although the Vichy authorities handed him over to the Germans in July 1940, Grynszpan was never tried for the murder of vom Rath. A trial was set for May 1942 but was indefinitely postponed. Goebbels' diary for 24 January 1942 says Grynszpan had claimed he had a homosexual relationship with his victim. In 1952 the journalist Graf Soltikov mentioned this version of the story in a newspaper article which earned him a writ from vom Rath's brother. In 1964, the suit was eventually dismissed, but Diewerge was now charged with withholding and falsifying evidence when questioned for the first time about this allegation – not about whether it was true or not. Herschel Grynszpan survived the war in a German prison, and settled in Paris after the war under an assumed name.

33. *Gefallen* means killed in action. The term '*März-Gefallene*' dates back to 1848 and refers to those who were shot by troops in Berlin during the March revolution in that year. Later, nationalist circles applied the term to those who were shot while demonstrating for the annexation of the Sudetenland by the German Reich on 4 March 1919. In 1933 the term (deliberately playing on the meaning of '*umgefallen*', literally, 'falling over', but also 'changing sides') pilloried those who, for opportunistic reasons, had joined the NSDAP in large numbers after the general elections of March 3, and after the Party had seized complete control of the Reich with the Enabling Act (*Ermächtigungsgesetz*) of 24 March.

34. Boberach (1984).

35. BA: R55/536.

36. BA: R55/559; Hans Hinkel was captured at the end of the war by Polish forces who mistook him for Paul Hinkler, chief

of the secret state police before Himmler and Heydrich took it over, and incarcerated him for several years. He died a broken man and severely ill in 1960.

37. In Hitler's political testament of 29 April 1945, he named Goebbels as his successor as Reich chancellor, and Dr. Werner Naumann as the new propaganda minister. Two days later, Goebbels took his own life. Naumann managed to slip through the Soviet lines and reach territory occupied by the western Allies. Here he submerged under an assumed name, working as a bricklayer in southern Germany. At the end of the de-nazification process, Naumann re-surfaced. His intention to stand for the 1953 federal elections was only prevented when a court deprived him of his active and passive voting rights.

38. Springer.

39. BA: R2/4907.

40. BA: R55/439.

41. Lochner, *Goebbels Diaries*, 11 November 1943.

42. BA: R55/1025

43. BA: R55/546

44. Picker (1965).

Chapter 2: Foreign Policy by Radio

1. Toni Winkelnkemper's brother, Peter (1902–1944), was lord mayor of Cologne, 1941–44.

2. On his return from the front, Dittmar was appointed, on 1 December 1941, press chief to Seyss-Inquart, the *Reichskommissar* in the occupied Netherlands. He took his own life at the end of the war.

3. BA: R55/439; R78/1000a; RA/Sonder-archiv, Moscow: Fond 1363, ProMi-Findbuch 1, No. 108.

4. FA: Dietze Archive.

5. Günther Weisenborn (1902–1969) was a friend of Harro Schulze-Boysen and his wife Libertas. Both were leading members of a Soviet-sponsored underground organization referred to by the Gestapo as the Red Chapel. It was founded in 1938 and became particularly active after the German invasion of Russia. After six weeks' observation the Gestapo

broke up the Red Chapel in August 1942, arresting over six hundred people, of whom nearly sixty were sentenced to death in subsequent trials. Günther Weisenborn was sentenced to three years' imprisonment and was liberated by Soviet troops in 1945.

6. FA: Dietze Archive.
7. AA-PA: R.67501.
8. FA: Dietze Archive.
9. Dr. Martin Schönicke (b. 1907, Party member from 1926) was responsible for programme production and became, in October 1944, the RRG's programme director.
10. FA: Dietze Archive.
11. FA: Affidavit by Hans König, April 1947.

Chapter 3: Short-Wave Propaganda to North America

1. Horst Cleinow was born in St. Petersburg in 1907 and raised in Berlin. He was fluent in English, French, Spanish and Persian.
2. Rolo (1943).
3. Pohle (1955).
4. FA: Dietze statement.
5. See pp. 43–82.
6. Taking her background into account, a British court bound her over to be of good behaviour for two years. The Times, 28 February 1946.
7. PRO: HO45/25814.
8. BDC.
9. AA-PA R.67586.
10. Some parts of the following section are based on the research of William Greenough Schofield, in his book, Treason Trail, and John Carver Edwards, in his book, Berlin Calling – American Broadcasters in Service to the Third Reich, to which studies the authors make due acknowledgement.
11. In addition to the principal figures considered in this chapter, the North America zone was, of course, manned by a number of other German repatriates and American Nazi propagandists. Among them were Frank Cleber, Inge Sylvia Doman (a secretary at the Foreign Ministry who, for thirteen months, doubled for Mildred Gillars as an announcer), Irene Dolores Fritsching, daughter of a former chancellor in the German embassy in Washington, DC, and girl-friend of Martin Monti, Marvin Herold Fritz, Ernst 'Ernesto' Grosskorth; Julius Krause; Jack Leibl and his father Hans Leibl; Wilhelm 'William' Linge; Pawel Matween; Alfred Ernst George 'Red' Miller; Ingrid Schumacher (b. Philadelphia, 1926); Edith Schwennesen; the brothers Charles and Edward Vieth Sittler, and Joachim Weidhaas. Weidhaas was fairly typical. Born to German parents in St. Louis, Missouri, in 1916, he was an electrical engineer who had come to Germany under contract to a construction firm in the summer of 1938. As a foreign national he lost his job at the beginning of the war but found employment at the American embassy in Berlin until December 1941, when he was interned at Bad Nauheim for repatriation to the USA. Having married a German woman in December 1940 and fathered a son, he applied to stay in Germany, and, in June 1942, joined the USA zone.

12. Clarence B. Odell/Robert H. Billigmeier, 'Aliens in Germany, 1939', in Department of State Bulletin No.
13. William L. Shirer, Berlin Diary, 26 September 1940.
14. IWM: BBC Digest, 22 October 1939.
15. IWM: BBC Digest, 20 February 1940.
16. IWM: BBC Digest, 14 January 1940.
17. IWM: BBC Digest, 20 January 1940.
18. Matrix nos. RRG 64699-710.
19. IWM: BBC Digest, 29 February 1940.
20. IWM: BBC Digest, 13 August 1940.
21. Shirer, Berlin Diary.
22. IWM: BBC Digest, 2 March 1940, 17:30 BST, Zeesen short-wave for North America, and 3 March 1940, 04:50 BST, Zeesen short-wave for the British Isles.
23. Edwards (1991).
24. AA-PA: R.67476.
25. IWM: BBC Digest, 14 January 1940.
26. IWM: BBC Digest, 19 Januray 1940.
27. AA-PA: R.67581.
28. IWM: BBC Digest, 31 October 1941.
29. IWM: BBC Digest, 22 December 1942.
30. Boberach (1984).
31. See pp. 126–28.
32. IWM: BBC Digest, 28 August 1942.

33. DRA/Sonderarchiv, Moscow: Fond 1363, ProMi-Findbuch 1, No. 145.

34. *Washington Post*, 25 February 1949.

35. Ulrich Haupt was born in Chicago on 30 October 1915, the son of German immigrant parents. Raised in Los Angeles where he became involved in the cinema, he played the leader of a settlers' party, Bull Flakes, in the 1930 Fox movie The Big Trail (*Die grosse Fahrt*) a German-American co-production directed by Raoul Walsh. In 1931, Haupt moved to Berlin to enrol at an art school, but having seen the great Gustaf Gründgens as Mephisto and Hamlet, decided instead to work on the stage. Gründgens accepted him as a pupil at the *Staatliche Schauspielschule* in Berlin. He made his début in 1935 as Romeo in Danzig. From 1937 he was a member of the Bavarian State Theatre (*Bayerisches Staatsschauspiel*) ensemble in Munich, until in 1940 Gründgens invited him to Berlin. After the war, Haupt returned to the United States, but settled again in Germany in 1951, becoming a distinguished classical actor and theatre director. He died in Munich on 22 November 1991.

36. BA: R78/1492-1583.

37. IWM: BBC Digest, 25 April 1941.

38. IWM: BBC Digest, 20 May 1941.

39. Schotte, Chandler's immediate superior, for example, earned only 900 marks a month, while Houben, programme controller of the entire short-wave system, received 1,100 marks.

40. IWM: BBC Digest, 10 March 1942.

41. IWM: BBC Digest, 22 February 1942.

42. AA-PA: R.67586.

43. AA-PA: R.67586.

44. IWM: BBC Digest, 21 April 1941.

45. AA-PA: R.67486.

46. Sington & Weidenfeld (1943).

47. William L. Shirer (1941); William L. Shirer, 'Propaganda Front', *New York Herald Tribune*, 31 May 1942.

48. IWM: BBC Digest, 18 September 1942.

49. Baillie (1959).

50. IWM: BBC Digest, 16 September 1942.

51. IWM: BBC Digest, 27 January 1943. Best's association of the term 'holocaust' with a *Jewish* 'conspiracy' against *Gentiles* will strike the present-day reader as very strange.

52. IWM: BBC Digest, 30 June 1944.

53. IWM: BBC Digest, 17 January 1945.

54. *Chicago Tribune*, 28 October 1941.

55. *Chicago Tribune*, 21 February 1942.

56. *Chicago Tribune*, 9 March 1942.

57. *P.M.*, 18 March 1942.

58. *Chicago Tribune*, 15 September 1942.

59. *Editor & Publisher*, 9 December 1944.

60. IWM: BBC Digest, 21 September 1944.

61. FA: Dietze statement.

62. *See* pp. 99–110.

63. Laughlin.

64. The Pound-Joyce correspondence is housed at the Beinecke Rare Book and Manuscript Library, Yale University.

65. 'I should think he will defend himself mightily, if in no very orthodox fashion. I wonder if he will resort to Economic Poetry. Poor old coot! [...] I always thought that he had many screws loose: this time there may have been method in his madness: but I dare say that he will be sent to an institution, from which he will be lucky if he emerges'. William Joyce to his wife Margaret, from Wandsworth prison, 5 and 26 December 1945. (FA).

66. Tytell.

67. The *Standarte Kurt Eggers*, named after a right-wing poet, was a unit established at the beginning of 1940 to provide the Waffen-SS with press and photo services of their own, separately from what the *Propagandakompanien* did for the German forces in general. This SS *Standarte* (regiment) gradually developed into a fairly independent psychological warfare unit of the German army, with practically all the propaganda expertise and facilities of the High Command at its disposal. Volunteers from twenty nations served with *Kurt Eggers*, mainly trying to steer the Germans' often misguided efforts to undermine their own nations' fighting morale in more effective directions. *SS-Standartenführer* (Colonel) Gunter d'Alquen (*b.* 1910) – a member of the Hitler Youth from 1925, of the Party from 1927 and from 1935 editor-in-chief of the SS-tabloid *Das Schwarze Korps* – was commanding officer and *SS-Obersturmbannführer* (Lieutenant-Colonel) Otto Kriegbaum (1912–1945) his deputy. *SS-Obersturmführer*

(Lieutenant) Konrad Buchholz (1902–1948) headed the broadcasting section and was liaison officer with the RRG.

Chapter 4: Fighting Great Britain on Medium-Wave

1. Herbert Schroeder (1940).
2. *Bremen I*, which used the frequency of the former Kattowitz (Katowice) station in annexed Poland, was the unlikely product of pre-war cooperation between the Reichspost and some British entrepreneurs; for details *see* p. 95. The old Bremen station was maintained under the name of Unterweser for the German home service.
3. Towards the end of 1943, the German European Station Calais acquired an opposite number in Sefton Delmer's British 'black' propagands station, *Soldatensender Calais*.
4. *The Saturday Review*, 1 February 1896, p. 118. The author was the young (Sir) Peter Chalmers Mitchell (1864–1945), biologist and for many years secretary of the Zoological Society of London. His ideas caused a furore in Germany, but (as he recalled in his memoirs) 'little stir' at home.
5. PRO: FO395/625, P445/6/150.
6. FA: Dietze agendas.
7. *See* Ch. 8.
8. The *New York Daily News* seems to have introduced this term on 23 October 1939, when it headlined a report on the war with 'The War is Phoney' (W.J. West).
9. BA: R78/1495.
10. Deutsche Welle/Schwipps, 1971.
11. *The Camp* was launched in July 1940, and by 1942 had a circulation of about 5,000.
12. On 16 June 1944, a note in Dietze's agenda reads: 'Baillie-Stewart in Vienna – Lale Andersen – Kapelle Jaritz'. During the 1930s Leo Jaritz (*b.* 1908) led a popular dance orchestra in Vienna. In 1943 he was released from the military to form a big band to frame propaganda broadcasts with swing-inclined music. Besides a number of draft-exempted Austrian musicians, the *Wiener Tanzorchester des Europasenders des Reichs-Rundfunks* included several foreign musicians released from internment and forced labour camps to augment this orchestra. During 1944–45, the collective personnel included: Leo Jaritz, the Belgian Bob Pauwels, Joschi Wimmer, N. Zdychinetz and Georg Pargas (trumpet); Fred Gollasch, Mladen Gutescha from Yugoslavia, 'Swing-Jule' Lippinsch from Latvia and the Italian Tino Passi (trombone); Ludwig Babinsky and the Bulgarian N. Kalatieff (alto-sax); Fritz Meinschadt and the Greek N. Kukulis (tenor-sax); Gyala Kutti and N. Moschutti, apparently also a foreigner (piano); Ernst Stumvoll, and later the Armenian Meg Tevelian (guitar); Fritz Kornher (string-bass); the Frenchman Arthur 'Tutur' Motta and Charly Fischer (drums). The orchestra played almost exclusively instrumental numbers which were broadcast by the DES station *Donau* to the eastern front and especially to the Balkans. Ludwig Babinsky, the later leader of the orchestra, once recalled: 'It was anything goes – the hotter, the more way out, the better.' The *Wiener Tanzorchester des Europasenders* did not record commercially, but some titles cut on Decelith acetates have survived. (Kraner/Schulz; Schulz, 1991).
13. *The Times*, 11 January, 1946.
14. *See* p. 99.
15. BA: R55/230.
16. BA: R55/230.
17. BA: R55/230.
18. *The Times*, 2 November 1945.
19. *The Times*, 2 November 1945.
20. *The Times*, 10 November 1945.
21. *The Times*, 2 November 1945.
22. Trial transcript, 10 December 1945.
23. On 24 August 1939 both Houses of Parliament had been recalled to pass the Emergency Powers (Defence) Bill, a comprehensive measure giving the government exceptional powers in the event of war. A section of the act provided for the detention of security suspects. In a broadcast from Berlin, William Joyce later commented on the Emergency Powers regulation 18.b: 'Never before has a government taken similar powers, no matter how difficult the situation.

Even the illusion of democracy has been dropped, and Churchill is determinded to force the people of Britain to defend him and his kind to their last drop of blood.' (IWM: BBC Daily Digest, 24 May 1940).

24. FA: Margaret Joyce letters.

25. BA: R78/1495.

26. Duff Cooper, the new Minister of Information, appointed a Home Morale Emergency Committee on 22 May 1940, to deal with the 'five menaces to public calm': fear, confusion, suspicion, class feeling and defeatism. The ministry's agents, dubbed 'Cooper's Snoopers', researched public opinon.

27. Boelcke (1966).

28. Imperial War Museum.

29. IWM: BBC Daily Digest , NBBS, 29 July 1940.

30. See Ch. 7 for the story of the 'clandestine' stations.

31. The term 'Fifth Column' originated at the start of the Spanish Civil War, when General Emilio Mola told journalists that, in addition to the four nationalist columns converging on republican-held Madrid, there was a 'fifth' column inside the city itself, meaning secret supporters hiding in the capital.

32. IWM: BBC Daily Digest , NBBS, 1 September 1940.

33. For example, *Struwwelhitler – A Nazi Story Book* by Doktor Schrecklichkeit, 'a parody on the original Struwwelpeter by Robert and Philip Spence, presented by them to the *Daily Sketch* War Relief Fund, which supplies wireless sets, games and woollen comforts to our Fighting Services, and clothing, bedding, boots and food to air raid victims'.

34. Towards the end of the war, on 21 December 1944, Joyce was enrolled in the *Sturm Wilhelmplatz* of the *Volkssturm*, the German equivalent of the Home Guard (which he had once ridiculed in his broadcasts). 'An official was filling out forms: "Any military service?" "Yes, British Army" – It was calmly filled in without an eyelash being batted, after nearly five years war. [...] About the same time, he was awarded the *Kriegsverdienstkreuz* (war merit cross) 1st class, presented by some Radio big bug, not, of course, the Old Man

[Hitler] – he was too busy.' FA: Margaret Joyce letters.

35. *The Times*, 20 September 1945.

36. *Daily Telegraph*, 8 February 1995.

37. Alan Hamilton, *The Times*, 8 February 1995.

38. William Joyce's younger brother, Edwin Quentin Joyce, had worked for the Air Ministry until he was detained and interned as a security risk for the remainder of the war.

39. Collection Bergmeier.

40. FA: Margaret Joyce letters.

41. Collection Bergmeier.

42. 'Jonah Barrington' was born Cyril Carr Dalmaine (1904–1986) and 'educated at Eastbourne College and the Royal Academy of Music. He taught at Uppingham and Christ's Hospital before taking up the post of chorus master at the British Broadcasting Corporation in 1931. In 1934 he became radio critic of the *Daily Express* and played an important role in the evolution of this comparatively new species. He remained with the *Express* until 1941 and later wrote for the *Sunday Chronicle* and the *Daily Sketch*. [...] Besides writing about the wireless, Barrington was also a regular performer on the medium [...]. His own musical compositions, as Cyril Dalmaine, included "Children Ballet", "The Ogre of Fontainebleau", "Suffolk Meditations" and "Victoriana".' (*Daily Telegraph*, obituary, 24 September 1986).

43. The *Daily Express* listening post, 'Radio Towers', was Lord Beaverbrook's private short-wave receiving station on a hill on his Checkley Court estate, near Leatherhead, Surrey.

44. According to *US: Mass Oberservation's Weekly Intelligence Service* of 29 March 1940, the nickname 'Harry Hamburg' had begun to catch on before Barrington's 'christening'.

45. Barrington (1948).

46. Barrington (1940).

47. Cit. in Asa Briggs (1970).

48. Kellersmann (1990).

49. Columbia DB.1883.

50. F. Tennyson Jesse and H.M. Harwood (1941).

51. BA: R55/1270.

52. The RRG's internal telephone directory of October 1942 mentions Peter

Adami, Margarete Guth and Helen Sensburg as staff on the European Stations' English service, besides a string of additions during the course of 1943: Maurice André, Claude Baudin, Helene Beckmann, James Blair, Sonja Kowanko, Mrs. Lüttich (in fact Mrs. Ella Neher, who was born Lüttich), Marina Manatzki, John O'Reilly, Jaques Piche, Dr. Poepping, Luise Schallies and Theodor Thony. All appear to have been on the staff of the English zone, although it is not clear in what capacity. In addition, there were contract workers, radio announcers and speakers.

53. *The Times*, 7 September 1945.
54. The Times, 7 September 1945.
55. *The Times*, 10 September 1945.
56. *The Times*, 7 September 1945.
57. *The Times*, 10 September 1945.
58. BA: R55/311.
59. When interrogated by British military intelligence in Paris in 1945, Wodehouse described Barnekow (who had returned to Germany only in 1939) as more American than German, and a confirmed anti-Nazi.
60. DRA/Sonderarchiv, Moscow: Fond 1363, ProMi-Findbuch 1, No. 40.
61. Cit. in Donaldson (1982).
62. Official British files on Wodehouse, at the Public Record Office, were due to be released late in 1996, after this book was in the press. See *The Times*, 10 September 1996.
63. PRO: HO45/25830.
64. PRO: HO45/25830.
65. BA: R55/1270.
66. *The Sunday Times*, 25 August 1996.
67. *The Times* covered the case of John Amery on 31 July, 13 September, 10 October and 29 November 1945.
68. *The Daily Telegraph*, 8 February 1995.
69. *The Times*, 8 February 1995.
70. David Millward also referred to an undated intelligence report: 'It was his attempts to recruit British prisoners of war into the German army which incensed the British government, who compared his activities to those of Sir Roger Casement, in the 1914–18 war'.
71. FA: *Eidesstattliche Erklärung* (affidavit) by Eduard Dietze.

72. In a memo of 10 June 1942, the European Stations reported the following commentators in its Irish service: 'Mrs. Susan Hilton, *alias* 'Susan Sweeney', (*b.* 1915 in Trichinopoly, India), rescued by the German raider 'Atlantis' after sinking the British ship 'Kemmendine' in which she was travelling; Mrs. Ella Neher, *alias* 'Ella'; Sonja Kowanko alias 'Linda Walter'; and the Wehrmacht NCO Werhahn *alias* 'Oscar Förster'. See BA: R55/1270. During her time in Germany, Susan Hilton published her memoirs, *Eine Irin erlebt England und den Seekrieg* (An Irish Woman's Experience of England and the War at Sea) (Hamburg: Falken-Verlag, 1942).
73. Geoffrey Elborn, *Francis Stuart – A Life*, (Dublin, 1990).
74. Stuart (1984).
75. *Picture Post*, 11 April 1942.
76. The Lutz Templin orchestra recorded 'We'll Meet Again', the Vera Lynn favourite, for the RRG on 1 October 1942; *see* App. I. Also *see* Mittler (1981).
77. 'Cab Calloway' was pianist-vocalist Bully Buhlan and Ilja Glusgal was the band's drummer. In spite of being Jewish, Schumann continued working as a musician in Berlin until 1943, when he was deported to Theresienstadt and thence to Auschwitz. The 'Groschenkeller' (Penny Cellar) in Kantstrasse, founded in the 1920s by the writer Franz Jung, was a haunt for jazz freaks during the late 1930s and early 1940s.
78. This story, from Mittler's own account, seems doubtful since, by this time, Oster himself was already under suspicion and was removed in April 1943, eventually being dismissed from the army and executed.
79. FA: Edith Dietze diaries, 28–29 August 1942.
80. Schmidt-Scheeder (1990).
81. The leaflet in question (AI-024-1-44) is titled 'At Nettuno'.
82. *Der Spiegel*, 9/1949, 'Seltsamer Haufe'.
83. Imperial War Museum: BBC Daily Digest of Foreign Broadcasts, 26 November 1943.
84. Leaflet AI-043-2-44.
85. Cit. in Michel Gérard, *Catalogue des Tracts Aériens Lancés sur les Français*,

1939–45; Paris: privately published, 1971–72.

86. Text of German propaganda leaflet used in operation '*Skorpion West*' during the spring of 1945.

87. Text of German propaganda leaflet used in operation '*Südstern*' in February 1945.

88. Text of German propaganda leaflet used in operation '*Skorpion West*' in 1944.

89. Texts of German propaganda leaflets used in operation '*Südstern*' in December 1944.

90. FA: '*Wirkungsbericht für die Monate Oktober und November*', 1 December 1944.

91. Cit. in Boelcke (1977).

92. *Der Spiegel*, 9/1949, 'Seltsamer Haufe'

93. BA: R55/311.

94. FA: Dietze statement.

95. Churchill is credited with this term, speaking about the east-west conflict at Fulton, Missouri, on 5 March 1946: 'An iron curtain has descended across the Continent. The Communist parties, which were small in all eastern states in Europe, have been raised to pre-eminence and power far beyond their numbers, and are seeking everywhere totalitarian control. [...] This is certainly not the liberated Europe we fought to build up. Nor is it one which contains the essential of a permanent peace.' But he was not the first to employ this metaphor, which has its roots in the theatre. Matthias Erzberger, of the German Centre Party, described the U-boats, in the Reichstag on 5 October 1916, as drawing 'an iron curtain around the British Isles and relentlessly sinking every vessel'. Colonel Nicolay, chief of Intelligence of the German High Command in the first World War, referred to the 'iron curtain of the hostile fronts' in his book *Nachrichtendienst, Presse und Volksstimmung im Weltkrieg*. On 30 January 1928, Gustav Stresemann, the German foreign minister, said: 'What we want and wish is that no iron curtain should exist between France and Germany'. Early in February 1945, at the time of the Yalta conference, Goebbels published an article '*Hinter dem Eisernen Vorhang*' ('Behind the Iron Curtain') in the weekly *Das Reich*, saying: 'Over the whole of south-eastern Europe an iron curtain of Bolshevik

fait-accompli has come down'.

96. See Foreign Office broadcast analysis of 7 May 1945, PRO: FO371/46807.

97. FA: Recording of broadcast.

98. FA: Recording of broadcast.

99. FA: Dietze statement.

Chapter 5: Propaganda Swing

1. Picker (1951 and 1965).

2. BA: R55/695.

3. A 'revolutionary' term that was favoured by the Nazis because it gave to what had been a legitimate, constitutional change of government the more romantic character of a 'new epoch', while at the same time justifying the increasingly arbitrary nature of Hitler's subsequent régime.

4. Hussong (1933).

5. Krenek's opera also prompted objections by implying that the New World, and its music, provided a liberation for Europe.

6. Paul Schwers, '*Die Frankfurter Jazz-Akademie im Spiegel der Kritik*', in *Allgemeine Musikzeitung*, 54/1927.

7. Reinmar von Zweter, in *Der Artist*, July 1936; Friedrich Bartels, 'Die berufstätige Frau', in *Ziel und Weg*, 3/1933.

8. *Amtsblatt des Thüringischen Ministeriums für Volksbildung*, Weimar: Jahrgang 9, 6/1930.

9. *Funk*, 17 March 1933.

10. *Funk-Stunde*, Presse Information, 8 March 1933.

11. *Mitteilungen der RRG*, 14 October 1935.

12. *Mitteilungen der RRG*, 25 February 1936; *Musik*, 28/1936.

13. *Neues Wiener Tageblatt*, 4 April 1941.

14. Cit. in Boelcke (1966).

15. Fröhlich (1987).

16. Cit. in Pohle (1955).

17. *Das Archiv*, July 1939.

18. BA: NS18/199, NS18/242.

19. Goebbels, '*Der Rundfunk im Krieg*', in *Zeit ohne Beispiel*.

20. BA: R58/1090.

21. BA: R55/695.

22. BA: R55/695.

23. BA: R55/695, R55/1224.

24. BA: Minutes of broadcasting planning meeting, 24 November 1941.

25. BA: broadcasting planning meeting, 2 December 1941.

26. BA: broadcasting planning meeting, 18 March 1942.
27. BA: R55/695.
28. Goebbels' Diaries, 27 February 1942.
29. BA: R55/1224, R55/1254.
30. The ten groups and their heads areas follows: A: Light Dance and Entertainment Music (Georg Haentzschel); B: Sophisticated Entertainment Music (Franz Grothe); C: General Popular National Entertainment (Werner Plücker); D: Cabaret (Günther Schwerkoldt); E: Entertainment Programmes for the Front (Heinz Goedicke); F: Popular Light Classical Music (Fritz Ganss); G: Serious, but generally accessible Music (Rudolf Schulz-Dornburg); H: Musical Soloists (Michael Raucheisen); J: Spoken Word Programmes (Theodor Loos); K: Difficult, because little-known, Classical Music (Gerhard von Westermann).
31. The assessment related to the period 5–11 June 1942; Boberach (1984).
32. Cit. in *Film und Funk*, 19 March 1942.
33. BA: R56I/41.
34. BA: R55/200.
35. BA: R55/242.
36. BA: R56I/34.
37. BA: R56I/34.
38. BA: R56I/34.
39. BA: R55/242, R56I/34.
40. BA: R55/242.
41. BA: R55/695.
42. BA: R55/1224.
43. *Das Podium der Unterhaltungsmusik*, 6 August 1942.
44. *Das Podium*, 15 July 1943.
45. *Das Podium*, 20 August 1942.
46. BDC.
47. BA: R56I/34.
48. BA: R56I/34.
49. BA: R56I/34.
50. Words and music by the British folklorist, the Rev. Sabine Baring-Gould and Sir Arthur Sullivan.
51. Grammophon 10704.
52. From information provided by Kleindin to Bergmeier during a series of interviews and communications.
53. Dr. Klaus Krüger, '*Es begann... Abends in der kleinen Bar*'; *Fox auf 78*, Nr. 5, December 1986.
54. Drummer Fritz Brocksieper once mistakenly recalled that this was Rudolf Arndt, the trombonist.
55. The White Ravens band, including alto-saxophonist Franz 'Teddy' Kleindin, once turned up at the studio to record two sides, which were never commercially released. Kleindin to Bergmeier; Hans-Joachim Berringer, '*Die Weissen Raben – Paradiesvögel der Berliner Tanzmusik*'; *Fox auf 78*, Nr. 7, Summer 1989.
56. Kleindin, personal information.
57. BDC.
58. *Der Artist*, Nr. 2545, 27 September 1934.
59. Kleindin, personal information.
60. *Das Deutsche Podium*, Nr. 15/16, April 1937, to Nr. 41, 15 October 1937.
61. Wittersleben, personal information.
62. Kellersmann (1990).
63. Lotz, personal information. Meyer at that time was also working for several other recording orchestras, including those of Hans Rehmstedt, Erhard Bauschke and Oskar Joost.
64. AA-PA: R.67476.
65. AA-PA: E.67477.
66. AA-PA: R.67476.
67. AA-PA: R.67477.
68. Plack was responsible for foreign visitors and collaborators.
69. Norman Baillie-Stewart, (1967).
70. AA-PA: R.67484.
71. IWM, BBC Monitors.
72. IWM, BBC Monitors. For a later version of the propaganda text of 'The Lambeth Walk', recorded by 'Charlie and his Orchestra' in December 1942, *see* App. II.
73. IWM, BBC Monitors.
74. IWM, BBC Monitors.
75. BA: R78/1000a, BDC.
76. BA: R78/1000a, BDC.
77. FA: "Wirkungsbericht für den Monat September 1944", dated 8 October 1944.
78. *See* App. I, 24 March 1942.
79. Florian Steinbiss & David Eisermann, *Propaganda Swing: Dr. Goebbels' Jazz-Orchester*; Bonn, 1989.
80. Wolfgang Muth, '*Jazz in der Zeit des Faschismus II – Swing und Propaganda*'; Sonntag, Nr. 26.
81. BA: R55/695.
82. BA: R55/230; R56I/27.
83. Kleindin, personal information.
84. This must be a slip; Ella Fitzgerald never recorded this number.
85. Friedrich Meyer, personal information.

86. BA: R56I/34.
87. Ernst van 't Hoff (1908–1955) was born Johan van 't Hof (van het Hof) to a German mother and Dutch father in Zandvoort, Netherlands. Early in his career he changed his name to Ernst, later adding an 'f' to his surname to harmonize Dutch pronunciation with German spelling. The issue was further complicated when the German records were wrongly labelled Ernst van *t*'Hoff, for van *ten* Hoff, instead of van *'t* Hoff, for van *het* Hoff.
88. Horst H. Lange (1966). Also see Gerhard Ruckert to Wolfgang Muth in *Swing Heil: Jazz im Nationalsozialismus* (Berlin, 1989).
89. Gerd Peter Pick of the Televox company, himself a jazz fan, recorded this session of which four titles were released in 1986 on Harlequin HQ-2051.
91. BDC.
92. Back in Holland, van 't Hoff organized a new formation, and on 22 May 1942 the orchestra was back on the air with a live broadcast over Hilversum I. At the end of the year, Hilversum II was integrated into the network of Berlin-controlled European stations as 'Calais II'. This station's rôle was to back up with music the English-language spoken-word programmes supplied *via* cable link from Berlin. Early in 1943, two jazz orchestras, as well as a light entertainment and a symphony orchestra were organized. Van 't Hoff and Dick Willebrandts were put in charge of the jazz formations. In addition, Hilversum hired *The Ramblers* (as *Het Dansorkest van Theo Uden-Masman*) and several other bands. From early 1943, these formations were on the air providing music from the former KRO studios for Nazi propaganda broadcasts against Britain. Most titles were recorded on Decelith discs for re-use, many of which have survived the war in the collection of a former studio technician. From the beginning, van 't Hoff had a running battle with the occupation authorities over the choice of music. On 25 January 1944 he was again arrested for infringing programme guidelines. Eventually, at the end of March 1944, he lost his job security when the Nazi authorities refused to renew his contract and work permit. After the war, the *Ereraad* (honour council), a semi-official Dutch commission that screened citizens for their collaboration under the German occupation, classified van 't Hoff and Dick Willebrandts as 'undesirable persons'.

92. Actually, the DTU was formed in Berlin and transferred to Prague in November 1943.
93. Otto Tittmann, personal information to Rainer Haensel.
94. Kleindin, personal information.
95. Kleindin, personal information. Henkel was, in fact, Paul Henkel who had replaced Rudi Wegener in the Kurt Hohenberger band early in 1938.
96. Kleindin, personal information.
97. Published in Loulakis' privately circulated periodical.
98. Barazzetta (1960).
99. Gerardo Brughere, personal information to Dr. Kimmo Luomanmäki; liner note 'Lecuona Cuban Boys' Harlequin CD-07, 1991.
100. BDC.
101. BDC.
102. Tittmann and Kleindin, personal information; official records say that Koblens died in Berlin-Wilmersdorf on 2 December 1942.
103. BDC.
104. Brocksieper, personal information.
105. Rainer E. Lotz, *Discographie der deutschen Tanzmusik, Band 4* (Bonn: Birgit Lotz Verlag, 1995).
106. Otto Tittmann, private information to Rainer Haensel.
107. Běhounek, '*Lebenserinnerungen*', unpublished typescript (Bonn, n.d.).
108. Wittersleben to Steinbiss (n.d)

Chapter 6: Farcical Feuding: the Nazi Propaganda Battle

1. IMT, Vol. XVII.
2. On 4 January Blomberg had married, as his second wife, a working-class girl on whom the Berlin vice squad (*Dezernat für Sittlichkeitsverbrechen*) produced a file, alleging solicitation and enclosing nude photographs, which was duly

brought to Göring's attention. In the case of von Fritsch, a would-be blackmailer had, in 1933, confused the army C-in-C with another officer in an attempt to enmesh him in a rent-boy scandal. The Gestapo, although aware of the error, fed this 'evidence' to von Fritsch's enemies, who had been looking for a way to discredit and remove him.

3. Brauweiler returned to his former position as deputy head of the ministry's Foreign Press Division under Dr. Bömer. On 15 May 1941, at a reception at the Bulgarian embassy in Berlin, Bömer was heard to brag about his forthcoming appointment as under-secretary of state: 'I shall be attached to Alfred Rosenberg, who is going to be governor-general of Russia. It won't be long now. [...] The Russians will be smashed within four weeks.' This spectacular gaffe, referring to the imminent invasion of the Soviet Union, resulted in the People's Court sentencing Bömer to two years imprisonment. He was released after six months for a period of probation on the eastern front, where he was killed in action in August 1942. Whether word of this massive indiscretion was passed to the Kremlin by the Bulgarian embassy is still not known. After Bömer's departure in June 1941, Brauweiler became the division's head. *See* BA-Potsdam: 30.17 ORA/VGH.

4. In November 1941 Dr. Wilhelm Christian Hauck (*b.* 1902) succeeded Cleinow, who had become *Intendant* of the German Short-Wave Station, and at the end of 1942, Dr. Heinz Pridat-Guzaris, former chief editor of the radio archives, took over as general manager of Radio-Union when Hauck was drafted into the army.

5. Lale Andersen was born Elisabeth Carlotta Helena Eulalia Bunnenberg (or Buntenberg) in Bremerhaven on 23 March 1908. Her husband's name was Wilke. Her debut was in Berlin in 1931. During 1933–34 she was engaged at the Zürich Schauspielhaus, followed by a stint at the 'Simplicissimus' in Munich, where in 1934 she, as Lale Andersen, introduced the song 'Lili Marleen', by Hans Leip to the music of Rudolf Zink. It became preeminently her song, and she also introduced its revised version,

with music by the pianist Norbert Schultze, at the 'Kabarett der Komiker' in Berlin early in 1939. This version was recorded both by Andersen for Electrola in July that year and by Mimi Thoma on 30 September 1941 (*see* App. I). After the war, Andersen continued her career, and died in Vienna on 29 August 1972.

6. 'Lady of the Lamplight' was the English lyric written for German radio by Norman Baillie-Stewart, not the version popularized for British audiences by Tommy Connor. *See* Künneke.

7. Prince Eugène of Savoy (1663–1736), Austrian commander and a potent symbol of German hegemony in south-east Europe (e.g., battle cruiser 'Prinz Eugen', SS-Panzer Division 'Prinz Eugen').

8. PRO: HO45/25801.

9. The Security Service (SD) had turned down Interradio's initial request for the release of Ward, dated 25 January 1943. (DRA/Sonderarchiv, Moscow: Fond 1363, ProMi-Findbuch 1, No. 108); PRO: HO45/25826.

10. PRO: HO45/25826.

11. BA: R55/1253.

12. Ewald Krümmer surfaced after the war as mayor (1956) and lord mayor (1961) of Iserlohn. From 1963 he was a member of the *Bundestag*, the federal parliament, and died in 1968.

13. After the war Heinrich Hunke became a senior civil servant (*Ministerialdirigent*) in the Ministry of Finance of Lower Saxony, and on supervisory and governing boards of several companies and institutions.

Chapter 7: Voices from Nowhere – the 'Concordia' Story

1. *See* Chs. 2 and 3.

2. Jacques Doriot was one of the leaders of the French Fascist movement. *See* p. 115.

3. BA: R55/1024.

4. BA: R55/1024.

5. BA: R55/1024.

6. *New York Times*, 5 August 1945.

7. On 9 October 1939, in his directive No. 6, Hitler ordered the campaign in the west to be prepared as early as possible and before the onset of winter. Time, he

held, would not be on Germany's side.

8. BA-Potsdam: 50.01/827.
9. BA-Potsdam: 50.01/827.
10. BA-Potsdam: 50.01/827.
11. Howe (1982).
12. Karl I. Albrecht, *Der verratene Sozialismus – Zehn Jahre als hoher Staatsbeamter in der Sowjetunion* (Berlin: Nibelungen Verlag, 1938).
13. Cit. in Boelcke (1966).
14. Dr. N. Muehlen, 'Observations on Nazi Propaganda and Public Opinion in France' sent to the BBC by John Wheeler-Bennett, 18 March 1941, cit. in Briggs (1970).
15. BDC.
16. Jacobsen (1968).
17. Hetzler's unit at the RRG included Ernst 'Ernesto' Meissner, a German from Brazil, as administrator, Walter Hohmann as chief editor (*Hauptsprachleiter*), and Dr. Joachim Schwalbe and Heinz Thorlichen as editors (*Sprachleiter*). A Mr. Bothien – a language-genius, according to Hetzler – was important on the listening posts, with Anna Jankowski, who was fluent in both French and Russian.
18. *See* 'Mystery of Anti-British Radio Station', *The Times*; 'Mystery of Bogus Radio Station', *Daily Telegraph*, both 27 February 1940.
19. Wave lengths were frequently altered to improve a station's reception or carry extra services.
20. IWM, BBC Digest: 27 February 1940.
21. PRO: HO45/25827.
22. PRO: HO45/25827.
23. *The Times*, 6 November 1945.
24. PRO: HO45/25833.
25. PRO: HO45/25833.
26. PRO: HO45/23833.
27. BA-Potsdam: 50.01/827.
28. BA-Potsdam: 50.01/827.
29. *See* p. 242.
30. IWM, BBC Digest, 18 September 1940.
31. IWM, BBC Digest, 11 July 1940.
32. IWM, BBC Digest, 13 July 1940.
33. Delmer (1962).
34. PRO: HO45/25833.
35. BA-Potsdam: 50.01/827.
36. IWM, BBC Digest, 23 September 1940.
37. IWM, BBC Digest, 21 August 1940.
38. *See* p. 219.
39. Collection Bergmeier.
40. *The Times*, 10 October 1945.
41. PRO: HO45/25742.
42. FA: Margaret Joyce files.
43. BA-Potsdam: 50.02/827.
44. PRO: HO45/25798.
45. PRO: HO45/25798.
46. The Big Six of the British Free Corps were: *Oberscharführer* (Sergeant) Thomas Haller Cooper, *nom-de-guerre* 'Peter Böttcher/Butcher', the Number One throughout the existence of the Corps; *Oberscharführer* Thomas Louis Freeman, *nom-de-guerre* 'Buck Rogers', responsible for discipline until June 1944, and the only member of the BFC to be cleared of any guilt after the war, as he was found to have 'joined with the object of escaping and of sabotaging the movement'; *Oberscharführer* John Eric Wilson (*b*. Blackpool, 1921), *nom-de-guerre* 'John "Tug" Montgomery', who succeeded Freeman, sentenced to ten years imprisonment by a Chelsea court-martial in 1946; *Unterscharführer* (Corporal) Roy Courlander, *nom-de-guerre* 'Roy Regan'; *Unterscharführer* Francis George MacLardy (*b*. Waterloo, Merseyside, 1915), *nom-de-guerre* 'Anthony Wood', responsible for propaganda, sentenced by Chester court martial in January 1946 for life, later remitted to fifteen years imprisonment; *Unterscharführer* Edwin Barnard Martin (*b*. Riverside, Ontario, 1919), *nom-de-guerre* 'Edwin Bartlett', in charge of security; court-martialled at Farnborough, Hampshire, and sentenced to twenty-five years' penal servitude.
47. *The Times*, 11 December 1945.
48. *The Times*, 27 August 1945.
49. DRA/Sonderarchiv, Moscow: Fond 1363, ProMi-Findbuch 1, No. 56.
50. *See* p. 42.
51. BA-Potsdam: 50.01/827; listing dated 11 July 1942, and report by Winkelnkemper dated 26 July 1942.

Chapter 8: The 'Battle Stations' and Radio Arnhem

1. FA: Dietze statement.
2. FA: Dietze statement.
3. BA: R55/1205, memo Dr. Halm,

14 October 1944.

4. BA: R55/1205, letter Dr. Helms, 17 October 1944.

5. The RRG's delegate in the Netherlands should not be confused with his namesake, the head of the ProMi's East Division, *Dr.* Eberhard Taubert (1909–1976).

6. RIOD: GKzbV 50e.

7. FA: Eschenberg.

8. FA: letter Winkelnkemper to Goebbels, 8 January 1945.

9. RIOD: Doc 1674-a-3.

10. FA: '*Wirkungsberichte für die Monate Oktober und November*', 1 December 1944.

11. The military commentary was compiled and presented by Johan(nes) Paardekooper (*b.* 1905), a Dutchman who spoke several languages fluently. He had been foreign correspondent for the Catholic newspaper *De Maasbode*, Rotterdam, since 1930. After serving briefly with the Dutch army and being held in a German PoW camp, he rejoined his newspaper in May 1940. When the Germans closed it down in February 1941, Paardekooper joined the short-wave station of the Amsterdam *Wereldomroep* (world radio) and, when the Dutch radio system was reorganized in April of that year, he was transferred to the *Nederlandsche Radio Omroep* in The Hague until that too was closed down in July 1944. On 14 October 1944 Paardekooper was '*dienstverpflichtet*' to work at Radio Arnhem. After the war, the *Rijksrecherche* of the Bijzondere Gerechtshof accepted that Paardekooper had been coerced into working for the German battle station, that he had tried to present balanced reports and that because of his limited cooperation he had prevented a Nazi hardliner from being given his programme slot. (Ministerie van Justitie, The Hague: *proces-verbaal van verhoor*; RIOD: 1674-a-5).

12. FA: letter Winkelnkemper to Goebbels, 8 January 1945.

13. Ministerie van Justitie, The Hague: *proces-verbaal van verhoor*.

14. FA: manuscript 'Forces Hour', 9 February 1945, by Helen Sensburg. The German military had used this theme before in Italy, in the form of leaflet titled 'Diary of Death' (No. *397/12–44) by the propaganda operation *Südstern* in December 1944.

15. FA: manuscript 'Forces Hour', 18 February 1945, by Helen Sensburg.

16. FA: manuscript 'Forces Hour', 3 March 1945, by Helen Sensburg.

17. RIOD: 1674-a-3.

Appendix I: Annotated Discography

Both disc and tape were the sound recording techniques available to the RRG during the war. Wax discs were only used for sound tests and in order to create a sample recording, because the surface wore off after being played a few times. Sound was cut into the wax directly by needle. Wax was easy to handle as the masters needed no industrial processing. The principal sound carrier for broadcasting material – and all commercial recordings – was shellac. When the base material, a resin-like secretion of tropical scale insects which Germany used to import from India, became scarce due to war restrictions, the RRG introduced a substitute called Decelith, a calcareous material, for the recording of all material intended for internal use only.

European broadcasting companies, including the RRG, commonly used 30cm (12") discs which were recorded from the inside to the outer rim, on one side only, for in-house use. This method had some technical advantages but was primarily meant to prevent private misuse.

Besides discs, the RRG had been using plastic tape with a ferrous coating since 1938 for the sound recording of its programmes, and speeches and commentaries in particular. This technology had been developed by AEG. Compared with the wire technology which was then still used by all foreign stations for the recording of broadcasts, the magnetic tape produced recordings of superior quality of up to twenty minutes duration, and could be edited like movie film, i.e. sequences could be cut and pieced together from different sources. On 15 September 1941, the RRG introduced pre-magnetized high-frequency tape, and half-a-year later, on 14 April 1942, a portable Magnetophon recorder was introduced.

When the Allies occupied Radio Luxembourg in September 1944, the BBC journalist Maurice Gorham was one of the first to inspect the facilities which the Germans had left behind:

> It was on this trip to Luxembourg that I saw and heard the Magnetophon, the magnetised tape recording system that the Germans had used for every sort of broadcast, including Hitler's speeches. Etienne Amyot, as a musician, said it was indistinguishable from a live broadcast and to me it certainly was, besides being very much easier to handle than disc. In those days Magnetophon machines could have been had almost for the asking, and when I went back I began a campaign to get the BBC to install them. But our engineers had just launched their improved disc recording, and it was impossible to get them really interested in the Magnetophon until practically all the equipment had disappeared.

Most 'Charlie' titles were recorded between 09:00 and 12:00 hours in studio IX of the Deutsche Grammophon company, Alte Jakobstrasse 32, Berlin. In the afternoon the musicians used to augment the Willi Stech orchestra for broadcasting work on the home service while others were tied to regular contracts at Berlin bars and restaurants.

The recordings were processed at the company's factory in Hanover, Podbielski-Allee. When in 1943 most of its labour force was called up and the capacity of Hanover could no longer be fully utilized, Deutsche Grammophon transferred the processing of all official orders, including those from the RRG, to the Esta factory in Prague.[†]

The label gives no information as to the source of these records – not even a label name. The records are therefore mostly referred to by the iconography used, i.e. the 'music clef label' (*Notenschlüssel* – red colour), the 'lyre label' (blue colour) and the 'clarinet and mandoline label' (maroon colour). For the last documented release, 0252/0253, the lyre design was once again used, but this time in the maroon colour which had previously been used for the clarinet and mandoline label.

It may be speculated that the change in label design reflects a change in responsibility, probably from the ProMi which may have started the series using the lyre label, to the Foreign Ministry which introduced the clarinet and mandoline label after it had gained nominal control of foreign-language propaganda in September 1939,[††] and took over the whole music project towards the end of 1940.

Label details vary. For example, the diameter of the lyre label and the lyre depicted on 15cm records has four strings whereas the one on 25cm records has five.

These records are all of standard 78 rpm speed, with outside start, and bear no order numbers for the simple reason that there was no catalogue from which to order them. The sides are identified by sequential numbers – in the case of lyre-labelled releases, in Roman numerals. All matrix details, which are normally pressed near the run-off groove of shellac discs, have been carefully erased as they would have disclosed the origin of the records. Oddly enough, given the circumstances, some labels are printed with composer credits and copyright information. This may have been a kind of a gesture towards the broadcasting authorities in neutral countries.

Some of the earlier records are of 15cm (6") diameter, but the majority are standard 25cm (10") diameter. No 30cm (12") records are known, although this was the normal size for inside-start acetates cut in and used by radio stations, normally on the flexible Decelith, as well as for special pressings made for the RRG.

All 'Charlie' records are extremely rare as they were never commercially released and were only distributed, in small quantities, to radio stations in Germany, in occupied territories and in neutral countries. They have been found in Amsterdam, Brussels, Paris, Belgrade, Zagreb, Vienna, Copenhagen and Oslo. According to a memorandum by the head of the RRG sound archive, Dr. Fritz Pauli, dated 23 March 1944,[†††] the print-run was forty copies per matrix number for all new recordings as well as re-pressings.

They may also have been distributed in some of the so-called 'holiday camps' – selected prisoner-of-war camps, where receptive prisoners were segregated from their fellow-prisoners and subjected to political and ideological indoctrination. An unfounded story circulated among record collectors after the war, according to which 'Charlie' records were pressed on unbreakable plastic and parachuted over Britain to be picked up by unsuspecting passers-by and undercover agents, who supposedly placed them on the doosteps of private homes when the occupants had gone to church!

In addition to what may be termed this 'popular' series, The RRG recorded other propaganda titles by a variety of vocalists and orchestras for re-broadcasting, as shown in the

---

† BA: R561/41 †† *see* chapter 5 ††† BA: R561/41

discography. These records have recently come to light in the sound archive of what used to be Radio Berlin in the former German Democratic Republic, and in the archive of the Czech radio, which had been part of the RRG's network of European stations during the war. These are 25cm or 30cm pressings, single-sided, with inside start, as was the practice with radio records. The plain white label of these records is usually hand-written, sometimes typed, never printed, and shows artist or band name only, and the title.

The RRG ledgers show further details, including recording studio and date, full title credits, and the source of the recording, for example, 'KWS' or 'DKS' for the German Short-Wave Station, 'DS' for *Deutschlandsender* or 'Bln' for *Reichssender Berlin*, followed by a matrix number. The matrix numbers are not in strict sequence as number blocks had apparently been pre-allocated to various broadcasting stations, perhaps as a means of controlling the consumption of shellac in wartime.

All shellac recordings by 'Charlie and his Orchestra' are systematically listed and annotated in the following discography. The following abbreviations are used: Gr = Grammophon. Po = Polydor, Br = Brunswick and b/c = broadcast. For completeness' sake, the commercial records by the Lutz Templin orchestra and associated studio formations are included as well. If a recording was considered imperfect or faulty a further attempt, or 'take' was recorded. They are identified by a suffix to the matrix number. Thus, -1 or -2 signal the respective attempt. In the case of Grammophon a 'plain' matrix number indicates the first take, -½ the second take and -¾ the third take. Both types of suffixes were in use and are shown in this discography as they appear on the archival records, or in the recording ledgers, respectively. However, Berlin live broadcasts monitored and recorded on acetate by the BBC Monitoring Service and in the United States by the Princeton Listening Center are not included in this section, although some samples are cited at the end in order to complete the picture.

The spelling of titles, composer credits and other information is taken from the actual record labels themselves. If no composer/lyricist was given, this is indicated by '(—)' in the discography; if the record was not available for inspection, the space is left blank. 'NP' stands for non-propaganda lyrics and 'voc' for vocal/vocalist.

(Anon.)

Erhard Bauschke *leader*; probably Willi Lipka, Hans Wieczorek, Max Müssigbrodt *trumpet*; Rudi Ahlers, E. Wrobel *trombone*; Otto Sill *alto-sax/clarinet*, Alfred Prellwitz *alto-sax/clarinet/violin*, Günther Grunwald *tenor-sax*, Kurt Wege *tenor-sax/baritone-sax*; Günther Gabriel *piano*; Fred Dömpke *guitar/bandoneon*, Hans Belle *guitar*; Otto Buchal *drums*; unidentified *male tenor vocal-1*, unidentified *male bass vocal-2*.

Berlin; 11 October 1939

(1)	British Soldier's Song (—)	Engl voc 1	Lyra I/II (15cm)
RID2119.A1	British Soldier's Song (—)	Engl voc 2	[Anon.] Nr. 19a (25cm)
RID2119.B1	British Soldier's Song (—)	Engl voc 2	[Anon.] Nr. 19b (25cm)

- *The details of this session are known from the diaries of guitarist Fred Dömpke, courtesy of his biographer Jan Grundmann. There is no entry for these sides in the available recording ledgers.*
- *This session lasted for two hours, and two different versions were recorded: The vocalist on Lyra I is a tenor, whereas the vocalist on record No. 19 may be termed a bass.*
- *Aurally, both sides of record No. 19 play the identical take.*

[session continued]

- *The label of No. 19 carries no name or picture; both sides have an identical plain white label with the full lyrics printed on it; what appear to be stamper numbers are pressed into the run-off part of the sides; the side numbers are printed on the label.*
- *This 'foxtrot' rendering would have made the famous hymn tune, with its martial rhythm, almost unrecognisable to British or American listeners. It suggests that neither singer nor producer was familiar with* 'Onward Christian Soldiers', *and so missed the opportunity for any satirical or propagandistic effect.*

(Anon.)

Erhard Bauschke *leader*, personnel & instrumentation probably similar to before; add Dick Buisman *bass*.

Berlin; 26 May 1939

8590 – GR9   Could Be. Foxtrot (Donaldson)   Lyra II/I (15cm)

- *This reissue of a recording of the Walter Donaldson composition by the Bauschke orchestra, arranged by Günther Gabriel, had been commercially released on Gr/Po 11161. It appears as Lyra II, on the B-side of Lyra I. The original 25cm recording was edited (the first bars were cut out) for reissue on the blue colour 15cm lyre label.*

In about October 1939, operatic baritone Karl Schmitt-Walter recorded six titles in French for the RRG. A limited number of these shellac pressings seem to have been distributed to the various *Reichssender*. The four sides in French which were released on the red music clef label are anonymous; in all probability they were also recorded at that time.

Schmitt-Walter (1900–1985) studied in Nuremberg and Munich, and after engagements at provincial opera houses, worked in Berlin from 1935. After the war, Schmitt-Walter was engaged at the Munich opera, with guest roles in New York, and was a professor at the music high school in Munich.

(Anon.)

Karl Schmitt-Walter *baritone vocal*;
- RRG nos. 56132 & 56133 unaccompanied;
- RRG no. 56134 accompanied by Dr. Rosen *piano*;
- RRG no. 56135 accompanied by Dr. Rosen *piano* and a small orchestra of the Reichssender Berlin under the direction of Willy Steiner (1910–1975);
- RRG no. 56136 unidentified accompaniment;
- RRG no. 56137 accompanied by the band of the *Wachregiment der Luftwaffe* directed by Hans Teichmann.

Berlin, Reichssender; *c.* October 1939

56132	Französische Lieder: 'Soldat De France'	KSchW (French voc)	RRG 56132
56133	Französische Lieder: 'A Bas La guerre Pour L'Angleterre'	KSchW (French voc)	56133
56134	Französische Lieder: 'A Bas La Guerre Pour L'Angleterre'	KSchW (French voc)	56134
56135	Französische Lieder: 'Adieu Mon Père, Adieu Ma Mère'	KSchW (French voc)	56135
56136	Französische Lieder: 'A Bas La Guerre Pour L'Angleterre'	KSchW (French voc)	56136
56137	Französische Lieder: 'A Bas La Guerre Pour L'Angleterre' [1st verse only]	KSchW (French voc)	56137

(Anon.)

Karl Schmitt-Walter *baritone-vocal*, accompanied by Dr. Rosen *piano*.

Berlin; *c.* October 1939

(4)	Adieu Mon Père Du Film Sonore 'La Guerre Absurde' (Paroles et musique Pierre Lapaix)	KSchW (French voc)	Notenschlüssel IV/V (15cm) (music clef)
(5)	J'en Ai Marre (Paroles et musique Pierre Lapaix)	KSchW (French voc)	V/IV (15cm)
(6)	Adieu Mon Père Du Film Sonore 'La Guerre Absurde' (Paroles et musique Pierre Lapaix)	KSchW (French voc)	VI/VII (25cm)
(7)	J'en Ai Marre (Paroles et musique Pierre Lapaix)	KSchW (French voc)	VII/VI (25cm)

- *VI and VII are transfers from 15cm records IV and V, not separate mx. nos. or alternative takes.*
- *Three records, i.e. sides number III and VIII-XII, are untraced.*

(Anon.)

Unidentified big band, including strings and celeste; unidentified *English-language male choir*.

Berlin; *c.* October 1939

(13)	Boomps-A-Daisy	Engl choir	Lyra XIII/XV (25cm?)
(14)	Boomps-A-Daisy		XIV/XVI (25cm?)

- *Side numbers VIII-XII are untraced.*

Reichsmusikzug des Reichsarbeitsdienstes mit Chor – Leitung: Obermusikführer Herms Niel

Herms Niel *leader*; military brass band, unidentified personnel and instrumentation; unidentified *German male choir*.

Berlin; 19 October 1939

8741 – 1GR9	Matrosenlied (Herms Niel)	German choir	unissued
8741 – 2GR9	Matrosenlied (Herms Niel)	German choir	unissued
8741 – 3GR9	Matrosenlied (Herms Niel)	German choir	unissued
8741 – 4GR9	Matrosenlied (Herms Niel)	German choir	unissued
8741 – 5GR9	Matrosenlied (Herms Niel)	German choir	Gr/Po 11357 (25cm), Lyra XVIII/XVII (15cm)
8741 – 6GR9	Matrosenlied (Herms Niel)	German choir	unissued

- *Original title of 'Matrosenlied' is 'Wir fahren gegen Engel-land'.*
- *On November 6, 1939, take 8741-5GR9 was duplicated and given the new number 8741-5GRD9, on November 14, 1939, take 8741-5GR9 was duplicated again and give the new number 8741-7GRD9; on November 17, 1939, take 8741-5GR9 was duplicated for the third time and two new numbers were allocated, 8741-9GRD9 for the sapphire-cut version and 8741-11GRD9 for the needle-cut version; take 8741-11GRD9 was released on 25cm Grammophon 11357 for local consumption and Polydor 11357 for export purposes and presumably transferred to the 15cm Lyra XVIII/XVII. (There is no available information on the use of takes 8741-8GRD9 and 8741-10GRD9.)*

(Anon.)

- 'Siegfried Line' accompanied by Fred Dömpke *accordion*, unidentified *bass, drums*.
- 'Seelord' (original title 'Das kann doch einen Seeman nicht erschüttern') with the Schuricke Terzett of Rudi Schuricke *tenor-voice*, Karl Golgowski, Horst Rosenberg; *German vocal trio*, accompanied by Fred Dömpke *accordion*, unidentified *bass, drums*.

Berlin; 29 November 1939

(15)	Siegfried Line (—)	Engl voc	Lyra XV/XIII (25cm?)
(16)	Siegfried Line (—)		XVI/XIV (25cm?)
(17)	Das muß den ersten Seelord doch erschüttern (M. Jary)	RST German voc 3	XVII/XVIII (15cm)

- *The details of this session are known from the diaries of guitarist Fred Dömpke, courtesy of his biographer Jan Grundmann. There is no entry for these sides in the available recording ledgers.*
- *Naturally, the war started a spate of patriotic songs and in 1939, within a couple of days, two British song-writing teams published songs on the 'Siegfried Line', the German's fortified defence-in-depth entrenchment behind the Western Front, during World War I. In 1938, when Hitler's construction of the 'Westwall' was publicised all over the world, the British press for some reason caught on to the old name. Ross Parker, Hugh Charles and St. John Cooper were the team behind 'I'm Sending You The Siegfried Line (To Hang Your Washing On)', while Michael Carr and Jimmy Kennedy were the authors of '(We're Gonna Hang Out) The Washing On The Siegfried Line'.*
- *This is the first of a total of four recordings of a parody on 'The Siegfried Line' by a German propaganda band. The suggestion has been made that the vocalist here was William Joyce ('Lord Haw-Haw'), but it has not been possible to substantiate this.*
- *Rudi Schuricke and Karl Golgowski both confirmed their participation to collector Hans-Joachim Schröer, Berlin.*

Charlie and his Orchestra

Lutz Templin *leader*; probably Rimis van den Broek, Charly Tabor, unidentified poss. Fernando Diaz or Helmuth Friedrich or Fritz Petz *trumpets*; Willy Berking, Henk Bosch *trombones*; Mario Balbo, Bob van Venetië *tenor-sax/clarinet*, Benny de Weille, Teddy Kleindin *alto-saxes/clarinets*; Franz Mück *piano*; Meg Tevelian *guitar*; Cesare Caivaion *bass*; Fritz Brocksieper *drums*; Walter Leschetitzky, 2 or 3 unidentified *string-section-1*; Charlie Schwedler, unidentified *vocals*; Lutz Templin, Willy Berking, Franz Mück, Friedrich Meyer-Gergs *arrangements*.

Berlin; c. autumn 1940

(26)	Nice People (—)	1	voc CS	Lyra XXVI/XXVII
(27)	Thanks For The Memory (—)	1	vos CS	XXVII/XXVI
(28)	Stormy Weather (—)	1	voc CS	XXVIII/XXIX
(29)	It's A Long Way To Tipperary (—)	1	voc CS/unidentified	XXIX/XXVIII

- *This is the first batch of recordings released as by 'Charlie and his Orchestra', probably indicating that cabarettist Karl 'Charlie' Schwedler had joined the propaganda orchestra as a vocalist and frontman.*
- *Side numbers IXX-XXV are untraced.*
- *The above and all following records are of 25cm (10") diameter.*

(Anon.)

Lutz Templin *leader*; personnel and instrumentation probably as before, including Walter Leschetitzky, 2 or 3 unidentified *string-section-1*; Charlie Schwedler *vocals*.

Berlin; *c.* autumn 1940

(30?)	Home Town	NP	voc CS	Lyra ? XXX/XXXI
(31?)	Sing, Baby, Sing		voc CS	? XXXI/XXX
(32)	They All Laughed (from 'Shall We Dance')		voc CS	XXXII/XXXIII
(33)	Sing, Baby, Sing (L. Pollack – Yellen)		voc CS	XXXIII/XXXII
(34)	When Day Is Done (—)	1	voc CS	XXXIV/XXXV
(35)	You're Driving Me Crazy (—)		voc CS	XXXV/XXXIV

- *XXXII and XXXV are 'anon.', i.e. without artist credit on the label.*
- *'Home Town' is a straight version, with no propaganda lyrics.*

(Anon. – Lyra XLVII/XLVI)
Charlie and his Orchestra

Lutz Templin *leader*; personnel and instrumentation probably as before, including Walter Leschetitzky, 2 or 3 unidentified *string-section-1*; Charlie Schwedler, Eva 'Evelyn' Leschetitzky *vocals*.

Berlin; *c.* autumn 1940

(42)	I Want To Be Happy. Foxtrot (Vincent Youmans)	1	voc CS	Lyra XXXXII/XXXXIII
(43)	Hold Me. Foxtrot (Little, Oppenheim, Schuster)	1	voc CS/EL	XXXXIII/XXXXII
(44)	You Can't Stop Me From Dreaming Foxtrot (Friend – Franklin)	1	voc CS	XXXXIV/XXXXV
(45)	With A Smile And A Song (Morey – Churchill)	1	voc CS	XXXXV/XXXXIV
(46)	Remember Me?		voc CS	XLVI/XLVII
(47)	Yours And Mine		voc CS	XLVII/XLVI
(48)	Good Night, Sweetheart		voc CS	XLVIII/XLIX
(49)	I'll See You In My Dreams		voc CS	XLIX/XLVIII

- *Lyra issues XXXVI-XXXXI are untraced.*
- *On 'Hold Me' Charlie sings in duet with a female vocalist whom he addresses as 'Evelyn'. According to bass-player Otto Tittmann, who joined the Templin orchestra at a later stage, this was Eva Leschetitzky, wife of the violinist, who can be heard playing hot violin on this take. Lutz Templin plays a tenor-sax solo on 'Hold Me', too.*

Charlie and his Orchestra

Lutz Templin *leader*; probably Rimis van den Broek, Charly Tabor, unidentified, poss. Fernando Diaz or Helmuth Friedrich or Fritz Petz *trumpets*; Willy Berking, Henk Bosch, unidentified poss. Ferri Juza *trombones*; Benny de Weille *clarinet/alto-sax*, Mario Balbo, Bob van Venetië, Eugen Henkel *clarinets/tenor-saxes*; Franz Mück *piano*; Meg Tevelian *guitar*; Cesare Caivaion or Paul Henkel *bass*; Fritz Brocksieper *drums*; Charlie Schwedler *vocals*.

		Berlin; *c.* late 1940
Indian Love Call (R. Friml)	voc CS	K & M 0101/0102
The Sheik Of Araby (Snyder)	voc CS	0102/0101
I'm Putting All My Eggs In One Basket (—)	voc CS	0103/0104
The King's Horses (Noel Gay & Harry Graham)	voc CS	0104/0103
St. Louis Blues (Haudy) [*sic*]	voc CS	0105/0106
Slumming On Park Avenue (—)	voc CS	0106/0105

• *These are the first recordings on the maroon clarinet & mandoline label (German: Klarinette & Mandoline).*

Charlie and his Orchestra

Lutz Templin *leader*; probably Nino Impallomeni, Charly Tabor and/or Alfredo Marzaroli *trumpets*; Willy Berking, Henk Bosch and/or Ferri Juza *trombones*; Benny de Weille *clarinet/alto-sax*, Mario Balbo *tenor-sax/clarinet*, 2 unidentified poss. Bob van Venetië, Eugen Henkel *saxophones/clarinets*; Franz Mück *piano*; Meg Tevelian *guitar*; Rudi Wegener *bass*; Fritz Brocksieper *drums*; Charlie Schwedler *vocals*; Friedrich Meyer-Gergs *arrangements*.

		Berlin; *c.* mid 1941
By By Blues [*sic*]	voc CS	K & M 0107/0108
Thanks Mr. Roosevelt	voc CS	0108/0107
Tea For Two (V. Youmans, Colline & Merry)	voc CS	0109/0110
I'll Never Say 'Never Again' Again (H. Woods)	voc CS	0110/0109
I've Got A Feeling You're Fooling	voc CS	0111/0112
The Washing On The Siegfried Line	voc CS	0112/0111

Charlie and his Orchestra

Lutz Templin *leader*; probably Nino Impallomeni, Charly Tabor, Alfredo Marzaroli *trumpets*; Willy Berking, Henk Bosch, Ferri Juza *trombones*; Teddy Kleindin *clarinet/alto-sax*, Detlev Lais *tenor-sax*, Mario Balbo *tenor-sax/clarinet*, unidentified poss. Francesco Paolo Ricci *tenor-sax/clarinet*; Primo Angeli *piano*; Meg Tevelian *guitar*; probably Rudi Wegener *bass*; Fritz Brocksieper *drums*; Charlie Schwedler *vocals*; Friedrich Meyer-Gergs *arrangements*.

		Berlin; *c.* mid 1941
Auf Wiedersehn, My Dear (—)	voc CS	K & M 0113/0114
Alone (—)	voc CS	0114/0113
Dinah (—)	voc CS	0115/0116
Daisy (—)	voc CS	0116/0115
I'm Playing With Fire (—)	voc CS	0117/0118
Goody Goody (—)	voc CS	0118/0117
I'm Feeling Like A Million	voc CS	0119/0120
Boo-Hoo	voc CS	0120/0119

Jazz-Orchester Templin (ledgers)
Lutz Templin Tanz-Orchester (Polydor)

Lutz Templin *leader*; probably Nino Impallomeni, Charly Tabor, Alfredo Marzaroli *trumpets*; Willy Berking, Henk Bosch, Ferri Juza *trombones*; Lutz Templin *tenor-sax*, Mario Balbo *tenor-sax/clarinet*, Benny de Weille *alto-sax/clarinet*, Heinz Berger *bass-clarinet*, unidentifed *flute*; Franz Mück or Primo Angeli *piano*; Meg Tevelian *guitar*; Rudi Wegener *bass*; Fritz Brocksieper *drums*; Friedrich Meyer-Gergs *arrangements*.

Berlin; 28 March 1941

8933 – GD9	Bei dir war es immer so schön. Langsamer Foxtrot (Theo Mackeben)	Gr/Po unissued
8933½GD9	Bei dir war es immer so schön. Langsamer Foxtrot (Mackeben)	Gr/Po 47535A
8934 – GD9	Du gehst durch all' meine Träume. Langsamer Foxtrot (Peter Kreuder)	Gr/Po unissued
8934½GD9	Du gehst durch all' meine Träume. Langsamer Foxtrot (Kreuder)	Gr/Po 47536A
8935 – GD9	Sahara. Foxtrot (Friedrich Meyer)	Gr/Po unissued
8935½GD9	Sahara. Foxtrot (Friedr. Meyer-Gergs)	Gr/Po 47536B

- *Recording ledgers state: 'Kombination: Nr. 1-4, Nr. 2-3'.*
- *Recordings of the Deutsche Grammophon using the -GD and -GR suffixes were recorded in studio 9.*
- *All issued sides were probably released on both the Grammophon (Germany) and Polydor (export) labels.*
- *Soon after this session, on 22 June 1941, arrranger-pianist Meyer-Gergs was drafted into the army. From June 1942 until October 1944, he was stationed at Radio Belgrade, then at the Reichssender Vienna until the end of the war.*

Jazz-Orchester Lutz Templin (ledgers)
Lutz Templin mit seinem Tanz-Orchester (Grammophon)
Lutz Templin Tanz-Orchester (Polydor)

Lutz Templin *leader*; probably Nino Impallomeni, Charly Tabor, Alfredo Marzaroli *trumpets*; Willy Berking, Jos Breyre, and Henk Bosch or Ferri Juza *trombones*; Detlev Lais *tenor-sax*, Mario Balbo *tenor-sax/clarinet*, Teddy Kleindin *alto-sax/clarinet*, and unidentified, Bob van Venetië or Eugen Henkel *saxophone/clarinet*; Primo Angeli *piano*; Meg Tevelian *guitar*; Rudi Wegener *bass*; Fritz Brocksieper *drums*; Adolf Steimel *arrangements*.

Berlin; *c.* 10 May 1941

8991 – GD9	Junger Mann aus gutem Hause. Foxtrot (Adolf Steimel)	Gr/Po unissued
8991½GD9	Junger Mann aus gutem Hause. Foxtrot (A. Steimel)	Gr/Po 47540A
8992 – GD9	Mein kleiner Teddybär, aus 'Anita und der Teufel' (Theo Mackeben)	Gr/Po unissued
8992½GD9	Teddy Bär. Foxtrot aus 'Anita und der Teufel' (Mackeben)	Gr/Po 47535B
8993 – GD9	Parade der kleinen weißen Mäuse (Parade Of The Little White Mice) Foxtrot (Caesar Fazioli, Bernh. Fazioli, Mickey Alpert)	Gr/Po unissued
8993½GD9	Parade der kleinen weißen Mäuse. Foxtrot (Caesar Fazioli, Bernh. Fazioli, Mickey Alpert)	Gr/Po 47540B

Karl Schotte, Gesang – Chor und Kapelle Hans Bund (ledgers)

Hans Bund *leader*; unidentified personnel and instrumentation; Karl Schotte *English vocals*, Jupp Hussels *German vocals, choir*.

Berlin, Reichssender, Studio 6; 22 July 1941

66341	Dreimal kurz – einmal lang	KS English voc/choir	RRG 66341
	(Werner Plücker – Musik von Martin Schönicke)		
66342	Dreimal kurz – einmal lang	JH German voc/choir	RRG 66342
	(Werner Plücker – Musik von Martin Schönicke)		

- *An indication that occasionally other orchestras were used for English-language propaganda broadcasts. This recording originated at the Berlin Reichssender and not at the short-wave station.*
- *The reference to the V-for-Victory theme from Beethoven's Fifth was part of the ProMi's effort to hijack the BBC's signal to German-occupied Europe.*
- *For Karl Schotte's rôle in the North America Zone see the index.*

Brasilianische Musik – Solé Aguilar, Tenor, mit Kapelle Lutz Templin (ledgers)

Lutz Templin *leader*; personnel and instrumentation probably as before; Ignacio Solé Aguilar *Portuguese vocals*.

Berlin, KWS, Studio 10; 22 July 1941

66456	Dizem Por Ahi. Samba von Waldemar de Abreu	2'51"	voc SA	RRG 66456
66457	Tens Razão. Valsa von Newton Teixeira	2'14"		66457
66458	Meu Mulato. Samba von Cyro de Souza	2'18"		66458
66459	Viver é Beijar. Valsa von Antenogenes Silva	2'36"		66459
66460	Fiquei Sentido. Samba von Milton de Oliveira – H. Lobo	2'49"		66460
66461	Sepulcro de um Coração. Samba von Claudionor Cruz	3'03"		66461
66462	Louca de Amor. Samba von Z. und R. Marques	2'12"	voc SA	66462
66463	Valsa da Saudade. von José Maria de Abreu	2'16"		66463
66464	Fiquei Louco. Samba von O. Silva – A. Saldanha – W.Silva	2'13"		66464
66465	Ultima Serenata. Valsa von Antenogenes Silva	2'51"		66465
66466	Lagrimas Sentidas. Samba von M. Viera u. Alvarengha	2'20"	voc SA	66466
66467	Sevilhana. Valsa von J.M. Abreu	2'09"	voc SA	66467
66468	Quando Eu Penso Na Bahia. Samba-Jongo von Ary Barroso	3'02"		66468
66469	Porque Voce Voltou. von Nassaro u. J. Ruy	3'11"	voc SA	66469

- *These titles complete the Templin discography.*
- *It is not known whether the texts contain any propaganda.*
- *Details as per RRG ledgers. Further information on the ledger cards: 'Abteilung 9: Musik' (Bln. 66341/42 and KWS.66456 – 66469); 'Keine Kosten bei Wiederholung' ['No charge for repeats'] (KWS.66456 – 66469); and the handwritten, post-war information 'nicht vorhanden' ['does not exist'].*

Jazzorchester Templin (ledgers)
Lutz Templin Tanz-Orchester mit Gesang (47569)
Lutz Templin m.s. Tanz-Orchester (47572)

Lutz Templin (*leader*); probably Nino Impallomeni, Charly Tabor, Alfredo Marzaroli *trumpets*; Willy Berking, and Henk Bosch or Ferri Juza *trombones*; Mario Balbo, Eugen Henkel *tenor-saxes/clarinets*, Benny de Weille, Cor Koblens *alto-sax/clarinet*; Franz Mück *piano*; Meg Tevelian *guitar*; Rudi Wegener *bass*; Fritz Brocksieper *drums*; Charlie Schwedler *vocals*; Lutz Templin, Willy Berking, Eugen Henkel, Franz Mück *arrangements*.

Berlin; 15 September 1941

9088–GD9	Für ein süßes Mädel Foxtrot aus dem Tonfilm 'Kleines Mädchen – große Sorgen' (Michael Jary – Text: Bruno Balz)	voc CS	Gr/Po unissued
9088½GD9	Für ein süßes Mädel Foxtrot aus dem Tonfilm 'Kleines Mädchen – große Sorgen' (Michael Jary – Text: Bruno Balz)	voc CS	Gr/Po 47569B
9089–GD9	Tadellos! Foxtrot (Templin – Text: Franz Baumann)	voc CS	Gr/Po unissued
9089½GD9	Tadellos! Foxtrot (Templin – Text: Franz Baumann)	voc CS	Gr/Po 47569A, 47572B

Jazzorchester Templin (ledgers)
Lutz Templin Tanz-Orchester. Gesang: Horst Winter und Frauenterzett (47569)

Lutz Templin l*eader*; personnel and instrumentation probably as before; Horst Winter *vocals*, 'Frauenterzett', probably Elisabeth Christ, Irmgard Burma, Anna Tevelian *female vocal trio*; Lutz Templin, Adolf Steimel *arrangements*.

Berlin; 16 September 1941

9090-GD9	Heute Nacht kam heimlich das Glück zu mir Langsamer Foxtrot (Text und Musik: Templin – de Weille)	voc HW/voc 3	Gr/Po unissued
9090½GD9	Heute Nacht kam heimlich das Glück zu mir Langsamer Foxtrot (Text und Musik: Templin – de Weille)	voc HW/voc 3	Gr/Po unissued
9092-GD9	Die Männer sind schon die Liebe wert Foxtrot (Adolf Steimel – Text: von R.M. Siegel)	voc HW/voc 3	Gr/Po unissued
9092½GD9	Die Männer sind schon die Liebe wert Foxtrot (Adolf Steimel – Text: von R.M. Siegel)	voc HW/voc 3	Gr/Po unissued
9093-GD9	Liebling, was wird nun aus uns beiden? Foxtrot aus dem Tonfilm 'Immer nur – du' (Friedrich Schröder – Text: Fritz Beckmann)	voc HW/voc 3	Gr/Po unissued
9093½GD	Liebling, was wird nun aus uns beiden? Foxtrot aus dem Tonfilm 'Immer nur – Du' (Friedrich Schröder – Text: Fritz Beckmann)	voc HW/voc 3	Gr/Po 47569A

- *Matrix 9090-GD was remade on 13 January 1942 as matrix 9320-GR9.*
- *Matrix 9091-GD was not allocated in the recording ledgers.*
- *Matrix 9092-GD was remade on 13 January 1942 as matrix 9319-GR9.*

Mimi Thoma m. kleinem Orchester. Leitung: Lutz Templin

Lutz Templin *leader* with small formation, probably from above personnel, including Primo
Angeli *piano*; Mimi Thoma *vocals*.

Berlin; 30 September 1941

9112–GD9	Lied eines jungen Wachtpostens (Lili Marleen) (Norbert Schultze – Text von Hans Leip)	voc MT	Gr/Po unissued
9112½GD9	Lied eines jungen Wachtpostens (Lili Marleen) (Norbert Schultze – Text von Hans Leip)	voc MT	Gr/Po 47575A
9112¾GD9	Lied eines jungen Wachtpostens (Lili Marleen) (Norbert Schultze – Text von Hans Leip)	voc MT	Gr/Po unissued
9112⅝GD9	Lied eines jungen Wachtpostens (Lili Marleen) (Norbert Schultze; Text von Hans Leip)	voc MT	Gr 47575A, 47152 47666, 48434
9113–GD9	Lieber Soldat (Text und Musik: F. Wilczek)	voc MT	Gr/Po unissued
9113½GD9	Lieber Soldat (Text und Musik: F. Wilczek)	voc MT	Gr/Po 47575B
9113¾GD9	Lieber Soldat (Text und Musik: F. Wilczek)	voc MT	Gr/Po unissued
9113⅝GD9	Lieber Soldat (Text und Musik: F. Wilczek)	voc MT	Gr 47575B
9114–GD9	Lieber guter Mond (Text und Musik: Dolf Bokler)	voc MT	Gr/Po unissued
9114½GD9	Lieber guter Mond (Text und Musik: Dolf Bokler)	voc MT	Gr 47598, 47643A

• *Diseuse Mimi Thoma (b. Munich, 1909) started her career at the 'Simplicissimus' cabaret
  where she featured for many years. Her attempts at a comeback after the war were
  unsuccessful. She died in Cologne on 16 May 1968. (Leimbach).*

Mimi Thoma

Mimi Thoma *vocals*, accompanied by Primo Angeli *piano*.

Berlin; 30 September 1941

9115–GD9	Mamatschi! Lied im Volkston (Text und Musik: Oskar Schima)	voc MT	Gr/Po unissued
9115½GD9	Mamatschi! Lied im Volkston (Text und Musik: Oskar Schima)	voc MT	Gr 47563A, 21113

Jazz-Orchester Templin (ledgers)
Lutz Templin m.s. Tanz-Orchester (57572)
Lutz Templin m.s. Tanz-Orchester m. Gesang: Horst Winter (47473A)
Lutz Templin m.s. Tanz-Orchester. Gesang: Horst Winter mit Frauenterzett (47573B)

Lutz Templin *leader*; probably Rimis van den Broek, Charly Tabor, Alfredo Marzaroli
trumpets; 2 unidentified, Willy Berking and/or Jos Breyre, and/or Henk Bosch or Ferri Juza
trombones; Mario Balbo, Bob van Venetië or Francesco Paolo Ricci *tenor-saxes/clarinets*,
Benny de Weille, Cor Koblens *alto-sax/clarinet*; Franz Mück *piano*; Meg Tevelian *guitar*;
Rudi Wegener *bass*; Fritz Brocksieper *drums*; Horst Winter *vocals*, 'Frauenterzett', probably
Elisabeth Christ, Irmgard Burma, Anna Tevelian *female vocal trio*; Lutz Templin, Willy
Berking, Adolf Steimel, Eugen Henkel, Franz Mück *arrangements*.

Berlin; 4 October 1941

9123–GD9	Was Dir fehlt ist etwas gute Laune Lied und Foxtrot (Adolf Steimel, Albert Bennefeld)		Gr/Po unissued
9123½GD9	Was Dir fehlt ist etwas gute Laune Lied und Foxtrot (Adolf Steimel, Albert Bennefeld)		Gr 47572B

[session continued]

9124–GD9	Hm – Hm, Du bist so zauberhaft	voc HW/voc 3	Gr/Po unissued
	Foxtrot (Leopold Korbar, Schwenn – Schaeffers)		
9124½GD9	Hm – Hm, Du bist so zauberhaft	voc HW/voc 3	Gr 47573B
	Foxtrot (Leopold Korbar, Schwenn – Schaeffers)		
9125–GD9	Kleiner Hampelmann.	voc HW/voc 3	Gr/Po unissued
	Foxtrot-Intermezzo (Ralph Maria Siegel)		
9125½GD9	Kleiner Hampelmann.	voc HW/voc 3	Gr 47573A
	Foxtrot-Intermezzo (Ralph Maria Siegel)		

Brocksieper (test)
Brocksieper m. Solisten (Brocksieper, Lais, Angeli) (ledgers)

Detlev Lais *tenor sax*; Primo Angeli *piano*; Fritz Brocksieper *drums*.

Berlin; 14 October 1941

9137–GD9	Brocksi-Foxtrot. Foxtrot (Brocksieper)	Gr/Po unissued
9137½GD9	Brocksi-Foxtrot. Foxtrot (Brocksieper)	Gr test
9138–GD9	So ist es. Foxtrot (Angeli)	Gr/Po unissued
9138½GD9	So ist es. Foxtrot (Angeli)	Gr test

• *From now on, Fritz Brocksieper, the drummer of the Templin orchestra, recorded a number of titles with a band-within-the-band. Since he insisted on principle that his session musicians should be credited on the record label, the recording ledgers often include the names and the instruments played.*
• *'Brocksi' was remade on 11 February 1942 as 'Die Trommel und ihr Rhythmus', as well as 'So ist es'.*

Ekaterina Wankowa-Kolarowa m. Orchester. Leitung: Lutz Templin (bulg.) Lutz Templin mit seinem Tanz-Orchester. Gesang: Ekaterina Wankowa-Kolarowa (bulg.)

Lutz Templin *leader*; probably Rimis van den Broek or Nino Impallomeni, Charly Tabor, Alfredo Marzaroli *trumpets*; 2 unidentified, Willy Berking and/or Jos Breyre, and/or Henk Bosch or Ferri Juza *trombones*; Mario Balbo, Bob van Venetië or Francesco Paolo Ricci *tenor-saxes/clarinets*, Benny de Weille, Cor Koblens *alto-sax/clarinet*; Franz Mück or Primo Angeli *piano*; Meg Tevelian *guitar*; Rudi Wegener *bass*; Fritz Brocksieper *drums*; Ekaterina Wankowa-Kolarowa *vocals*.

Berlin; 18 October 1941

9147–GD9	Stern von Rio (Engel-Berger)	voc EWK	Gr/Po unissued
9147½GD9	Stern von Rio (Engel-Berger)	voc EWK	Gr/Po?
9148–GD9	Warum bist du so bald von mir gegangen?	voc EWK	Gr/Po unissued
	Langsamer Foxtrot (Vasin)		
9148½GD9	Warum bist du so bald von mir gegangen?	voc EWK	Gr/Po?
	Langsamer Foxtrot (Vasin)		

• *Vocalist Ekaterina Wankowa-Kolarowa was born in Bulgaria.*
• *It is not known whether any of these sides was actually issued.*

Jo Evens mit Orchester. Dirigent: Lutz Templin

Lutz Templin *leader*, probably with similar personnel and instrumentation; Jo Evens *vocal.*

Berlin; 10 November 1941

9168 – GD9	Lass mich doch heute nicht so allein (Heino Gaze, Schulz-Gellen)	voc JE	Gr/Po unissued
9168½IX	Lass mich doch heute nicht so allein (Heino Gaze, Schulz-Gellen)	voc JE	Gr 47571
9169 – GD9	Wann kommt der Tag (Franz Neukum, Charlie Amberg)	voc JE	Gr/Po unissued
9169½IX	Wann kommt der Tag (Franz Neukum, Charlie Amberg)	voc JE	Gr 47571

• *Diseuse Jo Evens was born Joan Evans to American parents in Cologne on 4 April 1912. She was discovered by composer Heino Gaze. Jo Evens was married to an American with whom she returned to the United States in 1946. (Leimbach).*

Karl Schotte, Gesang, mit Kapelle Templin (ledger)

Lutz Templin *leader*; personnel and instrumentation probably as before; Karl Schotte *vocal.*

Berlin, KWS, Studio 10; 12 November 1941

67396	Politisches 49 Lied Melodie nach einem englischen Lied 'Oh My Darling Clementine' neuer Text von Karl Schotte	3'15"	voc KS	RRG 67396

Iska Geri, mit Templin-Orchester (ledgers)
Iska Geri, Vortragskünstlerin, mit Orchester. Leitung: Lutz Templin (47597)

Lutz Templin *leader*; probably Nino Impallomeni, Charly Tabor or Alfredo Marzaroli *trumpets*; Willy Berking *trombones*; Benny de Weille *clarinet*; Franz Mück or poss. Primo Angeli *piano*; Meg Tevelian *guitar*; Rudi Wegener *bass*; Fritz Brocksieper *drums*; Iska Geri *vocals*; Lutz Templin, Willy Berking, Eugen Henkel, Franz Mück *arrangements.*

Berlin; 27 November 1941

9221 – GD9	Tanzmusik (Heino Gaze – Text: Schulz-Gellen)	voc IG	Gr/Po unissued
9221½IX	Tanzmusik (Heino Gaze – Text: Schulz-Gellen)	voc IG	Gr 47597A
9222 – GD9	Ferdinand! (Heino Gaze – Text: Schulz-Gellen)	voc IG	Gr/Po unissued
9222½IX	Ferdinand! (Heino Gaze – Text: Schulz-Gellen)	voc IG	Gr 47597B

• *Actress and cabaret artist Iska Geri was born Hilde Predöhl in Stettin on 28 April 1923, and grew up in Frankfurt on Main where she trained in singing, drama and ballet. She started touring with puppet shows and private theatre companies. Her radio debut was in Berlin in 1937. In 1940, Willi Schaeffers discovered Iska Geri for the 'Kabarett der Komiker'. In the same year, she debuted in film. Iska Geri was married to actor Gerd Froebe. (Leimbach).*

Jo Evens mit Orchester. Dirigent: Lutz Templin (ledgers)
Jo Evens mit Orchesterbegleitung. Leitung: Lutz Templin (47596)

Lutz Templin *leader*; personnel and instrumentation probably as before; Jo Evens *vocal*.

Berlin; 2 December 1941

9236–GD9	Das Leben beginnt erst, wenn man verliebt ist (Theo Mackeben – Text: Aldo v. Pinelli)	voc JE	Gr/Po unissued
9236½IX	Das Leben beginnt erst, wenn man verliebt ist (Theo Mackeben – Text: Aldo v. Pinelli)	voc JE	Gr 47611, 47671
9237–GD9	In deinen Briefen (Charlotte Baerenz, Text und Musik)	voc JE	Gr/Po unissued
9237½GD9	In deinen Briefen (Charlotte Baerenz, Text und Musik)	voc JE	Gr 47596B

Charlie and his Orchestra

Lutz Templin *leader*; probably Nino Impallomeni, Charly Tabor, Alfredo Marzaroli *trumpets*; Willy Berking and/or Jos Breyre, Henk Bosch or Ferri Juza *trombones*; Mario Balbo, Francesco Paolo Ricci or Bob van Venetië *tenor-saxes/clarinets*, Benny de Weille, Cor Koblens *alto-saxes/clarinets*; Primo Angeli *piano*; Meg Tevelian *guitar*; Rudi Wegener *bass*; Fritz Brocksieper *drums*; Charlie Schwedler *vocals*.

Berlin; late 1941

F.D.R. Jones (—)	voc CS	K & M 0132/0133
After You've Gone (—)	voc CS	0133/0132
Who'll Buy My Bublitchky (—)	voc CS	0134/0135
I've Got A Pocketful Of Dreams (—)	voc CS	0135/0134
Shuffle Off To Buffalo	voc CS	0136/0137
Where The Poppies Bloom Again [*sic*]	voc CS	0137/0136
Change Partners	voc CS	0138/0139

• *Side numbers 0121-0131 are untraced.*

Charlie and his Orchestra

Lutz Templin *leader*; probably Rimis van den Broek, Charly Tabor, Alfredo Marzaroli *trumpets*; Willy Berking and/or Jos Breyre, and/or Henk Bosch or Ferri Juza *trombones*; poss. Detlev Lais *tenor-sax, guest soloist*, Mario Balbo, Bob van Venetië or Francesco Paolo Ricci *tenor-saxes/clarinets*, Benny de Weille, Cor Koblens *alto-sax/clarinet*; Franz Mück *piano*; Meg Tevelian *guitar*; Rudi Wegener *bass*; Fritz Brocksieper *drums*; Charlie Schwedler *vocals*.

Berlin; 12 January 1942

9310–GR9	Lilla Marleen [*sic*] (—)	NP	voc CS	K & M 0140/0141
9311–GR9	Yes We Have No Bananas (Fr. Silvey) [*sic*]		voc CS	unissued
9311½GR9	Yes We Have No Bananas (Fr. Silvey) [*sic*]		voc CS	?
9312–GR9	Alexanders Ragtime Band (J. Berlin) [*sic?*]		voc CS	0139/0138

[session continued]

9313 – GR9	Little White Lies (Donaldson)	voc CS	?
9314-GR9	Ramona (Mabel Wayne)	voc CS	?
9315 – GR9	Let's Put Out The Lights (—)	voc CS	0146/0147
9316 – GR9	Bei mir bist Du schön (—)	voc CS	unissued
9316½GR9	Bei mir bist Du schön (—)	voc CS	0147/0146
9317 – GR9	All Over The Place (—)	voc CS	?
9318 – GR9	The Man With The Big Cigar (—)	voc CS	0141/0140

- *'Lilla Marleen' is sung straight.*
- *In an interview with Lotz, Fritz Brocksieper aurally identified Detlev Lais as the tenor sax soloist on 0141.*
- *Entries in the recording ledgers: 'Wachsverbrauch: 28 Stück 25cm.' [Wax consumption...] 'Kopplungen: 1-9, 3-5, 4-8, 6-7.' [A/B sides...] '"Yes We Have No Bananas": Kopplung mit "Change Partners" schon aufgenommen.'*

Jazz-Orchester Lutz Templin (ledgers)
Lutz Templin m.s. Tanz-Orchester. Gesang: Horst Winter und Frauenterzett (47570)

Lutz Templin *leader*; personnel and instrumentation probably as before, incl. Detlev Lais *tenor-sax*; Horst Winter, Detlev Lais *vocals*, 'Damen-Terzett', prob. Elisabeth Christ, Irmgard Burma, Anna Tevelian *female vocal trio*; Lutz Templin, Adolf Steimel *arrangements*.

Berlin; 13 January 1942

9319 – GR9	Heute Nacht kam heimlich das Glück zu mir Langsamer Foxtrot (Templin – de Weille)	voc HW/voc 3	Gr/Po 47570B
9320 – GR9	Die Männer sind schon die Liebe Wert Foxtrot (Adolf Steimel; Text: R.M. Siegel)	voc HW/voc 3	Gr/Po 47570A
9321 – GR9	Morgen scheint wieder die Sonne. Foxtrot (R. Stauch)	voc DL/voc 3	Gr/Po unissued?
9321½GR9	Morgen scheint wieder die Sonne. Foxtrot (R. Stauch)	voc DL/voc 3	Gr/Po 47660?

- *Matrix 9319-GR9 is a remake of 9090-GD9, and 9320-GR9 of 9092-GD9.*

Brocksieper-Tanzquartett (ledgers)
Brocksieper-Quartet [*sic*] (Brunswick)

Franz Kleindin *tenor-sax*; Georg Haentzschel *piano*; Willibald Winkler *bass*; Fritz Brocksieper *drums*.

Berlin; 11 February 1942

9327 – GD9	Die Trommel und ihr Rhythmus. Foxtrot (Fritz Brocksieper)	Gr/Po unissued
9327½GD9	Die Trommel und ihr Rhythmus. Foxtrot (Fritz Brocksieper)	Br 82238A
9328 – GD9	Ich wüßt so gern. Foxtrot (Georg Haentzschel)	Gr/Po unissued
9328½GD9	Ich wüßt so gern. Foxtrot (Georg Haentzschel)	Br 82238B

- *'Die Trommel und ihr Rhythmus' is a remake of matrix 9137, recorded on 14 October 1941 as 'Brocksi Fox'.*
- *Deutsche Grammophon had cooperated with the American Brunswick-Balke-Collender company since 1928, and with its successor, the American Brunswick Corporation from 1935.*

Tanz-Orchester Lutz Templin (ledgers)
Charlie and his Orchestra (Klarinette & Mandoline label)

Lutz Templin *leader*; probably Nino Impallomeni, Charly Tabor, Alfredo Marzaroli *trumpets*; 2 unidentified, Willy Berking and/or Jos Breyre, Henk Bosch and/or Ferri Juza *trombones*; poss. Detlev Lais *tenor-sax guest soloist*, Mario Balbo, Bob van Venetië or Francesco Paolo Ricci *tenor-saxes*, Benny de Weille, Cor Koblens *alto-saxes/clarinets*; Primo Angeli or Franz Mück *piano*; Meg Tevelian *guitar*; Rudi Wegener *bass*; Fritz Brocksieper *drums*; Charlie Schwedler *vocals*.

Berlin; 12 February 1942

9353–GR9	Makin' Woopee! [*sic*] (—)	voc CS	K & M unissued
9353½GR9	Makin Woopee [*sic*] (—)	voc CS	0148/0149
9354–GR9	I'm Sending You The Siegfried Line (—)	voc CS	unissued
9354½GR9	I'am Sending You The Siegfried Line [*sic*] (—)	voc CS	0150/0151
9355–GR9	So You Left [*sic*] (—)	voc CS	0152/0153
9356–GR9	The Continental (—)	voc CS	0149/0148
9357–GR9	Laugh, Clown, Laugh (—)	voc CS	0153/0152
9358–GR9	The Moon Got In My Eyes (—)	voc CS	0154/0155
9359–GR9	By, By, Blackbird [*sic*] (—)	voc CS	0151/0150
9360–GR9	Say's My Heart [*sic*] (—)	voc CS	0155/0154

- *The following soloists were aurrally identified by Fritz Brocksieper in an interview with Lotz: Nino Impallomeni (trumpet) & Detlev Lais (tenor-sax) on 0150; Tip Tischelaar (piano) on 0151; however, at the time of this recording, Tischelaar played and recorded in The Hague as a member of the Ernst van 't Hoff orchestra.*
- *Entries in the recording ledgers: 'Wachsverbrauch: 23 Stück 25cm.' [wax consumption] 'Die Aufnahmen sind wie folgt zu koppeln: Nr.1 mit 4; Nr. 2 mit 7; Nr. 3 mit 5; Nr. 6 mit 8."*

Brocksieper-Tanz-Quartett (ledgers)
Brocksi-Quartett (Brunswick 82241)
Brocksi-Kvartetten (Norwegian Brunswick BS603066)

Detlev Lais *tenor-sax*; Primo Angeli *piano*; Walter Dobrzynski *bass*; Fritz Brocksieper *drums*.

Berlin; 5 March 1942

9379–GR9	Rip-Tip-Tap. Foxtrot (Franz Mück)	Gr/Po unissued
9379½GR9	Rip-Tip-Tap. Foxtrot (Franz Mück)	Br 82241A, BS603066A
9380–GR9	So ist es ... Langs. Foxtrot (Primo Angeli)	Gr/Po unissued
9380½GR9	So ist es ... Langs. Foxtrot (Primo Angeli)	Br 82241B,
	Det var det! Slowfox (Primo Angeli)	Br BS603066B

- *Personnel and instrumentation as per recording ledgers.*
- *Matrix 9380 is a remake of 9138-GD, recorded on 14 October 1941; according to the ledgers, only one take was recorded, but take -½ was actually issued.*

Templin-Tanzorchester (ledgers)
Lutz Templin m.s. Tanz-Orchester (Grammophon)
Lutz Templin Tanz-Orchester (Polydor)

Lutz Templin *leader*; probably Nino Impallomeni, Charly Tabor, Alfredo Marzaroli *trumpets*; 2 unidentified, Willy Berking and/or Jos Breyre, Henk Bosch or Ferri Juza *trombones*; Mario Balbo, Bob van Venetië or Francesco Paolo Ricci *tenor-saxes/clarinets*, Benny de Weille, Cor Koblens *alto-saxes/clarinets*; Primo Angeli or Franz Mück *piano*; Meg Tevelian *guitar*; Rudi Wegener *bass*; Fritz Brocksieper *drums*; Otto Gerd Fischer *vocals*; Lutz Templin, Willy Berking *arrangements*.

Berlin; 9 March 1942

9357–GD9	Pampas. Foxtrot (Otto Berking) [*sic*]	Gr/Po unissued
9357½GD9	Pampas. Foxtrot (Otto Berking) [*sic*]	Gr/Po 47634A
9358–GD9	Lieblich und süß. Langs. Foxtrot (L. Templin)	Gr/Po unissued
9358½GD9	Lieblich und süß. Langs. Foxtrot (L. Templin)	Gr/Po 47634B?
9359–GD9	Wer ist jung? Foxtrot aus dem Tonfilm voc OGF 'Fronttheater' (Werner Bochmann; Text: Schulz-Gellen)	Gr/Po unissued
9359½GD9	Wer ist jung? Foxtrot aus dem Tonfilm voc OGF 'Fronttheater' (Werner Bochmann; Text: Schulz-Gellen)	Gr/Po 47660

Fritz Stamer, Klavier (Amerikanische Lieder)

Fritz Stamer piano.

Berlin, Haus des Rundfunks, Saal 10, Kurzwellensender; 9 March 1942

65717	Pausenzeichen (Amerikanische Nationalhymne) [interval signal – American National Anthem]	RRG 65717
65718	a) Onward Christian Soldiers (Sir A. Sullivan) b) Bei mir bist du scheen (—)	65718
65719	Old Black Joe (Stephen S. Foster)	65719
65720	Star Spangled Banner (Nationalhymne) (Francis Scott Key)	65720
65721	America (S.F. Smith)	65721
65722	John Brown's Body ('unbekannt') [unknown]	65722
65723	South Of The Border ('unbekannt') [unknown]	65723
65724	Carry Me Back To Old Virginny (James Bland)	65724
65725	Old Kentucky Home (Stephen S. Foster)	65725
65726	a) Oh, My Darling Clementine (—) b) She'll Be Coming Around The Mountain (—)	65726

• *In 1942 and 1943 pianist Fritz Stamer recorded several popular American tunes for use by the North America zone of the RRG's Short-Wave Station – another example of Germany's English-language propaganda effort.*

Mitwirkende des Orchesters Willi Stech unter der Leitung von Lutz Templin (ledgers)

Lutz Templin *leader*; unidentified personnel and instrumentation of members of the Willi Stech orchestra.

Berlin, Deutschlandsender, Studio 5; 24 March 1942

65729	Abendsonne (Lutz Templin)	3'03"	RRG 65729
65730	Abendsonne (Lutz Templin)	3'03"	65730

- *Details as per RRG ledgers.*
- *This recording shows the close cooperation between the Templin orchestra at the Short-Wave Station and the Willi Stech orchestra at the Deutschlandsender.*
- *Further information on the ledger cards: 'Abteilung 9: Musik' and 'Keine Kosten bei Wiederholung' ['No charge for repeats'].*

Brocksi-Kwartet (*sic*, in ledgers)
Brocksi-Quartett (Brunswick 82245)

Fernando Diaz *trumpet*; Primo Angeli *piano*; Cesare Cavaion *bass*; Fritz Brocksieper *drums*.

Berlin; 2 April 1942

3979 – GD9	Ernst und heiter. Schneller Foxtrot (Leschetitzky)	Gr/Po unissued
3979½GD9	Ernst und heiter. Schneller Foxtrot (Leschetitzky)	Br 82245A
3980 – GD9	Kosende Hände. Langsamer Foxtrot (Leschetitzky)	Gr/Po unissued
3980½GD9	Kosende Hände. Langsamer Foxtrot (Leschetitzky)	Br 82245B

- *Personnel and instrumentation as per recording ledgers.*

Charlie and his Orchestra

Lutz Templin *leader*; probably Rimis van den Broek, Alfredo Marzaroli, Herre Jager *trumpets*; Jos Breyre, Henk Bosch *trombones*; Mario Balbo, Bob van Venetië or Francesco Paolo Ricci *tenor-saxes/clarinets*, Benny de Weille, Cor Koblens or Tinus Bruijn *alto-saxes/clarinets, saxes double on flutes 1*; Primo Angeli *piano*; Meg Tevelian *guitar*; Otto Tittmann *bass*; Fritz Brocksieper *drums*; Charlie Schwedler *vocals*.

Berlin; *c.* 2nd half May 1942

Blue Skies Are Around The Corner (—)	1	voc CS	K & M 0156/0157
Japanese Sandman (—)	1	voc CS	0157/0156
I Found A Million Dollar Baby (—)		voc CS	0158/0159
Avalon (—)		voc CS	0159/0158
But Where Are You (—)		voc CS	0160/0161
Blue Moon (—)		voc CS	0161/0160
Honey (—)		voc CS	0162/0169

- *In an interview with Lotz, Fritz Brocksieper aurally identified Rimis van den Broek (trumpet), Cor Koblens (alto-sax) and Primo Angeli (piano) as soloists on 'Japanese Sandman'.*

Brocksieper-Quartett

Rimis van den Broek *trumpet*; Primo Angeli *piano*; Willibald Winkler *bass*; Fritz Brocksieper *drums*.

Berlin; 20 May 1942

9503–GR9	Mir ist's so leicht. Schneller Foxtrot (W. Leschetitzky)	Gr/Po unissued
9503½GR9	Mir ist's so leicht. Schneller Foxtrot (W. Leschetitzky)	Br 82249A
9504–GR9	Leise klingt's über's Wasser (Rimis van den Broek)	Gr/Po unissued
9504½GR9	Leise klingt's über's Wasser (Rimis van den Broek)	Br 82249B

- *The music trade journal 'Das Podium der Unterhaltungsmusik' reviewed this session on 24 February 1943 in these terms: 'The Brocksieper Quartet can also notch up great performances, like the horn player's showy capers on stopped trumpet in his own number 'Leise klingt's über's Wasser' ['Softly Sounding 'cross The Water'] (R.v.d. Broek) and Leschetitzky's over-the-top but still fresh-seeming 'Mir ist's so leicht' ['Easy For Me'].'*

Lale Andersen, Gesang – Doppelquartett der Singgemeinschaft Rudolf Lamy mit Kapelle Templin (ledgers)

Lutz Templin *leader*; probably Rimis van den Broek, Alfredo Marzaroli, Herre Jager *trumpets*; Jos Breyre, unidentified, Henk Bosch or Folke Johnson *trombones*; Mario Balbo, Bob van Venetië or Francesco Paolo Ricci *tenor-saxes/clarinets*; Benny de Weille, Cor Koblens or Tinus Bruijn *alto-saxes/clarinets*; Primo Angeli or Tip Tichelaar *piano*; Meg Tevelian *guitar*; Otto Tittmann *bass*; Fritz Brocksieper *drums*; Walter Leschetitzky, 3 unidentified *string-section 1*; Lale Andersen, Doppelquartett der Singgemeinschaft Rudolf Lamy (Double Quartet of the Rudolf Lamy Choir) *vocals*, Bruno Seidler-Winhler, *arrangement*.

Berlin, KWS, Studio 11; 2 June 1942

68902	Lilli Marlen [*sic*] (englische Fassung) 3'21" 1 NP voc LA/choir RL von Norbert Schultze deutscher Text von Hans Leip engl. Übersetzung von Norman Daily Stewart [*sic*] arrang. von Bruno Seidler-Winkler	RRG-KWS 68902

- *Recording details as per RRG ledgers.*
- *Further information on the ledger card: 'Abteilung 9: Musik' 'Eigentum der 'Electrola-Ges.m.b.H.' – 20 Verszeilen', 'Keine Kosten bei Wiederholung'.*
- *Rudolf Lamy (1905–1962) had founded his choir in Berlin in 1934.*

Lale Andersen und Orchester Templin (ledgers)
Orchester Templin. Lale Andersen (test)
Lale Andersen With Charlie and his Orchestra (Klarinette & Mandoline label)

Lutz Templin *leader*; personnel and instrumentation probably as before; Lale Andersen, ensemble *vocals*.

Berlin; 5 June 1942

9483–GD	Blue Moon (R. Rodgers; Text: L. Hart)	1 NP voc LA	K & M unissued
9483½GD	Blue Moon (R. Rodgers; Text: L. Hart)	1 NP voc LA	0164/0163
9484–GD	Lili Marlen (N. Schultze)	NP voc LA/Ens	unissued
9484½GD	Lili Marlen (N. Schultze)	NP voc LA/Ens	0163/0164

- *Both titles are sung straight, with no propaganda texts.*

Charlie Schwedler, Gesang, mit Kapelle Templin (ledger)

Lutz Templin *leader*; personnel and instrumentation probably as before; Charlie Schwedler *vocal*.

Berlin, KWS, Studio 11; 29 June 1942

69080	Rommel Is Coming	voc CS	RRG 69080
	Zusammenstellung nach Musiken von Haydn, Norbert Schultze,		
	Herms Niel. Text von Norman Fallie-Stuwart [sic]		
	bearb. von Franz Mück, Lutz Templin und Charlie Schwedler		

- *Details as per RRG ledger.*
- *Further information on the ledger card: 'Abteilung 9: Musik', 'Manuskript 16 Verszeilen' [16 lines of text in manuscript], 'Keine Kosten bei Wiederholung' [No charges for repeats].*

Lutz Templin m.s. Tanz-Orchester. Gesang: Frauen-Terzett (Grammophon)
Lutz Templin Tanz-Orchester (Polydor)

Lutz Templin *leader*; probably with personnel and instrumentation as before; 'Frauen-Terzett', i.e. female trio *vocal 3*.

Berlin; *c.* July 1942

9518 – GR9	Für eine Stunde Leidenschaft. Foxtrot		Gr/Po unissued
9518½GR9	Für eine Stunde Leidenschaft. Foxtrot		Po 47732A
9519 – GR9	Maiglöckchen. Foxtrot (Richartz – Amberg)	voc 3	Gr/Po unissued
9519½GR9	Maiglöckchen. Foxtrot (Richartz – Amberg)	voc 3	Gr 47669B
9520 – GR9	Schau'n vom Himmel die Sterne ...	voc 3	Gr/Po unissued
	Tango (Grabau – H. Zander Lübeck)		
9520½GR9	Schau'n vom Himmel die Sterne ...	voc 3	Gr 47669A
	Tango (Grabau – H. Zander Lübeck)		

Brocksieperquartett (ledgers)
Brocksi-Quartett (Brunswick 82256)
Brocksi-Kvartetten (Norwegian Brunswick BS603076)

Eugen Henkel *tenor sax*; Fritz Schulze *piano*; Otto Tittmann *bass*; Fritz Brocksieper *drums*.

Berlin; 5 August 1942

002 – VX	Rampenlicht. Schneller Foxtrot (Eugen Henkel)	Gr/Po unissued
002½VX	Rampenlicht. Schneller Foxtrot (Eugen Henkel)	Gr/Po unissued
002¾VX	Rampenlicht. Schneller Foxtrot (Eugen Henkel)	Br 82256A,
	I Rampelyset. Foxtrot (Eugen Henkel)	Br BS603076A
003 – VX	Habe Vertrau'n. Langsamer Foxtrot (Heinz Weiss)	Gr/Po unissued
003½VX	Habe Vertrau'n. Langsamer Foxtrot (Heinz Weiss)	Br 82256B,
	Stol Pa Mig. Slowfox (Heinz Weiss)	Br BS603076B

- *Personnel and instrumentation as per recording ledgers.*
- *This session lasted for three hours.*
- *The music trade journal 'Das Podium der Unterhaltungsmusik' reviewed this session on 24 February 1943 in these terms: 'Eugen Henkel's harmonically often startling foxtrot 'Rampenlicht' ['In The Limelight'] is fairly wild stuff, but at least innovative. The Brocksieper Quartet – which also plays Weiss's 'Habe Vertau'n' ['Trust Me'] – is a small and very competent bunch of artists who know their business when it comes to virtuoso effects, particularly tenor-saxist and composer E. Henkel."*

Horst Winter und seine Kapelle

Horst Winter *vocals/leader, poss. clarinet*; unidentified personnel and instrumentation; according to the recollections of Horst Winter his orchestra always included Franz Mück *piano* and, at one time or another, Willy Berking *trombone*; Benny de Weille *alto-sax/clarinet*; Hans Klagemann *bass*; and Harry van Dijk *drums*; as well as 'many Dutch and Belgian musicians'. However, from April 1942, Mück, Berking and Klagemann were employed by the DTU and no longer available for outside work, and it may be assumed that Winter drew his orchestra from the same pool of radio musicians as Lutz Templin and Willi Stech did. Possibly Elisabeth Christ, Irmgard Burma, Anna Tevelian *female vocal trio*.

Berlin; 13 August 1942

9628 – GR9	African Song (Zubal – Diettrich)	Engl. voc HW/voc 3	Po 4268
9628½GR9	African Song (Zubal – Diettrich)	Engl. voc HW/voc 3	unissued
9629 – GR9	Introduction (Zubal – Diettrich)		Po 4268

- *Above titles are included in this discography as an example of the many facets of Germany's propaganda effort. The label design of this 25cm (10") record is the normal Polydor label used for export, but printed in faint golden letters on white paper with the additional imprint 'Interradio', presumably referring to the Foreign Ministry's broadcasting subsidiary which may have placed the order for these recordings. Other records of this type carry the label information 'Zentralstelle für Deutsche Kultursendungen im Ausland' (Central Agency for German Cultural Broadcasts in Foreign Countries).*
- *'Introduction' repeats the first few bars of the "African Song" four times, and was probably used to sign programmes on and off.*
- *Only one copy of this record is known to exist in a private collection.*
- *The ledger card for this session carries a reference to matrix 9625-GR9 of 11 August 1942, by Walter Pilger (harmonica), possibly indicating that it was originally planned to record a remake of the Pilger session of 11 August on the 13th.*

Charlie and his Orchestra

Lutz Templin *leader*; arranger probably Nino Impallomeni, Alfredo Marzaroli, Herre Jager *trumpets*; Jos Breyre, unidentifed, Henk Bosch or Folke Johnson *trombones*; Mario Balbo, Bob van Venetië or Francesco Paolo Ricci *tenor-saxes/clarinets*, Benny de Weille, Cor Koblens *alto-saxes/clarinets*; Tip Tichelaar *piano*; Meg Tevelian *guitar*; Otto Tittmann *bass*; Fritz Brocksieper *drums*; Walter Leschetitzky, 3 unidentified *string-section 1*; Charlie Schwedler *vocals*, unidentified female *spoken introduction 2*.

Berlin; 27 August 1942 (09:00-15:00)

9630 – GR9	You've Got Me This Way (Jimmy Mettugh) [*sic*]	1 NP	voc CS	K & M 0170/0165
9631 – GR9	You're The Top (Cole Porter)	1	voc CS	0171/0167
9632 – GR9	You Started Something (R. Rainger)	1	voc CS/voc 2	0165/0170
9633 – GR9	Love Is All (P. Tomlin)	1	voc CS	0166/0168
9634 – GR9	Angel (Peter de Rose)	NP	voc CS	0167/0171
9635 – GR9	Kiss The Boys Goodbye (Victor Schertzinger)	NP	voc CS	0168/0166
9636 – GR9	The Waiter And The Porter And The Upstairs Maid (Johnny Mercer)		voc CS	0169/0162

[session continued]

- *'You've Got Me This Way', 'Angel' and 'Kiss The Boys Goodbye' are sung straight, with no propaganda texts.*
- *Entries in the recording ledgers: 'Wachsverbrauch: 21 Stück 25cm.' [Wax consumption...] 'Nr. 4 zusammen mit dem freien Titel der letzten Sitzung, Nr. 1 mit 2, Nr. 3 mit 6, Nr. 5 mit 7.' [No. 4 coupled with spare title from last session, No. 1 with take 2, No. 3 with take 6, No. 5 with take 7]*
- *Although the records were normally coupled in consecutive numbers, the sides from this and the 6 October session were coupled out of sequence.*

Brocksi-Quartett

Jos Breyre *trombone*; Primo Angeli *piano*; Otto Tittmann *bass*; Fritz Brocksieper *drums*.

Berlin; 28 September 1942 (16:30-19:30)

9630 – GD9	Peinlich. Foxtrot (Weiss, Pfützner)	Gr/Po unissued
9630½GD9	Peinlich. Foxtrot (Weiss, Pfützner)	Br 82274A ?
9631 – GD9	Mary's Traum. Foxtrot (J. Breyre)	Gr/Po unissued
9631½GD9	Mary's Traum. Foxtrot (J. Breyre)	Br 82274B ?

- *Personnel and instrumentation as per recording ledgers.*
- *The correct name of the joint composer may be Pfrötzschner, rather than Pfützner.*

Jazz-Orchester Templin (ledgers)
Lutz Templin Tanz-Orchester (Polydor)

Lutz Templin *leader*; personnel and instrumentation probably as on 27 August 1942, incl. Primo Angeli for Tichelaar *piano*; Franz Mück, Lutz Templin *arrangement*.

Berlin; 29 September 1942 (11:00-15:30)

9632 – GD9	Schade, dass wir auseinandergeh'n. Foxtrot (Peter Igelhoff u. Otto Fuhrmann)	arr LT	Gr/Po unissued
9632½GD9	Schade, dass wir auseinandergeh'n. Foxtrot (Peter Igelhoff – Otto Fuhrmann – arr. L. Templin)	arr LT	Po 47732B
9633 – GD9	Immer wieder tanzen. Foxtrot (Fr. Mück)	arr FM	Gr/Po unissued
9633½GD9	Immer wieder tanzen. Foxtrot (Franz Mück)	arr FM	Po 47705A
9634 – GD9	Rhythmus in Dosen. Foxtrot (L. Templin)	arr LT	Gr/Po unissued
9634½GD9	Rhythmus in Dosen. Foxtrot (Lutz Templin)	arr LT	Po 47705B

Brocksi-Quartett

Eugen Henkel *tenor-sax*; Fritz Schulze *piano*; Otto Tittmann *bass*; Fritz Brocksieper *drums*.

Berlin; 30 September 1942 (16:30-19:00)

9635 – GD9	Improvisation. Foxtrot (P. Angeli)	Gr/Po unissued
9635½GD9	Improvisation. Foxtrot (P. Angeli)	Br 82274A, 82275A
9636 – GD9	Ewig denke ich an dich. Foxtrot (P. Angeli)	Gr/Po unissued
9636½GD9	Ewig denke ich an dich. Foxtrot (P. Angeli)	Bru 82275A

- *Personnel and instrumentation as per recording ledgers.*

Karl Schotte, Sprechgesang – Singgemeinschaft Rudolf Lamy mit Tanzkapelle Lutz Templin (ledgers)

Lutz Templin *leader*; arranger, personnel and instrumentation probably as on 27 August 1942; Karl Schotte *vocal*, Singgemeinschaft Rudolf Lamy *choir*.

Berlin, KWS, Studio 11; 1 October 1942

69896.a	Smiling Through [*sic*] (Felix Powell) [*sic*]	55"	voc KS/choir	RRG 69896
	Text von Karl Schotte, bearb. von Lutz Templin			
69896.b	Smiling Through [*sic*] (Felix Powell) [*sic*]	55"	voc KS/choir	69896
	Text von Karl Schotte, bearb. von Lutz Templin			
69896.c	Smiling Through [*sic*] (Felix Powell) [*sic*]	55"	voc KS/choir	69896
	Text von Karl Schotte, bearb. von Lutz Templin			
69897.a	Smiling Through [*sic*] (Felix Powell) [*sic*]	55"	voc KS/choir	69897
	Text von Karl Schotte, bearb. von Lutz Templin			
69897.b	Smiling Through [*sic*] (Felix Powell) [*sic*]	55"	voc KS/choir	69897
	Text von Karl Schotte, bearb. von Lutz Templin			
69897.c	Smiling Through [*sic*] (Felix Powell) [*sic*]	55"	voc KS/choir	69897
	Text von Karl Schotte, bearb. von Lutz Templin			

- *The Arthur Penn song 'Smilin' Through' (1919), a hit during the early 'twenties, was revived in the 1932 MGM movie of the same name.*

Gesangsterzett mit Tanzkapelle Lutz Templin (ledgers)

Lutz Templin *leader*; arranger personnel and instrumentation probably as on 27 August 1942; Elisabeth Christ, Irmgard Burma, Anna Tevelian *female vocal trio*.

Berlin, KWS, Studio 11; 1 October 1942

69898.a	Will Meet Again [*sic*] (Jim Parker) [*sic*]	1'07"	voc 3	69898
	Text von Charles, bearb. von Lutz Templin			
69898.b	Will Meet Again [*sic*] (Jim Parker) [*sic*]	1'07"	voc 3	69898
	Text von Charles, bearb. von Lutz Templin			
69899.a	Will Meet Again [*sic*] (Jim Parker) [*sic*]	1'07"	voc 3	69899
	Text von Charles, bearb. von Lutz Templin			
69899.b	Will Meet Again [*sic*] (Jim Parker) [*sic*]	1'07"	voc 3	69899
	Text von Charles, bearb. von Lutz Templin			

- *Details as per RRG ledgers.*
- *The authors of the Vera Lynn favourite 'We'll Meet Again', were Ross Parker and Hugh Charles.*
- *Further information on the ledger cards: 'Abteilung 9: Musik' (69896 – 69699); 'Manuskript 8 Verszeilen' (69896/97) and 'Manuskript' (69898/99); 'Kosten werden nachgemeldet' (69896 – 69899).*
- *These short pieces were probably used to sign programmes on and off.*

Charlie und sein Orchester (ledgers)
Charlie and his Orchestra (Klarinette & Mandoline label)

Lutz Templin *leader*; probably Nino Impallomeni or Rimis van den Broek, Alfredo Marzaroli, Herre Jager or Eberhard Schmid-Schulz *trumpets*; Jos Breyre, unidentified, Henk Bosch or Folke Johnson *trombones*; Mario Balbo, Bob van Venetië or Francesco Paolo Ricci *tenor-saxes/clarinets*, Jean Robert *tenor-sax/baritone-sax/clarinet*, Benny de Weille, Cor Koblens or Tinus Bruijn *alto-saxes/clarinets*; Primo Angeli or Tip Tichelaar *piano*; Meg Tevelian *guitar*; Otto Tittmann *bass*; Fritz Brocksieper *drums*; Walter Leschetitzky, 3 unidentified *string-section 1*; Charlie Schwedler, ensemble *vocals*.

Berlin; 6 October 1942 (11:00-16:00)

9639 – GD9	Pretty Little Busybody	1	NP voc CS		K & M unissued
	(Al Lewis, Larry Stock, Vincent Rose)				
9639½GD9	Pretty Little Busybody	1	NP voc CS		0172/0173
	(from McLewis, L. Stock and Vincent Rose) [*sic*]				
9640 – GD9	A Song Of Old Hawaii	1		voc CS	0173/0172
	(from Gordon Breeher and Johnny Noble) [*sic*]				
9641 – GD9	Bom [*sic*] (from Charles Trenet)	1		voc CS	0174/0176
9642 – GD9	Little Sir Echo (Hello)	1		voc CS/Ens	unissued
	(Adele Girard and Joe Marsala)				
9642½GD9	Little Sir Echo (Hello)	1		voc CS/Ens	0175/0177
	(Adele Girard and Joe Marsala)				
9643 – GD9	Night And Day (from Cole Porter) [*sic*]	1	NP voc CS/Ens		0176/0174
9644 – GD9	You Say The Sweetest Things (Harry Warren)		NP voc CS/Ens		0177/0175

• *Entry in the recording ledgers: 'Wachsverbrauch: 20 Stück 25cm.'*
• *'Pretty Little Busybody', 'Night And Day' and 'You Say The Sweetest Things' are sung straight, but the rest have propaganda texts.*
• *Gordon Beecher is the composer of 'A Song Of Hawaii'.*

Nina von Sprecher mit kl. Orchester. Leitung: Lutz Templin

Lutz Templin *leader* with small formation, probably from above personnel; Nina von Sprecher *vocals*

Berlin; 13 October 1942 (14:00-18:00)

9667 – GD9	Mein Herz denkt und fühlt. Vortragslied	voc NvS	Gr/Po unissued
	[speech song] (Nina von Sprecher, Text und Musik)		
9667½GD9	Mein Herz denkt und fühlt. Vortragslied	voc NvS	Gr 47707
	[speech song] (Nina von Sprecher, Text und Musik)		
9668 – GD9	Hörst du mich. Tangolied	voc NvS	Gr/Po unissued
	(Nina von Sprecher, Text und Musik)		
9668½GD9	Hörst du mich. Tangolied	voc NvS	Gr 47707
	(Nina von Sprecher, Text und Musik)		

Charlie and his Orchestra. Canto e letra: Carlos Henriques (ledgers)

Lutz Templin *leader*; probably Nino Impallomeni or Rimis van den Broek, Alfredo Marzaroli, Herre Jager or Eberhard Schmid-Schulz *trumpets*; Jos Breyre, unidentified, Henk Bosch or Folke Johnson *trombones*; Mario Balbo, Bob van Venetië or Francesco Paolo Ricci *tenor-saxes/clarinets*, Jean Robert *tenor-sax/baritone- sax/clarinet*, Benny de Weille, Tinus Bruijn *alto-saxes/clarinets*; Primo Angeli *piano*; Meg Tevelian *guitar*; Otto Tittmann *bass*; Fritz Brocksieper *drums*; Carlos Henriques *Portuguese vocals 1, English vocals 2.*

Berlin; November 2, 1942 (09:00-13:30)

9666 – GR9	It's A Long Way (engl. Soldatenlied)	2'54" arr LT	voc CH 1,2 K&M	unissued
9666½GR9	It's A Long Way (engl. Soldatenlied)	2'50" arr LT	voc CH 1,2	?
9667 – GR9	Siegfried-Line (Typ Peter; Maurice Co)	2'15"	voc CH 1	?
9668 – GR9	Lili Marlen (Norbert Schultze)	2'54"	voc CH 1	?
9669 – GR9	Daisy (engl. Volkslied)	2'14"	voc CH 1,2	?
9670 – GR9	Continental	2'44"	voc CH 1	unissued
9670½GR9	Continental	2'43"	voc CH 1	?
9671 – GR9	Bye, Bye, Blackbird	2'46"	voc CH 1	?

- *Entry in the recording ledgers: 'Wachsverbrauch: 18 Stück 25cm.' [Wax consumption...]*
- *The titles from this session may have been released on K & M 0178-0183, which are untraced.*
- *The 1912 marching song 'It's A Long Way To Tipperary' was written by Jack Judge and Harry Williams and was interpolated in the 1914 Broadway musical 'Chin-Chin'.*
- *Two 'Siegfried Line' songs were published within a few days of each other in 1939, but neither of them with credits to a Peter or a Maurice. Ross Parker, Hugh Charles and St. John Cooper were the team behind 'I'm Sending You The Siegfried Line (To Hang Your Washing On)', while Michael Carr and Jimmy Kennedy were the authors of '(We're Gonna Hang Out) The Washing On The Siegfried Line'.*

Kapelle Lutz Templin (ledgers)

Lutz Templin *leader*; personnel and instrumentation probably as before

Berlin, KWS; c. late 1942

70350	Ausschnitt aus dem 'Lied von der Siegfriedline' (Jimmy Kennedy)	voc ?	RRG 70350
70351	Ausschnitt aus dem 'Lied von der Siegfriedline' (Jimmy Kennedy)	voc ?	70351

- *Details as per RRG ledgers.*
- *This is probably a vocal recording, although no vocalist is given in the ledgers.*

Orchester Templin (Test)
Polydor Tanczenekar vezényel: Templin. Ania Suli énekel (47716A, 47717)
Polydor Tanczenekar vezényel: Templin. Barabás Sári énekel (47716B)
Brunswick Tanzorchester (Brunswick)

Lutz Templin *leader*; probably Nino Impallomeni, Alfredo Marzaroli, Herre Jager or Eberhard Schmid-Schulz *trumpets*; Jos Breyre, unidentified, Henk Bosch or Folke Johnson *trombones*; Mario Balbo, Bob van Venetië or Francesco Paolo Ricci *tenor-saxes/clarinets*, Jean Robert *tenor-sax/baritone-sax/clarinet*, Benny de Weille, Tinus Bruijn *alto-saxes/clarinets*; Ernst Zeebe *violin 1*; Primo Angeli or Tip Tichelaar *piano*; Meg Tevelian *guitar*; Otto Tittmann *bass*; Fritz Brocksieper *drums*; Barabás Sári, Ania Suli, real name Anna Szüle *Hungarian vocals*; Lajos Martiny *arrangements*; Chappy Orlay-Obendorfer *session supervisor*.

prob. Berlin, poss. Budapest, Hungary; early November 1942

9672 – GR9	Hin und her (Tedd ide, tedd oda)		Gr/Po unissued
9672½GR9	Tedd ide, tedd oda		Po 47715/230,
	Hin und her		Br 82302
9673 – GR9	Mert a nagy szerelmek. Slowfox	voc AS	Gr/Po unissued
	(Szöveg és zene: E.O. Chappy)		
9673½GR9	Mert a nagy szerelmek. Slowfox	voc AS	Siemens 47116A
	(Szöveg és zene: E.O. Chappy)		
9674 – GR9	Tudom-miért? Foxtrot	voc BS	Gr/Po test
	(Szöveg és zene: E.O. Chappy)		
9674½GR9	Tudom-miért? Foxtrot	voc BS	Siemens 47716B
	(Szöveg és zene: E.O. Chappy)		
9675 – GR9	Száz volt, ki ramdevura csábitott	voc AS	Gr/Po unissued
9675½GR9	Száz volt, ki ramdevura csábitott	voc AS	Siemens 47715
9676 – GR9	Mintha ma látnám öt. Dal	voc AS 1	Gr/Po unissued
	(Szöveg és zene: E.O. Chappy)		
9676½GR9	Mintha ma látnám öt. Dal	voc AS 1	Siemens 47717A
	(Szöveg és zene: E.O. Chappy)		
9677 – GR9	Pardon, téves a kapcsolás	voc AS	Siemens 47718
9677½GR9	Pardon, téves a kapcsolás	voc AS	Siemens 47718
9710 – GR9	Kedvesem visszavárlak. Dal (Dünnwald-Segesdy) voc AS		Gr/Po unissued
9710½GR9	Kedvesem visszavárlak. Dal (Dünnwald-Segesdy) voc AS		Siemens 47717B
	Széz gyönyory vagy	voc	Gr test
	Menj islen veleo	voc	Gr test

• *It is presently not known whether the reported Grammophon test pressing of 9674 is actually the unissued take 1.*
• *Siemens & Halske had taken over Deutsche Grammophon in 1940.*

Brocksie-Quartett

Nino Impallomeni *trumpet*; Primo Angeli *piano*; Otto Tittmann *bass*; Fritz Brocksieper *drums*.

Berlin; *c.* November/December 1943

9784½GR9	Verrückte Beine. Foxtrot (Impallomeni)	Br 82277A

Charlie und sein Orchester (ledgers)
Charlie and his Orchestra (Klarinette & Mandoline label)

Lutz Templin *leader*; probably Nino Impallomeni, Alfredo Marzaroli, Herre Jager or Eberhard Schmidt-Schulz *trumpets*; Jos Breyre, unidentified, Henk Bosch or Folke Johnson *trombones*; Mario Balbo, Bob van Venetië or Francesco Paolo Ricci *tenor-saxes/clarinets*, Jean Robert *tenor-sax/baritone-sax/clarinet*, Benny de Weille, Tinus Bruijn *alto-saxes/clarinets*; Primo Angeli *piano*; Meg Tevelian *guitar*; Otto Tittmann *bass*; Fritz Brocksieper *drums*; Walter Leschetitzky, 3 unidentified *string-section 1*; Charlie Schwedler, ensemble *vocals*.

Berlin; 15 December 1942 (09:00-14:00)

9741 – GD9	Elmer's Tune (—)	2'40"	1	NP	voc CS/Ens	
						K & M unissued
9741½GD9	Elmer's Tune (—)	2'40"	1	NP	voc CS/Ens	0188/0189
9742 – GD9	Whistle While You Work (—)	2'35"	1		voc CS	0186/0187
9743 – GD9	At Least You Could Say 'Hello' (—)	3'15"	1	NP	voc CS	unissued
9743½GD9	At Least You Could Say 'Hello' (—)	3'15"	1	NP	voc CS	0187/0186
9744 – GD9	Picture Me Without You (—)	2'40"	1		voc CS	0189/0188
9745 – GD9	Carry Me Back To Old Virginy [*sic*] (—)	3'23"	1	NP	voc CS/Ens	0184/0185
9746 – GD9	Sleepy Time Gal (—)	3'20"	1		voc	0185/0184

• *'Elmer's Tune', 'At Least You Could Say "Hello"' and 'Carry Me Back To Old Virginy' are sung straight, with no propaganda texts.*
• *'Elmer's Tune' was re-recorded in 1943, with a propaganda text and re-titled 'Submarines'.*

Charlie und sein Orchester (ledgers)
Charlie and his Orchestra (Klarinette & Mandoline label)

Lutz Templin *leader*; personnel and instrumentation probably as before; *string section 1*; Charlie Schwedler, ensemble *vocals*; Franz Mück *arrangement*.

Berlin; 22 December 1942 (09:00-14:00)

9748 – GD9	Who's Afraid Of The Big Bad Wolf? (—) arr FM	1	voc CS K & M	unissued
9748½GD9	Who's Afraid Of The Big Bad Wolf? (—) arr FM	1	voc CS	0190/0191
9749 – GD9	The Lambeth Walk (—)	1	voc CS/Ens	0192/0193
9750 – GD9	I'll Never Smile Again (—)	1 NP	voc CS	unissued
9750½GD9	I'll Never Smile Again (—	1 NP	voc CS	0194/0195
9751 – GD9	Aurora (—)	1	voc CS/Ens	unissued
9751½GD9	Aurora (—)	1	voc CS/Ens	0195/0194
9752 – GD9	Last Night (—)	1 NP	voc CS	unissued
9752½GD9	Last Night (—)	1 NP	voc CS	0191/0190
9753 – GD9	Y, Y, Y, Y Lowe You Very Much [*sic*] (—)		NP voc CS	0193/0192

• *Entry in the recording ledgers: 'Wachsverbrauch: 26 St. 25cm.' [Wax consumption...]*
• *The Franz Mück arrangement was identified by Fritz Brocksieper (Brocksieper to Lotz).*
• *'I'll Never Smile Again', 'Last Night' and 'Y, Y, Y, Y Lowe You Very Much' are sung straight, with no propaganda texts.*

Charlie und sein Orchester (ledgers)
Charlie and his Orchestra (Klarinette & Mandoline label)

Lutz Templin *leader*; personnel and instrumentation probably as before; *string section 1*;
Charlie Schwedler *vocals*.

Berlin; 18 January 1943 (09:00-13:30)

9811–GD9	Three Little Fishes [*sic*] (—)	2'05" 1	voc CS	K & M 0196/0200
9812–GD9	On The Sentimental Side (—)	2'45" 1	voc CS	0197/0198
9813–GD9	I've Got You Under My Skin (—)	3'15" 1 NPvoc CS		0198/0197
9814–GD9	You Stepped Out Of A Dream (—)	3'15" 1 NPvoc CS		0199/0201
9815–GD9	It's A Lovely Day To-morrow [*sic*] (—)	2'20" 1 NPvoc CS		0200/0196
9816–GD9	Why'd Ya Make Me Fall In Love (—) 2'30"		voc CS	0201/0199

- *Entry in the recording ledgers: 'Wachsverbrauch: 17 Stück 25cm.' [Wax consumption...]*
- *'I've Got You Under My Skin', 'You Stepped Out Of A Dream' and 'It's A Lovely Day Tomorrow' are sung straight, with no propaganda texts.*

Lutz Templin mit seinem Tanz-Orchester

Lutz Templin *leader*; personnel and instrumentation probably as before; Adolf Steimel, Willy
Berking *arrangements*.

Berlin; 19 January 1943 (13:30-17:30)

105–GX9	Ich hab' dich und du hast mich. Foxtrot a.d. Tonfilm 'Wir machen Musik' (Peter Igelhoff, Adolf Steimel)	Gr/Po unissued
105½GX9	Ich hab' dich und du hast mich. Foxtrot a.d. Tonfilm 'Wir machen Musik' (Peter Igelhoff, Adolf Steimel)	Po 47753A
106–GX9	Sing mit mir. Foxtrot a.d. Tonfilm 'Hab' mich lieb' (Franz Grothe)	Po 47753B
107–GX9	Ping-Pong! (Willy Berking)	Gr/Po unissued
107½GX9	Ping-Pong! (Willy Berking)	Gr 47754, Siemens 14023A

Brocksieper-Solisten-Orchester (Brunswick 82282)
Brocksieper Solistork. (Norwegian Brunswick BS603077)

Fritz Brocksieper *drums*, directing the Lutz Templin orchestra, personnel and instrumentation
probably asbefore; Pi Scheffer arrangement.

Berlin; 27 January 1943 (13:30-16:45)

9833–GD9	Excentric [?] Foxtrot (Pi Scheffer	Gr/Po unissued
9833½HGD9	Excentric. Foxtrot (Pi Scheffer)	Br 82282, BS603077A

- *The title of 9833-GD9 is not entered in the recording ledgers.*
- *The address of arranger Pi Scheffer is given as 'Conzestr. 471, Amsterdam-Oost' in the ledgers.*

Brocksi-Quartett

Probably: Eugen Henkel *tenor-sax*; Primo Angeli *piano*; Otto Tittmann *bass*; Fritz Brocksieper *drums*.

Berlin; 27 January 1943 (13:30-16:45)

9834–GD9	Verrückte Beine (Nino Impallomeni)	Gr/Po unissued
9834½GD9	Verrückte Beine (Nino Impallomeni)	Gr/Po unissued?

- *The four sides recorded on 27 January 1943, are noted as 'Probeaufnahme Witte' in the ledgers.*

Fritz Stamer, Klavier

Fritz Stamer *piano*.

Berlin, Haus des Rundfunks, Saal 10, Kurzwellensender; 29 January 1943

70540	Amerikanische Nationalhymne (—) [American National Anthem]	RRG 70540

- *This title is included in this discography as another example of Germany's English-language propaganda effort. Stamer had previously recorded this and similar material on 9 March 1942.*

Brocksi-Quartett

Eugen Henkel *tenor-sax*; Primo Angeli *piano*; Otto Tittmann *bass*; Fritz Brocksieper *drums*.

Berlin; 30 January 1943 (09:30-13:00)

9836–GD9	Liebeslaunen. Foxtrot (E. Henkel)	Gr/Po unissued
9836½GD9	Liebeslaunen. Foxtrot (E. Henkel)	Br 82276A
9837–GD9	O, La La, Madame! Foxtrot (Heinz Weiss)	Gr/Po unissued
9837½GD9	O, La La, Madame! Foxtrot (Heinz Weiss)	Br 82276B

- *Personnel and instrumentation as per recording ledgers.*

Charlie und sein Orchester (ledgers)
Charlie and his Orchestra (Klarinette & Mandoline label)

Lutz Templin *leader*; probably Nino Impallomeni, Alfredo Marzaroli, Eberhard Schmidt-Schulz *trumpets*; Jos Breyre, Robby Zillner *trombones*; Mario Balbo, Bob van Venetië *tenor-saxes/clarinets*, Jean Robert *tenor-sax/baritone-sax/clarinet*, Benny de Weille, Renato Carneval *alto-saxes/clarinets*; Primo Angeli *piano*; Meg Tevelian *guitar*; Otto Tittmann *bass*; Fritz Brocksieper *drums*; Walter Leschetitzky, 3 unidentified *string-section 1*; Charlie Schwedler *vocals*.

Berlin; 8 February 1943 (09:00-13:00)

9870–GD	Ain't Mis'behavin' [*sic*] (—)	NP	voc CS	K & M 0202/0203
9871–GD	I Double Dare You (—)		voc CS	0203/0202
9872–GD	Lover Come Back To Me (—)	1 NP	voc CS	0204/0205
9873–GD	Please Take A Letter (—)	1	voc CS	0205/0204
9874–GD	Deep Purple (—)	1	voc CS	0206/0207
9875–GD	There's Honey On The Moon To-Night (—)		voc CS	0207/0206

- *Entry in the recording ledgers: 'Wachsverbrauch: 16 Stück 25cm.' [Wax consumption...]*

Brocksieper-Spezial-Ensemble (ledgers)
Brocksieper-Solistork (Norwegian Brunswick BS603077)

Fritz Brocksieper *drums*, directing a small formation of the Templin orchestra.

Berlin; 11 February 1943 (09:15- ?)

9880–GD9	Barcarole. Foxtrot (Primo Angeli)	Gr/Po unissued
9880½GD9	Barcarole. Foxtrot (Primo Angeli)	Br 82282, BS603077

Brocksie-Quartet (*sic*, in ledgers)
Brocksi-Quartett (Brunswick 82345)

Probably: Alfredo Marzaroli *trumpet*; Primo Angeli *piano*; Otto Tittmann *bass*; Fritz Brocksieper *drums*.

Berlin; 11 February 1943 (09:15- ?)

9881–GD9	Sicherlich. Foxtrot (A. Marzaroli)	Gr/Po unissued
9881½GD9	Sicherlich. Foxtrot (A. Marzaroli)	Br 82345B

Nina von Sprecher m. Orchester. Leitung: Lutz Templin (ledgers)

Lutz Templin *leader*; personnel and instrumentation probably as before; Nina von Sprecher *vocals*.

Berlin; 12 February 1943 (19:00-22:00)

9886–1GD	Von Zeit zu Zeit ein kleiner Seitensprung (Musik und Text: Nina von Sprecher)	voc NvS	Gr/Po unissued
9886–2GD	Von Zeit zu Zeit ein kleiner Seitensprung (Musik und Text: Nina von Sprecher)	voc MvS	Gr ?
9887–1GD	Abends allein... (Musik und Text: Nina von Sprecher)	voc NvS	Gr/Po unissued
9887–2GD	Abends allein... (Musik und Text: Nina von Sprecher)	voc NvS	Gr ?

• *Entry in the recording ledgers: 'Wachsverbrauch: 8 Stück 25cm.' [Wax consumption...]*

Charlie und sein Orchester (ledgers)
Charlie and his Orchestra (Klarinette & Mandoline label)

Lutz Templin *leader*; probably Nino Impallomeni, Alfredo Marzaroli, Eberhard Schmidt-Schulz *trumpets*; Jos Breyre, Robby Zillner *trombones*; Mario Balbo, Bob van Venetië *tenor-saxes/clarinets*, Jean Robert *tenor-sax/baritone-sax/clarinet*, Renato Carneval *alto-sax/clarinet*; Primo Angeli *piano*; Meg Tevelian *guitar*; Otto Tittmann *bass*; Fritz Brocksieper *drums*; Walter Leschetitzky, 3 unidentified *string-section 1*; unidentified *flutes 2*; unidentified *Latin percussion 3*; Charlie Schwedler *vocals*.

Berlin; 15 February 1943 (09:00-13:00)

9888–1GD9	Miss Annabelle Lee (—)	2'20"			voc CS	K & M unissued
9888–2GD9	Miss Annabelle Lee (—)	2'20"			voc CS	0208/0209
9889––GD9	South Of The Border (—)	2'50"	1,2,3		voc CS	0209/0208
9890–1GD9	Home On The Range (—)	2'45"	2	NP	voc CS	unissued
9890–2GD9	Home On The Range (—)	2'45"	2	NP	voc CS	0210/0211

[session continued]

9891 – 1GD9	I Hear Music (—)	2'50"	2	NP	voc CS	unissued
9891 – 2GD9	I Hear Music (—)	2'50"	2	NP	voc CS	0211/0210
9892 – 1GD9	Hold Tight (—)	2'45"			voc CS	unissued
9892 – 2GD9	Hold Tight (—)	2'45"			voc CS	0212/0213
9893 – 1GD9	Cachita (—)	2'35"	2,3	NP	voc CS	unissued
9893 – 2GD9	Cachita (—)	2'35"	2,3	NP	voc CS	0213/0212

- *The Latin percussion included a Cuban bongo player. Flute players were contracted from outside (Fritz Brocksieper to Steinbiß, interview, Munich, 19 September 1987).*
- *Entry in the recording ledgers: 'Wachsverbrauch: 29 Stück 25cm.'[Wax consumption]*
- *'Home On The Range', 'I Hear Music' and 'Cachita' are sung straight, with no propaganda texts.*

Lutz Templin Jazzorchester (ledgers)
Jazzorch. L. Templin (test)
Lutz Templin mit seinem Orchester (Polydor 48149)
Lutz Templin mit seinem Tanz-Orchester (Siemens)

Lutz Templin *leader*; personnel and instrumentation probably as before.

Berlin; 22 February 1943 (13:30-18:00)

9905 – 1GD9	Ich mach' aus meiner Liebe kein Geheimnis. Foxtrot (Heino Gaze)	Gr/Po unissued
9905 – 2GD9	Ich mach' aus meiner Liebe kein Geheimnis. Foxtrot (Heino Gaze)	Po 48149B
9906 – 1GD9	Hoppla-Hopp. Foxtrot (Walter Leschetitzky)	Gr/Po unissued
9906 – 2GD9	Hoppla-Hopp. Foxtrot (Walter Leschetitzky)	Gr/Po unissued
9906 – 3GD9	Hoppla-Hopp. Foxtrot (Walter Leschetitzky)	Gr/Po unissued
9906 – 4GD9	Hoppla-Hopp. Foxtrot (Walter Leschetitzky)	Gr 47754, Siemens 14023B
9907 – 1GD9	Maria-Elena. Foxtrot (—)	Gr/Po unissued
9907 – 2GD9	Maria-Elena. Foxtrot (—)	Gr test

- *Matrix 9906-3GD9 is unconfirmed.*

Lutz Templin mit seinem Tanz-Orchester

Lutz Templin *leader*; personnel and instrumentation probably as before; Adolf Steimel, Willy Berking *arrangement*.

Berlin; *c.* late February 1943

105 – GX9	Ich hab' dich und du hast mich. Foxtrot aus dem Tonfilm 'Wir machen Musik' (Peter Igelhoff – Steimel)	Gr/Po unissued
105½GX9	Ich hab' dich und du hast mich. Foxtrot aus dem Tonfilm 'Wir machen Musik' (Peter Igelhoff – Steimel)	Siemens 47753A, 14081
106 – GX9	Sing mit mir. Foxtrot aus dem Tonfilm 'Hab mich lieb' (Franz Grothe)	Siemens 47753B, 14081
107-GX9	Ping-Pong! Foxtrot (W. Berking)	Gr 47754, Siemens 14023A

Brocksie-Quartett (*sic*, ledgers)
Brocksi-Quartett (Brunswick 82284)

Jean Robert *tenor-sax*; Primo Angeli *piano*; Otto Tittmann *bass*; Fritz Brocksieper *drums*.

Berlin; 1 March 1943 (14:00-17:00)

114 – GX9	Ich sing' mir eins. Foxtrot (W. Leschetitzky)	Br 82284A
114½GX9	Ich sing' mir eins. Foxtrot (W. Leschetitzky)	Gr/Po unissued
115 – GX9	Silhouetten. Langs. Foxtrot (Tevelian)	Br 82284B
115½GX9	Silhouetten. Langs. Foxtrot (Tevelian)	Gr/Po unissued

• *Personnel and instrumentation as per recording ledgers.*

Charlie and his Orchestra

Lutz Templin *leader*; probably Nino Impallomeni, Alfredo Marzaroli, Eberhard Schmidt-Schulz *trumpet*; Jos Breyre, Robby Zillner *trombones*; Mario Balbo, Bob van Venetië *tenor-saxes/clarinets*, Jean Robert *tenor-sax/baritone-sax/clarinet*, Renato Carneval *alto-sax/clarinet*; Primo Angeli *piano*; Meg Tevelian or Max Gursch *guitar*; Otto Tittmann *bass*; Fritz Brocksieper *drums*; Charlie Schwedler *vocals*.

Berlin; 16 March 1943 (09:00- ?)

9945 – 1GD9	Flat Foot Floogie (—)	3'05"	voc CS	K & M unissued
9945 – 2GD9	Flat Foot Floggie (—)	3'05"	voc CS	0214/0215?
9946 – 1GD9	Jingle Jangle Jingle (—)	2'45"	voc CS	unissued
9946 – 2GD9	Jingle Jangle Jingle (—)	2'45"	voc CS	0215/0214?
9947 – 1GD9	Mexican Magic (—)	2'50" NP	voc CS	unissued
9947 – 2GD9	Mexican Magic (—)	2'50" NP	voc CS	0216/0217
9948 – 1GD9	Hang Your Heart On An Hickory Limb [*sic*] (—)	2'40" NP	voc CS	unissued
9948 – 2GD9	Hang Your Heart On An Hickory Limb [*sic*] (—)	2'40" NP	voc CS	O217/0216
9949 – 1GD9	When You Wish Upon A Star (—)	2'40"	voc CS	unissued
9949 – 2GD9	When You Wish Upon A Star (—)	2'40"	voc CS	0218/0219?
9950 – 1GD9	La-Sha [*sic*?]	3'10"	voc CS	unissued
9950 – 2GD9	La-Sha [*sic*?]	3'10"	voc CS	0219/0218?

• *Entry in the recording ledgers: 'Wachsverbrauch: 31 Stück 25cm.' [Wax consumption...]*
• *K & M 0214/0215 & 0218/0219 remain untraced.*
• *'Mexican Magic' and 'Hang Your Heart On A Hickory Limb' are sung straight, with no propaganda.*
• *'La-Sha' may be a misspelling of the 1938 song 'Sha-Sha', popularized by the Andrews Sisters.*

Brocksie-Jazz (ledgers)
Brocksieper Solisten-Orchester (Bru 82287)

Fritz Brocksieper *drums*, directing the Templin orchestra, personnel and instrumentation probably as before.

Berlin; 19 March 1943 (09:00-12:30)

9960 – GD9	Globetrotter. Foxtrot (Templin)	Br 82287A
9960½GD9	Globetrotter. Foxtrot (Templin)	Gr/Po unissued
9961 – GD9	Melodie. Foxtrot (Leschetitzky)	Gr/Po unissued
9961½GD9	Melodie. Foxtrot (Leschetitzky)	Br 82287B

Templin-Orchester (ledgers)

Lutz Templin *leader*; personnel and instrumentation probably as before; unidentified, possibly Karl Schmitt-Walter *French vocals*.

Berlin; 24 March1943 (19:00-22:00)

9973 – 1GD9	France Réveille-Toi. Marche (Rosen)	French voc	K & M unissued
9973 – 2GD9	France Réveille-Toi. Marche (Rosen)	French voc	0220/0221?
9974 – 1GD9	Jeanneton (Rosen)	French voc	unissued
9974 – 2GD9	Jeanneton (Rosen)	French voc	0221/0220?

- *Entry in the recording ledgers: 'Wachsverbrauch: 12 Stück 25cm.' [Wax consumption...]*
- *K & M 0220/0221 unconfirmed.*

Charlie und sein Orchester (ledgers)

Lutz Templin *leader*; personnel and instrumentation probably as before; Charlie Schwedler *vocals*.

Berlin; 30 March 1943 (14:00-16:00)

9980 – 1GD9	Ooooooh Bum (—)	2'55"	voc CS	K & M unissued
9980 – 2GD9	Ooooooh Bum (—)	2'55"	voc CS	0224/0225?

- *Entry in the recording ledgers: 'Wachsverbrauch: 5 Stück 25cm.' [Wax consumption...]*
- *K & M 0224/0225 unconfirmed.*

Charlie und sein Orchester (ledgers)
Jazzorchester Charlie (ledgers)
Charlie and his Orchestra (Klarinette & Mandoline label)

Lutz Templin *leader*; personnel and instrumentation probably as before; Charlie Schwedler, Eva 'Evelyn' Leschetitzky *vocals*; Lutz Templin *arrangement*.

Berlin; 5 April 1943 (14:00-17:15)

9852 – GR9	I'm Stepping Out With A Memory To Night (—)	2'40"	voc CS	K & M 0225/0224?
9853 – GR9	Mac Pherson Is Rehearsin' [*sic*] (—)	2'50"	NP voc CS	0222/0223
9854 – GR9	I Can't Give You Anything But Love (—)	2'18"	voc CS/EL	0223/0222
9855 – GR9	The Nango (Nyango) (—)	2'58"	voc CS	?

[session continued]

9856–GR9   We Three (—)   3'00"   voc CS   ?

- *Entry in the recording ledgers: 'Wachsverbrauch 14 Stück 25cm.' [Wax consumption...]*
- *On 'Mac Pherson Is Rehearsin' Charlie sings a duet with a female vocalist whom he addresses as 'Evelyn'. According to Otto Tittmann, this was Eva Leschetitzky again, the wife of the violinist.*
- *'Mac Pherson Is Rehearsing' is sung straight, with no propaganda text.*

Brocksieper Solisten-Orchester

Fritz Brocksieper *drums*, directing the Templin orchestra, personnel and instrumentation probably as before. Hans Vlig van der Sijs *arrangement.*

Berlin; c. April 1943

9875–GR   Taktik (H. van der Sys)   Br 82325

Brocksi-Quartett

Nino Impallomeni *trumpet*; Primo Angeli *piano*; Otto Tittmann *bass*; Fritz Brocksieper *drums*.

Berlin; c. April 1943

9876–GD   Harmonie (N. Impallomeni)   Br 82277B, 82314B

Charlie and his Orchestra

Lutz Templin *leader*; probably Nino Impallomeni, Alfredo Marzaroli *trumpets*; Jos Breyre, Robby Zillner *trombones*; Mario Balbo, Bob van Venetië *tenor-saxes/clarinets*, Jean Robert *tenor-sax/baritone-sax/clarinet*, Renato Carneval *alto-sax/clarinet*; Primo Angeli *piano*; Max Gursch *guitar*; Otto Tittmann *bass*; Fritz Brocksieper *drums*; Charlie Schwedler *vocals*.

Berlin; c. mid-1943

Stardust (—)	NP	voc CS	K & M 0226/0227
Daisy (—)		voc CS	0227/0226
Two Blind Loves (—)	NP	voc CS	0228/0229
Submarines (—)		voc CS	0229/0228
United Nations Air Men (—)		voc CS	0230/0231

- *'Daisy' is a remake of the 2 November 1942, recording of this title; 'Submarines' is a propaganda remake of the 15 December 1942 recording of 'Elmer's Tune'; 'United Air Man' is a remake of the late 1940 recording of 'Slumming On Park Avenue'.*
- *'Stardust' and 'Two Blind Loves' are sung straight, with no propaganda texts.*

Charlie and his Orchestra

Lutz Templin *leader*; small formation consisting of *trumpet*; *trombone*; *tenor-sax*, *alto-sax*, *clarinet*; Primo Angeli *piano*; Otto Tittmann *bass*; Fritz Brocksieper *drums*; Charlie Schwedler *vocal*.

Berlin; c. mid-1943

I Got Rhythm (—)	NP	voc CS	K & M 0231/0230

- *Sung straight, with no propaganda text.*

Wilhelm Strienz, Bariton, mit Kapelle Lutz Templin (ledger)

Lutz Templin *leader*; personnel and instrumentation probably as before; Wilhelm Strienz *vocal*, Willi Lachner, *arrangement*.

Berlin, DÜS, Studio 11; 6 May 1943

| 71411 | Die Heimat grüßt (Olaf Andresen) | 2'44" NP | voc WSt | RRG 71411 |
| | bearb. von Willi Lachner | | | |

• *Details as per RRG ledger. Further information on the ledger card: 'Abteilung 9: Musik', 'Manuskript', 'Keine Kosten bei Wiederholung' [No charge for repeats].*

Horst Günther, Gesang, mit Kapelle Lutz Templin

Lutz Templin *leader*; personnel and instrumentation probably as before; Horst Günther *Afrikaans vocal*.

Berlin, DÜS, Studio 10; 3 June 1943

| 71222 | Es klopft mein Herz bum-bum | 3'20" NP? | voc HG | RRG 71222 |
| | (Frank Fux)Verlag Peter Schaeffers | | | |

• *Details as per RRG ledger. Further information on the ledger card: 'Abteilung 9: Musik', 'Keine Kosten bei Wiederholung' [No charge for repeats].*
• *Most Afrikaans broadcasts and recordings were accompanied by other orchestras.*

Fritz Stamer, Klavier

Fritz Stamer *piano*.

Berlin, Haus des Rundfunks, Saal 11; 17 June 1943

71483	Star Spangled Banner (Francis Scott Key)	1'14"	RRG USA 71483
	Star Spangled Banner	1'14"	
	Star Spangled Banner	1'14"	
71484	Home Sweet Home (—)	1'08"	71484
	Home Sweet Home	1'08"	
	Home Sweet Home	1'08"	

• *Fritz Stamer had recorded this type of material for the RRG's USA zone before. These short pieces were probably used to sign programmes on and off.*

Charlie und sein Orchester (ledgers)
Charlie and his Orchestra (Klarinette & Mandoline label)

Lutz Templin *leader*; personnel and instrumentation probably as before; Charlie Schwedler *vocals*.

Berlin; 28 June 1943 (09:00- ?)

10024–1GD	That's My Weakness Now (—)	3'15"	voc CS	K & M unissued
10024–2GD	That's My Weakness Now (—)	3'15"	voc CS	?
10025-1GD	'War Mongers' (—)	3'05"	voc CS	unissued
10025-2GD	'War Mongers' (—)	3'05"	voc CS	?

[session continued]

10026 – 1GD	You Go To My Head (—)	2'45" NP	voc CS		unissued
10026 – 2GD	You Go To My Head (—)	2'45" NP	voc CS		0240/0241
10027 – 1GD	I Hear A Dream (—)	2'50" NP	voc CS		unissued
10027 – 2GD	I Hear A Dream (—)	2'50" NP	voc CS		0241/0240
10028 – 1GD	The Modern English Girl (—)	2'55"	voc CS		unissued
10028 – 2GD	The Modern English Girl (—)	2'55"	voc CS		?
10029 – 1GD	Alexander's Ragtime Band (—)	3'15"	voc CS		unissued
10029 – 2GD	Alexander's Ragtime Band (—)	3'15"	voc CS		?

- *'Alexander's Ragtime Band' is a remake of the 12 January 1942, recording.*
- *'You Go To My Head' and 'I Hear A Dream' are sung staight, with no propaganda texts.*
- *Apparently, 'War Mongers' and 'The Modern English Girl' are German propaganda versions of unidentified American or British originals.*

Templin-Tango-Orchester (ledgers)

Lutz Templin *leader*; personnel and instrumentation probably as before; Nina Konsta *vocals*.

Berlin; 29 June 1943 (09:00-12:30)

10030 – 1GD9	Ich bin betrogen (—)	3'10"	voc NK	Gr/Po unissued
10030 – 2GD9	Ich bin betrogen (—)	3'10"	voc NK	?
10031 – 1GD9	Immer zusammen [?] (—)	3'10"	voc NK	unissued
10031 – 2GD9	Immer zusammen [?] (—)	3'10"	voc NK	?
10032 – 1GD9	Wenn du mich verlierst (—)	3'00"	voc NK	unissued
10032 – 2GD9	Wenn du mich verlierst (—)	3'00"	voc NK	?
10033 – 1GD9	Heute abend bin ich traurig (—)	2'40"	voc NK	unissued
10033 – 2GD9	Heute abend bin ich traurig (—)	2'40"	voc NK	?

- *Entry in the recording ledgers: 'Wachsverbrauch: 17 Stück 25cm.' [Wax consumption...]*
- *According to the ledgers, the songs were sung in Greek, although the titles are noted in German (perhaps translated from the Greek?).*

Brocksieper-Jazz-Ensemble

Fritz Brocksieper *drums*, directing the Templin orchestra, including Primo Angeli *piano/harpsichord 2*; Hans Vlig van der Sijs, Willy Berking *arrangements*.

Berlin; 1 July 1943 (09:00-15:00)

10037 – GD9	Cymbal-Promenade (v.d. Sijs)	arr HvdS	2	Gr/Po unissued
10037½GD9	Cymbal-Promenade (v.d. Sijs)	arr HvdS	2	Br 82314, 82355B
10038 – GD9	Romanze (van der Sys)	arr HvdS		Gr/Po unissued
10038½GD9	Romanze (van der Sys)	arr HvdS		Br 82325

[session continued]

10039 – GD9	Kein Problem (Willy Berking)	arr WB	Gr/Po unissued
10039½GD9	Kein Problem (Willy Berling)	arr WB	Br 82343B, 82356B

- *At the time of the recording, matrix 10039 was entered in the ledgers as untitled ('Titel wird noch bekanntgegeben' – [title to be announced'.).*
- *On 15 September 1943, Deutsche Grammophon wrote to Brocksieper, 'presently in Stuttgart', that they are unable to release the titles 'Cymbal-Promenade', 'Romanze' and 'a number without a title' in Germany. 'With these particular recordings, you have breached the conditions which we laid down. We shall discuss this matter with you in person.' In spite of this, at least one title was released in Germany at the time and reviewed by the notorious Herbert Gerigk: 'One can hardly believe one's ears: a newly advertised recording which we requested for review as an example of modern dance music, turns out to contain all those elements usually desccribed as Jewish and degrading. What the Brocksieper Soloists' are offering as so-called eccentric foxtrot is nothing but illicit jazz music from a world that is not ours and has nothing in common with that of the German people. How can it happen that such degenerate music gets recorded and released?" (Herbert Gerigk, 'Neuaufnahmen in Auslese', in* Musik im Kriege *Nr. 3/4 (June/July 1943).*
- *The title 'Cymbal-Promenade' was first released after the war.*

The last entry for the GD-series in the recording ledgers of Deutsche Grammophon are matrices 10059-GD and 10060-GD, which were recorded by Fred Dömpke on 16 July 1943. A block of matrices ranging from 10061-GD through 10092-GD was allocated to recordings made in Brussels by Jean Omer, John Ouwerx, Stan Brenders and Delphine Boeyen in October 1943. Matrices 10093-GD to 10099-GD were again recorded in Berlin by an Ukrainian choir on 29 October 1943. The 1943 recording ledgers of the GR-series have not survived.

Lale Andersen

Lale Andersen *vocal*, male *vocal 3*; accompanied by unidentified *violin 1; tenor sax 2; piano; guitar; drums.*

Berlin; 2 July 1943

(1)	Roll On The Funnel [*sic*] (—) [= Es geht alles vorüber]	2 NP	voc LA/voc-3 RRG	b/c acetate
(2)	If You Were The Only Girl In The World (—)	2 NP	voc LA	b/c acetate
(3)	When The Lilacs Bloom Again (—) [= Wenn der weisse Flieder wieder blüht]	2 NP	voc LA	b/c acetate
(4)	And So Another Lovely Day Is Over (—) [= Und wieder geht ein schöner Tag zu Ende]	1 NP	voc LA	b/c acetate

- *All titles from this session are sung straight, with no propaganda lyrics, and were recorded for use in the 'ANZAC Tattoo' radio broadcast programmes, as per handwritten label inscription.*
- *The start of the vocal on 'If You Were The Only Girl In The World' is faulty ('Anfang verjault').*
- *The session supervisor can be heard saying: 'Well, has she persuaded you?'*

Lale Andersen

Lale Andersen *vocal*, accompanied by unidentified *accordion; piano; guitar; bass; drums*.

Berlin; *c.* 12 August 1943

(5)	Unter der roten Laterne von Sankt Pauli (—)	NP voc LA	RRG b/c acetate
(6)	Unter einem Regenschirm am Abend (—)	NP voc LA	b/c acetate
(7)	Mache dir um mich doch bitte keine Sorgen (—)	NP voc LA	b/c acetate

- *All titles from this session are sung straight, with no propaganda lyrics, again for use on* 'ANZAC Tattoo' radio broadcasts, as per handwritten label inscription.

Lale Andersen (test)
Lale Andersen. Ltg. Friedrich Pasch (test)

Dr. Friedrich 'Fritz' Pasche *leader*; unidentified personnel and instrumentation, including *strings 1*; Lale Andersen *vocals*.

Berlin; *c.* September/October 1943

	If You Were The Only Girl (—)	1 NP voc LA	K & M 0244/0245 (test)
	Under An Umbrella In The Evening (—)	1 NP voc LA	0245/0244 (test)
	When The Scented Lilac Blooms Again (—)	1 NP voc LA	0246/0247 (test)
	Three Little Words (—)	1 NP voc LA	0247/0246 (test)

- *Dr. Fritz Pasche had directed the orchestra which accompanied Lale Andersen on commercial recordings for Telefunken on 29 December 1938 and Electrola on 27 March 1939; the handwritten information on above test recordings give his name as Friedrich Pasch.*
- *On the test pressing of 0244/0245 the title 'If You Were The Only Girl' is qualified 'schlecht' (poor), and 'Under An Umbrella In The Evening' as 'geht' (passable) handwriten on the blank label.*
- *Above titles are sung straight, with no propaganda texts.*
- *All titles from this session probably remained unissued.*

Lale Andersen And Orchestra (label)

Unidentified personnel and instrumentation, including *strings 1*; Lale Andersen, male choir *vocals*.

Berlin; *c.* October 1943

10093-1GR9	Lili Marleen (—)		NP voc LA/choir	K & M unissued
10093-2GR9	Lili Marleen (—)		NP voc LA/choir	0250/0251
10094-1GR9	Home May Be A Word (—)	1	NP voc LA	unissued
10094-2GR9	Home May Be A Word (—)	1	NP voc LA	0251/0250

- *All titles are sung straight, with no propaganda texts.*

Lale Andersen m. Orchester. Leitung Wilhelm Greiss (*sic*, ledgers)
Lale Andersen And Orchestra (Lyra label)

Wilhelm Greihs *leader*; unidentified personnel and instrumentation, including *strings 1*; Lale Andersen *vocals*.

Berlin; 12 November 1943 (09:00–14:30)

10144 – GD9	Under An Umbrella In The Evening (Unter einem Regenschirm am Abend) (Steinbrecher; engl. Text: Stewart)	1 NP voc LA	Lyra 0253/0252
10145 – GD9	Roll On The Big Boat (Es geht alles vorüber) (Fred Raymond; engl. Text: Stewart)	1 NP voc LA	0252/0253
10146 – GD9	Three Little Words (Norbert Schultze; engl. Text: Stewart)	1 NP voc LA	0254/0255
10147 – GD9	And So Another Lovely Day Is Over (Und wieder geht ein schöner Tag zu Ende) (Gerhard Winkler; engl. Text: Stewart)	1 NP voc LA	0255/0254

- *Originally the recording ledgers gave the date for this session as 12 September, however, this was corrected to read 12 November 1943.*
- *In the recording ledgers these sides are rubber stamped '11. Mai 1944' for unknown reasons.*
- *'Under An Umbrella In The Evening' and 'Three Little Words' are remakes of the September/October 1943 recordings of these titles.*
- *On 2 July 1943, the recording engineer had given the song 'Roll On The Big Boat' the title 'Roll On The Funnel'.*
- *The writer of the English lyrics for these current German hits was Norman Baillie-Stewart.*
- *All titles are sung straight, with no propaganda texts.*
- *For 0252/0253 the original lyre design was used again, but in maroon colour; 0254/0255 exists as a blank-label test pressing only.*

Lale Andersen mit Ufatanzorchester. Leitung: Wilhelm Greiss (*sic*, ledgers)

Wilhelm Greihs *leader*; unidentified personnel and instrumentation, probably including *strings 1*; Lale Andersen *vocals*.

Berlin; 13 November 1943 (09:00–12:00)

10149 – GD9	When The Scented Lilac Blooms Again (Wenn der weisse Flieder wieder blüht) (Franz Doelle; engl. Text: Stewart)	1 NP voc LA	Lyra unissued ?
10150 – GD9	If You Were The Only Girl In The World (engl. Titel) (Derrickson & Brown)	1 NP voc LA	unissued ?

- *In the recording ledgers these sides are rubber stamped '11. Mai 1944'.*
- *Entry in the recording ledgers: 'Wachsverbrauch: 8 Stück 25cm.' [Wax consumption...]*
- *When The Scented Lilac Blooms Again' is a re-make of the September/October 1943 recording of this title.*
- *The English lyrics of the popular Franz Doelle melody are by Norman Baillie-Stewart.*

These were in all probability the last sides recorded in Berlin for propaganda purposes, and may never have been issued.

At a time, when the so-called '*Kuckucksruf*' (cuckoo call[†]) was almost continuously alerting German radio audiences on medium-wave to Allied air raids, the Lutz Templin orchestra at the Reichssender in Stuttgart were playing jazz for foreign listeners on shortwave. Although no shellac recordings were made, the RRG cut a few selections on flexible 30cm (12") Decelith acetates. Careless handling and storage has led to many of these priceless originals being destroyed or lost.

Brocksi-Quintett

Nino Impallomeni *trumpet*; Jean Robert *tenor-sax/clarinet 1*; Martin Fey *piano*; Max Gursch *guitar*; Otto Tittmann *bass*; Fritz Brocksieper *drums*; Jos Breyre, Fritz Brocksieper *arrangements*.

Stuttgart, Reichssender; 17 April 1944

—	Swinging Tom-Tom (Fritz Brocksieper) [incomplete take]		RRG b/c acetate
—	Swinging Tom-Tom (Fritz Brocksieper) [alternate take, late start]		b/c acetate
—	Kosende Hände (Lovely Hands) (Walter Leschetitzky) [false start]	1	b/c acetate
—	Kosende Hände (Lovely Hands) (Walter Leschetitzky) [false start]	1	b/c acetate
—	Crazy Rhythm (—)		b/c acetate
—	Shoe Shine Boy (—)	1	b/c acetate

• *Personnel and instrumentation identified by Fritz Brocksieper.*

Orchester Lutz Templin

Lutz Templin *leader*; probably Nino Impallomeni, Alfredo Marzaroli *trumpets*; Jos Breyre, Robby Zillner *trombones*; Mario Balbo, Bob van Venetië *tenor-saxes/clarinets*, Jean Robert *tenor-sax/baritone-sax/clarinet*, Renato Carneval *alto-sax/clarinet*; Primo Angeli *piano*; Max Gursch *guitar*; Otto Tittmann *bass*; Fritz Brocksieper *drums* Lutz Templin, Jos Breyre, Fritz Brocksieper *arrangements*.

Stuttgart, Reichssender; 24 August 1944

—	Theme: Unter'n Linden (—)	arr LT	RRG b/c acetate
—	Piano Bridge (—)		b/c acetate
—	Die Trommel und ihr Rhythmus (—)	arr JB	b/c acetate
—	Happy Birthday To You (—)		b/c acetate

• *The Walter Kollo composition 'Unter'n Linden' was the signature tune of Charlie Schwedler's cabaret broadcast series.*
• *'Die Trommel und ihr Rhythmus' was composed by Fritz Brocksieper and 24 August was his birthday. During rehearsal the band breaks into 'Happy Birthday To You'. Trombonist Robby*

---

† When Allied bombers had been sighted over the Reich, a melodious two-tone signal would break into the music on the radio, which would then continue while the signal was repeated a few minutes later. At the third call, the music would cut out and a announcer would inform listeners that enemy formations had entered grid so-and-so on the map and were on such-and-such a course. This enabled listeners to follow the approach of the bombers from square to square.

[session continued]

Zillner can be heard saying: 'Der Fritz hat sich aber angestrengt', and saxophonist Mario Balbo comments: 'Die Sendung muß wiederholt werden' (This broadcast has got to be remade); Fritz Brocksieper admits: '1:0 für euch!' (OK, you won!). The carefree atmosphere of this session seems to belie the fact that all this happened during a live broadcast towards the end of the war. But, as Brocksieper recalled the situation, the inevitable happened: Allied planes attacked Stuttgart, the band stopped broadcasting and the party was continued in the bomb shelter ...

BBC monitors recorded some further snippets of German propaganda broadcasts:

(Anon.)

Orchestra of unidentified personnel and instrumentation.

probably Berlin; 7 May 1944

Theme 'Calling Invasion Forces' radio b/c

(Anon.)

Male *vocal*, male *choir*, unidentified *piano accompanyist.*

probably Berlin; 7 May 1944

There Was A Young Man voc 'Calling Invasion Forces' radio b/c

(Anon.)

Male *vocal*, accompanied by unidentified personnel and instrumentation.

probably Berlin; 7 May 1944

I Want To Be Happy voc 'Calling Invasion Forces' radio b/c

• *These broadcasts were monitored in Britain. Their exact origin is uncertain, but the sound of the band seems to indicate a Dutch source.*

(Anon.)

Female, probably Evelyn Künneke *vocal,* accompanied by unidentified personnel and instrumentation.

probably Berlin; 17 May 1944

Atlantic Wall (incomplete) female voc 'Calling Invasion Forces' radio b/c

(William Joyce)

William Joyce *radio announcer.*

probably Berlin; 17 May 1944

Headline News 'Calling Invasion Forces' radio b/c

(Anon.)

Unidentified male, not Charlie Schwedler *vocal,* accompanied. by unidentified personnel and instrumentation.

probably Berlin; 17 May 1944

Atlantic Wall (incomplete) female intro/male voc 'Calling Invasion Forces' radio b/c

•*These broadcasts were monitored in Britain. Their exact origin is uncertain, but the presence of William Joyce seems to indicate a Berlin broadcast which may have been relayed by some station in occupied western Europe.*

A Gestapo file card dated 4 October 1944, contains the following data. (*Geheimes Staatsarchiv*, Potsdam; BDC):

File Card Nr.	541
	Templin, Lutz
	Stuttgart, Funkhaus
	Born: 16/6/01 in Düsseldorf
Musician:	Europasender: Kapelle Lutz Templin
Nachteilige Notierungen in politischer Hinsicht liegen nicht vor [rubber stamped]	
[Nothing of a negative political nature reported]	
Reichssicherheitshauptamt − IV Ma − Berlin, den 4. Okt. 1944	

In 1943, Deutsche Grammophon transferred the processing of all official orders from Hanover to the Esta factory in Prague, after most of the company's work-force had been called up. Later that year, on 28 September 1943, the company's pressing plant in Hanover was bombed and out of action for three months. In January 1944, all but seventy workers of the Hanover plant were drafted into the war industry. Finally, on 30 January 1944, the Berlin studios of Deutsche Grammophon were completely destroyed by bombs, and make-shift recording facilities were installed at the former Zentraltheater, Alte Jakobstrasse[†].

Dieter Tasch recalled the take-over of the Deutsche Grammophon company in Hanover by the Allies:

When on 10 April 1945, forces of the American 9th Army occupied Hanover, and the first jeeps burst through the blockaded gates and drove on to the yard along the 'Podbi' [Podbielski-Allee], a considerable part of the manufacturing capability was still in working order. Eighty-two of the presses were usable. The grinding-mill, boiler-house and the plating works were more or less intact. The matrix store had survived. [...]

Units of American soldiers searched the works a few times. [...] People who began clearing the rubble took the precaution of incinerating the stacks of labels for the propaganda records that were stored here. One bunch of Americans, undeterred at being told that it had all been gone over several times already, quit their search the moment they heard their own hits coming over the speakers. Someone on the Deutsche Grammophon staff had stashed away stacks of the Brunswick pressings which the Nazis had banned and was playing them to the Yanks, who began to jive to the music.

Brits in khaki combed the Deutsche Grammophon works down to the last cupboard several times. They may have been in uniform, but it was clear from the knowledge they revealed in their pointed questions that they were recording experts. [...] One of us Germans who was being questioned had had dealings with our British competitors pre-war and inquired after some of the HMV bosses − it soon came out that these Britons belonged to that firm.

One British unit which had stumbled on the propaganda records gave orders for the Germans to take pressings from all matrices of this kind of material. British military police kept a close watch on the proceeding. For months afterwards, a British officer was posted in the works with the job of playing and reporting on every one of these propaganda records.

---

† Tasch

44 A selection of record labels in use by various broadcasting organisations.

Appendix II: Propaganda Lyrics

The texts in this appendix have been transcribed directly from the recordings, so it should be noted that, if in many cases the original English lyrics do not appear, it is because (for whatever reason) they were not part of the recording. Where more than one verse of the original appeared on the recordings, these have been deleted and indicated by '*etc*'. The same applies to Charlie's prompts – shown here in capital letters – with which the singer usually switches to the propaganda parody text. Sometimes even these prompts are missing, and in such cases, where the original lyric has been included, the transition from that to the parody is indicated in the transcript by '*'.

The two final numbers in the Appendix date from 1944 and are examples of musical texts copied by British monitors from broadcasts by a German 'battle station' signing as 'Calling Invasion Forces', shortly before D-Day. These are not part of the recording sequences by 'Charlie and his Orchestra', although some of Charlie's material seems to have been included in the programmes.

British Soldier's Song

Onward conscript army
you have naught to fear,
Isaac Hore-Belisha
will lead you from the rear.
Clad by Monty Burton,
fed on Lyons pies,
fight for Yiddish conquest
while the Briton dies.
Onward conscript army,
marching on to war,
fight and die for Jewry,
as we did before.

You must die for Poland,
pay your debt of thanks
to your benefactors:
International banks!
To place again the Germans
beneath the Jewish star
onward towards the shambles:
'Goy cattle that you are'.
Poor? Persecuted Jewry
will finance war again.
Forward to the slaughter
for the Hebrews' gain.

Lyra I – 11 October 1939
Original title – Onward Christian Soldiers. M. Sir Arthur Sullivan (1892–1900) T. Rev. Sabine Baring-Gould (1834–1924)

This is the earliest German 'propaganda song' for British listeners, recorded five weeks after the outbreak of war. Clearly the work of a competent English rhymster, these satirical verses may have already been current in the late 1930s among British Fascists.

Isaac Hore-Belisha – Sir Leslie Hore-Belisha, 1893-1957. Secretary of State for War in the Chamberlain cabinet, 1937-40. As a Jew charged with modernization of the British Army, he encountered antagonism among certain serving officers, and was mocked by local Fascists as 'Horeb-Elisha'. Best remembered as the Minister of Transport, 1934-37, who first placed 'Belisha beacons' on pedestrian crossings. Created baron, 1954

Montague Burton, Lyons, Marks & Spencer – Landmark British businesses, founded by Jewish entrepreneurs.

Driven to the shambles
like a flock of sheep
by lying propaganda,
by their plans laid deep.
So for Israel Moses Sieff   *Israel Moses Sieff* – The founder of
you must fight and die   Marks & Spencer.
that Marks & Spencer's neon signs
may still light up our sky.
Forward, on to Poland
ten million men shall fall
that Judah's reign of terror
may hold us all in thrall.

Siegfried Line

Lyra XV – 29 November 1939
Original title – The Washing On
The Siegfried Line. M: Michael Carr
T: Jimmy Kennedy (1939)

We're going to hang out the washing on the Siegfried
    Line –
have you any dirty washing, mother dear?
We're going to hang out the washing on the Siegfried
    Line,
for washing day is here.

Whether the weather is wet or fine –
we'll just rub along without a care.
We're going to hang the washing on the Siegfried
    Line,
if the Siegfried Line's still there.

YOU HAVE HEARD THE FIRST VERSE OF AN AMUSING
SONG. BY KIND PERMISSION OF THE COMPOSER WE
NOW GIVE THE VERSES WHICH HE DESIRES TO
SUBSTITUTE IN THE SECOND EDITION; COPYRIGHT:
BELISHA AND REUTER!

This is the first of four German
recordings of a parody of the British
morale-boosting hit. A variant was
rushed out within days, entitled 'I'm
Sending You The Siegfried Line (To
Hang Your Washing On)', by the
British song-writing team of Ross
Parker, Hugh Charles and St. John
Cooper. Later, in 1942, Charlie
Schwedler also produced and
recorded his own version of this (*See*
page 320).

We'd like to get our jobs back at the home front line,
can [...?...] deliver on your pension, mother dear!
We like to get our jobs back at the home front line
from Jew boys in the rear.

Whether our children eat or starve -
Jews just love belong [..?..] without a care.
We'd like to get our jobs back ar the home front line,
for we think we've done our share!

It's alright, hanging washing on the Siegfried Line,   *The Siegfried Line* – Originally the
if you've got a change of clothing you can spare.   German name for one of the
It's alright, hanging washing on the Siegfried Line,   fortification lines behind Germany's
if the Yiddish clothes would wear.   western front in the First World
War. The name became familiar in
the Allied press when it eventually
crumbled in the Allies' 1918

Whether the weather is wet or fine,
they just seem like shoddy [..?..] Jewish ware.
We'll try to hang the washing on the Siegfried Line,
if our clothes last out till there.

We are not so sure that laundring is our proper job,
if it is, we like to wash our things at home!
We are not so sure that laundring is our proper job
so far away from home.

Whether Belisha pays his Bob or not,
or just lets us pay the lion's share.
We are not so sure that laundring is our proper job,
'cause the wages aren't quite fair!

Das muss den Ersten Seelord doch erschüttern

Wie gerne Churchill uns blockiert!
You see, it looks now black.
Das deutsche U-Boot torpediert
ihm seinen Frühstücksspeck.

Ihn selber trifft ein jeder Schuss,
die Welt zu rulen ist jetzt Schluss!
Die Nordsee ward ein deutsches Meer!
Nu kiekste hinterher!

Das muss den Ersten Seelord doch erschüttern!
Jeder Streich macht ihn weich, macht ihn kleen!
Wir werden ihn auch weiterhin zerknittern,
siehste woll, siehste woll, Chamberlain!

Am Meeresgrund three mighty ships,
wir kriegen ihn noch an den Schlips!
Das wird den Ersten Seelord doch erschüttern!
Siehste woll, siehste woll, Chamberlain!

Am Meeresgrund three mighty ships,
wir kriegen ihn noch an den Schlips!
Das wird den Ersten Seelord doch erschüttern!
Siehste woll, siehste woll, Chamberlain!

offensive. When Hitler announced the construction in 1938–39 of the 'Westwall', a modern line of defences on German soil, the British press promptly dubbed it the new 'Siegfried Line'.

Lyra XVII – 29 November 1939
Original title – Das kann doch einen Seeman nicht erschüttern
M: Michael Jary – T: Bruno Balz (1939)

Gerhard Fliess' macaronic parody of the top German hit of 1939 (popularized by the trio of Hans Brausewetter, Josef Sieber and Heinz Rühmann in the movie '*Paradies der Junggesellen*') was intended as a home-front booster in the early 'Phoney War' months. It is included here out of interest, as performed by the Schuricke Terzett in the Lyra series.

English summary – [Churchill, the First Lord of the Admiralty, is here confused with the First Sea Lord, a naval appointment.] Churchill likes blockading us, but now things look black. A German U-boat has sunk his bacon. No more Ruling the Waves! Now the North Sea's the 'German Ocean' again! That'll shake the First Sea Lord; Down he goes; As we told you, Chamberlain! At the bottom: Three Mighty Ships! We'll get him by the throat. That'll shake the First Sea Lord; As we told you, Chamberlain!

A German U-boat – This refers to the feat of submarine commander Günther Prien who took U-47 into the supposedly impregnable base at Scapa Flow on 14 October 1939, sank the battleship HMS Royal Oak and got away safely.

Nice People

Lyra XXVI – autumn 1940
Original title – Nice People
M: Angelo Musolino – T: Henry Jerome (1938)

Nice people, with nice manners –
but got no money at all!
They've got such nice habits –
they tease rabbits,
but got no money at all!
Their father keeps their mother,
their mother keeps their brother,
and when they're running short of cash
they borrow from each other...
Nice people, with nice manners –
but got no money at all!

ENGLISH YOUTH IS STRONG AND HEALTHY, AND THEY WILL GIVE THE GERMANS A REAL FIGHT. ESPECIALLY THE UPPER CLASSES HAVE PRODUCED YOUNG FINE OFFICERS AND MEN – SAYS CHURCHILL. WELL, HERE IS THE VERSION THAT FITS PERFECTLY TO WHAT THE YOUNG FINE SONS OF ENGLAND REALLY ARE.

The intended audience for this skit on the 'decadent' British upper class is more likely to have been the USA than the UK. Replacing Chamberlain as prime minister at the beginning of the Blitzkrieg in 1940, Churchill became the primary propaganda target. He was caricatured as an inveterate German-hater – a whisky-guzzling, cigar-chomping, overbearing and philistine war-monger – not far from the British left-wing view of him in the 1930s.

Nice people, with no manners –
thinking only of money, that's all!
They've got such funny habits –
they don't like rabbits,
they're a sick and tired generation, that's all!
Their fathers sail big shippies,
their mothers buy diamond clippies,
and when they're running short of cash
they are doing their confidence trickies ...
Nice people, with dusty manners –
they've got no sense of duty at all!

A sick and tired generation – Anthony Eden, Duff Cooper and others in Churchill's circle were habitually depicted as decadent, rich and snobbish hangers-on in stuffy, out of date outfits and top hats.

Nice people, with Eton education –
but their brains? Just their top hats, that's all!
They've got such funny habits –
they're afraid of rabbits,
they think the world is just their turban, that's all.
Their fathers give them money,
their mothers think they're a honey,
and when they're running short of cash
they are doing something funny ...
They think they're nice people,
with very nice manners –
but those high-head guys are no use at all!

Thanks For The Memory

Thanks for the memory
of rainy afternoons,
swinging Harlem tunes,
and motor trips,
and burning lips,
and burning toast and prunes –
How lovely it was!

Thanks for the memory
of candlelight and wine,
castles on the Rhine,
your cosy chair,
and parties where
we sang 'Sweet Adeline' –
How lovely it was!

Many's the time that we feasted,
and many's the time that we fasted.
Oh well, it was swell, while it lasted.
We did have fun –
no harm was done.

And thanks for the memory
of sunburn on the shore,
nights in Singapore –
You might have been a haddock,
but you never were a bore!
So, thank you so much!

AND NOW I'LL DEDICATE THIS TO ENGLAND:

Thanks for the memory
that is in every German's mind
when you broke the ties
that bind and dictated a peace
called Treaty of Versailles –
How rotten that was!

Thanks for the memory
of British aims divine,
French negroes on the Rhine,
your food blockade and misery
all over the German Reich –
What an injustice that was!

Many's the time that you feasted,
and many's the time that we fasted.
For you it was swell, while it lasted.

Lyra XXVII – autumn 1940
Original title – Thanks For The
Memory. M: Ralph Rainger – T: Leo
Robin (1937)

This 1937 Oscar-winning number
has been given a 'victimized little
Germany' slant that plays on the
British perception, fairly common in
the 1920s and 1930s, that Britain
had weakly allowed the (often
disliked) French to press extravagant
claims on defeated Germany. Now,
in 1940, France had got her
cumuppance, and the British had
better be reasonable.

the ties that bind – the German
perception of an affinity between the
two nations – two empires 'made for
each other' – was not reciprocated.

French negroes on the Rhine – a
racist gibe at French colonial
occupation troops after 1918.

your food blockade – the British
economic blockade of Germany,
1914–18, remembered resentfully.

You did have fun –
but too much harm was done!

Well, thanks for the memory
that gives us strength to fight
for freedom and for right.
It might give you a headache, England,
that the Germans know how to fight –
and hurt you so much!

Stormy Weather

Don't know why
there's no sun up in the sky.
Stormy weather,
since my gal and I ain't together
keeps raining all the time.

etc.

HERE IS MR. CHURCHILL'S LATEST SONG:

Don't know why
I cannot blockade the sky.
Stormy weather,
since my ships and the German planes got together
I'm beaten every time.

Life is bare,
gloom and mis'ry everywhere.
Stormy weather –
just can't keep my poor ships together,
they're sinking all the time.
O, blimey, they're sinking all the time!

When I walked into Norway
the Germans came along and met me.
My hair has turned to grey
now that the French are against me.

All I do is call my Royal Navy for action
to attack French ships in their peaceful base.
Can't go on – even my truest friends are gone.
Nasty weather -
just can't keep my poor self together –
I'm beaten all the time,
I'm beaten all the time!

Lyra XXVIII – autumn 1940
Original title – Stormy Weather
M: Harold Arlen – T: Ted Koehler
(1933). Written for Cab Calloway, the
song became an Ethel Waters trademark, until adopted by Lena Horne.

my poor ships – Refers to shipping
losses inflicted by the Luftwaffe and
U-boats.

Norway – Early in May 1940, British
forces abandoned Namsos and
Andalsnes in central Norway to the
invading German forces, and a month
later, coinciding with the German
offensive in the west, gave up Narvik
in the far north.

the French are against me, etc. – The
Pétain government at Vichy broke off
relations with Britain following the
Royal Navy's disabling of the French
fleet in their base at Mers El-Kébir
(Oran) and elsewhere in the
Mediterranean on 3 July 1940.
Anti-British feeling in France was
fanned by the Germans when British
naval forces, with Free French partici-
pation, raided the port of Dakar in
French West Africa on 29 September.

It's A Long Way To Tipperary

It's a long way to Tipperary,
it's a long way to go.
It's a long way to Tipperary
to the sweetest girl I know.

Goodbye, Piccadilly,
farewell, Leicester Square!
It's a long, long way to Tipperary
but my heart's right there.

HERE IS THE NEW VERSION OF THAT FAMOUS WAR
SONG NOW VERY POPULAR AMONG THE ENGLISH
SOLIDERS:

Who reserved already cabins
to sail for Canada?
Who is ready to go?
Who are the heroes that risk their life
for a trip to Canada?
Churchill, Eden, Cooper, Halifax and Co.!

Goodbye, Piccadilly,
Farewell, Leicester Square!
English gold and English Peers
go over the ocean
and we soldiers got no fare.

It's impossible to beat the Germans
we found out, that's why they go!
Those wise guys
told us a lot of nonsense -
Churchill, Eden, Cooper, Halifax and Co.!
Goodbye, Piccadilly,
fare thee well, Leicester Square!
English gold and English politics
go over the ocean -
Brother, have you got a dime to spare?

Lyra XXIX – autumn 1940
Original title – It's A Long Way To
Tipperary. M: Jack Judge – T: Harry
Williams (1912)

to sail for Canada, etc. – Press stories
from America spoke freely of
privileged Britons crossing the
Atlantic before the Germans
invaded, and of plans for the royal
family and the government to take
refuge in Canada if they did.

Eden, Cooper – See note to 'Nice
People'.

Halifax – Charlie Schwedler
clumsily includes Lord Halifax
among the Churchill cronies, when
in fact he had been Chamberlain's
ally at the Foreign Office over
appeasement. Churchill replaced
him with Anthony Eden as foreign
secretary on 22 December 1940, and
despatched Halifax to Washington
as ambassador.

They All Laughed

They all laughed at Christopher Columbus
when he said the world was round.
They all laughed when Edison recorded sound.
They all laughed at Wilbur and his brother
when they said that man could fly.
They told Marconi
wireless was a phony –
it's the same old cry.

Lyra XXXII – autumn 1940
Original title – They All Laughed
M: George Gershwin – T: Ira
Gershwin (1937)

They laughed at me wanting you,
said I was reaching for the moon
But all you came true –
now they have to change their tune.
They all said we never could be happy,
they laughed at us, and how –
but ho-ho-ho, who's got the last laugh now?
Ha-ha-ha, who's got the last laugh now?
*

The odds were a hundred to one against Germany.
Certain people thought that the New Reich would
    never succeed.
But the war mongers in England
never really knew Germany.
That was very stupid indeed.
Far from the history we have learned
how many, many times the worm had turned.

They all laughed at Germany and its leader
when he said that Germany will rise.
They all laughed and wished the war at any price.
They all laughed at Göring's four year plan
and when he said that German boys can fight.
But they said, baloney, the Germans planes are phony –
It's the same old cry.

They laughed at Germany wanting colonies,
said, she was reaching for the moon!
Now it's a joke to deny German victory –
wise guys have to change their tunes.
They all said, the Germans would get their licking,
they laughed at them, and how!
Ho-ho-ho, who's got the last laugh now?
But ha-ha-ha, who's got the last laugh now?

Although a fairly straightforward boast-fest short, on subtlety, this number might have fed a sense of defeatism in the post-Dunkirk, pre-Blitz period among some British listeners who remembered what the papers had been saying in 1938–39.

Göring's four-year plan – The second four-year plan, aiming at economic self-sufficiency for Germany, was launched in 1936, with Göring in charge.

Germany wanting colonies – The claim for the return of Germany's pre-1918 colonies in Africa and the Pacific was a joker usually kept well up the propagandists' sleeve. Presumably it is mentioned at this time for extra effect on British listeners.

Sing, Baby, Sing

When trouble troubles you –
sing, baby, sing!
Do like the birdies do –
sing, baby, sing!

THE BRITISH MINISTER OF INFORMATION SAYS:

Englishmen, don't you talk so much about the war,
air-raids, and the bad things that you are going through!
Talk about the weather, golf, or football,
and sing, always, sing –
you will help the national defence!

Lyra XXXIII – autumn 1940
Original title – Sing, Baby, Sing
M: Lew Pollack – T: Jack Yellen
(1936)

Hitler knew that supremacy in the air was the precondition for a successful landing in Britain. He issued directive No. 16 for the build-up to 'Operation Sea Lion' on 16 July 1940, and on 31 July the date for crossing was provisionally set for 15 September. On 1 August, Hitler ordered the intensification of the air attacks (directive No. 17). British

HERE IS AN ENGLISHMAN'S REPLY:

When air-raids drive one crazy –
sing, sing, sing!
Let's all do boomps-a-daisy –
get hot, and swing!

The Germans roar over our shore –
we can't win this blasted war.
We are tired and hungry and we are not eating',
but Churchill wants us tweet-tweet-tweetin'.

THAT WISE GUY DUFFY COOPER SAYS:

A song a day might keep those German planes away.
Hard luck, Mister Cooper –
we don't want to sing!
Stop your talking and stop that war and then
we'll sing, oh baby, and how we'll sing!

sources date the Battle of Britain from 8 August; the Germans named 13 August Eagle Day ('Adlertag'), when some 1,500 German aircraft were launched against targets in Britain. However, Hitler deferred 'Sea Lion' several times, until he had to fall back on calling the preparations a 'deception' (17 September) or a way of 'applying political and military pressure' (12 October).

Mister Cooper – Duff Cooper, at this time in charge of the Ministry of Information.

When Day Is Done

When day is done and shadows fall, I dream of you.
When day is done, I think of all the joys we knew.
A yearning returning to hold you in my arms
won't go love, I know love, without you night has lost
   its charm.

etc.

LONDON'S PEOPLE IN THEIR SOLITUDE:

When day is done and shadows fall we dream of peace.
We can't go on believing in Churchill's victories –
we don't stand for this bluff any more,
the whole world laughs at him.
This hopeless war is Churchill's war.
It's not too late we'll get rid of him.

Day and night we have alarms,
big fires all over town –
London life has lost its charm.
These air raids get us down.

Churchill's politic [*sic*] kills civilians,
he's world's enemy number one.
We know that terrible things are still before us –
this charming war has just begun.

Lyra XXXIV – autumn 1940
Original title – When Day Is Done
M: Robert Katscher – T: Buddy
DeSylva (1926)

This Blitz-period lyric tempts British listeners to dump Churchill and negotiate for peace rather than pay the price of a long war of attrition.

You're Driving Me Crazy

Lyra XXXV – autumn 1940
Original title – You're Driving Me Crazy. Walter Donaldson (1930)

Yes, you, you're driving me crazy!
What did I do, what did I do?
My tears for you make ev'rything hazy,
clouding the skies of blue.
How true were the friends who were near me to cheer
   me –
believe me, they knew.
But you were the kind who would hurt me,
desert me when I needed you.
Yes, you, you are driving me crazy.
What did I do to you?

HERE IS WINSTON CHURCHILL'S LATEST TEAR JERKER:

An explicitly anti-Semitic lyric that also plays on an American isolationist prejudice that Churchill is trying to trap Roosevelt into coming to Britain's aid in the war.

Yes, the Germans are driving me crazy!
I thought I had brains,
but they shattered my planes.
They built up a front against me,
it's quite amazing,
clouding the skies with their planes.

The Jews are the friends who are near me to cheer me –
believe me, they do.
But Jews are the kind that now hurt me,
desert me, and laugh at me too.

Yes, the Germans are driving me crazy!
My last chance, I'll pray,
to get in this model, USA.
This new pact also is driving me crazy –
Germany, Italy, Japan –
it gives me a pain!

this new pact – Refers to the 'Tri-Partite Pact' (*Dreimächtepakt*) signed between Germany, Italy and Japan in Berlin on 27 September 1940, as an extension of the pre-war 'Anti-Comintern Pact' between them. The prime aim was to deter Roosevelt with the threat of a potential two-ocean war in both the Pacific and the Atlantic.

I'm losing my nerves, I'm getting lazy –
A prisoner forced to remain in England to reign.
The Jews are the friends who are near me,
they still cheer me, believe me, they do.

But Jews are not the kind of heroes who would fight
   for me –
now they are leaving me too.
Yes, the Germans are driving me crazy.
By Jove, I pray: Come in, USA!

I Want To Be Happy

I want to be happy,
but I won't be happy
till I make you happy, too!

etc.

HERE IS MR. CHURCHILL'S APPEAL TO THE USA:

I want to be happy,
but I won't be happy
till I get the Americans in this war, too!

Life's not worth living –
USA, you must be birth giving,
I need money, ships, and help from you!

When skies are grey
you know that I say, they're blue.
Don't let bad news bother you!

I want to be happy,
but I won't be happy
till I get the United States in this muddle, too!
I want to be happy,
so will you please make me happy?
Come in my darling USA, I love you so!

Just give me all your money –
don't think it's rather funny,
England always pays her debts as you know!

Now that skies are grey,
I seem to remember you:
Aren't you the people that fought once for me, too?

You see, if England is in a bad way
her memory clears up straight away,
she remembers that great country, America –
its the lastest thing to do!

Lyra XXXXII – autumn 1940
Original title – I Want To Be Happy
M: Vincent Youmans – T: Irving
Caesar (1925). From the musical
'No, No, Nanette', revived by Anna
Neagle in the 1940 movie version.

The propaganda theme here for
American listeners is the same as in
'You're Driving Me Crazy', only
more so.

Just give me all your money –
Churchill's letter to President
Roosevelt of 8 December 1940 had
pleaded for American support in
Britain's perilous financial situation.

Hold Me

(*Charley*) NOW CHARLIE – YOU SING IT:

Hold me, honey won't you hold me,
hold me, never let me go.
Take me, honey won't you take me –
never to forsake me 'cause I love you so!

Lyra XXXXIII – autumn 1940
Original title – Hold Me
M: Ira Schuster – T: Jack Little,
David Oppenheim (1932)
Revamped version of one written by
Art Hickman and Ben Black for 'The
Ziegfeld Follies of 1920'.

etc.

Thrill me, let your kisses thrill me,
just like you alone can do.
Hold me tenderly, and enfold –
never try to hold me from you!

(*Evelyn*) Now Charlie – you sing it!

Hold me, honey won't you hold me,
hold me, never let me go.
Take me, honey won't you take me –
never to forsake me 'cause I love you so!

Thrill me, let your kisses thrill me,
just like you alone can do.
Hold me tenderly, and enfold me –
never try to hold me from you!

After numerous English propaganda tunes sent
to the USA, here is Englnad's latest tune to
the Americans:

Help me, Yankee, won't you help me,
oh, help me with an awful lot.
Aid me, with your money aid me,
you're the only one could save me –
a German put me on the spot!

Oh, thrill me, let your dollars thrill me,
without your dough, nothing I can do.
Help me, send more ships and planes to me –
after the war, I might be able to give everything back
  to you!

The propaganda version targets the
same American isolationist nerve as
the two preceding numbers.

You Can't Stop Me From Dreaming

You can stop me from kissing you,
you can stop me from cuddling, too;
you can treat me mean, honey, that's all right.
But I'll get even with you to-night,
'cause you can't stop me from dreaming!

etc.

I'll dedicate this to England:

Germany is beating you,
you deny it, but it's true.
You tell the world that you're all right,

Lyra XXXXIV – autumn 1940
Original title – You Can't Stop Me
From Dreaming. Dave Franklin,
Cliff Friend (1937). Chick Bullock
and Dick Robertson popularized the
rather sweet original. Frances Hunt,
with the Teddy Wilson orchestra,
recorded an interesting swing
version.

Like the propaganda version of
'They All Laughed', a straightforward 'in-yer-face' lyric for British
listeners, but also attuned to
American isolationist ears.

but the German blockade is holding you tight
and all your ships are sinking!
You can't stop the Germans, you're in their hands,
you'll have to listen to their commands.
Keep on denying German victories, that's all right,
the Germans get even with you and fight.
They're wide awake and they are not dreaming!

Your idea divine
to march to the Rhine
didn't come true –
How you must be feeling blue!
You can't stop Germany from beating you,
Germany is the boss now and you are through.
You double crossed many countries, all right,
but Europe gets even with you and fights.
Mister Churchill and your politicians are dreaming!

With A Smile And A Song

With a smile and a song
life is just like a bright sunny day –
your cares fade away
and your heart is young.

etc.

HERE IS THE LATEST BRITISH PROPAGANDA SONG,
SUNG BY DUFF COOPER:

Where's your smile? There's nothing wrong!
Life is just like a bright sunny day –
we haven't got a care
in the world and the outlook is grand.

Oh no, there's nothing wrong!
Every town will be built up again,
we're progressing every day,
and our army is strong.

There's no use in grumbling
when the bombs come down tumbling.
Don't say, you can't go on,
after rain there'll always be sunshine!

Just keep quiet and fight through,
everything I will promise to you –
just keep going along.
Don't show the world there is something wrong!

Lyra XXXXV – autumn 1940
Original title – With a Smile And A Song. M: Frank Churchill – T: Larry Morey (1937). From the 1937 Disney animated movie 'Snow White and the Seven Dwarfs'.

There's nothing wrong! – A touch of irony for British listeners – rare, but all the more effective.

Indian Love Call

When I'm calling you, will you answer, too?
That means, I offer my love to you to be your own.
If you refuse me, I will be blue
and waiting all alone.

etc.

HERE IS ENGLAND'S LOVE CALL TO AMERICA:

When I'm calling you, who, who, who — who, who, who
will you answer, too? Who, who, who — who, who?
That means, I offer my colonies just as a loan.
If you refuse, I will be through, just fighting all alone!

I hear the sound of German guns on my shore,
they don't seem to respect my splendid isolation any
    more!
I sacrifice my whole Empire, just to flirt with you.
Send planes and second-hand ships to me —
and my naval bases belong to you.

K & M 0101 — late 1940
Original title — Indian Love Call
M: Rudolf Friml — T: Otto Harbach,
Oscar Hammerstein II (1924)
Introduced in the 1924 operetta
'Rose Marie' and popularized by the
Paul Whiteman orchestra

*I offer my colonies just as a loan. ...
Send planes and second-hand ships to
me* — an early reference to
Churchill's deal with Roosevelt in
September 1940, under which the
US supplied Britain with fifty
obsolete destroyers in exchange for
99-year leases on eight British bases
on the American side of the Atlantic.

The Sheik Of Araby

I'm the Sheik Of Araby,
your love belongs to me.
At night, when you're asleep
into your tent I creep.
The stars that shine above
will light a way to love.
You'll rule this land with me —
the Sheik of Araby!

HERE IS MR. CHURCHILL'S LATEST SONG:

I'm afraid of Germany,
her planes are beating me.
At night, when I should sleep,
into the Anderson I must creep.
Although I'm England's leading man,
I'm led to the cellar by ten.
A leader in the cellar each night —
that's the only damned way I can fight!

Made in Germany —
that trademark is beating me.
Everything this people do
is successful and really comes through.
Although I lie and I shout,

K & M 0102 — late 1940
Original title — The Sheik Of Araby
M: Ted Snyder — T: Harry B. Smith,
Frances Wheeler (1921). Inspired by
the 1921 silent movie 'The Sheik',
starring Rudolph Valentino.

A refreshingly satirical cameo of
Churchill after dark.

into the Anderson ... — The Anderson
shelter — a simple bomb shelter
composed of arched corrugated-steel
units that was supplied by the
government and could be put
together by anyone in the back
garden and banked up with earth —
commemorates Sir John Anderson,
secretary of state for home defence
and minister of national security,
September 1939 — October 1940.

Made in Germany, that trademark ...
— a light touch, for once, as most
people would have associated 'Made
in Germany' with a quality
industrial product.

I don't know what it's all about.
My charming war is a tragedy –
I'm at the mercy of Germany!

I'm Putting All My Eggs In One Basket

I'm putting all my eggs in one basket,
I'm betting everything I've got on you.
I'm giving all my love to one baby,
Lord help me, if my baby don't come through.

I've got a great big amount
saved up in my love account,
honey, and I've decided –
love divided
in two won't do!
So, I'm putting all my eggs in one basket,
I'm betting everything I've got on you.

HERE IS MR. CHURCHILL'S LATEST SONG TO THE
AMERICANS:

I'm putting all my eggs in one basket,
I'm betting everything I've got on you.
I'm giving my British Empire to you, Yankee,
Lord help me, if my victory won't come through.

I've spent a great big amount,
gone is my lovely bank account,
Yankee, I've decided –
your dollars must be divided
in two or I'm through!
So, I'm putting all my eggs in one basket,
I'm betting everything I've got on you.

K & M 0103 – late 1940
Original title – I'm Putting All My
Eggs In One Basket. Irving Berlin
(1936). Introduced by Fred Astaire
and Ginger Rogers in the movie
musical 'Follow The Fleet'.

The aim is to sow equal degrees of
suspicion in the minds of both
British and US listeners.

The King's Horses

The King's horses, the King's men
marched down the street and then marched back again.
The King's horses and the King's men
they're in colour, they're in gold,
all dolled up, it's a joy to behold.

etc.
*

The King's horses and the King's men
marched down to France and marched back again.
The King's horses and the King's men
they were out to march to the Rhine
and hang out their washing on the Siegfried Line.

K & M 0104 – late 1940
Original title – The King's Horses
(And The King's Men). M: Noël Gay
– T: Harry Graham (1930)

A belated sneer at the 'Dunkirk
spirit'.

The King's horses and the King's men
they couldn't do a thing to beat the foe,
you might think so, but, oh dear, no –
all the men are feeling low
'cause they couldn't put some pep into Churchill's show.
It's their duty now and then,
make a glorious retreat and be decorated again,
the King's horses and the King's men.

St. Louis Blues

A NEGRO FROM THE LONDON DOCKS SINGS THE BLACK-OUT BLUES:

I hate to see the evenin' sun go down,
hate to see the evenin' sun go down,
'cause the German, he done bombed this town.

Feelin' tomorrow, like I feel today,
feelin' tomorrow, like I feel today,
I'll pack my trunk, make my getwaway.

That Churchill badman with his wars and things
pulls folks 'round by his apron strings.
Wasn't for Churchill and his bloody war,
I wouldn't feel, yeah, so doggone sore.

Got the black-out blues, yeah, blue as I can be –
that man got a heart like a rock cast in the sea.
He just won't let folks live as they want to be –
doggone it.

K & M 0105 – *c.* late 1940
Original title – St. Louis Blues
William Christopher Handy (1914)

An unusual example of the
propagandist putting a human face
on a racist stereotype.

like I feel today – From 7 September
1940, the Luftwaffe bombed London
on sixty-five consecutive nights. The
heaviest Blitz experienced so far was
carried out on 15 September.

Slumming On Park Avenue

Let's go slumming, take me slumming,
let's go slumming on Park Avenue.
Let us hide behind a pair of fancy glasses
and make faces when a member of the classes passes.

etc.

HERE IS THE LATEST SONG OF THE BRITISH AIRMEN:

Let's go bombing, oh, let's go bombing,
just like good old British airmen do.
Let us bomb the Frenchmen, who were once our allies!
England's fight for liberty,
we make them realize from the skies.

Let's go shelling, where they're dwelling,
shelling Nanette, Fifi and Loulou.

K & M 0106 – *c.* late 1940
Original title – Slumming On Park
Avenue. Irving Berlin (1937)
From the 20th Century-Fox movie
'On the Avenue', starring Alice Faye,
Dick Powell and The Ritz Brothers.

Let us bomb the Frenchmen – another
reference to the attack on the French
fleet at Mers El-Kébir on 3 July 1940
(see also 'Stormy Weather'). The
sneering tone might have only
irritated British listeners during the
Blitz months, but the target audience
was probably in America, anyway.

Let us go to it, let's do it,
let's sink their food ships, too.
Let's go bombing, it's becoming quite the thing to do!

Tea For Two

Picture you upon my knee:
Just tea for two, and two for tea,
just me for you, and you for me — alone.
Nobody near us to see us or to hear us;
no friends or relations.
On weekend vacations,
we won't have it known
that we own a telephone,
dear!

etc.
*

We're mighty strong in Germany,
which causes England's jealousy.
She doesn't like our unity,
she wants to rule the seas — alone.
No one should like us,
everyone should fight us.
No friends or relations,
no weekend vacations.
She won't have it known
that we even own
a dime for a glass of beer.

England's humanity, it's a fake!
The world's soon awake, that will be our break,
our birthday cake — whoopee!
Come on, have fun in Germany,
we will raise a world's family.
Let's all live in harmony,
oh can't you see how happy we would be?

K & M 0109 — *c.* mid 1941
Original title — Tea For Two
M: Vincent Youmans — T: Irving
Caesar (1924). Introduced by Louise
Groody and John Barker in the
musical 'No, No, Nanette'.

The 1940 recordings by Bing Crosby
and Connie Boswell may have
tempted the Nazi propagandists to
take this song into their repertoire.
The tone is confident and relatively
unthreatening.

England's humanity, it's a fake! —
This line points to the target
audience being American.

I'll Never Say 'Never Again' Again

I'll never say 'never again' again,
'cause here I am in love again,
head over heels in love again — with you!

etc.

HERE IS A NEW VERSION SENT TO US BY AN
DISILLUSIONED ENGLISHMAN:

We'll never say 'never again' again,

K & M 0110 — mid 1941
Original title — I'll Never Say 'Never
Again' Again. Harry Woods (1935)

Harry Allen's jazz version of April
1935 was followed later that year by
Chick Bullock's New York recording,
and by Connie Boswell's with the
Ambrose orchestra in London.

The 'disillusioned Englishman' of
mid-1941 is presumed to have been
shaken by a sequence of bad news:
the German occupation of
Yugoslavia and Greece (including

'cause here we are at war again,
up to our necks in war again with you.

We'll never say 'never fight wars' again,
'cause here we are at war again,
it's just the thing that Churchill made us do!

We thought to war we'd said 'goodbye',
'cause war ain't fun, and that's no lie.
We like to live, and we hate to die,
but it's all up now, and that, too, is no lie!

We'll never say, 'never again' again,
'cause here we are at war again,
up to our necks in war again –
and we can't pull through!

the airborne invasion of Crete,
20–28 May), and the loss of Tobruk
to the Afrika-Korps.

We thought to war we'd said 'good-bye' – an appeal to pacifist
sentiment.

Auf Wiedersehn, My Dear

Come, let us stroll down lovers' lane
once more to sing love's old refrain.
Soon we must say Auf Wiedersehn,
Auf Wiederseh'n, my dear.
Here in your arms I can't remain,
so, let me kiss you once again,
soon we must say: Auf Wiederseh'n,
auf Wiederseh'n, my dear.

etc.

AND HERE IS THE BRITISH FAREWELL TO GREECE:

Come let us view our countryside
where once the English did reside.
How soon they said: Auf Wiederseh'n,
Auf Wiederseh'n, dear Greece.
Here on your shores we can't remain
to be defeated once again,
so we must say: Auf Wiederseh'n,
Auf Wiederseh'n, dear Greece.

We'll put our ships to sea,
under cover of night time,
and to the islands flee –
we won't be staying there a long time.
Soon times will change again
and we'll be glad to meet again,
and so: Goodbye, Auf Wiederseh'n,
Auf Wiederseh'n, dear Greece.

K & M 0113 – mid-1941
Original title – Auf Wiederseh'n, My
Dear. Milton Ager, Al Goodheart,
Al Hoffman, Ed Nelson (1932)

By the end of April 1941 the British
and Commonwealth forces – with
Greek units – had been evacuated
from mainland Greece. The events
in south-east Europe leading up to
this had been set in motion by
Mussolini's ill-advised invasion of
Greece from Albania in October
1940. With the capture of Crete by
German paratroopers in May 1941,
Hitler's control over the European
continent seemed complete. A
dangerous complacency is apparent
in the cheap sneering tone of this
and the following lyric ('Alone'), for
the successful German campaigns in
Yugoslavia and Greece had fatefully
forced the invasion of the Soviet
Union to be delayed by at least a
month. The price which the
Wehrmacht had to pay was failing
to capture Moscow before the
freezing winter of 1941–42 set in.

Alone

Alone, alone, with a sky of romance above.
Alone, alone, on a night that was meant for love.
There must be someone waiting, who feels the way I do!
Whoever you are, are you, are you alone?

etc.

THIS SONG WAS SUNG DURING GERMAN AIR-RAIDS
OVER GREECE:

Alone, alone, with the sky black with planes in flight.
Alone, alone for the sake of the Jews we fight!
Why listen to old Churchill who never held a gun.
He'd rather sit back — or run, or run!
Alone, alone, we are left but he does not care.
Alone, alone with our heads caught within his snare.
We should have known much better, so now we
    cannot moan —
Alone, alone, with a sky black with planes — alone ...!

K & M 0114 — *c.* mid 1941
Original title — Alone
M: Nacio Herb Brown — T: Arthur
Freed (1935). Introduced by Kitty
Carlisle and Allan Jones in the Marx
Brothers' 1935 movie 'A Night at the
Opera'.

old Churchill, who never held a gun —
a gibe almost as coarse, and as
misjudged, as the refrain from the
popular British soldiers' ditty, '*and
Goebbels has no balls at all!*' But
then, who expected the Man in the
Street to really know anything about
his leaders?

Dinah

Dinah — is there anyone finer
in the State of Carolina?
If there is one and you know her:
just show her to me! ...
Ev'ry night, why do I shake with fright?
Because my Dinah might
change her mind about me.
Dinah — if she wandered to China,
I would hop an ocean liner,
just to be with Dinah Lee.
*
Weiner — do you know when he's the whiner?
Do you know a bigger whiner?
If you do and you know him,
phone up and say:
Weiner, what he says is quite amazing!
Oh, he loves to go on hazing
all the folks in USA.

Ev'ry night, why does he shake with fright?
Because some dynamite
might sink his hull in a day.
Weiner — he might wander to China,
even hop an ocean liner,
just to get to the USA!

K & M 0115 — mid 1941
Original title — Dinah. M: Harry
Akst — T: Samuel M. Lewis, Joe
Young (1925). 'Sweet Mama
Stringbean', Ethel Waters,
introduced this number at the New
Plantation Club, NYC.

wander to China — On 29 December
1940, Roosevelt asked Congress to
recognize that the United States
were effectively the 'arsenal of world
democracy'. On 11 March 1941, he
signed the 'Lend-Lease Bill' by
which the president was authorized
to deliver weapons and equipment to
all states whose defence might be in
the interest of the United States.

Weiner — the topical news story that
provided this reference has not been
identified.

Daisy

Daisy, Daisy, give me your answer, do!
I'm half crazy all for the love of you.
We won't have a stylish marriage,
I can't afford a carriage,
but you'll look sweet
upon the seat
of a bicycle built for two.

HERE IS CHURCHILL'S LATEST APPEAL TO ROOSEVELT:

Frankie, Frankie, the Germans are driving me nuts!
From Narvik down to Egypt they took all my landing
    spots.
They've done such a lot of bombing,
the docks are completely done in.
Now, I'm afraid
it will be too late,
for heaven's sake, hurry up!

Frankie, Frankie, give me your answer, do!
I'm half crazy waiting for news from you.
Britannia won't have a carriage
for the Anglo-American marriage,
if you don't send
on the Lease-and-Lend
a shipload of dollars, too!

K & M 0116 – mid-1941
Original title – Daisy (A Bicycle
Built For Two)/Daisy Bell
Harry Dacre (1892). Popularized in
the London music halls by Kate
Lawrence.

the Anglo-American marriage –
While aiming to undermine the
confidence of British listeners, the
lyric also plays on American
isolationist suspicion that Churchill
is tricking Roosevelt into
involvement in the war in Europe.

I'm Playing With Fire

I'm playing with fire –
I'm gonna get burned.
I know it, but what can I do?
I know my heart must be content
to go where it is sent,
although I may be singed when I'm through –
But what can I do?

etc.

HERE IS WHAT THE EAST THINKS OF THE PRESENT
SITUATION:

England is playing with fire –
she's gonna get burned!
She knows it, but what does she do?
She says, her people must be content
that for Churchill's sins they may repent.
When they're through,
there'll be plenty of praying to do!

K & M 0117 – mid 1941
Original title – I'm Playing With
Fire. Irving Berlin (1933)

Although the Italians had scored
some initial successes in 1940 with
their occupation of British
Somaliland (August) and of Sidi
Barani in Egypt (September), the
British regained the initiative in
Egypt by December and early in
1941 in Ethiopia and Somalia. This
lyric probably dates from *after* the
intervention of the Afrika Korps
under Rommel had wrested the
initiative into German hands from
March 1941 onwards (*'Egypt is
troubling her, too!'*).

what the East thinks – in other
words, the lyric tries to give a lead to
public opinion in the Middle East
and India.

England is playing with fire —
she's already been burnt,
and Egypt is troubling her, too!
Sure, she's loosing her pride
with her eyes open wide.
England is playing with fire —
she knows it! — Does America too?

Goody Goody

K & M 0118 — mid 1941
Original title — Goody-Goody
M: Matty Malneck — T: Johnny
Mercer (1935). Benny Goodman
recorded a swing version in January
1936, with vocals by Helen Ward.

So you met someone who set you back on your heels —
goody, goody!
So you met someone and now you know how it feels —
goody, goody!
So you gave him your heart too,
just as I gave mine to you;
and he broke it into little pieces —
now, how do you do?

So you lie awake just singing the blues all night —
goody, goody!
So you think that love's a barrel of dynamite —
hooray and hallelujah!
You had it coming to ya,
goody, goody for him,
goody, goody for me;
and I hope you're satisfied, you rascal you!
*
Who is that guy who set you back on your heels?
Winnie Churchill!
Who never fought in France and doesn't know how it
    feels?
Winnie Churchill!
Not a word he said came true,
he is always teasing you.
He breaks the Empire into little pieces -
what are you going to do?

*who never fought in France ... You
declared this war* — both are clumsy
errors which would ring false even
at the time.

Who lies awake, just dreaming of revenge all night?
Winnie Churchill!
He would like to put the whole world on a barrel of
    dynamite.
Hooray and hallelujah!
Winnie — You had it coming to ya!
You declared this war
and you will be licked like never before!
Now I hope you're satisfied, you rascal you!

Trying to reach listeners who might
be disillusioned with Churchill's
management of the war.

Who'll Buy My Bublitchky

HERE'S LADY WINTERBOTHAM'S SONG TO HER
HUSBAND:

I love the Bolshevikis, the lovely Bolshevikis —
I'm telling you, Ducky, they're very nice.
I'm going Bolsheviki, let's all go Bolsheviki,
they're lovely people, Ducky, take my advice.

Mayfair goes Bolsheviki, the King goes Bolsheviki —
don't be a fool, Ducky, why don't you try?
I'll make you a Bolsheviki, an English Bolsheviki,
a gentleman Bolsheviki, with an Eton tie!

K & M 0134 — autumn 1941
Original title — Who'll Buy My
Bublitchky? (The Pretzel Vendor
Song) Lester O'Keefe, Gregory Stone
(1938)

The tune is based on traditional
Yiddish material. Among the few bands
that ever recorded the number are the
Ziggy Elman and Benny Goodman
orchestras with swing versions.

On the day of the German invasion
of the Soviet Union, 22 June 1941,
Churchill pledged Britain's support
for this unexpected new ally.

I've Got A Pocketful Of Dreams

I'm no millionaire,
but I'm not the type to care,
'cause I've got a pocketful of dreams.

It's my universe,
even with an empty purse,
'cause I've got a pocketful of dreams.

etc.

LISTEN TO FRANKLIN ROOSEVELT:

I will win this war,
even from American shore,
'cause I've got a pocketful of schemes!

I claim the universe
to fatten out my purse,
'cause I've got a pocketful of dreams!

Gonna save the world of Wall Street,
gonna fight for Russia, too.
I'm fightin' for democracy,
I'm fightin' for the Jew.

Lucky, lucky me —
I can live in luxury,
'cause I've got a pocketful of schemes!

K & M 0135 — autumn 1941
Original title — I've Got A Pocketful
Of Dreams. M: James V. Monaco —
T: Johnny Burke (1938)

This number, targeting American
isolationists with FDR-phobia, is the
first one to put words into the mouth
of the president.

gonna fight for Russia, too —
American arms and war-materials
deliveries to the USSR started on 2
August 1941.

Change Partners

The English pray in ev'ry church for Stalin and his gang,
although they've murdered people again and again.
That's the English idea of Christianity!
How can they be friends so close
and show decent people their face?
The world knows what has taken place -
England is a traitor to Christianity!

She allied with murders [sic] for the sake of getting to
    the Rhine.
how they would love to hang their dirty washing'
on the Siegfried Line!
England, what has become of you?
With this actor you will meet
Franklin Roosevelt and Stalin Joe –
and even the devil won't prevent your defeat!

K & M 0138 – autumn 1941
Original title – Change Partners
Irving Berlin (1938). Introduced by
Fred Astaire and Ginger Rogers in
the RKO movie 'Carefree'.

A curious mix of hypocritical piety
with gloomy threats.

*you will meet Franklin Roosevelt and
Stalin Joe* – the USA was not at war
with Germany and Italy until after
Pearl Harbor (7 December 1941).
However, at the time of this
recording, the singer is already
assuming that Roosevelt's meeting
at sea with Churchill in August (the
'Atlantic Charter' signing) marks
him as an enemy.

Alexander's Ragtime Band

Come on and hear, come on and hear
the latest news from Soviet land.
Come on and hear, come on and hear
Stalin, Roosevelt, and Churchill go hand in hand.
They've recreated members of the Comintern,
the Internationale, and now they've gotta learn.
Red flags are flying all over London town –
poor London town!

Comrade Winnie, comrade Frankie, is it really true
that you've been made commissars of the awful GPU?
It won't be long
and King George will have hammer and sickle in his
    crown –
Yeah man!
Come on and hear, come on and hear
the latest news from Soviet land.

It won't be long
and King George will have hammer and sickle in his
    crown –
Yeah man!
Come on and hear, come on and hear
the latest news from Soviet land.

K & M 0139 – 12 January 1942
Original title – Alexander's Ragtime
Band. Irving Berlin (1911)

It's only five weeks since Pearl
Harbor, and in the recording studio
the singer belts out the line '*Stalin,
Roosevelt and Churchill go hand in
hand*', making it sound as if this –
for Hitler – fatal coalition could be
shown as some kind of plus for
German propaganda. We have here
an example of how an ill-considered
attempt at political irony can
misfire.

*They've recreated members of the
Comintern* – the Communist
International (Comintern) was not
actually dissolved by Stalin until 22
May 1943.

Lilla Marleen [sic]

Listen to the bugle, hear its silv'ry call,
carried by the night air, telling one and all:
Now is the time to meet your pal,
to meet your gal, to meet your pal,
as once I met Marlene,
as once I met Marlene.

Underneath the lantern by the barrack gate,
there I met Marlene, every night at eight.
That was a time in early spring
when birds all sing, then love was king
of my heart and Marlene's,
of my heart and Marlene's.

Waiting for the drum beats' tingling retreat,
walking in the shadows, where all lovers meet.
Yes, those were days of long ago.
I love her so, I couldn't know
that time would part – Marlene,
that time would part – Marlene.

Then I heard the bugle calling me away;
by the gate I kissed her, kissed her tears away.
And by the flickering lantern's light
I held her tight – 't was our last night,
my last night with Marlene,
my last night with Marlene.

Still I hear the bugle, hear its silv'ry call,
carried by the night air, telling one and all:
Now is the time to meet your pal,
to meet your gal, to meet your pal,
as once I met Marlene,
as once I met Marlene.

K & M 0140 – 12 January 1942
Original title – Lili Marleen (Lied eines jungen Wachtposten)
M: Norbert Schultze – T: Hans Leip (1939) English version for the Reichsrundfunk by Norman Baillie-Stewart.

Eduard Dietze reported to Winkelnkemper in 1944[1]: The song 'Lili Marlen' comes up again and again in our programmes for the British and American forces, particularly in 'Jerry Calling'. *Colliers* magazine for September[2] this year carries a feature under the headline 'We're Saving Money for Hitler' in which it says: 'You will at last be able to hear Lili Marlene [sic]. For months, publishers have been eager to bring out Lili Marlene here, with American lyrics, but were not permitted to do so until the [Alien Property] Custodian's office determined if the song were copyrighted and, if so, who owned it. Thanks to our invasion of Italy, an Italian version of Marlene found its way to Washington, and on this sheet was the necessary information as to German as well as Italian copyright. If the public likes Lili Marlene as well as Yank and Hun soldiers do, the man named Schultze who wrote it might get quite a hunk of American money after the war'.

1. FA: '*Wirkungsbericht für den Monat September 1944*', dated 8 October 1944
2. In fact *Collier's*, 29 July 1944

The Man With The Big Cigar

Who is that man with the big cigar
whose greatest friend is the USSR?
He's known around from near and far
that actor man with the big cigar.

He puffs away every night and day
with a twinkle in his eye,
and all the while, behind that smile,
lurks many an untold lie!

K & M 0141 – 12 January 1942
Original title – The Man With The Big Cigar. Art Noël, Don Pelosi (1941)

The rhymster responsible for this version stands in a class apart from the majority of Charlie Schwedler's satires. This is surely by a native-born English speaker, and the name of Norman Baillie-Stewart suggests itself.

'*V*' *stands for vanquished* – On 19 July 1941, the BBC launched its famous 'V

Down Whitehall way you'll see his car,
he's here, he's there,
he's everywhere,
the friend of the USSR!

'V' stands for vanquished,
it's the slogan of his land,
and he'll fight until it's finished
and there's no one left to stand!

He'll keep the Red Flag flying,
though hammered black and blue,
for he's getting more than he bargained for,
that fat friend of the Jew!

So, keep your chins up one and all
and remember what I say:
If Britons were to Britons true,
they'd send that man away!

Who is that man with the big cigar?
He's here, he's there,
he's everywhere,
that man with the big cigar!

for Victory' campaign, directed by
'Colonel Britton', the *nom-de-guerre*
of Douglas Ritchie of the European
Service. The opening bars of
Beethoven's fifth symphony, representing the letter 'V' in morse code,
framed the 'Colonel's' broadcasts, and
'V'-*graffiti* began appearing all over
occupied Europe. Immediately, the
ProMi tried to hijack the symbol by
declaring it represented the German
word *Viktoria*, from the stirring old
Prussian march, '*Preussens Gloria*'.
Here, however, the 'V' message has
been inverted, and becomes 'vanquished ... the slogan of [Churchill's]
land' – confusing!

The German 'secret station', NBBS,
tried a more devious ploy, making out
they were supporting the
'P'-for-Peace campaign inside Britain
(of which no trace was found).
Undeterred, the NBBS advised its listeners: 'Most of you know the letter
'P' campaign. You have probably seen
this letter written in your locality.
The idea is very simple. It is to keep
peace in the public mind. War is
widely advertised and we think peace
should have publicity too.'

Let's Put Out The Lights

AN OLD ENGLISH PROVERB IS: 'EARLY TO BED AND
EARLY TO RISE MAKES A MAN HEALTHY, WEALTHY
AND WISE.' NOW, HERE IS WHAT THE AVERAGE
ENGLISHMAN THINKS OF THE PRESENT SYSTEM OF
GETTING HEALTHY, WEALTHY AND WISE:

No more whisky, if you're blue.
No more steak and onions, too!
What's to do about it?
Let's put out the lights and go to sleep!

No more money in the banks.
The Russians get our guns and tanks.
What's to do about it?
Let's put out the lights and go to sleep!
The food gets dearer every day
and the shops are closing.
Mister Gloom is on his way
and the Russians losing.

No more butter, eggs and cheese,
no more: Tea and coffee, please!

K & M 0146 – 12 January 1942
Original title – Let's Put Out The
Lights (And Go To Sleep)
Herman Hupfeld (1932)

The food gets dearer every day – By
the time of this recording, there had
been food rationing in Britain for
two years, with the allowance of
some food items measured by the
price. Meat rations in Germany were
cut to 400g a week on 2 June 1941,
and on 5 April 1942, to 300g. The
USA started food rationing on 29
March 1943, and at the end of May
1943, German meat rations shrank
to 250g a week.

and the Russians losing – Although
the advance had stalled in extreme
wintry conditions close to the
outskirts of Moscow, it was stabilized
late in December 1941, when Hitler

What's to do about it?
Let's put out the lights and go to sleep!

The food gets dearer every day
and the shops are closing.
Mister Gloom is on his way
and the Russians losing.

took over operational command in
person. A Soviet counter-attack on the
new lines was being fought off at the
very time this piece was being
recorded. However, the Wehrmacht's
thrusts on the southern front to the
Volga and the Caucasus were to
dominate the year ahead (1942). At
the end of the road lay Stalingrad.

Bei mir bist Du schön

HERE IS THE ANTHEM OF THE INTERNATIONAL
BROTHERHOOD OF BOLSHEVIKS:

Es ist alles futsch!
C'est tout à fait égal!
I don't give a damn! –
means: Nitchevo!
And this 'nitchevo',
in case you don't know,
is: Nil, nothing, naught,
or just an '0'.

We bear it on our banners
of the World Comintern,
such things as sickles and hammers –
tell the world, it must learn!
And so, nitchevo,
mankind is our foe!
We don't care a damn,
so – nitchevo!

Bei uns ist es scheen,
please let us explain:
We comrades of Cain
sont très très chic.
We fight for the left,
with murder and with theft.
To fight for the right
would not be right!

Our land is bella bella –
it will soon be the world,
because in London and in New York
the Red Flags unfurled.
We sing: Nitchevo,
so that you may know
that life in our world,
is nitchevo!

K & M 0147 – 12 January 1942
Original title – Bei mir bist du schön
(please let me explain). M: Sholom
Secunda – T: Jacob Jacobs, Saul
Chaplin (1937). Popularized by the
Andrews Sisters, and a Benny
Goodman standard

There is a strange irony in finding
this Yiddish-American hit being
played back by the German short-
wave station as a parody-nihilistic,
far-left anthem. The original
version, based on Yiddish folk
material from eastern Europe, must
have seemed to Goebbels the
epitome of 'Jewish-Nigger Jazz'
which he specifically banned in
Germany, only two months before
the pogroms of 10 November 1938.

the World Comintern – dissolved by
Stalin eighteen months later.

'nitchevò' – (Russian) it's nothing, 'I
don't give a damn'.

Bei uns ist es scheen – 'scheen'
rhymes in Yiddish style with
'explain', as in the original first line,
'bei mir bist Du schön'.

Makin Woopee [*sic*]

THE JEWS OF THE USA HAVE ASKED EDDIE CANTOR
TO WRITE A NEW VERSION OF HIS FAMOUS OLD-TIMER
'MAKIN' WHOOPEE'. IN ONE OF HIS LATEST
PROGRAMMES ON THE AIR HE SANG THE FOLLOWING
SONG:

Another war, another profit,
another Jewish business trick!
Another season,
another reason
for makin' whoopee!

A lot of dough, a lot of gold,
the British Empire is free and sold!
We're in the money,
thanks to Frankie
we're makin' whoopee!

Washington is our ghetto,
Roosevelt is our king,
democracy is our motto –
think, what a war can bring!

We throw our German names away,
we are the kikes of USA.
You are the goys, folks,
we are the boys, folks –
we're makin' whoopee!

K & M 0148 – 12 February 1942
Original title – Makin' Whoopee
M: Walter Donaldson – T: Gus Kahn
(1928). Introduced by Eddie Cantor
(Edward Israel Isskowitz) in the
1928 Broadway musical 'Whoopee',
after which it became his trademark.

Roosevelt is our king – classic anti-
Semitic conspiracy theory. Hitler
having declared war on the USA (11
December 1941), the propaganda
brakes were off. The ProMi
calculated that anti-Jewish themes
could be fruitfully employed in
dividing American public opinion.

we are the kikes – American racist
slang for Jews.

The Continental

Japanese action, dangerous rhythm –
It's so terrific in the Pacific!
The Japanese are doing very well –
They've taken Hong Kong and Manila;
their navy and air force is swell.
The talk of the world is the Pacific,
the Japanese are in the big news.
They fight aggression in the Pacific,
they fight Roosevelt and his Jews.
'My ships', whispers Franklin so helplessly,
'We're anything but strong!'

It's so terrific in the Pacific!
The Japanese have taken Singapore –
terrific, Pacific, terrific!
USA – Did you know that before:
The Japanese fight while you're plotting!

K & M 0149 – 12 February 1942
Original title – The Continental
M: Con Conrad – T: Herb Magidson

This upbeat celebration of the
Imperial Japanese combined-ops
blitzkrieg in the Far East gave the
German propagandists some welcome
relief from the depressing stagnation
on the German eastern front in the
winter of 1941–42. The rapid
German advance had come to a halt
50km before Moscow, besieged
Leningrad was holding out, Rostov
was not taken, and Murmansk could
not be reached. Reports of Japanese
successes had to fill the vacuum on
the German news.

Hong Kong and Manila ... Singapore –
surrendered 25 December 1941, 15
February 1942 and 26 December
1941 respectively. (Recording this

It's democratic, so democratic!
The Japanese act while you're wondering!
It's democratic, so democratic!
You know, before this land is through
that what Frankie prophesized would never come true.
You'll find, while you're talking,
the Japanese got a spirit in their heart and soul,
a certain spirit that you can't control,
'cause you do the British Continental all the time.
Japanese action, dangerous rhythm!

number on February 12, 1942,
Charlie seems to have slightly
jumped the gun in the case of
Manila.)

I'm Sending You The Siegfried Line

Mrs. Smith is telling all the neighbours here today:
'Young Bert has written home to say
no presents on the way!'
Everybody gathered 'round to hear the letter read
and they didn't half get excited for this is what it said:
'Dear Ma, I'm feeling rather done,
my washing on the Siegfried Line has done a bunk
     and gone.
Tell Pa that Hitler's had the fun –
he left behind the Siegfried Line by cooking my bit of
     fun.
I couldn't bring a little souvenir for Mary
'cause I met a German soldier who sent me back to
     Tipperary.
Love from your ever-loving son.
My washing on the Siegfried Line has done a bunk
and gone.'

K & M 0150 – 12 February 1942
Original title – I'm Sending You
The Siegfried Line (To Hang Your
Washing On). Ross Parker, Hugh
Charles, St. John Cooper (1939)

This is the rival version mentioned
in the annotation to the very slightly
earlier 'We're Going to Hang Out
The Washing On The Siegfried
Line' on page 294. On 2 November
1942, an anti-British version of the
above was recorded in Portuguese,
but may not have been issued.

So You Left [*sic*]

LADY SKINNER'S HUSBAND HAS JOINED THE
COMMUNISTS. SHE'S FURIOUS ABOUT IT. NOW LISTEN
TO HER, SWINGING HER APPEALS:

So you left me for the leader of the Soviets!
You don't like my social parties any more!
Though you broke my heart in two,
I'll be waiting here for you
till your Soviet days are over with and through.

Communism is now spreading over England
and we'll all be bloody Communists one day!
But my Comrades don't forget,
England is not beaten yet!
Why play traitor and why join the Soviets?

K & M 0152 – 12 February 1942
Original title – So You Left Me (For
The Leader Of A Swing Band)
Archie Gottler, Harry Kogen (1938)

Though you think you're mighty cute,
I think you're just a brute,
the Soviets got you dipsy-doodle-oo.
When you learn of all their faults,
you'll learn to do the English Waltz.
Come back to me and I'll waltz with you!

I am worried about the leader of the Soviets,
'cause they call him Killer Diller Swingeroo.
If that Killer Diller means
what I think it really means,
then I'm all prepared to come and rescue you!

Laugh, Clown, Laugh

FDR's FAMOUS SMILE INSPIRED AN AMERICAN TO
WRITE A SONG ABOUT IT. HERE IT IS, DEDICATED TO
FRANKLIN ROOSEVELT HIMSELF:

Even though you're only make-believing –
laugh, clown, laugh!
Even though something inside is grieving –
laugh, clown, laugh!
Don't let the Japanese make you sad and mellow,
just be a real Pulcinello fellow –
Yes, sir!

You're supposed to brighten up the war
and laugh, Frankie, laugh!
Paint a lot of smiles around your face
and laugh, Frankie, laugh!
Forget the New Deal, war and defeat –
hahahahahaha!
Be a Pagliaccio
and laugh, Frankie, laugh!

K & M 0153 – 12 February 1942
Original title – Laugh, Clown,
Laugh. M: Ted Fiorito – T. Samuel
M. Lewis, Joe Young

Berlin had not been let into the
Japanese government's war plans, so
the attack on Pearl Harbor came like
a bolt from the blue for the Nazi leadership. Guidelines for Germany's propaganda towards the United States
had to be laid down in a hurry and
were issued on 15 December 1941:
1).Do not attack the American people,
but only President Roosevelt, who is
responsible for the war. Roosevelt
pursues a policy of personal and
financial power. Roosevelt and the
Jews. Roosevelt deceives the
American people through the press
and radio. 2) Argue that the
American people have nothing to
gain in this war. 3) Rival groupings
in conflict within the United States to
be played off against one another.
4) The American people to be got to
realise they face an unbeatable
Europe consolidated in a New Order.

Finally, it was emphasized that, in
implementing these guidelines,
'Allowance must be made for
American listeners' lack of sophistica-
tion and their ignorance in respect of
European affairs.'

By, By, Blackbird [*sic*]

HERE IS MR. CHURCHILL'S LATEST SONG DEDICATED
TO GREAT BRITAIN:

I never cared for you before,
Hong Kong, Burma, Singapore –
bye, bye, Empire!

K & M 0154 – 12 February 1942
Original title – Bye, Bye, Blackbird
M: Ray Henderson – T: Mort Dixon
(1926)

Not a bad shot at undermining
confidence in Churchill's war
leadership at the start of the last
year of Axis advances in Russia,
Egypt and the Far East.

India I may loose, too,
then I only have the London Zoo —
bye, bye, Empire.
There's no one here who loves and understands me,
nothing but heaps of bad news they all hand me.
The Yankees are still out of sight,
I can't make out wrong from right —
Empire, bye, bye!

Blue Skies Are Around The Corner

Grey skies are around the corner,
peep 'round the corner and see,
just 'round the corner
there'll be those grey skies!
Grey skies — there's nothing bluer ...
Perhaps you'll feel sorry to see
thunder and lightning at sea
under those grey skies!

Troubles will come,
such troubles, you know,
don't you ever wonder any more!
Look at those grey skies,
they're not telling lies.
That's what Churchill's there for!
Grey skies are around the corner —
everything's gonna go wrong ...

Never a break in those dull grey skies!

K & M 0156 — second half of May 1942
Original title — Blue Skies Are
Around The Corner. Ross Parker,
Hugh Charles (1938).

From the Axis viewpoint at this
date, the war looked winnable:
Tobruk and Sebastopol had been
taken, the Afrika Korps had reached
el Alamein, convoys on their way
through Arctic waters were being
severely mauled before reaching
Russia, and the German advance
towards the Volga and the Caucasus
had begun.

That's what Churchill's there for —
his unlucky touch spells doom for
Britain.

Japanese Sandman

Watch the Japanese Sandman,
like a bolt from the blue.
He is no second-hand man —
he'll take no old days from you!

He will bring you some sorrow,
long before your are through,
and he'll give you tomorrow
what was coming to you.

Then you'll be a bit wiser,
in the dawn, when you wake.
He'll throw mud in your eyes, sir,
and the Empire he'll take!

K & M 0157 — second half of May 1942
Original title — The Japanese
Sandman. M: Richard A. Whiting —
T: Raymond B. Egan (1920)

See also '*Avalon*', page 323, where
the message is the same — the British
must say good-bye to India, along
with Malaya and the rest of the
Empire already occupied by the
Japanese. But on 4 June 1942, the
Battle of Midway was to mark the
beginning of the turn of the tide in
the Far East.

Watch the Japanese Sandman,
changing old days for new.
He is no second-hand man –
your mistakes you will rue!

I Found A Million Dollar Baby

The day that Churchill came to power
was just the most convenient hour.
He came as a million dollar baby
in the ten cent English war.

The war continued for an hour,
he lost some battles, three or four,
because this million dollar baby,
ran a ten cent English war!

He supported China
while Roosevelt made him eyes.
He kept backing China
until the Japs got wise.

Incidentally, if Churchill keeps himself in power
and carries on with his own war,
you'll pay a million dollar forfeit
with the Empire on the floor!

K & M 0158 – second half of May 1942
Original title – I Found A Million-
Dollar Baby (In A Five-And-Ten-
Cent Store). M: Harry Warren –
T: Billy Rose, Mort Dixon (1931)

backing China until the Japs got wise –
At the end of April 1942, the rapidly
advancing Japanese reached and cut
the Burma Road. To try to make up
for the loss of this lifeline to
Nationalist China, the British, with
US support, built up an air shuttle
between Assam and Chungking.

a million dollar forfeit – Britain will
be bankrupt, and the Empire up for
sale.

Avalon

I found my love in Avalon, beside the bay.
I left my heart in Avalon and sailed away.
I dream of her in Avalon from dusk till dawn,
and so I think, I travel on to Avalon.

Listen England! Listen Empire! Listen England!

You lost the fight at Singapore, beside the bay.
you lost your all at Singapore and sailed away!
Your dream of wealth and Singapore has led to war.
Goodbye to Hindustan's fair shore and Singapore!

K & M 0159 – second half of May 1942
Original title – Avalon. M: Vincent
Rose – T: Buddy DeSylva, Al Jolson
(1920)

Avalon, beside the bay – a harbour on
Santa Catalina island, south of Los
Angeles, echoing a mythical island
in the Arthurian legends, where it
merges with Glastonbury.

Hindustan – the Japanese reached
the Burma-India border in May
1942, and although the Congress
party called for civil disobedience in
the summer, the Japanese did not
succeed in turning the political crisis
in India to their military advantage.

But Where Are You

The days go by and Churchill's blue,
says: Here I am – but where are you?
The USA is fighting too,
and we are here – but where are you?

K & M 0160 – second half of May 1942
Original title – But Where are You?
Irving Berlin (1936)

in the Atlantic – in August 1941, while
the US was still neutral, Roosevelt
and Churchill met and proclaimed the
'Atlantic Charter'. The US navy

Have you forgotten the day that we met?
It was in the Atlantic – how could you forget?
The plans we planned have not yet come true!
Roosevelt, why aren't you here? Just where are you?

agreed to take over the defence of the
Denmark strait between Iceland and
Greenland, and to 'shadow' British
convoys in the North Atlantic.
why aren't you here? – apparently
unnoticed by Charlie, the first US
troops had landed in Northern Ireland
in January 1942, and in February 1942
the first units of US Army Air Force
bombers were stationed in the UK.

Blue Moon

ENGLAND HAS LEFT HER BOLSHEVIK ALLIES FIGHTING
ALONE. ALL SHE HAD TO OFFER WAS A CANTERBURY
PRAYER:

Red Star – I saw you fighting alone.
It touched the strings of my heart
without a sigh or a groan.

Red Star – you knew just what I was there for.
You heard me saying a prayer
for someone I really could care for.

And then there suddenly appears before me,
another one my arms could not hold.
I heard somebody whisper 'Singapore'
and when I looked – the tide of battle rolled.
Red Star – I regret that you're alone.
It's simply breaking my heart –
both of us can't hold our own!

K & M 0161 – second half of May 1942
Original title – Blue Moon
M: Richard Rogers – T: Lorenz Hart
(1934)

A BBC report of prayers offered for
the Soviet Union in Canterbury
Cathedral early in 1942 is the
starting point for this gloat over the
two allies' reverses.

Honey

I'm in love with you, honey.
Say you love me too, honey.
No one else will do, honey,
it seems funny, but it's true.

THIS IS SIR STAFFORD CRIPPS' SERENADE TO HIS
BROTHER STALIN:

I'm in love with you, Stalin.
Say you love me too, Stalin.
No one else would do, Stalin,
you're Bolshee, but I'm through!

Love you from the stars, Stalin.
But you've got a heart, Stalin.
Though you are a rotten Bolshee –
Stalin, I'm one, too!

K & M 0162 – second half of May 1942
Original title – Honey. M: Richard
A. Whiting – T: Seymor Simons,
Haven Gillespie (1928)

Sir Stafford Cripps – Cripps
(1889–1951) was sent by Churchill
as ambassador to Moscow, May 1940
until January 1942. He was a left-
wing Labour politician who had
advocated a united front with the
Communists in 1936. In April 1942
Cripps was in the news when he was
sent to India by the War Cabinet on
an unsuccessful mission to negotiate
with the Congress party leaders, in
anticipation of a Japanese invasion
and a possible rebellion against
British rule.

You Started Something

HELLO CHURCHILL! I THINK YOU STARTED
SOMETHING! NOW LISTEN TO CHARLIE, GIVING YOU
THE WORDS:

You started something, yes, you did,
and you thought it very easy
to declare a charming war
and beat the Nazis –
You fool!

You started something, yes, but now,
as your British Empire's shrinking
you just can't prevent
your precious ships from sinking –
You fool!

You believe in fairy-tales,
all your retreats
are victories.
You believe, your dream came true –
to rule, to rule.

You started something, yes, you did,
but we'll put you out of practice,
the Nazis, yes, the Nazis
and the Axis –
You fool!

K & M 0165 – 27 August 1942
Original title – You Started
Something. M: Ralph Rainger –
T: Leo Robin (1941)

we'll put you out of practice – the
buoyant, jeering tone of this and the
next number, '*Love Is All*', seems to
have been encouraged by the
atmosphere engendered by a series
of events during this period: the
débâcle of the Anglo-Canadian raid
on Dieppe some ten days previously
(19 August 1942) and by the
German occupation of the Maikop
oil-fields in the Caucasus on 8
August – not forgetting the
showpiece planting of the swastika
ensign on Mt. Elbruz (5630m) by
German Alpine troops on 21 August.

Love Is All

'Second front! Second front
is all I want, second front!'

Joe Stalin is yelling at Churchill:
'Second front! Second front!
Where or when? Second front!
Any old front, at any cost, hurry up!'

The British at Dieppe tried
a landing full of fight.
They returned with bleeding noses
and long faces – All right!

'Second front! Second front!
Where or when? Second front!'
Stalin cries, Churchill sighs:
'Second front!'

K & M 0166 – 27 August 1942
Original title – Love Is All. M: Pinky
Tomlin – T: Harry Tobias (1940)

The propaganda version of the lyric
spares British listeners no embarrassment in the aftermath of the
Dieppe raid (19 August 1942). As the
German Sixth Army approached
Stalingrad on the Volga, the Soviets
stepped up their public pressure on
the Allies to open the Second Front
in western Europe. All through 1942
Germany's foreign-language
propaganda harped on Anglo-
American unwillingness to take the
risk, and kept nourishing Soviet
suspicions. Meanwhile, during
August, Roosevelt and Churchill,
with their staffs, laboured to agree
on the details of the Allied landing
in French North Africa, finally
scheduled for 8 November 1942.

'Second Front! Second front!
Where or when? Second front!'
Stalin cries, Churchill sighs:
'Second front!'

The Waiter And The Porter And The Upstairs Maid

K & M 0169 – 27 August 1942
Original title – The Waiter and the
Porter and the Upstairs Maid
Johnny Mercer (1941)

The people in Great Britain
are getting Bolshevistic.
So one begins to get just a little afraid,
they are so Stafford Crippsey pals with old Stalin –
like the waiter and the porter and the second story maid.

Stafford Crippsey pals – *See* note for
'*Honey*', page 324.

Remember good old London with all the decent
    people,
those football matches, cricket, and bank holidays?
The King was ruling England then,
the King and his people –
not the waiter, and the porter, and the upstairs maid!
Now everybody's poisoned with that Soviet idea.
They clench their fists, and shouting
and Stalin they cheer.
The Yankees are teaching
them how to get hot, hot diggity-dog?

*that Soviet idea ... The Yankees are
teaching them* – a double swipe at
the political, social and cultural
impact on Britain of her two
overpowering allies.

If ever you're invited to some English party,
you're gonna watch some harlequinade.
They are completely crazy,
Americanized, and lazy –
the waiter and the porter and the upstairs maid!
The waiter and the porter and the upstairs maid!

You're The Top

K & M 0171 – 27 August 1942
Original title – You're The Top
Cole Porter (1934)

A SERENADE TO YOUR GIRLFRIEND – BY KIND
PERMISSION OF COLE PORTER:

You're the top –
you're a German flyer.
You're the top –
you're machine-gun fire,
you're a U-Boat chap
with a lot of pep.
You're grand –
you're a German Blitz,
the Paris Ritz,
an army van.

You're the Nile,
an attack by Rommel.
You're the mile
that I'd walk for a Camel.
I'm a Soviet Czech [check / cheque ?]
a total wreck –
a fluff!
But it's, baby: I'm the bottom – You're the top!

a Soviet...– the word is aurally indistinguishable.

You're the top –
you're Mahatma Gandhi.
You're the top –
you're Napoleon brandy,
you're a German raid
by Messerschmitts at night.
You're a Stuka noise,
Goering's voice,
you're Nazi might.

You're Swiss cheese,
you're a bottle of whisky,
you're strip-tease –
that is rather risqué.
I'm completely nuts,
like General Smuts –
a flop!
But it's, baby: I'm the bottom – You're the top!

General Smuts – Jan Smuts (1870–1950), prime minister of South Africa, whose advice Churchill sought on the appointment of a new commander-in-chief of the Eighth Army facing Rommel at El Alamein at the beginning of August 1942.

Smiling Through

Pack up your troubles in your old kit bag!
(*chimes*)
Some day the world will be at peace again!
So – smile, smile, smile!
Some day goodwill among us all will reign!
There's a proper smile!
Don't forget behind the clouds the sun waits
all the while!
So, some day the world will be at peace again!
So – smile, smile, smile!
Some day the world will be at peace again!
So – smile, smile, smile!

RRG 69896 – 1 October 1942
Original title – Smilin' Through
Arthur Penn (1919)

'Pack Up Your Troubles' was well known to Germans in a version that was less jaunty than the English original – with a melancholic refrain: *'Weit ist der Weg zurück ins Heimatland, so weit, so weit..'* British visitors to youth camps in Germany would find it ranked high as an English folk song, and were expected to perform it.

the world will be at peace again – these words were to come true, but history tells us that two major turning- points in the war were approaching: on 17 October 1942, the German Sixth Army began its final onslaught at Stalingrad before being encircled and crushed, and on 23 October the British Eighth Army began its offensive to drive Rommel back from El Alamein – and out of Africa.

Will Meet Again [*sic*]

We'll meet again! Don't know where, don't know when,
but I know we'll meet again some happy [?sunny] day.
Keep smiling through, just as you always do,
till the blue skies drive the dark clouds far away.

Keep smiling through, just as you always do,
till the blue skies drive the dark clouds far away.

RRG 69898 – 1 October 1942
Original title – We'll Meet Again
Ross Parker, Hugh Charles (1939)
For ever associated with Vera Lynn,
the 'Forces' Sweetheart'

Charlie sings Britain's own hymn of
wartime yearning – straight. Like
Norman Baillie-Stewart's English version of '*Lili Marleen*' (page 316),
there's no parody, no propaganda, no
political moral to distort his rendering
of '*We'll Meet Again*'.

A Song Of Old Hawaii

There's a graveyard of a dozen ships,
sunk beneath the harbour of Hawaii.
That's where Kimmel lost his admiral's skills,
sleeping in the harbour of Hawaii.
There was a silver moon,
a symphony of stars, a propeller tune,
and a hum of birds from Mars.
There were bombers roaring in the heaven,
heading for the harbour of Hawaii.

K & M 0173 – 6 October 1942
Original title – A Song Of Old Hawaii
Gordon Beecher, Johnny Noble (1938)

Kimmel – Admiral Husband E.
Kimmel, commander–in–chief (1
February 1941) of the US fleet in the
Pacific, based at Pearl Harbor, near
Honolulu. He was made the
scapegoat for the devastating
Japanese attack on 7 December 1941
and dismissed on 17 December.

a hum of birds from Mars – the
propaganda songsmith's unusually
poetic sound-image for the approaching Japanese bombers and fighters.

Bom [*sic*]

Boom! Why did my heart go boom?
Me and my heart go boom-di-di-boom,
'cause I found you.

Boom! When you are nearest, boom!
I could see love in bloom, di-di-boom,
all around you.

Was it at seven
or half past eleven,
or cruising about the Pacific?
I only know
that I can't let you go:
Your effect upon me is terrific!

Boom! When we're a bride and groom,
oh, won't my heart go boom, boom-di-di-boom,
'cause I love you.

K & M 0174 – 6 October 1942
Original title – Boom (Why Does
My Heart Go Boom?). Charles
Trenet, Ray Goetz (1938)

cruising about the Pacific – this
'modern Yankee sea shanty' is
clearly addressed to American
listeners, though the shipping losses
referred to are those in the Battle of
the Atlantic. By August 1942,
sinkings by U-boats exceeded
500,000 tons in the Atlantic. By the
autumn, U-boat packs were able to
strike on their own initiative when
they got the chance.

A MODERN YANKEE SEA SHANTY:

Boom! Why did my ship go boom?
Me and my ship go boom, boom-di-di-boom,
and founder.

Boom! No land is near it, boom!
U-Boats don't care about boom, boom-di-di-boom,
all around her.

Was it eleven
or seventy-seven,
or cruising about the Pacific?
I only know
that wherever I go,
their effect upon me is terrific!

Boom! When there're those U-Boats bloom out of the
    gloom,
and boom, boom-di-di-boom –
oh, I'm sinking!

Little Sir Echo (Hello)

Poor Mr. Churchill, how do you do?
Hallo, hallo, hallo, hallo!
Your famous convoys are not coming through!
Hallo, hallo, hallo, hallo, hallo, hallo, hallo, hallo!

German U-Boats are making you sore.
You're a nice little fellow,
but don't talk too much:
With speeches one can't win the war.

Poor Mr. Churchill, how do you do?
Hallo, hallo, hallo, hallo!
You're always licked, not a victory came through!
Hallo, hallo, hallo, hallo!

Dunkirk, Tobruk, Dieppe, Hong Kong, Singapore!
You're a nice little fellow,
but by now you should know
that you never can win this war!

Hallo lalalalala – Hallo lalalala

Hallo, hallo, hallo!

K & M 0175 – 6 October 1942
Original title – Little Sir Echo
Adele Girard, Joe Marsala (1939)

The jaunty, almost patronizing, tone of this fate-tempting number illustrates the *hubris* that lies in wait for a propagandist who begins to believe what he's trying to make the other side accept: only five weeks after this recording, an Anglo-American armada sailed undetected by the Axis to North Africa and put an invasion force ashore, the first step in taking the war back onto European soil – in Italy.

Sleepy Time Gal

K & M 0185 – 15 December 1942
Original text – Sleepy Time Gal
M: Richard A. Whiting, Ange
Lorenzo – T: Joseph R. Alden,
Raymond B. Egan (1925)

Sleepy Time Gal, you're turning night into day.
Sleepy Time Gal, you dance the evening away.
Before the silvery star drifted out of sight,
please give me one more kiss, then let us whisper:
    Good-night.

It's getting late dear, and your pillow is waiting,
Sleepy Time Gal, when you're dancing it through.
Sleepy Time Gal, I'll find a cottage for you.

You'll learn to cook and sew.
What's more, you'll love it, I know,
when you're a stay-at-home,
play-at-home,
eight-o'clock Sleepy Time Gal.

HERE IS AN APPEAL TO CHURCHILL FROM HIS OLD
FRIEND JOE STALIN:

Sleepy Time Pal, you're turning night into day.
Sleepy Time Pal, your Empire's fading away.
While you're at sleep, your ships fade out of sight;
you call it help, when the Arabs you fight.
It's getting late dear, and I think I'm beaten,
Sleepy time Pal, while you're talking, it's true
Sleepy Time Pal, I do the fighting for you.

But now I'm telling you:
We Soviets are worn and through,
we want a million planes, a million tanks,
a million guns –
Sleepy Time Pal!

you call it help, when the Arabs you fight – a rather stale jibe that refers back to the ousting of Rashid Ali al-Ghailani's régime in Iraq by British forces in May-June 1941 (actually, just before Hitler's invasion of Russia).

I think I'm beaten ... we Soviets are worn and through – but at the time of this recording, the attempt to relieve the German Sixth Army at Stalingrad was about to be abandoned by Hitler. Left to its fate it capitulated on 31 January 1943 – ten years and one day after Hitler's appointment as chancellor of Germany.

Whistle While You Work

K & M 0186 – 15 December 1942
Original title – Whistle While You Work. From the Disney full-length cartoon movie 'Snow White and the Seven Dwarfs'. M: Frank Churchill – T: Larry Morey (1937)

We sail the seven seas!
La-la-la-la-la-la-la –
We're here, we're there,
we're everywhere!
We go just where we please!

Our crew is very tough!
We're regular guys,
real sailor boys!
We like the sea when rough!

We've got you on the run!
Gross register ton,
you're sinking fast into the sea!
The waves are ruled by Germany!

We sail the seven seas!
La-la-la-la-la-la-la —
We're here, we're there,
we're everywhere!
We're like the busy bees!

We sink all ships at sight!
La-la-la-la-la-la-la —
The rougher the weather,
the tougher the better —
it aids us in our fight!

We are the submarines!
It's so romantic
in the Atlantic!
We're are always full of beans!

We're hunting convoys down
from twilight until dawn.
We are the modern wolves at sea!

The waves are ruled by Germany!
We sail the seven seas!
La-la-la-la-la-la-la —
We'll sink US and British ships
until the day of peace!

Gross register ton — this rather
foreign-sounding term punctuated
claims of Allied shipping losses in
Germany's English-language
broadcasts like a refrain throughout
the war. It is the equivalent of the
German term *Bruttoregistertonne*.

We sink all ships at sight! — a savage
boast, unlikely to endear the
Germans to British listeners, that
reflects the heavier line being taken
in propaganda as long as the naval
high command still believed in the
possibility of winning the Battle of
the Atlantic.

until the day of peace! — the
withdrawal of U-boats from the
south Atlantic, in the face of
cooperation there between Britain
and the still neutral US, had actually
been ordered twelve months before
this recording was made. By March
1944 the U-boats would be recalled
even from the North Atlantic, in
readiness for the defence of Europe
against the expected Allied invasion.

Picture Me Without You

Picture USA without a Jew —
Roosevelt without ballyhoo!
Picture Winnie Churchill without a licking!
Picture India without pig-sticking!
Picture Canterbury without a prayer!
Picture old New York without a mayor! —
Mix them together and what have you got?
Just the picture of the whole damn lot!

Picture Russia without lice and fleas!
Picture British officers without VC's!
Picture Halifax without a Bible!
Picture any war without a rifle!
Picture the BBC without a lie!
Picture Anthony Eden without that tie! —
Mix them together and what have you got?
Just a purée without a pot!

K & M 0189 — 15 December 1942
Original title — Picture Me Without
You. M: Jimmy McHugh — T: Ted
Koehler (1935)

New York without a mayor — Fiorello
LaGuardia (1882–1947), reformist
mayor for twelve years, elected 1933,
1937, 1941.

Halifax without a bible — Lord
Halifax (1881–1959), viceroy of
India (as Lord Irwin) 1925-31, foreign secretary 1938-40, British
ambassador to Washington 1940-46.
A prominent 'High Anglican' layman
of the Church of England — although
the 'Bible' tag suggests the author
mistook him for an 'Evangelical'.

Anthony Eden without that tie — continental Europeans and some
Americans were hypnotized by the
perfect knotting of the British foreign secretary's neckwear.

Who's Afraid Of The Big Bad Wolf?

Listen to the BBC, BBC, BBC!
Listen to the BBC!
Tra-la-la-la-la!
Who's preaching world democracy?
Democracy, democracy!
Who wants to make free people free?
Tra-la-la-la-la!

First they won the war in France,
then they said they had no chance
each time the German did advance!
How could they have a chance?
They told stories so divine:
Often marched across the Rhine,
Germans eat only rats and mice!
But in England all was fine –

Bye, bye, Churchill, BBC, BBC, BBC,

your tricks won't work with Italy!
Tra-la-la-la-la!
Why not give us different news?
Different news, different news!
Skip those Soviets, skip those Jews!
Tra-la-la-la-la!

K & M 0190 – 22 December 1942
Original title – Who's Afraid Of The
Big Bad Wolf? Ann Ronell, Frank
Churchill (1933)

In Axis-occupied countries people
secretly listened to the BBC, and in
spite of jamming and severe penal-
ties, the BBC even seems to have had
a sizeable audience within the Reich.
The Nazi leadership were increasingly concerned about this psychological invasion of their territory. The
BBC policy in wartime was to let the
facts speak for themselves – however
carefully presented in a confident picture of the Allied cause in general
and the British war effort in particular. One device was to play snatches
from recordings of speeches by Nazi
leaders, to prove them liars by their
own words. Faced with Germany's
initial military successes, British
broadcasters took the line that was
that ' the Germans might win every
battle but the last'. This number suggests that by the recording session of
22 December 1942, the satirical
inventiveness of the German propa-
ganda-lyricists was indeed flagging.

your tricks won't work with Italy – six
months later the Allies landed in
Sicily, and on 8 September 1943, the
Italians changed sides in the war.

The Lambeth Walk

When you tune in London way
ev'ry evening, ev'ry day,
you'll find some guy
talking the wishful talk. Oi!

Ev'ry little comment'ry
with its little subtlety
you'll hear them all
talking wishful talk. Oi!

Ev'rything's BBC'sy
hear what you darn well pleasy,
hear how the speakers lie there,
cry there, die there!

When you tune in London way
ev'ry evening, ev'ry day,
you'll find some guy
talking the wishful talk. Oi!

K & M 0192 – 22 December 1942
Original title – The Lambeth Walk
M: Noël Gay – T: Douglas Furber,
Arthur Rose (1938) From the
musical 'Me And My Girl'.

Berlin had previously broadcast several
parodies of this number in January and
February 1940. One version is
mentioned by Sington and Weidenfeld
(*see* Bibliography), from a 1941
broadcast of 'The Club of Notions'
presented by Mildred Gillars (*q.v.*),
with Charlie Schwedler featuring as
'Naughty-Naughty', an Englishman
'who was constantly, but of course
unsuccessfully, trying to invent a secret
weapon which would beat Germany.
The striking of Big Ben provided
'background atmosphere', and a chorus
of inane Britishers was made to sing, to
the tune of the 'Lambeth Walk':
  Listen in to Schenectady
  They are just like Daventry
  They lay it on thick
  Which gives us a kick! Oi –

Ev'rything's BBC'sy,
hear what you darn well pleasy,
hear how the speakers lie there,
cry there, die there!
When you tune in London way
ev'ry evening, ev'ry day,
you'll find some guy
talking the wishful talk. Oi!

Aurora

You waste million after million –
ohohohoh, oh Frankie –
Wasting billion after billion –
ohohohoh, oh Frankie!
How can you spend America's money?
Ohohohoh, oh Frankie!
The Yankees won't think it's so funny!

Ohohohoh, oh Frankie!
You're buying this, you're buying that
without the people's dough!
You steal an island here and there,
you're getting rather low!
You preach democracy,
a way of making money –
ohohohoh, Frankie!

If you want to beat the Axis –
ohohohoh, oh Frankie –
you will need a lot of practice!
Ohohohoh, oh Frankie!
MacArthur and Eisenhower –
ohohohoh, oh Frankie -
getting shower after shower!
Ohohohoh, oh Frankie!
You lose ships here,
you lose ships there,
those U-Boats make you sore!
Axis sailors just don't care,
they're sinking ships more and more!
Oh, no, my Chickadee,
you've usually oversee/overseas [?] –
Ohohohoh, oh Frankie!

K & M 0195 – 22 December 1942
Original title – Aurora
M: Mario Lago, Roberto Roberti –
T: Harold Adamson (1941)

This asssortment of routine gibes at
Roosevelt sits uneasily with the
actual course of the war at the time
of the recording.

MacArthur – Although forced to
abandon the Philippines to the
Japanese in March 1942, General
Douglas MacArthur was now based
in Australia as Allied C.-in-C. in the
south-west Pacific. By December
1942, the Japanese in Papua-New
Guinea were already on the
defensive, and the tide was about to
turn against them in the Pacific
generally.

Eisenhower – General Dwight D.
Eisenhower – the future American
president – was named commander-
in-chief of US troops in the
European theatre of operations on 15
June 1942, and later that year,
commander-in-chief of the Allied
forces that were landed in North
Africa on 8 November.

Three Little Fishies [*sic*]

K & M 0196 – 18 January 1943
Original title – Three Little Fishes
(Itty Bitty Poo) Saxie Dowell (1939)

Down in the Atlantic on a nasty afternoon
swam some Yankee shippies, in a great big convoy, too.
Mr. Knox said: Swim, swim, you're safe.
So they swam, and they swam, happy and brave.
Boob-boob-didem-dodem-whopee-hooray!
Boob-boob-didem-dodem, we're on our way,
Boob-boob-didem-dodem, with no delay.
The Yankees are coming, hip-hip-hooray!

'Whooee!', yelled a little ship: 'We're soon in Africa,
that's the place I always, always longed to go!'
'Yes', said a second ship: 'It's so marvellous to me.'
Another tiny ship said: 'We rule the seven seas!'
Suddenly, my God, there was a awful blow.
Everybody yelled: 'That must be U-Boats, though!'
Crash! Boom! It's a maze!
What a jam, and they swam all over the place!

All the little shippies had to go down.
German sailors had a swinging day and really went to
 town!
And the moral of this story: Don't believe in Mr. Knox!
Yankees, look out, look out for more shocks!
Boob-boob-didem-dodem-waden-choo.
Boob-boob-didem-dodem-waden-choo.
Boob-boob-didem-dodem-waden-choo.
Stay at home, little shippies, and then you'll be safe!

Mr. Knox – W. Frank Knox, although
a Republican journalist and politician,
was US secretary of the Navy from
July 1940 until his death in April
1944. He was responsible for the
modernization, expansion and supply
of the American fleet during the war
in the Pacific.

On The Sentimental Side

K & M 0197 – 18 January 1943
Original title – On The Sentimental
Side. M: James V. Monaco – T:
Johnny Burke (1938)

THE SONG OF THE US HOME FRONT:

If you wonder why we're fighting
even though we pray for peace:
It's because we have to do it
for the sake of Lend and Lease!

I suppose we should refuse to
if we had an ounce of pride,
but I guess we can't help fighting
on the Anglo-Jewish side!

Though we act gay,
call and cough and clap and yell –
that line just doesn't wear well,
it fools nobody!

We'll be glad when war is over
and the world is satisfied.
What's it matter who's the leader
on the Continental side!

What's it matter... — a hint here of the shift towards a pacifistic, we're-all-in-this-together, anti-war line that German propaganda adopted after the Allied invasion of Europe in 1944 — for example, the Radio Arnhem themes.

Why'd Ya Make Me Fall In Love

THIS IS WHAT A WELL-KNOWN BROADWAY VOCALIST IS ASKING HIS PRESIDENT NOW:

Why'd ya make me go to fight?
Why'd ya mention Yankee might?
Why'd ya make me go to fight for you
when I thought that war was blind?
Why'd ya make me change my mind?
Why'd ya make me go to fight for you?
Fine thing, Mister Smarty!
Fine thing, thought you had a party.
Why'd ya make me fall so hard?
Should have stayed in your own back yard!
Why'd ya make me go to fight for you?

HEY FRANK, WHY SHOULD I FIGHT FOR YOU?

K & M 0201 — 18 January 1943
Original title — Why'd Ya Make Me Fall In Love? Walter Donaldson (1938)

The message is addressed to American listeners who might be disappointed by US setbacks against the Afrika Korps in Tunisia, and the slow progress generally in the Mediterranean theatre. While this recording was being made, the Casablanca conference (Roosevelt and Churchill) was taking place, 14–26 January 1943.

I Double Dare You

LISTEN TO MADEMOISELLE LA FRANCE

I double dare you to come over here!
I double dare you to venture too near!
Take off your high hat and quit that ragging,
turn off the clap-trap and keep your hair on!
Can't you take a dare on?

I double dare you to venture a raid!
I double dare you to try and invade!
And if your loud propaganda means half what it says,
I double dare you to come over to me!
I, I double dare you!

K & M 0203 — 8 February 1943
Original title — I Double Dare You
M: Terry Shand — T: Jimmy Eaton (1937)

In March 1942 Henry Stimson, America's secretary for war, and General George Marshall, the American chief-of-staff, had presented a plan for a landing in northern France. In April presidential adviser Harry Hopkins discussed alternatives for a second front with Churchill. Later that month Roosevelt sent a note to Stalin, saying he was working on plans to relieve the pressure on the Soviet Union. A few weeks later, during Molotov's visit to Washington, the US raised Soviet hopes for a landing in 1942. In July the western Allies agreed instead on the strategically more prudent course of landing in North Africa, before the end of 1942.

to venture a raid! ... try and invade! — The opening of a second front in mainland France while the mass of the Wehrmacht was forced on the defensive in Russia haunted the Nazi leadership. What propaganda could not prevent, propaganda could perhaps delay, if it succeeded in sufficiently unnerving public opinion in the west. Encouraged by the outcome of the Dieppe raid (19 August 1942), Berlin's English-language broadcasts harped ever more insistently, from now until D-Day, on the theme of a bloodbath on the beaches that would be more terrible than the remembered casualties in Flanders, 1914–18.

Please Take A Letter

COMMANDING OFFICER ROOSEVELT TO LIEUTENANT CHURCHILL:

K & M 0205 – 8 February 1943
Original title – Please Take A Letter, Miss Brown. M: Eddie Burnett, George N. Terry – Paul Cunningham (1940)

Please take a letter, Winnie!
It's strictly confidential
and may prove consequential,
with someone so essential to my schemes
that I refrain to greet his name.

Please take a letter, Winnie!
Just address it: My lieutenant!
Then say: I have discovered
a debt he hasn't covered,
so it seems!

Just like a guy who lost the game!
A sly lieutenant, you should know,
what war has done to me.
And I think it's very à propos
you offer sympathy!

Why are you crying, Winnie?
If it's true you are expressing,
then, Winston, I'm confessing:
It's you, I was oppressing from the start!
So, please, take this letter to heart!

Winnie – Whether it was deliberate irony, or textual confusion, which sketched this cruel picture of a subservient Winston Churchill taking down the president's letter to a 'sly lieutenant' which turns out to carry a rebuke meant for himself, we do not now know. The singer's introductory words, however, strangely echo the prime minister's own self-attached label, 'former naval person', in his historic correspondence with the president, which at the time could hardly have been known about in the corridors of the ProMi.

There's Honey On The Moon To-Night

K & M 0207 – 8 February 1943
Original title – There's Honey On The Moon Tonight. M: J. Fred Coots – T: Haven Gillespie, Mack David (1938)

There's money on the Franklin fight –
it's a cinch that he'll lose it!
Where there's trouble he woos it,
begs and prays for it, too!

There's money on the Franklin fight —
all the odds are against him!
All begin to lambast him
and make him feel blue!

It'll take more than a boat,
a motorcar, or a plane
to win back part of the slightest part
of what that man has lost on the game!

There's money on the Franklin fight —
it's a cinch that he lose it!
Where there's trouble he woos it,
begs and prays for it, too!

the Franklin fight – the propaganda ministry is here clutching at a straw: calculating that Roosevelt might fail to win the fight for a fourth term in November 1944, in which case America's will to fight the Axis in Europe might flag. The German radio (like some American isolationists) called Roosevelt power-crazy, and reminded voters that they had a choice. The Republican challenger (Thomas E. Dewey, governor of New York state) polled 22 million votes to the president's 25.6 million, but lost by 99 votes to the latter's 432 in the electoral college.

Miss Annabelle Lee

Who's wonderful? Who's marvellous? —
Little Miss BBC!
Who's kissable? Who's lovable? —
Little Miss BBC!

Ain't she a pretty baby?
Oh, what would I give
just reportin' her and supportin' her!
Don't forget that she's exclusive!

Who's dignified? Who's glorified? —
Little Miss BBC!
What makes 'em fall? She has it all!
Listen and you'll see!

So you ain't telling me a thing, boy,
so I'm telling you:
Who's wonderful? Who's marvellous? —
Little Miss BBC!

K & M 0208 – 15 February 1943
Original title – Miss Annabelle Lee
M: Lew Pollack, Harry Richman –
T: Sidney Clare (1927)

Intended for US listeners, this is a folksy swipe at the BBC as a snooty British icon of Allied war propaganda.

South Of The Border

A SWAN SONG SUNG BY A WELL-KNOWN ENGLISH CAPITALIST:

Western Atlantic, America way,
that's where I'll come to live
if you will give me sanctuary.
Away from the war zone
my thoughts ever stray —
Western Atlantic, America way!

K & M 0209 – 15 February 1943
Original title – South Of The Border
(Down Mexico Way) M: Michael
Carr – T: Jimmy Kennedy (1939)

War is a fine thing if you have money,
just for the ten per cent
on what you lent
to your country.
But now it's fiasco!
And U-Boats – they play
in the Atlantic, America way!
Churchill cries when he thinks of torpedoes:
All his scheming is wholly in vain,
ships capsized as they're hit by torpedoes –
and with convoys it's the same!

Across the Atlantic, I'm going one day,
when things have got too hot
and England's lot is misery!
My conscience will tell me that I mustn't stay
but cross the ocean, America way!
Ayeyi-yi-yi, Ayeyi-yi-yi, Ayeyi-yi-yi –

U-boats – they play in the Atlantic, America way! – U-boat sinkings of shipping nearly doubled in February 1943, and in the first twenty days of March the Admiralty recorded that 'the Germans never came so near to disrupting communication between the New World and the Old'.

Hold Tight

Red Front, Red Front, Red Front, Red Front –
pooradiyackzicky!
Want some Communism, bugs and lice,
they're very nice!

Red Front, Red Front, Red Front, Red Front –
pooradiyackzicky!
Want some Communism, bloodshed and force,
and then, of course:
I like murder, purges, too!

I like my tasty smell of blood!
When I come home from work at night
I give my favourite yell:
Hell! –

Red Front, Red Front, Red Front, Red Front –
pooradiyackzicky!
Want some Communism, murder and vice,
it's very nice!

K & M 0212 – 15 February 1943
Original title – Hold Tight – Hold Tight (Want Some Seafood, Mama) Leonard Kent, Jerry Brandow, Edward Robinson, Leonard Ware, Willie Spottswood (1938)

Already – with the destruction of the German Sixth Army at Stalingrad in January – the initiative in the east has passed to the Russians, and the only message that Europe will hear from Berlin from now on is 'Panic Stations!' as Soviet military power grinds westward. This number appeals directly to entrenched anti-communism in the United States.

I Can't Give You Anything But Love

LISTEN TO FRANKLIN D. ROOSEVELT

I can't go on building ships and ships,
Winnie!
Oh those U-Boats – better find some tips,
Winnie!

K & M 0223 – 5 April 1943
Original title – I Can't Give You Anything But Love. M: Jimmy McHugh – T: Dorothy Fields (1928)

Wait a while,
walk a mile,
you're sure to find happiness,
and I guess,
you get the tankers that you long for.

Gee, I'd like to see you go to hell,
Winnie!
I wanna buy – what have you got to sell,
Winnie?
The Yanks are businessmen,
you know that well,
Winnie!
I can't go on building ships and ships.

I can't sent those Soviets tanks and tanks,
Winnie!
I get into troubles with my banks,
Winnie!
Dream a while,
scheme a while,
you're sure to find happiness,
and I guess,
every thing will be in clover.

Gee, I'd like to see your Empire mine,
Winnie!
Soon we'll sing together Auld Lang Syne,
Winnie!
Never mind your troubles,
throw'em away,
Winnie!
United Nations – hip-hip-hip-hooray!

United Nations – this is Charlie's first acknowledgement of the existence of Roosevelt's brain child. The organization was originally identical to the twenty-six members of the western alliance, who on 1 January 1942 signed the 'Declaration of the United Nations' in which their war aims against Germany, Italy and Japan were set out.

Daisy

LISTEN TO FRANKLIN D. ROOSEVELT:

Stalin, Stalin, give me an answer, do!
I'm half crazy, having bad news from you.
You promised a great offensive,
it turned out to be defensive!
Don't run away,
make your soldiers stay!
For heaven's sake, hold that line!

Stalin, Stalin, your alliance drives me mad!
Communism sweeps my country.
I'm in an awful state:
My Jewish friends go crazy,

K & M 0227 – mid-1943
Original title – Daisy (A Bicycle Built For Two)/Daisy Bell. Harry Dacre (1892) *See also* page 312.

This is Charlie's second go at a propaganda version of the evergreen 'Bicycle Built for Two'.

hold that line! – reflecting the official line on the situation on the Orel-Kursk front in July 1943, where the German offensive had run out of steam, and the Russians were counter-attacking heavily. It was expected that the Germans would regain the initiative, as often before – but the reverse was to be the case. By October, the entire German line from the Dvina to the Sea of Azov had been thrust back 200–300km to the west.

my workmen getting lazy –
the USA, far away,
is just like a Soviet state!

I'm in an awful state – implying the
strength of subversive left-wing
influence in the USA.

Submarines

Why are the ships always sinking
and blinking at sea?
What makes the British start thinking
of their cup of tea?
It's now the season to reason.
Explain what it means:
German submarines! –

What makes the sailors go crazy
wherever they crew?
What makes the market go down?
What frightens the Jew?
What takes the kick of the chicken,
the pork from the beans?
German submarines! –

Listen, listen!
Can't you hear the sound they're never missin'?
Torpedoes, torpedoes,
hitting at day, and hitting at night!

Who sinks the trawler, the tanker,
the ship full of meat?
Who sinks destroyers and cruisers,
the pride of the fleet?
It's now the season to reason.
Explain what it means:
German submarines!

K & M 0229 – mid-1943
Original title – Elmer's Tune
Elmer Albrecht, Sammy Gallopp,
Dick Jurgens (1941). Charlie and his
Orchestra had already recorded this
number under its original name as
an instrumental swing version.

This quite well-crafted propaganda
text would have been *written* in the
early months of 1943, when the
menace of German submarines to
Allied convoys and warships reached
its peak, but by the time it got to the
recording studio, Germany had
withdrawn from, and effectively
lost, the Battle of the Atlantic.

United Nations Air Men

Let's go bombing!
Oh, let's go bombing.
like United Nations air men do –
in the night when peaceful citizens are sleeping –
far from any AA-gunfire we are keeping!

Let's go shelling
where they're dwelling!
Let's shell Churchill's women, children, too!
Let us go to it! Let's do it! Let's bomb neutrals, too!
Let's go bombing! It's becoming quite the thing to do!

K & M 0230 – mid-1943
Original title – Slumming On Park
Avenue. Irving Berlin (1937)

This is Charlie's second propaganda
version to the music of 'Slumming on
Park Avenue' (page ••• [37]) and also
the last of his recordings known to
have survived in the K & M series.
After the Allies had called for the
unconditional surrender of Germany,
Italy and Japan at the January 1943
Casablanca conference, Goebbels
extracted an ecstatic 'Yes' from his
frenzied audience in favour of 'total
war' at the Berlin Sportpalast rally on

Let's go shelling
where they're dwelling!
Let's shell Churchill's women, children, too!
Let us go to it! Let's do it! Let's bomb neutrals, too!
Let's go bombing! It's becoming quite the thing to do!

18 February 1943. On June 10 –
around the time of this recording –
the Allies began the combined round-
the-clock saturation bombing of
German cities, as also resolved at
Casablanca.

like United Nations airmen do – a sly
twist here: instead of linking the new
'United Nations' to grand plans for a
post-war peace-keeping organization
the label is attached to a bombing
offensive against civilians in the
target cities instead.

There Was A Young Man From Chicago

Radio broadcast monitored 7 May
1944. No original recording traced.

There was a young man from Chicago
who served as a war transport cargo.
He kept thinking why
he should hide now or die
when the mine placed them under embargo.
That was a beautiful rhyme!
Sing us another one, do!
'nother one do!

There was a young workman from Leeds
whose wage never covered his needs.
When they talked of invasion
for the hundredth occasion,
he said: 'That's just talk – We want deeds!'

(orchestra plays '*I Want To Be Happy*' without vocals)

– Listen I've got the sweetest girl in the world!
really, she got teeth like stars!
– Like stars, how's that?
– Ha, ha, they come out at night!

This snatch of a pre-D-Day
broadcast by 'Calling Invasion
Forces' was monitored in Britain.
The musical number had been
recorded by Charlie with a
propaganda lyric in the autumn of
1940.

Atlantic Wall

Radio broadcast monitored 17 May
1944. A female vocalist declaims
over an orchestral accompaniment.
No German recording traced.

To the cause and Germany:
We are looking forward to your landing days!
Germany is calling you: Everythin' will be perfect in
    every way!
You will all be welcomed at the Atlantic Wall!
Yet in bonny Stalags you like it the most!
When duty calls, when duty calls:
Don't forget that we are waiting for you!

The mines are bursting, it seems on land and on the sea!
Along the towering Atlantic Wall

In December 1941 construction had
begun on Germany's new Atlantic
coast defences, stretching 5,300km
from the Pyrenees to North Cape.
The 'Atlantic Wall' was to connect
15,000 bunkers and heavy artillery
emplacements, manned by a force of
some 150,000. But by the time –
three weeks after this broadcast –
that it was put to the test, only 5,000
of the bunkers had been completed,

they play their game for me.
My weapon is brand new,
and magic is for you:
The magic of the Atlantic Wall
that'll be a hot surprise for you!

If a thousand planes are roaring over my head,
they will drop in vain their bombs on my concrete shed,
as soon as engines roar
and heavy guns galore!
Of those who approach the Atlantic Wall
there will be no one living left ashore!

and of the designated 547 gun positions only 299 had a concrete shell. Allied air raids had also prevented most of the 64 radar posts from becoming operational.

'*No one living left ashore*' – remained an empty boast. This is another pre-D-Day number from 'Calling Invasion Forces'.

Sources and Bibliography

1. Unpublished Sources

Běhounek, Kamil, 'Lebenserinnerungen' (Bonn, typescript, n.d.)

Clark, James, 'Open Wounds – A Berlin Memoir 1939-1945' (London, typescript, August 1992)

Deutsche Grammophon AG, 'Aufnahme-Blätter, GD-Serie, 1934–1945' (Berlin/Hanover, typescript)

Deutsche Grammophon AG, 'Aufnahme-Blätter, GR-Serie, 1934–1943' (Berlin/Hanover, typescript)

Deutsche Grammophon AG, 'Aufnahme-Blätter, GX-Serie, 1939–1943' (Berlin/Hanover, typescript)

Deutsche Grammophon AG, 'Aufnahme-Blätter, KK-Serie, 1945–1950' (Berlin/Hanover, typescript)

Dietze, Eduard Roderich, business agendas 1938–1945 (Berlin)

Dietze, Eduard Roderich, 'Personal Remarks' (13 unnumbered pages) (Apen, 24–25 April 1946)

Dietze, Eduard Roderich, 'Statement' (36 numbered pages) (Apen, 24–26 April 1946)

Diller, Ansgar, 'Der Frankfurter Rundfunk 1923–1945' (Frankfurt University dissertation, 1973)

Dömpke, Fred, 'Schallplatten-Aufnahmen bei div. Firmen. Beginn: Sept. 1933 bis 22.3.1943' (unpublished manuscript in the collection of Jan Grundmann, Hamburg)

Fudge, Russell Oliver, 'The Armed Forces Radio Service. An Evaluation Of AFRS', Contribution to the U.S. Army's Troop Informational and Educative Program (George Washington University, Washington DC, dissertation, 1949)

Joyce, Margaret, correspondence with J.A. Cole (Hamburg, 1961)

Kleindin, Franz 'Teddy', correspondence and conversations with Horst Bergmeier (Munich, 1992–93)

Klingler, Walter, 'Nationalsozialistische Rundfunkpolitik 1942-1945 – Organisation, Programm und die Hörer' (Mannheim University: Master's thesis, 1983)

Kupsch, Dr. Richard, cine-interview with Michael and Doreen Forman (Berlin, April 1992)

Oehme, Frank, Meyer-Rähnitz, Bernd & Schütte, Joachim, '*Die 78er Schallplatten des Verlages Lied der Zeit, Berlin (einschließlich der Radiophon- und einiger Regina-Matrizen)*', (Dresden, manuscript dates 1994, forthcoming from Birgit Lotz Verlag, Bonn)

Schröder, Heribert, 'Tanz- und Unterhaltungsmusik in Deutschland 1918-1933 – Studien zu ihrer Rezeption und zur Sozialgeschichte des Unterhaltungsmusikers' (Bonn University, Master's thesis, October 1961)

Schütte, Joachim, 'Katalog der Amiga Lied der Zeit Schallplatten 1945–1985' (Ennigerloh, typescript, n.d.)

Steinbiss, Florian & Eisermann, David, 'Goebbels' Swing-Orchester – Jazzmusik als national-sozialistische Propaganda' (Radio Bremen, broadcast typescript, n.d.)

Steinbiss, Florian & Eisermann, David, 'Propaganda-Swing' (Bonn, typescript, n.d.)

Steinbiss, Florian & Eisermann, David, 'Interview mit Fritz Brocksieper' (Munich, typescript, 19 September 1987)

Stuart de Lay, Jr., 'Theodore, An Historical Study of the Armed Forces Radio Service to 1946' (University of Southern California, Los Angeles, dissertation, May 1951)

2. Books

Andersen, Lale, *Der Himmel hat viele Farben – Leben mit einem Lied* (Stuttgart: 1972)

Baillie, Hugh, *High Tension* (New York: Harper, 1959)

Baillie-Stewart, Norman, *The Officer in the Tower* (London: Leslie Frewin, 1967)

Baird, Jay W., *The Mythical World of Nazi War Propaganda, 1939–1945* (Minneapolis: University of Minnesota, 1974)

Balfour, Michael, *Propaganda in War 1939–1945 – Policies and Publics in Britain and Germany* (London: Routledge and Kegan Paul, 1979)

Barazzetta, Giuseppe, *Jazz inciso in Italia* (Milan: Messaggerie Musicali, 1960)

Bardura, Heinz, *Stuttgart im Luftkrieg 1939–1945* (Stuttgart: Union Druckerei, 1967)

Barrington, Jonah, *Lord Haw-Haw of Zeesen* (London: Hutchinson, 1940)

Barrington, Jonah, *And Master of None* (London: Walter Edwards, 1948)

Berendt, Joachim Ernst, *Das Jazzbuch. Entwicklung und Bedeutung der Jazzmusik* (Frankfurt am Main: Fischer Taschenbuch No. 48, first edn. 1953)

Boberach, Heinz (ed.), *Meldungen aus dem Reich – Die geheimen Lageberichte des Sicherheitsdienstes der SS 1938–1945* (Herrsching: Pawlak, 1984)

Boelcke, Willi A. (ed.), *Kriegspropaganda 1939–1941 – Geheime Ministerkonferenzen im Reichspropagandaministerium* (Stuttgart: Deutsche Verlagsanstalt, 1966)

Boelcke, Willi A., *Die Macht des Radios – Weltpolitik und Auslandsrundfunk 1924–1976* (Frankfurt: Ullstein, 1977)

Bolz, Rüdiger, *Synchronopse des Zweiten Weltkriegs – Hermes Hand-Lexikon* (Düsseldorf: Econ, 1983)

Boveri, Margaret, *Der Verrat im XX. Jahrhundert – Für und gegen die Nation* (Hamburg: Rowohlt, 1956)

Boveri, Margaret, *Treason in the Twentieth Century* (London: MacDonald, 1961)

Brard, Olivier & Nevers, Daniel, *Le Jazz en France – Jazz and Hot Dance Music Discography, Vols. 1–3* (Paris: M.A.D., 1989–1991)

Briggs, Asa, *The History of Broadcasting in the United Kingdom – Vol. 3, The War of Words* (London: Oxford University Press, 1970)

Brown, Anthony Cave (ed.), *The Secret War Report of the OSS* (New York: Berkley, 1976)

Bruce Lockhart, Sir Robert H., *Comes the Reckoning* (London: Putnam, 1947)

Buchbender, Ortwin & Hausschild, Reinhard, *Geheimsender gegen Frankreich - Die Täuschungsoperation 'Radio Humanité' 1940* (Herford: Mittler, 1984)

Cole, John Alfred, *Lord Haw-Haw and William Joyce: The Full Story* (London: Faber & Faber, 1964, new edn. 1987)

Conrad, Gerhard, *Posaunen-Dob – Kleine Biographie Walter Dobschinskis* (Menden: Jazzfreund-Publikation Nr. 13, 1983)

Crone, Michael, *Hilversum unter dem Hakenkreuz – Die Rundfunkpolitik der Nationalsozialisten in den besetzten Niederlanden 1940–1945* (Munich: K.G. Saur, 1983)

Danzi, Michael, *American Musicians in Germany 1924–1939. Memoirs of the jazz, entertainment, and movie world of Berlin during the Weimar Republic and the Nazi era – and in the United States, as told to Rainer E. Lotz* (Schmitten: Ruecker, 1986)

Day, Donald, *Onward Christian Soldiers* (Torrance, Ca.: Noontide, 1982)

Delmer, Sefton, *Black Boomerang* (London: Secker & Warburg, 1962)

Deutsche Welle, Köln (ed.), Schwipps, W., & Runge, W., *Mit 8 kW rund um die Welt – Geschichte des Kurzwellenrundfunks in Deutschland 1929–1932* (Berlin: Haude & Spener, 1969)

Deutsche Welle, Köln (ed.), Schwipps, W., & Lubbers, H., *Morgen die ganze Welt – Deutscher Kurzwellensender im Dienste der NS-Propaganda / Geschichte des Kurzwellenrundfunks in Deutschland 1933–1939* (Berlin: Haude & Spener, 1970)

Deutsche Welle, Köln (ed.); Schwipps, W., & Goebel, Gerhart, *Wortschlacht im Äther – Der deutsche Auslandsrundfunk im Zweiten Weltkrieg – Geschichte des Kurzwellenrundfunks in Deutschland 1939–1945* (Berlin: Haude & Spener, 1971)

Diller, Ansgar, *Rundfunkpolitik im Dritten Reich* (Munich: Deutscher Taschenbuchverlag, 1980)

Donaldson, Frances, *P.G. Wodehouse – The Authorized Biography* (London: Weidenfeld & Nicolson, 1982)

Drechsler, Nanny, *Die Funktion der Musik im deutschen Rundfunk, 1933–1945* (Pfaffenweiler: Centaurus, 1988)

Dümling, Albrecht und Girth, Peter (eds.), *Entartete Musik – Dokumentation und Kommentar* (Düsseldorf: Der kleine Verlag, 1988 & 1993)

Eck, Hélène, *La Guerre des Ondes. Histoire des radios de langue francaise pendant la Deuxième Guerre Mondiale* (Paris: Colin, 1985)

Edwards, John Carver, *Berlin Calling – American Broadcasters in Service to the Third Reich* (New York: Praeger, 1991)

Elborn, Geoffrey, *Francis Stuart – A Life* (Dublin: Raven Arts Press, 1990)

Erdmann, Karl Dietrich, *Handbuch der deutschen Geschichte* (Munich: Deutscher Taschenbuch Verlag, 1980)

Ewen, David, *American Popular Songs from the Revolutionary War to the Present* (New York: Random House, 1966)

Eyle, Wim van, (ed.), *Jazz & geimproviseerde muziek in Nederland – Handboek voor de Nederlandse Jazzwereld* (Utrecht: Spectrum, 1978)

Eyle, Wim van, (ed.), *The Dutch Jazz & Blues Discography 1916–1980* (Utrecht: Spectrum, 1981)

Fleming, Peter, *Invasion 1940: An Account of the German Preparations and the British Counter-Measures* (London: Rupert Hart-Davis, 1957)

Frank/Altmann, *Kurzgefasstes Tonkünstler-Lexikon, 15. Auflage* (Wilhelmshaven: Heinrichshofen's Verlag, 1974)

Fröhlich, Elke (ed.), *Die Tagebücher von Joseph Goebbels – Sämtliche Fragmente, Teil 1* (Munich: K.G. Saur, 1987)

Goebbels, Joseph, *Die deutsche Kultur vor neuen Aufgaben – Signale der neuen Zeit* (Munich: Eher, 1934)

Goebbels, Joseph, *Vom Kaiserhof zur Reichskanzlei. Eine historische Darstellung in Tagebuchblättern (Vom 1. Januar 1932 bis 1. Mai 1933)* (Munich: Eher, 4th edn. 1934)

Goebbels, Joseph, *Das eherne Herz – Reden und Aufsätze aus den Jahren 1941/42* (Munich: Eher, 1943)

Gombrich, E.H., *Myth and Reality in German War-Time Broadcasts* (London: The Athlone Press, 1970)

Gorham, Maurice, *Sound & Fury – 21 Years at the BBC* (London: Percival Marshall, 1948)

Graves, Charles, *Londoner's Life* (London: Hutchinson, 1943)

Grundmann, Jan, *Jazz aus den Trümmern – Discographie der Eigenaufnahmen der Deutschen Grammophon 1945/48* (Menden: Jazzfreund-Publikation Nr. 17, 1982)

Grundmann, Jan, *Hot Bandoneon – Swingin' Guitar. Die Fred Dömpke Bio-Discographie* (Menden: Jazzfreund-Publikation Nr. 30, 1986)

Hale, Julian, *Radio Power – Propaganda and International Broadcasting* (London: Elek, 1975)

Hall, John William (ed.), *The Trial of William Joyce – Volume 68 of 'Notable British Trials Series'* (London: William Hodge, 1946)

Heiber, Helmut (ed.), *Das Tagebuch von Joseph Goebbels 1925/26 mit weiteren Dokumenten* (Stuttgart: Deutsche Verlagsanstalt, n.d.; 2nd. edn. 1961)

Herzstein, Robert Edwin, *The War That Hitler Won – Nazi Propaganda* (London: Hamish Hamilton, 1979)

Hildebrand, Klaus, *Deutsche Außenpolitik 1933–1945 – Kalkül oder Dogma?* (Stuttgart: 1980)

Honig, Piet Hein, & Rodek, Hanns-Georg (eds.), *100001 – Encyclopedie van de internationale Showbusiness in de 20e Eeuw* (Diepenveen: Showbizdata Nederland, 1990)

Howe, Ellic, *The Black Game* (London: Michael Joseph, 1982)

Huesmann, Günther & Lotz, Rainer E. 'Brocksieper, Fritz', in S. Sadie (ed.), *The New Grove Dictionary of Jazz, Vol. 1 A to K* (London & New York: Macmillan, 1988)

Hughes, Spike, *Opening Bars* (London: Jazz Book Club, 1946)

Hussong, Friedrich, *Kurfürstendamm – Zur Kulturgeschichte des Zwischenreichs* (Berlin: Scherl Verlag, 1933)

Jäckel, Eberhard (ed.), *Hitler – Sämtliche Aufzeichnungen 1905–1924* (Stuttgart: Deutsche Verlagsanstalt, 1980)

Jacobsen, Hans-Adolf, *Nationalsozialistische Aussenpolitik 1933 –1938* (Frankfurt/Berlin: Alfred Metzner Verlag, 1968)

Joyce, William, *Dämmerung über England* (Berlin: Internationaler Verlag, 1940)

Joyce, William, *Twilight over England* (The Hague: Uitgevers-Maatschappij 'Oceanus', 1942)

Kater, Michael H., *Different Drummer – Jazz in the Culture of Nazi Germany* (New York: Oxford University Press, 1992)

Kellersmann, Christian, *Jazz in Deutschland 1933–1945* (Menden: Jazzfreund-Publikation Nr. 40, 1990)

Kernfeld, Barry (ed.), *The New Grove Dictionary of Jazz* (London: Macmillan, 1988)

Kinkle, Roger D., *The Complete Encyclopedia of Popular Music and Jazz 1900–1950* (New Rochelle, N.Y.: Arlington House Publishers, 1974)

Klarsfeld, Beate, *Die Geschichte des PG 2633930 – Kiesinger* (Darmstadt: Josef Melzer, 1969)

Kordt, Erich, *Nicht aus den Akten ... Die Wilhelmstrasse in Frieden und Krieg. Begegnungen und Eindrücke 1928–1945* (Stuttgart: Union, 1950)

Kraner, Dietrich Heinz & Schulz, Klaus, *Jazz in Austria – Historische Entwicklung und Diskographie des Jazz in Oesterreich* (Graz: Universal Edition, 1972)

Kühn, Volker, *Deutschlands erwachen – Kabarett unterm Hakenkreuz 1933–1945* (Berlin: Quadriga, 1989)

Künneke, Evelyn, *Sing Evelyn sing – Revue eines Lebens* (Hamburg: Rowohlt, 1985)

Lange, Horst H., *Die deutsch Jazz-Discographie. Eine Geschichte des Jazz auf Schallplatten von 1902 bis 1955* (Berlin/Wiesbaden: Bote & Bock, 1955; 2nd. edn. Berlin: Colloquium, 1978; 3rd. edn. Berlin: Panther, 1992)

Lange, Horst H., *Die Geschichte des Jazz in Deutschland. Die Entwicklung von 1910 bis 1960 mit Discographie* (Lübbecke: Uhle & Kleimann, 1960)

Lange, Horst H., *Jazz in Deutschland – Die deutsche Jazz-Chronik 1900–1960* (Berlin: Colloquium, 1966)

Laqueur, Walter, *Weimar – Die Kultur der Republik* (Frankfurt: Ullstein, 1977)

Laughlin, James, *Pound As Wuz – Essays and Lectures on Ezra Pound* (Saint Paul: Greywulf Press, 1987)

Lean, Tangye E., *Voices in the Darkness* (London: Secker & Warburg; 1943)

Leimbach, Berthold, *Tondokumente der Kleinkunst und ihre Interpreten 1898–1945* (Göttingen: Leimbach, 1991)

Lerg, Winfried B., *Die Entstehung des Rundfunks in Deutschland* (Frankfurt am Main: Josef Knecht)

Liddell Hart, Basil H., *History of the First World War* (London: Cassell, 1970)

Lochner, Louis P. (ed.), *Joseph Goebbels – Tagebücher aus den Jahren 1942–1943 mit anderen Dokumenten* (Zurich: Atlantis-Verlag, 1948)

Longerich, Peter, *Propagandisten im Krieg – Die Presseabteilung des Auswärtigen Amtes unter Ribbentrop* (Munich: R. Oldenbourg, 1987)

Lotz, Rainer E., & Neuer, Ulrich, *The Armed Forces 'Jubilee' Radio Transcription Broadcasts, Vols. 1 & 2* (Frankfurt: Ruecker, 1985)

Lotz, Rainer E., 'Templin, Lutz', in S. Sadie (ed.), *The New Grove Dictionary of Jazz, Vol. 2 L–Z* (London & New York: Macmillan, 1988)

MacKenzie, A.J., *Propaganda Boom* (London: The Right Book Club, 1938)

Magnus-Andersen, Litta, *Lale Andersen – Die Lili Marleen: Das Lebensbild einer Künstlerin* (Munich: 1981)

Mazzoletti, Adriano, *Il Jazz In Italia* (Roma: Laterza, 1983)

Milward, Alan S., *The German Economy at War* (London: The Athlone Press, 1965)

Mittler, Wolf, *Anzac Tattoo – Eine Reise durchs Niemandsland* (Percha: R.S. Schulz, 1987)

Münzenberg, Willi, *Propaganda als Waffe* (Paris: Editions du Carrefort, 1937)

Otto, Heinrich W.E., *Germany Calling – Lord Haw-Haw's Radio War. Facts, Figures, Stories about William Joyce* (Melbourne: Heliocentric, 1987)

Oven, Wilfried von, *Mit Goebbels bis zum Ende. Vols. I & II* (Buenos Aires: Dürer-Verlag, 1949–50)

Pernet, Robert, *Jazz in Little Belgium* (Brussels: Sigma, 1967)

Pernet, Robert, *La Discographie du Jazz Belge* (Brussels: Editions I.M.C., 1983)

Pernet, Robert, & Schroeder, Jean-Pol (ed.), *Dictionnaire du Jazz à Bruxelles et en Wallonie* (Liège: Mardaga, 1991)

Pfitzner, Hans, *Gesammelte Schriften. Vols. 1–3* (Augsburg: Filser, 1926–29)

Picker, Henry, *Hitlers Tischgespräche im Führerhauptquartier 1941–1942* (Bonn: 1951 and Stuttgart: Athenäum, 1965)

Pohle, Heinz, *Der Rundfunk als Instrument der Politik – Zur Geschichte des deutschen Rundfunks 1923–1938* (Hamburg: Hans Bredow Institut, 1955)

Polster, Bernd (ed.), *'Swing Heil'– Jazz im Nationalsozialismus* (Berlin: TRANSIT, 1989)

Prieberg, Fred K., *Musik im NS-Staat* (Frankfurt: Fischer, 1982)

Prieberg, Fred K., *Musik und Macht* (Frankfurt: Fischer, 1991)

Pryce-Jones, David, *Unity Mitford – A Quest* (London: Weidenfeld & Nicolson, 1976)

Rauschning, Hermann, *Germany's Revolution of Destruction* (New York and London: Heinemann, 1939)

Reuth, Ralf Georg (ed.), *Joseph Goebbels Tagebücher 1924–1945*, 5 Vols. (Munich/Zurich:

Piper, 1992)

Roberts, E. Beckhofer (ed.), *The Trial of William Joyce, with some notes on other recent trials for treason* (London: Jarrolds, 1946, Vol. 5 of 'The Old Bailey Trial Series')

Rolo, Charles J., *Radio Goes To War* (London: Faber & Faber, 1943)

Roosevelt, Kermit (ed.), *War Report of the OSS – Vol. 2: The Overseas Targets* (New York: Walker & Company, 1976)

Rühle, Gerd, *Das Dritte Reich – Dokumentarische Darstellung des Aufbaus der Nation, 1933–1938*, 6 Vols. (Berlin: Hummel Verlag, 1934–1938)

Rust, Brian & Forbes, Sandy, *British Dance Bands on Record 1911 to 1945* (Harrow, Middlesex: General Gramophone Publications, 1989)

Rust, Brian, *Jazz Records 1897–1942* (Chigwell, Essex: Storyville Publications, 1975)

Rust, Brian, with Debus, Allen G., *The Complete Entertainment Discography from the mid-1890s to 1942* (New Rochelle, N.Y.: Arlington House, 1973)

Rutherford, Ward, *Hitler's Propaganda Machine* (London: Bison Books, 1978)

Rutledge, Brett (pseud.), *The Death of Lord Haw-Haw – No. 1 Personality of World War 2* (New York: Random House, 1940)

Schäfer, Dietrich, *Deutsche Geschichte* (Jena: G. Fischer, 1916)

Scheel, Klaus, *Krieg über Ätherwellen – NS-Rundfunk und Monopole 1933–45* ([East] Berlin: VEB Deutscher Verlag der Wissenschaften, 1970)

Schmidt-Scheeder, Georg, *Reporter der Hölle* (Stuttgart: Motorbuch Verlag, 1990)

Schnabel, Reimund, *Missbrauchte Mikrophone – Deutsche Rundfunkpropaganda im Zweiten Weltkrieg* (Wien: Europa, 1967)

Schofield, William Greenough, *Treason Trail* (New York: Rand McNally, 1964)

Short, K.R.M. (ed.), *Film & Radio Propaganda in World War II* (London: Croom Helm, 1983)

Schröder, Herbert, *Ein Sender erobert die Herzen der Welt – Das Buch vom deutschen Kurzwellenrundfunk* (Essen: 1940)

Schröder, Heribert, *Tanz- und Unterhaltungsmusik in Deutschland 1918–1933* (Bonn: Verlag für systematische Musikwissenschaft; Band 58 der Orpheus-Schriftenreihe zu Grundfragen der Musik, herausg. von Martin Vogel, 1990)

Schröter, Heinz, *Unterhaltung für Millionen – Vom Wunschkonzert zur Schlagerparade* (Düsseldorf: Econ, 1973)

Schütte, Joachim, *Discographie des RBT-Orchesters und der anderen Formationen des Berliner Rundfunks* (Menden: Jazzfreund-Publikation Nr. 3, 1977)

Sears, Richard S., *V-Discs – A History and Discography* (Westport and London: Greenwood, 1980)

Seth, Ronald, *Jackals of the Reich – The Story of the British Free Corps* (London: New English Library, 1972)

Shirer, William L., *Berlin Diary – The Journal of a Foreign Correspondent 1934–1941* (New York: Knopf, 1941)

Sington, Derrick & Weidenfeld, Arthur, *The Goebbels Experiment – A Study of the Nazi Propaganda Machine* (London: John Murray, 1943)

Slade, Marquis de, (pseud.), *Yeomen Of Valhalla* (Mannheim: privately published, n.d. – First Series: Behind The Siegfried Line, Vol. 1)

Slade, Marquis de (pseud.), *The Frustrated Axis* (Witten: privately published, 1978 – First Series: 'Behind The Siegfried Line', Vol. 2)

Soley, Lawrence C., *Radio Warfare – OSS and CIA Subversive Propaganda* (New York: Praeger, 1989)

Spaeth, Sigmund, *A History of Popular Music in America* (London: Jazzbook Club, 1961)

Spitzenverband deutscher Musik SPIDEM (ed.), *Chronik deutscher Unterhaltungsmusik* (Bonn: SPIDEM, 1991)

Steinhoff, Johannes, Pechel, Peter & Showalter, Dennis, *Voices From the Third Reich — An Oral History* (London: Grafton, 1991)

Stern-Schubarth, Edgar, *Die Propaganda als politisches Instrument* (Berlin: Trowitzsch & Sohn, 1921)

Stockorst, Erich, *Fünftausend Köpfe — Wer war was im Dritten Reich* (Velbert: blick + bild, 1967)

Stuart, Francis, *Black List — Section H* (London: Martin Brian & O'Keeffe, 1975)

Stuart, Francis, *States of Mind — Selected Short Prose 1936–83* (Dublin: Raven Arts Press, 1984)

Tennyson, F. and Harwood, H.M., *London Front: Letters written to America, August 1939–July 1940* (London: Constable, 1941)

Thimme, Hans, *Weltkrieg ohne Waffen — Die Propaganda der Westmächte gegen Deutschland, ihre Wirkung und Abwehr* (Stuttgart, Berlin: Cotta: 1932)

Tytell, John, *Ezra Pound — The Solitary Volcano* (New York: Doubleday, 1987)

Verkijk, Dick, *Radio Hilversum 1940–1945* (Amsterdam: De Arbeiderpers, 1974)

Vronskaya, Jeanne with Chuguev, Vladimir, *A Biographical Dictionary of the Soviet Union, 1917–1988* (London: K.G. Saur, 1989)

Weale, Adrian, *Renegades: Hitler's Englishmen* (London: Weidenfeld & Nicolson, 1994)

Weinbrenner, Hans-Joachim (ed.), *Handbuch des Deutschen Rundfunks 1938* (Heidelberg-Berlin-Magdeburg: Kurt Vowinckel Verlag, 1938)

Weinbrenner, Hans-Joachim (ed.), *Handbuch des Deutschen Rundfunks 1939/40* (Heidelberg-Berlin-Magdeburg: Kurt Vowinckel Verlag, 1939)

Wendtland, Karlheinz, *Geliebter Kintopp — Sämtliche deutscher Spielfilm von 1929-1945* (Berlin: Verlag Medium Film, 1989)

West, Rebecca, *The Meaning of Treason* (London: Macmillan, 1949)

West, W.J. (pseud.), *Truth Betrayed* (London: Duckworth, 1987)

Wheeler-Bennett, John, *The Forgotten Peace* (New York: Morrow, 1939)

Wistrich, Robert, *Wer war wer im Dritten Reich — Ein biographisches Lexikon* (Frankfurt: Fischer, 1988)

Wolf, Dieter, *Die Doriot-Bewegung — Ein Beitrag zur Geschichte des französischen Faschismus* (Stuttgart: 1967)

Wulff, Joseph, *Musik im Dritten Reich* (Gütersloh: Mohn, 1963)

Wulff, Joseph, *Presse und Funk im Dritten Reich* (Güthersloh: Mohn, 1964)

Zwerin, Mike, *La Tristesse de Saint Louis — Swing under the Nazis* (London: Quartet, 1985)

3. Articles & Periodicals

Anon., [Charles Mitchell], 'A Biological View of our Foreign Policy', *Saturday Review*, 1/2, 1896

Anon., 'Hitler's Hit Parade', *Time*, 9 May 1988

Ahlander, Lars, 'Nazist-Jazz. Paradox för export', *Göteborgs Posten*, 2 April 1989

Bergmeier, Horst, 'The unknown Ernst van 't Hoff', *Doctor Jazz Magazine*, 109, July 1985

Bergmeier, H. & Lotz, R., 'Rudi Rischbeck — der singende Geiger', *Fox auf 78*, 5, Munich, Autumn 1988

Berringer, Hans-Joachim, 'Die weissen Raben — Paradiesvögel der Berliner Tanzmusik', *Fox auf 78*, 7, Summer 1989

Börner, Herbert, 'Der Anteil der Ortsempfänger an der Ausbreitung des deutschen

Rundfunks 1923–1945', *Beiträge zur Geschichte des Rundfunks*, 2/3, [East] Berlin,1976

Clough, Patricia, 'When Goebbels let the Nazi big band swing', *Independent*, 19 April 1988

Crossroads News – Weekly Red Cross Events; Stuttgart, Vol. 1, 1946

Cunningham, Alan, 'Swingtime for Hitler', *Mail on Sunday*, London, 30 August 1987

Delden, Ate van, 'Josse Breyre – Europe's trombone talent', *Doctor Jazz Magazine*, 123, March 1989

Die Wildente – Informationen; PK Mitteilungsblatt; Hamburg: 1955–1966

Eschenberg, Gerda, 'Ich war 'Mary von Arnheim', Hamburg: *Hör zu*, 50–52, 1948

Faber, Tom, 'Jean Robert overleden – een tijdgenoot van Adrian Rollini', *Doctor Jazz Magazine*, 95, March 1981

Fischer, Eugen Kurt, 'Das Brucknerstift St. Florian – Ein Beitrag zur Geschichte des Rundfunks im Dritten Reich', *Publizistik*, 3, 1960

Ganschow, Eberhard, 'Wer war Charlie and his Orchestra?', *Rhythmus* 78, 10, Wuppertal, n.d. (November 1970)

Ganschow, Eberhard, 'Charlie and his Orchestra, II', *Rhythmus* 78, 11, Wuppertal, n.d. (October 1971)

Gerigk, Herbert, 'Die Jazzfrage als eine Rassenfrage', *Musik im Kriege 2*, 3/5, June/July 1944

Graef, Jack de, 'Belgische Jazz-Lexicon', Braschaat, *Jazzspiegel*, Belgium, 7–9 September 1968

Humblot, Catherine, 'L'orchestre du Dr. Goebbels', *Le Monde*, 24–25 November 1991, p.9

Jost, Ekkehard, 'Jazz in Deutschland – Von der Weimarer Republik zur Adenauer-Aera', *That's Jazz – Der Sound des 20. Jahrhunderts; catalogue of exhibition*, Darmstadt, 29 May–28 August 1988

Klingler, Walter, 'Das Bruckner-Stift St. Florian', *Studienkreis Rundfunk und Geschichte*, Mitteilungen, 4, Cologne, 1981

Kutsch, Arnulf, 'Die Sowjets und der Rundfunk nach 1945', *Studienkreis Rundfunk und Geschichte*. Mitteilungen, 3, Cologne, 1984

Lange, Horst H., 'Artfremde Kunst und Musik unerwünscht – Jazz im Dritten Reich', *That's Jazz – Der Sound des 20. Jahrhunderts; catalogue of exhibition*, Darmstadt, 29 May–28 August 1988

Latour, Conrad F., 'Goebbels "Ausserordentliche Rundfunkmassnahmen" 1939–1942', *Vierteljahreshefte für Zeitgeschichte*, 4, 1963

Lerg, Winfried B., 'Edgar Stern-Rubarths "Propaganda als politisches Instrument" von 1921', *Gazette*, 1964

Lerg, Winfried B. 'Deutscher Auslandsrundfunk im zweiten Weltkrieg – Bemerkungen zu einer William-Joyce-Biographie', *Rundfunk und Fernsehen*, 1, Hamburg, 1966

Lerg, Winfried B., 'Vom Kulturinstrument zum Führungsmittel – Rundfunkkontrolle in Deutschland bis 1945' (2. Teil), *Studienkreis Rundfunk und Geschichte*, Mitteilungen, 3, Cologne, 1981

'Lord Haw-Haw to be buried in Eire', *The Daily Telegraph*, London, 20 August 1976

Möller, Bernd-Andreas, 'Lang- und Mittelwellenrundfunk in Nazideutschland, 1933–1945, sowie den annektierten Gebieten 1938–1945', *Beiträge zur Geschichte des Rundfunks*, 3, [East] Berlin,1985

Müller, Michael, 'Warum nicht über Goebbels schmunzeln?', *Süddeutsche Zeitung*, 6–7 March 1976

'Nazis' propaganda swung to the big band sound', *The Age*, 20 April 1988

Reichsrundfunk; Berlin, Vol. 1941/42 – 1943/44

Richter, Erich, 'Entwicklung und Wirken des faschistischen Rundfunks':
  • Teil 1: 'Der Prozess der Faschisierung im Rundfunk der Weimarer Republik,

Beiträge zur Geschichte des Rundfunks, [East-] Berlin, 3, 1968
- Teil 2: 'Die Faschisierung des deutschen Rundfunks nach der Machtübernahme durch die Nazis', *Beiträge zur Geschichte des Rundfunks*, 4, 1968
- Teil 3: 'Die Auslandsarbeit des deutschen faschistischen Rundfunks bei der Vorbereitung und Durchführung des zweiten Weltkrieges', *Beiträge zur Geschichte des Rundfunks*, 2, 1969
- Teil 4: 'Der Nazi-Rundfunk im Kriegseinsatz', *Beiträge zur Geschichte des Rundfunks*, 3, 1969
Schebaum, Willy, 'Entscheidung im Aether – Stationen der Rundfunkgeschichte', *Beiträge zur Geschichte des Rundfunks*, 3, 1973
Scheel, Klaus, 'Die letzten Wochen des Nazirundfunks 1945', *Beiträge zur Geschichte des Rundfunks*, 1, 1969
Schröder, Herbert, 'Wir rufen Europa!', *Reichs-Rundfunk*, 7 October 1943
Schröder, Heribert, 'Zur Kontinuität nationalsozialistischer Maßnahmen gegen Jazz und Swing in der Weimarer Republik und dem Dritten Reich', *Colloquium, Festschrift Martin Vogel*, Bad Honnef, 1988
Schütte, Joachim, 'Platten aus Ruinen – Radiophon, die unbekannte Schallplattenmarke der frühen Nachkriegszeit', *Fox auf 78*, 10, Munich, Autumn/Winter 1991/92
Schulz, Klaus, 'Der Neubeginn des Swing in Wien', *der Jazzfreund*, Menden
Schulz, Klaus, 'Französische Musiker in der Wiener Jazzszene 1942–44', *der Jazzfreund*, June 1991
Steinbiss, Florian & Eisermann, David, 'Wir haben damals die beste Musik gemacht', *Der Spiegel*, 16, Hamburg, 1988
Steinbiss, Florian & Eisermann, David, 'Le Jazz – Armée Secrète des Nazis', *Emois*, 8, February 1988
Steinbiss, Florian & Eisermann, David, 'La orquesta de Charlie – Una banda que interpretaba "jazz" con letras nazis durante la II Guerra Mundial', *El Pais*, 129, Madrid, 3 April 1988
Steinbiss, Florian, & Eisermann, David, 'Goebbels' Band Played 'Propaganda Swing', *San Francisco Chronicle*, Sunday Punch, 22 May 1988
Steinbiss, Florian & Eisermann, David, 'Hmmm – Big Band Swing? The amazing story of the Nazi band', *Milwaukee Journal*, 2 June 1988
Steinbiss, Florian & Eisermann, David, 'Nazi Swing – Third Reich big band turned jazz to propaganda', *Chicago Tribune*, Section C, 3 June 1988
Tasch, Dieter, 'Die "Grammophon" in Hannover – 100 Jahre Schallplattengeschichte', *100 Jahre Schallplatte – Von Hannover in die Welt*, Beiträge und Katalog zur Ausstellung vom 29 September 1987 bis 10 Januar 1988 im Historischen Museum am Hohen Ufer, Hannover (Hamburg: Polygram Deutschland, 1987)

4. Record Liner Notes

Lange, Horst H., *Die grossen Tanzorchester 1930-1950 – Lutz Templin* (Polydor 243762-30, 1978)
Lotz, Rainer E., *Charlie & His Orchestra: Propaganda Swing. Vol. 1* (Discophilia 13UTC1-1, 1975)
Lotz, Rainer E., *Charlie & His Orchestra: Propaganda Swing. Vol. 2* (Discophilia 13UTC1-2, 1975)
Lotz, Rainer E., *German Propaganda Swing – Charlie & His Orchestra 1940–1941. Vol. 1* (Harlequin HQ-2058, 1987)

Lotz, Rainer E., *German Propaganda Swing – Charlie & His Orchestra 1940–1943. Vol. 2* (Harlequin HQ-2059, 1988)

Lotz, Rainer E., *German Propaganda Swing – Charlie & His Orchestra 1940–1944. Vol. 3* (Harlequin HQ-2067, 1988)

Lotz, Rainer E., *German Propaganda Swing – Charlie & His Orchestra 1941–1942* (Harlequin HQCD-03, 1990)

Lotz, Rainer E., *Charlie & His Orchestra. Vol. 2: I Got Rhythm* (Harlequin HQCD-09, 1991)

5. Films, Television and Radio Broadcasts, Taped Interviews

Blakeway, Denys, *Germany Calling – The War In The Ether* (London: BBC Radio 4 broadcast, Parts 1 & 2, 1991)

Eisermann, David, *Germany Calling – Die englisch-sprachige Radiopropaganda der Nationalsozialisten* (script: 30 March 1992 – Brandenburg: Ostdeutscher Rundfunk, October 1992)

Pointon, Michael, *Swingtime for Hitler* (London: BBC radio broadcast, 1987)

Sarkovicz, Hans & Crone, Michael, (eds.), *Der Kampf um die Ätherwellen – Feindpropaganda im Zweiten Weltkrieg* (Munich: Michael Roggisch, 1991 – Sammlung Historica Tondokumente: 6 Audiokassetten (420 min) mit Begleitbuch)

Steinbiss, Florian & Eisermann, David, *Interview mit Traute & Heinrich Wittersleben* (Warder: August 1989)

Steinbiss, Florian & Eisermann, David, *Propaganda Swing: Dr. Goebbels' Jazz-Orchester* (Bonn: Constant Flow Productions, 1989, 60 min, German language)

Steinbiss, Florian & Eisermann, David, *Propaganda Swing: Dr. Goebbels' Jazz-Orchestra* (Bonn: Constant Flow Productions, 1991, 60 min PAL, English language)

Stenke, Wolfgang, *Die Stimme seines Herrn: William Joyce - Spachrohr der nationalsozialistischen Radiopropaganda* (script: 28 and 30 March 1993, Westdeutscher Rundfunk und Sender Freies Berlin)

Index